GOVERNING
THE
POSTINDUSTRIAL
CITY

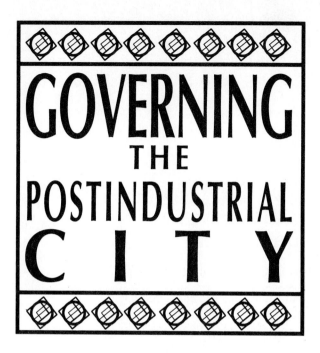

GOVERNING
THE
POSTINDUSTRIAL
C I T Y

Marcus D. Pohlmann

Rhodes College

Longman

New York & London

Governing the Postindustrial City

Longman, 10 Bank Street, White Plains, N.Y. 10606

Associated companies:
Longman Group Ltd., London
Longman Cheshire Pty., Melbourne
Longman Paul Pty., Auckland
Copp Clark Pitman, Toronto

Sponsoring editor: David J. Estrin
Development editor: Susan Alkana
Production editor: Victoria Mifsud
Cover design and illustration: Kevin C. Kall
Text art: Execustaff
Production supervisor: Richard C. Bretan

Library of Congress Cataloging-in-Publication Data

Pohlmann, Marcus D.
    Governing the postindustrial city / Marcus D. Pohlmann.
        p.   cm.
    Includes bibliographical references (p.   ) and index.
    ISBN 0-8013-0665-5
    1. Municipal government—United States.   2. Municipal finance—
United States.   I. Title.   II. Title: Governing the
post-industrial city.
    JS341.P595   1993
    320.8'5'0973—dc20   92-23830
                                                                    CIP

1 2 3 4 5 6 7 8 9 10-AL-9695949392

To Justin Michael Pohlmann,
whose generation must rise
to these challenges

Contents

Illustrations

FIGURES

TABLES

Preface

This book is a critical introduction to contemporary urban politics in the United States. To understand that politics, there is not only a detailed analysis here of formal and informal political processes but also consideration of the social and economic contexts within which a city's political decisions are made. In addition, the book will explore the interrelationships between these social and economic realities and the distribution of political power.

The central theme is that urban political institutions, the roles of the actors who occupy them, and the ultimate distribution of political power have evolved considerably over the course of U.S. history. They have been significantly affected by the economic and social realities of postindustrialism. Specifically, in the postindustrial era, technological changes in production, transportation, and communication allow many corporations and better-off individuals and families to move to more attractive environs. Thus, host cities face a dilemma. They must provide taxing and spending incentives that will prove attractive to the increasingly mobile corporations and wealthier individuals while maintaining expenditures to support the central city poor and the bureaucracy that provides various city services. Cities have become increasingly dependent on state and federal funding to provide these services, even though their clout in those legislative arenas has declined. Moreover, all city activities are carried out under the watchful eye of an ever more pervasive mass media and without the strong political party organizations that in the past served as effective countervailing forces to the interests of the wealthy.

This book is concerned primarily with large U.S. cities, meaning those that have populations currently exceeding 200,000. In particular, the focus is on the basic similarities of the governments in some large cities such as Atlanta, Chicago, Detroit, New York, and Los Angeles. These similarities allow the development of an archetypal "postindustrial city." Significant variations among them will be noted as the book proceeds. If the historical discussion is accurate, what is true for large, previously industrialized cities will be true to some degree for all U.S. cities—even those that did not emerge until after the postindustrial era began.

OVERVIEW BY CHAPTER

Chapter 2 provides a conceptual framework for the ensuing analysis. Chapters 3 through 6 survey in detail the economic, social, and political evolution of America's largest cities. Chapters 7 through 11 examine the institutions and individuals that have contributed to the political policy-making process in what are often increasingly troubled cities. These chapters look at the current structures, functions, and relative power of these institutions and actors. Chapter 12 summarizes the dilemmas faced and considers alternative policy routes as these cities attempt to cope more effectively with the realities of postindustrialism.

ACKNOWLEDGMENTS

First, I would like to thank Ira Katznelson and Charles V. Hamilton whose teaching and writings helped inspire this work. In particular, I would like to thank Demetrios "Jim" Caraley, my primary mentor in the field. Although some of our conclusions diverge significantly, I am deeply indebted to Jim for his incisive instruction concerning the inner workings of the urban governmental process. Because I learned so much from him, it is hard to begin to fully credit every fact and idea. Nonetheless, I simply want to acknowledge Jim and reiterate that much of what I know about urban politics I learned from him. Having said that, I also want to make clear that he is in no way responsible for any errors or omissions contained in this book.

Second, I wish to thank my editor, David Estrin. Not only is David a superb editor, he is also a terrific human being (despite his bad taste in baseball teams). I am very grateful to George Galster and the late Phillip Meranto for their contributions to earlier versions of this material, as well as to the following reviewers for their invaluable critiques of this manuscript at various stages:

Margery Marzahn Ambrosius, Kansas State University

Claire Felbinger, Cleveland State University

Richard Rich, Virginia Polytechnic Institute

Rowan Miranda, University of Illinois at Chicago

Max Neiman, University of California, Riverside

In addition, Susan Alkana, and Victoria Mifsud were helpful during the editorial and production processes, and I am indebted to them as well.

Last, but certainly not least, I would like to thank Sarah Gotschall and Ashley Brian for their assistance in verifying facts and references, as well as

Carola O'Connor and Libby Rich for their help in compiling the book's sizable bibliography. I would also like to thank Rhodes College for granting me the research leave that allowed me to finish this project on schedule. Finally, I would like to express my deepest gratitude to Barbara Pohlmann, whose love and support are such essential pillars in my life.

PART I
Overview

CHAPTER 1

Introduction

William Jeffries is the first African American to be elected mayor in this large industrialized city. The city he inherits faces tremendous problems. A number of its largest industries have either moved elsewhere or are threatening to do so. Meanwhile, the city's population has dipped significantly over recent years, and this has reduced electoral clout in statewide and national elections—meaning a decreasing likelihood of favorable consideration in the state capitol as well as in Washington. In addition, there is racial polarization. A majority of the population is of African American descent, reflecting a steady out-migration of better-off whites to the suburbs or beyond. Many of the remaining blacks and whites are poor because they are not employable, they are unemployed, or they are left with service-sector positions that pay scarcely better than minimum wage and provide few fringe benefits.

Although a large portion of the mayor's votes came from this lower-income constituency, the out-migration of businesses and higher-income residents as well as the decline of influence in external legislatures have left little money in the public coffers with which to serve those most in need. When a bit of discretionary revenue does become available, Mayor Jeffries, like his predecessors, will have little choice but to use it to create an urban atmosphere attractive to potential wealthy investors. He will feel compelled to build office buildings rather than shelters for the homeless, football stadium skyboxes rather than modern public schools, and so on with the hope that some opportunities eventually will trickle down. The increasing ability of the wealthy to invest virtually anywhere on earth has left the mayor competing with cities around the globe. As a result, even more political power has shifted to the owners of this capital—simply a contemporary urban fact of life.

How did we arrive at this present juncture? And just how widely has this phenomenon spread—particularly in the United States?

URBANIZATION

Where and how populations come together generally reflect the economic necessities supporting these arrangements. The history of societies can be divided into three phases: (1) preindustrial, (2) industrial, and (3) postindustrial. Following are definitions of these periods and a general description of how they evolve in any nation where economic development has not been centrally planned by its government. Time frames vary by country and by regions within a country depending on when industrialization and urbanization actually occurred.

Time Frames

A *preindustrial* society revolves around its agricultural base. Its principal cities remain relatively small and are located at logical transshipment points to serve as efficient trading and commercial centers. Most city dwellers tend to be employed as independent artisans or shopkeepers, although a few are likely to be wealthy merchants. Governance in these societies tends to be conducted in a relatively informal way by those with the greatest material interests in governmental policies, such as the wealthiest local landowners and merchants.

When the society acquires the technology necessary to perform large-scale manufacturing, it is said to be *industrial.* When industrialization occurs, factories need to be near specific natural resources, work forces, and markets. Thus, large cities arise in locations that allow manufacturers to obtain necessary materials, workers, markets, intercity trading facilities, and commercial services such as banking and insurance. These cities grow in size as more people arrive in search of employment opportunities that industrialization has created for managers and skilled and unskilled workers. More formal political mechanisms are needed to help structure these new complexities into an orderly environment for industrial production and trade.

The *postindustrial* period can be distinguished by technological developments such as automated assembly lines, automobiles, airplanes, computers, and telecommunications. These technologies enable companies to locate away from workers, markets, waterfronts, and related businesses. As a result, these corporations become mechanized and mobile, with serious implications for the society's cities in general, and specifically for their work forces and political power structures.

The first and most obvious indicator of postindustrial development is a marked decline in a previously industrialized city's population. With their manufacturers and related industries no longer tied to that particular location, firms often opt to locate in the more attractive outlying areas. As expected, those workers who can afford it often follow. The advantages for both businesses and individuals include more space, less congestion, less crime, and lower taxes. Unless liberal state annexation laws allow a city to continue to annex these outlying havens, the older city's number of residents will decline as postindustrialism gathers momentum.

Not only do the city's population and economic growth begin to shrink, but the nature of employment changes for those left in the wake of these developments. At best, the older cities once again become commercial centers, with the manufacturing that remains being more mechanized and employing fewer people in well-paying factory positions. Another indicator is polarizing of city occupations, leaving a number of positions for managers and professionals at the top and more low-paying service positions at the bottom, for example, cleaning, cooking, waiting tables, stocking shelves, emptying bedpans, and so on. Also, many of the professional/manager class will choose to live outside the city and commute to their jobs. As a result, the median income of city residents will begin to fall given that service jobs generally pay less than manufacturing positions.

The structure of political power will begin to change. Those who can invest are now able to put their money in a number of places, and cities will compete to attract that investment. Thus, potential investors normally will get their industrial parks, subsidies, tax breaks, or whatever project they desire. A post-industrial city's political officials simply will seldom be in a position to say no. However, such a shift in priorities also will lead to periodic unrest among those left stranded at the bottom of the socioeconomic ladder, so government occasionally will have to provide them with assistance. Consequently, a "bureaucratic state" will develop as an increasing number of governmental employees will be required to provide these various services. At the same time, governmental officials need to remember that the interests of investors will come first. Table 1.1 shows the evolution of a city through its three phases.

THE CITY

History of the City's Development

Historically, cities are a relatively new phenomenon. There has been life on earth for more than a million years, but human beings formed cities only within approximately the last 7,000 years and to any real extent only in the last 2,500.

TABLE 1.1 Urban Evolutionary Periods

	Phase		
	Preindustrial	*Industrial*	*Postindustrial*
Economy	commerce, home enterprises	expanding, immobile, labor-intensive manufacturing	commerce, service, and slower-expanding, more capital-intensive manufacturing
Work force	merchants, artisans, shopkeepers	factory owners, managers, artisans, unskilled laborers	corporate owners, managers, professionals, service laborers
City functions	trading center	site of industrial resources, markets and transportation; immigrant "staging area"	commercial center, services, "dumping ground" for the economically marginal
City governance	informally by economic elites	more formal structures and mass participation	elite-dominated bureaucratic state

The early growth of cities seems to have corresponded to such innovations as the domestication of grain, the invention of the plow, the use of irrigation, and the development of storage containers, power generation, and the coinage of money. Thus fewer farmers were able to provide more food for a larger number of people, and greater specialization, division of labor, trade, and commerce became possible. Cities began to serve as small-scale production and consumption centers as well as becoming the location for markets, meetings, and information. They were where many of the economic elites lived.

In 1800 only 2.4 percent of the world's population lived in cities larger than 20,000 people and that figure had increased to only 5 percent by 1900.[1] Yet by 1900, new forces had been set in motion that would soon lead a clear majority of the world population to live in cities.

Nineteenth Century.   As the nineteenth century developed, significant changes occurred in many parts of the world: populations grew rapidly, governments began to stabilize, and transportation advancements increased mobility. Farm laborers were replaced by machines such as the steam-powered tractor and the mechanical thresher. Farm owners themselves were plagued by droughts, insects, and other crop perils. Without governmentally stabilized costs and prices, the farm owners began to search for more reliable forms of livelihood. Even more important, industrialization had begun, providing many with alternate occupations; as manufacturers located their factories where they could most efficiently acquire necessary resources, process them, and distribute the final product, these industries took root in urban areas that provided access to key resources, services, and markets.[2]

In addition to these industrial advantages cities offered promises of a better life. There were job opportunities and a variety of consumer items as well as a host of social and cultural possibilities that required support services and large clienteles, for example, fine arts, libraries, museums, schools, colleges, and the press. Cities also offered formal and informal occupational, ethnic, racial, and religious organizations.

Twentieth Century.   In scarcely more than a century, industrialization ushered in the urbanization of much of the world. As the twentieth century dawned, Great Britain became the first urbanized nation—a nation having more of its people living in cities than in the country. Today, nearly half the world's population lives in cities, and it is no longer unusual to find cities populated by as many as a million people. Mexico City has more than 20 million; São Paulo, Bombay and Calcutta, Rio de Janeiro, and Seoul more than 10 million each; and a growing number have more than 6.5 million: Moscow, New Delhi, Tokyo, New York City, Shanghai, London, and Istanbul.[3]

With the growth of cities came increasing urban problems. Sewage and garbage accumulation, overcrowding, poverty, and shortage of livable housing have plagued cities since the days of ancient Greece and Rome. In addition, another thread that seems continuously to run through urban history is that people who can afford it generally attempt to escape urban pollution, congestion, poverty, and related problems by moving to the outskirts of the cities.[4] These developments coupled with important technological innovations set the stage for the postindustrial period.

U.S. Cities

> The tradition of privatism has meant that the cities of the United States depended for their wages, employment, and general prosperity upon the aggregate successes and failures of thousands of individual enterprises, not upon community action. It has also meant that the physical forms of American cities, their lots, houses, factories, and streets have been the outcome of a real-estate market of profit-seeking builders, land speculators, and large investors. Finally, the tradition of privatism has meant that the local politics of American cities have depended for their actors, and for a good deal of their subject matter, on the changing focus of men's private economic decisions.[5]

The general picture Sam Bass Warner paints of cities in the Unites States appears to be true of virtually all societies with private enterprise, as opposed to collectivized economies. Where and how the U.S. population has come together certainly reflects the private economic decisions underlying these arrangements.

History of U.S. Cities. In the United States, the roots of urbanization reach back to the earliest days of colonial settlement. Most colonial Americans first made their homes in waterfront towns and villages, not on individual farms, because these communities offered physical security, sustenance, and a semblance of the living arrangements the settlers had left in the old country. Nonetheless, as the nation expanded, the large majority of the population, following agrarian-related opportunities, moved to inland villages and the countryside surrounding them. As a result, by 1690 only 9 to 10 percent of Americans lived in cities, and by 1790 that figure dipped to 5.1 percent.[6]

In 1776, Philadelphia was the largest colonial city, with approximately 40,000 people. New York had a little over 30,000, and Boston 18,000. No city's population would exceed 100,000 until 1820, and only three had reached that size by 1840.[7]

The industrial revolution, however, began to stir in the 1820s. It grew with the help of significant improvements in water and overland transportation and also with a major population increase in the nineteenth century. Industrialization and urbanization seemed to nurture each other. By 1830, the proportion of Americans living in cities had returned to its 1690 level, and between 1820 and 1930, the United States became an urbanized nation. A veritable "urban explosion" occurred between 1820 and 1860, with city population increasing 797 percent, while the national population increased only 226 percent. In 1820, only 12 cities had more than 10,000 people, and those 12 cities held some two-thirds of the nation's urban population. By 1860, however, more than 100 cities had populations in excess of 10,000 people, and 9 had more than 100,000 residents each.[8]

Individual cities, such as Pittsburgh, Cincinnati, and St. Louis, saw their populations increase some two to three times in the course of the 1840s alone. The population density of New York City soared to 137 people per acre by 1850. From 1862 to 1864, 60 factories were built each year in Philadelphia. By 1900, 28 cities held over 100,000 people. Chicago is the most striking example. Labeled the "shock city of the twentieth century," Chicago's population increased from 50 in 1830 to 3.3 million a century later. New York City, on the other hand, annexed Brooklyn in 1898 and immediately became the second largest city in the Western world (London being the largest).[9]

Nationwide, the percentage of Americans living in urban areas rose from 6 percent in 1800 to 40 percent by 1900. It reached a majority (51.4 percent) in 1920,[10] and had grown to nearly 75 percent by 1980. The 1990 census noted that a majority of the U.S. population resided in 39 metropolitan areas, each with more than 1 million inhabitants.

As for geographic distribution, a full 70 percent of the population lived in the Northeast region as late as 1910, nearly two-thirds of them in cities. Elsewhere, the transcontinental railroad contributed to the fact that more than one-half of those in the Far West lived in connecting cities, while the figures were closer to one in five for those living in the South and Southwest.[11]

Table 1.2 shows two of the most important trends: the urban explosion and the gradual shift in population to the Sun Belt—the Far West, the Southwest, and the South. Comparing the size of the 10 largest cities over a period of time, it is clear that urbanization really began to appear with industrialization in the 1820s and that it continued into the twentieth century. Also, by noting the location of these cities, interregional trends can be observed. For example, virtually all 10 cities were located on the eastern seaboard in 1790. The move inland became apparent with the growth of such cities of the Frost Belt as Cincinnati, Cleveland, Detroit, and Chicago. Then, between 1920 and 1990, the emergence of Los Angeles, Houston, Dallas, San Diego, Phoenix, and San Antonio provided a clear indication of the population shift to the Sun Belt.

During the years of this growth, the character of these cities also was changing. From little more than trading posts in the late eighteenth century, they were becoming huge metropolitan centers, economically, socially, and politically complex. The early cities soon had to contend with traffic congestion and accidents, garbage-strewn streets, fire, theft, impure water, epidemics, poverty, and illiteracy. Even in the late twentieth century many cities continue to be plagued with these troubles, but on a larger scale. Pollution, congestion, crime, poverty, and inadequate education, housing, and health care have proven to be very difficult problems indeed.

Postindustrial Cities. The mechanization and mobility of industries in the postindustrial period have cost many unskilled workers the opportunity to hold more promising industrial jobs. As a result, urban ghettos that once served as "processing centers" for less-skilled immigrants preparing themselves for economic advancement have tended to become "repositories" for workers with little "economic value."[12] Yet, as chapter 6 will detail, many postindustrial urban

TABLE 1.2 Rank and Size (by Population in Thousands) of America's 10 Largest Cities, 1790–1990

Rank	1790 Population		1830 Population		1870 Population		1920 Population		1990 Population	
1	New York	33.1	New York	202.5	New York	942.3	New York*	5,620.0	New York	7,322.6
2	Philadelphia	28.5	Baltimore	80.6	Philadelphia	674.0	Chicago	2,701.7	Los Angeles	3,485.4
3	Boston	18.3	Philadelphia	80.4	Brooklyn	420.0	Philadelphia	1,823.8	Chicago	2,783.7
4	Charleston, S.C.	16.3	Boston	61.3	St. Louis	310.9	Detroit	993.7	Houston	1,630.6
5	Baltimore	13.5	New Orleans	46.0	Chicago	299.0	Cleveland	796.8	Philadelphia	1,585.6
6	Salem, Mass.	7.9	Charleston, S.C.	30.2	Baltimore	267.4	St. Louis	772.9	San Diego	1,110.6
7	Newport, R.I.	6.7	Cincinnati	24.8	Boston	250.5	Boston	748.0	Detroit	1,028.0
8	Providence, R.I.	6.3	Albany, N.Y.	24.2	Cincinnati	216.2	Baltimore	733.8	Dallas	1,006.9
9	Gloucester, Mass.	5.3	Brooklyn	20.5	New Orleans	191.4	Pittsburgh	588.3	Phoenix	983.4
10	Newburyport, Mass.	4.8	Washington, D.C.	18.8	San Francisco	149.5	Los Angeles	576.7	San Antonio	935.9

*New York City incorporated Brooklyn in 1898.

SOURCE: Adapted from David Goldfield and Blaine Brownell, *Urban America: From Downtown to No Town* (Boston: Houghton Mifflin, 1979), pp. 14–19; and U.S. Department of Commerce, Bureau of the Census, *Census of the Population* (Washington, D.C.: Government Printing Office, 1990).

residents have not passively accepted their increasing obsolescence and isolation. They rebelled in the 1930s and again in the 1960s; and this seems to have helped to prompt the government to increase levels of both public employment and social services.

From the postindustrial city's perspective, however, with businesses leaving and many of those people who could afford it following suit, the local share of a number of services became a drain on a shrinking city tax base. Therefore, when capital interests demanded more government incentives to encourage them either to stay in the city or to move there from somewhere else, city governments had little choice but to try to comply. Thus, social services were cut and problems festered even while financial incentives were being increased for the wealthy. Economic changes significantly intensified such political imperatives.[13]

Table 1.3 summarizes the general urban evolutionary experience nationwide. One should recognize, however, that each individual city has proceeded at its own pace. Some regions of the country have evolved more slowly than others. The bulk of the Sun Belt, for instance, has only recently urbanized—attracting population growth and capital investment that previously would have occurred in the older industrial cities. The full brunt of the postindustrial experience awaits these emerging cities down the evolutionary road.

FOCUS

This book will focus on large U.S. cities, meaning those that have populations that currently exceed 200,000. In particular, it will focus on the governing arrangements in the largest of these cities, cities such as Atlanta, Chicago, Detroit, New York, and Los Angeles. All of the cities are distinguishable from one another; but the analysis will concentrate on their basic similarities. These similarities will allow the development of an archetypal postindustrial city, although significant variations will also be noted. Lastly, what is true for large previously industrialized cities will likely to be true to some degree for all U.S. cities—even those that did not emerge until after the postindustrial era had begun.

TABLE 1.3 Urban Evolution in the United States

	Phase		
	Preindustrial	*Industrial*	*Postindustrial*
Dates	colonization to 1820	1820 to 1930	1930 to the present
% in urban areas	5 to 10 percent	10 to 50 percent	50 to 75 percent
Growth regions	Northeast	Northeast, Midwest	South, Southwest, West
City governance	informal elite "committees" and town meetings	political machine	"reformed" bureaucratic state
City finances	solvent, with mostly voluntary services	solvent, despite increases in maintenance and relief services	solvency problems, with revenues declining as service needs increase

THEME

The central theme is that these cities' political institutions, the roles of the actors who occupy them, and the ultimate distribution of political power have evolved considerably over the course of U.S. history; but in particular they have been affected significantly by the economic and social realities of postindustrialism.

Technological changes in production, transportation, and communication have allowed many corporations and better-off individuals and families to move more easily to more attractive environs. Thus, their host cities face a dilemma. They must provide taxing and spending incentives that will prove attractive to the increasingly mobile corporations and wealthy individuals, while at the same time maintain expenditures to support the city poor and to provide various city services. They have become increasingly dependent on state and federal funding in order to obtain these things, even though their clout in those legislative arenas has declined. Moreover, this must be done under the watchful eye of a more pervasive mass media, and it must be done without the strong political party organizations that have helped their governmental predecessors be more effective countervailing forces to those interests of the wealthy.

NOTES

1. J. John Palen, *The Urban World* (New York: McGraw-Hill, 1987), p. 4.
2. For example, see Douglas Brown, *Introduction to Urban Economics* (New York: Academic Press, 1974), chap. 3.
3. Mark Hoffman, ed., *The World Almanac and Book of Facts* (New York: World Almanac, 1992), pp. 734–821.
4. For a good summary, see Brown, *Introduction to Urban Economics,* pp. 12–19. See also Peter Ucko, Ruth Tringham, and G. W. Dimleby, eds., *Men, Settlement, and Urbanism* (Cambridge, Mass.: Schenkman, 1972); Lewis Mumford, *The City in History* (New York: Harcourt Brace, 1961); Palen, *The Urban World.*
5. Sam Bass Warner, *The Private City* (Philadelphia: University of Pennsylvania Press, 1968), p. 4.
6. Palen, *The Urban World,* chap. 3.
7. United States Bureau of the Census figures quoted in John Harrigan, *Political Change in the Metropolis* (Boston: Little, Brown, 1989), p. 24.
8. Palen, *The Urban World,* chap. 3.
9. Ibid, chap. 3; U.S. Department of Commerce, Bureau of the Census, *Census of the Population* (Washington, D.C.: Government Printing Office, decennial from 1790); U.S. Department of Commerce, Bureau of the Census, *Census of Manufacturers* (Washington, D.C.: Government Printing Office, decennial from 1790).
10. In 1920, a city was defined as having a population of more than 2,500 people. Massachusetts and Rhode Island had "urban" majorities before this. See Howard Chudacoff, *The Evolution of American Urban Society* (Englewood Cliff, N.J.: Prentice-Hall, 1975), p. 179.
11. Adna Ferrin Weber, *The Growth of Cities in the Nineteenth Century* (New York: Macmillan, 1899), pp. 20–39; U.S. Department of Commerce, Bureau of the Census, *Census of the Population.*

12. This conceptualization is fleshed out in chapter 2 below.
13. It should be noted that many of these data and much of the discussion were presented previously in Marcus Pohlmann, *Political Power in the Postindustrial City* (New York: Stonehill, 1986). For further reference, see Weber, *The Growth of Cities in the Nineteenth Century*; Blake McKelvey, *American Urbanization* (Glenview, Ill.: Scott, Foresman, 1973); Brown, *Introduction to Urban Economics;* chap. 2 of this book; Chudacoff, *The Evolution of American Urban Society*; Charles Glaab and A. Theodore Brown, *A History of Urban America* (New York: Macmillan, 1976); Peter Gluck and Richard Meister, *Cities in Transition* (New York: New Viewpoints, 1979); David Goldfield and Blaine Brownell, *Urban America: From Downtown to No Town* (Boston: Houghton Mifflin, 1979); Mumford, *The City in History*; Zane Miller, *The Urbanization of Modern America* (New York: Harcourt Brace Jovanovich, 1973); Palen, *The Urban World*; and Sam Bass Warner, *The Urban Wilderness* (New York: Harper & Row, 1972).

CHAPTER 2

Theoretical Context

A theory, quite simply, is a "set of related propositions that suggest why events occur in the manner that they do."[1] A common example would be Newton's theory of gravity. To explain the relationship of objects in the universe, Newton suggested that a force called gravity makes all components of the universe attracted to each other. The level of force depends on the amount of matter in the particular bodies and the distance between them. With this theory he could explain why a large rock is more difficult to pick up than a small rock.

A political theory, on the other hand, attempts to explain the various components of the process for deciding how things of value are to be allocated in a society—for example, what factors consistently affect who will sit in decision-making positions, what range of alternatives they will consider, what they will decide, how those decisions will be implemented, and who will benefit from them.

Much political science analysis has been built on two fundamental political theories: pluralism and systems theory. These approaches, however, often have left the discipline incapable of adequately examining how decisions made in the political arena may be shaped by underlying social and economic structures. Even elite theorists, who focus on the disproportionate power held by social, economic, and political elites, tend to ignore the structures that shape their behavior. The impact of these structures on political behavior must be examined if one is to understand the total political process.

The purpose of this chapter is twofold. First, I will briefly discuss the pluralist, systems, and elite theory approaches, as well as some of the shortcomings inherent in them. Second, I will outline a theoretical framework that allows systematic analysis not only of the governmental decision-making process, but also of the underlying structures that may be constraining political decisions of both the city's elite and its mass citizenry.

My alternative framework melds components of systems, pluralist, and elite theories with Marxian and liberation theories. Then I synthesize the urban-related concepts of urbanologist George Sternleib, economist James O'Connor, political scientist Frances Fox Piven, and sociologist Richard Cloward within my alternative analytical framework. This more complex analytical construct should allow a fuller examination of the urban political process.

PLURALISM

Pluralism involves analyzing political conflict as it is organized around interest groups, where political decisions are seen as arising out of the clash of groups of individuals who have come together to pursue perceived common political purposes. Some of the standard-bearers of this analytical approach are Arthur Bentley, Earl Latham, David B. Truman, and Nelson Polsby.[2]

Yet, a traditional pluralist approach fails to recognize groups such as African Americans, Hispanics, low-income people, the homeless, or gays as meaningful political interest groups appropriate to study. Nor does it consider the possibility of institutionalized barriers to their effective participation. Such myopia springs from key presuppositions concerning what constitutes an empirically relevant interest group and how the political process actually functions.

Interests

Interests are defined as needs people are aware that they have. Thus, the word tends to become valuable as a political science concept only when used as a verb—that person has decided that he or she "needs" something. It is seen as having little empirical value in its noun form—one has a "need" for indoor plumbing regardless of whether or not one realizes this. The latter type of need is avoided or discounted in traditional pluralist theory because it involves the analyst in projecting a need onto someone else, an act entailing too much chance for observer bias. When a person writes a letter to an elected official requesting something, this act is an expressed political interest appropriate to study. On the other hand, when that same person loses his or her job because the company has moved overseas, that person's need for governmental protection from such arbitrary abandonment is not deemed to be an appropriate subject for "value-neutral" behavioral analysis. The reason is that the analyst has projected a need onto that unemployed worker and has thus become more an advocate than a purely detached observer.

Interest Groups

Political interest groups comprise people sharing commonly felt needs interacting with one another for the purpose of affecting public policy. Pluralist David B. Truman defined them this way:

Interest group refers to any group that, on the basis of one or more shared attitudes, makes certain claims upon other groups in the society for the establishment, maintenance, or enhancement of forms of behavior that are implied by the shared attitudes.[3]

By that definition, low-income city residents do not have a common "interest" appropriate to study. They would not have such an interest until all of them had at least one conscious purpose in common.

In addition, they are not an empirically relevant "group" either. Truman put it this way:

> The significance of a . . . group in producing similar attitudes and behaviors among its members lies, not in their physical resemblance or in their proximity . . . but in the characteristic relationships among them. These interactions, or relationships, because they have a certain character and frequency, give the group its molding and guiding powers. . . . A minimum frequency of interaction is, of course, necessary before a group in this sense can be said to exist.[4]

Truman argues that to be an interest group, all members must not only be conscious of a commonly held opinion, but they must also come together on a regular basis to promote that shared interest. If this does not happen, they really are not an interest group appropriate for study as such.

Power Resources

Power resources available to these various political interest groups—time, money, prestige, contacts, media access, and the right to vote and petition elected representatives—are clearly distributed in an uneven fashion. Nevertheless, inequitable distribution is not a structural bias worthy of analysis in its own right. First, those with the largest accumulation of power resources do not automatically have the most political power; for example, candidates who raise the largest amounts of money do not always win their elections. Strategy and circumstances are also important, and the resource wealthy cannot monopolize these. Second, because everyone has access to at least some power resources, any group is capable of becoming competitive if it can effectively pool an adequate number of such resources; for example, the poor can use their numbers to generate a substantial voting bloc and their spare time to swamp officials with messages.

Openness

The political system is considered to be "open" because of the variety of input channels available to interest groups. Not only do all participants have at least some of the resources necessary to compete, but the political process has so many access points that all voices will be heard if they speak up. These access points include elections, thousands of officials to contact, radio call-in shows, and newspapers columns devoted to letters to the editor, not to mention the constitutionally protected "right of the people peaceably to assemble and to petition the government for a redress of grievances."

Government

Government is seen as a relatively unbiased arbiter, refereeing the competition between conflicting groups according to essentially neutral rules. The elected officials will either strive to determine and implement the expressed needs of their constituencies or they will soon find themselves looking for alternative employment. Therefore, even if these officials are virtually all well-to-do white males, they still can and will respond fairly, for example, to African American females who head households—if those women effectively pool their resources.

Elections

Any notion of an abstract "public interest" is discounted as that would require unanimous consent. Nevertheless, elections are seen as an important means for determining the "collective wish" at any one point in time, recording the outcome of the political competition between individual groups.

Equilibrium

Diverse groups flock to the political process to do battle over scarce public resources. That conflict creates "disequilibrium" within the political system, leaving the elected officials to find a compromise that will appease the various groups and return the system to equilibrium.

Overall, then, traditional pluralists argue that the dispersion of power resources and the multiple opportunities for influencing government guarantee that the system will be relatively open to all. Therefore, political scientists need not concern themselves with the possibility that underlying structures include some and exclude others in significant ways before the political game even begins. If the political–economic system was biased in that manner, it might make some sense to explore why categories of people, identifiable by nothing other than their consistent deprivations, so regularly fail to receive the prizes bestowed by that system. But if the system is open and all people are basically aware of their own interests, then the researcher need only focus on the government's efforts to appease organized groups seeking government favor. Drawing on such pluralist propositions, systems theory concerns itself only with that type of expressed political conflict.[5]

SYSTEMS THEORY

Systems theorists Gabriel Almond and G. Bingham Powell define a system as possessing two distinctive characteristics: (1) separate and distinguishable components—differentiation—and (2) interaction among those components in order to perform certain functions—integration.[6] By this definition, a political system would be a set of differentiated units interacting to perform certain political functions. An example would be the city council and the mayor interacting to provide police and fire protection, assist the poor, stimulate local commerce, and so on. David Easton's conceptualization of the system is shown in figure 2.1.

Inputs arise from the political environment and include popular support (e.g., recognizing the laws as legitimate and obeying them) and popular demands (e.g., the National Association for the Advancement of Colored People [NAACP] lobbying against a particular redistricting proposal). Conversion ultimately amounts to public policy-making, by which political actors (e.g., the mayor and city council) respond to various inputs by converting them into policies. Outputs are these authoritative decisions themselves (e.g., a decision not to pass a corporate income tax). Feedback is public reaction to these outputs. That reaction may be positive, settling the matter, or it could be negative, leading to further inputs on the issue and/or a decline in support of the governmental officials in power and possibly the political system itself.[7]

These bare bones of Easton's model provide a widely accepted picture of how a political system operates. However, it is a deceptively simplistic depiction of what constitutes a "political" phenomenon. A more searching question is, What is to be included under the category *politics*? And the obvious corollary is, What is and is not public policy, and thus is or is not appropriate for a political scientist to analyze?

Empirical Dilemmas

Easton suggests that politics, or public policy-making, occurs when political officials make authoritative policies for an entire political community.[8] It seems simple, but to appreciate the ambiguities that still remain, consider which of the following acts constitute public policy by this definition.

FIGURE 2.1   David Easton's Political System Model

SOURCE: From *The Political System* by David Easton. University of Chicago Press. Copyright 1953, © 1971 by David Easton. All rights reserved.

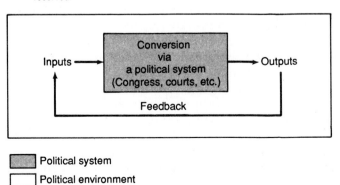

▨ Political system
▢ Political environment

1. The city council passes the city's budget.
2. The mayor successfully fires the city's police chief.
3. An official at the board of elections scrutinizes the nomination petitions of black candidates more closely than those of white candidates.
4. The mayor of Detroit does not even seriously consider requiring General Motors to abide by the letter of local pollution laws, as he fears such pressures could cause the company to relocate elsewhere.
5. The board of directors of General Motors decides that the auto company will increase its manufacturing abroad instead of in Detroit—a decision with serious implications for thousands of local workers.

The decisions of the mayor and the city council would seem to qualify as public policy-making as these individuals are representatives elected to positions of public authority who make binding decisions for the political community. By the same logic, the board of elections employee has been delegated public authority by elected officials. But what about the last two cases?

Peter Bachrach and Morton Baratz carefully develop the argument that the alternatives government decides against, or will not even consider, are often equally as political and important as their ultimate decisions to act.[9] Detroit's decision not even to consider enforcing its pollution laws thus would be viewed as an important public policy affecting many in the city of Detroit. It is simply a negative, rather than a positive, output, and it may reflect underlying structural biases.

As for the final example, Frederick Wirt says:

The . . . oligopoly of private resources acts as a major force on the community.
. . . The injection of . . . outside capital sources does affect such major decisions . . . as: who shall work and for what returns; how such returns will be spent locally; what will be an available . . . tax source to support local public services; how traffic will move; and what public services will be needed. . . .
The decision to insert or withdraw business resources, then, is a decision certainly as important in scope and consequence as many others treated by students of community power.[10]

The decisions made in the boardrooms of General Motors, EXXON, Chase Manhattan Bank, and U.S. Steel—or at the executive meetings of local labor unions, for that matter—often are policies that significantly affect large segments of the urban population. They may also be authoritative in the sense that the public accepts these organizations' prerogatives to make such decisions; yet, they are not particularly "open" to much direct popular input.

In summary, systems theory defines the political system as institutions such as the legislative body, chief executive, and bureaucracy interacting with one another to process inputs and emit outputs in a way that will enable them to maintain adequate support from the citizenry. Dissatisfied segments of that citizenry, as pluralism suggests, can always align to form interest groups and freely pressure government for a change of policy. Nonetheless, strict adherence to this standard combination of traditional pluralism and systems theory leaves the researcher incapable of addressing the type of important policy-related questions raised by examples 4 and 5 above. These exercises of political power cannot be measured by looking only at overtly grouped input and the policy responses of the governmental branches. Consider the following two general cases in point, which focus on potential structural biases stemming from the interrelationship between America's political and economic systems.

Example: Class and Political Participation.   Income is quite unevenly distributed in the United States (table 2.1). For example, families in the top quintile make nearly as much money as the other 80 percent of the families combined, and this distribution has remained remarkably consistent over time.[11] In addition, many of the families in the lower 80 percent are able to achieve their incomes only by having two or three wage earners or by receiving cash grants from governmental public assistance programs.[12] Thus, there appear to be obvious income classes in the United States, and those classes seem to have distinct interests in the degree to which government does or does not reinforce this economic inequality.

One might reasonably expect to see a rather large group of low-income Americans becoming quite active politically in an attempt to alter a system that permits—and possibly even reinforces—such a maldistribution of income. Yet as Lester Milbraith and M. L. Goel conclude,

> It is almost universally true that the more prosperous persons are more likely to participate in politics than the less prosperous. . . . [And] the relationship between income and unconventional political participation is similar to the relationship between SES [socioeconomic status] and conventional political participation.[13]

What do such developments indicate about the political system in America? A traditional analyst could be expected to argue as follows. If large segments of the population are experiencing economic injustices, little precludes these people from seeking political redress by actively participating in the input processes. How can one suggest that the entire system may be structurally biased simply because the conversion process is not responding to interests some analysts claim people

TABLE 2.1   Family Income as a Percentage of National Income, 1947–1989

Population Quintile	1947	1950	1955	1960	1965	1970	1975	1980	1985	1989
Top fifth	43	43	42	41	41	41	41	42	43	45
Second fifth	23	23	23	24	24	24	24	24	24	24
Third fifth	17	17	18	18	18	18	18	18	17	17
Fourth fifth	12	12	12	12	12	12	12	11	11	10
Bottom fifth	5	5	5	5	5	5	5	5	5	4

SOURCE: U.S. Department of Commerce, Bureau of the Census, *Current Population Reports* (Washington, D.C.: Government Printing Office, 1947–1990); U.S. House of Representatives, Committee on Ways and Means, *1991 Green Book* (Washington, D.C.: Government Printing Office, 1991); unpublished data.

have? If these people really felt that certain governmental actions were in their best interests, they would be attempting to utilize the input channels available to bring about such policies. If political participation is unimpeded, and especially if no single elite continually dominates these open competitions, there is what reasonably can be viewed as a political system capable of adequately reflecting the community's various political interests.

But what if, no matter how open the procedures, the political race is biased from the start, significantly affecting who the winners and losers are likely to be before the contest even begins? Although technically open to every citizen, the input process certainly does appear to be more open to some than to others. As Milbraith and Goel and numerous other analysts of American political participation have concluded, the poor spend so much time eking out a living, they have little time for politics.[14] Lower status also makes them less likely to have direct contact with the decision makers in the course of their day-to-day lives, while lower income leaves them less money with which to purchase special consideration by making large campaign contributions. In addition, the dominant American political value system may well be leading the vast majority of American wage earners to accept their subordinate economic position as not being politically rectifiable. Thus, the political system may indeed be far more likely to reproduce, rather than rectify, the inequalities of the economic structure upon which it is built. To ignore the possibility of such structural biases seems to be empirically myopic.

Example: Urban Renewal.   Homes in and near the central business district are razed and their predominantly low-income residents displaced. The land is then sold below market value to venture capitalists. Meanwhile, the displaced poor are often never relocated. Between 1949 and 1961, 126,000 housing units were destroyed, displacing 113,000 families and 36,000 individuals; yet, only 28,000 new housing units were built in their stead.[15]

Analyzing such an issue in order to understand who has how much political power in a community, most traditional analysts would begin with the proposition that to minimize the introduction of the researcher's own values into a study, the analyst must first assume that people are the best judges of their own political interests. People's political activity, or lack thereof, can thus be seen as a reasonably accurate reflection of those interests. Consequently, the results of a relatively unimpeded competition in the political process should provide an acceptable reflection of the various political interests in that community.

For example, a city council is chosen by means of the standard American electoral process. The council confronts the issue of urban renewal. It proceeds to hold public hearings on the question of whether to raze an inhabited slum block to make way for the erection of a new corporate headquarters. After the hearings, the council votes to raze the neighborhood. Traditional analysts would then approach this political decision by first assuming that the council has effectively refereed a relatively fair competition between various interests in the city. If the procedures are judged to be physically unimpeded, it is assumed that the process was open enough not to close out any interest group from the outset.

But what if the majority of the council members are local business owners or are otherwise beholden to local business owners either because of this group's large campaign contributions or because of the overall importance of their investments to the community? If that were true, is it not possible that the final council decision might have been primarily a reflection of narrow elite interests rather than the broader interests of the community as a whole? And if such elitism is occurring in most of the city's public policy-making arenas, just how "open" is the political process in this community?

ELITE THEORY

Elite theorists recognize a certain degree of competition between interest groups; however, they reach very different conclusions about how open and fair the competition is. While power does not always equate precisely with one's amount of power resources (e.g., a resource-laden businessman may not realize that he has a fundamental interest at stake in a given political decision and thus may not commit his resources to the fray), the two correlate often enough to suggest strongly that those with the most political power resources generally will dominate governmental decisions.

Thus, a combination of resource-rich corporate elites and governmental officials, most drawn from the upper strata of society, will share many interests and work in unison to frame the political agenda in a way to guarantee that their interests will be served. They also will be capable of manipulating the mass public to the view that these elite interests represent what is best for the community as a whole.[16]

Floyd Hunter studied Atlanta in the 1950s and concluded that some 40 such people dominated local politics, speculating that they made their major decisions in hotel rooms, on golf courses, and similar restricted places.[17] In Houston, there is a long-standing rumor that the elites of that city would meet in Suite 8F of the Lomar Hotel to shape the city's crucial governmental decisions.[18]

Although they go beyond the traditional pluralist-systems framework and recognize the significantly unequal distribution of political power, elite theorists continue to focus on the decisions of private and governmental elites. But what if underlying structures all but preordain the decisional results virtually regardless of who holds these positions? For example, in a competitive private enterprise environment, any head of General Motors will have to continue to look for locations that will reduce production costs. And any mayor of Detroit will have little choice but to do whatever is necessary to appease General Motors given the city's reliance on that corporation for its economic well-being.

Most elite theorists seem reasonably comfortable with the pluralists' operational definition of political interest groups. To address questions of structural bias directly requires some objective determination of people's interests, which is an analytical jump most social scientists are unwilling to make. And that brings us to "structural analysis," which allows for the possibility that economic, social, and political rules and relationships may shape the political outcome no matter who lobbies or who actually makes the political decisions.

MARXIAN THEORY

> In the social production of their life, men enter into definite relations . . .
> of production which correspond to a definite stage of development of their
> material productive forces. The sum total of these relations of production
> constitutes the economic structure of society, the real foundation, on which
> rises a legal and political superstructure and to which correspond definite forms
> of social consciousness.[19]

Karl Marx hypothesized that societal institutions such as the political system
inevitably function to reinforce underlying economic class relationships. Thus,
if a society is organized under a capitalistic economic system—one in which a
small owning class controls business capital and uses it primarily to make profits
for themselves while everyone else receives wages for working for them—then
the political system will function to help maintain the ongoing domination of
the capitalist class over the subordinate mass of working people.

Marx's argument can be outlined in the following seven propositions:

1. The evolution and structure of any society arise from the dominant
   method of economic production, e.g., feudalistic, capitalistic, or socialistic. In other words, the historical development of a society's social and
   political relationships—its "superstructure"—will reflect and reinforce
   the domination and subordination existing in the economy.
2. Production under capitalism is accomplished when those who own the
   means of production engage workers in wage contracts. As a consequence,
   human labor becomes a commodity to be bought and sold in the marketplace. And when owners sell the resulting products for more than they
   paid workers to produce them, providing themselves with a return on
   invested capital, they are seen to be exploiting those workers by not
   allowing them to realize the full market value of their work.
3. Products are then distributed via the marketplace, utilizing the principle
   of supply and demand. Thus, production comes to be determined by the
   potential profitability of any given product, and consumption is based
   on one's ability to pay and not necessarily on one's needs.
4. Capitalistic enterprises must continue to expand in order to survive in
   a competitive marketplace. This expansion requires a relentless search
   for cheaper labor and materials, the production of as many potentially
   profitable items as possible, and the cultivation of every conceivable
   market for those products. All of this is done with little concern for the
   actual needs of society.
5. Owners and nonowners end up competing for scarce resources.
6. Paradoxes arise: resources are depleted; industrialization under capitalism has made people both interdependent and at the same time competitive with one another; a maldistribution of wealth and products
   leaves mansions at one end of town and slums at the other, while
   division of labor and subordination in the workplace mutilate people's

creative potential and leave them alienated from their work, and thus from themselves.

7. The nonowning classes are increasingly likely to become more aware of their common plight, as well as more united and better organized; however, revolution does not occur immediately or automatically. Cultural, social, and political institutions and values continue to reflect and reinforce the maldistribution of wealth and power in the society, as shown in institutions such as privately funded electoral campaigns and privately owned means of mass communication (the media), or beliefs that poverty results from one's own inadequacies, or that human beings are naturally individualistic and greedy, or that blacks are genetically inferior.[20]

An analogy often used to help explain the relationship between capitalism's political and economic systems is that of a coiled spring. Think of a large and powerful coiled spring being held down by the force of a person's hand. The coiled spring symbolizes the inherent tension in the underlying economic class relations: workers against owners. If the repressing hand, symbolizing superstructural devises, begins to weaken, at some point the spring will be unleashed. That release would represent the class tensions being forcefully resolved as the working class throws off the yoke of the capitalist class.

Two very important premises are in operation here. Marx is suggesting, first, that a class structure is inevitable under capitalism. Specifically, there will not only be a small owning class and a large nonowning class, but there will also be societal barriers all but precluding anyone from crossing those class lines. People are highly likely to remain in the class within which they are born, no matter how talented or hardworking they are. Second, if this class structure truly exists, it will possess inherent tensions. By this Marx means that it is in the best interest of the working class to control the means of production themselves rather than to work for a small class of owners. Should the workers become aware of this, political conflict will occur, and the political system may no longer be able to keep the workers from seizing a more proportionate share of control over the means of production.[21]

LIBERATION THEORY

But even Marx does not go far enough. Besides the political impact of economic structures such as the economic class system, there are other potentially significant underlying factors that also must be considered. Social structures such as racism, sexism, and homophobia cannot be ignored. Stokely Carmichael, Charles V. Hamilton, Catherine MacKinnon, and Richard Mohr remind us that these structural barriers may well shape political outcomes at least in part independently of the economic arrangement.[22]

Whether the force is the African American liberation movement, the women's liberation movement, or the gay liberation movement, they share certain fundamental concepts. Each begins by noting that regardless of economic position, a person's race, gender, or sexual preference may limit his or her political influence. Prejudices imbedded in the dominant ideology may predispose people to undervalue someone's potential contribution before that person even enters the political arena. The subordinate positions that evolve, then, stem from discrimination and are not the result of some natural reality. Thus, all these movements seek to unveil and combat individual and institutionalized oppression by a dominant group, whether this group is whites, males, or heterosexuals.

Liberationists attempt not only to dismantle the external constraints imposed by some portions of the dominant group, but also seek to reduce the degree to which their own members have internalized the value structure that helps perpetuate their subordination. Those members have come to believe some of the myths about their own limitations. Thus, the liberationists will seek to raise the consciousness of both their own members and those in the dominating group.[23]

AN ALTERNATIVE THEORETICAL APPROACH

At this point, it is important to return to Easton's model. If political analysis is to occur wholly within his original schema, with its inputs, outputs, and feedback, it will be difficult to consider underlying structures and their relationship to politics. Easton, however begrudgingly, limits his definition of a political system to the operation of the conversion mechanisms, and he proceeds to differentiate his political system from his political environment. Yet, Marx, for example, claims that the political system is intricately intertwined with the economic system, functioning primarily to reflect and reinforce an underlying economic class structure. And the liberation theorists note similar constraints imposed by underlying social hierarchies.

Rather than simply ignoring those possibilities, I define political environment to include people's relations to both the productive apparatus and entrenched social structures. How much wealth does one own? What is one's occupation? What is one's social status? Is one discriminated against because of certain social traits? The answers to these and similar questions have potential political relevance.

A political system is further defined to include the entire political environment. This means that a political decision will be any decision that affects the allocation of value, and these political decisions will be weighed in light of various social and economic realities. Thus, in response to the queries posed above, it will indeed be appropriate to study a General Motors decision to increase its manufacturing abroad, a decision with serious implications for thousands of local workers. And we will probe why the mayor of Detroit may not insist that General Motors abide by the letter of local pollution laws.

Therefore, anything with even remote potential relevance to the authoritative allocation of things of value in a society will be an appropriate subject of political analysis under this empirical framework. Politics simply cannot be separated from economic or social relations.

Easton's revised model is shown in figure 2.2. The revision allows analysis of any authoritative decision or nondecision that significantly affects the city as well as analysis of possible structural impediments to effective input into those decisions. Within this framework we can examine the input mechanisms of political parties and the mass media, as well as analyze the functioning of the traditional conversion mechanisms, such as the city council, mayor, and bureaucracy. The analysis is done in light of the potential constraints imposed on these political participants by the underlying economic, social, and political structures.[24]

The Postindustrial Urban Fiscal Crisis

For a better understanding of the link between the political, social, and economic systems in late twentieth-century urban America, it is important for us to incorporate a conceptual explanation of how the development of a postindustrial economy has affected urban politics. The work of George Sternlieb, James O'Connor, Frances Fox Piven, and Richard Cloward is helpful in this understanding.

The previous chapter showed the technological changes in production, transportation, and communications have given rise to the postindustrial economy. The next chapter will detail how these changes have made it possible for increasingly centralized and internationally dominant U.S. corporations to search this country and abroad for more profitable industrial environments. Numerous corporations, no longer tied to a particular geographic location, are now free to move to a less expensive environment. In addition, those individuals and families who can afford it have been choosing to live in the suburbs, even when they continue to work in the city. Thus as a good many industries mechanize or leave the postindustrial city, the ranks of the urban poor increase while their economic opportunities decline.

Sternlieb uses the metaphor of a child's sandbox to explain the changing city:

> A sandbox is a place where adults park their children in order to converse, play, or work with a minimum of interference. . . . There is some reward for children in all this. The sandbox is given to them as their own turf. Occasionally,

FIGURE 2.2 David Easton's Political System Model—Revised

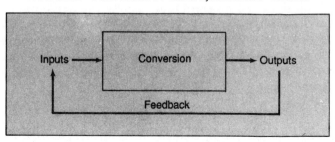

Political system (which includes the political environment)

fresh sand and toys are put in the sandbox, along with an implicit admonition
that things are furnished to minimize the level of noise and nuisance. If the
children do become noisy and distract their parents, fresh toys may be brought.
If the occupants of the sandbox choose up sides, and start bashing each other
over the head, the adults will come running, smack the juniors more or less indis-
criminately, calm things down, and then, perhaps, in an act of semi-contrition,
bring fresh sand and fresh toys, pat the occupants of the sandbox on the head,
and disappear once again into their adult involvement and pursuits.[25]

Sternleib suggests that a major function of America's cities has been changing.
Instead of serving as "processing centers" for less-skilled immigrants who came
to them hoping to begin their way up the economic ladder, the cities were becoming "sandboxes" wherein a growing bureaucracy preoccupied itself with "tending
to" those who had become increasingly marginal to the American economy.[26]

Meanwhile, cities face ever greater demands for services while their tax bases
decrease. To complicate matters further, the increasing mobility of capital and
better-off residents has created significant constraints on governmental policy.
City officials know well that departing firms take with them their share of the
tax base while the new unemployed are no longer available as a tax source. This
condition has obvious implications for the level of services that can continue to
be offered to the population as a whole; also, the need for social services will
have increased as a result of the layoffs. In order to remain solvent in the face
of such departures, the government is generally forced either to raise taxes or
to cut service levels, both of which are likely to drive away even more taxpayers.

O'Connor has developed a theory that helps explain the political dimension
of these events. He argues that capitalist economies require two contradictory
functions of their governments. He calls the first the "accumulation" function.
Here government attempts to guarantee an adequate supply of venture capital
and productive labor so that the capital-owning class can and will invest in ways
that will lead to stable economic growth. These enticements can include offering
corporations tax abatements and subsidies (social investment) as well as providing
roads, sewers, and so on (social consumption). He also refers to the "legitimation"
function. In this case, government compensates those who become economically
dislocated so that the necessary level of social harmony can be maintained, as by
providing maintenance services and social welfare programs (social expenditures).
As the ownership of capital becomes more concentrated, the capitalist class can
coerce the government into socializing even more of the costs of capital accumulation
and production while the benefits remain largely private. This situation requires the
government to spend more and more on social expenditures to retain legitimacy
with the nonowners. The growing outlay results in an ever increasing fiscal strain
on the city government as its revenues become more limited.[27]

The work of Piven and Cloward puts O'Connor's contradictory functions
into a historical context. Because the health of capitalist economies ultimately
depends in large part on the profitability of their private corporations, Piven and
Cloward suggest that governments in capitalist societies tend to reduce legitimation expenditures in favor of accumulation spending whenever possible. At a

certain point, however, the lower classes will no longer stand for this. They rebel both in the streets and at the ballot box. Government responds with repression, but it is also forced to alter its priorities. Thus social expenditures are increased both to quell the unrest and to legitimate the system; yet once the turmoil subsides, this aid is gradually once again redirected into accumulation expenditures.[28]

The following adaptation of Piven and Cloward's thesis offers a context within which certain past as well as more recent urban-related political events can be viewed.

Regulating the Poor

Phase 1: Without adequate governmental assistance in the postindustrial period, quality of life declines for the American underclasses; this is particularly true for the increasingly dependent urban poor.

Phase 2: A national movement emerges, such as the labor movement of the early twentieth century or the Civil Rights movement beginning in the 1940s. This activity gradually politicizes more and more of the oppressed, raises their consciousness, and provides a vehicle for organized protest.

Phase 3: Resentment and anger build, and the situation becomes volatile as in a Salvation Army breadline where unemployed men and women stand for hours or in a black ghetto where numerous unemployed teenagers are hanging out on a hot summer evening.

Phase 4: A "spark incident" occurs, often involving real or alleged police brutality, and some of the most economically and politically frustrated lash out in mass unrest, as did the unemployed in the 1930s or ghetto blacks in the 1960s.

Phase 5: Government responds with repression, but also with a liberalization of welfare requirements in an attempt to appease the unruly with large doses of direct relief. Examples are components of the New Deal and the Great Society.

Phase 6: As the domestic unrest subsides, direct relief is reduced, and limited work relief tends to be substituted.

Phase 7: Mounting demand for accumulation expenditures and acquiescence on the part of the previously disruptive poor lead to governmental belt tightening and a shift toward more loosely targeted block grants, such as Community Development Block Grants rather than programs designed primarily for the indigent.

Phase 8: Soon even the block grants begin to disappear.

(The cycle returns to Phase 1 and begins again.)[29]

It is important to remember that this is not simply a repetitive cycle. Rather, the disturbances intensify with each round and so does the fiscal predicament of government as it tries to quell the unrest. The problems seem to be inherent both in the class structure generated by the present economic system and the nature of the postindustrial economy.

Wealth remains very concentrated, and interclass mobility remains very difficult for those not owning capital. As postindustrial developments further reduce economic opportunities, nonowners of capital find themselves even further locked out of what little mobility is available. A permanent underclass results, yet it becomes increasingly better informed and better organized, especially when concentrated in segregated inner-city enclaves. So, each time the members of the underclass rebel, new legitimation expenditures tend to be added to those remaining from the last round of placations.

In addition, as corporate capital becomes concentrated, competition decreases between individual business firms; but as technological advances increase the mobility of this concentrated capital, competition increases among governmental units for the privilege of having such capital invested within their jurisdictions. In the process, accumulation expenditures escalate as well.

The fiscal crisis of the city generally appears first in those metropolises where social problems are most heavily concentrated and therefore where legitimation spending is proportionately highest. So far, this phenomenon has tended to occur in the oldest and largest industrial cities of the Frost Belt.[30] Their local resources have been overwhelmed rather quickly, and thus these cities have sought help from the state and federal levels of government. The state and federal levels, however, soon face fiscal problems of their own. The federal government has accumulated trillions of dollars in debt, spending hundreds of billions a year merely to pay the interest on the debt; accordingly, it tries to shift costly social programs to the states, jeopardizing often precarious state solvency as it attempts to balance its own budget. With each new round of underclass turbulence, it becomes increasingly more difficult for the city, state, or federal governments to stimulate capital investment in their jurisdictions and to appease their periodically rebellious, deprived classes.

The United States has passed through two of these regressively cyclical patterns in the postindustrial period and is conceivably entering a third. In the first, 1930–1960, massive amounts of New Deal relief followed considerable civil unrest, but these were reduced after a decline in domestic violence. In the second, 1960–?, the impact of both postindustrialism and racism on urban ghettos had been all but ignored for decades. This neglect culminated in the ghetto disturbances that occurred between 1962 and 1968. The Great Society programs were then instituted to address this unrest, stacked on top of what remained of the New Deal. Yet as the turbulence tapered off, these programs also were reduced. Thus a third round appears inevitable. As severe urban unemployment and poverty persist, ghetto unrest seems destined to erupt again. This time, however, for a number of reasons, it may be far more broadly based and require structural alterations in the political-economic system to be quelled.

Corporate capital has become more concentrated and more mobile and thus more capable of successfully demanding increased accumulation assistance from government. At the same time, both the central-city poor and the bureaucracy, which has arisen to provide legitimation services, have begun to organize themselves to protect their periodic gains. Inescapably, city governments are locked in a vicious cycle. They are required to spend more and more money to boost capital accumulation; yet it is increasingly difficult for them to retrieve the social expenditures surrendered during the previous rounds of civil unrest. Commenting on these conflicting demands on cities' ever scarcer revenues, the chief Washington lobbyist for the National League of Cities concludes, "This is a death spiral."[31]

CONCLUSION

Today's standard political science approach to public policy-making is to focus on the political behavior of individuals and groups within the existing political apparatus, utilizing variants of systems theory. Thus, the political, economic, and social structures get separated, and political activity is analyzed in an empirical vacuum of sorts. The justification is contained in a theory called pluralism, which as traditionally applied presumes enough openness in the political system that the analyst need not be concerned about structural biases favoring some groups of people over others.

This chapter took a critical view of the empirical myopia inherent in that traditional theoretical approach. In its place, a different theoretical framework was suggested, integrating pluralist theory, systems theory, elite theory, Marxian theory, and liberation theory. This integration allowed for a broader focus that encompassed potential links between politics and underlying economic, social, and political structures. The chapter also added the conceptualizations of Sternleib, O'Connor, Piven, and Cloward to help apply this framework to the urban level.

The result was a hybrid in which a community's political environment was defined to include economic and social structures; and the political system then was enlarged to include all of that political environment. With this expansion, interrelationships among economic, social, and political structures can now be analyzed as well.

NOTES

1. Kenneth Hoover, *The Elements of Social Scientific Thinking* (New York: St. Martin's Press, 1992), p. 34.
2. For example, see Arthur Bentley, *The Process of Government* (Chicago: University of Chicago Press, 1908); Earl Latham, "The Group Basis of Politics," *American Political Science Review* 46 (June 1952); David B. Truman, *The Governmental Process: Political Interests and Public Opinion* (New York: Knopf, 1971); Nelson Polsby, *Community Power and Political Theory* (New Haven: Yale University Press, 1980). Also see Robert Dahl, *Pluralist Democracy in the United States* (Chicago: Rand-McNally, 1967). For an explicit defense of this position, see Robert Dahl's articles in the *American Political Science Review* 52 and 60 (June 1958 and June 1966).
3. Truman, *The Governmental Process,* p. 33.
4. Ibid., p. 24.
5. For critical analysis of traditional pluralism, see Robert Dahl and Charles Lindbloom, *Politics, Economics, and Welfare* (Chicago: University of Chicago Press, 1976); Charles

Lindbloom, *Politics and Markets* (New York: Basic Books, 1977); Robert Dahl, *Dilemmas of Pluralist Democracy* (New Haven: Yale University Press, 1982); Michael Parenti, "Power and Pluralism," *Journal of Politics* 32 (August 1970); John Manley, "Neo-Pluralism," *American Political Science Review* 75 (June 1983); Kenneth Dolbeare and Murray Edelman, *American Politics* (Lexington, Mass.: D C Heath, 1981), pp. 40–41.

6. Gabriel Almond and G. Bingham Powell, *Comparative Politics: A Developmental Approach* (Boston: Little, Brown, 1966).

7. David Easton, *The Political System* (New York: Knopf, 1953); David Easton, *A Framework for Political Analysis* (Englewood Cliffs, N.J.: Prentice-Hall, 1965).

8. Ibid.

9. Peter Bachrach and Morton Baratz, "Two Faces of Power," *American Political Science Review* 56 (December 1962); Peter Bachrach and Morton Baratz, "Decisions and Nondecisions: An Analytical Framework," *American Political Science Review* 57 (September 1963).

10. Frederick Wirt, *Power in the City: Decision-Making in San Francisco* (Berkeley: University of California Press, 1974), p. 329.

11. Lester Thurow, *Zero-Sum Society* (New York: Basic Books, 1980); George Sternlieb and James Hughes, *Income and Jobs: USA* (New Brunswick, N.J.: Center for Urban Policy Research, 1984); *New York Times,* February 6, 1991.

12. Ibid.

13. Lester Milbraith and M. L. Goel, *Political Participation* (Chicago: Rand-McNally, 1977), pp. 96–97. Also see Sidney Verba and Norman Nie, *Participation in America* (New York: Harper & Row, 1972), part I and chap. 20.

14. For example, see Milbraith and Goel, *Political Participation,* p. 97.

15. For a more detailed discussion, see the National Commission on Urban Problems, *Building the American City* (New York: Praeger, 1969), p. 153; Martin Anderson, *The Federal Bulldozer* (Cambridge, Mass.: MIT Press, 1964); Bernard Frieden and Marshall Kaplan, *The Politics of Neglect* (Cambridge, Mass.: MIT Press, 1975); Susan Fainstein, Norman Fainstein, Richard Child Hill et al., *Restructuring the City* (White Plains, N.Y.: Longman, 1983); Nancy Kleniewski, "From Industrial to Corporate City: The Role of Urban Renewal," in William Tabb and Larry Sawers, eds., *Marxism and the Metropolis* (New York: Oxford University Press, 1978); Dennis Judd, *The Politics of American Cities* (Boston: Little, Brown, 1988), p. 273.

16. For examples, see Floyd Hunter, *Community Power Structure* (Chapel Hill: University of North Carolina Press, 1953); Jack Newfield and Paul DuBrul, *The Permanent Government* (New York: Pilgrim Press, 1981); C. Wright Mills, *The Power Elite* (New York: Oxford University Press, 1956); G. William Domhoff, *Who Rules America Now?* (New York: Simon and Schuster, 1983); G. William Domhoff, *Higher Circles: The Governing Class in America* (New York: Random House, 1971); G. William Domhoff, *The Bohemian Grove and Other Retreats: A Study in Ruling Class Cohesiveness* (New York: Harper & Row, 1975); Thomas Dye, *Who's Running America?* (Englewood Cliffs, N.J.: Prentice-Hall, 1983); Richard Hamilton, *Class and Politics in the United States* (New York: Wiley, 1972).

17. Hunter, *Community Power Structure.*

18. See *New York Times,* October 30, 1989.

19. Karl Marx, from his preface to "A Contribution to the Critique of Political Economy," as quoted in Robert Tucker, ed., *The Marx-Engels Reader* (New York: Norton, 1978), p. 4.

20. This outline was drawn from summaries presented in David Gordon, ed., *Problems in Political Economy* (Lexington, Mass.: D C Heath, 1977), pp. 3–10; Kenneth Dolbeare and Patricia Dolbeare, *American Ideologies* (Boston: Houghton Mifflin, 1976), chap. 8; Tabb and Sawers, *Marxism and the Metropolis,* pp. 3–17. This synthesis originally appeared in Marcus Pohlmann, *Political Power in the Postindustrial City* (New York: Associated Faculties Press, 1986).

   For more detailed discussion of Marx's theory of the state and its relationship to capitalism's economic class system, see Karl Marx and Frederick Engels, *Articles from the Nene Rheinische,* trans. S. Rvazanskava, ed. B. Isaacs (Moscow: Progress Publishers, 1964); D. Easton and K. H. Guddat, *Writings of the Young Karl Marx on Philosophy and Society* (New York: Doubleday, 1967); Karl Marx, preface to *A Contribution to the Critique of Political Economy*; Karl Marx, *The Grundrisse,* trans. Martin Nicolaus (Baltimore: Penguin, 1973); and Karl Marx and Frederick Engels, *The German Ideology,* ed. and trans. S. Rvazanskava (Moscow: Progress Publishers, 1964). For good secondary discussions of these views, see David McLellan, *The Thought of Karl Marx* (New York: Harper & Row, 1971), chaps. 4 and 6; John McMurtry, *The Structure of Marx's World View* (Princeton, N.J.: Princeton University Press, 1978), chaps. 3 and 4.

21. See Karl Marx, *The Poverty of Philosophy,* ed. Frederick Engels (Moscow: Progress Publishers, 1966); Karl Marx, *The Grundrisse*; Karl Marx, *Das Kapital,* ed. Frederick Engels (Moscow: Progress Publishers, 1965), especially vols. 1, 3, 4. For summaries of Marx's overall thinking, see McLellan, *The Thought of Karl Marx*; Tucker, *The Marx-Engels Reader.*

22. For example, see Stokely Carmichael and Charles V. Hamilton, *Black Power: The Politics of Liberation in America* (New York: Vintage, 1967); Catherine MacKinnon, *Toward a Feminist Theory of the State* (Cambridge, Mass.: Harvard University Press, 1989); Richard Mohr, *Gays/Justice* (New York: Columbia University Press, 1988).

23. For summary overviews of these conceptual frameworks, see Dolbeare and Dolbeare, *American Ideologies,* chaps. 10–11; Kenneth Hoover, *Ideology and Political Life* (Pacific Grove, Calif.: Brooks/Cole, 1987), chap. 8; Terence Ball and Richard Dagger, *Political Ideologies and the Democratic Ideal* (New York: HarperCollins, 1991), chap. 8.

24. A version of this theoretical synthesis was first presented in Marcus Pohlmann, *Black Politics in Conservative America* (White Plains, N.Y.: Longman, 1990), chap. 2.

   For other examples of such structural constraint models as they have been applied to urban politics, see Manuel Castells, *The City and the Grassroots* (Berkeley: University of California Press, 1983); Ira Katznelson, *City Trenches* (Chicago: University of Chicago Press, 1981); Pohlmann, *Political Power in the Postindustrial City*; Paul Peterson, *City Limits* (Chicago: University of Chicago Press, 1981); Bryan Jones and Lynn Bachelor, *The Sustaining Hand* (Lawrence: University of Kansas, 1986); Clarence Stone, *Regime Politics* (Lawrence: University of Kansas, 1989).

25. George Sternleib, "The City as Sandbox," *Public Interest* 25 (Fall 1971): 14–21.

26. Ibid., p. 17.

27. James O'Connor, *The Fiscal Crisis of the State* (New York: St. Martin's Press, 1973).

28. Frances Fox Piven and Richard Cloward, *Regulating the Poor: The Functions of Public Welfare* (New York: Vintage, 1971).

29. Ibid.; *New York Times,* March 13, 1992.

30. See Pohlmann, *Political Power in the Postindustrial City.*

31. Frank Shafroth, quoted in *Washington Post,* March 24, 1991, p. A6.

PART II

The Evolution of American Cities

CHAPTER 3

Economic Relationships

From that first moment of bigness, from about the mid-19th century onward, the successes and failures of American cities have depended upon the unplanned outcomes of the private market's demand for workers, its capacities for dividing land, building houses, stores, and factories, and its need for public services. . . . What the private market could do well American cities have done well; what the private market did badly, or neglected, our cities have been unable to overcome.[1]

—Sam Bass Warner

As Sam Bass Warner concludes, the fate of U.S. cities has been tied to the vagaries of private economic decisions and developments. *Economics* refers to how a society's goods and services are produced and distributed. In a private enterprise economy where most means of production are controlled by individual owners, the fate of everyone is tied to whatever those owners decide will be the best way to maximize their profits. Thus, new technologies continually are developed to reduce the costs of producing goods (e.g., robotized assembly lines) and services (e.g., checkout scanners in grocery stores) as well as to market these goods and services to the public (e.g., stylized individual automobiles). Such technological change can have sweeping impacts on where people will live, how they will be employed, what they will produce, what their standards of living will be, how secure their lives will be, and even how political power will be distributed.

In a very real sense, urban history in the United States has revolved around the process of private industrialization. In the *preindustrial* period, cities tended to be small commerce centers with relatively homogenous populations and minimal governmental services. *Industrialization* brought an urban explosion as factories sprang up in waterfront cities and diverse populations flocked to work in them. This population shift required a much more formal governmental system to provide far more public services in order for the urban economic machine to function smoothly. Then, *postindustrialism* left the previously industrialized cities holding the proverbial bag and many of these cities began to decay, with significant implications for their residents.[2]

In a private enterprise system in which economic change normally just happens rather than being governmentally planned, people soon resign themselves to riding the roller coaster of private economic decisions and changes. Some of the most basic of these private economic events profoundly affected the evolution of urban economies in the United States. The economic arrangement that has evolved forms the underlying economic structure in the current political environment.

PREINDUSTRIAL PERIOD

In the U.S. setting, the preindustrial period lasted until the early nineteenth century. The national economy remained predominantly agricultural during this era, with most of the country's population living and working on small farms in the countryside. The cities that sprang up often were little more than trading centers for this farm-based economy.

National Developments

The preindustrial urban economy was based primarily on commerce. Without the process of incorporation to allow a number of individuals to pool their capital, most commercial ventures remained rather small. Nonetheless, trading was spurred by developments such as paper currency, insurance, credit facilities, and advertising. Soon these commercial businesses began to grow and diversify. By the late eighteenth century, people also began to manufacture goods for market purposes, with the work often being done in individual homes on a contract basis or to be sold in small shops run by the producers themselves.[3] Despite the emergence of small-scale manufacturing, commerce remained the order of the day. Cities in the East, for example, were engaged in seven times more commerce than manufacturing.[4] As the frontier shifted west and river cities developed along major waterways such as the Mississippi and Ohio Rivers, this commerce-to-manufacturing mix tended to persist.[5]

Prior to the Revolutionary War, commerce was tied to British mercantilism. Americans were forced by law and encouraged by tax breaks to export large quantities of raw materials to Great Britain and to import many of Britain's finished products. In the process, Britain gained both economically and politically. Not only did the mother country secure a stable supply of raw materials (especially foodstuffs), as well as a significant market for its products, but it was also easier for the British to maintain political control with American life and trade centered in a manageable number of places.

Cities

The cities where these economic events occurred were both "clustered" and "pedestrian" in nature. They were clustered in the sense that their populations had settled as close as possible to such facilities as military forts and sea and river ports; and because walking was the most common mode of transportation, residential areas rarely stretched farther than two miles beyond the commercial center of these pedestrian cities. There were, however, some noteworthy differences between waterfront and inland towns.

The waterfront towns were larger, and they were the first to experience some of the key changes taking place in society at large. In particular, both the economy and urban land use were becoming more specialized. As the economy expanded, a merchant no longer needed to serve as his or her own shipbuilder, banker, insurer, attorney, importer, exporter, wholesaler, and retailer. These jobs were being performed more and more by specialists, as were a number of crafts such as cabinetmaking, baking, joining, and coopering. Soon this specialization came to be reflected in the city environment. The downtown area was the location of markets, banks, and other commercial services; the waterfront was for warehouses and shipping. In terms of residential location, the wealthy lived closest to the city center while the less wealthy lived farther out.[6]

The invention of the Conestoga wagon helped to facilitate overland travel, which contributed to the proliferation of inland cities. These landlocked towns were considerably smaller and less complex than their coastal counterparts, and they were often little more than trading outposts at first. As late as 1817, shipping time between two cities such as New York and Cincinnati was 52 days.[7] Inland trade was quite limited as a result, slowing the growth of these inland cities. Nonetheless, technological developments soon would begin to eradicate the differences between the two city forms and to spur urbanization.

INDUSTRIAL PERIOD

As private entrepreneurs discovered ways to produce and distribute goods on a much larger sale, the prospects of massive profits fueled an economic revolution. From a predominantly agriculturally based society, the country soon became an industrialized and urbanized one.

National Developments

Howard Chudacoff has defined industrialization as the "coordinated development of economic specialization, mass mechanized production, mass consumption, and mass distribution of goods and services."[8] As the nineteenth century opened, economic specialization clearly had already begun, and the potential existed for greater consumption. The invention of steam power had helped to revolutionize commerce. The adoption of the system of government established in the U.S. Constitution helped stabilize commerce by allowing for more trade regulation. Owners of wealth could now pool their resources through the process of incorporation, while at the same time allowing the legal liability of their joint businesses to be separate from that of the individual investors.[9] Concurrently, the development of a more formalized and extensive banking system further spurred the accumulation of capital by allowing venture capitalists to borrow and invest other people's money. All these developments, ultimately combined with war-inflated profits and protective tariffs, helped to launch industrialization. Soon American manufacturers were mass producing steel, woolen goods, farm machinery, and processed foods; and large cities were providing them with access to labor, materials, ancillary services, and local, intercity, and international markets.[10]

The development of canals and railroads also significantly expanded opportunities for industrialization, as they reduced reliance on existing waterways and thus allowed more resources and finished products to be shipped to and from more places and far more quickly. For example, there were 2,800 miles of railroad track in 1840, some 30,600 by 1860, and 254,000 in 1916. By 1916, trains carried more than three-quarters of all intercity freight and nearly all the intercity passengers.[11]

The number of people employed in manufacturing jobs increased by 127 percent between 1820 and 1840, as these individuals left their farms or small town trades to work for a wage in the emerging factories.[12] And that was just the beginning: those working for a wage increased from 7.7 million in 1849 to 48 million by 1929.[13] By the turn of the century, there were some 40,000 corporations in the country, and manufacturing accounted for more than one-half of all commodities produced.[14] Industrial giants were beginning to appear: United States Steel, General Electric, International Harvester, and American Telephone and Telegraph.

Cities

Creating sizable manufacturing firms and clustering a number of these large infant industries in single places was economical for at least three primary reasons: economies of scale, trade efficiency, and agglomeration.[15] *Economies of scale* exist when a "proportionate change in all inputs leads to a greater proportionate change in output."[16] In other words, a given manufacturer can make more money with a larger production operation. To build one car per day on a small assembly line will cost more per unit than to build 100 on a much larger line. By minimizing duplication, the firm can minimize the need for land, expensive equipment, and maintenance and administrative personnel.

Trade efficiency was achieved by locating factories along main waterways and railroad lines. Thus, raw materials could be received and finished products shipped at lower costs. In addition, it was most profitable for retail distributors to be located close together so as to provide easier access for customers, as in department stores clustering together in the center of the city.

Agglomeration was the logical process by which related industries located near one another. Transportation and communication costs could be minimized by having suppliers and distributors close by. By locating in cities, industries had ready access to such private-sector services as banks and insurance companies as well as government services such as education, police, fire, and sanitation.

Urbanization also gave firms access to a large and diversified work force which generally was able to remain employed year-round despite seasonal and cyclical variations in the production and sales of any particular firm. In addition, it offered a large and diverse local market that helped to overcome fluctuations in popular demand. Last, the intense interpersonal interaction characteristic of cities also helped to spawn innovation.[17]

Large cities, then, were born along primary transportation arteries, and they contained a variety of manufacturers, service suppliers, distributors and the work force necessary to provide the labor. As monopolization of industries proliferated in the latter nineteenth century, there was a tendency for major manufacturing to concentrate in a handful of very large cities—each with its own network of suppliers and markets.[18]

Yet even before industrialization or monopolization were well under way, a transportation revolution had begun to spur decentralization of both people and businesses away from the increasingly congested and expensive city center. The bicycle began to replace the horse as a means of intracity travel, while the horse-drawn streetcar eventually gave way to electrified trolleys. Soon commercial "strips" emerged along the trolley lines and remained the sites of much urban retail trade until shopping malls emerged in the postindustrial period. In addition, electrified travel expanded city boundaries to roughly a six-mile radius.[19] Finally, cable cars, subways, and elevated trains developed as means of mass transportation within the city; and before long, a number of the "fringe settlements" that had been emerging throughout the period actually began to incorporate as separate cities. Despite a stirring of suburbanization between 1890 and 1930, there remained enough urban growth to support both city and suburbs.[20]

Intercity transportation was spurred by the development of the steamboat, a web of canals, and the rapid growth of the railroad. As the nineteenth century drew to a close, the invention of suspension bridges, the use of asphalt and brick for paving, and above all, the internal combustion engine were setting the stage for another very significant innovation: the automobile.

POSTINDUSTRIAL PERIOD

Beginning in the 1930s and really accelerating after the 1960s, the scene began to change. Veritable revolutions in transportation, communication, and manufacturing technology would reshape the urban landscape in very significant ways. Owners of venture capital would be able to invest their money virtually anywhere on earth, and most individual businesses would be far freer to move to more profitable locations without disrupting their production or distribution schemes. Technological developments would fundamentally alter the manufacturing process so that an ever larger portion of the labor force would find work in the service sector of the economy. All these changes gradually would have significant economic implications for large U.S. cities.

National Developments

As figure 3.1 indicates, the number of Americans owning automobiles increased tremendously over the first half of the twentieth century. This trend also corresponded to the federal government's enthusiasm for building highways. Following

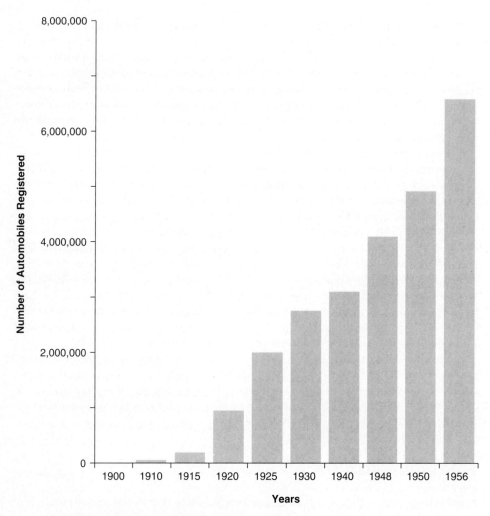

FIGURE 3.1 U.S. Automobile Registrations, 1900–1956

SOURCE: Sam Bass Warner, *The Urban Wilderness* (New York: Harper & Row, 1972), p. 43; Charles Glaab and A. Theodore Brown, *A History of Urban America* (New York: Macmillan, 1976), p. 252.

a number of congressional studies during the 1930s and such events as the General Motors Futurama exhibit at the 1939 New York World's Fair, highway construction mushroomed after World War II. In particular, it was spurred by the 1956 Federal Aid Highway Act.

Consequently, the development of the automobile and the proliferation of highways significantly accelerated the decentralization of the nation and its individual metropolitan centers. The development of air travel and advanced telecommunications further fueled this dispersion. It was becoming increasingly possible for a business to have access to many of the advantages only cities had long been able to provide without locating within the confines of a large waterfront city, or any city at all for that matter.

The mechanization of production was of equal importance. Machines were developed that could accomplish many of the tasks previously done by human hands. With the development of robotics, even more specialized human tasks could be performed mechanically.[21] In addition, computers could be programmed to do much of the record keeping and billing that used to require large clerical staffs. "Artificial intelligence programming" also began to be developed whereby a computer could actually engage in problem solving by a process of random calculations until the problem was solved.[22] Thus, even some white-collar positions were in jeopardy.

Mechanization made much of the manufacturing process capital intensive instead of labor intensive, leaving more of the available jobs in nonmanufacturing areas—for example, professional and personal services in such fields as medicine, insurance, and retail sales. Where manufacturing was still the most common form of employment as late as 1979, it would be surpassed by trades and services by the mid-1980s.[23] By that time, more people would be employed by McDonald's restaurants than by either General Motors of United States Steel. By 1990, the number of jobs in health care was growing at a rate three times faster than the growth of the population as a whole.[24] Meanwhile, industrial employment shifted from heavy industry (steel and automobiles) to lighter high-technology industries (electronics, computers, aerospace, and chemicals) and the manufacturing of consumer goods (appliances, furnishings, and sports equipment).

These shifts had a marked impact on the wages of American workers. Clearly a number of highly skilled positions have been created in this more service-oriented economy; examples are physical therapists, lawyers, and computer programmers. Their work involves extensive training and knowledge and tends to draw the kinds of wages, benefits, skill development, and opportunities for advancement that place these workers in the primary labor market. However, this is a labor status that also has been attainable by many unionized blue-collar workers in the past as unionized manufacturing industries allowed many unskilled workers to earn a good living and at the same time develop skills and advance.

Unfortunately, far more of the new positions fall into what has been called the secondary labor market, such as jobs at fast food restaurants, discount stores, and private hospitals. These jobs often pay little more than minimum wage; offer few, if any, benefits (health insurance, paid vacation and holidays, retirement plan); involve little to no skill development or opportunities for significant advancement; and are often only part-time.[25]

Overall, the postindustrial economy has tended to create jobs at the top and bottom of the employment scale. There are ever fewer stable bottom rungs upon which underskilled workers or even small-scale entrepreneurs can begin their way up the ladder of economic success.[26]

Since reaching a peak of roughly 34 percent in the late 1940s, the proportion of U.S. workers belonging to labor unions has declined steadily and is now less than half that—even less if government workers are excluded.[27] Corporate mobility leaves many workers afraid to organize, while companies are becoming much less inhibited about firing striking union workers and replacing them with nonunion "scabs."[28] This trend, combined with the changing nature of much of the employment itself, has meant a significant alteration in the wage picture.

Focusing on the period from 1973 to 1982 and considering only constant-dollar income distributions, George Sternleib and James Hughes found growth in jobs paying more than $35,000 per year and less than $15,000 per year, but a significant decline in those paying between $15,000 and $35,000. In these years, the United States lost more than a million manufacturing jobs that paid an annual average wage of $17,000, while it added an even larger number of nonmanu-facturing positions paying about $12,000. Thus, the proportion of workers making between 80 percent and 120 percent of the average wage has been declining significantly in recent years as the distribution skews toward the top and bottom of the scale.[29] Real-dollar wages for production and nonsupervisory personnel have been eroding across the nation as a whole, with nearly one-half of all new jobs created between 1979 and 1985 paying a family head poverty-level wages at most.[30]

As additional indicators of this phenomenon, the number of part-time workers has been growing at twice the rate of the total work force; lump-sum cash bonuses rapidly have been replacing fixed wage increases, leaving base pay rates the same. Related to this trend, an ever smaller percentage of the work force is covered by cost-of-living adjustments, which tie wage increases to the rises in the federal government's Consumer Price Index.[31] Not too surprisingly, standards of living have begun to decline. The proportion of people owning their own homes, for example, has been dropping steadily: home ownership by household heads between the ages of 30 and 34 fell from 60.2 percent in 1973 to 53.6 percent in 1989, and from 23.4 percent to 17.6 percent for those under 25 years of age.[32] Meanwhile, the number of persons not covered by health insurance has risen by approximately one-third during this same period.[33]

Cities

As a result of the transportation, communication, and technological developments described above, the number and size of inland cities continued to increase rapidly throughout the twentieth century. In addition, the configuration of most cities changed. From small pedestrian cities clustered around a fort or waterfront, they were becoming distended metropolises extending more than 20 square miles, functionally segregated, and reaching outward in a star-shaped fashion along the various transportation lines. Consequently, the more affluent workers were no longer required to live in the congested and deteriorating inner ring immediately surrounding the downtown area.

Businesses, on the other hand, were freer to escape the various costs of locating in the downtown sector of the older cities, costs related to congestion, crime, taxes, government regulation, and the higher price of land. Many industrial firms could and did move to the suburbs; the transportation and communications revolutions allowed them the benefits of agglomeration, economies of scale, and trade efficiency without clustering in the center of the older waterfront cities. In 1930, three-quarters of all metropolitan manufacturing occurred within central cities rather than in the suburbs. By 1980 it was just the opposite, with only one-quarter based in the city.[34]

As further indications of the suburbanization trend, by 1980 four out of five United Auto Worker bargaining units were located in suburban plants while some 80 percent of U.S. steel was being produced in the suburbs.[35] In addition, the central city segment of metropolitan retail sales has declined from 95 percent in 1920 to less than 50 percent. In cities such as Boston, Detroit, Pittsburgh, St. Louis, and Washington, D.C., the figure is less than 20 percent. In Newark, it is only 10 percent. Political scientists John Bollens and Henry Schmandt note that this trend is visible across all regions of the country.[36]

Following the second world war, *multilocational* corporations also began to proliferate. A beer manufacturer that had once brewed all its beer at one central urban location and shipped the finished product to its various markets via refrigerated train cars now began to produce and ship from any number of separate breweries located in cities across the country.[37] In addition, a number of these firms were becoming *multinational* as well, producing and distributing to a global market from factories scattered around the world. This trend came to be most apparent after World War II, when U.S. investors began investing heavily in a number of the recovering war-torn nations abroad. It really began to accelerate in the mid-1970s as economic competition from a recovered Japan, Western Europe, and even the Third World began to cut into the profits of large U.S.-based companies. Competition from abroad set off what Barry Bluestone and Bennett Harrison have called the "hypermobility of [U.S.] capital," with aggressive searches for production settings that provide cheaper and more abundant resources, less expensive and more pliant labor, and a high degree of political stability with little chance of government expropriation.[38] Furthermore, some of the last remaining legal impediments to such mobility have recently been removed by National Labor Relations Board and federal court decisions.[39]

The resulting shifts in capital have come in a variety of ways. The overt physical relocation of an entire plant is relatively rare, although it does happen on occasion. For example, a South Korean firm arranged to purchase equipment from an abandoned automobile plant in Pennsylvania so that it could reconstruct the plant at home in anticipation of increased Asian demand for automobiles.[40] Less drastic and more common are such techniques as redirecting profits and depreciation allowances, gradually relocating pieces of physical capital, laying off workers while contracting out their work to cheaper plants, and resorting to shutdowns or bankruptcy.[41]

One aspect has been consistent. These ever more mobile corporations and the investors who own them have less and less loyalty to particular cities, no matter how long they have been producing there, no matter how much support they have received from the city's people and government over the years, and no matter how dependent upon them the local communities have become. If more money can be made elsewhere, the economic marketplace dictates that they shift investments regardless of the implications for the city, state, or even nation they are leaving behind.[42]

U.S. firms have been ceding more and more of our cities' labor-intensive manufacturing to foreign nations. As President Jimmy Carter's Urban and Regional Policy Group concluded,

Foreign industrial competition has grown in America and has had a growing impact on the domestic economy and cities. The United States is losing manufacturing jobs to foreign countries, especially in labor-intensive industries. . . . Air freight today is fast and relatively cheap, so foreign workers can perform labor-intensive steps related to production, while domestic workers carry out the skilled or capital-intensive steps.[43]

Corporate Rationale for Relocation.   Whether it be to the surrounding suburbs, another state, or a foreign country, industrial corporations have given a variety of reasons for why they chose, or will choose, to invest elsewhere. These reasons include such "push" factors as worker incompetence and high wages; no room to expand; and crime, taxes, and government regulation, especially antipollution laws that are more restrictive in already polluted areas.[44] The president of Republic Steel speaks of the "monstrous growth" of government regulation. A senior vice-president of Procter and Gamble cites "urban terrorism." The chairman of McGraw-Hill wants a "more intelligent trade-off between taxes paid and the quality of services rendered." An executive vice-president of Union Carbide complains about the "so-called high school graduates who can't even read." The chairman of the Masonite Corporation adds that "policies which hold companies responsible for all past social inequities or responsible for the correction of the same, under threat of sanctions or fines, do not encourage a company willingly to assume the risk of central city residency."[45]

Meanwhile, "pull" factors lure companies to alternative locations. These factors include more and cheaper land on which to expand, less crime, a more temperate climate, less restrictive zoning, lower and more regressive taxes, a significantly lower rate of unionization, and lighter population densities that allow for a larger amount of pollution given existing pollution regulations.

Suburban governments are able to keep their tax burdens lower than those of their adjacent central cities by having private garbage and trash collections, volunteer fire departments, and similar nongovernmental services. In particular, most benefit from having a much larger tax base and a far smaller poverty population requiring *legitimation* spending. They also may be able to hold down corporate taxes by utilizing their sizable residential property-tax base.[46]

On the other hand, the gap between city and suburban rents and clerical salaries has been declining, and some of the larger suburbs are beginning to experience urbanlike problems of congestion and crime as services are less extensive and necessary infrastructure has not kept pace with their overall growth.[47] Rather than suggesting a return to the cities, however, such suburban push factors may simply add further fuel to the inclination of corporations to expand overseas where wages and government regulation are often considerably lower. In terms of wages, for instance, the average factory wage in South Korea, Brazil, Mexico, Hong Kong, Taiwan, and Singapore combined is less than $3 per hour, compared to $13.09 in the United States.[48]

Urban Metamorphosis.   As a result of these trends, urban economies have undergone a considerable metamorphosis. Manufacturing and retail centers have been giving way to office complexes, specialty services, entertainment facilities, convention centers, and government buildings. In addition, although the city may well get the corporate headquarters, the suburbs are getting the divisional headquarters, regional sales offices, and research and development laboratories.[49] Where new shopping malls have been erected and grand hotels refurbished in the central business district, much of this has been done with the help of city subsidies and tax breaks.[50]

U.S. cities currently fall at a variety of places along this evolutionary continuum. Older cities like New York, Chicago, Boston, Philadelphia, Cleveland, and San Francisco have made the transition from an industrial economic base to one more reliant on service, finance, and government employment. Newer cities like Phoenix and San Diego actually began at this stage for all intents and purposes. Meanwhile, older cities like Detroit, Buffalo, Youngstown, and Gary are still undergoing industrial decline but have yet to make as full a transition to a more service-based economy.[51]

Despite the concern that has arisen over the continuing flight of population and industrial corporations away from the older industrialized cities, David Birch sees a potential "silver lining." Putting the question of job availability aside for the moment, he claims that there is no clear relationship between the growth or decline of a city's population and its fiscal health:

> Declining urban areas may be saved by the city dwellers who desert them. It may just be that our cities would be better places in which to live and work if their densities and population could fall to half of their present levels. . . . Few would argue that the extraordinarily high densities of the cities . . . are desirable. Most of the people who live in these cities spend their spare time plotting escape routes, and many are now following these routes.[52]

Quite obviously, it all depends upon who is left in the central city and what is left for those living there.

The reality is that those living in may of the older industrial cities have become poorer amid deteriorating economic circumstances. Those moving out have clearly been financially more well-to-do than the mass of those remaining. In New York City, for example, city residents made 71 percent of what their suburban counterparts did in 1969, but only 64 percent a decade later; and this relative decline was even more extreme in cities such as Newark, St. Louis, Baltimore, Cleveland, Milwaukee, and Philadelphia.[53] Nationwide, per capita income in large cities is now less than 60 percent that of their suburbs.[54]

Jobs. In the 1930s, approximately three-quarters of all U.S. manufacturing occurred within a corridor of large cities which ran from Chicago and Louisville in the West to Boston and Baltimore in the East. But between 1948 and 1972, St. Louis lost 6,000 retail and 869 manufacturing businesses. In the year 1970 alone, it saw 43 corporations move to its suburbs. Between 1958 and 1972, New York City lost 32 percent of its plants; Detroit, 29 percent; Baltimore, 24 percent; and so on. Between 1970 and 1972 alone, Boston lost 75 factories; Cleveland lost Stouffer Food's Frozen Food Division, National Screw and Manufacturing, National Copper and Smelting, and the headquarters of the B. F. Goodrich

Chemical Company, among others; Detroit lost S. S. Kresge, Delta and Pan American Airlines, R. L. Polk Publishers, and Circus World Toys, to name only a few.[55]

In turn, manufacturing jobs were lost: New York City lost 18 percent of its manufacturing jobs between 1960 and 1970. When Philadelphia lost 100 blue-collar manufacturing jobs, 70 of them had been held by city residents. When it added 100 white-collar office jobs, however, only 30 were held by city residents.[56] Wilbur Thompson concluded that

> in broad terms, the large metropolitan areas have been evolving into two easily identifiable, although heavily overlapping, economies. The central city is more and more a place of business and professional service—the workplace of lawyers, consultants, financiers, and officials of all kinds; the suburbs are more and more the heart of the manufacturing district.[57]

Putting it another way, Sternlieb stated, "There is a mismatch between the people who live in cities and the new kinds of functions cities have taken on."[58] So, what does that leave for many of the lesser-skilled urban residents?

UNEMPLOYMENT   Although unemployment rates vary considerably by city (see figure 3.2 for unemployment rates in 12 select cities[59]), unemployment has become a way of life for many of today's urban dwellers. Except for the years in the 1960s immediately following Lyndon B. Johnson's War on Poverty efforts, cities have absorbed a disproportionate share of national unemployment since the end of World War II. In our sample of 12 select cities, for instance, 8 of them have unemployment rates that exceed the national average (see figure 3.2). It is also important to note that unemployment figures actually understate the problem.

SUBEMPLOYMENT   In the old central cities in particular, unemployment figures can be doubled if "discouraged workers"—those no longer looking for work— are included.[60] In addition, there is the trend toward involuntary part-time work, particularly common in retail stores and restaurants. These positions allow employers to pay lower wages and provide fewer benefits than they do for their full-time employees. The federal Bureau of Labor Statistics estimates that the number of such jobs increased 121 percent between 1970 and 1990.[61]

Many city residents lack the skills increasingly required for work in the primary labor market; they often do not have access to the transportation necessary to reach the growing number of such positions that have come to be located in outlying areas.[62] Thus, those of them fortunate enough to have found work often toil in the less attractive secondary sector of the labor market. Here they are employed primarily by private service-producing businesses where unionization is rare, wages are low, benefits are often all but nonexistent, and their job futures are tenuous at best.

A U.S. Bureau of the Census survey of residents in 51 urban areas found 60 percent of those who are employed not making enough for a "decent standard of living," half of them not earning even poverty-level incomes. The survey also

FIGURE 3.2 Unemployment Rate, 1990

SOURCE: U.S. Department of Commerce, Bureau of the Census, *Census of the Population* (Washington, D.C.: Government Printing Office, 1990).

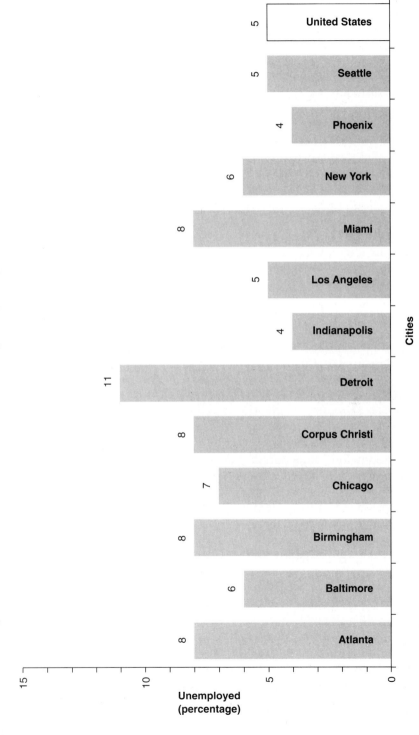

found that in New York City, for example, when the unemployed, discouraged workers, involuntary part-timers, and those underemployed are combined, "subemployment" was in the vicinity of 40 percent to 67 percent.[63]

Sweatshops, home work, and child labor, most banned by law earlier in this century, are quietly beginning to reappear as urban residents feel compelled to take whatever employment is available. Workplace regulations requiring such things as minimum wages, maximum hours, opportunities to organize labor unions, and a prohibition on child labor disappear rather quickly in the small and crowded makeshift factories hidden away in abandoned buildings or among individuals compelled to do their work at home. The workers involved in these largely illegal enterprises are estimated to number in the hundreds of thousands, thousands of whom are children. The apparel industry is one of the biggest culprits, and undocumented aliens are among the most vulnerable employees. An indication of the regulatory backsliding in this area was the Reagan Administration's lifting in 1988 of the federal ban on the home manufacture of most types of jewelry and clothing.[64]

Thus, there is far less likelihood of today's ghetto residents working their way out of the urban underclasses. This is true despite the documented willingness of most of them to work.[65]

Poverty.   While more people are leaving the cities than are coming to live in them, the average income of those who leave clearly exceeds that of both those who come and those who have remained. This trend is estimated to have cost cities at least $48 billion in taxable income between 1970 and 1976 alone.[66] The 1980 census figures indicated that middle-income blacks had also begun to depart, leaving the cities with even higher proportions of impoverished inhabitants. As Peter Gluck and Richard Meister stated, "Those cities that have been unable to expand find themselves with an increasing lower-class population and decreasing sources of revenue."[67]

Nationwide, poor people have come increasingly to be concentrated in central cities.[68] As a result, by the mid-1980s more than one out of every five central-city residents lived below the federal government's poverty level, that is, below the $10,178 a family of four was seen as needing for a minimally comfortable standard of living in 1984. A significantly higher percentage lived below this level in a number of the older industrialized cities (see figure 3.3). And, a 1989 study by the National League of Cities indicated that the poor were becoming poorer and less likely to escape their plight.[69]

As to the question of whether the nation has been making progress toward eliminating poverty, there is a considerable amount of debate.[70] Nonetheless, both sides in the debate agree on at least three points: (1) "relative poverty" (inequality of income) has changed very little, if at all, in recent years; (2) the "hard-core poor" (households headed by a single woman, the elderly, the unskilled, and/or the undereducated—especially if the family or person is African American) have remained locked in trying circumstances; and (3) the government's very definition of poverty excludes many who could reasonably be placed in that category.[71]

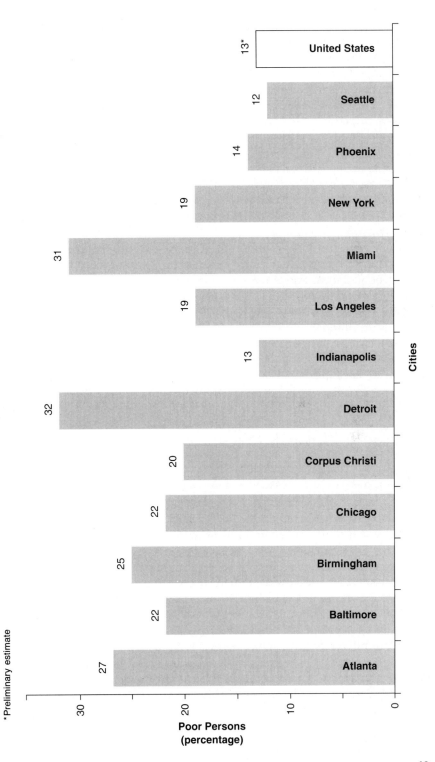

FIGURE 3.3 Poverty Rate, 1990

SOURCE: U.S. Department of Commerce, Bureau of the Census, *Census of the Population, 1990* (Washington, D.C.: Government Printing Office, 1990).

*Preliminary estimate

49

Even using the government's definition of poverty, the 1980 President's Urban and Regional Policy Group Report indicated that poverty had been declining everywhere in the nation during the 1970s *except* in the large central cities where real incomes had actually decreased. In addition, the metropolitan areas of the United States saw white poverty decline by 5 percent during this period while the level of black poverty increased by 21 percent. Marshall Kaplan, who was then the deputy assistant secretary for urban policy in the Department of Housing and Urban Development, stated that "all of this suggests a permanent underclass"; and it is in the ghettos of the oldest and largest central cities that this "permanent underclass" all too often is found.[72]

Back to the Cities?   Many, however, are placing considerable faith in what is called a variety of things from "revitalization" to "gentrification."[73] In general, *revitalization* has come to mean the conversion of previously declining areas into viable business, service, and/or recreational places. Examples include the Navy Pier in Chicago, the Quincy Market in Boston, Harbor Place in Baltimore, Union Station in St. Louis, and the South Street Seaport in New York City.[74]

By *gentrification,* analysts most commonly refer to the rehabilitation of neighborhoods, a process in which they are converted from lower-income enclaves to middle- and upper-income residential areas. Examples of this phenomenon include Bolton Hill in Boston, Society Hill and Queens Village in Philadelphia, the West End of St. Louis, and Georgetown, Capitol Hill, and Adams-Morgan in Washington, D.C.[75]

The overall success of such transformations has, however, come into question. As Richard Nathan concluded:

> We entered this research . . . with an idea that some of the older cities have improved social and economic conditions as a result of neighborhood invest-ment . . . . But when you look at all of the cities as a whole, there's no evidence the conditions of the cities are improving.[76]

Sternleib and Kristina Ford have referred to the successes as small;[77] and the Congressional Joint Economic Committee found that in the nation's 30 largest cities, for every neighborhood renovated in recent years, several others have slipped into disinvestment and decay.[78] Michael Schill and Nathan Glazer conclude that the potential for further gentrification is seriously limited by a shortage of renewable housing as well as the diminishing attractiveness of these cities due to the overall declines in their economies and services.[79]

Sternleib suggests that two distinct "towns" have developed within America's older postindustrial cities. The first is the "new town" that is small and largely populated by young, upwardly mobile people not needing extensive municipal services (its size exaggerated because this is where most tourists and urbanologists spend their time); the second is the "old town" with its poor, unemployed, aged and/or minority populations.[80]

> The folks who can afford to buy co-ops and condos are part of the new city. This is a new world city, it's not a manufacturing city. It's a city of services,

it's a city of fun and games. And they're making out like bandits. They represent the 21st century. Left behind, both in lifestyle and income, are the folks who either have fallen off the train or are in the caboose. And, unfortunately, that's a majority of the city.[81]

Results of City Changes.   Cities have begun once again to serve largely as commercial centers, this time often functioning primarily as marketplaces and sites for corporate headquarters and services. In particular, heavy manufacturing has become more decentralized, less labor intensive, and often employing more white-collar than blue-collar workers. By 1988, less than one-fifth of the American work force was employed in any kind of manufacturing at all.[82]

The entire restructuring process has left unskilled and semiskilled inner-city workers with significantly fewer opportunities for gainful employment. As Sternleib observed, rather than serving as "staging areas" for lesser-skilled immigrants preparing to mount the ladder of economic opportunity, large cities and their ghettos were becoming vast "refuse dumps" for economically marginal labor.[83]

Certainly U.S. cities vary in terms of their evolutionary advance.[84] As an indication, note the variation in the occupational mix of our 12 select cities (see figure 3.4). Corresponding to this, the government's prerecession unemployment rate for these cities varied from 4 percent in Indianapolis and Phoenix to 11 percent in Detroit, with a related variation in individual poverty rates from 12 percent in Seattle to 31 percent in Miami. Nonetheless, the basic economic trends described above are slowly becoming apparent in virtually all large cities, no matter what their age, size, or region.

AN URBAN CLASS SYSTEM?

Structure of Ownership

Regardless of a city's economic stage, just who has owned the farms, manufacturing firms, and nonindustrial businesses throughout this sweep of United States history? What has been the structure of ownership in the American economy?

Concentration of Capital.   From early in the history of the United States wealth has been concentrated. At the time of the American Revolution, 10 percent of the property owners controlled half the taxable assets in Portsmouth, New Hampshire; 40 percent in Newburyport, Massachusetts; 44 percent in Albany, New York; 57 percent in Boston; 62 percent in Charleston, South Carolina; 47 percent in New York City; and nearly 90 percent in Philadelphia.[85]

By the nineteenth century, industrialists like the Rockefellers, Carnegies, and Du Ponts were pioneering "vertically integrated" giant corporations that combined acquisition of raw materials, manufacturing, packaging, marketing, and financing. They also used advertising to spur demand as well as to increase their share of the market. For example, advertising budgets increased from $27 million in 1880 to $95 million in 1900.[86] By 1941, 1,000 manufacturing firms controlled

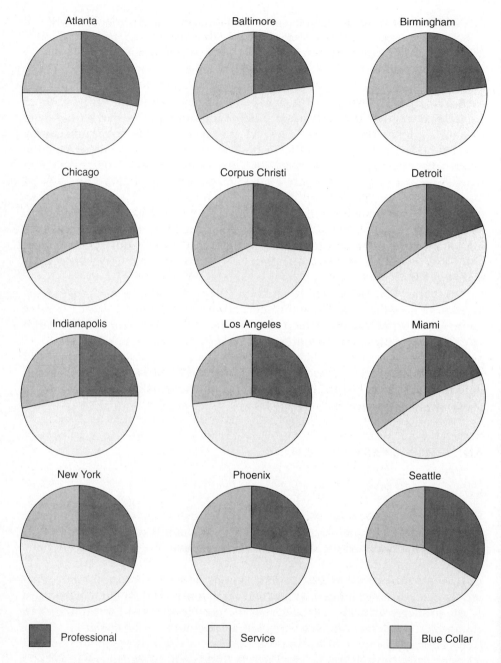

FIGURE 3.4 Occupational Mix, 1980

SOURCE: U.S. Department of Commerce, Bureau of the Census, *Census of the United States* (Washington, D.C.: Government Printing Office, 1980).

roughly two-thirds of the nation's manufacturing assets. Approximately 200 do so today.[87] Many of the nation's key economic decisions have therefore been made by the owners of a relatively small number of corporations.

The Owners.   For such a small number of firms to have so much economic clout would mean less if ownership of these firms was spread relatively equally across the nation's population. That is not the case. Looking at the national economy as a whole, fewer than one in five U.S. adults has ever directly owned any stock, while the top 1 percent hold more than half of all corporate stock and the top 5 percent of American families own nearly two-thirds of it.[88]

Those with the largest accumulation of a corporation's stock can dominate that corporation's decision making, even if they do not own all the shares. This occurs because voting is proportionately weighted according to the number of shares owned (as opposed to the one person–one vote principle) and because owners of smaller numbers of shares tend rarely to band together to counterbalance such power. Additionally, there has been the innovation of "management shares," which count more than ordinary ones. Henry Ford, for instance, was able to control 40 percent of Ford Motor Company's voting rights (and thus dominate the company) even though he actually owned only 20 percent of the company's stock.[93] Consequently, we get the term *controlling shares,* meaning that the person possesses enough votes to direct company decisions in the direction desired.

The Du Pont family, for example, has held the controlling shares of General Motors, Coca-Cola, Boeing Aircraft, and Penn Central Railroad. The Rockefellers have owned similar amounts of corporate stock, including dominant shares in the nation's leading oil companies headed by EXXON as well as four of its largest banks headed by Chase Manhattan. The Mellon family has had comparable reign over Alcoa and Carborundum.[89] In the late 1960s, Robert Sheehan found that either individuals or members of a single family held controlling shares in nearly 150 of the nation's top 500 corporations, and a full 70 of the family-named companies were still controlled by their founding families.[90] Maurice Zeitlin notes that all Americans owning more than $1 million worth of stock would fit easily in one average-size professional football stadium.[91]

Even with the breakup of some of the large family estates, William Domhoff notes that where three families each had their own companies before, now all three may own stock in each others' companies, increasing their common interests. In addition, they have numerous opportunities to come together in groups such as trade associations, social clubs, political action committees, and the boards of various profit-making and nonprofit organizations.[92]

The Nonowners.   Much of this wealth was built on the backs of a badly exploited work force. Factory work for men, women, and children in the industrial period meant very low wages, long hours, dull work, and unsafe working conditions.[94] One worker described a typical work day: "Up before day at the clang of the bell—and out of the mill by the clang of the bell—into the mill and at work, in obedience to that ding-dong of a bell—just as though we were so many living machines."[95] Life was hard, mobility difficult, and even the organization of labor unions was impeded by spatial separation, blacklists, violent repression, and an abundant supply of newly arriving immigrants. Then, just as much of that began to change in the 1930s, along came the beginnings of postindustrialism.

In the postindustrial period, private economic decisions continued to have enormous impacts on the lives of individual city residents. Some of these were positive, such as the personal mobility that accompanied the development of the various transportation innovations and the amount of information available as a result of the telecommunications revolution. However, a number of these private decisions wreaked havoc on individuals and communities as well.

Consider the layoffs that occurred as steel companies conceded much of the world's steel production to more modernized foreign firms, closed down many U.S. steel plants, and reinvested their capital outside the steel industry. Of the thousands of workers laid off from Chicago's South Works between 1978 and 1984, fully one-half found it impossible to obtain adequate alternative employment. Combining the unemployed and the reemployed, average household income dropped from $22,000 to $12,500; 11 percent were evicted from their homes; one-quarter felt compelled to find cheaper residences; and an additional one-third fell behind on their mortgage or rent payments and faced the possibility of eviction.[96]

As one might expect, the related economic havoc can be widespread when a company relocates or closes. Neighborhoods deteriorate. Property values plummet. Community networks begin to disintegrate. Charitable gifts and tax bases diminish. Health worsens, especially when medical insurance is eliminated. Retirement plans are curtailed. And suicide rates soar.[97]

Harvey Brenner found that for every 1 percent increase in national unemployment, there is a corresponding increase of 650 murders, 920 suicides, 4,000 admissions to state mental institutions, 3,300 admissions to state or federal prisons, and 37,000 premature deaths (27,000 from cardiovascular problems); furthermore, child abuse is three times greater in families where the breadwinner is unemployed. Brenner also found corresponding increases in automobile accidents, infant deaths, and cigarette smoking and other forms of drug abuse. He concluded that if unemployment was classified by the Public Health Service instead of the Labor Department, it would be considered a "killer disease."[98]

The urban results of such private decisions steadily became more visible. Although the wealthy of the pedestrian city originally lived near the center of town so as to be close to government buildings, churches, and the commercial center, and those less prosperous had to travel a bit farther to reach downtown, the classes were far less residentially segregated than they were soon to become. There was also a significant amount of residential mobility. As late as the 1840s, for example, 40 percent of Boston's population moved each year. By 1900, today's geographical sorting by class was nearly in place. Many of the wealthy had escaped to estates on the outskirts of the city. Middle-income people tended to live in the newer residential areas between the center of town and the periphery. Quite unlike the early days, neither experienced much contact with the poor who generally lived in the shanties, cellars, warehouses, and tenements amid the crowding, deterioration, disease, and crime of the inner ring.[99]

Chudacoff has summarized this postindustrial reality as follows:

> As affluent whites dispersed into more comfortable regions of the periphery, they loaded central cities with severe burdens. . . . Residential sprawl pushed with it commercial and service establishments, leaving behind the lowest jobs, cheapest housing, and poorest educational and health facilities. These were the conditions that all migrants, poor and unskilled, faced when they arrived in central cities.[100]

A Class System?

The concentration of ownership has left most urban residents at the mercy of decisions made by that small group of owners. However, does this entire situation actually qualify as a "class system"?

A class system exists when these economic relationships begin to calcify. In the above context, the *owning class* is the group that owns the controlling shares of a community's major corporations. *Nonowners* are those who do not, and consequently are dependent on the former group. This becomes a class system if there is virtually no likelihood that one could move from the nonowning to the owning class or vice versa. For a person to be born, live, and die a member of the nonowning class, as did his or her parents and grandparents, becomes evidence of the intergenerational reproduction of class position and thus of a class system. It comes about when one inherits one's parents' values, connections, wealth, and other attributes, making it very likely that one will also inherit their class position.

Is that the reality in the United States? Geographic mobility and the open spaces to the West offered economic opportunities to many of the earliest working-class laborers, artisans, and mariners—even though such opportunities were far less accessible to the poorest inhabitants living in shanties on the outer rims of the cities. As Chudacoff described the colonial period, "The situation of a rising standard of living and mobility up and down the social scale, however limited, applied to about four-fifths of the colonial urban dwellers—a sizable majority. But the remainder, consisting of Negroes and Indians, slave and free, formed a permanent, inescapable lower class."[101] Nevertheless, industrialization and the ensuing monopolization of capital created an even more clearly defined class structure as a large-scale "proletariat" also developed.

Paul Menchik concluded an extensive study of contemporary inheritance and found that if one is born to parents who are 10 times wealthier than someone else's, one is likely to die at least 8 times wealthier than that other person.[102] Focusing exclusively on males, the U.S. Department of Commerce found that nearly two out of three sons will end up working at a job of the same general status as their fathers. When the white collar category is limited to managers and professionals, almost three in four sons will remain outside that group, just as their fathers did.[103] Income is related to education; a college graduate makes an average of 50 percent more than a high school graduate and so on.[104] But, the U.S. Department of Commerce also has found that the more income a child's parents have, the more likely that child will be to have the opportunity for further education.[105]

There certainly appears to be a semblance of an economic class system in the United States, and it seems to play itself out most rigidly in settings like the older industrial cities. Given the economic evolution that has taken place in these environs, those at the top of the ownership pyramid seem even more secure and in control, while the bulk of urban residents seem to have fewer opportunities than ever to emerge from their subordinate positions.

Urban planning theorist John Friedmann summarizes the dilemma in more philosophical terms.

> Over the last two centuries, *economic space* has been subverting, invading, and fragmenting the *life* spaces of individuals and communities.
> Life space is at once the theater of life, understood as a convivial life, and an expression of it. . . . . Life spaces exist at different scales [and] are typically bounded, territorial spaces. . . . . Places have names. They constitute political communities.
> In contrast, economic space is abstract and discontinuous, consisting primarily of locations (nodes) and linkages (flows of commodities, capital, labor, and information). As an abstract space, it undergoes continuous change and transformation.
> Economic space is open and unlimited; it can expand in all directions. Indeed, its continuous expansion is vital to the reproduction of capitalist relations as a whole. Expansion occurs ruthlessly. . . . .
> We can see the result in the dissolution of life spaces and their progressive assimilation to economic space. The capitalist city has no reverence for life. It bulldozes over neighborhoods to make way for businesses. It abandons entire regions, because profits are greater somewhere else. Deprived of their life spaces, people's lives are reduced to a purely economic dimension as workers and consumers—so long, at least, as there is work.[106]

CONCLUSION

Whether or not one agrees fully with all of Friedmann's conclusions, there is no denying the evolution of some important economic structures in the urban political environment. Cities furthest along the road of postindustrial advance find that technical developments have altered their local economies in some very fundamental ways. Businesses have mechanized; a number have located outside the city limits, yet are still producing and distributing pretty much as before. Meanwhile, the jobs left for the remaining urban population tend to be at the high and low ends of the employment scale, with far fewer primary labor market jobs available for unskilled and semiskilled workers seeking to climb the economic ladder of success and ultimately achieve the American dream.

Thus, the postindustrial city ends up with a tiny owning class, a larger professional cadre, a shrinking number of people between those two groups, and what may well be a permanent urban underclass—intergenerationally locked into urban ghettos with little prospect for escape. Even worse, the ranks of that latter group appear to be growing as postindustrial urban economies continue to be ruled by the dictates of private-sector profitability. Chapter 4 will weigh the effects of these and other developments on the social structure of the city. Chapters 5 and 6 will begin the discussion of the political implications.

NOTES

1. Sam Bass Warner, *The Private City* (Philadelphia: University of Pennsylvania Press, 1968), p. x.
2. For general references see J. John Palen, *The Urban World* (New York: McGraw-Hill, 1987); Paul Kantor and Stephen David, *The Dependent City* (Glenview, Ill.: Scott, Foresman, 1988).
3. Sam Bass Warner, *The Urban Wilderness* (New York: Harper & Row, 1972).
4. Alan Pred, *The Spatial Dynamics of United States Urban-Industrial Growth* (Cambridge, Mass.: Harvard University Press, 1966), pp. 146–152.
5. Ibid.
6. Warner, *The Private City*; George Rogers Taylor, *The Transportation Revolution, 1815–1860* (New York: Rinehart, 1951).
7. Taylor, *The Transportation Revolution,* p. 443.
8. Howard Chudacoff, *The Evolution of American Urban Society* (Englewood Cliffs, N.J.: Prentice-Hall, 1981), p. 84.
9. See Paul Samuelson and William Nordhous, *Economics* (New York: McGraw-Hill, 1985), chap. 20.
10. For example, see Pred, *The Spatial Dynamics,* and Jeanne R. Lowe, *Cities in a Race with Time* (New York: Random House, 1967).
11. Warner, *The Urban Wilderness,* p. 89.
12. Charles Adrian and Charles Press, *Governing Urban America* (New York: McGraw-Hill, 1977).
13. Alfred Watkins, *The Practice of Urban Economics* (Beverly Hills, Calif.: Sage, 1980), p. 204.
14. Pred, *The Spatial Dynamics,* p. 16.
15. Pred, *The Spatial Dynamics,* chap. 2; and Edwin S. Mills, *Urban Economics* (Glenview, Ill.: Scott, Foresman, 1972), chap. 1.
16. Mills, *Urban Economics,* p. 13.
17. Jane Jacobs, *The Economy of Cities* (New York: Random House, 1969).
18. David Gordon, "Capitalist Development and the History of American Cities," in William Tabb and Larry Sawers, eds., *Marxism and the Metropolis* (New York: Oxford University Press, 1978), p. 39; Kantor and David, *The Dependent City.*
19. See Sam Bass Warner, *Streetcar Suburbs* (Cambridge, Mass.: Harvard University Press, 1962); John Bollens and Henry Schmandt, *The Metropolis* (New York: Harper & Row, 1982), p. 38.
20. See Dennis Judd, *The Politics of American Cities* (New York: HarperCollins, 1988), p. 173.
21. *New York Times,* October 20, 1984; March 4, 1985; March 7, 1985; April 17, 1986; April 22, 1986; November 10, 1986; *Memphis Commercial Appeal,* June 14, 1986, p. B10.
22. *New York Times,* June 6, 1985; *Christian Science Monitor,* January 3, 1986, pp. 14–15.
23. *New York Times,* August 15, 1986; April 16, 1992.

24. *New York Times,* March 5, 1990.

25. Louis Uchitelle, "Service-Sector Wage Issues," *New York Times,* December 19, 1986; Peter Passell, "Earning Plight of Baby Boomers," *New York Times,* September 21, 1988.

26. Robert W. and Mary Grisez Kweit, *People and Politics in Urban America* (Pacific Grove, Calif.: Brooks-Cole, 1990), p. 38; Robert Reich, *The Work of Nations* (New York: Knopf, 1990); John Kasarda, "Urban Change and Minority Opportunities," in Paul Peterson, *New Urban Reality* (Washington, D.C.: Brookings Institution, 1985); *New York Times,* May 27, 1992.

27. U.S. Department of Commerce, Bureau of the Census, *Statistical Abstracts of the United States* (Washington, D.C.: Government Printing Office, 1991), p. 425. And for trends, see city data from the U.S. Department of Labor, compiled in Samuelson and Nordhous, *Economics,* p. 633.

28. *New York Times,* September 30, 1986.

29. George Sternleib and James Hughes, *Income and Jobs* (New Brunswick, N.J.: Center for Urban Policy Research, 1984), chap. 5; Thierry Noyelle, "The Implications of Industrial Restructuring for Spatial Organization in the United States," in Frank Moulaert and Pokius Wilson-Salimas, eds., *Regional Analysis and the New International Division of Labor* (Boston: Kluwer-Nijhoff, 1982), pp. 120–122; Frank Levy, "The Vanishing Middle Class and Related Issues," *PS* 20 (Summer 1987): 650–655; *New York Times,* February 3, 1986; May 2, 1986; July 31, 1987; September 4, 1989; May 27, 1992.

30. Barry Bluestone and Bennett Harrison, "The Grim Truth about the Job 'Miracle,' " *New York Times,* February 1, 1987; May 26, 1991; May 12, 1992.

31. *New York Times,* December 11, 1988.

32. *National Journal,* July 28, 1990, p. 1857; June 29, 1991, pp. 1614–1619.

33. Sternleib and Hughes, *Income and Jobs*; *New York Times,* June 18, 1991.

34. *New York Times,* November 26, 1986; Alan Pred, *City-Systems in Advanced Economics* (London: Hutchinson, 1977), p. 164.

35. John H. Mollenkopf, *The Contested City* (Princeton, N.J.: Princeton University Press, 1983), p. 26.

36. Bollens and Schmandt, *The Metropolis,* pp. 80–81. Also see Harold Brown and Bennett Hymer, "Racial Dualism in an Urban Labor Market," in David Gordon, ed., *Problems in Political Economy* (Lexington, Mass.: D C Heath, 1977); *Akron Beacon Journal Magazine,* May 15, 1983, p. 7; *New York Times,* July 28, 1984.

37. Michael Storper, "Toward a Structural Theory of Industrial Location," in John Rees, J. D. Geoffrey, and Howard Hewinger, eds., *Industrial Location and Regional Systems* (Brooklyn: J. F. Bergin, 1981), pp. 9–21.

38. Barry Bluestone and Bennett Harrison, *The Deindustrialization of America* (New York: Basic Books, 1982), especially chaps. 2, 5, and 6. Also see William Goldsmith, "Bringing the Third World Home," in Larry Sawers and William Tabb, eds., *Sunbelt/Snowbelt* (New York: Oxford University Press, 1984); John Culbertson, "Importing a Lower Standard of Living," *New York Times,* August 17, 1986; Michael Storper and Richard Walker, "The Spatial Division of Labor," in Larry Sawers and William Tabb, eds., *Sunbelt/Snowbelt* (New York: Oxford University Press, 1984), pp. 19–22; Raymond Vernon, *Storm Over the Multinationals* (Cambridge, Mass.: Harvard University Press, 1977); Ernest Mandel, *Late Capitalism* (London, New Left Books, 1975); Folker Froebel, Jurgen Heinrichs, and Otto Kreye, *The New International Division of Labor* (Cambridge, England: Cambridge University Press, 1980).

39. *New York Times,* January 25, 1984; April 11, 1984; June 20, 1985.

40. *National Journal,* January 13, 1990.

41. Bennett Harrison and Barry Bluestone, "The Incidence and Regulation of Plant Closings," in Larry Sawers and William Tabb, eds., *Sunbelt/Snowbelt* (New York: Oxford University Press, 1984), pp. 368–402; *New York Times,* November 26, 1986.

42. *New York Times,* March 26, 1990.

43. The President's Urban and Regional Policy Group Report, *A New Partnership to Conserve America's Communities* (Washington, D.C.: Government Printing Office, March 1979), p. 24.

44. For an early discussion of the "push" and "pull" conceptualization, see Charles Glaab and A. Theodore Brown, *A History of Urban America* (New York: Macmillan, 1976), chap. 6.

45. U.S. Congress, Joint Economic Committee, "Trends in the Fiscal Conditions of Cities, 1978–80" (Washington, D.C.: Government Printing Office, 1980); National League of Cities survey cited in *Nation's Cities,* 10 (February 1972): 15. Also see Leonard Lund, *Factors in Corporate Location Decisions* (New York: The Conference Board, 1979); Eva Mueller and James N. Morgan, "Location Decisions of Manufacturers," *American Economic Review,* 52 (May 1962): 204–217; M. L. Greenhut and M. R. Colberg, *Factors in the Location of Florida Industry* (Tallahassee: Florida State University, 1962); V. Fuchs, *Changes in the Location of Manufacturing in the United States Since 1929* (New Haven, Conn.: Yale University Press, 1962).

46. For example, see Charles Schultze, Edward Fried, Alice Rivlin, et al., *Setting National Priorities: The 1973 Budget,* as adapted in Roger Alcaly and David Mermelstien, eds., *The Fiscal Crisis of American Cities* (New York: Vintage, 1977), p. 195.

47. For example, see Memphis, *Commercial Appeal,* October 15, 1989.

48. *New York Times,* June 26, 1987.

49. Edgard Hoover and Raymond Vernon, *Anatomy of a Metropolis* (Garden City, N.Y.: Anchor Books, 1959), chap. 3; Charles Levin, "Economic Maturity and the Metropolis' Evolving Physical Form," in Gary Tobin, ed., *The Changing Structure of the City* (Beverly Hills, Calif.: Sage, 1979), p. 25; Thomas Till, "Manufacturing Industry: Trends and Impact," in Amos Hawley and Sarah Mills, eds., *Nonmetropolitan American in Transition* (Chapel Hill: University of North Carolina Press, 1981), p. 197.

50. Bollens and Schmandt, *The Metropolis,* pp. 82–83.

51. John Mollenkopf, *The Contested City* (Princeton, N.J.: Princeton University Press, 1983).

52. David Birch, quoted in *New York Times,* December 10, 1978.

53. See Brian Berry, *The Human Consequences of Urbanization* (New York: St. Martin's Press, 1973).

54. See *Washington Post,* March 24, 1991, p. A6.

55. Bollens and Schmandt, *The Metropolis,* p. 79.

56. See *New York Times,* October 22, 1986; T. M. Stanbeck and T. J. Noyelle, *Cities in Transition* (Totowa, N.J.: Allanheld and Osman, 1982); S. Sheingold, *Dislocated Workers* (Washington, D.C.: Budget Office, 1982); M. C. Barth, "Dislocated Workers," *Journal of the Institute of Socioeconomic Studies* 7 (Spring 1982).

57. Wilbur Thompson, "A Preface to Suburban Economics," in Louis Masotti and Jeffrey Hadden, eds., *The Urbanization of the Suburbs* (Beverly Hills, Calif.: Sage, 1973), p. 411.

58. George Sternleib, quoted in *New York Times,* October 8, 1979.

59. These 12 cities have been drawn from our pool of large cities—a sample selected to vary by characteristics such as size, age, and region, and one that will be used for points of comparison throughout the remainder of the book.

60. The President's Urban and Regional Policy Group, *A New Partnership,* p. 43; *New York Times,* February 29, 1981; March 8, 1981; April 19, 1983; January 8, 1992.

61. See *New York Times,* June 18, 1991.

62. See Kweit and Kweit, *People and Politics,* chap. 3; Kasarda, "Urban Change"; *New York Times,* August 10, 1986.

63. As cited in William Spring, Bennett Harrison, and Thomas Vietorisz, "The Crisis of the Underemployed," in Gordon, *Problems in Political Economy.*

64. See *New York Times,* September 6, 1986; November 16, 1987; November 11, 1988; February 5, 1990; February 8, 1990; June 21, 1992.

65. *New York Times,* April 21, 1983, for a survey of the attitudes of unemployed black teenagers. Also see Harvey Hilaski, "Unutilized Manpower in Poverty Areas of Six Major Cities," *Monthly Labor Review* 94 (December 1971): 45–52; and Paul Ryscavage and Hazel Willacy, "Employment of the Nation's Poor," *Monthly Labor Review* 91 (August 1968): 15–21.

66. See Vincent Barabba, "The National Setting: Regional Shifts, Metropolitan Decline, and Urban Decay," in George Sternlieb and James Hughes, *Postindustrial America* (New Brunswick, N.J.: Center for Urban Policy Research, 1976).

67. Peter Gluck and Richard Meister, *Cities in Transition* (New York: New Viewpoints, 1979), p. 150.

68. See *New York Times,* March 12, 1989. Also see the President's Urban and Regional Policy Group, *A New Partnership,* pp. 35 and 43; Douglas Brown, *Introduction to Urban Economics* (New York: Academic Press, 1974), p. 243; David Gordon, "Characteristics of the Poor," in Gordon, *Problems in Political Economy,* pp. 293–295; U.S. Department of Commerce, Social and Economics Statistics Administration, Bureau of the Census, "Low Income Families in 1969, by Type, Age, and Race of Head: 1970" (Washington, D.C.: Government Printing Office, 1970).

69. Mark Allen Hughes, *Poverty in Cities* (New York: National League of Cities, 1989).

70. For examples of various points of view on this question, see Robert Plotnick and Felicity Skidmore, *Progress against Poverty* (New York: Academic Press, 1975); Thomas Pettigrew, *Racially Separate or Together* (New York: McGraw-Hill, 1971); Lester Thurow, as quoted in *New York Times,* November 29, 1975; *New York Times,* December 2, 1975; November 27, 1983. Also see Lee Rainwater, "Perceptions of Poverty and Economic Inequality," in David Gordon, *Problems in Political Economy* (Lexington, Mass.: D C Heath, 1977).

71. Nonfarm poverty is defined by the Bureau of Labor Statistics (BLS) as a minimum subsistence "standard budget" (food, housing, clothing, medical care, transportation, etc.), for example, rental housing without air conditioning, use of mass transportation instead of a private car, and so on. The Social Security Administration Index is derived by taking the cost of a subsistence level of food and multiplying that figure by three. It is considerably more conservative than the BLS standard.

    As for estimates of the number of poor people excluded by such definitions, see the sources cited in note 70 above as well as Michael Harrington, "The Betrayal of the Poor," *Atlantic,* January 1970; Alan Haber, "Poverty Budgets," *Poverty and Human Resources Abstracts,* 1, no. 3, 1966; and Lee Rainwater, *What Money Buys* (New York: Basic Books, 1974).

72. As reported in *New York Times,* September 29, 1980.

73. Paul Porter, *The Recovery of American Cities* (New York: Sun River, 1976); Hoover and Vernon, *Anatomy of a Metropolis,* p. 198; Shirley Broadway Laska and Daphne Spain, eds., *Back to the City* (New York: Pergamon Press, 1980); *New York Times,* October 11, 1987. And for contrasting points of view, see Phillip Clay, *Neighborhood Renewal* (Lexington, Mass.: Lexington Books, 1979); Brian Berry, "Islands of Renewal in Seas of Decay," in Paul Peterson, ed., *New Urban Reality* (Washington, D.C.: Brookings Institution, 1986); George Sternlieb and James Hughes, "The Uncertain Future of the Center Cities," *Urban Affairs Quarterly* 18 (June 1983); George Sternlieb and James Hughes, eds., *Revitalizing the Northeast* (New Brunswick, N.J.: Center for Urban Policy Research, 1978); Donald Rosenthal, ed., *Urban Revitalization,* vol. 18, Urban Affairs Annual Reviews (Beverly Hills, Calif.: Sage, 1980).

74. Gregory Lipton, "Evidence of Central City Revival," *Journal of the American Institute of Planners* 45 (April 1977): 136–147; *New York Times,* September 30, 1985.

75. Thomas Black, "Private Market Housing Renovation in Central Cities," in Shirley Broadway Laska and Daphne Spain, eds., *Back to the City* (New York: Pergamon Press, 1980); or Harvey Marshall and Bonnie Lewis, "Back to the City," *Journal of Urban Affairs* 4 (Winter 1982).

76. As quoted in *Cleveland Plain Dealer,* July 8, 1980, p. A4.

77. George Sternlieb and Kristina Ford, "Some Aspects of the Return to the Central City," in Herrington Bryce, ed., *Revitalizing the Cities* (Lexington, Mass.: D C Heath, 1979). Also see Gary Tobin and Dennis Judd, "Moving the Suburbs to the City," *Social Science Quarterly* 63 (December 1982); George Sternlieb and James Hughes, "Back to the Central City: Myths and Realities," in George Sternlieb and James Hughes, eds., *America's Housing: Prosperity and Problems* (New Brunswick, N.J.: Center for Urban Policy Research, 1980); Department of Housing and Urban Development, Office of Policy Development and Research, *Displacement Report* (Washington, D.C.: Government Printing Office, 1979); and Dennis Judd, "Urban Revitalization," in Gary Tobin, ed., *The Changing Structure of the City* (Beverly Hills, Calif.: Sage, 1979).

78. U.S. Congress, Joint Economic Committee, "Is the Urban Crisis Over?" (Washington, D.C.: U.S. Government Printing Office, March 20, 1979), p. 37. Also see J. John Palen and Bruce London, eds., *Gentrification, Displacement, and Neighborhood Revitalization* (Albany, N.Y.: SUNY Press, 1983); Michael Schill and Nathan Glazer, eds., *Revitalizing America's Cities: Neighborhood Reinvestment and Displacement* (Albany, N.Y.: SUNY Press, 1983); Sternlieb and Ford, "Some Aspects"; Larry Long, "Back to the Countryside and Back to the City in the Same Decade," in Shirley Broadway Laska and Daphne Spain, eds., *Back to the City* (New York: Pergamon Press, 1980), pp. 61–76; Peter Salins, "The Limits of Gentrification," *New York Affairs* 5 (1979): 61; and Roy Bahl, *Financing State and Local Government in the 1980s* (New York: Oxford University Press, 1984), pp. 170–174.

79. Schill and Glazer, *Revitalizing America's Cities.*

80. U.S. Congress, Joint Economic Committee Report, April 26, 1979.

81. George Sternlieb, quoted in *New York Times,* June 3, 1984. Also see Berry, "Islands of Renewal"; Paul Levy and Dennis McGrath, "Saving Cities for Whom?," *Social Policy* 10 (November/December, 1979): 20–28; Neil Pierce, "Industrial Blackmail in the Cities," *P.A. Times,* December 1, 1980.

82. U.S. Department of Commerce, *Statistical Abstracts of the United States,* p. 400.

83. For further reference, see George Sternlieb, as quoted in the *New York Times,* August 15, 1981; Alexander Ganz, "Out Large Cities: New Light on Their Recent

Transformations" (Cambridge, Mass.: MIT Laboratory for Environmental Studies, 1972), especially pp. 11–36; Seymour Sacks, "The Cities as the Center of Employment," in Herrington Bryce, ed., *Urban Governance and Minorities* (New York: Praeger, 1976); David Gordon, "Capital Development and the History of American Cities," in William Tabb and Larry Sawers, eds., *Marxism and the Metropolis* (New York: Oxford University Press, 1984); George Sternlieb and James Hughes, "New Regional and Metropolitan Realities of America," *Journal of American Institute of Planners* (July 1977); George Sternlieb, "The City as Sandbox," *Public Interest* 82 (Fall 1971): 14–21; *New York Times,* July 28, 1984.

For empirical evidence concerning the "staging area" period, see such works as Tom Kessner, *The Golden Door* (New York: Oxford University Press, 1977), and Stephan Thernstrom, *The Other Bostonians* (Cambridge, Mass.: Harvard University Press, 1973).

84. E. Barbara Philips and Richard LeGates, *City Lights* (New York: Oxford University Press, 1981), chap. 16.

85. Warner, *The Private City,* p. 9; and Jackson Turner Main, *The Social Structure of Revolutionary America* (Princeton, N.J.: Princeton University Press, 1965), pp. 35–36.

86. As cited in Zane Miller, *The Urbanization of Modern America* (New York: Harcourt Brace Jovanovich, 1973), pp. 66–67.

87. Senate Subcommittee on Antitrust and Monopoly, "Economic Concentration," (Washington, D.C.: Government Printing Office, 1979), p. 173; U.S. Department of Commerce, Bureau of the Census, *Statistical Abstracts of the United States* (Washington, D.C.: Government Printing Office, 1986–92); Bluestone and Harrison, *The Deindustrialization of America,* pp. 118–132.

88. See Marcus Pohlmann, *Black Politics in Conservative America* (White Plains, N.Y.: Longman, 1990), p. 63.

89. See New York Stock Exchange Survey (November 1983) as reported in *New York Times,* December 1, 1983; Gabriel Kolko, *Wealth and Power in America* (New York: Praeger, 1972); James D. Smith and Stephen D. Franklin, "The Concentration of Wealth, 1922–1969," *American Economic Review* 64 (May 1974): 164; Edward S. Greenberg, *The American Political System* (Boston: Little, Brown, 1983), p. 36; Neil Jacoby, *Corporate Powers and Social Responsibility* (New York: Macmillan, 1973), pp. 36–37; Pohlmann, *Black Politics in Conservative America,* p. 69; Gerald Zilg, *Du Pont: Behind the Nylon Curtain* (Englewood Cliffs, N.J.: Prentice-Hall, 1974); Peter Collier and David Horowitz, *Rockefellers: An American Dynasty* (New York: Holt, Rinehart and Winston, 1976); Thomas Dye, *Who's Running America?* (Englewood Cliffs, N.J.: Prentice-Hall, 1983), pp. 45–46.

It should also be noted that this discussion refers primarily to direct ownership, although a large number of people indirectly hold shares through banks, insurance companies, and pension funds. However, most of the latter group have not controlled those shares in a way that poses any threat to the dominant power of those who directly possess large individual holdings.

90. Robert Sheehan, "Proprietors in the World of Big Business," *Fortune,* June 15, 1967, pp. 178, 182.

91. Maurice Zeitlin, "Who Owns America?," *The Progressive* 42 (June 1978): 15.

92. See G. William Domhoff, *Who Rules America?* (Englewood Cliffs, N.J.: Prentice-Hall, 1967), p. 40; Domhoff, *Who Rules America Now?* (New York: Touchstone, 1983), chap. 2.

93. Lee Iacocca, *Iacocca: An Autobiography* (New York: Bantam, 1984), p. 110. Also see *New York Times,* March 19, 1985; July 15, 1985; December 17, 1986; April 12, 1991; Domhoff, *Who Rules America Now?,* pp. 59–78.

94. Raymond Mohl, "Poverty in Early America," *New York History* 50 (January 1969); James Henretta, "Economic Development and Social Structure in Colonial Boston," *William and Mary Quarterly* 22 (January 1965); Upton Sinclair, *The Jungle* (New York: Signet, 1906); Jackson Turner Main, *The Social Structure of Revolutionary America* (Princeton, N.J.: Princeton University Press, 1965); David Goldfield and Blaine Brownell, *Urban America: From Downtown to No Town* (Boston: Houghton Mifflin, 1979), pp. 228–240; Chudacoff, *The Evolution of American Urban Society,* especially pp. 14, 15, and 116–123.

95. Benita Eisler, *The Lowell Offering: Writings of New England Mill Women, 1840–1945* (Philadelphia: Lippincott, 1977), p. 161, as quoted in Phillips and LeGates, *City Lights,* p. 452. Also see Sinclair, *The Jungle.*

96. *New York Times,* October 31, 1984. And for national data in this regard, see *New York Times,* January 25, 1986; February 7, 1986.

97. For example, see Bluestone and Harrison, *The Deindustrialization of America,* chap. 3.

98. Douglas Fraser et al., *Economic Dislocations: Plant Closings, Plant Relocations, and Plant Conversion,* report prepared for the U.S. Congress, Joint Economic Committee (Washington, D.C.: Government Printing Office, 1979), p. 1; *Chicago Tribune,* April 23, 1983; July 8, 1984. Also see articles by Duane Hagan, Dennis Ahlburg, and Morton Shapiro in *Hospital and Community Psychiatry* (May 1983); Bluestone and Harrison, *The Deindustrialization of America.*

99. Harvey Zorbaugh, *The Gold Coast and the Slum* (Chicago: University of Chicago Press, 1929); Miller, *The Urbanization of Modern America,* pp. 79–84; Charles Glaab and A. Theodore Brown, *A History of Urban America* (New York: Macmillan, 1976), pp. 149–150.

100. Chudacoff, *The Evolution of American Urban Society,* p. 248.

101. Ibid., p. 15.

102. Paul Menchik, *Conference on Research in Income and Wealth* (New York: National Bureau of Economic Research, 1979).

103. See U.S. Department of Commerce, Bureau of the Census, Current Population Surveys, *Occupational Changes in a Generation Survey* (Washington, D.C.: Government Printing Office, 1973).

104. U.S. Department of Commerce, Bureau of the Census, *Statistical Abstracts of the United States, 1986* (Washington, D.C.: Government Printing Office, 1986).

105. National Center for Education Statistics, Digest of Education Statistics (1979), p. 93; U.S. Department of Commerce, Bureau of the Census, "Characteristics of American Children and Youth," *Current Population Reports* (Washington, D.C.: Government Printing Office, 1982).

106. John Friedmann, "Life Space and Economic Space," manuscript (Los Angeles: UCLA, 1981), quoted in Bluestone and Harrison, *The Deindustrialization of America,* p. 20.

CHAPTER 4

Social Relationships

[The cities have always been] a useful place to store America's homeless, to house new immigrants and to stack up the chronically poor and uneducated. Can't have all those off-brands wandering around Kennebunkport.[1]
—*Mike Royko*

The United States of America is a nation of immigrants. The only truly native Americans have long since been run off the land and consigned to Indian reservations. Everyone else, at some point in their family histories, immigrated here from an established country abroad. Millions of them, many of whom were poor peasants or unskilled laborers, left their native lands to seek haven in the United States. Many were seeking economic opportunities. Others fled from class barriers, religious persecution, military conscription, and/or economic downturns. In essence, these immigrants were being pushed by hardships and pulled by perceived opportunities. Yet, one group came under very different circumstances: most African Americans were forcibly removed from their homelands and arrived enchained as slaves.

Cities in the industrializing era tended to serve as processing centers for wave after wave of poor, lesser-skilled immigrants beginning their way up the economic ladder of material success. The newest arrivals normally would huddle together in ethnic ghettos and were looked down upon by many of the longer residing "natives." Nevertheless, economic opportunities offered them a way out. In the postindustrial period, on the other hand, this is changing. Economic exit avenues have been disappearing. Social polarization has been calcifying. Such economic and social realities have been posing real problems for the latest waves of immigrants, but in particular for the seemingly least accepted of all the relatively recent arrivals to United States cities: African Americans. This social milieu is an important part of the urban political environment. To better understand that component, this chapter will begin by tracing the various waves of ethnic immigration. It will then focus on significant social pathologies that seem endemic to the postindustrial city.

THE PREINDUSTRIAL PERIOD

Large cities are a relatively recent historical phenomenon. In 1550, Paris was the largest city in Europe, with a population of some 300,000.[2] Two centuries later, at the dawn of U.S. independence, London was the largest European city, having approximately 750,000 people.[3] The United States would not have a city with even 100,000 residents before the nineteenth century.[4] Thus, in this country the preindustrial period was essentially a pre-urban period.

It is important to note the immigrations that provided the social context for the ultimate urbanization of America. Some 10,000 years ago the earliest American immigrants, Native Americans, came across Siberia and entered the continent via what is now Alaska. Far more recently, beginning in the seventeenth century and extending into the nineteenth, the next major waves of ethnic immigration tended to come from Western and Northern Europe. The English made their initial permanent settlements in the Northeast and later moved to the South as well. The Spanish congregated in the Southwest and Far West. The French favored the Gulf Coast. The Irish tended to stay in the Northeast. The Germans, Dutch, and Scandinavians, later assisted by the development of the railroad, tended to move to the Midwest. These earliest immigrants usually lived on farms or in small commercial towns.[5]

THE INDUSTRIAL PERIOD

In addition to political instability and religious persecution, economics played a particularly significant role in spawning immigration during the industrial period. Crop failures like the Irish potato famine of the 1840s and opportunity-constricting population booms like those in Western Europe in 1825 and 1840–1845 and in Southern and Eastern Europe in 1860–1865 and 1885–1890 accelerated what was already a sizable exodus from Europe.[6] As American capital came largely from Europe—at least it did so prior to the twentieth century—surges in European investment also prompted immigration by creating jobs in the United States. Large numbers of immigrants followed the injections of foreign capital in the years between 1878 and 1892 and between 1897 and 1913. Some skilled craftsmen, trailing these cycles of investment, even sailed back and forth between Europe and America.[7]

From the time the immigration floodgates opened at the beginning of this era until they began to be closed forcibly at the end of the period, some 50 million people entered the United States. Nearly nine million entered in the decade between 1900 and 1910 alone.[8]

U.S. Cities

The cities bore the brunt of this immigration. The urbanization of the United States was being fueled not only by recent immigrants but also by a rather steady movement of previous immigrants from farms to cities, pushed by job reductions because of mechanization in agriculture and pulled by factory job opportunities in large cities. In 1910, approximately one-third of city residents had recently migrated there from farms in the United States.[9] As a result of these two influxes of people, one from without and one from within, the population of U.S. cities increased a full sevenfold between 1860 and 1910. Whereas only 15 percent of the U.S. population lived in cities at the beginning of this urbanizing industrial era, a majority did by 1920.[10]

Mainly for the economic reasons discussed in the last chapter, it was the largest cities that grew the fastest. Where there were only 3 cities with more than 100,000 people at the beginning of this era, there would be 28 by the turn of the century. Meanwhile, the gradual settlement of the western frontiers and the evolution of rail travel led to the emergence of western "gateway cities" such as St. Louis. By 1871, there were 81 such cities, which encompassed a total of 172,000 people.[11]

Ethnic Groups.   As an indication of the urban impact posed by immigration from abroad, in 1890 only one-third of native-born Americans lived in cities. By contrast, two-thirds of American immigrants did. As of 1910, 79 percent of all newly arriving immigrants lived in cities as did 72 percent of all existing white residents who were born in a foreign country.[12] These recent immigrants comprised majorities in virtually all the large cities by the end of this period. More than three-quarters of New York City residents were first- or second-generation immigrants, while the figure exceeded 60 percent in cities such as Boston, Newark, Buffalo, Philadelphia, Pittsburgh, Cleveland, Chicago, Detroit, Milwaukee, and San Francisco.[13] With the large cities being in their formative stages, these recently arriving ethnics would have an enormous impact on all aspects of urban life throughout the industrial era and beyond.

The "old immigrants" were primarily of Western and Northern European stock while the "new immigrants" came disproportionately from Southern and Eastern Europe. Between 1830 and 1880, the first wave of industrial era immigration tended to be Germans, Irish Catholics, and Scandinavian Protestants. As late as 1880, some 85 percent of the American population had come from Britain, Germany, and Scandinavia. As industrialization flourished, however, Poles, Italians, Greeks, Russians, and other Eastern and Southern Europeans, not to mention Chinese and Japanese, literally poured into every industrialized area in the land. Between 1880 and 1920, some 23.5 million immigrants arrived in the second wave of this era's immigration. By the turn of the century, 50 percent were coming form Italy, Russia, and Austria-Hungary alone. Meanwhile, the cities became home for more than five-sixths of the native-born Irish and Russians, more than 70 percent of the English, Scots, Australians, Greeks, and Chinese, two-thirds of the Germans, and three-fifths of the Swedes.[14]

This tremendous tide of ethnic immigration into the cities proceeded almost entirely at its own pace until regulations began to appear in the 1870s. The Chinese Exclusion Act of 1882 severely restricted immigration from China while the Immigration Act of 1921 also placed strict limits on a variety of other nationalities. In addition, potential immigrants would come to be screened by a host of criteria such as their skill levels, criminal records, political views, and the likelihood they would be persecuted for their religious or political beliefs if they remained in their native country.

Just as immigration from abroad began to slow, African Americans began to migrate in large numbers from the rural South to the northern industrial cities. A "third wave" had begun. Pushed by diminishing agricultural job opportunities and increasingly violent racism in the rural South, and attracted by manufacturing positions in northern cities especially during World War I, the "Great Migration" began to stir. In Chicago, for instance, the African American population more than tripled between 1900 and 1920, growing from 30,000 to 110,000.[15]

Social Relationships and Pathologies.   Seeking solidarity and support while confronted with exclusionary discrimination, the most recent immigrants generally lived together in relatively tight-knit communities called ethnic ghettos. This was the general pattern whether it was the Irish of the first wave, the Eastern and Southern Europeans of the second, or the racial minorities of the third. Edward Burgess, Robert Park, and others studied Chicago's *urban ecology* in the 1920s and actually coined terms such as *invasion* and *succession* to describe the neighborhood transitions from one group to the next.[16]

The good news was that the cities became rich mosaics of ethnic neighborhoods, each with its distinguishable language, signs, restaurants, groceries, and social clubs. Vestiges of these are often still visible today. The bad news was that the cities soon were overwhelmed. Beneath the glitter of the "silk-stocking" affluent districts, huge numbers of immigrants lived in slums plagued by poverty, filth, and overcrowding. By the mid-nineteenth century the lower wards of New York City contained 164 people per acre, 29,000 of whom lived in cellars. By 1894, such tenement districts had 986 persons per acre, many of them paupers— the unemployed, aged, widowed, disabled, and their children—and often more than 80 percent of this poorest class were immigrants.[17]

Not only were the cities besieged by immigrant poor; they also were unable to adapt to the rapid rate of industrialization and urbanization in general. Streets were clogged with garbage, refuse, and horse dung. Open ditches ran beside them carrying kitchen water as well as human wastes. Epidemics of typhoid, dysentery, typhus, cholera, yellow fever, malaria, and tuberculosis were rampant. In one year Philadelphia lost 10 percent of its population (more than 4,000 people) to yellow fever. The death rate climbed from 1 per 46.5 persons in 1810 to 1 per 29 in 1859. Prostitution, youth gangs, brawling, and riots were commonplace and highly visible as the overall crime rate rose rapidly.[18] It did not go unnoticed that the bulk of the convicted criminals were immigrants. Soon, immigrants were being blamed for everything from pollution and disease to moral decay.[19]

The American press over a considerable period of time has reflected a good bit of this sentiment:

> This country is undergoing an invasion of venomous reptiles . . . , long-haired, wild-eyed, badsmelling, atheistic, reckless foreign wretches, who

never did an hour's work in their lives, and who thus need to be crushed like snakes in the grass before they have a chance to bite.[20]

. . . lower classes of intemperate dissolute and filthy people huddled together like swine in their polluted habitations.[21]

. . . rag-tag and bob-tail cutthroats of Beelzebub . . . , the very scum and offal of the earth.[22]

Americans are pretty well agreed that the Italian and Russian immigrants are of a kind which we are better without.[23]

The striking Irishmen are a mongrel mass of ignorance and crime and superstition, as utterly unfit for its duties as they are for common courtesies and decencies of civilized life.[24]

Let us whip these Slavic wolves back to the European dens from which they issue, or in some way exterminate them.[25]

Those who made up the largely Anglo-Saxon "old guard" of the cities were appalled by this invasion, and those who could afford it were some of the first to retreat to the urban outer rim in order to escape these ethnic hordes. Meanwhile, the rural citizenry, many living only at a subsistence level themselves, resented the fact that the immigrants often seemed to have greater economic opportunities than they. Soon nativist organizations arose: the American Protective Association, the American Patriotic League, the Patriotic Sons of America, the Minutemen, the Know-Nothing Party, and the Ku Klux Klan. They led organized assaults against the newcomers that ranged from discriminatory laws such as "exclusionary acts" and immigration restrictions, to overt job discrimination such as signs declaring that "Irish Need Not Apply" or newspaper advertisements with different black and white wage rates. There were also restrictive housing covenants, and the immigrants were subjected to physical violence as well. Beyond nativist reactions, there was some interethnic rivalry and hostility, too.

In terms of violence, as early as 1741, 13 blacks were burned at the stake, 8 hung, and 71 banished from New York for "conspiring"; in the 1840s, Protestant mobs attacked Roman Catholic churches; and after World War I, in such cities as East St. Louis and Chicago, insecure whites killed dozens and injured hundreds of blacks whom they viewed as competitors for the limited number of available jobs.[26]

Thus, those who did not return to their original homelands—some 20 percent to 40 percent apparently did return[27]—tended to band together in ghettos. This concentration allowed them to maximize their economic and political resources and to gain as well the social support and protection available in more homogeneous areas.[28] For those who stuck it out, the industrial era urban ghettos often did serve as staging areas from which they, or at least some of their offspring, ultimately were able to improve their economic lot and move on—either to the West, to a more respectable city neighborhood, or to the outlying regions in their urban area.

THE POSTINDUSTRIAL PERIOD

The revolutions in transportation and communication technology turned the urban economy on its head and led to the development of postindustrialism. The increased mobility of capital allowed corporations to locate and relocate with much more flexibility, leaving no city's manufacturing base secure. In addition, the nature and security of individual jobs were changing as manufacturing became far less labor intensive. The postindustrial ghetto dweller was not nearly as likely as his or her immigrant predecessors to find a job in the far more promising primary labor sector.

But besides the economic implications, these technological changes made it much easier for the more affluent to locate outside the central cities with their mounting social problems. Soon many cities actually were losing population, a significant reversal of the tremendous urbanization that had been occurring for nearly a century. And, those who remained were notably poorer and in more need of governmental services.

Rather than "staging areas" for impending economic advancement, the cities were more and more becoming "holding tanks" for the economically superfluous. And, the economically superfluous often tended to be the most recent ghettoized poor—in this case, racial minorities.

U.S. Cities

The United States continues to be a highly urbanized nation. A majority of the U.S. population now lives in 39 metropolitan areas, crammed onto well less than 10 percent of the nation's land. In the decade of the 1980s, a full 90 percent of the nation's population growth occurred in metropolitan areas.[29] Nonetheless, it was not until 1970 that more people lived in the suburbs than in the cities. There also has been some definite variation among individual cities. For example, consider population trends in our 12 select cities (see figure 4.1).

The population variation shown in figure 4.1 indicates regional differences. The Sun Belt cities are simply in a different evolutionary stage than older ones. While more and more people are moving from Frost Belt cities to their suburbs (or out of the region entirely), a significant amount of urbanization continues to occur in the Sun Belt. In our sample of 12, for example, the 4 cities indicating population growth can be found in the Sun Belt.

There were only 96 metropolises in the entire nation in 1930, yet there were 284 by the 1990 census. Most indicative is that the bulk of this growth has occurred outside the old manufacturing corridor running from Chicago and Milwaukee east to Boston and New York City. By 1930, 60 percent of the cities that had attained populations of 100,000 people or more could be found in the Northeast. Since then, 80 percent of cities reaching that population plateau were in the Southeast or Southwest, cities like Austin, Tulsa, Colorado Springs, and Raleigh-Durham. In the 1980s, the fastest growing metropolitan areas were Orlando, Phoenix, San Diego, Dallas-Fort Worth, Atlanta, and Los Angeles. In 1984, Los Angeles surpassed Chicago to become the nation's second largest city.[30]

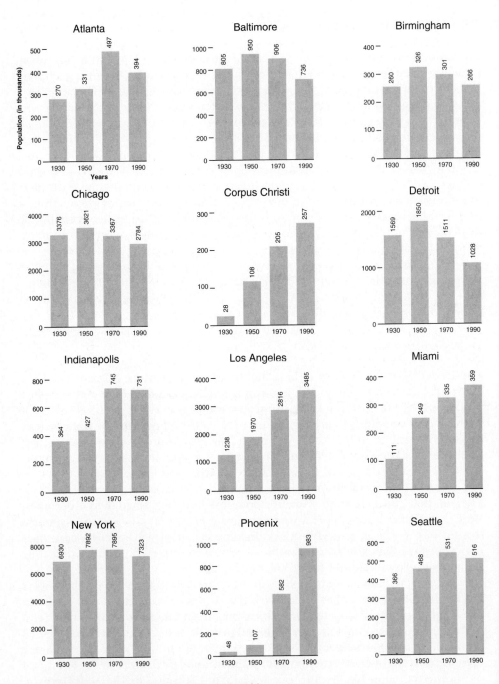

FIGURE 4.1 Population Trends, 1930–1990

SOURCE: U.S. Department of Commerce, Bureau of Census, *Census of the Population, 1930–1990* (Washington, D.C.: Government Printing Office, 1930, 1950, 1970, and 1990).

Ethnic Groups.   The United States continues to allow some one-half million people per year legally to immigrate into the country, besides making regular exceptions for political refugees (those with a well-founded fear of persecution if they return to their homelands). Such immigration amounts to more than one-quarter of our annual population growth, and that proportion has been increasing. Thus, roughly one American out of every six is first-generation foreign born, and 90 percent of those individuals live in cities. In the New York City and Los Angeles metropolitan areas, nearly one in four residents was foreign born.[31]

The 1970s was the decade with the second largest wave of ethnic immigration in the nation's history. Inflated by the number of Southeast Asian refugees accepted after the Vietnam War, the United States added 4.4 million immigrants. Then in the 1980s, besides allowing the continued immigration of refugees from what were deemed to be repressive nations around the globe, Congress extended amnesty to millions of previously undocumented Hispanic aliens, making it one of the most immigration-receptive decades as well. Additionally, somewhere between 800,000 and 2 million undocumented aliens are estimated to settle here each year—generally in the older industrial cities.[32]

The majority of Americans are descendants of European ancestors, with roughly one-third having come originally from Germany, Ireland, Russia, Poland, Italy, or France. Nonetheless, as table 4.1 indicates, this profile began to change in the period from 1920 to 1970 as the majority of new immigrants no longer came here from Europe. Since 1970, more than three-quarters of all immigrants have come from either Asia or Latin America.[33]

The combination of African Americans and Hispanics alone, generally referred to as minorities or racial minorities, currently makes up more than half of many of our urban populations. As figure 4.2 indicates, these two groups combined to make up majorities or near majorities in all but three of our dozen select cities. In addition, their proportion in all 12 cities has been growing steadily.

African Americans.   Following their legal emancipation from slavery, most African Americans stayed in the South, either migrating to the cities or remaining in the rural areas as tenant farmers and farmhands. Toward the end of the nineteenth century, however, the boll weevil, cotton gin, and overall mechanization of southern agriculture thrust many of them out of work. In addition, they continued to be plagued by blatant forms of discrimination as well as by night riders and lynch mobs. When the plummeting of cotton and tobacco prices during the Great Depression destroyed many of the existing opportunities to sharecrop, the prospect of a better life in northern cities became alluring. Word of better conditions came in advertisements run in Chicago's widely circulated black newspaper, *The Defender,* or in letters written by relatives who had already made the move. With the availability of transportation, many made the trek to the industrial cities of the North despite extensive efforts by southern political and economic elites to keep them where they were.[34] The combination of opportunities and escape was proving attractive in much the same way that this promise had attracted other immigrant groups before them.[35]

TABLE 4.1 Immigration by Countries and Continents, 1821–1970 (in thousands and percentages)

	Total	Great Britain	Ireland	Germany	Central Europe	Russia	Italy	Asia	Balance of World
1821–1870	7,214	1,475	2,309	2,332	8	3	26	106	875
Percent	(100)	(20)	(33)	(32)	(—)	(—)	(—)	(1)	(12)
1871–1920	26,278	2,495	1,967	3,161	4,067	3,276	4,171	700	6,441
Percent	(100)	(10)	(7)	(12)	(15)	(12)	(16)	(3)	(25)
1921–1970	11,508	929	368	1,299	566	163	976	725	6,482
Percent	(100)	(8)	(3)	(11)	(5)	(2)	(9)	(6)	(56)

SOURCES: U.S. Department of Commerce, Bureau of the Census, *Historical Statistics of the United States* (Washington, D.C.: Government Printing Office, 1960), pp. 56–59; U.S. Department of Justice, Immigration and Naturalization Service, *Report of the Commissioner: 1970* (Washington, D.C.: Government Printing Office, 1971), pp. 63–64; as adapted from Sam Bass Warner, *The Urban Wilderness* (New York: Harper & Row, 1972), p. 168.

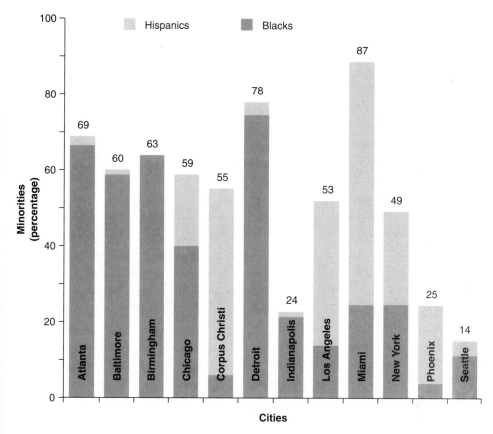

FIGURE 4.2 Percentage Minority, 1990

SOURCE: U.S. Department of Commerce, Bureau of the Census, *Census of the Population, 1990* (Washington, D.C.: Government Printing Office, 1990).

Although at the turn of the century 90 percent of all African Americans lived in the South and only 17 percent lived in cities, this proportion soon changed. In general terms, figure 4.3 captures the results of the "Great Migration" to the North.

Blacks migrated along the least expensive routes. From Maryland to Florida they generally traveled by coastal steamer and railroad to destinations in the Northeast such as New York City and Newark; from Virginia and the upper South many went to Washington, D.C.; those living west of the Alleghenies rode riverboats and the railroad. From Alabama, Mississippi, and Tennessee they settled in such cities as St. Louis, Chicago, Cleveland, and Detroit. One regional exception was that rural blacks from Arkansas, Louisiana, and Texas were more inclined to go to Sun Belt cities such as Dallas, Fort Worth, Houston, Los Angeles, and Oakland.[36]

In the 60 years between 1910 and 1970, more than 6.5 million African Americans migrated to the North, almost exclusively to northern cities. In 1916

FIGURE 4.3 Regional Distribution of the African American Population, 1920–1990

source: U.S. Department of Commerce, Bureau of the Census, *Census of the Population* (Washington, D.C.: Government Printing Office, 1920, 1940, 1960, 1990).

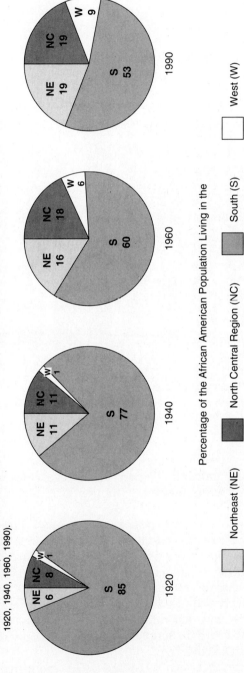

Percentage of the African American Population Living in the

Northeast (NE)

North Central Region (NC)

South (S)

West (W)

and the first six months of 1917, as a case in point, 50,000 African Americans arrived in Chicago, most on free tickets provided by local industries in need of wartime workers and/or strikebreakers. Yet, there has been considerable black urbanization in the South as well. The shift of African Americans from farms to the city continues to this day in urban places such as Atlanta, Houston, and Jacksonville.[37]

From an almost exclusively rural existence in the nineteenth century, more than one-quarter of all African Americans resided in urban areas by 1910 and more than three-quarters do today—more than one-half in central cities and approximately one-fifth in suburbs.[38] Slightly more than 12 percent of the U.S. population, they make up more than one-quarter of the population in the nation's largest central cities, with one-third of them concentrated in 14 such cities.[39]

Recently there have been some indications of an emerging reversal in these migration patterns. The proportion of African Americans residing in the South actually has increased since 1980.[40] Nationwide, they are moving to the suburbs at a faster rate than whites.[41] In addition, there is evidence of some movement outside metropolitan areas entirely to escape the poor schools, gangs, drugs, and crime of the inner city.[42] This migratory reversal has been most apparent in cities that do not have large and established black middle classes, cities like Milwaukee, Detroit, St. Louis, Buffalo, Pittsburgh, and San Francisco as opposed to New York, Chicago, and Atlanta where sizable black middle-class populations seem to help stabilize their African American communities.[43]

Nevertheless, much of the suburbanization has been to all-black inner-ring suburbs adjacent to black urban ghettos. Despite some movement outward, most inner-city ghettos continue to become ever blacker; and even where there has been out-migration, those blacks have been more than replaced by poor Hispanics.[44] Additionally, racial minorities are an increasing proportion of a number of urban populations because whites have been departing at faster rates than they have.

Thus, African Americans and Hispanics have come to make up more than one-third of the central city population, and a third of them live below the federal government's poverty level.[45] Many estimate that this latter population actually has been undercounted, meaning that there are even more low-income racial minorities in a number of these cities, and thus they make up an even larger proportion of these cities' overall populations.[46]

Hispanics.   Hispanics have been one of the two most rapidly growing ethnic groups in the United States, increasing in number by more than 50 percent in the 1980s alone. They now represent more than 8 percent of this country's population, and they have a birthrate higher than non-Hispanic white or black Americans.[47] Hispanic Americans represent roughly the fifth-largest Spanish-speaking population in the world, after those in Mexico, Spain, Argentina, and Colombia.[48]

They are also more geographically concentrated and more urbanized than most of America's other ethnic groups. Geographically, a majority of Hispanic Americans live in either Texas or California, with most of the rest residing in New York, Florida, Illinois, Colorado, Arizona, and New Mexico. Within these states, approximately 85 percent live in metropolitan areas, three out of five in the central cities. San Antonio and El Paso, Texas, now have Hispanic majorities, as do Miami and Hialeah, Florida.[49]

Like other immigrant groups, Hispanics have come to the United States in various waves, from various places, and for various reasons. The basic population can be subdivided into Mexicans, Puerto Ricans, Cubans, and others—the latter group coming largely from Central and South American countries. Each has its own unique history and settlement pattern.[50]

MEXICANS In the mid-nineteenth century, a sizable group of Mexicans became American citizens with the annexation of a large plot of land following the Mexican-American War. However, Mexican immigration did not begin in significant numbers until the end of the industrial period, and it has been difficult to monitor because over the years a good bit of this entry has not been through governmentally sanctioned channels.

The Mexican Revolution began in 1909, prompting about one-quarter of a million Mexicans to flee to the United States between then and the late 1920s. During the Great Depression, however, many returned to Mexico, often as a result of deportation. Between 1929 and 1934, for example, some 400,000 returned. The 1930 census showed 639,000 Mexican Americans, but that number had shrunk to 377,000 by 1940.[51] The second major wave occurred in the 1940s and 1950s, initially prompted by a need for labor during World War II. Once again, the surge was followed by a spate of deportations, this time numbering as many as four million. Finally, the current wave commenced in the 1960s and continues to this day, despite continual efforts at deporting those without proper documentation.[52]

At present, approximately 62 percent of Hispanic Americans are of Mexican descent. Most live in California and various southwestern states, although a number followed migrant farm routes as far north as Ohio, Wisconsin, and Minnesota. Some 81 percent reside in metropolitan areas. San Antonio, for instance, now has a Mexican American majority, while Chicago appears to be the city outside the Sun Belt region with the largest Mexican American population.[53]

PUERTO RICANS Puerto Ricans are the second largest subgroup, representing roughly 13 percent of all Hispanic Americans. They are also the poorest, with nearly one-half living below the poverty line. Ninety-five percent reside in metropolitan areas, 60 percent in New York City alone. Most of the rest live in other cities of the Northeast. Although the New York City contingent increased from 500 to 70,000 between 1910 and 1940, most arrived after World War II. They came in search of economic opportunities and also out of a curiosity about life in the United States. This was facilitated in large part by the introduction of regular air service between U.S. cities and Puerto Rico. Puerto Ricans have U.S. citizenship because Puerto Rico has been a U.S. territory since the Jones Act of 1917, but many move back and forth between the mainland and Puerto Rico, and a number have retained a stronger identity with their native island.[54]

CUBANS   Cuban Americans make up the next largest segment of the Hispanic American population, roughly 6 percent of that group. Like Mexicans and Puerto Ricans, Cubans are an overwhelmingly urban people. Some 95 percent of Cuban Americans live in metropolitan areas, in particular Miami and Union City, New Jersey. Yet, many of the similarities stop there. They are a very different group with a very different history. Most are reasonably skilled middle-class people who left the island of Cuba for political reasons after Fidel Castro took power in the late 1950s. Given this history, Cuban Americans tend to be far more politically conservative than Americans of either Mexican or Puerto Rican heritage.

Most Cubans originally came to the United States in one of two major waves. Some 200,000 arrived in the decade between 1963 and 1973, many via a series of "freedom fights." Then, another 125,000 came during the Mariel boat lift in the spring of 1980 when Castro allowed a variety of people to emigrate, including a number of criminals, mental patients, and seriously ill individuals.[55]

OTHER HISPANICS   The remainder of the Hispanic American population has been drawn from a host of Central and South American countries, such as Nicaragua, Haiti, El Salvador, and Chile. Most have been fleeing poverty and political turmoil, and many have come to large U.S. cities. This group has been harder to count, however. Many have not come from countries that were considered the most politically repressive, and thus they did not qualify as readily for refugee status. Nevertheless, a number have come anyway, and many have joined the ranks of the estimated 3 to 12 million undocumented aliens presently residing in the United States.[56]

Asians.   The earliest Asian Americans came largely from China and Japan, but more recently they have come disproportionately from Korea, the Philippines, Vietnam, Thailand, and the Middle East.[57] A major turning point occurred in 1965 when President Lyndon Johnson ended extensive restrictions on Asian immigration that had been in effect since the turn of the century.[58] Entering at a rate of approximately 275,000 per year, their population more than doubled in the decade of the 1980s, increasing to more than 7 million people. Since 1980, Asians have been the nation's fastest growing ethnic group.[59]

As of the 1990 census, approximately 23 percent of Asian Americans were of Chinese descent, 19 percent were from the Philippines, and 11 percent were from East Asia and Korea, respectively. Meanwhile, Japanese Americans, an Asian American majority as recently as 1960, now make up only 19 percent of that population.[60]

Geographically, Asians have settled disproportionately in the Sun Belt, many taking advantage of the growth of jobs in new high-technology industries.[61] In particular they have settled on the West coast, one-third of them in California alone. They also have become a heavily urbanized population, with some 92 percent residing in metropolitan areas and a majority in central cities. As an example of this growth, there was only one Los Angeles census tract with an Asian American majority in 1950. By the 1980s, there were more than 50, including the largest Korean population outside Korea. Chinese Americans are a majority in the Los Angeles suburb of Monterey Park, and Filipinos make up a majority of the San Francisco suburb of Daly City. Asian Americans may soon be a majority of San Francisco's population. Some 83 languages currently are spoken on the streets of Los Angeles, and 60 within Hollywood High School alone.[62] Detroit, on the other hand, has the largest Arab American population in the country. Estimates of that population range from 80,000 to 200,000 people, largely Iraqis, Palestinians, and Syrians. Nationwide, there are approximately 2.5 million Arab Americans.[63]

Socioeconomically, the average member of one of the longer-standing Asian groups is well educated and has prospered. The 1980 census found the median family income of Japanese Americans to be $27,350, while it was $22,973 for Arab Americans, $22,560 for Chinese Americans, and only $20,800 for American whites.[64]

Native Americans.   Not all of this country's two million Native Americans have remained isolated in rural Indian reservations. An increasing number can be found in small ethnic enclaves located in a limited number of U.S. cities. Minneapolis and Los Angeles have identifiable Native American ghettos. Yet, like blacks and Hispanics, this group tends to be disproportionately poor and socially outcast.[65]

Immigration Today.   As an indication of just how significant immigration remains and how varied it has become, consider the case of New York City. Roughly 100,000 immigrants per year have been coming to that city, more than compensating for the outflow of natives during the 1980s. At least 5,000 people have come from each of 18 separate countries during the past decade alone, led largely by a variety of Caribbean and Asian nations. Some demographers have even speculated that such immigration must be allowed to continue if the country as a whole is to counterbalance its much slower native population growth.[66]

Three other immigration-related phenomena deserve attention. One is the increasing difficulty in counting the immigrants. The second is reverse immigration. And the third is recent changes in immigration law.

Because of the tremendous size of the nation's overall population, coupled with ever increasing residential mobility, it has become extremely difficult to take an accurate snapshot of our population. The U.S. Bureau of the Census struggled against great odds to conduct the 1990 census, and this process may be even more difficult in future years. A number of estimates suggested that many low-income city dwellers, especially African Americans and Hispanics, were undercounted by as much as 10 percent in the 1980 national census. Such undercounting has tremendous implications for large city electoral representation as well as for state and federal grant monies. It occurs in part because lower-income residents tend to move quite often and may well live with friends and relatives for periods of time, more than occasionally in violation of public housing or public assistance regulations. They also tend not to have telephones or long-term employment locations. Thus, besides the sizable phenomenon of undocumented immigration, such rootlessness and low visibility among Hispanic and African Americans makes it hard to know the precise demographic parameters of the current racial and ethnic ghettos.[67]

A second phenomenon is reverse immigration. In the industrial era a considerable number of immigrants changed their minds and returned to their native lands after an often brief stay in the United States. That trend has continued into the postindustrial period. Of the roughly 30 million people known to have immigrated to this country between 1900 and the present day, approximately one-third of them have since departed. In addition, more than 100,000 people have been emigrating from the United States to other countries each year.[68]

Last, the immigration laws themselves continue to evolve. There were three major revisions between 1980 and 1990. The 1980 Refugee Act put far more emphasis on accepting those fleeing politically repressive regimes, or at least those politically repressive regimes that were not presently in favor with the government of the United States. As a consequence, large numbers of Vietnamese, Thais, and Cambodians were allowed to enter, as were many Soviet Jews. Then came the Immigration Reform and Control Act of 1986, which granted amnesty to approximately three to seven million undocumented aliens who could prove that they had lived and worked in the United States for the previous three years. The tradeoff was that employers would begin to be held legally liable for hiring undocumented aliens, facing thousands of dollars in fines and up to six months in prison if they did so. Finally, the 1990 Immigration Act put more emphasis on admitting wealthy and skilled individuals. The federal government reserved as many as 20 percent of all available slots for those either with badly needed skills or who promised to invest at least $1 million and create at least 10 jobs in this country.

Other Demographic Trends.   Beyond the changing ethnic composition of large city populations, two additional demographic phenomena cannot be ignored. They are the growth in the number of elderly people populating large U.S. cities and the increasing number of urban children being raised in one-parent households. Both phenomena are often indicators of long-term poverty, and thus they are not good signs for the cities.

Age.   Defining the elderly as those over 65 years of age, we find that some two-thirds of them live in urban areas, about equally split between central cities and suburbs.[69] Even more remarkable is the fact that the elderly have shifted from being a predominantly rural population in 1930 to an overwhelmingly urban one today. This urbanization has been on the increase in recent years.[70] Figure 4.4 indicates the extent of this phenomenon in our 12 select cities. Besides representing some variation among cities, those figures are the culmination of sizable increases that have occurred across the postindustrial era. For example, the median for our 12 cities increased from 4 percent in 1930 to 8 percent in 1950, and was 18 percent by 1990.

The primary significance of this change from the cities' perspective is that this population requires additional public services. Less and less inclined to drive as they age, for example, the elderly turn to mass transportation as a major mode

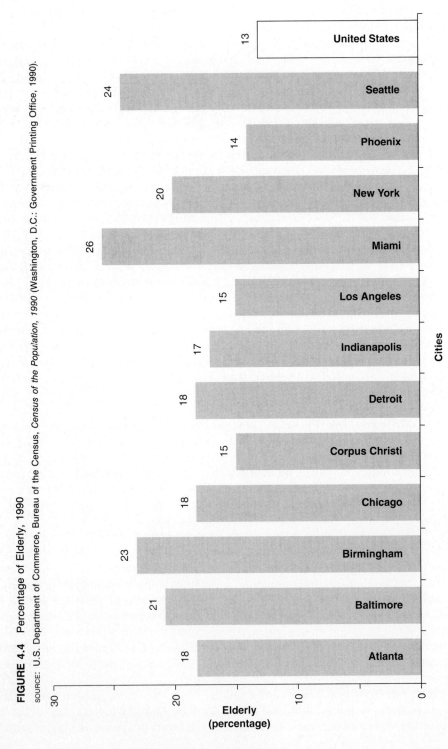

FIGURE 4.4 Percentage of Elderly, 1990

SOURCE: U.S. Department of Commerce, Bureau of the Census, *Census of the Population, 1990* (Washington, D.C.: Government Printing Office, 1990).

of travel. As a further complication, the cities have not been attracting a representative cross-section of the elderly, becoming instead the focus for a good many of the nation's elderly poor who require a host of social services. As life expectancy continues to increase and the large glut of Baby Boomers ceases having babies of their own (as shown in the decline in the number of school-age children nationwide), there is every reason to believe that the elderly will continue to make up a growing proportion of large city populations.[71]

A somewhat contrary development is at the other end of the age spectrum, however. The cities' increasing percentage of racial minorities has a higher reproduction rate and thus a significantly lower median age. In the nation's largest cities, the median age for whites is 33, while it is 25 for African Americans and 23 for Hispanics.[72] Given existing poverty rates in the black and Hispanic communities, this phenomenon does not bode well for the cities either, a point further reinforced by looking at changes in urban family structure.

Family Structure.   One last demographic trend of considerable urban significance is the sizable increase in one-parent families, particularly where the family head is female. The latter phenomenon correlates rather closely with poverty. Approximately one-half of all poor families nationwide are headed by a female, a figure far higher for poor black families and for poor urban families in general.[73] Central cities have twice as many female-headed families as do suburbs or nonmetropolitan areas;[74] and that number has been increasing steadily. Currently, roughly one in four urban children lives in a home without a father present.[75] Not only does this trend foreshadow the need for more and more public services as these indigent youth age, but William Julius Wilson also notes the links between the intergenerational perpetuation of the phenomenon and the creation of a nearly permanent service-dependent underclass.[76]

Social Relationships and Pathologies

The contour of metropolitan America has changed considerably in the post-industrial era. Core cities are now surrounded by a proliferation of people living in a variety of suburbs and unincorporated areas, with many of these areas beginning to develop urbanlike problems of their own. Such out-migration has in part been fueled by racial and ethnic group polarization—nothing new for the urban landscape. But besides the long-term social ramifications of such separation, it is also important to note what little is left for those trapped in urban ghettos at the bottom of today's socioeconomic hierarchy. With postindustrial economic shifts leaving ever fewer opportunities for legitimate socioeconomic advancement, large cities are increasingly plagued with social problems such as alarming crime and school dropout rates as well as inadequate housing and health care for their indigent residents.

Suburbanization.   A number of the oldest and largest industrial cities in the United States have witnessed a net loss in the number of their inhabitants while the national population continues to increase. During the industrial revolution, these cities absorbed more than their share of the growth in the nation's population. The country was urbanizing, and they clearly had become primary industrial and population centers. As both capital and people became more mobile, however, this trend finally began to peak and soon reversed itself. That reversal seems to have been slowed by accelerated wartime production in these cities during the 1940s; but the statistics leave little doubt that it has resumed with vigor since the end of World War II in both the older industrial cities and many of the cities that have emerged since the onset of postindustrialism.

By 1873 Chicago had a hundred suburbs containing a total of 50,000 people; between 1870 and 1900, Boston's suburbanites increased in number from 60,000 to 227,000. Nonetheless, as late as the 1920 census, less than 10 percent of the American public lived in suburbs.[77]

Cities had won a temporary reprieve throughout the industrial era, in part by aggressively annexing border areas before their populations united to incorporate themselves into separate suburban municipalities, but this was changing as postindustrialism dawned. An ever larger number of better-off whites were able to find a way to fend off annexation in order further to protect their escape from the people, problems, and taxes of the city. Today, although very gradually, the same phenomenon is beginning to occur in the more recently urbanizing Sun Belt.

In the course of the 1920s, the population of Beverly Hills grew 2,485 percent; Shaker Heights (Cleveland), 1,000 percent; Richmond Heights (St. Louis), 328 percent; Grosse Pointe Park (Detroit), 717 percent; and Elmwood (Chicago), 717 percent. Individual suburbs actually advertised in an effort to attract people, reminiscent of the competition between cities in the nineteenth century.[78]

The urban decline during the Great Depression left cities with insufficient quality housing to accommodate the baby and economic booms that followed World War II. Then, corresponding to the first major proliferation of automobiles, key federal programs accelerated the exodus to the suburbs. Urban renewal eliminated a good bit of lower-income housing to make way for downtown "revitalization." The Federal Housing and Veterans Assistance Acts made it possible for far more people to own their own homes, and the least expensive place to build this abundance of new homes was outside the city. In addition, the National Defense Highway Act, with its $2 billion per year in highway construction, made it far easier to reach the suburbs—even if one still worked in the city. Soon suburban areas were growing faster than the central cities.[79]

The population of the suburbs grew 2.5 times faster than that of the cities during the 1940s, and 5 times faster in the 1950s. Consequently, where three of five metropolitan residents still lived in center cities in 1950, more than three of five lived in the suburbs by 1990. Before long, shopping malls, entertainment centers, secondary business "strips," and a host of other service-related enterprises were following their patrons to these greener pastures.

The suburbs have become the fastest-growing areas in the nation (see figure 4.5). They have attracted central-city residents as well as a number of nonmetropolitan people who previously would have been likely to migrate into the central city. In addition, this national trend is understated when one remembers that cities have succeeded in annexing a good many of these residents in a number

FIGURE 4.5 Recent Trends in Areas of Residence 1950–1990

SOURCE: U.S. Department of Commerce, Bureau of the Census, *Statistical Abstracts of the United States* (Washington, D.C.: Government Printing Office, 1950, 1960, 1970, 1990).

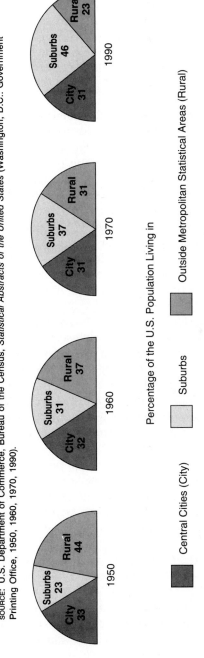

1950

1960

1970

1990

Percentage of the U.S. Population Living in

Central Cities (City)

Suburbs

Outside Metropolitan Statistical Areas (Rural)

83

of the sprawling metropolitan areas of the Sun Belt; for example, Houston encompasses more than 500 square miles and Oklahoma City more than 600.

As suburbanization has grown, five important recent developments deserve mention: (1) There is some indication that the traditional pattern of the better-off living farther from the center city has begun to reverse. (2) A number of suburbs have evolved into sizable cities themselves. (3) Suburbs are more and more distinguishable one from another by their demographic profiles, functions, and problems. (4) A phenomenon called the mega-county has begun to appear. And, finally, (5) an increasing number of metropolitan residents are opting to live outside the metropolis altogether.

One of the reasons the better-off residents traditionally moved away from the center city during the industrial era was to distance themselves from the noise, congestion, and pollution of the city's large factories. Yet, the high-tech industries of the postindustrial period do not exhibit most of these externalities, creating more of an incentive for the well-to-do once again to live closer to their work and play. When the median cost of a house reached $170,000 in the city of Boston, for example, high-tech industries ended up literally busing in blue-collar workers from outlying small towns and suburbs.[80] Yet, gentrification of the central city is still by far the exception rather than the rule. And net out-migration continues.

Some very sizable suburbs have developed. A number have become so large and both economically and socially diverse, that they have left demographers in search of a new lexicon. The 1990 census notes that 29 suburban communities now have populations of 100,000 or more. Five surround Dallas-Fort Worth alone. They are Arlington, Garland, Irving, Mesquite, and Plano. Other prominent suburb-cities include Lowell, Massachusetts, Stamford, Connecticut, and Scottsdale, Arizona. Some even have begun to spawn their own suburbs.[81]

There has long been considerable differentiation in the composition and function of suburbs, especially between inner-ring and outer-ring ones. Black suburbs developed in part as a response to early twentieth-century white violence in the cities. As an example, the development of Kinloch outside St. Louis followed the riots of 1917. At about the same time, blue-collar suburbs emerged with their own manufacturing industries.[82] Thus, as a result of key social and economic trends, some one-third of the metropolitan poor currently reside in a suburb.[83] Beyond attracting an increasing number of poor people, the older inner-ring suburbs often face the same problems of crime, poor schools, and population loss as do the core cities they surround. As John Bollens and Henry Schmandt put it, "In looking at the central city of today, we may be seeing the suburbs of tomorrow."[84]

Another trend is the evolution of megacounties. Often unincorporated, these are not cities nor are they suburbs. Instead they are expanses of residential and commercial development normally subject only to the jurisdiction of their surrounding county. Virtually all white racially, they contain many of the retail stores, restaurants, and entertainment centers frequented by those who live and now often work there. Examples include much of Du Page County (outside Chicago), Montgomery and Fairfax Counties (Washington, D.C.), Orange County (Los Angeles), Johnson County (Kansas City), Oakland County (Detroit), and Gwinnett and Cobb Counties (Atlanta).[85]

There is clear evidence that both suburban cities and megacounties are beginning to face the standard array of urban problems, including pollution, congestion, school crowding, and inadequate infrastructure (roads, water, and sewer lines). Nonetheless, most have been wealthy enough to cope, particularly given a proclivity to utilize private services.[86]

Last, although census data have yet fully to reflect it, studies are beginning to show that a considerable number of people have opted to move away from the immediate metropolitan area entirely, living in small towns within commuting distance.[87] Recent Gallup polling indicates a steady decline in the proportion of Americans preferring to live in central cities. Some one-half of all Americans would currently prefer to live in a small town or a rural area; and equally problematic for cities is the fact that even two-thirds of those still preferring a metropolitan residence want to be in the suburbs.[88]

Why have so many people found suburbia and small towns more attractive? Demetrios Caraley speaks of specific pull and push factors.[89] Pull factors would include yards and trees, roomier housing, newer and better schools, availability of governmental mortgage loans, and individual methods of transportation. Edward Banfield has argued that this decentralization was inevitable, given the development in methods of transportation, that is, trains, highways, and automobiles. These allowed people more easily to make status moves up the residential ladder; it was cheaper to build out rather than up; and it was only natural to want to own one's own home.[90] Beyond these incentives, there were push factors as well: deteriorating services, rising taxes, overall cost of living, accelerating blight, mounting crime rates, racial "invasion" of neighborhoods, and the fear of busing.

The 1920s marked the end of the physical expansion of the central cities— at least in the North. Their surrounding suburbs were almost all refusing annexation, and state laws protected them. The middle class could now escape the responsibility of supporting and servicing in-migrating groups. As Robert Goldston noted, "Suburbanites are suburbanites because they desire to be near enough to the city to enjoy its benefits, but not near enough to have to shoulder its burdens."[91] Again from the central city perspective, Robert Wood concluded that "the central city had become the receptacle for all the functions the suburbs did not care to support."[92]

Detroit is a case in point. Its population stood at nearly two million in 1950 but has been declining steadily since. The preliminary 1990 census count puts Detroit at roughly one million people, a decline of approximately 50 percent in just four decades. Following the white flight of the 1960s and 1970s, the city is now approximately 75 percent African American. Yet as Kurt Metzger, senior research analyst at Wayne State University's Center for Urban Studies observed, "People might have though it would end with white flight. But crime, drugs, and the overriding concerns of life and death are driving the black middle class away, too." Bette Buss, senior research associate at Michigan's Citizen's Research Council concludes that "more and more, Detroit is a city with a remnant population that can't afford to escape."[93]

An example of the beneficiary of such flight is DeSoto County, Mississippi. In 1950, it contained 24,599 people and was almost entirely rural, some 40 miles from the nearest big city, Memphis. By 1990, that population had nearly tripled as Interstate 55 pushed south and brought Memphis with it. Bill Smith, an economic analyst for the Center for Policy Research and Planning in Jackson, Mississippi, notes that now "when you drive into it, you'd never realize you've gone from one state to another or one town to another. The small farms have been almost wiped out."[94]

Meanwhile, the likelihood that the central cities' current ghetto residents can work their way out has declined considerably. Gluck and Meister concluded that only mass production during World War II and federal assistance prompted by the reliance of the national Democratic party on the urban vote, postponed these cities' "day of reckoning."[95] Thus were forged the circumstances facing the most recent waves of urban newcomers, especially the racial minorities.

> The years immediately following World War II witnessed an acceleration of the trend toward two separate racial societies, this time on a much broader spatial scale than had existed before. . . . It was an overwhelmingly white exodus primarily because even at the prevailing modest prices, home ownership was an economic impossibility for most urban blacks. Then, too, suburban jurisdictions, learning from the big cities, incorporated . . . exclusionary zoning.[96]

Racial Polarizations.   A group of Yonkers city councilpersons recently chose fines and jail terms rather than implement a federal judge's order to integrate low-cost apartments into single-family, all-white residential neighborhoods.[97] As another example of this growing separation, a number of Boston's black leaders gave up on integration altogether and led a movement toward having a number of predominantly black areas secede entirely from Boston and form their own black city.[98] The same move was attempted in East Palo Alto, California, as well.[99] However, these are only contemporary symptoms of a problem that began much earlier.

Between 1962 and 1968, more than 300 major civil disturbances shook many of the nation's largest inner cities. Frustrated blacks lashed out with arson, vandalism, and sniper fire directed at symbols of white authority, most notably in Chicago (1964), Watts (1965), Newark and Detroit (1967), and Washington, D.C. and Chicago again (1968). Hundreds were killed; thousands were injured; tens of thousands were arrested; and millions of dollars in property damage was done. Yet, this was neither the first nor last of such urban unrest. Similar disturbances had occurred in Chicago (1919), Detroit (1943), and would appear again in Miami (1980) and Los Angeles (1992).[100]

The Kerner Commission noted that between 1950 and 1966, 70 percent of the increase in the nation's white population occurred in the suburbs, while 86 percent of the black population increase occurred in the central cities. The commission warned that America was becoming two separate societies: one white, one black; one in the suburbs, and one in the cities.[101] Since that warning was issued, the separation has increased.

Residential segregation remains widespread and well documented. At present, Chicago, Cleveland, Detroit, Milwaukee, and Newark are deemed to be the most divided and have earned the classification "hyper-segregated."[102] Cities such as

Atlanta, Baltimore, Birmingham, Boston, Dallas, Fort Lauderdale, Houston, Indianapolis, Jacksonville, Los Angeles, Memphis, Philadelphia, Pittsburgh, and St. Louis are all more than 80 percent segregated; most others exceed 70 percent. Communities with extensive residential integration are still by far the exception, for example, cities with large local universities such as Gainesville, Riverside, Tallahassee, and San Jose.[103]

How has such extensive segregation come about? Although a certain degree of self-selection is no doubt a factor, there have been a number of racially segregationist practices that have contributed. Until the United States Supreme Court put an end to it in 1948, blacks were excluded from a number of all-white neighborhoods by restrictive covenants actually written into the deeds of the houses. Yet, despite other prohibitive Supreme Court decisions and the passage of the Fair Housing Act of 1968, segregation is still quite pervasive, leaving most blacks—including the black middle class—in predominantly black areas.[104] Today, real estate agents continue both consciously and subconsciously to steer members of one race into racially homogeneous neighborhoods. Government contributes by siting social services and public housing in predominantly black low-income areas, and zoning laws effectively keep most blacks out of middle- and upper-income areas by restricting the size and type of house that can be built in these neighborhoods.[105] As a discomforting symbol of this separation, cities have increasingly been inclined to block off streets at the end of gentrified neighborhoods, creating artificial cul-de-sacs in order to restrict access to those wealthier residential areas.[106]

Richard Sabaugh, city councilman in the white Detroit suburb of Warren, stated: "The image of Detroit is of a decaying, crime-ridden city headed by a mayor who makes racist remarks. We view the values of people in Detroit as completely foreign. We just want to live in peace. And we feel anybody coming from Detroit is going to cause problems. . . . It's all as one complex—blacks, Coleman Young, crime, drugs, Detroit. People feel they've been driven out once, and it could happen again."[107]

> When Rosa Parks refused to move to the back of the bus in 1955, there was still the belief that the end of the Jim Crow laws would mean the end of second-class status. The laws would change and life would change. Well, in America's cities we've met the future, and it's the past. Black families live in the urban equivalent of sharecroppers' shacks and their children go to segregated schools.[108]

Not only are whites and blacks geographically separated; they still attend separate schools for the most part despite court-ordered desegregation efforts. In New York City only 3 percent of whites attend public schools, leaving the average black student attending a school that is 60 percent black, 27 percent Hispanic, and 3 percent Asian.[109]

Blacks and whites also remain far apart socioeconomically. Blacks remain twice as likely as whites to be unemployed or among the working poor and three times as likely to live below the poverty level and in overcrowded housing. Black income is roughly 40 percent less than that of whites, and the gap has been increasing of late. When blacks and Hispanics are combined, they make up a clear majority of the urban poor, with central city blacks three times as likely to be poor as central city whites. Some 60 percent of black households headed by a single woman live below the poverty level, more than 60 percent of black teenagers are out of work, and scarcely more than 50 percent of all black males have employment. Those who are employed are overrepresented in lower-echelon blue-collar and domestic-service positions, in lower-paying industries, and in the public sector.[110] As a shocking upshot to all of this, the NAACP has estimated that at current rates the year 2000 will find 70 percent of existing black men dead, in jail, or addicted to drugs or alcohol.[111] The *New England Journal of Medicine* notes that a black man in Harlem has less chance of seeing his 65th birthday than does a man in Bangladesh.[112]

Overt racist violence has plagued black Americans for more than a century beyond the Emancipation Proclamation. They have faced night riders, lynchings, and the storming of black neighborhoods by white mobs. Although somewhat less frequent, these blatantly violent acts continue and in many ways simply represent the tip of a very large iceberg of racism.

Mobile, Alabama (March 1981)
A black man, accused of killing a white police officer, is set free because of a mistrial. Two admitted Klan members seek revenge by randomly abducting a 19-year-old black youth. They beat him with a tree limb as he pleads for his life, and when he is finally beaten into submission, they strangle him, cut his throat three times, tie a rope around his neck, and hang him from a tree to demonstrate "Klan strength in Alabama."[113]

Steubenville, Ohio (April 1981)
Another 19-year-old black male is murdered in an apparent act of racist violence. In this instance, the youth is shot in the head for allegedly dating a white girl.[114]

Detroit, Michigan (May 1981)
For over two years a black woman is harassed by a group of whites for choosing to live in a predominantly white neighborhood. They throw baseballs through her windows and paint KKK insignia on her garage. Then three whites, aged 19 to 23, throw a pipe bomb through her bathroom window. When she attempts to throw it back outside, it explodes and leaves her maimed.[115]

Brooklyn, New York (June 1982)
Three middle-aged black transit workers finish their shift at midnight. They stop to buy a snack on their way home. When leaving the store, they are harassed by a number of whites. When their car fails to start, the group of whites swells. Amid chants of "niggers go home," the car is smashed with blunt objects. Two of the transit workers flee, but the driver is pulled from the car and beaten to death.[116]

Boston, Massachusetts (June 1982)

A black woman moves into the white neighborhood of Dorchester. As she walks to and from her home, she endures racial taunts, stone throwing, and hard shoves. Finally, a gasoline bomb is hurled through her window.[117]

Chicago, Illinois (November 1984)

A black family moves into an all-white enclave called The Island, next to Cicero and Oak Park. Approximately a dozen whites, armed with guns, spend an entire night hurling bricks, bottles, pipes, and tire irons through their windows. Unable to call police because phone service has not yet been installed, the family huddles behind their furniture until they are able to flee down a back alley at daybreak. Throughout the nightlong attack, no neighbors come to their rescue, while police cars apparently cruise past on three different occasions and do nothing to stop it.[118]

Philadelphia, Pennsylvania (November 1985)

A black family and an interracial couple move into the predominantly white area of Elmwood. Vandalism begins almost immediately, and it culminates in 400 whites congregating outside their homes and chanting for them to leave.[119]

Queens, New York (December 1986)

At approximately midnight, faced with near-freezing temperatures, three black men leave their stalled car to seek shelter. As they walk through the all-white Howard Beach area, three white youths shout racial slurs at them, words are exchanged, and gestures are exchanged shortly thereafter at a pizza parlor. The white youths then proceed to a party and round up eight friends, saying, "There's some niggers in the pizza parlor —let's go kill them." Armed with bats and sticks, they chase and beat the black men; one flees onto a highway and is struck dead by a car.[120]

Peekskill, New York (November 1987)

A black insurance adjuster is confronted by three bat- and pipe-wielding white men on the outskirts of town. He is chased until he is finally rescued by a passing motorist. Five days later, his family's home is firebombed.[121]

Portland, Oregon (November 1988)

A 27-year-old Ethiopian is beaten to death after being dropped off in front of his apartment in southeast Portland. His white assailant, who testified in court that he killed the young man "because of his race," hit him so hard with a baseball bat that the bat split.[122]

Brooklyn, New York (August 1989)

A 16-year-old black youth, having come to all-white Bensonhurst with three black friends to check out a used car he had seen advertised in the paper, found himself surrounded by some 20 to 30 jeering whites armed with baseball bats and a gun. This group mistakenly thought that the black youths had come to attend a party being hosted by a white woman, and in the course of the confrontation shot and killed the 16-year-old. Standing on a nearby corner shortly thereafter, a white teen stated that "black people don't belong here. This is our neighborhood."[123]

African Americans have faced the fear, hostility, and violence of the indigenous population. Instead of "Little Italys," they have lived in areas referred to as "Niggertowns," "Smoketowns," "Black Bottoms," "Buzzard Rows," and "Coon Alleys."[124] Unlike other ethnic groups, they have had a far more difficult time looking, thinking, and acting like Anglo-whites.[125] Residential mobility has proven to be very difficult, and in a rapidly changing economy, blacks have had an extremely hard time improving their social position.

Therefore, even though World Wars I and II supplied periods of economic reprieve, the die already was cast. Truly bad times lay ahead.

CASE STUDY   Toledo, Ohio

In 1980, Toledo had a population of 345,000, of whom 61,000 were blacks. Most of [the blacks] settled here in the 1940s and 1950s moving from farms in Mississippi and Alabama to take jobs in what was then a booming industrial area where a person without training could walk a block or two and find a factory job.

All that has changed for blacks and whites over the last few years as plant after plant has closed. The city is now rebuilding its downtown around new office buildings, a convention center, hotels, and shops on the Maumee River. . . .

But the city is living under fear that its largest manufacturer, the Jeep Corporation, which employs 6,000 people, will close, as it has threatened to do in a war of nerves with the United Automobile Workers.

Like most cities, Toledo has experienced a series of civil rights advances, from fair housing efforts that have opened new neighborhoods for minority people to the entry of blacks into business and politics.

But growth of black poverty areas and confinement of most blacks within a few square miles of the city south of downtown has created tensions. Recently, a 27-year-old white man, Kirk R. Taeberner, was sentenced to 9 to 15 years in prison for firing a sawed-off shotgun into the home of a black family that moved into a white neighborhood. He said the motive had been to "send a little message" to blacks.

In 1970, 10,531 Toledo blacks lived in poverty neighborhoods. By 1980 the number had grown to 16,019, and by all estimates it is much higher now.

"We are in deep trouble," said the Reverend Floyd Rose, a former president of the local chapter of the NAACP. "We have lost our children. When they get to high school age they are not in school and they are not in jobs, they are on the streets."

Speaking to the loss of community, he said that 20 years ago many of the businesses in the black neighborhoods here were owned and run by blacks but were now owned and run by Asians.

A few blocks away at the Kitchen for the Poor, Mr. Savage, the minister, told of other reasons for distress. "Growing numbers are on welfare," he said. "There is public housing here but there is a long waiting list. The cheapest you can rent a house for is about $300 a month, which those on welfare cannot afford. What they do is get up enough for a security deposit and the first month's rent and stay there as long as they can before they are evicted. It is constant moving from one house to another."[126]

Additional Social Discord.   Prejudice and discrimination have not been reserved exclusively for African Americans. Hispanics have endured much stereotyping and discriminatory treatment as well, particularly as many are presumed to be job-threatening illegal aliens.[127] There is mounting evidence that the 1986 Immigration Act only has increased this animosity,[128] but it does not stop with racial minorities, either. In a move reminiscent of the early twentieth century, the United States House of Representatives seriously considered a 1990 bill that would have required any company with 50 or more employees to pay between $500 and $1,000 for every foreign worker they hired. The money was to be used to retrain American workers.[129]

Although not directed at "foreigners" as such, physical attacks on gays also have been on the rise. In a recent rather typical incident in New York's Greenwich Village, seven young men ranging in age from 23 to 30 accosted three gay men, ultimately slashing the face of one, beating another, and threatening to throw the third into the Hudson River.[130]

Last, there are tensions beyond those that exist between mainstream white "natives" and the more recent urban arrivals. Amid postindustrial squalor and the competition for scarce resources, racial and ethnic minorities have been turning on each other as well. There has been a long-standing tension between African Americans and many of the Hispanics in Miami. There is ill-will between blacks and Asians that has surfaced in a number of incidents in which alleged Asian mistreatment of black customers has culminated in emotion-charged boycotts of Asian stores. Such episodes occurred in Washington, D.C. in 1986, Philadelphia in 1986, New York City in 1990, and Los Angeles in 1991.[131]

Other Pathologies.   In the wake of the individual and corporate abandonment of many U.S. cities lies a whole host of social problems for those who remain. Beyond the intergroup animosities discussed above are school dropout rates, crime, homelessness, and inadequate health care.

School Dropouts.   Virtually since the dawn of urbanization, city residents had been more likely than the rest of the country to have finished high school. As late as 1940 that was still the case. Yet, as postindustrialism has progressed, city residents are now less likely than others to finish school (see figure 4.6). Of course, there is clear variation according to a city's stage of postindustrial decline. The dropout rate ranges from a quarter or less in cities like Indianapolis, Phoenix, and Seattle to more than one third in cities like Chicago, Detroit, Baltimore, and Miami.

FIGURE 4.6 High School Dropout Rate, 1990

SOURCE: U.S. Department of Commerce, Bureau of the Census, *Census of the Population, 1990* (Washington, D.C.: Government Printing Office, 1990).

*Preliminary estimate

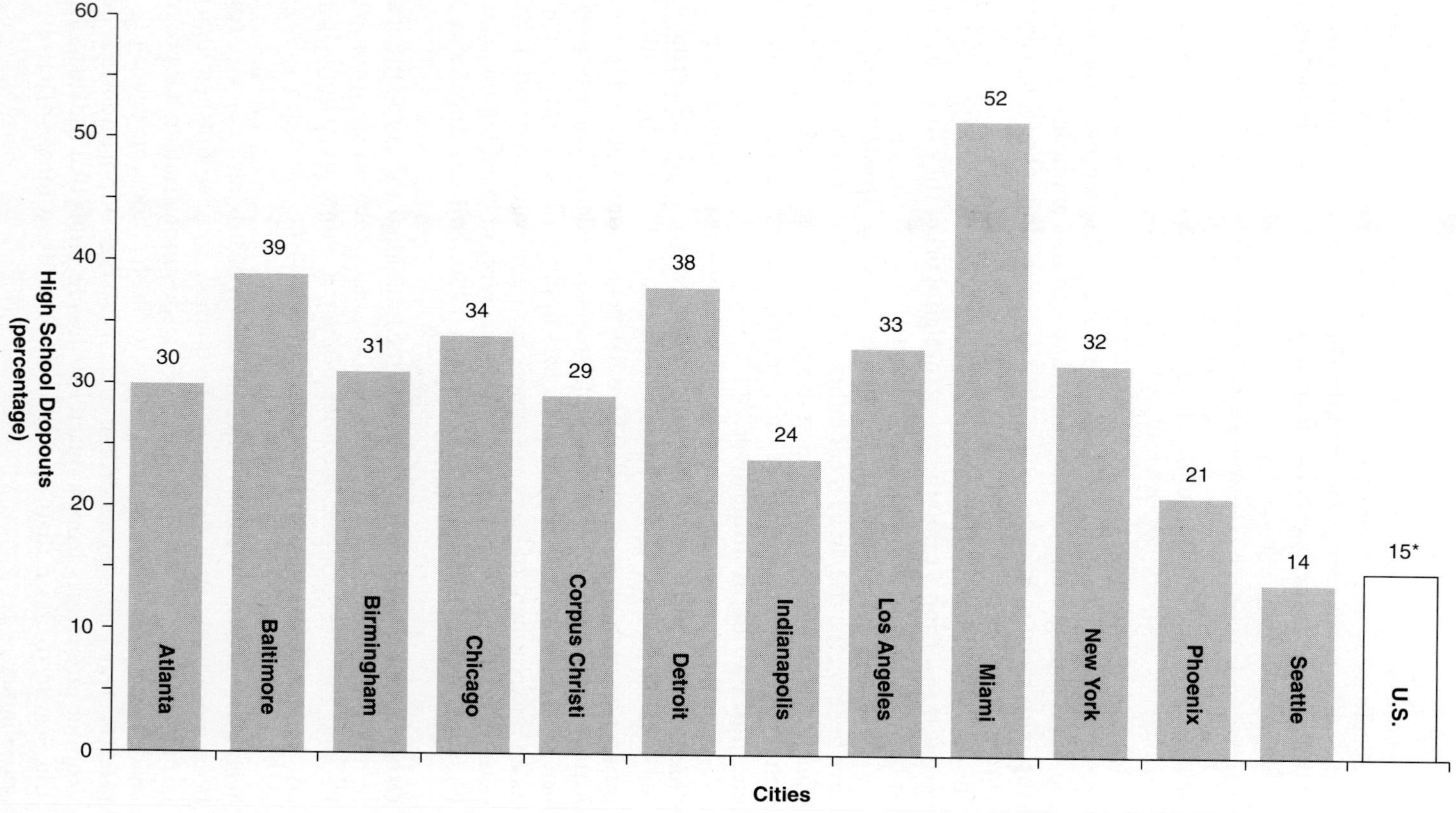

High School Dropouts (percentage)

Cities

City	Percentage
Atlanta	30
Baltimore	39
Birmingham	31
Chicago	34
Corpus Christi	29
Detroit	38
Indianapolis	24
Los Angeles	33
Miami	52
New York	32
Phoenix	21
Seattle	14
U.S.	15*

But even for the graduates, the quality of inner-city schools is often questionable.[132] Thus, with more and more inhabitants of the cities lacking even a suspect high school diploma and with job prospects for the underskilled vanishing rapidly, a good many of the residents of the ghetto have come to rely on government either for a job or for special training increasingly necessary to enter the secondary labor market. Lately, the government has been eliminating many of its jobs and job-training programs.[133] So what is left for these ghetto inhabitants?

> . . . go downtown and get a job? Oh, come on . . . I make $40 to $50 a day selling pot. You want me to go down to the garment district and push one of those trucks through the street and at the end of the week take home $40 or $50 if I'm lucky?[134]

Crime. As crime statistics imply, a sizable number of inner-city residents apparently are turning to the "irregular" job market. Harvey Brenner, doing research for the Congressional Joint Economic Committee, found clear correlations between unemployment and social and individual pathology, including violent crime.[135] Although bad in the early days of urbanization, before police and other services were regularized and expanded, crime may well be becoming worse today.

> The level of violence has no equal since at least the 1920s and invites comparison with benighted periods of mayhem in the 19th century. . . . [W]hen old accounts are discounted for exaggeration, this era may emerge as the worst ever. . . . [W]here once it was largely bottled up in a few notorious districts, it now rages throughout the city.[136]

Whereas crime rates have risen steadily across the United States since 1960, they literally have soared in the inner cities; and they actually understate the problem, given victim and bureaucratic underreporting.[137] In Washington, D.C., for example, the RAND institute estimated that approximately one in four young inner-city men are dealing drugs.[138] In New York City, even the official robbery rates have increased more than tenfold since the early 1950s, and gunshots are reported on an average of more than 200 times a day.[139] Drive-by shootings, reminiscent of the "Roaring '20s," have become increasingly frequent, leaving rivals as well as innocent bystanders lying dead.[140] This time, instead of fighting over illegal alcohol, however, much of the violence apparently stems from the traffic of illegal drugs. Both users and sellers seem prone to violence, particularly when cocaine and crack cocaine are involved. As Judith Miller Jones and Jane Koppelman put it, "Crack has hit the social fabric of the ghetto like a nuclear bomb."[141]

In East Oakland, children must be taught what to do when the shooting starts. When they hear the crack of gunfire begin, they must turn off the lights to avoid being silhouetted in the windows. In addition, it is best to run and hide in the safest places available. "We better head for the bathtub, Nanny," says 6-year-old Miesha when she hears the telltale crackle.[142]

The crime rates depend to a large extent on the particular city's stage of postindustrial decline. Figure 4.7 indicates the highest crime rates are in older Frost Belt cities such as Detroit, Baltimore, Chicago, and New York and in older Sun Belt cities such as Atlanta and Miami in particular, with Birmingham being a peculiar exception. The rates are lowest in newer cities such as Corpus Christi, Phoenix, and Indianapolis. In between is the more recently industrialized city of Seattle. Yet, 11 of the 12 cities have violent crime rates well above the national average. Thus, the absolute and relative crime levels of many such cities scarcely place them in a position of comparative advantage as they attempt either to attract or to retain industrial corporations and more financially secure inhabitants.

Crime statistics have a certain abstractness to them that fails to capture the tragedy involved. Consider, instead, a concrete case in point. A young single mother of a teenage boy is employed part of the time as a domestic worker in the home of a suburban physician and his family, a reasonably long bus ride from her place of residence in a public housing project. One night she is accosted and brutally raped on her way home from the bus stop. Yet despite the fact that she can identify her assailants, she dares not report the incident to the police. She has well-founded fears that other members of their street gang will seriously harm her son if she does. Such is the rule of law in the projects.

Urban crime now reaches far outside the projects. A five-month-old baby is shot in the head by a stray bullet as he lies sleeping in bed with his grandmother. A nine-year-old girl, asleep in her family's car, is killed in a crossfire. A middle-income female jogger is raped and nearly beaten to death, apparently just for the sport of it. In a botched robbery attempt, an advertising executive is shot and killed in a pay telephone booth.[143]

"People here accept the violence as normal," said Reverend John Brogan, a priest at the Saint John Cantius Church in East New York. As an example, he notes the time "we were setting up for a church dance, taking chairs to the school. There was a shootout at the corner. We just stopped carrying the chairs until it was over. What else can you do?"[144]

Statistics are beginning to suggest devastating psychological effects on inner-city children exposed to such day-to-day violence. The trauma appears to stem from fear, and it surfaces in the form of depression, anxiety, nightmares, emotional numbness, behavioral problems, and low self-esteem. Some children even exhibit a form of posttraumatic stress disorder, where they reenact a particularly horrifying event in repetitive joyless play.[145]

Homelessness.   Another urban pathology that has grown enormously and become increasingly visible is homelessness. In virtually any large city in the country the homeless can be seen huddled in doorways, sleeping on park benches, cowering in alleyways, rummaging through trash bins, and begging on street corners. These are some of America's most unwanted. Most of them must scrounge daily for something to eat as well as a place to sleep. They have followed a variety of paths to arrive where they are.

Estimates of numbers of homeless range from 230,000 to four million, depending on how the term is defined. One group is the "literally homeless," those with absolutely no place to live at that moment. These people sleep either

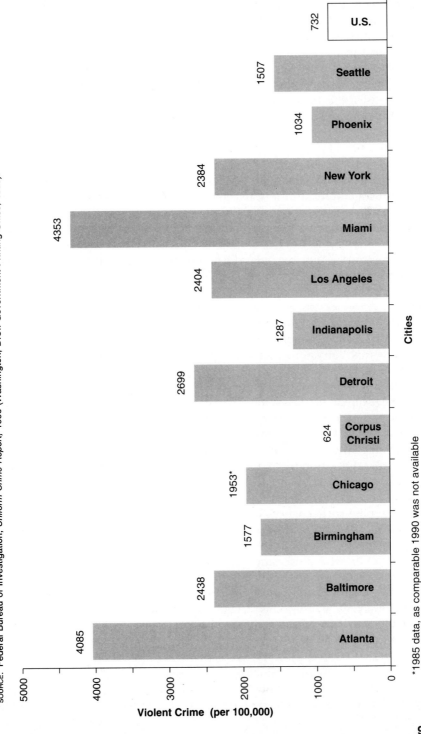

FIGURE 4.7 Violent Crime Rates, 1990

SOURCE: Federal Bureau of Investigation, *Uniform Crime Report*, 1990 (Washington, D.C.: Government Printing Office, 1990).

*1985 data, as comparable 1990 was not available

Cities

Violent Crime (per 100,000)

City	Rate
U.S.	732
Seattle	1507
Phoenix	1034
New York	2384
Miami	4353
Los Angeles	2404
Indianapolis	1287
Detroit	2699
Corpus Christi	624
Chicago	1953*
Birmingham	1577
Baltimore	2438
Atlanta	4085

on the streets or in one of a limited number of publicly or privately provided shelters. The other major group is the "hidden homeless," those living in someone else's home because they cannot provide one for themselves.[146] In 1985, New York mayor Ed Koch began placing homeless families in dormitory-like shelters rather than welfare hotels in order to dissuade such families from leaving the homes of friends and relatives who had been accommodating them.[147]

Many of these people are mentally ill, cast adrift by the deinstitutionalization movement of the 1960s and 1970s. Many are drug and alcohol addicted. Some are competent and employable but are simply irresponsible. Some have just been unlucky. A few actually have chosen a life "on the road." Yet, as the phenomenon has been receiving more systematic analysis, a number of surprises have surfaced in terms of proportionality. Kathleen Dockett found that three-quarters of the District of Columbia homeless were not mentally ill and 90 percent had no history of institutionalization in any psychiatric hospital.[148] Martha Burt and Barbara Cohen, interviewing a sample of 1,700 homeless people across 20 cities, found that a full one-quarter had jobs and still could not afford shelter; their average monthly income was $137; and a growing proportion of them were mothers with small children.[149] Most recently, the number of homeless two-parent families also has begun to mount.[150]

Using 1980 census data, Peter Rossi estimated that there were at least 17 million "extremely poor" people in the United States. He defined extremely poor to mean less than $4,396 per year. If rent were $200 per month, such individuals would be left with a daily budget of $1.50 for all else. This finding led him to conclude that "given the increased size since 1980 of the extremely poor population, it is remarkable not that we have so many homeless people in America, but that we have so few."[151]

The problem has been exacerbated of late by massive cuts in federal housing assistance for the poor and the destruction of many single-room-occupancy hotels to make way for more lucrative private real estate development in downtown areas. Some cities have attempted to take up a degree of the slack, but most are not in a fiscal position to do much more than make a small dent in the problem. That leaves the emergency shelters; and not only are they inadequate in number, but many are so filthy, overcrowded, and dangerous that potential residents often prefer to take their chances on the streets.[152]

Rather than demanding a political solution to this human tragedy or even showing much compassion, most urban dwellers either try to ignore the homeless or, of late, express increasing impatience with them. In a number of cities, a backlash actually has begun to occur. Citizens are not demanding that city governments find an adequate way to feed, shelter, clothe, and rehabilitate these people; instead, they are fighting the placement of shelters in their neighborhoods and demanding an end to the intrusion of begging and the visual blight created by their street encampments or mere presence.[153]

Inadequate Health Care.   Since the ghetto unrest of the 1960s, besides providing food stamps and increased public assistance monies in general, government has made a much more concerted effort to guarantee health care services for inner-city residents. The Medicaid insurance program has been the primary vehicle for such care, with the federal, state, and a few local governments sharing the costs. Nevertheless, the entire effort appears to be in trouble.

Health care costs have soared across the country, a problem further complicated by the expense of treating increasing numbers of drug addicts and victims of violent crime as well as providing long-term care for patients with acquired immune deficiency syndrome (AIDS). As a result, the cost of Medicaid health insurance for the poor has become burdensome for government at all levels.[154] To address this fiscal pressure, Medicaid has begun to cut back on procedures it will cover as well as the amount it will pay for covered services. This policy, coupled with the normal bureaucratic red tape involved in collecting from such a large agency, has led an increasing number of physicians to stop treating Medicaid patients altogether.[155]

In addition to problems with the Medicaid process itself, a number of people make too much money to qualify for it; yet, they do not receive health insurance with their jobs and do not make enough money to afford an individual health plan. These people, some 35 million in number, or 14 percent of the U.S. population, are completely uninsured and vulnerable to potentially devastating medical bills.[156] Of the 5.2 million people in Cook County, Illinois, 700,000 qualify for Medicaid and 850,000 have no medical insurance whatsoever.[157]

These numbers have left center-city hospitals overwhelmed, particularly those public hospitals that do not have the luxury of transferring Medicaid or "charity" cases elsewhere to avoid the financial burden. Even so, the 1,000-bed Cook County Hospital, which treats 30 emergency room patients each hour, must frequently reroute prospective patients elsewhere because it is totally full.[158] In Harlem Hospital, it is not unusual to find patients sleeping in hallways because there are no more rooms, or to find frail elderly women with asthma waiting patiently for three days in order to get into the emergency room's cardiopulmonary resuscitation unit.[159] The average emergency room wait for a bed in a county hospital is more that 5 hours and can be up to 10 days. Meanwhile, these hospitals lose an average of $40 million annually on non-reimbursed treatment.[160]

Central-city health indicators remain shameful. Using infant mortality as one of the best of such indicators, a number of America's postindustrial cities exhibit levels as bad or worse than some Third World countries. Defining infant mortality as death within the first year after birth, the numbers are 13 out of 1,000 in New York City, 16 in Chicago, 17 in Philadelphia, 19 in Newark, 20 in Detroit, and 21 in Washington, D.C. These figures mean that 2 of every 100 babies born will never reach their first birthday, and the figures are far worse in the inner cities.[161]

Similarly, thousands of ghetto women are dying unnecessarily from cancer because they are not receiving adequate care. Without routine mammograms, breast cancers go undetected.[162] When pap smears are not taken regularly, or when their results are not read in a timely fashion, cervical cancer is untreated.[163] Poverty is not just inconvenient, or even painful; it can actually kill. It kills people every day in America's inner cities.[164]

CONCLUSION

Cities have remained a magnet for virtually all recently arriving immigrants, long serving as launching pads in which many immigrants developed the economic and social skills necessary to begin their way up the ladder of material well-being and social acceptance. At least, that was true for a large number of the Irish ghetto dwellers of the early industrial era as well as a good many Italians, Poles, Jews, and others in the latter part of that period.

In the postindustrial era, however, much of this tendency has changed. The most recent ghetto dwellers, especially racial minorities, are finding very few bottom rungs available on the economic ladder of success. Instead, they have become increasingly likely to remain locked in dead-end secondary labor market jobs that offer little hope of economic or social advance.

Cities that have not become magnets for high-tech industries, regional services, and corporate headquarters are facing significant abandonment. Many areas that in the past would have been the sites of vibrant racial and ethnic neighborhoods today are often vacant lots collecting trash, or rows of abandoned buildings collecting drug addicts, street gangs, and the homeless. Liquor stores, thrift shops, pawn shops, and adult theaters have replaced many of the department stores that used to line inner-city commercial strips. Even worse, the violence of these core areas is driving away all but those so poor that they have virtually no means of escape.

Thus, the archetypical postindustrial city really becomes two cities. First, there are well-insulated middle- and upper-class neighborhoods, with their tree-lined streets, cul-de-sacs, private security patrols, and private schools. Related to these are the office complexes and retail and entertainment areas where the better-off residents work, shop, and play. Then there is the other city. Here are the core neighborhoods described above, what little is left of the old racial and ethnic ghettos. Whether in New York's South Bronx or Minneapolis's Near Side, survival is about the best that can be hoped for in these desolate islands of poverty, violence, and despair.

Richard Nathan, author of numerous urban studies for the Brookings Institution, speaks directly to the postindustrial economic and social realities that frame much of today's urban politics. He concludes that the cities are deteriorating despite some variation in the advance of this urban distress and despite some statistical improvements resulting from urban abandonment.[165] He concludes that "all in all, the picture is grim. Urban problems are getting worse at precisely the time the nation is doing less about them."[166] It is to that political response that we now turn.

NOTES

1. *Chicago Tribune,* July 27, 1990.
2. See Charles Adrian and Charles Press, *Governing Urban America* (New York: McGraw-Hill, 1977), p. 8.

3. Population estimate for the year 1779, from Adrian and Press, *Governing Urban America.*

4. John Palen, *The Urban World* (New York: McGraw-Hill, 1975), pp. 47–49.

5. For example, ibid., chap. 3; Howard Chudacoff, *The Evolution of American Urban Society* (Englewood Cliffs, N.J.: Prentice-Hall, 1975), chap. 1.

6. See Charles Glaab and A. Theodore Brown, *A History of Urban America* (New York: Macmillan, 1976), chap. 6; Chudacoff, *The Evolution of American Urban Society,* chap. 4.

7. Ibid.

8. John Bollens and Henry Schmandt, *The Metropolis: Its People, Politics, and Economic Life* (New York: Harper & Row, 1982), p. 41; Zane Miller, *The Urbanization of Modern America* (New York: Harcourt Brace Jovanovich, 1973), p. 81.

9. Glaab and Brown, *A History of Urban America,* p. 136. The decline in farm population has been rather steady since the dawn of the industrial era. Today only approximately 2 percent of the U.S. population still lives on farms.

10. See Blake McKelvey, *The Urbanization of America, 1860–1915* (New Brunswick, N.J.: Rutgers University Press, 1963); Adna Ferrin Weber, *The Growth of Cities in the Nineteenth Century* (New York: Macmillan, 1899); Chudacoff, *The Evolution of American Urban Society,* p. 179.

11. Glaab and Brown, *A History of Urban America,* pp. 23–30, 113–144; Roderick McKenzie, *The Metropolitan Community* (New York: McGraw-Hill, 1933), chaps. 4–5.

12. Glaab and Brown, *A History of Urban America,* p. 25; Miller, *The Urbanization of Modern America,* p. 81.

13. Chudacoff, *The Evolution of American Urban Society,* p. 91.

14. McKelvey, *The Urbanization of America, 1860–1915*; Miller, *The Urbanization of Modern America.* For good synopses of Irish, Italian, Jewish, and Polish immigrant circumstances, see John Harrigan, *Political Change in the Metropolis* (Boston: Little, Brown, 1989), chap. 3.

15. Halford Fairchild and Belinda Tucker, "Black Residential Mobility," *Journal of Social Issues* 38 (1982): 54; Nicholas Lehman, *The Promised Land* (New York: Knopf, 1990).

16. Palen, *The Urban World,* chap. 4.

17. For a detailed description of industrial slums, see Glaab and Brown, *A History of Urban America,* chap. 4.

18. Glaab and Brown, *A History of Urban America,* chaps. 4–7. For a brief, colorful account, see Charles Lockwood, "Gangs, Crime, Smut, Violence," *New York Times,* September 20, 1990.

19. Palen, *The Urban World,* p. 58.

20. Quoted in John Higham, *Strangers in the Land* (New York: Atheneum, 1963), pp. 54–55.

21. New York's John Pintard, quoted in Glaab and Brown, *A History of Urban America,* p. 70.

22. Quoted in Higham, *Strangers in the Land,* pp. 54–55.

23. Quoted in Roy Lubove, *The Progressives and the Slums* (Pittsburgh: University of Pittsburgh Press, 1962), p. 58.

24. Quoted in Herbert G. Gutman, "Work, Culture, and Society in Industrializing America, 1815–1919," *American Historical Review* 78 (June 1973): 548.

25. Ibid.

26. For further reference concerning early discrimination, see Madison Grant, *The Passing of the Great Race* (New York: Scribner's, 1921); Raymond Mack, "Economic Factors in an Industrial Shop," *Social Forces* 32 (May 1954): 351–356; Herbert Gans, *The*

Urban Villagers (New York: Free Press, 1962); Chudacoff, *The Evolution of American Urban Society,* chap. 4; Palen, *The Urban World,* pp. 208–212; Higham, *Strangers in the Land.*

27. Richard Krickus, *Pursuing the American Dream* (New York: Anchor Books, 1976), pp. 58–59; and Chudacoff, *The Evolution of American Urban Society,* p. 98.

28. Sociologist Robert Park pioneered the concept of "urban ecology" to attempt to describe the entire process of social group sorting in cities. For example, see Robert Park, "The City: Suggestions for the Investigation of Human Behavior in the Urban Environment," *American Journal of Sociology* 20 (March 1916): 577–612; Robert Park, Ernest Burgess, and Roderick McKenzie, *The City* (Chicago: University of Chicago Press, 1925).

29. *New York Times,* February 21, 1991.

30. See Harrigan, *Political Change in the Metropolis,* pp. 29–30; *New York Times,* February 21, 1991. Also see Barbara Roberts, *The Dynamic West: A Region in Transition* (Portland, Ore.: Westrends, 1989).

31. U.S. Department of Commerce, Bureau of the Census, *Census of the Population* (Washington, D.C.: Government Printing Office, decennial). Most recently there appears to have been a trend toward limiting legal immigration to educated and wealthy Europeans, Asians, and Latin Americans, most of whom choose to live in suburbs and small towns. For example, *New York Times,* February 29, 1983; May 31, 1992.

32. See President's Urban and Regional Policy Group Report, *A New Partnership to Preserve America's Communities* (Washington, D.C.: Government Printing Office, March 1979), p. 22.

33. U.S. Department of Commerce, Bureau of the Census, "Characteristics of the Population by Ethnic Origins," *Current Population Reports,* Series P-20 (Washington, D.C.: Government Printing Office, occasional); *New York Times,* May 31, 1992.

34. See Dennis Judd, *The Politics of American Cities* (Boston: Little, Brown, 1988), chap. 8.

35. For further reference on black migration to the North, see Robert E. Grant, *The Black Man Comes to the City* (Chicago: Nelson-Hall, 1972); H. C. Hamilton, "The Negro Leaves the South," *Demography* 1 (January 1964): 294; August Meier and Elliot Rudwick, *From Plantation to Ghetto* (New York: Hill and Wang, 1969); Lehman, *The Promised Land;* Karl and Alma Taueber, *Negroes in the Cities* (Chicago: Aldine, 1965).

36. *Report of the National Advisory Commission on Civil Disorders,* reprint (New York: Bantam, 1968), pp. 116–118.

37. Bollens and Schmandt, *The Metropolis,* pp. 44–49; Glaab and Brown, *A History of Urban America,* p. 124.

38. Bollens and Schmandt, *The Metropolis,* pp. 44–49.

39. Ibid., pp. 45–46.

40. *National Journal,* May 26, 1990, p. 1283; *New York Times,* July 6, 1991.

41. Bollens and Schmandt, *The Metropolis,* p. 48.

42. *New York Times,* December 4, 1989.

43. *Wall Street Journal,* May 22, 1990.

44. *National Journal,* August 12, 1989, p. 2025.

45. U.S. Department of Commerce, Bureau of the Census, *Census of the Population* (Washington, D.C.: Government Printing Office, 1990).

46. *New York Times,* July 25, 1990; July 28, 1990.

47. See Clarence Stone, Robert Whelan, and William Murin, *Urban Policy and Politics in a Bureaucratic Age* (Englewood Cliffs, N.J.: Prentice-Hall, 1986), p. 24; *New York Times,* March 11, 1991; May 31, 1992.

It is difficult to get a precise measure of the number of Hispanic Americans. Many list themselves as "White" or in the "Other" category. There is also a sizable number of undocumented Hispanic aliens and the U.S. Census Bureau has a difficult time counting lower-income populations.

48. Joan Moore, *Mexican-Americans* (Englewood Cliffs, N.J.: Prentice-Hall, 1971).
49. *New York Times,* December 13, 1982.
50. *New York Times,* May 26, 1991.
51. Robert Kweit and Mary Grisez Kweit, *People and Politics in Urban America* (Pacific Grove, Calif.: Brooks-Cole, 1990), pp. 76–78.
52. U.S. Department of Commerce, Bureau of the Census, "Persons of Spanish Origin in the United States, March 1982," *Current Population Reports,* Series P-20, #396 (Washington, D.C.: Government Printing Office, 1985); Bollens and Schmandt, *The Metropolis,* pp. 50–52; Stone, *Urban Policy and Politics,* pp. 33–34; Leo Grebler, *The Mexican-American People* (New York: Free Press, 1970).
53. Ibid.
54. Stone, *Urban Policy and Politics,* p. 36; Bollens and Schmandt, *The Metropolis,* pp. 50–52; U.S. Department of Commerce, Bureau of the Census, "Persons of Spanish Origin in the United States, 1982"; Kweit and Kweit, *People and Politics in Urban America,* 70–73.
55. Bollens and Schmandt, *The Metropolis,* pp. 50–52. Also see U.S. Department of Commerce, Bureau of the Census, "Persons of Spanish Origin in the United States, 1982."
56. Bollens and Schmandt, *The Metropolis,* p. 42.
57. See *New York Times,* March 2, 1990; March 11, 1991; Ronald Takaki, *Strangers from a Different Shore* (Boston: Little, Brown, 1989).
58. *New York Times,* February 24, 1991.
59. *New York Times,* March 11, 1991; February 29, 1992.
60. *New York Times,* June 12, 1991.
61. Ibid.
62. Stone, *Urban Policy and Politics,* p. 19. Also see *New York Times,* June 2, 1991.
63. Douglas Massey and Nancy Denton, "Trends in Residential Segregation of Blacks, Hispanics, and Asians, 1920–1980," *American Sociological Review* 52 (December 1987): 802–825; *National Journal,* February 9, 1991, p. 359; *Atlantic* 261, no. 1 (1988): 31–56; Bollens and Schmandt, *The Metropolis,* p. 52; Stone, *Urban Policy and Politics,* p. 19.
64. U.S. Department of Commerce, Bureau of the Census, *Census of the Population* (Washington, D.C.: Government Printing Office, 1980).
65. Harrigan, *Political Change in the Metropolis,* pp. 34–35; *New York Times,* March 11, 1991.
66. *New York Times,* July 30, 1990. Some of these most recent émigrés have already begun to move on. See *New York Times,* September 4, 1990.
67. *New York Times,* July 24, 1987; March 18, 1988; and March 13, 1990.
68. *New York Times,* March 13, 1985.
69. Bollens and Schmandt, *The Metropolis,* p. 56.
70. *New York Times,* April 2, 1984.
71. Bollens and Schmandt, *The Metropolis,* p. 57.
72. Ibid.
73. Lawrence Herson and John Bolland, *The Urban Web* (Chicago: Nelson-Hall, 1990), p. 399. Also see Harrell Rodgers, Jr., *Poor Women, Poor Families* (Armonk, N.Y.: M.E. Sharpe, 1990).

74. U.S. Department of Commerce, Bureau of the Census, *Poverty in the United States, 1985* (Washington, D.C.: Government Printing Office, 1985).
75. Bollens and Schmandt, *The Metropolis,* p. 55.
76. William Julius Wilson, *The Truly Disadvantaged* (Chicago: University of Chicago Press, 1987).
77. U.S. Department of Commerce, Bureau of the Census, *Census of the Population* (Washington, D.C.: Government Printing Office, 1920).
78. Ibid., p. 255.
79. Leo Schnore, "Urban Structure of Suburban Selectivity," *Demography* 1 (January 1964); Gary Tobin, "Suburbanization and the Development of Motor Transportation," in Barry Schwartz, ed., *The Changing Face of the Suburbs* (Chicago: University of Chicago Press, 1976); Patrick Ashton, "The Political Economy of Suburban Development," in William Tabb and Larry Sawers, eds., *Marxism and the Metropolis* (New York: Oxford University Press, 1984), pp. 72–73; Robert Wood, *Suburbia* (Boston: Houghton Mifflin, 1958); Sam Bass Warner, *The Urban Wilderness* (New York: Harper & Row, 1972), p. 144; and Glaab and Brown, *A History of Urban America,* p. 248; Judd, *The Politics of American Cities,* chap. 9.
80. *Christian Science Monitor,* March 26, 1985, p. 5; *New York Times,* July 26, 1987.
81. *New York Times,* February 23, 1991.
82. Judd, *The Politics of American Cities,* p. 146.
83. Herson and Bolland, *The Urban Web,* p. 397.
84. Bollens and Schmandt, *The Metropolis,* p. 41.
85. *Time,* June 15, 1987; *Wall Street Journal,* February 2, 1988; Herson and Bolland, *The Urban Web,* pp. 441–444.
86. Ibid.; *New York Times,* February 23, 1991.
87. Glenn Fuguitt, Paul Voss, and J. C. Doherty, "Growth and Change in Rural America" (Washington, D.C.: Urban Land Institute, 1979); Barbara Phillips and Richard LeGates, *City Lights* (New York: Oxford University Press, 1981), p. 150; John Herbers, *The New Heartland: America's Flight beyond the Suburbs and How It Is Changing Our Future* (New York: Times Books, 1986).
88. *Gallup Polls* (Wilmington, Del.: Scholarly Resources, annual) March 1985, and others.
89. Demetrios Caraley, *City Governments and Urban Problems* (Englewood Cliffs, N.J.: Prentice-Hall, 1977), chap. 1. Also see Gallup Poll cited in the *New York Times,* May 16, 1981.
90. Edward Banfield, *The Unheavenly City Revisited* (Boston: Little, Brown, 1974), chap. 2.
91. Robert Goldston, *Suburbia: Civic Denial* (New York: Macmillan, 1970), p. 22.
92. Wood, *Suburbia,* p. 106.
93. Statistics and quotes from an article in the *New York Times,* September 6, 1990.
94. Bill Smith, quoted in Felicity Barringer, "What America Did after the War: A Tale Told by the Census," *New York Times,* September 2, 1990, pp. E1–5.
95. Peter Gluck and Richard Meister, *Cities in Transition* (New York: Viewpoints, 1979), chap. 7.
96. David Goldfield and Blaine Brownell, *Urban America: From Downtown to No Town* (Boston: Houghton Mifflin, 1979), p. 320.
97. *New York Times,* August 4, 1988.
98. *New York Times,* August 10, 1986; November 9, 1986; December 10, 1989.
99. *New York Times,* December 10, 1989. Also see D. Garth Taylor, Paul Sheatsley, and Andrew Greeley, "Attitudes towards Racial Integration," *Scientific American* 238 (June 1978).

100. *Report of the National Advisory Commission on Civil Disorders* (Washington, D.C.: Government Printing Office, 1968); Joe Feagin and Harlan Hahn, *Ghetto Revolts* (New York: Macmillan, 1973).
101. *Report of the National Advisory Commission on Civil Disorders* (Washington, D.C.: Government Printing Office, 1968).
102. See *New York Times,* March 19, 1991.
103. Karl Taeuber, *Racial Segregation, 28 Cities, 1920–1980,* Center for Demography and Ecology, University of Wisconsin, Working Paper 83–12, March 1983; W. A. U. Clark, "Residential Segregation in American Cities," *Population Residency and Policy Review* 5 (1986): 95–127. Also see Douglas Massey and Nancy Denton, "Hypersegregation in United States Metropolitan Areas," *Demography* 26 (August 1989): 373–391; Douglas Massey and Mitchell Eggers, "The Ecology of Inequality," *American Journal of Sociology* 52 (March 1990): 1153–1188; Wade Roof, ed., "Race and Residence in the United States," *Annals of the American Academy of Political and Social Sciences* 441 (January 1979).
104. There are a few truly integrated suburbs, such as University City (St. Louis), Shaker Heights (Cleveland), and Hillcrest Heights (D.C.), but these are still by far the exception.
105. The practice of "restrictive covenants" was ruled unconstitutional by the Supreme Court of the United States in *Shelly v. Kramer,* 334, US1 (1948). For contemporary practices, see Herson and Bolland, *The Urban Web,* pp. 405–415; Judd, *The Politics of American Cities,* pp.179–191, 282–288; Frederick Wirt, *On the City's Rim* (Lexington, Mass.: D C Heath, 1972); Michael Danielson, *The Politics of Exclusion* (New York: Columbia University Press, 1976); Schwartz, *The Changing Face of the Suburbs*; James Hughes, *Suburbanization Dynamics and the Future of the City* (New Brunswick, N.J.: Center for Urban Policy Research, 1974).
106. Such cul-de-sacs are quite evident, for instance, in the Central West End of St. Louis and Shaker Heights outside Cleveland. See *New York Times,* June 27, 1987. For a general analysis of housing discrimination, see Rachel Bratt, Chester Hartman, and Ann Myerson, *Critical Perspectives on Housing* (Philadelphia: Temple University Press, 1986).
107. *New York Times Magazine,* July 29, 1990, p. 26.
108. Anna Quindlen, *New York Times,* September 7, 1991.
109. *New York Times,* June 24, 1989; June 24, 1988.
110. *New York Times,* May 11, 1984; January 26, 1987; March 12, 1989; Herson and Bolland, *The Urban Web,* p. 397. Also see earlier studies such as Firdaus Jhabvala, "The Economic Situation of Black People," in David Gordon, ed., *Problems in Political Economy: An Urban Perspective* (Lexington, Mass.: D C Heath, 1977); Lloyd Hogan, "Blacks and the American Economy," *Current History* 67 (November 1974); Douglas Charnahan, Walter Gove, and Omer Galle, "Urbanization, Population Density, and Overcrowding," *Social Forces* 53 (September 1974): 62–72; Palen, *The Urban World,* pp. 201–224; and *Time,* April 6, 1970; Katherine Bradbury, Anthony Downs, and Kenneth Small, *Urban Decline and the Future of American Cities* (Washington, D.C.: Brookings Institution, 1982), pp. 187, 214–215; Richard Hamilton, *Class and Politics in the United States* (New York: Wiley, 1972), pp. 155–180.
111. *New York Times,* June 26, 1987.
112. See *New York Times,* December 24, 1990.
113. *New York Times,* February 2, 1984.
114. Manning Marable, *How Capitalism Underdeveloped Black America* (Boston: South End Press, 1983), p. 241.

115. Ibid., pp. 240–241.
116. *New York Times,* June 23, 1982; March 4, 1983.
117. *New York Times,* June 2, 1982.
118. *New York Times,* November 18, 1984. For another Chicago area example, see *New York Times,* July 14, 1992.
119. *New York Times,* December 1, 1985.
120. *New York Times,* December 24, 1986; January 5, 1987; September 23, 1987.
121. *New York Times,* December 14, 1987.
122. *New York Times,* May 3, 1989.
123. *New York Times,* August 25–26, 1989.
124. See Glaab and Brown, *A History of Urban America,* pp. 124–125.
125. See Andrew Greeley, *Ethnicity in the United States* (New York: Wiley, 1974), pp. 14–16.
126. *New York Times,* January 26, 1987. For a comparable case study of Milwaukee, see Isabel Wilkerson, "How Milwaukee Boomed But Left Its Blacks Behind," *New York Times,* March 17, 1991.
127. George Borjas, *Friends or Strangers: The Impact of Immigration on the United States Economy* (New York: Basic Books, 1990).
128. See *New York Times,* January 12, 1990; March 30, 1990; *National Journal,* January 27, 1990.
129. *New York Times,* August 15, 1990.
130. See *New York Times,* July 27, 1990.
131. *New York Times,* November 25, 1990, p. E5; September 3, 1991; October 6, 1991; February 29, 1992.
132. Gordon, *Problems in Political Economy,* chap. 4.
133. For a critique of such job training programs, see Firdaus Jhabvala, "A Critique of Reformist Solutions to Discrimination," in David Gordon, ed., *Problems in Political Economy: An Urban Perspective* (Lexington, Mass.: D C Heath, 1977).
134. Quoted in Kenneth Clark, *The Dark Ghetto* (New York: Harper & Row, 1965), p. 13.
135. Harvey Brenner, "Estimating the Social Costs of National Economic Policy," in the Congressional Joint Economic Committee's *Achieving the Goals of the Employment Act of 1946,* 30th Anniversary Review, 1, Employment Paper no. 5 (Washington, D.C.: Government Printing Office, 1976).
136. Ralph Blumenthal summarizing the views of historian Richard Wade, criminologist Marvin Yablon and others in the *New York Times,* August 26, 1990. Also see *New York Times,* August 13, 1989.
137. U.S. Department of Justice, *Criminal Victimization in the United States* (Washington, D.C.: Government Printing Office, 1974).
138. Sam Staley, "Cities Are Learning—Revitalize or Else," *The World and I* 6 (June 1991): 27.
139. Ibid.; *New York Times,* August 6, 1990.
140. For numbers on bystander deaths, see *New York Times,* August 5, 1990; August 12, 1990.
141. Quoted in the *National Journal,* September 30, 1989.
142. *New York Times,* August 12, 1990. For other examples of coping techniques, see *New York Times,* August 9, 1990.
143. Sam Roberts, "Dodge City It Isn't. It's Deadlier," *New York Times,* August 6, 1990. Also see *New York Times,* August 7, 1990.
144. Quoted in *New York Times,* August 9, 1990.
145. See *New York Times,* February 21, 1991.

146. Mitchell Levitas, "Homelessness in America," *New York Times Magazine,* June 10, 1990; Peter Rossi, "The Urban Homeless: A Portrait of Urban Dislocation," *Annals of the American Academy of Political and Social Sciences* 507 (January 1989): 132–142; *New York Times,* April 12, 1991.
147. *New York Times,* December 17, 1985.
148. Results of a two-year study for the Economic Policy Institute, reported in the Memphis, *Commercial Appeal,* October 6, 1989, p. A1.
149. Martha Burt and Barbara Cohen, "Feeding the Homeless," prepared for the U.S. Department of Agriculture (September 1988). Also see Rossi, *The Urban Homeless.*
150. *New York Times,* January 22, 1986; October 30, 1986.
151. Peter Rossi, *Down and Out in America* (Chicago: University of Chicago Press, 1989).
152. *Time,* December 17, 1990, pp. 44–49; *New York Times,* October 30, 1986; December 25, 1985; January 22, 1985.
153. *New York Times,* December 25, 1985; July 8, 1990; June 13, 1991; September 2, 1991; January 20, 1992; Memphis, *Commercial Appeal,* December 2, 1990, p. B5.
154. *New York Times,* April 15, 1991; Memphis, *Commercial Appeal,* January 30, 1991, p. A2.
155. *New York Times,* September 11, 1991.
156. *New York Times,* April 28, 1991; March 26, 1992.
157. *Newsweek,* February 19, 1990.
158. *National Journal,* March 10, 1990, pp. 558–562.
159. *New York Times,* January 5, 1990.
160. See *New York Times,* January 30, 1991; August 27, 1991.
161. See *New York Times,* March 8, 1991; June 26, 1987; September 30, 1990; Chicago Tribune Staff, *The American Millstone* (Chicago: Contemporary Books, 1986).
162. *New York Times,* October 29, 1990.
163. *New York Times,* June 23, 1990.
164. *New York Times,* December 24, 1990; January 9, 1991.
165. For measures and examples of variation, see Roy Ball, *Financing State and Local Government in the Eighties* (New York: Oxford University Press, 1984); Richard Nathan and Charles Adams, "Four Perspectives on Urban Hardship," *Political Science Quarterly* 104 (Fall 1989): 483–508; *Christian Science Monitor,* December 26, 1985.
166. Quoted in *New York Times,* January 26, 1987.

CHAPTER 5

Political Relationships: Institutional and Historical Context

Chapters 3 and 4 surveyed the evolution of cities in the United States, emphasizing economic and social dimensions of this development. The purpose was to provide a broad historical and analytical context within which to place governmental actions. As shown in chapter 2, understanding the political environment is essential to understanding the political system. The following two chapters (Chapters 5 and 6) will present an overview of how the political process has responded to these economic and social realities, beginning with the basic institutional setting within which city governments operate.

INSTITUTIONAL SETTING

Cities operate within a complex intergovernmental web. Each city falls within the jurisdiction of both a home state and the federal government of the United States; most also are encompassed by at least one county as well. Seattle, for instance, shares political authority with King County, the state of Washington, and the national government in Washington, D.C.

These primary political units divide the political labor in a number of ways. As table 5.1 indicates, the largest responsibilities of the federal government are Social Security and national defense. States spend most providing education and welfare services, while localities (a category that includes all governmental entities below the state level) have the major role of providing elementary and secondary education. On the revenue side, the federal government is primarily reliant on income and Social Security taxes, the state on sales taxes, and localities on property taxes.[1]

Such aggregate figures can be deceiving, however, especially at the local level. Comparing the 1983 budgets of the cities of Chicago and New York, for example, we find what appears to be a tremendous difference in policy priorities. Chicago

TABLE 5.1   Governmental Budgets (1985)

Expenditures		Revenues	
Federal Government			
Insurance Benefits	28%	Personal Income Tax	32%
National Defense	26	Social Security Tax	24
Interest on Debt	14	Borrowing	22
Intergovernmental	10	Charges and Fees	10
Welfare	8	Corporate Income Tax	6
Health and Education	2	Other Taxes	6
Other	12		
State Governments (average)			
Intergovernmental	31%	Sales and Use Taxes	24%
Education	14	Intergovernmental	20
Welfare	13	Insurance Trust	15
Insurance Benefits	10	Personal Income Tax	14
Highways and Roads	7	Charges and Fees	14
Health	6	Corporate Income Tax	4
Interest on Debt	4	Property Tax	1
Police and Corrections	3	Liquor Stores	1
Natural Resources	2	Other	7
Other	10		
Local Governments (cities, counties, special districts, etc.)			
Education	36%	Intergovernmental	34%
Utilities	13	Property Taxes	25
Health	7	Charges and Fees	20
Interest on Debt	6	Utilities	10
Police and Corrections	6	Sales Tax	5
Roads and Streets	5	Personal Income Tax	2
Sanitation	4	Insurance Trust	2
Other	23	Other	2

SOURCE: U.S. Department of Commerce, *Statistical Abstracts of the United States*
(Washington, D.C.: Government Printing Office, 1986).

spent approximately $2 billion on a population of three million people, with its largest expenditure item being law enforcement (34%), followed by streets and sanitation (17%) and public services (14%). New York, on the other hand, spent $14 billion on seven million residents, with the bulk of its monies being spent on health and welfare (28%), education (21%), and public services (14%). Does that mean New Yorkers receive three times more services, or that Chicago cares less about schools and New York less about police protection? No. These figures mask the contribution of surrounding state and county governments as well as independent special school districts. New York City, for instance, has to pay one-quarter of its own welfare costs while the state of Illinois absolves Chicago of all that responsibility. In addition, Cook County provides for Chicago residents many of the health services that New York City must provide for its citizens without outside help.[2]

These variations demonstrate how interdependent the various levels of government have become. The policies of one may well have significant impacts on the others. New federal taxes on gasoline, cigarettes, beer, and wine most likely will reduce state excise revenues because state residents are likely to drive less, drink less, and smoke less as a result. The state of Tennessee estimated that it would lose more than $100 million over four years as a result of such federal tax increases.[3]

Intergovernmental Relations

Cities and Their States.   In 1923, when the United States Supreme Court handed down its decision in *Trenton v. New Jersey,* it made quite clear where cities stood legally vis-à-vis their respective states. Trenton had sued the state of New Jersey for violation of a contract, but the U.S. Supreme Court declared that cities are no more than creatures of their states—political subdivisions for the convenient exercise of certain policies. Therefore, they had no standing to sue in federal court. As neither cities nor localities are mentioned anywhere in the U.S. Constitution, they can look for very little help from the federal government if they run afoul of their respective states.

> The city is a political subdivision of the state, created as a convenient agency for the exercise of such of the governmental powers of the state as may be entrusted to it. . . . The state, therefore, at its pleasure may modify or withdraw all such powers, . . . expand or contract the territorial area, unite the whole or the part of it with another municipality, repeal the charter and destroy the corporation. All this may be done, conditionally or unconditionally, with or without the consent of the citizens, or even against their will.[4]

This decision meant that cities lacked U.S. Constitutional guarantees such as due process and equal protection under the laws. Their states were relatively free to treat them rather arbitrarily if they so desired, unless hemmed in by their own state constitutions. On occasion states have done just that. As extreme examples, Tennessee temporarily abolished Memphis as a separate political entity in 1879; around the same time, Alabama took similar action with Mobile and Selma.[5]

Municipal Incorporation.   Cities, then, owe their very existence to their state governments. Most states allow their legislatures to create cities, even without the approval of the affected residents. More common, however, is for a geographically contiguous group of people to determine that they would like to form a city and collectively govern themselves at the local level. At that point they must apply for a municipal charter from their respective state. In granting such a charter, the state is creating a "municipal corporation" with geographic boundaries, a governing structure, and some taxing authority. The newly incorporated municipality will have the independent legal status necessary to make ordinances, own and sell property, borrow and lend money, operate proprietorships, and assume legal liability for the actions of its governing officials. There are currently nearly 20,000 municipalities in the United States, and they contain approximately 150 million residents.[6]

City charters normally outline in considerable detail what the city has the authority to do. Just the index of the Los Angeles city charter, for example, is longer than the entire U.S. Constitution. Cities' subordinate position means they literally cannot open a peanut stand at the local zoo without state authorization.[7]

Home-Rule Charters.   Rather than become too closely intertwined in most local governmental decisions, most states routinely have come to grant variations of what are called home-rule charters. Such charters allow varying degrees of discretionary power to the city, meaning that it is authorized to make certain types of institutional changes without permission from the state capitol. Cities may be free to take on additional functions, establish a pension system for city workers, change the day on which they elect local officials, alter the size of their city council, and so on. Normally these changes are made by either the city council or a charter commission drawing up a proposed revision; the proposal is then put to the city electorate for a vote.

Typically, the larger the city, the more discretion it is granted by its state. State governments simply have many other things to do than to manage large, complex, and increasingly troubled cities. Nonetheless, there is considerable variation by state. Some of the states granting the broadest home-rule authority are California, Michigan, Missouri, and Texas.[8]

Even though states have become more generous with extensions of home-rule authority, they are less forthcoming with taxing authority. States generally have remained quite stingy in this regard. Cities may be free to take on more service responsibilities, but they will have to fund them out of existing revenues. This policy, of course, leaves the states with more access to whatever tax resources exist beneath the federal level.[9]

In addition, vagueness even in a home-rule charter leaves many city actions open to legal challenge by the state if it happens to disapprove. Some cities have been attempting to exercise home-rule provisions to ward off unwanted landfills, low-income housing, and so on.[10] If such practices are challenged, the legal burden of proof clearly rests with the city to show that it was meant to have the authority it was exercising. Even if the city wins, there is little preventing the state from changing the law afterwards.

This legal inferiority, as set out in the U.S. Supreme Court's constitutional interpretation in *Trenton v. New Jersey,* was an extension of the legal position taken some 50 years earlier by Iowa Judge John F. Dillon, referred to as ''Dillon's Law.'' Summarizing his position, Dillon stated:

It is a general and undisputed proposition of law that a municipal corporation possesses and can exercise the following powers and no others: First, those granted in express words; second, those necessarily or fairly implied in or incident to the powers expressly granted; third, those essential to the accomplishment of the declared objects and purposes of the corporation—not simply convenient, but indispensable. Any fair, reasonable, substantial doubt concerning the existence of power is resolved by the courts against the corporation, and the power is denied.[11]

Other State Discretion.   Besides the authority to pass regulatory statutes, state governments have at least four other means of regulating the behavior of cities. First, state agency officials often have administrative authority over various city agency activities, such as granting permits, requiring reports, issuing advice, or even abolishing the local agency and assuming its functions if necessary. Second, the state may launch a special investigation into a local government practice— for example, police corruption—and bring public pressure to bear through this mechanism. Far more common is the third method. This involves granting local government state monies and then both restricting how that money can be used (mandates) and threatening to withdraw the funds if the city does not do as the state wishes in related areas (often referred to as the carrot-and-stick ploy). Last, if pushed to this, most states retain the authority to revise or even revoke a city's charter, as demonstrated in the Tennessee and Alabama examples above, or to remove local officials and reappoint their successors. New York Governor Franklin Roosevelt did so with New York City Mayor Jimmy Walker's police chief in the 1920s.

Where the relationship between the states and the federal government is deemed to be *federalistic* in nature (with the states enjoying a degree of independence and sharing certain authority with their federal counterpart), that is certainly not the case between states and their cities. The city-state relationship is a *unitary* one, meaning that all authority flows one way: down. The more service burden the federal government shifts to the states and localities, the more the state's role in local politics increases.[12]

About the only real protection cities have is that provided by state constitutions. In 1984, for example, the voters of New Hampshire passed a constitutional amendment requiring the state government to provide necessary funds for any services it mandates local governments to perform.[13] A city is fortunate if such protections were written into the state constitution at some point in the state's history because state constitutions are normally far more cumbersome to alter than are regulatory statutes passed by state legislatures.[14]

Meanwhile, how are city officials and city residents to influence decisions of their nearly omnipotent state (and federal) governments?

Electoral Clout.   If city residents are to influence the decisions of elected representatives and their appointees, obviously it is important for them to affect who is elected and whether these individuals will be allowed to remain in office. A bright spot for city residents was the reapportionment of legislative representation stemming from such U.S. Supreme Court decisions as *Baker v. Carr* (1962)[15] and *Reynolds v. Simms* (1964).[16] Reapportionment gave them much more equitable representation in their state legislatures and in Congress. Prior to these decisions, voting for legislative seats by geographic territory rather than by population had left those legislative bodies dominated by nonurban areas.

In 1960, scarcely over one-quarter of the California population could elect a majority of the state's legislative seats: the six million residents of the Los Angeles area had roughly the same amount of representation as a rural county with 14,000 people. In Florida, some 80 percent of the population could elect only 11 percent of the legislators, with Dade County's 495,000 residents having three seats where Glades County's 2,199 people had one. Meanwhile, in Congress, the 20 most populous districts held nearly 14 million people, while the 20 least populous held only some 4.5 million.[17]

Ultimately the federal courts would require nearly complete population equity among districts, including local districts.[18] At one point, a New Jersey reapportionment plan was rejected even though there was only a seven-tenths of 1 percent variation in population between districts. Variations had to be justified as necessary to serve a legitimate governmental end. Following the 1970 census, for instance, 16 percent variation was allowed for "jurisdictional convenience," but, no state had more than a 3 percent variation after the 1980 reapportionments.[19]

As Chief Justice Earl Warren stated,

> Legislators are elected by voters, not farms or cities or economic interests. . . . And if a state should provide that the votes of citizens in one part of the state should be given two times, or five times, or ten times the weight of votes of citizens in another part of the state, it could hardly be contended that the right to vote of those residing in the disfavored areas had not been effectively diluted. . . . Diluting of the weight of votes because of place of residence impairs constitutional rights under the Fourteenth Amendment just as much as invidious discriminations based on race and economic status.[20]

Even as city residents were being freed from the inequities resulting from malapportionment, however, their newly attained political power was being undercut by population shifts. Suburbanization had been building since the dawn of postindustrialism and particularly since the end of World War II. By 1964, no single city any longer represented a majority of its state's population. And as of the 1970 census, more Americans lived in the nation's suburbs than in its cities.

In 1952, the citizens of New York City cast nearly one-half the votes in New York State, but by 1988, they cast less than a third of them. Chicago's share of the Illinois vote dropped from 41 percent to 23 percent over the same period; Baltimore's fell from 39 percent to 14 percent; Detroit's, from 29 percent to 8 percent; and St. Louis's, from 20 percent to 7 percent.[21]

The help that had arrived in the form of reapportionment was too little and too late. Elected officials at the state and federal levels already were becoming far less reliant on the votes of the urban populace. By the Ninety-Fifth Congress (1977–1978), for example, fewer than one-quarter of the seats were held by central-city representatives.

Cities and the Federal Government. Article IV of the U.S. Constitution states: "The Constitution and the laws of the United States which shall be made in pursuance thereof . . . shall be the supreme law of the land; and Judges in every State shall be bound thereby, anything in the Constitution or Laws of any State to the contrary notwithstanding." If a city does not even have the same constitutional status as a state, it is quite clear that cities are to be legally subordinate to the federal government as well.

Rather than give the federal government carte blanche to dominate the states, and by extension the localities, however, the founding fathers added the Tenth Amendment, which states: "The powers not delegated to the United States by the Constitution, nor [expressly] prohibited by it to the States, are reserved to the States respectively, or to the people." By implication, if the Constitution does not say the federal government may do it, the authority remains with the states. Thus being "convenient subdivisions" of their respective states, cities would seem to have some constitutional protection from federal interference—but note the word *expressly* in brackets. It was contained in some of the early drafts, but was ultimately eliminated. That exclusion set the stage for a considerable degree of "implied" authority that would come to be claimed by the federal government.

In the U.S. Supreme Court case of *McCulloch v. Maryland,* Chief Justice John Marshall summarized the concept of implied federal powers:

> Let the end be legitimate, let it be within the scope of the Constitution, and all means which are appropriate, which are plainly adapted to that end, which are not prohibited, but consistent with the letter and spirit of the Constitution, are constitutional.[22]

Since Congress has the authority to pass all laws that are "necessary and proper" to carry out its enumerated duties, it passed laws such as the civil rights and voting rights acts of the 1950s and 1960s in order to implement the forms of "equal protection" federal judges had come to read into the Fourteenth Amendment. It has seized on its authority to regulate interstate commerce in order to ban child labor, limit the work week, require minimum wages, regulate pollution, and use the FBI to battle the gambling and drug trades. It also has used its authority to "lay and collect taxes" as a way to pursue mobsters with the FBI and prosecute them in federal court for income tax evasion.

But how, for instance, has the federal government been able to dictate that cities abide by a 55-mile-an-hour speed limit, employ affirmative action plans in their police forces, or provide facilities for the handicapped? This authority has come indirectly from some rather innocuous looking language in Article 1, Section 8, which states that Congress may tax and spend for the general welfare. In practice that has meant that Congress has provided cities with money to build highways, buy sophisticated computers for their police departments, purchase new buses, and so on. In accepting such funding, cities often either agree to the specific mandates attached or they acquiesce under the threat of losing the monies they have come to rely on.

Grants-in-Aid.   Federal grants have taken three basic forms, presented here in descending order of federal restrictions on how the monies can be used. *Project* (or categorical) *grants* are finite amounts of money that require cities to apply, show need of the funds, and spend them only on a specified project, such as a bilingual education program, a subway system, park acquisition, public housing construction, or a sewage treatment plant. Urban Development Action Grants, as an example, were designed to spur commercial and industrial development in the more distressed cities by funding hotel renovations, industrial parks, and similar projects.

Block grants were created to combine several related categorical grants under one larger category, leaving the state or locality more leeway to shift monies around within the broader category as local needs require. As an example, the 1974 Community Development Block Grant program, the principal surviving federal grant program primarily for the cities, combined Urban Renewal, Model Cities, and five other federal programs. It included monies for streets, lighting, small business subsidies, slum clearance, and other such efforts.

Last, *federal revenue sharing* was established by the 1972 State and Local Fiscal Assistance Act. Before it was terminated in 1986, this act had returned some $85 billion in federally collected tax monies to the states and localities on a formula basis with very few restrictions on how the money could be used.

In terms of how the grants are to be distributed, there are two primary methods: formula and competition. *Formula grants,* by far the most common, provide funds on the basis of a predetermined formula. The legislation specifies the amount of money each qualifying jurisdiction will receive, such as $1,000 for each learning-disabled elementary school student. Open-ended formula grants such as Medicaid, school lunches, and Aid to Families with Dependent Children (AFDC) provide whatever funds are necessary to service those who qualify under the formula. Closed-ended formula grants such as certain educational programs, on the other hand, have fixed maximums (or ceilings). The alternative to a distributional formula is a *competitive process* in which a city applies for grant money and competes with other cities that also have applied for those particular monies.

Grant History.   Historically, federal funding of city projects has occurred in roughly three phases. In the first, prior to the 1930s, the federal government provided very little aid at all, with a few exceptions such as small amounts of money for harbors, flood control, and highway construction.

Then in phase two, from the 1930s through the 1960s, federal assistance proliferated, spurred on by civil unrest. Largely through categorical formula grants, the federal government began supplementing individual incomes, creating jobs, subsidizing the construction of an interstate highway system, paying for medical care and legal assistance, providing food stamps, and subsidizing everything from the building and rehabilitation of private homes to school meals, apartment rents, slum clearance, and the development of industrial parks. From spending $3 million through five grant programs at the turn of the century, the federal government accelerated to spending more than $100 billion on more than 500 programs. At the height of this period, New York City Mayor John Lindsay even called for the development of certain "federal cities" that would fall directly under the jurisdiction of the federal government, rather than within any particular state.[23]

Since the 1970s, the country has experienced what President Richard Nixon termed a period of "new federalism" in which political power began to shift from the federal to the state level. Larger and more flexible block grants were seen as a way to allow localities to regain some of the discretion that had eroded since the federal government began its flurry of spending in the 1930s. Federal revenue sharing with the states was to permit even more state and local leeway. Then, by the 1980s, the Reagan and Bush administrations began reducing the federal funding of many of these more flexible programs.

Federal aid to states and localities peaked in 1978 at more than 25 percent of their total revenues. That aid dropped by more than one-third between 1978 and 1982 alone. The next major reduction occurred when federal revenue sharing was terminated in 1986.[24] Urban Development Action Grants all but disappeared, and Community Development Block Grants were reduced considerably. As a consequence, large cities that had received approximately 20 percent of their total revenues from the federal government in 1970 were receiving less than 10 percent by 1990. These cuts meant that the states and localities would have to increase their taxes just to maintain the existing level of services.[25] It also meant there would be increasing reliance on the more regressive forms of taxation employed at the state and local levels, whereby sales and property taxes and user fees took the same percentage from all taxpayers regardless of their income levels.

State and Local Responses.   Despite recent funding cutbacks, the federal government continues to play crucial roles at the state and local levels. Thus, a number of lobbying groups have sprung up to articulate state and local interests, particularly in the nation's capital. Groups have formed such as the U.S. Conference of Mayors, the National League of Cities, the National Governors' Association, the National Conference of State Legislatures, the Council of State Governments, the National Association of Counties, and the State and Local Legal Center.

States and localities also have demonstrated their concern in a number of other ways. One is the attempt to amend the U.S. Constitution both to allow states to initiate constitutional amendments and to breathe more life into the Tenth Amendment by requiring federal judges to determine with greater precision what authority is reserved to the states (and by extension, to the cities). Resolutions calling for these constitutional amendments already have been passed in more than a dozen state legislatures and are pending in a sizable number of others.[26]

Local Governing Structures

Within the confines of their charters and certain decisions by the federal courts, cities have taken a wide variety of governmental and electoral forms over the course of U.S. history. At any particular point in time, it is difficult to find two urban areas that have identical governmental structures. Not only have some structures simply been found to be more efficient given certain geographic and demographic realities, but any structural arrangement is likely to provide advantages to some groups and disadvantages to others. Thus, the political winds of the day have also helped to shape these choices of form.[27]

Governmental Forms.   Overlapping the boundaries of any large city are a variety of governmental structures. Besides the legislative and executive arrangement that comprises the city's primary governmental unit, there are often various special districts, most prominent of which are school districts. Linking cities to surrounding populations, in addition to county government, there may well be a metropolitan government, or a council of governments, or at least informal agreements between the city government and surrounding governmental entities.

City Government.   Other than a number of small New England towns that still make some of their more important governmental decisions en masse in town meetings,[28] cities operate under the principle of representative democracy. Officials are elected to make legislative decisions, such as how to spend the city's money, as well as to make executive decisions concerning the implementation of legislative policy. This legislative and executive decision making has tended to be accomplished in one of three general ways.

MAYOR-COUNCIL   In a mayor-council system there is normally an independently elected mayor whose primary responsibility is to see that laws passed by the city council are implemented (see figure 5.1). City councils pass the laws including the imposition of taxes and the expenditure of subsequent tax revenues. Such councils range in size from as few as 9 in Detroit, Boston, and Pittsburgh to more than 40 in New York City, Chicago, and Nashville.[29]

Within this arrangement, however, there is considerable variation in mayoral authority. In theory, the strongest of "strong mayors" would serve an indefinitely renewable four-year term, regularly submit a full city budget proposal to the council (and thus set the council's agenda for them), would be allowed to veto legislation, and also would be delegated the authority to appoint and remove agency heads, reorganize bureaucratic functions, and transfer funds within or between departmental budgets without subsequent council approval. At the "weak mayor" end of this continuum would be a mayor who served a nonrenewable two-year term, had little formal authority other than to preside over city council meetings, and even had his or her agency heads elected independently and supervised by council committees or public boards. In reality, most mayors in mayor-council systems fall somewhere between these polar extremes, with the mayors of the very largest cities tending to fall at the stronger end of the formal authority scale. Exceptions are Los Angeles, Seattle, Atlanta, Chicago, and Milwaukee, whose mayors have less formal authority.

As an example of this distinction, consider a dilemma faced by Los Angeles Mayor Tom Bradley in the spring of 1991. When a handheld video camera caught a group of Los Angeles police officers mercilessly beating a prone black speeder with truncheons, there was considerable public pressure for something to be done. This situation was made even more delicate by the fact that the mayor and victim

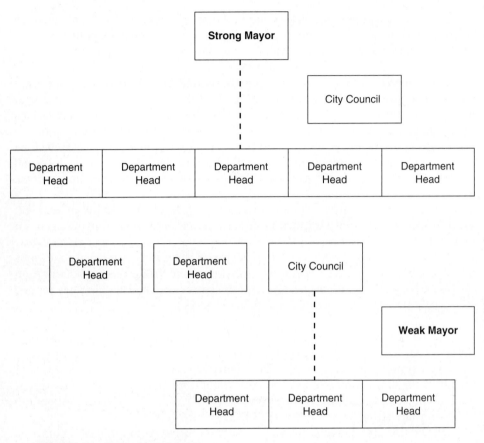

FIGURE 5.1 Mayor-Council System

were black while all the officers were white. Would it be enough simply to prosecute the officers, or would white police chief Daryl Gates also have to be removed? Bradley was not in a position to order either alternative. As the mayor in a weak mayor-council system, he lacked the formal authority to fire the prosecutor if he refused to prosecute or to fire the police chief if he refused to resign.[30]

COUNCIL-MANAGER   A council-manager arrangement normally has a relatively small city council that hires a manager to carry out the city's executive duties (see figure 5.2). That manager then serves at the pleasure of the council, meaning he or she can be fired at a moment's notice. As long as the manager remains in the council's good graces, however, that person normally can appoint and remove any of the city's department heads as well as propose the city's budget. These council-manager cities still have a mayor, but the mayor, whether chosen from the ranks of council or independently elected by voters, often does little besides performing ceremonial functions unless he or she also serves as a voting member of the city council.

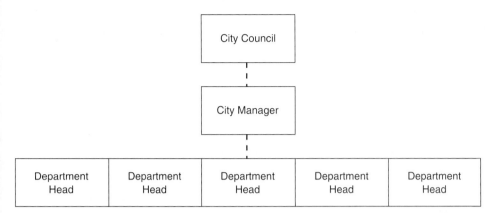

FIGURE 5.2 Council-Manager System

COMMISSION   In the commission form, no single individual serves as the chief executive over all the city's departments. Instead, a small number of commissioners (usually five) are independently elected to provide this administration (see figure 5.3). In some cities these individuals run for specific departmental chairs while in others they caucus after the election and then decide which department each shall supervise. The commissioners collectively comprise the city's legislative body, making the laws and passing the budget. Normally one of the commissioners carries the title of mayor, either elected to that position by the voters or by fellow commissioners; yet the mayor seldom has any additional authority other than to preside over legislative sessions and represent the city in ceremonial functions.

As table 5.2 indicates, the council-manager system is currently employed by a majority of U.S. cities with more than 100,000 people. These include cities as large as San Diego, Dallas, Kansas City, San Antonio, and San Jose. It is an especially popular form in cities with 100,000 to 200,000 residents, with nearly two-thirds of them opting for it. It is also more popular in the newer cities of the Sun Belt. Among the very largest cities in the nation, those with more than a half-million people, nearly 80 percent have chosen a mayor-council system. The commission system, on the other hand, reached its peak in popularity in about 1917 and remains in use in only eight cities whose populations exceed 100,000, although these include cities as large as Portland (Maine), Tulsa

FIGURE 5.3 Commission System

City Commissioner (Department Head)	City Commissioner (Department Head)	City Commissioner (Department Head)	City Commissioner (Department Head)	City Commissioner (Department Head)

Department Head	Department Head	Department Head

TABLE 5.2 Governmental Form by City Size, 1990

	Number of Cities Using		
Population Size	*Mayor-Council*	*Council-Manager*	*Commission*
100,000–199,999	36	71	4
200,000–499,999	22	24	4
500,000 and over	19	5	0
	77	100	8

SOURCE: *The Municipal Year Book* (Washington, D.C.: International City Managers' Association, 1990), Table 1/8.

(Oklahoma), Jackson (Mississippi), and Mobile (Alabama). Of our 12 select cities, Corpus Christi, Miami, and Phoenix use the council-manager form; all the others employ a mayor-council arrangement.[31]

Special Districts. The nation's more than 40,000 special districts are governmental units that provide services above and beyond what the city government provides, operating parallel to the city's governing structure. They are variously called authorities (e.g., transit authorities), boards (e.g., boards of education), corporations (e.g., health and hospital corporations), or districts (e.g., sanitation districts). The key characteristics of a special district are that it performs a particular function, has its own taxing and borrowing authority, and is governed by an independent governing board—with members either popularly elected or at least appointed for long terms of office. Although it may operate within the boundaries of an established city, it is essentially autonomous.

Nearly two-thirds of all special districts can be found in just 11 of the more populous states, such as California, Illinois, New York, and Pennsylvania.[32] Probably the best known of these are school districts and public housing authorities, but parks, water, sewers, sanitation, soil conservation, mosquito control, cemeteries, and mass transportation are other examples of services commonly provided in this manner. Some of the districts encompass more than one municipality, while some municipalities contain a number of special districts providing the same service, such as separate school districts. Two of the very largest special districts in the country are the Chicago Transit Authority and the Port Authority of New York and New Jersey, the latter operating airports, bridges, and tunnels in addition to some mass transit.

County Government. Some 3,000 separately elected and fiscally autonomous county governments also provide services enjoyed by city residents. Normally referred to as counties, they are called boroughs in Alaska, parishes in Louisiana, and judicial districts in Rhode Island. The county's boundaries may extend beyond the city limits, be completely coterminous with those of the city, or even be encompassed by the city. In New York City, for example, more than one county falls wholly within the city's boundaries. Whatever their configuration, these county governments routinely provide court services, keep area records, and conduct elections. Like city governments, however, they too are legally subordinate to the state.

Counties vary considerably, especially in size, population, functions, and governing structure. They range in size from San Bernardino (California), which is bigger than the states of Vermont and New Hampshire combined, to counties as small as Arlington (Virginia), which covers only 24 square miles. Some have less than 1,000 people while the largest have several million: Los Angeles County has seven million and Cook County, Illinois, has six million. The range of services provided also varies considerably, ranging from New England states, where counties generally do very little, to other regions, where a number of counties assume a lion's share of health and welfare responsibilities. (An example is Cook County.) Last, they are normally governed by a board of commissioners, although counties with county-managers or strong mayors, and even home-rule charters, are no longer uncommon.[33]

Exceptions include Connecticut, which does not have many such subdivisions, as well as cities like Baltimore and St. Louis, which do not fall within the jurisdiction of a county government.[34] In addition, there are roughly two dozen examples where cities have merged with their counties in a process generally referred to as consolidation.[35]

Most consolidation occurred prior to 1910. Since then, there has been some urban reluctance to share sizable amounts of political authority with a larger county, especially in those cities in which the African American or Hispanic population is just beginning to reach majority status.[36] There also has been reluctance among county residents living outside the city limits to shoulder any additional burden of inner-city services. In Memphis, for example, both city and suburban voters rejected consolidation in 1962; and although a majority of city voters voted for it in 1971, it was defeated in the suburbs by a 2 to 1 voting margin.[37] Nonetheless, there have been a few recent examples of city-county consolidation; some of these are Nashville and Davidson County (1962), Jacksonville and Duval County (1967), and Indianpolis and Marion County (1969). These are relatively new and less industrial cities, however. The differentials in socioeconomic status between their central cities and their surrounding suburbs are also smaller than those common in older industrial metropolitan areas.[38]

Yet, as the fiscal condition of postindustrial cities deteriorates, such consolidation may become more tempting. Although these mergers dilute city residents' voting power, they do reduce some governmental overlap and provide access to additional tax bases.[39]

In the interim, a more politically palatable alternative has been functional consolidation whereby the core city agrees to have one or more particular services provided countywide—either completely by the county government or in city-county partnership. Common examples include city-county hospitals, traffic commissions, libraries, animal shelters, and police technical services. Services such as planning, zoning, parks, welfare, and corrections increasingly are being surrendered exclusively to the counties.[40] Memphis, for example, was unable to accomplish full consolidation, but it turned over services such as corrections and its public hospital to the county.

Metropolitan Government.   Most metropolitan areas have a multiplicity of governments creating considerable confusion as well as some service duplication and other inefficiencies. In the Minneapolis–St. Paul metropolitan area, John

Harrigan and William Johnson found 273 separate governmental units: 7 counties, 140 cities, 49 school districts, 22 other special districts, and so on. Chicago now has more than 1,200, Philadelphia more than 800, and Pittsburgh more than 700. A typical big city resident can be served by as many as 10 local jurisdictions.[41] Such a proliferation of governing bodies has for some time given rise to a call for metropolitan government.[42]

A fully constituted metropolitan government would be the primary governmental unit for the entire metropolitan area, including the central city and its suburbs and in some cases encompassing more than one county. More typical is what is called a metropolitan service district, an additional layer of government established to provide services across the various governmental lines within the metropolis. These services often include highway construction, traffic control, mass transportation, hospitals, zoning regulation, economic development, and pollution control. In contrast to the situation under consolidation, autonomous city and suburban governments continue to provide certain other services within their own jurisdictions.

> A metropolitan government is desirable (1) when coordination of a function over the whole area is essential to effective service or control in any part of the area; (2) when it is desired to apply the ability to pay theory of taxation to the area as a whole, instead of allowing each part to support its own activities at whatever level its own economic base will allow; (3) when services can be applied more efficiently through large-scale operations; and (4) when it is necessary in order to assure citizens a voice in decisions that affect them at their places of work and recreation as well as at their places of residence.[43]

Metropolitan government is rare, however, for many of the same reasons city and county consolidation is unusual today. Residents of suburban St. Louis and Seattle soundly defeated such plans in the 1960s. Nonetheless, metropolitan areas such as Miami, Florida (Metropolitan Dade County Government, established in 1957), and Portland, Oregon (Metropolitan Service District, established in 1978), still have managed to have a significant number of their services provided at the metropolitan level under the control of 12- and 13-person commissions, respectively.[44] Outside the United States, one of the best examples of a fully constituted metropolitan governing arrangement is in Canada's Toronto metropolitan area. Here the central city and 12 surrounding municipalities have been functioning under a far-reaching metropolitan government since 1953.[45]

Councils of Governments.   Councils of Governments (COGs) are voluntary associations between separate governmental entities, normally comprising the chief executives of the participating governments and increasingly involving population-weighted voting. Because of their voluntary nature, however, they generally lack formal authority to enforce their decisions as well as authority independently to raise revenues. Nevertheless, they still can function as a forum for the exchange of information and ideas, and this communication can lead to both informal cooperation and more formal intergovernmental agreements.

Some of the more prominent ones are the Metropolitan Washington (D.C.) Council of Governments, the Association of Bay Area Governments (San Francisco), and the Supervisors' Inter-County Commission (Detroit).

COGs began to emerge in the late 1940s as suburbanization developed. The first major one was the New York Metropolitan Regional Council, formed in 1956. A sizable number of COGs developed between 1965 and 1975, especially where required by the mandates of a federal grant, such as the 1966 Demonstration Cities and Metropolitan Development Act. Today, most metropolitan areas have at least a semblance of a COG, but as few of these have independent taxing authority, they remain reliant on external governmental funding. This funding has all but disappeared of late, particularly if the COG was involved primarily in the delivery of welfare-related services.[46] An example is the Oklahoma City metropolitan council. It received more than 90 percent of its money from the federal government in 1976, but by 1988 that figure had dropped to 24 percent as its overall budget shrank from $2 million to $1 million.[47]

Intergovernmental Agreements.   Even less institutionalized are voluntary arrangements reached between neighboring local governments. Two cities, for example, may agree to build and operate a sewage system or a large airport. One city may provide another with a particular service, such as water, for a fee. Lakeland, California, as an extreme example, purchases police, fire, planning, and virtually every other service from Los Angeles County. Two communities may have a mutual assistance pact whereby they help each other in emergencies. These often include police or fire protection given when the other community's services cannot cope with the immediate problem. Similarly, a number of cities may agree that each will take certain steps to battle an overlapping problem such as pollution.[48]

Electoral Forms.   The formal role of the urban voter in these decision-making arrangements varies considerably from city to city. At one end of the continuum, beyond the New England town meeting, the voters may make a number of policies directly by means of initiative and referendum processes. At the other extreme, where many of the key decision makers are appointed rather than elected, the voter has only indirect input. In between is the norm, however, where the voters choose elected officials to decide for them; but even here, there is much variation. Cities vary as to whom the elected officials represent, how they are nominated, whether general elections are partisan or nonpartisan, and whether recall votes are permitted.

Initiatives.   Where initiatives are allowed, voters begin the process by first drafting their own proposed law. They then must circulate petitions until they have the number of signatures required for the initiative to be placed on the next election ballot. Once on the ballot, if approved by a majority of voters, the proposition becomes law just as if it had been passed by an elected legislative body. In some cities, this direct legislative authority is diluted in one of two ways. In the first, the city council may by authorized to draft their own substitute proposal, placing it on the ballot next to the voter-initiated one. If both receive majorities, the one with the most votes is enacted. Other cities allow for only indirect initiatives. In this system any voter-initiated law must either be ratified by the city council or be subject to repeal by the council within a designated period of time.

Referenda.   The initiative process allows voters to draw up and pass their own laws directly. Referenda, on the other hand, at least give them a chance to approve or disapprove laws passed by elected bodies. Such referenda may be (1) mandated by law, as is the case for many bond issues, charter amendments, or annexations; (2) required if enough voters sign petitions to call for one (generally called a petition or protest referendum); or (3) called by the legislative body, whereby that body voluntarily subjects its own law to voter review (an optional referendum) or at least asks for a nonbinding "advisory" vote.

As table 5.3 indicates, cities are most likely to allow optional referenda, while the majority of them also permit elected officials to be recalled by popular vote. Less common are cities that require referenda before certain bills can become law, and least common of all is the provision for popular initiatives. Thus, in most cities, voters are limited to providing input before and after the governmental decisions are made. They choose the decision makers and occasionally are allowed to pass on a piece of legislation produced by those elected officials.[49]

Electing Representatives.   Even if a city is liberal in allowing for initiatives and referenda, most of its major decisions will still be made by elected officials and the individuals they appoint. Thus, it is also important to examine how city voters choose these representatives, and thereby exercise at least indirect control over them.

CONSTITUENCIES   When candidates for an elective office such as member of the city council are voted on by all the city's voters, it is an at-large election. When such candidates are voted on by a particular subdivision within the city, it is a district (or ward) election.

The overwhelming majority of council-manager and commission cities choose their council members at-large, consistent with their emphasis on removing political decisions as far as possible from parochial political concerns.[50] The majority of mayor-council cities elect all or most of their council members from districts. Of the 16 mayor-council cities with populations larger than 500,000 in 1986, 9 elected all of their council members by district; 2 elected all of them at-large

TABLE 5.3   Provision for Initiative, Referendum, and Recall Votes by Governmental Form, 1988

	Percentage of Cities Permitting			
Governmental Form	*Initiatives*	*Optional Referenda*	*Mandatory Referenda*	*Recalls*
Mayor-Council	37	71	39	53
Council-Manager	59	83	45	70
Commission	37	76	46	59

SOURCE: *The Municipal Year Book* (Washington, D.C.: International City Managers' Association, 1988), p. 10.

(San Francisco and Detroit). The remaining four had mixed arrangements: Indianapolis had 4 at-large, 25 district; Jacksonville had 5 at-large, 14 district; Memphis had 6 at-large, 7 district; and Houston had 5 at-large, 5 district.[51]

In 1979, the U.S. Justice Department prodded the city of Houston into adopting a mixed system, as its 14-person at-large city council had only one black member in a city that was 40 percent black. Similar federal actions more recently have been directed against the at-large systems in cities such as Dallas and Memphis.[52]

In *Thornburgh v. Gingles* (1986),[53] the U.S. Supreme Court struck down an at-large election system as racially discriminatory based on the fact that so few blacks had been elected. The particular electoral process was outlawed even though there was no clear evidence of intent to discriminate on the part of those who designed it. This action was possible because the U.S. Congress had passed the 1982 Voting Rights Act Amendment that included a "discriminatory results" test explicitly allowing for such statistics-based challenges.

Even more recently and without federal prodding, Pittsburgh voters used a 1987 referendum vote to scrap an entirely at-large system in favor of a system with all nine councilmembers elected from specific districts. Prompted by the federal government or not, there has been a clear recent trend away from at-large arrangements.[54]

METHODS OF VOTING   Whether a city employs an at-large system, a district system, or a combination of the two, it also must decide how many representatives are to be chosen from each election unit. In most general terms, will the election unit be represented by only one person (a single-member district) or by more than one person (a multimember district)?

When a single-member scheme is chosen, the one major decision left to be made is the vote percentage required to win. The top vote getter may win the seat regardless of the percentage of the vote attained (a plurality election); a simple majority of the votes cast may be required, with a run-off between the top vote getters if no one attains that majority the first time around; or a larger majority of the votes cast may be required (e.g., 60 percent), again with a run-off provision.

As with at-large electoral schemes, runoff provisions have been challenged successfully as racially discriminatory in predominantly white cities beset by racial polarization. These arrangements have allowed many offices to continue to be held by whites, even when a black candidate may have received the most votes. This situation tends to occur in multiple-candidate contests in which the white vote splits between two or more white candidates. In a runoff between the top black and top white vote getter, the white majority would then routinely pull together to elect one of their own.[55]

In Memphis, as an example, the runoff process was challenged as racially discriminatory. In 1991, a federal judge struck that provision in subsequent mayoral contests. In the very next election, Memphis elected its first African American mayor by a plurality vote, even though two white candidates had received a narrow majority of the total votes cast.

In a multimember arrangement, voting can be conducted in one of several ways:

1. Candidates run for a seat on the council in general; the voter casts one vote for his or her preferred candidate and the top vote getters win the seats up for election that time.
2. Candidates run for a seat on the council in general; however, under this scheme the voter may cast the number of votes corresponding with the number of positions up for election, and the top vote getters win the seats. Detroit and San Francisco select their entirely at-large city councils by this method. One slight variation is that some systems permit the voter to cast one or more of these votes for a particular candidate (cumulative voting).[56]
3. Candidates run for a seat on the council in general, and the voter may cast votes for as many of the candidates as he or she approves of (approval voting). Again, the top vote getters win the seats. Although not presently employed in any large city, this is about the most consensual system available, with those ultimately chosen having the broadest bases of popular support.
4. Candidates run for a seat on the council in general and the voter prioritizes his or her preferences for the total number of positions to be filled. Thereafter, a formula is used to determine how many of these "weighted votes" are needed to be elected (the Hare system).[57]
5. Candidates run for a particular at-large seat of their choice; the voter casts one vote in each race, and the top vote getter in each race wins that particular seat (winner take all). Cities such as Memphis, Jacksonville, Houston, and Indianapolis use this system for selecting their at-large councilmembers and they fill each seat every election. An alternative is to stagger the terms of those councilmembers being elected from multi-member districts such as these, much as is done in the U.S. Senate.

PARTISAN VERSUS NONPARTISAN BALLOTS   If it is a partisan election, the candidate's political party affiliation appears adjacent to his or her name on the ballot: Democrat, Republican, Socialist, Libertarian, or any of a number of other political parties. If it is a nonpartisan election, on the other hand, no party designations are allowed on the ballot.

In a partisan city, candidates nominated by officially sanctioned political parties are automatically placed on the general election ballot. Most states determine which organizations qualify as an official party by requiring that they ran a candidate in the most recent gubernatorial election, and that their candidate received more than a certain percentage of the votes cast. On the other hand, additional candidates normally can be placed on the ballot by getting a fixed percentage of the registered voters to sign their nominating petitions. The number of signatures required is usually large enough, however, to make this latter route rather difficult.

In a nonpartisan city, a candidate secures a position on the general election ballot either by being one of the top finishers in a nonpartisan primary or simply by filing for such a position. To file, the candidate normally must pay a filing fee; in a number of cities, he or she also must acquire the signatures of a certain percentage of the city's registered voters.

Almost all the council-manager and commission cities employ the nonpartisan scheme. This is to reduce the introduction of parochial politics (as opposed to what is best for the city in general). Approximately one-half of all mayor-council cities also use this voting arrangement.[58] In part to reduce the spillover influence of state and national parties, local elections rarely are held at the same time as elections for state and national office.

NOMINATION PROCESS   For a candidate to get on the ballot in a nonpartisan primary election, he or she must follow essentially the same steps required of an independent candidate seeking a place on a partisan ballot or of any candidate simply filing his or her way onto a nonpartisan general election ballot. Again, a declaration of candidacy must be filed; a fee normally must be paid; and a number of signatures may have to be acquired as well, although not nearly as many as the independents must attain. Thereafter, a designated number of the highest vote getters advance to the nonpartisan general election.

In a partisan primary, candidates must personally be registered members of the particular party; they are then nominated at a convention of party leaders or they are chosen in a direct primary with a ballot access method similar to the nonpartisan scheme described above. If it is to be a direct primary, state law will indicate whether voting can be restricted to registered party members (a closed primary) or must be left open to any registered voter regardless of party affiliation (an open primary). In most large cities with partisan elections, the closed direct primary is the nomination method of choice. The winner of each party's nomination bears that party's label on the general election ballot.

THE RECALL OPTION   Either the city's charter or applicable state law will prescribe how vacancies are to be filled if an elected official resigns or dies. In a majority of cities voters also are allowed to reconsider their previous electoral choice if a relatively large fixed percentage of registered voters sign a petition calling for such a recall determination.[59] This method was used to recall mayors in Los Angeles (1909), Seattle (1910), Detroit (1929), Los Angeles (1938), and Seattle (1938). Petitions were also circulated in Detroit in 1967, but petitioners did not attain enough signatures to subject Mayor Jerome Cavanaugh to a formal recall vote. Seattle's Mayor Wes Uhlman was taken to a recall vote in 1975 but survived by a nearly 2 to 1 margin.[60] Much closer was the recall vote on Cleveland's Mayor Dennis Kucinich in 1978.

THE SPECIAL CASE OF WASHINGTON, D.C.

An interesting exception to many of these rules is the District of Columbia, normally referred to as Washington, D.C. When the state of Pennsylvania would not send troops to protect members of the Continental Congress from attacks by mutinous Revolutionary Army troops in 1783, the Congress moved the national government to a plot of land donated by the state of Maryland.[61] Thus, the nation's capital was placed in a city that would not be part of any county or state but instead would be directly under federal control.

In 1801, a "District of Columbia" committee was created in the U.S. House of Representatives to supervise the governance of the nation's capital city. And much more slowly than its state counterparts, the national legislature only recently has begun to extend degrees of home rule to the residents of the District. Not until 1974, for instance, did the city receive its first home-rule charter. Today, it has a strong mayor-council form of government and a city budget that exceeds $3 billion; but more than $500 million of its budget comes directly from the federal government, theoretically to compensate for the fact that federal properties are exempt from city property taxes.

Reliance on the federal government for a sizable portion of its budget has meant that the city is subject to numerous federal mandates, such as the prohibition on spending governmental monies to fund abortions. Congress also has retained authority to veto almost any city legislation within 30 days of its passage. Examples of such vetoes have included a residency requirement for city workers, the banning of embassies from residential neighborhoods, a gay rights bill, guaranteed life insurance for AIDS victims, prohibition against conducting city business with firms operating in South Africa, police being chosen randomly from a list of qualified candidates (rather than by test-score ranking), and provisions of a "constitution" passed by city voters in 1982 that included job and loan guarantees for all city residents as well as a right to strike for the city's public service unions. Congress has also vetoed such minor decisions as allowing metered taxicabs, closing a fire station, and renaming certain streets.[62]

Julius W. Hobson, the city's chief congressional lobbyist, lamented,

> Any District issue is easy game for any member (of Congress) who wants to tee off on something, or help out a union or an industry or an organization, or who just doesn't like Washington or its people. . . . We live in a goldfish bowl, surrounded by members of Congress, none of whom are our own full-fledged representatives.[63]

In 1961, Washington, D.C., residents finally were given three electoral votes and thus could begin to influence presidential elections. Ten years later, they were granted their first congressional representation, a single nonvoting member in the House of Representatives. Then, in 1990, they took matters into their own hands and chose the first of two "shadow Senators" to represent them unofficially in the U.S. Senate.

The most far-reaching reform would be for the District to succeed in its efforts to achieve statehood. Its residents pay more than $1 billion per year in federal taxes even though they have no voting representation in the Congress. This, it can be argued, amounts to taxation without representation. Signs have been erected along approachways to the city that read "Welcome to the Nation's Last Colony: All Residents Must Leave Their Rights at the Border. D.C. Statehood Now!"[64]

Proponents also claim that the concept of a separate and dependent capital is outmoded. There were only 14,000 residents when the District was first established; consequently, the number of people being disenfranchised seemed somewhat trivial. Today, there are more than 600,000 residents, and not even one-third of them work for the federal government. As for fiscal independence, the city already raises more than 80 percent of its own revenues locally, and it could supplement that income by adding a commuter tax and billing the federal government for a number of services currently provided. In addition, if Washington were given statehood, proponents note that there would be at least four other states with fewer people: Alaska, Wyoming, Vermont, and Delaware.[65]

What are the prospects of statehood? In 1978 Congress initiated a constitutional amendment that would have made the District a "city-state." However, that amendment was ratified in only 16 of the necessary 38 state legislatures and expired in 1985. More recently, bills have been introduced in Congress that would create the state of New Columbia by federal legislation. Federal lands would be separate and not under the new state's control; the city's mayor and council would be replaced by a governor and a 25-member unicameral state legislature; and, of course, the new state would be entitled to the minimum of two U.S. senators and one representative in the U.S. House of Representatives. A majority of the American public appears to support statehood, as do a sizable number of interest groups including the AFL-CIO, the American Jewish Congress, Common Cause, the American Trial Lawyers Association, and the National Education Association.[66]

Opposition to the constitutional amendment and to the more recent congressional legislation has come largely from Republicans in the state and federal governments. Much of that opposition reflects fears that the city's population, which is overwhelmingly black and disproportionately poor, would elect two liberal Democratic senators and a liberal Democratic representative to Congress. In a system replete with checks and balances, such opposition is likely to preclude Washington's becoming a state, short of serious civil unrest or another comparable crisis.

The Bias of Rules

In politics there is seldom such a thing as a neutral rule. This reality can be seen most vividly in the struggles that inevitably occur when rule changes are being considered. In almost every instance, some groups stand to gain and others to lose as a result of the alteration. The partisan and ideological battles over the congressional representation of Washington, D.C., residents is a classic example.

Consider this from the perspective of the wealthy, the group I argue has always been dominant and is becoming even more so. Their interests are more likely to be secure when governing officials are insulated from the electorate, as when devices like nonpartisan elections put most emphasis on name recognition and individual ability to raise large campaign funds, making political parties less capable of aggregating the interests of the nonwealthy. Unless they actually do the governing directly themselves, the wealthy will be less threatened if the political authority of the elected officials is more broadly dispersed, as in a weak-mayor system. In a governing structure where insulated decision makers are subject to extensive checks and balances among themselves, it will be difficult to concentrate the kind of political resources necessary to pose a major political challenge to the existing distribution of wealth. For such a challenge to occur, particularly outside the most severe of urban crises, the political system either would have to be altered or circumvented.

URBAN POLITICS

> Urban leaders looked over their expanded domain and set out to control its physical growth so that it would enhance, not interfere, with its economic growth. . . . In devising their policies, they assumed that their interests for economic growth were synonymous with the community's interests. They therefore measured their policies for ordering growth by the standard of benefit to the business community, for what benefited business, benefited all.[67]

Although the form of American urban government has changed markedly over the years, its primary function has not. In each period, necessity has dictated that first priority be given to maintaining a healthy local economy. Without that, there are not enough jobs to provide work, not enough products to buy, and not enough revenues in the public coffers. Thus municipal governments have concentrated on providing an orderly environment as well as using tax abatements and the like to facilitate the accumulation of capital within their jurisdictions.

The economic elites themselves made most of the decisions in the limited governments of the small preindustrial commercial centers. Then as rapid urbanization caused a host of problems to disrupt business and to spill over into more affluent neighborhoods, the popularly elected governments of the industrial cities added more maintenance and social-welfare services. Finally, in the postindustrial era as these services expanded, their bureaucracies and recipients became organized and more demanding. The city governments came to be increasingly squeezed between these demands and the necessity to keep corporate taxes low and corporate services high; and all of this occurred in the face of trends that were making other environs more attractive and accessible to businesses and more affluent individual taxpayers.[68]

Preindustrial Period (pre-1820)

Like their European counterparts, America's preindustrial municipal governments strived to maintain both economic stability and social order. They could not stop the droughts or other perils to crops that plagued the agricultural economy; but when permitted by the British Parliament and suspicious rural-dominated colonial legislatures, they could be of assistance in providing for the common defense and regulating trade. Even after the American Revolution, their functions remained quite similar. Besides coordinating largely voluntary police and fire systems, they established standards for weights and measures, licensed tradesmen, and set some wages and prices, primarily to protect local merchants. The total cost of all such governmental activity scarcely amounted to anything. In the early nineteenth century, New York City was spending roughly $1.00 per capita; and in 1821, the city of Cleveland spent $80.02 to provide public services for its 600 people.[69]

> [Local government] was asked to do little, did little, and generally was reluctant to do very much more, concerned as it was with the interests and values of taxpaying property holders.[70]

Most of these limited governments tended to operate rather informally; and the public, even once the right to vote began to be extended, generally seemed content to defer to local economic notables for leadership. Whether members of life-tenured "closed corporations" or of elected city councils, the area's leading citizens—merchants, bankers, doctors, lawyers, and landowners—dominated whatever political decisions were taken in what came to be referred to as the borough form of governance. Mayors, in particular, were kept weak, as most were elected by their city councils rather than by the voters, and they had little independent authority. Where municipal services existed, they often were overseen by council-created independent commissions. Fragmentation and elitism were the political order of the day.[71]

The one slight variation was to be found in New England where all propertied white males made such decisions in regular town meetings, and politics also was attached to a Puritan religious base. Nonetheless, as the "faithful" became diluted by immigration, the religious base gave way; and there are indications that economic elites were quite influential in the town meetings as well.[72]

As there was not much of a middle class during this era, those who were not landowners were often dependent and poor. These "paupers" of the preindustrial city either became indentured servants, were sent to asylums or almshouses, or were begrudgingly extended poor relief, work relief, or private charity. Before extending such sustenance, however, benefactors often attempted to "cure" the wretches with a healthy dose or two of "moral training." Yet despite this "education," as well as settlement and vagrancy laws which kept many indigents moving along, one-third of northern city dwellers were poor by the middle of the eighteenth century; whatever poorhouses were then in existence were filled; and local governments were spending sizable shares of their meager budgets on relief.[73]

Meanwhile, the large majority of African Americans remained in the South as plantation slaves. Not only had southern agriculture become highly dependent on slave labor, but northern textile mills benefited greatly by being able to buy cheap cotton. Consequently, federal and state government policy began to protect this arrangement. The federal government required runaway slaves to be returned, and that law was often actively enforced. Meanwhile the 1808 ban on slave importation went largely unenforced. Some northern states adopted exclusion laws, limiting a black person's ability to settle or even travel across those states. The post–Civil War Freedman's Bureau often would persuade former slaves to accept contracts to work on the plantations of their previous slavemasters, only to have the plantation owners lend them money and in the process keep them dependent and unable to leave.[74]

Industrial Period (1820–1930)

> In truth Pittsburgh is a smoky, dismal city at her best. At her worst, nothing darker, dingier, or more dispiriting can be imagined.[75]

Spurred by technological innovations, as well as government construction of canals and railroads, industrialization began to emerge. Soon people were pouring into the cities. As should have been expected, social problems increased accordingly. Crime, fires, and severe poverty were widespread, and epidemics of disease raged out of control. City government was simply not equipped to face the challenge. Police, fire, and public-health protection as well as social services remained sorely inadequate largely because the property-owning citizenry clung tightly to its private property, individual liberties, and fear of strong and intrusive government. It was acceptable for government to tax and spend and even go into debt to promote economic growth, such as building streets, canals, and railroads; however, maintenance and social welfare services generally remained ''private matters.''[76]

> Given the powerful forces that fostered political consensus within the merchant communities, the major sources of conflict were usually confined to the problems of overcoming local inertia and building support among these leaders in favor of a particular kind of civic venture. The problems of political leadership focused on convincing their peers through newspapers, public meetings, private conventions, city council debates and the like that it was in everybody's interest to do all they could to support and contribute to some specific public works, harbor improvement, railway venture, stock purchase, or whatever.[77]

Soon, however, it became more and more apparent that urban problems could no longer be ignored, in part because they obviously were disrupting economic stability. Maintenance services were expanded. For example, a rash of epidemics and the discovery of bacteriology finally prompted the creation of public water and sewage systems (as in Philadelphia in 1811 and Boston in 1823); severe fires spurred the enactment of building codes and the hiring of building inspectors and professional fire fighters (as in Cincinnati in 1853); and the proliferation of crime and rioting led to the expansion and formalization of the police force (as in Boston in 1838).[78]

By the mid-nineteenth century, cities were well on their way to adopting governmental structures similar to the national model. Mayors were popularly elected as chief executives; Boston and St. Louis began this practice in 1822, Detroit in 1824, and New York in 1834. Citizens also chose city councils to serve legislative functions. A number of these councils followed the national model closely and were even bicameral. Like the federal government at the time, the chief executive was kept comparatively weak so as to avoid anything that resembled the British monarchical rule still fresh in America's collective mind. Councils were dominant in the formation of policy, with mayors essentially limited to ceremonial functions, presiding over the council, giving legislative advice, occasionally vetoing legislation on behalf of the city as a whole, and loosely overseeing the implementation of passed legislation.[79]

Holding political office would become a full-time occupation for some of these officials, and governmental payrolls would explode. Between 1865 and 1875, the nation's 15 largest cities saw their populations increase 70 percent, yet their municipal debts rose 271 percent during the same period.[80] And that was before the advent of the political machine.

Industrialization brought with it very definite cycles of economic slumps and booms; and subsequently relief became systematized, at least in part to help sustain a reserve work force during the slumps so that they would be available to work during the boom periods. The less fortunate could thus turn to social workers, settlement houses, and the selective benefits soon to be offered by the political machine.[81]

Despite the growth in municipal services, city political structures continued to be jerry-built, weak, and essentially obsolete. In large part as yet another hedge against anything resembling a strong mayor, service administration remained in the hands of a confusing jumble of decentralized boards and commissions whose administrators were independent as the result of their long-term tenures. As an example of jerry-building, Jersey City's charter was amended 91 times in 40 years; weak and decentralized government was exemplified in the 30 separate boards that were administering public functions in Philadelphia.[82] In addition, the problems failed to disappear. As an example, the poverty and crime rates climbed in Cincinnati; in 1884, 57,000 arrests were made in its population of only 250,000.[83] Thus, the stage was set for someone or something to begin bridging these gaps, and it was the political machine, a strong mayor, and patronage that gradually helped to facilitate the centralization of politics and the stabilization of the economic, social, and political environments.

Despite the opposition of many economic elites, entrenched independent bureaucrats, and a public still somewhat wary of concentrated political authority, popular referenda finally began to deliver more authority to the mayor's office at least in part because the public apparently felt it had become too far removed from political control under the "board" arrangement.[84] One of the first such grants was authority given to the mayor to appoint and remove those who administered the city's programs. Not only did this shift bring more centralization to political authority and make it more popularly responsive, but it also opened the door for the development of the patronage system.

Patronage became the currency that held the political structure together, taking the form of jobs, contracts, special services, friendship, ethnic recognition, and the like. The constituent, often an undereducated immigrant fresh from the blatantly elitist politics of the homeland, was generally happy to provide electoral loyalty in return.[85] As South Boston boss Martin Lomasney noted, ''There's got to be in every ward somebody that any bloke can come to—no matter what he's done—and get help. Help, you understand, none of your law and justice, but help."[86]

And help the bosses of the political machines did indeed provide. In good times, they spent liberally on city streets, public buildings, and sewers as well as on a host of maintenance and social services.[87] In the health field alone, by 1920 New York City had 228 dispensary clinics, 60 baby health stations, 21 tuberculosis clinics, 26 multipurpose clinics, 34 independent dispensaries, 65 outpatient hospital departments, 4 children's dental clinics, and 6 dispensaries for college students, all of which treated some 1,250,000 patients annually.[88] Yet the bosses also spent money during bad times, such as during the depressions of 1873–1878 and 1893–1897. Consequently, the biggest cities wound up spending as much as a third of their budgets on debt service.[89]

Soon this form of political structure outlived its usefulness, at least for the economic elites of the cities.[90] A "reform" movement began, crystallizing in 1894 with the formation of the National Municipal League. Laws like the Pendleton Act were reducing patronage by creating a civil service system for governmental hiring; and electoral reforms, such as nonpartisanship and nominations by primary elections, would strip the political machines of much of their crucial nomination control in these largely one-party cities. An era was coming to an end.

Whether the machine was a vehicle by which the lower and working classes could gain real economic and political power or whether it was the shifty hand of a "demagogic plutocracy" used to placate and dupe the teeming masses[91] has been hotly debated ever since the days of Boss Tweed and Tammany Hall. Nevertheless, Howard Chudacoff concludes that at the very least, "boss politics, with its legions of foreign-born supporters and its proclivity toward extralegal activities, posed a threat to the established classes. . . . They feared the immigrant-dominated political machines were subverting social and political order . . . and they equated bad politics with bad business."[92] Thus even though the political machines nearly always cooperated with the business elites—for example, machine-approved members of the municipal police helped to crush the early labor movement—they apparently had become more threatening than useful.[93]

Reform governments emphasized open politics, and impersonal, efficient, and scientifically based bureaucratic administration. If, however, the economic elites thought the style and the demands of the machine-mobilized underclasses were getting out of hand during the economically prosperous industrial period with its "politics of plenty," they would feel even more threatened when forced to confront organized neighborhoods and unionized bureaucrats amid the postindustrial period's "politics of scarcity."[94] It is to that postindustrial period that we now turn.

NOTES

1. In terms of taxation trends, more than 40 states now employ an income tax, and their reliance on that source is increasing. At the local level, reliance on sources other than property taxes has been increasing as well. A majority of large cities now have a local sales tax, ranging from 1/2 to 3 percent; and more than 3,500 local jurisdictions also

have a personal income tax, normally a flat rate of from 1 percent to 3 percent. For example, see John Bollens and Henry Schmandt, *The Metropolis* (New York: Harper & Row, 1982), pp. 206–207.

2. *Chicago Tribune,* November 13, 1982; *New York Times,* May 11, 1982.

3. Memphis, *Commercial Appeal,* July 25, 1990, p. A2.

4. *Trenton v. New Jersey,* 262 U.S. 182, 185–186 (1923).

5. Howard Chudacoff, *The Evolution of American Urban Society* (Englewood Cliffs, N.J.: Prentice-Hall, 1975), p. 150.

6. U.S. Department of Commerce, Bureau of the Census, *Census of the Population* (Washington, D.C.: Government Printing Office, 1990).

7. Edward Banfield and James Q. Wilson, *City Politics* (Cambridge, Mass.: Harvard University Press, 1963), p. 65.

8. See Advisory Commission on Intergovernmental Relations, *Measuring Local Government Discretionary Authority* (Washington, D.C.: Government Printing Office, 1980).

9. William Cassella, Jr., "A Century of Home Rule," *National Civic Review* 64 (1975): 441–450.

10. For example, see *New York Times,* August 10, 1989.

11. John F. Dillon, *Commentaries on the Law of Municipal Corporations* (Boston: Little, Brown, 1911), p. 448.

12. David Nice, *Federalism* (New York: St. Martin's Press, 1987), pp. 145–151.

13. See *Christian Science Monitor,* January 2, 1986, p. 7. For more on state mandates, see Advisory Commission on Intergovernmental Relations, *State and Local Roles in the Federal System* (Washington, D.C.: Government Printing Office, 1982).

14. The majority of existing state constitutions have not been overhauled for a century or more and thus contain some rather peculiar provisions by contemporary standards. Some, for instance, actually restrict the positions married couples can assume in sexual relations, while approximately a dozen still make adultery a crime punishable by imprisonment. Although such archaisms normally lie dormant on the yellowed pages of these constitutions, they are occasionally enforced. In 1990, for example, there were four adultery arrests in southeastern Connecticut. (See *New York Times,* September 21, 1990.)

    These examples stand as evidence of just how intimidating it is to attempt to amend a state constitution, at very least requiring popular ratification through a referendum vote.

15. *Baker v. Carr,* 369 U.S. 186 (1962). This decision overturned Tennessee's apportionment of state legislative seats as violating the "equal protection clause" of the Fourteenth Amendment to the United States Constitution. Thus, districts were to be drawn in a way that would roughly equalize the number of persons in each, and the state would be required to reapportion with each decennial census.

16. *Reynolds v. Simms,* 377 U.S. 533 (1964). In this case, Alabama was required to elect both houses of its state legislature according to the proportionality principle set out in *Baker v. Carr.*

17. See Thomas Murphy and John Rehfuss, *Urban Politics in the Suburban Era* (Homewood, Ill.: Dorsey, 1976), pp. 28–49; *New York Times,* February 19, 1984.

18. For the extension of *Reynolds v. Simms* to local election districts, see *Avery v. Midland County,* 390 U.S. 474 (1968).

19. See *New York Times,* February 19, 1984.

20. *Reynolds v. Simms,* at 562, 566.

21. *National Journal,* August 12, 1989, pp. 2026–2030. For a case study, see Richard Lehne, *Reapportionment in the New York State Legislature* (New York: Municipal League, 1972).

22. *McCulloch v. Maryland,* 4 Wheat 316 (1819).

23. See John Lindsay, *The City* (New York: Norton, 1970); Nat Hentoff, "The Mayor," *The New Yorker,* October 7, 1967; May 3, 1969.

24. See *New York Times,* January 31, 1987. Also see Dennis Judd, *The Politics of American Cities* (Boston: Little, Brown, 1988), pp. 303–305.

25. *New York Times,* June 11, 1989 and May 21, 1990. For a historical review of federal urban policy in the postindustrial era, see Paul Kantor and Steven David, *The Dependent City* (Glenview, Ill.: Scott, Foresman, 1988), chap. 10.

26. See *New York Times,* June 26, 1990.

27. For a fuller discussion of both city governing and electoral forms, see Demetrios Caraley, *City Governments and Urban Problems* (Englewood Cliffs, N.J.: Prentice-Hall, 1977).

28. For example, see Jane Mansbridge, *Beyond Adversarial Democracy* (New York: Basic Books, 1980).

29. ICMA, "Profiles of Individual Cities," *Municipal Year Book* (New York: International City Managers' Association, 1981), pp. 7–42.

30. See *New York Times,* March 7, 1991; March 31, 1991.

31. See Thomas Dye and Susan McManus, "Predicting City Government Structures," *American Journal of Political Science* 20 (May 1976): 257–272.

32. U.S. Department of Commerce, Bureau of the Census, *Census of Governments* (Washington, D.C.: Government Printing Office, 1990).

33. See Vincent Marando and Robert Thomas, *The Forgotten Governments* (Gainesville: University of Florida Press, 1977).

34. There is a St. Louis County and a Baltimore County, but both are located adjacent to the cities bearing their names.

35. See Charles Adrian and Charles Press, *Governing Urban America* (New York: McGraw-Hill, 1977), p. 237.

36. In the above-mentioned consolidations, for example, the African American proportion of the governmental unit slipped from 40 percent to 25 percent in Nashville, 43 percent to 23 percent in Jacksonville, and 25 percent to 15 percent in Indianapolis. See U.S. Department of Commerce, *Census of the Population*; Bollens and Schmandt, *The Metropolis,* pp. 311–322.

37. Vincent Marando, "The Politics of City-County Consolidation," *National Civic Review* 64 (February 1975): 71–81; Vincent Marando, "City-County Consolidation," *Western Political Quarterly* 32 (December 1979): 409–422; Bollens and Schmandt, *The Metropolis,* pp. 311–322.

38. Other post–World War II mergers include Baton Rouge (Louisiana), Lexington (Kentucky), Columbus (Ohio), Las Vegas (Nevada), and Juneau (Alaska); For example, see Charles Adrian and Michael Fine, *State and Local Politics* (Chicago: Nelson-Hall, 1991), p. 231.

39. Parris Glendening and Patricia Atkins, "City-County Consolidations: New Views for the Eighties," *Municipal Yearbook, 1980* (Washington, D.C.: International City Managers' Association, 1980), p. 70.

40. See Adrian and Press, *Governing Urban America,* pp. 241–242.

41. John Harrigan and William Johnson, *Governing the Twin Cities Region* (Minneapolis: University of Minnesota Press, 1978), p. 4.

42. One of the earliest of these analyses was Robert Wood, *1400 Governments* (Garden City, N.Y.: Doubleday/Anchor, 1964).

43. Victor Jones, "Local Government Organization in Metropolitan Areas," in Coleman Woodbury, ed., *The Future of Cities and Urban Redevelopment* (Chicago: University of Chicago Press, 1953), part IV, p. 508.

44. Bollens and Schmandt, *The Metropolis,* pp. 324–339.
45. Terry Shevciw, "Canadian Experience with Metropolitan Government," *Municipal Yearbook, 1973* (Washington, D.C.: International City Managers' Association, 1973); Adrian and Press, *Governing Urban America,* pp. 240–241.
46. See Advisory Commission on Intergovernmental Relations, *Metropolitan Councils of Government* (Washington, D.C.: Government Printing Office, 1966); Joan Aron, *The Quest for Regional Cooperation* (Berkeley: University of California Press, 1969); Ann Bowman and James Franke, "The Decline of Substate Regionalism," *Journal of Urban Affairs* 6 (Fall 1984): 51–63; Charles P. Shannon, "The Rise and Emerging Fall of Metropolitan Area Regional Associations," in J. Edward Benton and David Morgan, eds., *Intergovernmental Relations and Public Policy* (New York: Greenwood, 1986).
47. David Morgan, *Managing Urban America* (Pacific Grove, Calif.: Brooks-Cole, 1989), p. 32.
48. See David Reynolds, "Progress Toward Achieving Efficiency and Responsible Political Systems in Urban America," in John Adams, ed., *Urban Policy Making and Metropolitan Dynamics* (Cambridge, Mass.: Ballinger, 1976); Gary Miller, *Cities by Contract* (Cambridge, Mass.: MIT Press, 1981); *New York Times,* July 15, 1991.
49. For a discussion of trends, see Heywood Saunders, "Voters and Urban Capital Finance," unpublished paper presented at the annual meeting of the American Political Science Association, San Francisco, September 1990.
50. The origins, operations, and biases of the council-manager system are discussed at far greater length in chapters 7 and 8 below.
51. See International City Managers' Association, *Municipal Year Book* (New York: ICMA, 1987), pp. 174–212.
52. For an empirical analysis of the entire phenomenon, see Susan Welch, "The Impact of At-Large Elections on the Representation of Blacks and Hispanics," *Journal of Politics* 52 (November 1990): 1050–1076.
53. *Thornburgh v. Gingles,* 106 U.S. 2752 (1986).
54. See Heywood Sanders, "The Government of American Cities," *Municipal Yearbook, 1982* (Washington, D.C.: International City Managers' Association, 1982), pp. 185–186; Peggy Helig and Robert Mundt, *Your Voice at City Hall* (Albany, N.Y.: SUNY Press, 1984).
55. For an empirical analysis of the runoff system's racial impact, see Charles Bullock and A. Brock Smith, "Black Success in Local Runoff Elections, *Journal of Politics* 52 (November 1990): 1205–1220.
56. Although not presently employed at the city level, cumulative voting was used to choose members of the Illinois legislature from 1870 to 1980.
57. A tremendous variety of proportional representation schemes are employed throughout the world, but most are designed to be used in highly partisan elections (normally in parliamentary systems), or at least in elections where people cast their ballots for a particular group rather than particular candidates. Under the "list plan," for instance, each party or group presents an ordered slate, wins a number of seats proportionate to their party/group percentage of the total vote, and then particular winners are assigned beginning at the top of their slate. See Wolfgang Birke, *European Elections by Direct Suffrage* (Layden: Sythoff, 1961); or E. Lakeman, *How Democracies Vote: A Study of Majority and Proportional Electoral Systems* (London: Faber and Faber, 1974).
    A few "proportional representation" arrangements have been tried in the United States, as in Boulder (1918–1950), Cleveland (1924–1934), Cincinnati (1926–1957), Toledo (1936–1952), New York (1937–1945), and Worcester (1950–1960). Some remnants are left in the Cambridge and New York City school board election systems.

However, these are rare exceptions and the system is virtually nonexistent in U.S. cities today. For a discussion of the New York City experience, see Martin Gottleib, "The 'Golden Age' of the City Council," *New York Times,* August 11, 1991.

58. William Dutton and Alana Northrup, "Municipal Reform and the Changing Pattern of Urban Politics," *American Politics Quarterly* 6 (October 1978): 429–452.

59. See *The Book of States, 1980–81* (Lexington, Ky.: Council of State Governments and the Legislatures' Association, 1981), p. 198.

60. See Caraley, *City Governments and Urban Problems,* pp. 98–99.

61. The first site was a 100-square-mile plot of land donated jointly by the states of Virginia and Maryland. Yet when Virginia residents rebelled in 1846, the Virginia portion was returned to the jurisdiction of the state of Virginia.

62. See *New York Times,* July 19, 1988.

63. Quoted in *New York Times,* July 19, 1990.

64. For a look at Washington, D.C.'s political-economic circumstances over the past decade, see *New York Times,* March 10, 1980; July 26, 1986; July 19, 1988; January 21, 1990; July 12, 1990; July 19, 1990; *Common Cause Magazine,* November/December 1987, pp. 24–27.

65. See *Common Cause Magazine,* November/December 1987, pp. 24–27.

66. Reagan administration pollster Richard Wirthlin found 80 percent of Americans feeling that D.C. residents should have the same rights as all other Americans, while a majority actually supported statehood. Poll cited in *Common Cause Magazine,* November/December, 1987, p. 24. That same article also lists a number of the interest groups supporting statehood.

67. David Goldfield and Blaine Brownell, *Urban America: From Downtown to No Town* (Boston: Houghton Mifflin, 1979), p. 166.

68. For two good general discussions, see Peter Gluck and Richard Meister, *Cities in Transition* (New York: Viewpoints, 1979); and Charles Glaab and A. Theodore Brown, *A History of Urban America* (New York: Macmillan, 1976), chap. 9.

69. Glaab and Brown, *A History of Urban America,* p. 17. For more on the governance of these preindustrial mercantile cities, see Kantor, *The Dependent City,* chaps. 3–5.

70. Michael Frisch, *Town into City* (Cambridge, Mass.: Harvard University Press, 1964), p. 44.

71. For more on elite domination of government during the preindustrial period, see Robert Dahl, *Who Governs?* (New Haven, Conn.: Yale University Press, 1960), p. 28; Richard Wade, *The Urban Frontier* (Chicago: University of Chicago Press, 1959), p. 78.

72. Paul Kantor, *The Dependent City* (Glenview, Ill.: Scott, Foresman, 1988), p. 41; James Zimmerman, *Participatory Democracy: Populism Revisited* (New York: Praeger, 1986), pp. 20–21.

73. Chudacoff, *The Evolution of American Urban Society,* pp. 11–12, 39–41; Blake McKelvey, *The Urbanization of America: 1860–1915* (New Brunswick, N.J.: Rutgers University Press, 1963), chap. 10; Goldfield and Brownell, *Urban America: From Downtown to No Town,* chap. 4.

74. Howard Zinn, *A People's History of the United States* (New York: Harper Colophon, 1980), chap. 9.

75. Willard Glazier, *Peculiarities of American Cities* (New York: Ferguson, 1885), p. 334, as quoted in William Schultze, *Urban Politics* (Englewood Cliffs, N.J.: Prentice-Hall, 1985).

76. Goldfield and Brownell, *Urban America: From Downtown to No Town,* chap. 8; Kantor, *The Dependent City,* chap. 5.

77. Kantor, *The Dependent City,* p. 59.

78. See Goldfield and Brownell, *Urban America: From Downtown to No Town,* chap. 8; Kantor, *The Dependent City,* chap. 5; Nelson Blake, *Water for the City* (Syracuse, N.Y.: Syracuse University Press, 1956); Frank Goodnow, *City Government in the United States* (New York: Century, 1904); Richard Hofstadter, *Social Darwinism in American Thought,* rev. ed. (New York: George Braziller, 1955); Sam Bass Warner, *The Urban Wilderness* (New York: Holt and Rinehart, 1972), p. 200; Glaab and Brown, *A History of Urban America,* pp. 80–81, 161–168.

79. Peter Gluck and Richard Meister, *Cities in Transition* (New York: New Viewpoints, 1979), chap. 3; Goldfield and Brownell, *Urban America: From Downtown to No Town,* chap. 8.

80. Gluck and Meister, *Cities in Transition,* pp. 41–42; Glaab and Brown, *A History of Urban America,* pp. 80–81, 161–168.

81. Frances Fox Piven and Richard Cloward, *Regulating the Poor* (New York: Vintage, 1971).

82. See Ernest Griffith, *History of American City Government* (New York: Praeger, 1974); Chudacoff, *The Evolution of American Urban Society,* p. 126.

83. Zane Miller, "Boss Cox's Cincinnati: A Study in Urbanization and Politics," *Journal of American History* 54 (March 1968): 823–838.

84. Ibid., chap. 3.

85. For a depiction of the inner workings of the political machine, see William Riordan, *Plunkitt of Tammany Hall* (New York: Dutton, 1963); or see Chudacoff, *The Evolution of American Urban Society,* chap. 5.

86. As quoted in Lincoln Steffens, *The Autobiography of Lincoln Steffens* (New York: Harcourt Brace, 1931), p. 618.

87. Sam Bass Warner, *The Private City* (Philadelphia: University of Pennsylvania Press, 1968); Bayard Still, "Patterns of Mid-Nineteenth Century Urbanization in the Midwest," *Mississippi Valley Historical Review* 28 (September 1941): 187–206; John C. Teaford, *The Municipal Revolution in America* (Chicago: University of Chicago Press, 1975); Clarence Stone, Robert Whelan, and William Myrin, *Urban Policy and Politics in a Bureaucratic Age* (Englewood Cliffs, N.J.: Prentice-Hall, 1979), part 2.

88. Warner, *The Urban Wilderness,* pp. 221–222.

89. For example, see Ernest Griffith, *A History of American City Governments* (New York: Praeger, 1974); Glaab and Brown, *A History of Urban America,* pp. 80–81, 161–168.

90. Samuel Hays, "The Politics of Reform in Municipal Government in the Progressive Era," in Harlan Hahn and Charles Levine, eds., *Urban Politics: Past, Present, and Future* (White Plains, N.Y.: Longman, 1980); Richard Wade, "The City in History—Some American Perspectives," in Werner Hirsch, ed., *Urban Life and Form* (New York: Holt, Rinehart and Winston, 1963); Kenneth Newton, "Feeble Governments and Private Power," in Lou Masotti and Robert Lineberry, eds., *The New Urban Politics* (Cambridge: Ballinger, 1976); Eugene Lewis, *The Urban Political System* (Hinsdale, Ill.: Dryden, 1973), p. 70; or Richard Bernard and Bradley Rice, "Political Environment and the Adoption of Progressive Reforms," *Journal of Urban History* 1 (February 1975): 149–174.

91. Robert Merton, "The Latent Function of the Machine," in Edward Banfield, ed., *Urban Government* (New York: Free Press, 1969); Daniel Gordon, "Immigrants and Urban Governmental Reforms in American Cities, 1933–1960," *American Journal of Sociology* 74 (September 1968): 158–171; or Robert Lineberry and Edmund Fowler, "Reformism and Public Policy in American Cities," *American Political Science Review* 61 (September 1967).

For examples of the opposite view, see James Scott, "Corruption, Machine Politics, and Political Change," *American Political Science Review* 63 (December 1969); Michael Rogin, *The Intellectuals and McCarthy* (Cambridge: MIT Press, 1967), p. 187; Harold Gosnell, *Machine Politics: Chicago Model* (Chicago: University of Chicago Press, 1934 and 1968); Lincoln Steffens, *The Shame of the Cities* (New York: McClure, Phillips, 1904; New York: Hill and Wang, 1957).

92. Chudacoff, *The Evolution of American Urban Society,* pp. 148–149.

93. Kantor, *The Dependent City,* chap. 7; Judd, *The Politics of American Cities,* chap. 3.

94. For more on industrial era politics, see Kantor, *The Dependent City,* chaps. 4–6.

CHAPTER **6**

Political Relationships: The Postindustrial City

The 1920s marked the last of the real boom years for the older industrial cities as well as the last significant chance for most of the in-migrating poor to begin fulfilling the American dream of rising from rags to riches. Among other things, the postindustrial era (1930–present) would be marked by a substantial increase in the mobility of capital and the more affluent people away from urban areas. Cities, and especially their poorer residents, would soon face varying degrees of abandonment.

Many cities also became markedly less successful at extending their boundaries, seeking thereby to retain the sizable portion of their tax base that was moving farther and farther from the center of town. Whereas the nation's 20 largest cities had annexed 1,602 square miles before 1930, they added only 83 in the next 40 years.[1] Suburbanites and rural-dominated state legislatures had put their collective foot down. The net result was reduced circumstances for the urban poor left in the wake of postindustrial social and economic change and increased difficulty for governments attempting to cope with their needs within an altered distribution of urban political power.

THE CRISIS CYCLE

What happens to a dream deferred?
   Does it dry up?
   like a raisin in the sun?
   Or fester like a sore—
   and then run?
   Does it stink like rotten meat?
   Or crust and sugar over—
   like a syrupy sweet?

Maybe it just sags
like a heavy load
or does it explode?[2]

As the postindustrial era dawned, the dream indeed came to be deferred for a considerable number of Americans—in particular, for the most recent immigrants living in the urban ghettos. The western frontier had already been settled for all practical purposes, and the development of the postindustrial economy left fewer and fewer opportunities for the underskilled to work their way out of the ghetto. Soon national economic and social crises would cause the dream to explode. Thereafter, once short-term governmental efforts to placate the economically and socially dislocated of the inner cities had subsided, the powder keg of discontent would erupt once again.

The Great Depression Era

As the Great Depression ushered in the 1930s, urban unemployment soared: there were more than a million unemployed people in New York City, 660,000 in Chicago, and unemployment rates of more than 50 percent in cities like Akron and Toledo. As much as one-third of the nation's work force was unemployed, and only a quarter of those jobless households was receiving any form of governmental assistance.[3]

City governments responded by increasing expenditures for relief as well as for public works and job training. Between 1929 and 1931, Detroit's relief expenditures grew from $2.4 million to $14.9 million, Milwaukee's from $0.6 to $2.9 million, and Philadelphia's from $0.6 to $3.5 million. By the end of 1930, the nation's 75 largest cites were spending approximately $420 million on public works, yet most was in vain. Property values plummeted; taxpayers voted themselves tax cuts; and tax delinquencies soared. By 1932, 40 percent of Detroit's taxes were delinquent and 70 percent of its budget was going to debt service. By the end of that year, cities had defaulted on some 600 payments, services were being slashed, and serious social unrest had begun.[4]

The turbulence generally took the form of either mass looting or clashes between large numbers of demonstrators and the police; it was almost always prompted by one or more of the following conditions: lack of employment, lack of food, housing evictions, and/or inadequate public relief. Among the incidents occurring in this period, 1,100 men mobbed two trucks delivering baked goods to a New York City hotel; thousands of unemployed workers stormed city halls in Cleveland, Detroit, New York City, Milwaukee, Boston, and other cities, clashing with police who had ordered them to disperse; local relief offices were invaded and administrators badgered into providing easier access to, and larger quantities of, welfare assistance. Thousands of people would turn out to block the eviction of tenants, often engaging in rent riots; and some large hunger marches turned into full-scale food riots.[5]

Frances Fox Piven and Richard Cloward concluded that "economic distress . . . produced unprecedented disorder and the specter of cataclysmic disorder."[6] At the time, Congressman Hamilton Fish warned, "If we don't give security under the existing system, the people will change the system. Make no mistake about that."[7]

In 1933, Franklin D. Roosevelt and a heavily Democratic Congress launched the New Deal, with its Federal Emergency Relief Administration (for direct relief), Civil and Public Works Administrations (for jobs), and Homeowners' Loan Corporation (to forestall evictions) among other programs. In addition, the settlement house concept and political-machine patronage gave way to Aid to Families with Dependent Children, Social Security, unemployment compensation, and so on— an ever more systematic plan for welfare assistance. The New Deal thus marked the beginning of a formalized national welfare state. With this development, however, American citizens gradually came to expect more and more help from their governmental institutions, including those of the cities, which meant that the cities would come to face a growing demand for services just as increasing numbers of taxpayers were beginning to move to the suburbs.

In the meantime, the social unrest subsided, and it was not long before a still heavily unemployed nation began gearing up for war. World War II fueled the gross national product (GNP), reduced unemployment, and diverted public attention from economic uncertainties at home. At the same time, relief was rapidly reduced during the 1940s and 1950s, setting the stage for the next round of unrest.[8]

The Civil Rights Era

In the mid-1960s, the "dream deferred" once again began to fester. For example, the nation's 12 largest cities had come to contain more than two-thirds of the non-southern black population, of which more than 85 percent lived together in ghettos. African Americans were unemployed at well over twice the national average; and those who had work were being paid an average of less than 60 percent of what their white counterparts were earning, a percentage that was actually shrinking. This left more than 40 percent of the black community below the government's poverty line; and those living in the urban slums often had to pay higher prices and usurious credit rates as well.[9]

It should have come as little surprise, then, that as the Civil Rights and Black Power movements raised black consciousness, and as television dangled "the good life" before peoples' eyes amid these dire slum conditions, another underclass rebellion erupted. This time the turbulence engulfed many of the nation's black urban ghettos. Between 1962 and 1968, some 164 outbreaks left more than a hundred people dead (90 percent of them black), thousands injured, thousands more arrested, and hundreds of millions of dollars worth of property damage. The largest outbreaks occurred in New York, Los Angeles, Newark, Detroit, and Washington, D.C.[10]

Amid the turmoil, President Lyndon Johnson and a heavily Democratic Congress launched a "War on Poverty," which included liberalized welfare-eligibility requirements, food stamps, Medicaid, Head Start, legal aid, community mental health centers, and model city programs. Zane Miller has stated that "Congress ground out urban-oriented programs unparalleled in their volume and variety."[11] Federal aid to urban areas increased 590 percent between 1961 and 1972, with 136 grant programs added between 1963 and 1967 alone.[12] Piven and Cloward noted that increases in relief services seem to have corresponded rather directly with rises in ghetto turbulence.[13] The national Democrats introduced these programs in an attempt to ameliorate the economic dislocations that had helped to set off ghetto unrest,[14] and also because the more politicized of the ghetto poor had become important components of governing Democratic party coalitions.[15]

Once again, however, as the violence subsided and war (this time in Vietnam) diverted national attention, such efforts were given a much lower priority.[16] Then, with the ascendance of more conservative presidential administrations in the 1970s and 1980s, a number of these programs were scaled back considerably.[17]

Cycles of Urban Unrest

> For most of our history the place of the urban poor has been comfortably "hidden" under the "rock" of urban profit. America becomes concerned with its urban poor when their condition can no longer be hidden; when they pose a barrier to economic growth and a threat to social order, thus exacerbating a developing crisis in the legitimacy of the city as a center for profit.[18]

With the sandbox in turmoil, the adults came running, wielding their sticks,[19] but also carrying bags of goodies. As Piven and Cloward commented, "Although the processes by which the relief expansion occurred were sometimes covert and circuitous, the moral seems clear: a placid poor get nothing, but a turbulent poor sometimes get something."[20]

Welfare programs have served the function of placating and restraining the periodically rebellious underclasses, but the level of unrest seems to increase with each round. The political organization and sophistication of the underclass improves as well, helping the poor become increasingly effective at retaining at least some of each round's governmental concessions.[21] In addition, this aid is administered by a largely unionized bureaucracy; and their unwillingness to lose these jobs imposes an added and rather effective constraint on elected officials desiring to scale down the programs.[22]

THE FISCAL RESULT

City governments have found themselves in a quandary. Corporations and tax-paying populations have departed for the suburbs and beyond, leaving behind an economically trapped, informed, and demanding underclass citizenry. Service demands increase at the time that those with wealth find it easier to flee from the central cities.[23]

James O'Connor's fiscal crisis theory can be applied to postindustrial city governments.[24] Assisting capital accumulation and providing legitimizing mainte-nance and social welfare services cost the cities greater and greater sums of money, dollars that the ever more tightly squeezed wage-earning taxpayer became less and less willing to give up in taxes. The costs of attempting to lure and/or keep industries, as well as maintaining some semblance of livelihood for ghetto populations lost in the economic shuffle, ultimately pinched the pocketbooks of taxpaying corporations and people, helping to drive them beyond the city limits. As this burden was shifted to the state and federal levels, there arose statewide tax cutting efforts, like California's Proposition 13 or Massachusetts's Proposition 2 1/2, as well as efforts to enact similar restrictions on the federal government.[25]

Expenditures

Postindustrial cities spend an increasing amount on maintenance services. Once roads, sewers, and waterworks have been built to serve a population of a given size, maintenance costs do not decrease simply because people leave. They generally increase as the physical plant ages, and they certainly increase in terms of cost per capita.[26]

In addition, more and better services are needed if an attractive business climate is to be cultivated and maintained. As part of that climate, cities also must offer more and more tax breaks and subsidies to potential investors.[27]

The people remaining tend to be "high-cost citizens." Demetrios Caraley identifies these as low-income families, the school-age children of the poor, the elderly, the addicted, the insane, AIDS victims, and others "who are direct consumers of expensive services and cash benefits like welfare payments, subsidized housing, etc."[28]

Finally, even when demand subsides a little it is highly difficult to reduce the city budget because the decline in the number of private-sector jobs has left the city as an employer of last resort; an organized and militant public work force has become effective at resisting retrenchment; and pension payments have become a large and fixed short-term expenditure.[29]

In order to provide services, reduce unemployment, and appease the unionized bureaucracies, public-sector jobs multiplied. Between 1967 and 1972, New York City lost 89,400 private-sector positions and added 57,500 public-sector ones. The figures were 7,000 and 3,900 for Baltimore; 53,000 and 18,400 for Philadelphia; and 26,000 and 2,300 for St. Louis. Thus in the decade between 1960 and 1970, public employment as a percentage of all jobs increased from 8.2 to 14 percent in New York; 9 to 12.2 percent in Detroit; and 6.9 to 9.8 percent in Philadelphia.[30] These work forces have not only proven very difficult to reduce; they have continued to grow in many cities.

Revenues

In the late 1970s, William Tabb estimated that each departing job took with it between $650 and $1,035 in local tax revenues.[31] When a city loses hundreds of thousands of jobs in a matter of a few years, there are bound to be tax revenue shortfalls, even if services are simply to be maintained at their previous levels. When the nation faces extended periods of substantial economic recession and/or inflation, city tax revenues shrink still further. Increased unemployment reduces revenues and necessitates more expenditures for public assistance programs; and as cities rely primarily on property taxes, they face the practical difficulty of continually reassessing privately owned property in order to keep up with inflation.

As for raising taxes, those city residents are already among the highest taxed in the nation; they not only tend to feel present taxes are too high[32] but have often attempted to do something about it. As an example, where nearly three-quarters of all school bond issues passed in 1965, that figure had dropped to roughly one-half 10 years later. These citizens have also "voted with their feet," moving out of the cities altogether and taking their tax base with them.[33]

The Bottom Line

> While the nation's large cities are plagued by many specific problems—crime, pollution, congestion, and poverty—the overriding urban problem . . . may well be the general inability of large city governments to make ends meet.[34]

The postindustrial cities borrowed heavily to appease their fleeing industries and affluent upper and middle classes, their unionized bureaucrats and the turbulent poor as the vicious cycle reached crisis proportions in the 1960s. Debts soared in the early 1970s, despite the fact that the combined contributions of the state and federal governments had more than doubled since 1950 and amounted to roughly 50 percent of these municipal revenues.[35] And, even though these deficits leveled off to some extent, the perception that the financial situation improved is deceptive. Some ways that cities conceal their true financial condition are presented in the following list.

Common Methods of Masking Fiscal Distress

Maintenance deferral	postponing needed maintenance of bridges, sewer lines, and waterworks, thus shifting costs to future taxpaying constituencies
Surrendering functions	shifting service-delivery responsibilities to counties and any other governmental unit that will take them
Off-budget financing	delivering services by means of public corporations, with their own independent borrowing and revenue-generating capacities

Cities have been able to hide their fiscal problems in at least three major ways. First, crucial long-term maintenance expenditures continue to be postponed. George Peterson has called this practice a "time bomb,"[36] and the Congressional Joint Economic Committee referred to it as "the single greatest problem facing our nation's cities."[37] The resulting deterioration of the cities' physical infrastructures can be seen in many ways: large amounts of pure water are lost because of leaking pipes or severe water-main breaks; inadequate sewers overflow causing sewage to be dumped into freshwater sources; ground water leaks into sanitation sewers and overloads treatment plants; storm sewers prove to be inadequate.[38]

The consequences of this expenditure-deferral process can be demonstrated with New York City's Williamsburg Bridge, one of the city's more than 1,400 structurally deficient bridges. If the city had spent about $2 million per year (in 1990 dollars) to maintain it, estimates are that it could have lasted another 100 years. Because routine maintenance was not done, the bridge must be rebuilt at a cost of $400 million, more than $200 million more than regular maintenance would have cost.[39] Such deferrals in essence amount to borrowing from future tax revenues and doing so in a very costly manner.

A second method of hiding fiscal problems has been to surrender a number of city functions. Surrounding counties have been absorbing many of the duties previously performed by the cities themselves. Thus, when it appears that some cities are faring better than others, their counties may be providing services that other cities have to provide largely for themselves. As a result, some of these counties have begun to stagger under the burden; one of these, Wayne County (Detroit), actually defaulted on its payroll in October of 1979.[40] Balanced city budgets and marginally shrinking city deficits should therefore not necessarily be viewed as indicators of success in these cities' battles against their fiscal crisis cycles.

Finally, there is off-budget financing. In this case, when voters refuse to approve the issuance of new revenue-raising city bonds, public corporations are created. These corporations are then able to sell revenue bonds without any form of voter approval, and neither the spending nor the borrowing of these agencies appears anywhere in the budgets of the governments that created them. Between 1972 and 1982, over $250 billion was borrowed by this method, $200 billion more than in the preceding decade.[41]

In the end, then, many postindustrial cities are fiscally unstable, no matter how well hidden from public view their true condition may be. This instability can quickly turn into a fiscal crisis, particularly if the city finds itself in an extended period of inflation and/or recession.[42] Such vulnerability has begun to shake investor confidence in government revenue-raising bonds. As the cities have struggled, these investors have opted for safer tax-sheltered investments such as revenue bonds of private industries, equipment leasing, and investments in countries where taxation is considerably lower.

Once investors begin to get nervous, for whatever reason, cities soon lose their ability to borrow easily on the open market. Among the first signs of borrowing difficulty is a marked decline in a city's bond rating (even though the rating process at best is inexact and subjective).[43] This development, however, generally means that one of two things is likely to follow: either the city will simply have to pay higher and higher interest rates if it hopes to continue necessary borrowing for long-term capital investments and short-term borrowing in anticipation of revenues; or the city may be closed out of the borrowing market entirely, leading it soon to the verge of default and possible bankruptcy.[44]

Policy Alternatives

Faced with expenditures that were outstripping their revenues, city politicians soon recognized that they needed to do one or more of the following: (1) increase locally generated revenues; (2) cut expenditures; or (3) attain more assistance from county, state, and federal governments.

Policy Alternatives for Reducing City Deficits

Increase local revenues	accumulation schemes, legalized gambling, commuter taxes, program-linked tax increases, employee pension funds
Cut expenditures	defer maintenance, surrender functions, use off-budget financing, privatize functions, increase reliance on private supplements
Increase external assistance	categorical grants, block grants, revenue sharing, urban impact statements, national accumulation schemes

Local Revenues.   Most recently, many cities have determined that the only way to break this cycle is to lure businesses back into the urban area as a way to generate revenue. For them, the accumulation function has been stressed—tax incentives and extra services for corporations. When they are successful, jobs are created, the need for public services declines, and there is a larger tax base with which to fund those services still required.[45]

A more immediate revenue-raising scheme has been to run, or allow and tax, various forms of legalized gambling. A majority of states have opted for lotteries, which generate millions of dollars per state by allowing a net gain of approximately 40 cents on every $1 ticket sold. Meanwhile, cities gradually have received local-option authority to raise funds from the proceeds of race tracks and now even casinos. As painless as this route appears to be, a number of studies suggest that it amounts to a form of regressive taxation, since the revenue comes disproportionately from those less able to afford it.[46]

Another revenue-raising scheme has been to impose taxes on nonconstituents. One of the most common forms is the commuter tax. By this device, cities tax the wages of suburbanites who live outside the city limits but commute into the city for their jobs. Cleveland, for instance, collects almost half its city tax revenues from such commuters.[47]

When taxes on constituents have to be raised, these increasingly are tied to specific popular purposes so as to reduce taxpayer resistance. One dollar per year is tacked onto automobile insurance premiums with the proceeds used for a special team of police and prosecutors to combat car theft. Marriage license fees are hiked to raise money to combat child abuse. Alcohol taxes are raised to increase drug and alcohol rehabilitation programs. A number of new taxes are tied to increases in educational spending. The list grows longer each year.[48]

Another method that is being used with increasing frequency is to tap employee pension funds. This can be done in a number of different ways. A proportion of their net interest can be extracted. Cities such as New York and Philadelphia effectively coerced their employee unions into lending them money at below-market rates under threat of large-scale layoffs. Most commonly, the city delays pension contributions by changing the accounting methods and assumptions they use to calculate their long-term obligations to the fund. For example, they increase the estimated return from the fund's investment portfolio and reduce the city's contribution accordingly.[49]

Local Expenditures.   Maintenance expenditures also have been reduced, often without a very visible reduction in service levels. First, upkeep costs are deferred. Second, more service responsibilities are shifted to public authorities and other governmental levels; services begin to be privatized—residents are required to arrange their own garbage collection when city sanitation departments are dissolved. Also, citizens who can afford it purchase private services such as schooling and home security protection.

The continued appropriation of scarce resources to the legitimation function is considered by many to be a misallocation of funds. Cutting services for the poor at such a time, however, seems likely only to increase the viciousness of the cycle by exacerbating such problems as poverty, crime, and racial tensions.

The one hope would seem to be increased help from external governmental sources. But decline in their populations has decreased central-city voting clout at the county, state, and national levels.

External Assistance.   In the 1960s, President Lyndon Johnson and Congress added a host of relief, education, job training, and urban redevelopment programs to the already sizable number of welfare state programs surviving from the 1930s. Soon, however, much of this assistance was reduced considerably, as the turbulence subsided and the electoral clout of many postindustrial cities continued to shrink.[50]

Following this intermittent and often clumsy effort to achieve the Great Society, these programs were altered and the emphasis was significantly shifted under two successive Republican administrations. Instead of categorical grants targeted narrowly toward the poorest areas of the nation, the Nixon and Ford administrations pushed block grants and revenue sharing through the Congress, allowing a far greater number of areas to compete for federal assistance.[51] As Piven and Cloward concluded, "Once the turmoil of the 1960s ebbed, the federal and state governments could and did reduce grants-in-aid to the older central cities, thereby widening the disparities in the city budgets even more."[52]

As the American economy struggled with rapidly increasing oil prices in the 1970s, some two-thirds of the states proceeded to enact taxation ceilings, the most prominent being California's Proposition 13 and Massachusetts's Proposition 2 1/2. A *stagflation*-plagued public (one facing economic stagnation and inflation at the same time) was not ready to launch another "war on poverty." In January 1978, only 41 percent of the self-styled liberals and 21 percent of the self-identifying conservatives favored any increase in government spending on domestic programs.[53]

The Carter Administration.   By November of 1978, besides retargeting more existing urban aid to distressed older cities as well as adding a few urban action grants and an administrative urban impact procedure (for weighing the impact of nonurban federal expenditures before adoption), the most that President Jimmy Carter could promise the nation's mayors was that he would not make "wholesale, arbitrary spending cuts" in assistance the cities were already receiving.[54] Shortly thereafter, a reelection-oriented Carter unveiled his balanced budget, which had been balanced at the expense of most program areas except the Defense Department. In 1980, the cities were to face cuts such as $100 million in antirecession grants to localities and $100 million in economic development programs, in addition to cuts in the areas of health, education, recreation, and public service jobs. Carter's 1981 budget promised more of the same: cuts of $1.1 billion in antirecession aid to localities, $1.7 billion in revenue sharing with the states, and further reductions in health, education, employment, and job training programs.

The Reagan-Bush Era.   Enter President Ronald Reagan. If the cities thought they had been financially underassisted during the Nixon, Ford, and Carter years, they were now to face even more federal austerity measures. Under the banner of supply side economics, both federal taxing and spending were reduced to free more venture capital for private entrepreneurs to invest. The intended result was to be enough economic growth to improve the lives of most Americans. In addition, the administration argued that federal aid to cities actually had been doing more harm than good. The cities, they claimed, would be much better off if they raised their own revenues and spent them where they saw fit.[55]

The view from outside Washington was not the same. Because many state and local governments tax only that income that the federal government also taxes, they stood to lose billions of dollars in revenues as a result of federal tax cuts. In the first year, for example, the state of Ohio lost as much as $100 million in corporate income tax revenues alone while the city of New York lost roughly $90 million. Cities were then forced to pay considerably higher interest rates to borrow money, both because the tax-free character of municipal bonds proved less enticing to those in the newly lowered tax brackets and because of such mechanisms as "All Savers' Certificates," designed to shore up the less competitive components of the banking industry by allowing them to issue tax-exempt savings certificates.[56]

The problems did not end there, however. In the alleged attempt to fight inflation by balancing the federal budget, the Reagan administration sought to offset its tax cuts with a host of cuts in expenditures. These, too, had a considerable impact on the cities and particularly their poorer residents.

In the first round of retrenchment alone, the Reagan administration succeeded in steering through Congress some $35 billion in spending cuts. A partial list of the welfare-related cuts follows on page 149.[57]

Shortly thereafter, the administration succeeded in steering through Congress even further cuts in a number of nonmilitary categories. Among these were reductions for low-income housing construction, urban aid, and various welfare programs.[58]

The underlying rationale for many of these cuts was expressed best by Charles Hobbs, deputy assistant to the President for policy development.

> The current national welfare system, although aimed at assisting poor people who cannot meet their own needs, provides unneeded benefits to many people who are not poor, reduces incentives for work and self-reliance and discourages strong family and community ties.[59]

The burden of the cuts fell on all governments below the federal level. Richard Condor of the National Association of Counties pointed out that although the

Reagan's First Round of Social Program Cuts, 1981

Aid to Families with Dependent Children	cut approximately 10 percent of its budget allocation by eligibility changes that struck 408,000 families from the rolls and reduced benefits for 279,000 others
Food Stamps	cut 875,000 families and reduced benefits for most others
School Lunches	cut $1.4 billion by no longer requiring that the lunches satisfy one-third of a child's daily nutritional needs
Medicaid	cut $600 million
Medicare	increased the share of the bills to be paid by the elderly themselves
Public Housing	limited new construction and raised the rent from 25 percent to 30 percent of a poor person's income
Public Service Jobs	cut all 306,000 of the Comprehensive Employee Training Act's (CETA) public service positions
Unemployment Insurance	cut the maximum number of weeks from 39 to 26, reducing benefits for 640,000 immediately

municipalities, counties, and states received only 14 percent of federal allocations, they were asked to absorb some two-thirds of the first cuts.[60] Even though revenue-sharing funds had grown to one-quarter of city budgets and one-half of county budgets, these allocations immediately were cut by 12 percent and ultimately eliminated altogether.[61]

As for the people, the brunt was borne by the working poor,[62] especially the black poor. Vernon Jordan called the Reagan policies a "clear and present danger" to blacks, pointing out that they had been required to shoulder a disproportionate share of the costs.[63] As the administration relaxed their affirmative action and antidiscrimination enforcements, lower-income women and minorities really felt the pinch.

Officials of the Reagan and subsequent Bush administrations argued that much would trickle down over the long term as a result of the supply-side policies of the early Reagan presidency, but about all they could suggest for the short run was that given reductions in mandates and taxes, the business community, private charities, and state governments should be in a position to pick up a good deal of this "public assistance" slack.

The first two groups, however, were quick to point out that they could not begin to fill the void left by even the initial round of federal cutbacks. Although private corporations had been making larger public contributions, many seemed to feel that they had begun to approach their limit.[64] In addition, the Urban Institute found that the reductions in the top tax rates imperiled millions of dollars in charitable contributions, for the wealthy no longer needed to find tax shelters for that part of their income.[65] As for the state governments, despite fiscal constraints of their own, a good number did step in to assume many of the responsibilities cast off by the federal government, yet that might well have proved impossible had not organized interests forced the president and Congress to modify some of their initial austerity measures.[66] Nonetheless, a senior congressional aide summed it up rather bluntly by stating, "I don't believe there's any stomach for new initiatives for the poor anymore."[67]

Meanwhile, the job prospects of the ghetto poor were unlikely to improve when corporations like Du Pont and U.S. Steel used their new venture capital to buy up other corporations—Conoco and Marathon Oil, respectively—rather than to increase labor-intensive industrial production.

The end result was predictable: the rich got significantly richer, the poor got significantly poorer, and there was little change for those in between. Trickle down, in fact, had become trickle up.[68]

A classic upshot of this governmental posture occurred in the severely poor Watts area of Los Angeles. Residents found it necessary to vote themselves a $148 per homeowner property tax increase just so they could have 300 more police officers to patrol their own crime-plagued neighborhoods.[69]

COMMUNITY POWER

As a result of these shifts, how has political power come to be distributed? To answer that question, it is essential to define political power. First, there is an important distinction between *political power* and *political authority. Political authority* is the legal right to make a politically significant decision; *political power* is the ability to get people to perform a political act they were not planning to perform. The latter is accomplished by (1) invoking authority, (2) persuading them that the act is in their best interest, (3) striking a bargain with them in which favors are traded, or (4) coercing them by use of physical force, if necessary.

The following examples help to illustrate these distinctions. When a city first elects a black mayor, that mayor may well want to appoint a black police commissioner. The mayor has the authority to do so. Nonetheless, the need to maintain cooperation throughout the ranks of a largely white police force may prevent that appointment from occurring, at least for a while. The mayor has the authority but not the power at that particular time. As another example, the city government of Detroit may have the authority to increase significantly corporate property taxes on companies such as General Motors. In point of fact, however, there are a variety of political and economic reasons this is unlikely even to be considered; thus, they do not have the political power to accomplish it.

A variety of entities operate in or on U.S. cities, wielding varying degrees of political authority and power. Besides the general public, there are political parties, the state and federal governments, local governmental institutions such as mayors, councils and bureaucracies, and private institutions such as the mass media and other concentrations of private capital. Among these, the owners of large amounts of private capital assume special importance because their interests appear to have become preeminent.

Urban Dependency

The main job of municipal government is to create a climate in which private business can expand in the city to provide jobs and profit.[70]

These words of New York City's former mayor Ed Koch echo the circumstances confronted by elected officials in virtually all postindustrial cities. The requisites of corporate profitability have become the ultimate parameters circumscribing the political decisions of the city's governing officials no matter who they happen to be. When David Dinkins succeeded Koch and became the first black mayor of New York City, he quickly came face-to-face with the reality outlined by his predecessor. Investment banker Kenneth Lipper immediately indicated that major developers had decided not to build anything new in the city "until the political situation clarifies itself."[71]

Even though many not owning capital may gain material benefits from a healthy economy, this entire process precludes a serious challenge to the basic structure of ownership and power. In the postindustrial city, if local government responds to other interests by implementing too many fundamentally redistributive public policies, it may drive much of the city's private-sector capital to suburbs, small towns, newer cities, or foreign soil.

The urban populace will continue to retain that ultimate democratic sanction, the right to elect and lobby the municipal officials who, at least in theory, govern the city. No matter who is elected, however, public officials normally will be compelled to put corporate interests first or risk corporate flight and the subsequent loss of both jobs and tax revenues.

Even within these parameters, should the city's fiscal position continue to worsen, there will be greater urgency to attract capital investors, and more money will be needed from federal, state, and local governmental sources to fund accumulation, maintenance, and legitimation functions. This increased dependence brings a corresponding centrifugal shift in governmental decision-making power, which for the urban citizenry means a further dilution of their democratic rights.[72]

All decisions that cause urban fiscal crises are private decisions, and . . . the most influential private decisions, the decisive ones, are corporate.[73]

Local Capital Interests.   The power held by the owners of urban capital is manifest in at least three forms. First, in the everyday pursuit of their own economic interests, the decisions of local corporate elites can be crucial to the economic well-being of a city as well as to the municipal government's capacity to serve that city. Second, the threat of disinvestment can influence the policy priorities of the local government. Third, as demonstrated in the New York City and Cleveland case studies below, blunt economic coercion can be employed by financiers upon whom deeply indebted cities are forced to depend. Overall, however, the thread that holds these three mechanisms together is the "power of the purse"—the possession of most of the city's private-sector capital.

Corporate Decisions and Threat of Disinvestment. In a very real sense, the economic fate of a city hangs on the investment decisions of its largest private corporations. Consider the following examples:

> Between 1950 and 1980, the declining city of Akron lost 23,634 jobs in the rubber industry, with Goodyear cutting nearly 75 percent of its work force between 1950 and 1977. Then, on January 10, 1978, Goodyear abruptly closed its passenger tire manufacturing operation, while at the same time purchasing Chile's largest tire producer.[74]

> In Youngstown, the Lykes Corporation essentially "milked" the capital out of Youngstown Sheet and Tube, ultimately leading to the closing of its Mahoning Valley plant and the rapid layoff of over 4,000 workers.[75]

> U.S. Steel's mammoth South Works on the southeast side of Chicago employed more than 18,000 workers in the 1940s, some 6,000 by 1978, and less than 1,000 by 1984.[76]

Such actual or potential corporate moves have significant impact on urban governance. These economic realities set the parameters for the governmental decisions that realistically are available. Because the health of a city is indeed dependent on the profitability of its private corporations, the corporate elite seldom have to lift a political finger for their interests to be given priority.

When there is a clear threat of capital disinvestment in a city, the city often will dole out large subsidies and tax breaks in hopes of retaining those private investments. In one such move approximately 40 percent of "New Pittsburgh" was made tax exempt. Such direct and indirect expenditures are made (1) without any clear evidence that they affect corporate investment decisions; (2) in the face of evidence that few of the jobs that result will go to previously unemployed local residents; (3) despite the immediate negative impact such reprioritization has on existing maintenance and legitimation programs; and (4) without any legally binding guarantees that the benefiting companies will be there long enough for the city to recover its investment.[77] Why, then, do cities engage in such desperate fiscal measures? This casting of rather scarce seeds hopefully into the wind is done in large part because many other cities are doing at least that much; it is a direct result of the intercity competition created by the increasing mobility of capital. As Bryan Jones and Lynn Bachelor point out, cities must do everything they can to present corporate America with the image that their city cooperates with business and is pro-growth.[78]

Roger Friedland and his associates also have noted that decisions concerning important accumulation expenditures are more likely to be shielded from open public debate than are their legitimation and maintenance counterparts. For example, social consumption in the form of capital improvements is generally funded by bonded indebtedness and administered through low-visibility special districts. On the other hand, most legitimation and maintenance functions are funded through direct taxation and administered through highly visible political organs. Thus, the latter are usually subject to far more open political debate and conflict.[79]

New York City recently allocated large amounts of public monies in their attempts to retain key local corporations. Chase Manhattan Bank was granted a $235 million package to keep it from moving across the Hudson River to New Jersey. The package included a $108 million property tax cut over 22 years, $35 million in discounted electricity, $49 million in sales tax cuts, $26 million in city-funded improvements at a new Brooklyn site, and $17 million in tax credits for employees. Comparable deals were struck with Drexel, Burnham and Lambert ($85 million), NBC ($100 million), and Shearson, Lehman and Hutton ($74 million).[80]

Consider the 3,500 lower-income residents of Detroit's half-white, half-black Poletown neighborhood. In 1980, General Motors threatened to locate 6,000 jobs elsewhere if already ailing Detroit would not raze the Poletown community so that a new $600-million Cadillac plant could be built there. The city had little choice. A number of residents became concerned, however, and formed the "Poletown Area Revitalization Task Force." They appealed to the mayor, the city council, and the courts—but to no avail. With the help of hundreds of millions of dollars in public subsidies, 465 acres were to be razed, on which sat 1,176 homes, 100 small businesses, 16 churches, 2 schools, and a hospital so that Cadillacs could soon roll off these publicly subsidized assembly lines. In return, GM promised 3,000 jobs, "economics permitting." As Mayor Coleman Young put it, "Jobs are our economic base, the key to our survival and future prosperity."[81]

The most important lesson in the last example, in terms of the themes of this study, is that in the Poletown debate, the only realistic alternatives for the city of Detroit concerned the number of concessions to make to General Motors. The municipal government ultimately used eminent domain to condemn and destroy an entire community. No one, however, seriously considered using eminent domain to condemn GM property in Detroit and seize it "for the public good." Why did this not occur? To begin with, the latter type of government seizure simply falls outside the present realm of acceptability as established by the dominant political culture in the United States. But beyond that, the mobile capital community could literally have "frozen out" the economy of Detroit in retaliation. In addition, by withholding capital investments, the owners of capital outside the city were capable of damaging the economies of both the state of Michigan and the United States, if need be, until such "destabilizing" public policy was "righted." As capital becomes increasingly more mobile and the cities more financially crippled, this corporate power will increase accordingly.[82]

The city's government officials often become glorified shills for the interests of private capital. First, they must spend whatever it takes to make the city attractive to private investors, and then they must convince the taxpayers that such costs are ultimately in their interest, too. As Houston's former two-term mayor, Fred Hofheinz, said in a recent mayoral campaign, "I think Houston needs someone who really understands the importance of entrepreneurial activity, who really knows how to sell something."[83]

Finally, wealthy elites have acquired even greater power in a somewhat more subtle way. In recent years, governments at all levels have attempted to hold down the cost of providing social services in order to avoid tax increases. The hope was that private philanthropy would step into the void left by these cutbacks.

In a number of cases that simply has not occurred. Even when it has, one side effect has been that the private philanthropists, instead of elected officials, have begun to shape a considerable amount of social policy. In addition, President Bush's vaunted "thousand points of light" comes to amount to "a thousand points of increased dependence." Instead of social services as rights created by elected officials, the poor are left begging at the doors of wealthier private individuals.[84]

External Governments.   Besides being constrained by local corporate interests, fiscally beleaguered cities also found their functions being assumed by governments at the county, state, and federal levels. As Detroit's Budget Director Wallace Stecher testified before Congress, "The basic structure of the local revenue base in America does not allow cities, at least the older core cities, to cope with the changing socio-economic conditions in which we live. Very simply, the matter of slipping out of our hands."[85]

The "metropolitanization" of politics, for example, has come to mean anything from city annexation of its surrounding territory, to the consolidation or federating of adjacent governments, to interlocal functional coordination, to single-service agreements between local governments. For many postindustrial cities, however, territorial annexation had all but stopped by the end of the nineteenth century, and consolidation votes kept failing, in large part because those in the outlying areas had little desire to pay higher taxes in order to subsidize services for the inner-city poor.[86] Nonetheless, variations of functional coordination and service agreements have proliferated in recent years, producing a variety of interlocal contracts and agreements, a mosaic of federally designated regional councils and numerous "councils of government."[87] As cities run out of money, more and more county governments assume administrative responsibility for a good many city services such as sewers, hospitals, the water supply, mass transportation, and jails.[88] This situation led Cuyahoga County's Democratic chairman to lament,

> The people who have been left out of the system in those industrial areas that are dying . . . are the poor, the minorities. They're the ones who need the most political leverage to improve their lives, but they lose leverage every time they give up another asset. So the mother city's political clout is being dissipated. It's following the money and education to the suburbs.[89]

Yet, the story does not stop there, for the fiscally troubled cities have also been forced to relinquish ever more political power to the state and federal governments. Beginning primarily in the Great Depression, which saw a number of cities actually slip into default and some even into bankruptcy, the roles of the state, and especially of the federal government, have increased tremendously, particularly in the areas of housing, health care, education, and welfare. By the mid-1970s, a number of declining postindustrial cities found themselves receiving more than half their revenues from these sources;[90] and this dependence has continued to grow.[91] The money has generally come with strings attached, such as direct orders and/or "conditions of aid."

At the state level, for instance, Connecticut recently passed new laws allowing state officials to override local objections to the siting of landfills for incinerator ash and empowering state courts to overrule certain local decisions on zoning and low-income housing. In order to reduce traffic congestion, the state of New Jersey now allows state and county planners to restrict access to highways at the sites of new housing and commercial developments and to establish transportation districts than can assess development fees. Meanwhile, New York's Board of Regents authorized parents of homeless children to defy local school districts and attend whichever school they wish.[92]

The federal government, on the other hand, has recently increased its mandates, even though additional federal monies often have not been forthcoming to fund compliance. Within the "new federalism" era, since the early 1970s, cities have been required to begin monitoring pollution from thousands of storm sewers, test for dozens of new chemicals in their water supplies, and control many new drinking water contaminants. School districts have been required to locate and remove asbestos from school buildings.[93] In addition, the federal government unilaterally has altered the coverage of expensive programs such as Medicaid, even though states and localities must pay half the bill.[94]

When tested legally, the U.S. Supreme Court normally has sided with the external governments, particularly in the postindustrial era. Consider the court-interpreted authority of the federal government as an example. Beginning with their decision in *Gibbons v. Ogden*,[95] the Court recognized broad congressional rights to regulate interstate commerce, and thus struck down New York's law granting a steamboat monopoly to a private company operating between New York and New Jersey. From there, such authority came to be extended into all sorts of state and local domains. Two relaively recent U.S. Supreme Court extensions have significant implications for state and local authority and fiscal well-being. In its 1985 decision *Garcia v. San Antonio*,[96] the Supreme Court ruled that state and local employees were subject to federal wage and hour laws. Then in 1988, in *South Carolina v. Baker*,[97] it ruled that Congress could eliminate the exemption of state bonds from federal taxes.[98]

G. Ross Stephens looked at the period from 1957 to 1986 to determine which levels of government provided what services and which had more governmental employees. He concluded that "the trend toward centralization has been particularly strong in the past 30 years," estimating that local autonomy had diminished by some 21 percent over this period.[99]

As the political arena expands, then, the urban populace witnesses a further dilution of what little control they ever had over political decisions that have come to play a larger and larger part in their lives. Even though state and federal programs may improve the material quality of their existence, at least for a while, such programs mean more political and economic dependence.

CASE STUDIES   New York City and Cleveland

As the fiscal crises of postindustrial cities deepen, the potential power of their local corporate interests has become actualized, with the corporate elite once again playing an overt role in shaping the cities' political futures. As demonstrated in the following case studies, local corporate interests, apparently concerned about governmental

Case Studies (continued)

"instability" and the "misallocation" of scarce resources on "unnecessary" legitimation services, began a major effort to reverse these trends in order to protect their
own investments.[100] When necessary, they actually appear capable of converting
their "power by implicit intimidation"—the threat to disinvest in these cities—into
more formal and legitimized political control.

This newest set of "reforms" was accomplished in New York City and Cleveland
when bankers were able to manipulate fiscal circumstances to the point where these
cities' governments were rendered virtually helpless. City officials were then pressured
into accepting significant changes in their public policies as well as in their policy-
making processes. These changes included cuts in public services, increases in
accumulation incentives, a new more formalized political role for the city's corporate
elite, and the removal of even more political power from the hands of locally elected
officials and thus from their constituents. Yet, rather than a show of strength, such
moves seem to indicate a degree of corporate desperation, because their political
power then lies naked for all to see.

New York City

In its most basic components, New York City's tale of fiscal woe was a standard
one. Between 1950 and 1970, the number of available jobs remained relatively stable;
but some 80 percent of all new positions in the 1960s were to be found in the public
sector. Then, between 1970 and 1978, nearly 600,000 jobs in the private sector
disappeared, including half of the city's manufacturing positions (450,000 in
manufacturing between 1971 and 1976 alone).[101] By 1980, only 15 percent of all
payroll employment was in manufacturing, half of what it had been in 1950.[102]

Meanwhile, the city was also losing population—10.4 percent, or more than
800,000 people, between 1970 and 1980. Most of this was "white flight"; in those
same years, the city lost nearly a third of its white population while the number
of blacks actually increased by more than 7 percent.[103] But as the city was becoming
blacker, it was also becoming older, poorer, and more crime prone. From 1950 to
1970, the number of elderly residents increased by 50 percent; the number of families
making less than the median national income increased from one-third to one-half
of the city's more than seven million people; and all of this boosted the proportion of
families receiving welfare to some one in seven (two-thirds of whom were not native
to the state and at least 90 percent of whom were eligible, not to mention those
who were not receiving the aid for which they were eligible). Amid this poverty,
violent crime increased by almost 700 percent between 1960 and 1977. This meant
that on the average, nearly 1 out of every 60 New York City residents would annually
fall victim to a violent crime.[104]

Subsequently, in an attempt to meet the service requisites of its needier inhabitants, the city increased its expense budget at an annual rate of 12.2 percent between
1961 and 1977 and more in the years following the ghetto unrest (1966–1971) than
in all the other 10 years combined. This growth came mostly in the area of social
services. Although the percentage of the city budget devoted to police, fire, and
sanitation actually decreased slightly between 1965 and 1975, the share going to
health, education, and welfare services increased from one-half to two-thirds. Thus,
the city came to be spending at least one-half of its $12 billion expense budget on
social welfare-type programs, a quarter of it on welfare alone.[105]

In the end, of course, the city's budget would not balance. Again focusing on
the decade prior to the crisis that would develop in 1975, despite a 33 percent

increase in local taxation and a doubling of aid from outside governmental sources, expenditures were still growing three times faster than revenues. The result was cumulative (illegal) deficit in the short-term expense budget that increased from $0.5 to $4.5 billion, not to mention a long-term capital budget debt that increased from $5 to $7.8 billion. Combined, these sums amounted to one-quarter of the entire nation's municipal debt, and a debt of $1,288 for every child, woman, and man in the city.[106]

The Corporate Coup. The banks soon began quietly to flood the market with billions of dollars worth of New York City securities. They disposed of these quickly, often without even charging commissions; and they also took small losses whenever necessary. Soon a panic was set off, the municipal bond market was glutted, and the city's bond rating plummeted, making it virtually impossible for the city to borrow. New York had been rendered helpless.[107]

Closed out of the borrowing market and nearly defaulting as each new payroll came due, the city turned to the state for help. On June 10, 1975, the state responded by declaring a debt moratorium and creating the Metropolitan Assistance Corporation (MAC), which was to control borrowing for the city as long as municipal officials proceeded to mend their misguided ways. The concept, structure, and authority of MAC essentially were devised by investment banker Felix Rohatyn and several other commercial bankers, who met at the Greenwich, Connecticut, residence of Metropolitan Life Insurance Company's Richard Shinn. The corporation's governing board was to include nine members, all of whom were to be appointed by the governor. As it turned out, eight of the original nine had either banking or brokerage connections.[108]

Yet the problems did not stop there, for even MAC-backed bonds proved difficult to sell. Thus, in order to make such investments more secure, an Emergency Finance Control Board (EFCB) was added to remove the city's fiscal fate even further from the hands of its "irresponsible" elected officials. This time the setting was the home of New York Telephone Company's William Ellinghaus, and the idea had been developed by Rohatyn, Chase Manhattan's William Butcher, Morgan's Walter Page, Citibank's Edward Palmer, and the sole elected official in the room—Governor Hugh Carey. They decided that the control board would consist of the governor, the state controller, the mayor, the city controller, and three public members appointed by the governor. The public members turned out to be Rohatyn, Ellinghaus, and David Margolis, the $364,000-a-year president of Colt Industries.[109]

Ultimately the control board, in consultation with MAC, was to submit a financial plan for the city, after reviewing the operating and capital budgets, all borrowing, all large vendor contracts, and all union contracts. Thereafter, the board was to monitor closely the city's adherence to the plan. In essence the members of the board were delegated the final authority over the city's budget. Beyond all this discretion, the board also was given legal title to the city's bank accounts as well as authority to review "political" decisions and to make whatever "suggestions" it saw fit. Needless to say, the elected municipal officials had been stripped of much meaningful authority over the public policies of the city.

As for comparable help from the federal government, New York State bowed to federal pressure and passed the "Debt Moratorium Act for New York City," placing up to a three-year moratorium on the repayment of some $1.6 billion in short-term city debt. Thereafter, President Ford finally endorsed a loan package of $3.6 billion to extend over the next three years, with each loan to be paid back at the end of every fiscal year. If a loan was not paid back on time, payment was to be extracted from the federal aid designated for the city.

Case Studies (continued)

Reliance on the state and federal governments for financial assistance, with the mandates and restrictions that entailed, left New York City's elected officials with control of approximately 30 percent of its budget. In addition, control of the city's elected officials, and thus of local residents, was reduced even further by the modus operandi of the city's new governmental levels. The meetings of both MAC and the EFCB were closed to the public, although minutes were kept and "guests" were occasionally present; these guests included such members of the corporate elite as Walter F. Wriston, William Salomon, Citibank's William Spencer, Morgan's Ellmore Patterson, and Chase's David Rockefeller.[110]

Policy Implications. The policy priorities of "the Super Government" were not difficult to predict. As local investors still held sizable amounts of city securities (e.g., local banks themselves held $1.2 billion in regular municipal bonds and $1.1 billion in MAC bonds) prompt repayment was high on the board's agenda.[111] As a matter of fact, the Emergency Finance Control Board legislation itself actually stated that debt service was to be the first priority. Therefore, to facilitate repayment as well as future borrowing, city policy was revised. The city work force was cut by 20 percent (61,000 jobs); a wage freeze was declared; property taxes and bridge tolls were increased; and after only a half-hour of discussion and no public debate, the mass transit fare was raised 43 percent, and free tuition was ended at the City University of New York merely for what Rohatyn called "the shock effect."[112]

As Jack Newfield and Paul DuBrul have pointed out, MAC and the EFCB never even considered asking the banks to forgive owed interest or to accept a restructuring of the debt; breaking the 20-year leases that the Lindsay administration had given, without competitive bidding, to a few favored landlords; collecting unpaid real estate taxes from landlords like Irving Maidman and Sol Goldman; raising the taxes on Consolidated Edison—a utility monopoly that had nowhere to move and that had been bailed out by the state with a $500 million sale and lease-back deal in 1974; depoliticizing the tax commission so that reduced real-estate assessments for "hardship" were no longer awarded to the likes of Prudential Insurance, Consolidated Edison, Chemical Bank, Rockefeller Center, and New York Telephone; or asking for an audit of all the Medicaid mills.[113]

Quite to the contrary, corporate accumulation became the name of the game. Once interest rates had soared to record levels and political power was in "safe" hands, the big lenders returned to the municipal bond market and recorded sizable profits. Dividends from city bonds, backed by either the state or federal government, were exempted from city, state, and federal taxes, and thus were yielding an annual interest rate that amounted to nearly 18 percent.[114] By 1977, the city was paying some $2.4 billion a year in interest alone. In addition, multimillion dollar tax abatement and public construction schemes were facilitating even more such accumulation.[115]

In 1978, the EFCB was renamed the Finance Control Board and extended until the year 2008, or until the city budget had been balanced for three consecutive years and all federal loans repaid. The Control Board also continued to have the final say over all city expenditures, contracts, labor agreements, borrowing, repayment plans, and internal monitoring; it was to hold the city to the standard of credit worthiness established by MAC; and if necessary, it had the authority to seize city bank accounts, stop city checks, and give direct orders to comply.

Cleveland

The tale for Cleveland is essentially the same, with only differences in scale, personalities, and a few tactics to distinguish it.[116]

Cleveland also was locked in the throes of a fiscal crisis cycle. It lost 23 percent of its business firms and 30 percent of its jobs between 1958 and 1972;[117] and it had been losing blue-collar positions for years.[118] It lost over one-third of its population between 1960 and 1980, most of which was white. At the same time, its black population grew to nearly 40 percent.[119] Violent crime was 13 times higher in 1975 than it had been in 1950, leaving city police with a backlog of more than 5,000 arrest orders.[120] Both city and county gross debts exceeded $400 per resident, including the city's (illegal) cumulative expense budget deficit of more than $52 million.[121]

Nevertheless, the city managed to avert disaster, in particular by gradually surrendering service functions to countywide and regional governance. In this way, it lost control over its mass transit, port authority, sewers, jails, and health and welfare systems between 1969 and 1979.[122] However, the day of reckoning finally arrived on December 15, 1978. On that date, Cleveland became the first major city to go into default since the Great Depression. What transpired before and after December 15 provides further support for the central theses of this chapter.

Ralph Locher was mayor in the mid-1960s, and his complacency about ghetto conditions clearly helped to provoke the 1966 disturbances in the Hough neighborhood. The smoke from that eruption had barely settled when Cleveland became the first large American city to elect a black mayor.[123] Carl Stokes actively sought to improve the lives of the city's poor, implementing such programs as Model Cities and his own "Cleveland Now."[124] He hoped to pay for these ventures by both raising taxes and making them more progressive. Thus, he put a property tax cut and an income tax increase to referendum, only to have the voters accept the cut and reject the increase. This action resulted in a $17 million city deficit the very first year thereafter.[125]

Republican Ralph Perk succeeded Carl Stokes as mayor, claiming he would put the city's fiscal house in order. Instead, the city's short-term debt more than tripled under the new mayor. In the period from 1972 through 1973 alone, the Perk administration "bonded the city to the limit" (according to state law, outstanding bonds could not exceed 5.5 percent of the city's property tax base without being cleared by popular referendum) and buried the city in long-term notes (which by law had to be converted into bonds within five years).[126] When an income-tax levy failed in 1974, the stage was set for real financial trouble in 1977–1978. In that fiscal year all these notes would have to be converted into bonds even though the city itself was already bonded to the limit. Resolving this crisis would require a considerable amount of cooperation on the part of both the general public (for additional tax revenues) and the financial community (for even more lending and refinancing).

Enter maverick populist Dennis Kucinich, running against the "corporate parasites," characterizing bankers as "blood-sucking vampires," calling the executives of the mammoth Cleveland Trust Bank "the worst of the robber barons," and declaring that "the banks must be brought under public control."[127] His other major issue was opposition to the proposed sale of "Muny Light." The publicly owned Municipal Light Company was dwarfed by the privately owned Cleveland Electric Illuminating Company (CEI), which served a full 80 percent of the Cleveland market; and Muny Light had run up a $40 million deficit by 1979 attempting both to provide cheaper power and to prevent a monopoly.[128]

Case Studies (continued)

The battle lines had been drawn. Before long, the corporate community began closing ranks, and the banks would maneuver themselves into a command position.[129] The corporate squeeze play was on; before it was over, Kucinich would be ousted; the state's role would be increased, diluting the political input of the urban populace; public service expenditures would be slashed; and the corporate elites would formalize and legitimize their political influence.

The Corporate Coup. In November 1977, Kucinich had defeated both the incumbent Perk and the Democratic party's candidate, Ed Feighan. Within months, however, a variety of political opponents were accusing him of fiscal mismanagement, of having appointed inexperienced and brazen members to his staff, and of having introduced political considerations into police administration. A recall effort was launched; and in the course of it, they city's banks for the first time refused to lend the city the money needed to refinance a debt. The city wished to sell $35 million worth of notes; but the banks, with $14 billion in assets, $2 billion invested in municipal bonds outside Cleveland, and $122 million in profit that very year, refused to lend.[130] Kucinich, narrowly surviving the recall, finally was successful in attaining the needed money. The banks, however, had tipped their hand, and the same strategy would be employed by them more firmly the following December when they steadfastly refused to refinance $15.5 million in debts.

Meanwhile, the media, the state of Ohio, and the federal government remained at arm's length as the city staggered toward default. Two reporters wrote stories quoting bank officials who said they would force Cleveland into default if necessary in order to defeat Kucinich. One of the reporters was subsequently fired, and the other was hounded into resigning.[131] A bill was introduced in the state legislature designed to help the city restructure its debt, but the bill was held up in committee. The federal government, moreover, refused to intervene, calling this a case of "unique and bizarre politics," bad management, and a situation in which there remained considerable latitude for bargaining and compromise.[132] Dennis Kucinich would have to face the bankers on his own.

In December, the banks made their more. The city owed $15.5 million to five different banks, and repayment of those specific loans was due on December 15. The city owed the largest amount to the Cleveland Trust Bank, $5 million, and at one point the bank apparently was willing to strike a deal. It would refinance the debt, help convince the other banks to do likewise, and even extend $50 million in new financing if the mayor would sign a resolution promising to sell Muny Light. Kucinich countered by offering 100 percent collateral (from property and income taxes) if the banks simply would refinance the $15.5 million about to come due. He even indicated that a private investor had offered to underwrite the city's debt and that his administration publicly had agreed to support an income tax hike. Nonetheless, Cleveland Trust refused, despite the mayor's warning that default would prompt the layoff of 15 percent of the city's work force (including 250 members of the police force, 150 members of the fire department, and 100 sanitation workers) and would preclude borrowing for such needed capital items as snow-removal equipment.[133]

Cleveland Trust was one of CEI's three biggest stockholders, holding some 782,798 shares (purchasing 91,000 more shares 10 days after the city defaulted), and three of Cleveland Trust's directors also sat on the board of CEI. In addition, Cleveland Trust held most of CEI's $140 million pension fund. But even though the

Federal Reserve Board saw no impropriety in this relationship and behavior, Kucinich did, and he refused to sell Muny Light.[134]

A desperate Mayor Kucinich made one last plea to the federal government, the state government, and the city council, but in vain. The federal government refused to advance the revenue-sharing money that was due on December 31. The state government disallowed any loans from the municipal union pension funds, and they also refused revenue advances. The city council would not even put an income-tax hike to referendum unless the mayor agreed to sell Muny Light. Thus, on December 15, 1978, the city of Cleveland went into default.

At that point, however, there was a twist. Rather than forcing the city into bankruptcy by demanding payment, thereby surrendering precious decision-making power to the courts, the banks simply did not move to collect. Through this maneuver, the city effectively was subordinated, and the banks were left in a much stronger position to "suggest" public policy priorities and to "encourage" city voters to elect more "responsible" candidates.

With the city in default and under virtual bank receivership, and with referenda pending on the sale of Muny Light and a hike in the income tax, local businesses suddenly agreed to prepay some of their taxes; the state acceded here, and the federal government delayed their demand for the $400,000 the city owed them for Comprehensive Employment and Training Act (CETA) abuses.

Nevertheless, Kucinich persisted. He proceeded to win his third and fourth electoral victories in scarcely more than a year, when the income-tax levy passed and the sale of Muny Light was voted down. He also attempted to improve the city's fiscal position by cutting 20 percent of the city work force and successfully repaying $5 million of the loans on which the city had defaulted. Yet the banks still refused to refinance the rest of those loans. They now demanded that the money be set aside in a default account, and talk turned to a financial control board.

Kucinich seized on the control board issue, and he opened fire once again. He asserted that "a state controlling board would put the people of Cleveland at the mercy of the very special interests who helped to force the politically motivated default."[135] But by November, still unable to elicit the support of either the state or the federal government, a beleaguered Dennis Kucinich was soundly defeated by Republican Lieutenant Governor George Voinovich.

Within two weeks of Kucinich's defeat, the state legislature passed an assistance package; and as the *New York Times* reported, "[State] Republicans acknowledged that they were waiting until a new city administration was in place, and the effect was to keep the cloud of default over Mr. Kucinich's head until Election Day."[136] This state legislation authorized the state auditor to declare a local fiscal emergency if a locality defaulted on a payment, or if the state legislature, mayor, or city council requested it. At that point, the city would have to produce a financial plan, including the members it was recommending to sit on the Financial Planning and Supervision Commission (FPSC)—the equivalent of New York City's Emergency Finance Control Board. If the plan was approved and certified by a special state commission, the city would receive access to a new debt instrument, Local Government Fund Notes. These would be sold by a state agent—comparable to New York's Metropolitan Assistance Corporation— and retired out of revenue owed to the city. The FPSC, which was to remain in place until all such notes were retired, was then to monitor the city's financial decisions and veto any actions that seemed contrary to the plan. The FPSC was to be composed of the mayor, city council president, two state administrators, and three public representatives, nominated by the mayor and appointed by the governor.

Case Studies (continued)

In December 1979, Mayor Voinovich applied for fiscal emergency status; when that was granted, he submitted his financial plan for approval. It named the following three persons as the public representatives: George Grabner (chairman and president of Lamson and Sessions Company), Robert Blyth (executive, National Citibank), and Jackie Presser (at that time, a vice-president of the Teamsters Union with reputed links to organized crime).[137] The plan was approved early in January 1980. State-assisted borrowing then began, and the FPSC itself first met on January 21, 1980.

At last, with the city now in "safe" hands and debt retirement a top priority, the banks proceeded to refinance the remaining $10.5 million in defaulted notes and lent the city another $27 million so it could refinance other debts. Furthermore, the banks did this even though a Voinovich administration audit had found the city's expense budget was some $111 million in the red, with a current-year deficit of some $30 million.[138]

CONCLUSION

Figure 6.1 summarizes the devolving, cyclical nature of urban fiscal woes. It attempts to capture key social and economic forces that seem to be driving post-industrial urban politics. And, to the degree that it accurately portrays those dynamics, it also reinforces the importance of understanding a broadly defined political environment if a political system is to be understood.

Technological changes have produced a postindustrial economy that has both facilitated and encouraged the flight of capital and well-to-do white people from many large cities. Left in their wake are increasing levels of unemployment, poverty, crime, and racial polarization. Service needs increase accordingly but at a time when these cities have not only smaller tax bases but also less electoral clout with which to acquire additional financial assistance at the state and federal levels. In a nearly futile attempt to reestablish a healthy degree of private investment in their cities, municipal governments let service levels decline and focus instead on spurring capital accumulation.

The loss of services and the subsequent deterioration of the overall quality of urban life combine to drive even more people to the suburbs and beyond. Eventually the situation becomes intolerable for many low-income individuals who are unable to escape their plight. Civil unrest occurs, and it is met with both repression and a further round of social expenditures. The turbulence, however, drives even more well-to-do people out of the city, while the shift in budgetary priorities makes the cities even less attractive places for capital investment.

The postindustrial era, at least within the context of the existing "free enterprise" economic system, appears destined to be marked by periodic and increasingly vicious spells of urban ghetto unrest. As governments strain to placate the socially and economically dislocated ghetto poor with more social services, they must at the same time appease an ever more mobile elite class by providing them with more tax breaks and services, or on occasion even the reins of formal

FIGURE 6.1 Vicious Cycle of the Urban Fiscal Crisis

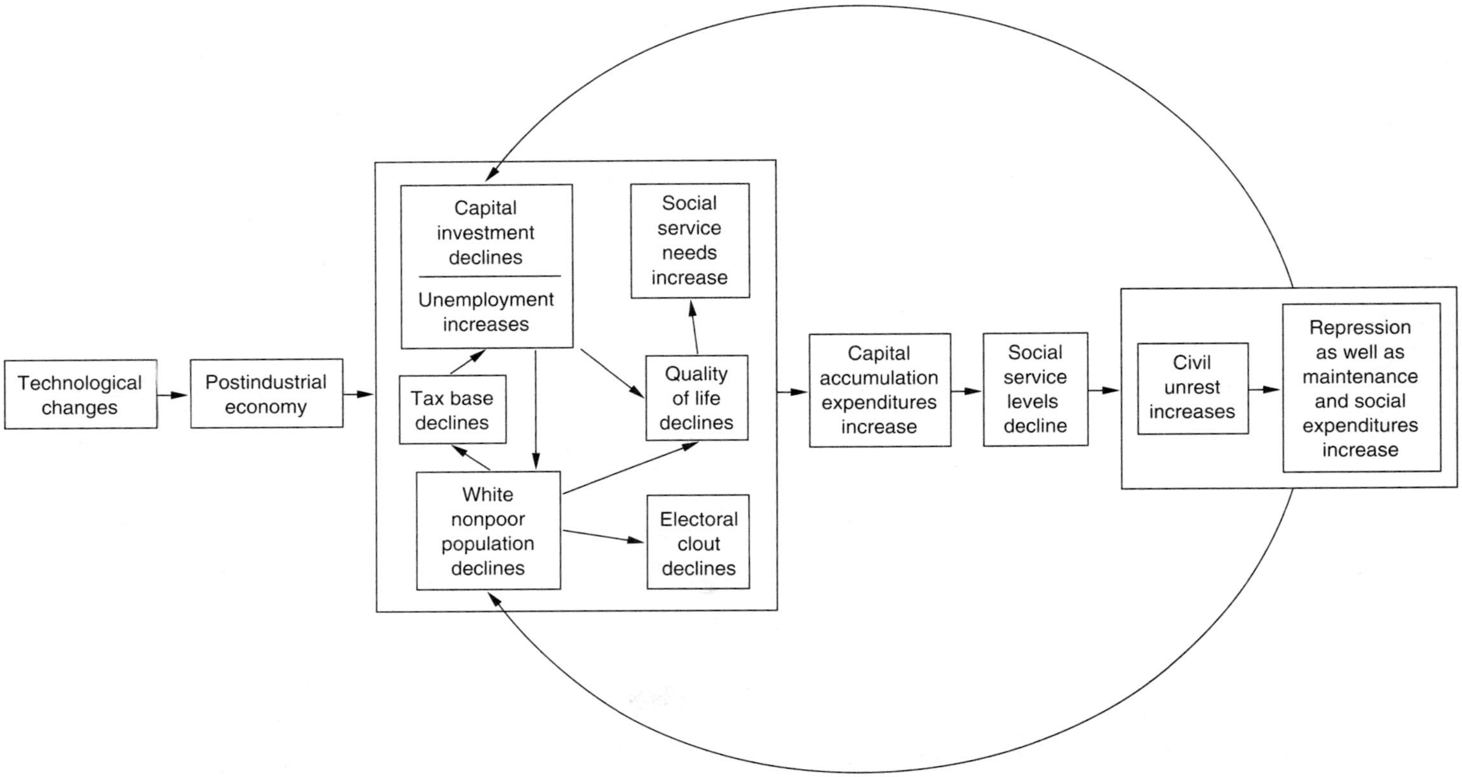

governmental authority themselves. We will now turn to the individual institutions of city government and look at their histories as well as at particular ways cities have been responding to these postindustrial dilemmas.

NOTES

1. Kenneth T. Jackson, "Metropolitan Government versus Suburban Autonomy," in Kenneth T. Jackson and Stanley K. Schultz, eds., *Cities in American History* (New York: Knopf, 1972), p. 453; John Bollens and Henry Schmandt, *The Metropolis* (New York: Harper & Row, 1982), pp. 303–311.

    Certain Sun Belt states have had exceptionally lenient annexation laws that have allowed a minority of large U.S. cities to annex sizable areas during this period; examples are Oklahoma City, Los Angeles, San Diego, Houston, Dallas, Fort Worth, San Antonio, Kansas City, Atlanta, Memphis, and Phoenix. At the other extreme, however, cities like Milwaukee, Minneapolis, and St. Louis became completely hemmed in by already incorporated areas and thus were unable to annex at all.

2. Langston Hughes, *The Panther and the Lash* (New York: Knopf, 1951).

3. Howard Chudacoff, *The Evolution of American Urban Society* (Englewood Cliffs, N.J.: Prentice-Hall, 1975), p. 210; Frances Fox Piven and Richard Cloward, *Regulating the Poor* (New York: Vintage, 1971).

4. Chudacoff, *The Evolution of American Urban Society,* pp. 211–212; David Goldfield and Blaine Brownell, *Urban America: From Downtown to No Town* (Boston: Houghton Mifflin, 1979), p. 367.

5. Piven and Cloward, *Regulating the Poor,* pp. 61–71; Frances Fox Piven and Richard Cloward, *Poor People's Movements* (New York: Vintage, 1979), pp. 49–60.

6. Piven and Cloward, *Regulating the Poor,* p. 67.

7. Hamilton Fish, quoted in Piven and Cloward, *Regulating the Poor,* p. 68.

8. Piven and Cloward, *Regulating the Poor,* pp. 71–77.

9. For probably the best compilation of these data, see *Report of the National Advisory Commission on Civil Disorders,* reprint (New York: Bantam, 1968), especially chaps. 6–9.

10. Ibid.

11. Zane Miller, *The Urbanization of Modern America* (New York: Harcourt Brace Jovanovich, 1973), p. 203.

12. Dennis Judd, *The Politics of American Cities* (Boston: Little, Brown, 1988), p. 307.

13. Piven and Cloward, *Regulating the Poor,* chaps. 8 and 9. For a cross-sectional affirmation of this phenomenon, see Michael Betz, "Riots and Welfare: Are They Related?," *Social Problems* 21, (1974): 345–355. For a general synthesis of available data, see Joe Feagin and Harlan Hahn, *Ghetto Revolts* (New York: Macmillan, 1973), pp. 239–259.

14. Piven and Cloward, *Regulating the Poor;* Charles Schultze, Edward Fried, Alice Rivlin, et al., "Setting National Priorities: The 1973 Budget," as adapted in Roger Alcaly and David Mermelstein, eds., *The Fiscal Crisis of the American Cities* (New York: Vintage, 1977).

15. Frances Fox Piven and Richard Cloward, "The Urban Crisis: Who Got What, When, and Why," in Frances Fox Piven and Richard Cloward, *The Politics of Turmoil* (New York: Pantheon, 1974); Judd, *The Politics of American Cities,* chap. 5; Martin Shefter, "Organizing for Armageddon," unpublished paper presented at the annual meeting of the American Political Science Association, Washington, D.C., August 1980.

16. John Donovan, *The Politics of Poverty* (New York: Pegasus, 1967).
17. Roy Bahl, *Financing State and Local Government in the 1980s* (New York: Oxford University Press, 1984), chap. 3.
18. David Perry and Alfred Watkins, "People, Profit, and the Rise of the Sunbelt Cities," in Joe Feagin, ed., *The Urban Scene* (New York: Random House, 1979), p. 143.
19. Feagin and Hahn, *Ghetto Revolts,* pp. 227–239.
20. Piven and Cloward, *Regulating the Poor,* p. 338. For a more recent study of this subject, see Roger Friedland, Frances Fox Piven, and Robert Alford, "Political Conflict, Urban Structure, and the Fiscal Crisis," in William Tabb and Larry Sawers, eds., *Marxism and the Metropolis* (New York: Oxford University Press, 1984), pp. 273–297. For the application of some private-sector "placebos," see Feagin and Hahn, *Ghetto Revolts,* pp. 245–246.
21. See Piven and Cloward, *Regulating the Poor,* pp. 261–276; John Mollenkopf, *The Contested City* (Princeton, N.J.: Princeton University Press, 1983); Clarence Stone, Robert Whelan, and William Murin, *Urban Policy and Politics in a Bureaucratic Age* (Englewood Cliffs, N.J.: Prentice-Hall, 1986); Harry Boyte, *The Backyard Revolution* (Philadelphia: Temple University Press, 1980); Clarence Stone, "Citizens and the New Ruling Coalition," in Herrington Bryce, ed., *Urban Governance and Minorities* (New York: Praeger, 1976); Douglas Yates, *Neighborhood Democracy* (Lexington, Mass.: Lexington, 1973); Alan Altschuler, *Community Control* (New York: Western, 1970); Milton Kotler, *Neighborhood Government* (Indianapolis: Bobbs-Merrill, 1969); Piven and Cloward, *Poor People's Movements*; Norman and Susan Fainstein, *Urban Political Movements* (Englewood Cliffs, N.J.: Prentice-Hall, 1974); and Shefter, "Organizing for Armageddon."
22. For example, see Norman and Susan Fainstein, "Introduction to Urban Bureaucracies," *American Behavioral Scientist* 15 (March/April 1972); Piven, "The Urban Crisis."
23. For example, see *New York Times,* June 30, 1987; *National Journal,* July 15, 1989; John Kasarda, "Caught in the Web," *Society* (1983).
24. James O'Connor, *The Fiscal Crisis of the State* (New York: St. Martin's Press, 1973). For an urban application of this concept, see Freidland et al., "Political Conflict," especially pp. 290–293.
25. Bollens and Schmandt, *The Metropolis,* pp. 223–224.
26. George Peterson, "Finance," in William Gorham and Nathan Glazer, eds., *The Urban Predicament* (Washington, D.C.: Urban Institute, 1976), pp. 47–51.
27. *New York Times,* December 18, 1991; *National Journal,* December 21, 1991.
28. Demetrios Caraley, *City Governments and Urban Problems* (Englewood Cliffs, N.J.: Prentice-Hall, 1977), p. 407. Also Marian and Howard Palley, *Urban America and Public Policies* (Lexington, Mass.: D C Heath, 1977), p. 51.
29. Frances Fox Piven, "The Urban Crisis: Who Got What, and Why," in Stephen David and Paul Peterson, eds., *Urban Politics and Public Policy* (New York: Praeger, 1977), pp. 318–338.
30. Peterson, "Finance." Also see Judd, *The Politics of American Cities,* chap 7.
31. William Tabb, "The New York City Fiscal Crisis," in William Tabb and Larry Sawers, eds., *Marxism and the Metropolis,* (New York: Oxford University Press, 1984), p. 333.
32. Floyd Fowler, Jr., *Citizen Attitudes toward Local Government Services and Taxes* (Cambridge, Mass.: Ballinger, 1974); *New York Times,* July 21, 1975.
33. Peterson, "Finance," p. 106. Also see James Pfiffer, "Inflexible Budgets, Fiscal Stress, and the Tax Revolt," in Alberta Sbragia, ed., *The Municipal Money Chase* (Boulder, Colo.: Westview, 1983), pp. 45–56; and *New York Times,* February 19, 1984. For

a summary of how urban services have increased disproportionately to revenues, see Bahl, *Financing State and Local Government in the 1980s,* chap. 5.

34. Schultze et al., "Setting National Priorities," p. 189.

35. U.S. Department of Commerce, Bureau of the Census, *Census of Governments* (Washington, D.C.: Government Printing Office, 1950–1990).

36. George Peterson, quoted in *New York Times,* March 18, 1979.

37. U.S. Congress, Joint Economic Committee, "Trends in the Fiscal Conditions of Cities, 1978–80" (Washington, D.C.: Government Printing Office, 1980).

38. *New York Times,* October 18, 1991.

39. *New York Times,* April 21, 1990; April 2, 1991; November 20, 1990; February 26, 1991.

40. For further examples of corresponding county indebtedness, see Marcus Pohlmann, *Political Power in the Postindustrial City* (New York: Associated Faculties Press, 1986), pp. 118–122.

41. James Bennett and Thomas DiLorenzo, *Underground Government: The Off-Budget Public Sector* (New York: Cato, 1983).

42. For concrete examples, see Bernard Ross and Murray Stedman, *Urban Politics* (Itasca, Ill.: Peacock, 1985), pp. 285–289.

43. Twentieth Century Fund Task Force on Municipal Bond Credit Ratings, *The Rating Game* (New York: Twentieth Century Fund, 1974); *New York Times,* December 20, 1990.

44. *New York Times,* June 30, 1987.

45. Lynn Bachelor, "Urban Economic Development," *Urban Affairs Quarterly* 16 (December 1981): 239–246.

46. See *New York Times,* February 16, 1988; August 25, 1988; May 31, 1989; *National Journal,* May 13, 1989, p. 1201; Charles Clotfelter and Philip Cook, *Selling Hope* (Cambridge, Mass.: Harvard University Press, 1989); Advisory Commission of Intergovernmental Relations, *Significant Features of Fiscal Federalism, 1985–86* (Washington, D.C.: Government Printing Office, 1988), vol. 2, pp. 88–90.

47. See *The World and I* 6 (June 1991): 34.

48. *New York Times,* November 27, 1990.

49. *New York Times,* July 21, 1991.

50. Donovan, *The Politics of Poverty.*

51. Jack Newfield and Paul DuBrul, *The Permanent Government* (New York: Pilgrim, 1981), chap. 3; Jeffrey Pressman, "Political Implications of the New Federalism," in Warren Oates, ed., *Financing the New Federalism* (Baltimore: Johns Hopkins University, 1975); see also Edward Fried, Alice Rivlin, Charles Schultze et al., *Setting National Priorities: The 1974 Budget* (Washington, D.C.: Government Printing Office, 1975), especially p. 19.

52. Piven and Cloward, *Poor People's Movements,* p. 356.

53. A *New York Times*/CBS poll, as cited in *New York Times,* January 22, 1978.

54. As reported in *New York Times,* November 28, 1978.

55. See the HUD report cited in *New York Times,* July 10, 1982.

56. See Robert Burchell, James Carr, Richard Florida et al., *The New Reality of Municipal Finance* (New Brunswick, N.J.: Center for Urban Policy Research, 1984). Also see *New York Times,* August 21, 1981; March 10, 1982.

57. *New York Times,* September 21, 1981. For details of the impact on specific programs, see *New York Times,* September 25, 1981 (school lunches); November 11, 1981 (housing); November 17, 1981 (health care).

58. See *New York Times,* October 8, 1981; December 2, 1981; December 30, 1981. Also Congressional Quarterly, *Current American Government* (Spring 1982): 31–32.

59. Quoted in *New York Times,* March 2, 1986.
60. *New York Times,* October 2, 1981.
61. See *Boston Globe,* December 6, 1981, p. 1; *New York Times,* March 12, 1981; March 6, 1982; *Washington Post,* March 24, 1991, p. A1.
62. *New York Times,* March 20, 1981; June 2, 1981; February 28, 1982; March 31, 1984; April 4, 1984; June 10, 1984; September 25, 1984.
63. *New York Times,* July 20, 1981; June 2, 1981; February 28, 1982; March 6, 1982; March 18, 1982.
64. *New York Times,* October 31, 1981; January 2, 1982.
65. *New York Times,* July 6, 1981; August 12, 1981; August 28, 1981; November 14, 1981; December 9, 1981; January 2, 1982; May 7, 1982; January 23, 1991.
66. *New York Times,* September 29, 1981; October 1, 1981; November 13, 1981; November 15, 1981; January 12, 1982; May 26, 1982; February 5, 1982; June 10, 1984.
67. *New York Times,* June 11, 1979.
68. *New York Times,* April 4, 1984; March 5, 1992; May 1, 1992; May 5, 1992; June 17, 1992. Denny Braun, *The Rich Get Richer* (Chicago: Nelson-Hall, 1990); Kevin Phillips, *The Politics of Rich and Poor* (New York: Random House, 1990); The Urban Institute, Policy and Research Report (Winter/Spring 1991): 1–3; Marcus Pohlmann, "Profits, Welfare, and Class Position: 1965-1984," *Journal of Sociology and Social Welfare* 15 (September 1988): 3–28; Clarence Stone, "Atlanta: Protest and Elections Are Not Enough," *PS* 19 (Spring 1986): 623.
69. *New York Times,* June 2, 1987; June 26, 1987.
70. *New York Times,* March 4, 1978.
71. *New York Times Magazine,* December 31, 1989, p. 46.
72. For a more detailed discussion of this conceptual view of political power, see Charles Lindbloom, *Politics and Markets* (New York: Basic Books, 1977); Paul Peterson, *City Limits* (Chicago: University of Chicago Press, 1981); Pohlmann, *Political Power in the Postindustrial City*; Paul Kantor and Stephen David, *The Dependent City* (Glenview, Ill.: Scott, Foresmen, 1988); Todd Swanstrom, *The Crisis of Growth Politics* (Philadelphia: Temple University Press, 1985); Bryan Jones and Lynn Bachelor, *The Sustaining Hand* (Lawrence: University of Kansas Press, 1986); William Domhoff, *Who Really Rules?* (New Brunswick, N.J.: Transaction, 1978); Harvey Molotch, "The City as a Growth Machine," *Journal of Sociology* 82, no. 2 (1986); Clarence Stone, *Regime Politics* (Lawrence: University of Kansas Press, 1989).
73. William Capitman, *Panic in the Boardroom* (New York: Anchor Books/Doubleday, 1973), p. 226.
74. *Cleveland Plain Dealer,* October 12–15, 1980; *National Catholic Reporter,* June 2, 1978; *The Progressive,* August 1980; *Fortune,* July 17, 1978, p. 56.
75. Ibid.
76. For additional case studies, see John Portz, *The Politics of Plant Closings* (Lawrence: University of Kansas Press, 1990).
77. *New York Times,* March 8, 1990; October 31, 1990; *National Journal,* March 10, 1990, p. 590.
78. Jones and Bachelor, *The Sustaining Hand,* chap. 13. Also Jones and Bachelor, "Local Policy Discretion and the Corporate Surplus," in Richard Bingham and John Blair, eds., *Urban Economic Development* (Beverly Hills, Calif.: Sage, 1984); Charles Lindbloom, "The Market as a Prison," *Journal of Politics* 44 (May 1982): 324–336.
79. Friedland et al., "Political Conflict." Also see Roger Friedland, *Power and Crisis in the City* (London: Macmillan, 1982).

80. *New York Times,* November 13, 1988.

81. This quote and most of the information on the controversy were drawn from the *New York Times,* September 15, 1980; December 10, 1980. Also see Jeanie Wylie, *Poletown: Community Betrayed* (Champaign: University of Illinois Press, 1990). For more examples of such urban efforts, see *National Journal,* March 18, 1989, pp. 634–640.

82. For more discussion of this subject, see Kenneth Newton, "Feeble Governments and Private Power," in Louis Masotti and Robert Lineberry, eds., *The New Urban Politics* (Cambridge, Mass.: Ballinger, 1976); Peterson, *City Limits*; Barry Bluestone and Bennett Harrison, *Capital and Communities* (Washington, D.C.: Progressive Alliance, 1980); William Tabb, "Economic Democracy and Regional Restructuring: An Internationalization Perspective," in Larry Sawers and William Tabb, eds., *Sunbelt/Snowbelt* (New York: Oxford University Press, 1984), pp. 403–416; Jones and Bachelor, *The Sustaining Hand*; Kantor and David, *The Dependent City.*

83. *New York Times,* October 30, 1989. Also see Kantor and David, *The Dependent City,* chaps. 11–12; Bernard Frieden and Lynn Sagalyn, *Downtown, Inc.* (Cambridge, Mass.: MIT Press, 1990).

84. Judd, *The Politics of American Cities,* pp. 110–113; Mollenkopf, *The Contested City.*

85. Wallace Stecher, Detroit budget director, testifying before the U.S. Congress's Joint Economic Committee, February 1976, quoted in Peterson, "Finance," p. 35.

86. For an example of how annexation laws can be biased in favor of wealthy property owners, see Calvin Larson and Stan Nikkel, *Urban Problems: Perspectives on Corporations, Governments, and Cities* (Boston: Allyn & Bacon, 1979), p. 125.

87. David Walker, "The Rise of Regional, County, and State Governments," in Bryce, *Urban Governance and Minorities*; Advisory Commission on Intergovernmental Relations, *Regional Decision-Making* (Washington, D.C.: Government Printing Office, 1973); *New York Times,* February 20, 1984; August 10, 1989.

88. *New York Times,* November 9, 1979; June 10, 1987.

89. *New York Times,* November 9, 1979, p. 16.

90. Peterson, "Finance," pp. 58–62; President's Urban and Regional Policy Group Report, *A New Partnership to Preserve America's Communities* (Washington, D.C.: Government Printing Office, March 1979), pp. 61–62; Advisory Commission on Intergovernmental Relations, *State and Local Roles in the Federal System* (Washington, D.C.: Government Printing Office, 1982); and Thomas Anton, Jerry Cawley, and Kevin Kramer, *Moving Money* (Cambridge, Mass.: Oelgeschlager, Gunn, and Main, 1980).

91. *New York Times,* January 21, 1979. Also see Kantor and David, *The Dependent City,* chap. 10.

92. *New York Times,* August 10, 1989.

93. Catherine Lovell and Charles Tobin, "Mandating—A Key Issue for Cities," *Municipal Yearbook* (New York: International City Managers' Association, 1980), pp. 73–79; J. J. Courtier and S. E. Dunn, "Federal Colonization of State and Local Government," *State Government* 50 (Spring 1977): 65–71; William Lyons and David Morgan, "The Impact of Intergovernmental Revenue on City Expenditures," *Journal of Politics* 39 (November 1977): 1088–1097; Edward Gramlich, "Intergovernmental Grants: A Review of the Literature," in Warren Oates, ed., *The Political Economy of Fiscal Federalism* (Lexington, Mass.: Lexington, 1979); Catherine Lovell, "Federal and State Mandating on Local Governments," National Science Foundation, Contract No. NSF/RA-790138 (Washington, D.C., 1979); Catherine Lovell and Charles Tobin, "The Mandating Issue," *Public Administration Review* 41 (1981): 318–331; the Advisory

Commission on Intergovernmental Relations, *The Federal Influence on State and Local Roles in the Federal System* (Washington, D.C.: Government Printing Office, 1981); Deil Wright, *Understanding Intergovernmental Relations* (Pacific Grove, Calif.: Brooks-Cole, 1982); Advisory Commission on Intergovernmental Relations, *State and Local Roles in the Federal System*; James Fossett, *Federal Aid to Big Cities: The Politics of Dependence* (Washington, D.C.: Brookings Institution, 1983); *New York Times,* February 19–20, 1984.

94. *New York Times,* August 30, 1989; March 24, 1992. Also see Kantor and David, *The Dependent City,* chaps. 16–17.

95. *Gibbons v. Ogden,* 22 U.S. 1 (1824).

96. *Garcia v. San Antonio Metropolitan Transit Authority* 469 U.S. 528 (1985).

97. *South Carolina v. Baker* 485 U.S. 505 (1988).

98. For a strict constructionist perspective on the limits of federal authority, see the interview with Assistant Attorney General Charles J. Cooper in the *New York Times,* November 16, 1986.

99. G. Ross Stephens quoted and study findings reported in *New York Times,* August 10, 1989.

100. John Mollenkopf, "The Crisis of the Public Sector in America's Cities," in Roger Alcaly and David Mermelstein, eds., *The Fiscal Crisis of the American Cities* (New York: Vintage, 1977), pp. 122–127; Piven, "The Urban Crisis."

101. Bernard Gifford, "New York City and Cosmopolitan Liberalism," *Political Science Quarterly 93* (Winter, 1978–1979): 563–564.

102. Ibid.; *New York Times,* March 14, 1981; December 12, 1984.

103. U.S. Department of Commerce, Bureau of the Census, *Statistical Abstracts of the United States, 1981* (Washington, D.C.: Government Printing Office, 1981).

104. *New York Times,* November 16, 1975; Ira Katznelson and Mark Kesselman, *The Politics of Power* (New York: Harcourt Brace Jovanovich, 1975), chap. 12; Federal Bureau of Investigation, *Uniform Crime Reports,* (Washington, D.C.: Government Printing Office, 1960–1977).

105. Theodore Kheel, "A Strategy for Survival," *New York Magazine,* September 1, 1975; Katznelson and Kesselman, *The Politics of Power,* chap. 12.

106. Donald Haider, "The New York City Congressional Delegation," *City Almanac,* March 1973; Katznelson and Kesselman, *The Politics of Power,* chap. 12; U.S. Department of Commerce, *City and County Data Book* (Washington, D.C.: Government Printing Office, annual); U.S. Department of Commerce, *Statistical Abstracts of the United States.*

107. Jack Newfield and Paul DuBrul, *The Abuse of Power* (New York: Pilgrim Press, 1981), chap. 1.

108. Ibid., pp. 178–179. See pp. 179–182 for biographical sketches of these nine members.

109. Ibid., p. 179.

110. *New York Times,* November 17, 1980; Newfield and DuBrul, *The Abuse of Power,* p. 183.

111. Newfield and DuBrul, *The Abuse of Power,* p. 183.

112. Ibid., pp. 184–190; Shefter, "Organizing for Armageddon," pp. 9–10.

113. Newfield and DuBrul, *The Abuse of Power,* pp. 186–187.

114. Tabb, "The New York City Fiscal Crisis," pp. 255–257; Gifford, "New York City and Cosmopolitan Liberalism," pp. 563–564.

115. Eli Silverman, "New York City Revenues: The Federal and State Role," in Roger Alcaly and David Mermelstein, eds., *The Fiscal Crisis of the American Cities* (New York: Vintage, 1977); *New York Times,* November 28, 1983; September 22, 1984;

May 12, 1983; May 5, 1983; February 2, 1982; January 19, 1982; October 1, 1981; October 22, 1979.

116. The information used in this section has been drawn largely from UPI and *Cleveland Plain Dealer* accounts; Carl Stokes, *Promises of Power* (New York: Simon and Schuster, 1973); Edward Whelan, "Mayor Ralph J. Perk and the Politics of Decay," *Cleveland Magazine,* September 1975; Edward Whelan, "The Making of a Mayor, 1977," *Cleveland Magazine,* December 1977; and Bob Holden, "Kucinich's New Urban Populism," *Seven Days,* March 16, 1979.

Other useful information concerning the evolution of Cleveland's political economy can be found in such sources as William Gamson Rose, *Cleveland: The Making of a City* (Cleveland: World Publishing, 1950); Carl Stokes, "Cleveland Now" *American City* 84 (September 1968); Estelle Zannes, *Checkmate in Cleveland* (New York: University Press Book Service, 1972); Louis Masotti and Jerome Corsi, *Shoot-Out in Cleveland* (Washington, D.C.: Government Printing Office, 1969); Peter Phipps, "How the City Withers Away," *Cleveland Magazine,* June 1972; Phillip Porter, *Cleveland, Confused City on a Seesaw* (Columbus: Ohio State University Press, 1976).

117. U.S. Department of Commerce, *Census of Manufacturers* (Washington, D.C.: Government Printing Office, 1958; 1972); Cleveland City Planning Commission, *Jobs and Income* (Cleveland: City Government Printing Office, 1975).

118. Donald Haider, "Fiscal Scarcity," in Masotti and Lineberry, *The New Urban Politics*; President's Urban and Regional Policy Group Report, p. 18; U.S. Department of Commerce, *City and County Data Book*; U.S. Department of Commerce, *Statistical Abstracts of the United States.*

119. U.S. Department of Commerce, *City and County Data Book*; U.S. Department of Commerce, *Statistical Abstracts of the United States*; Chudacoff, *The Evolution of American Urban Society,* p. 91.

120. Federal Bureau of Investigation, *Uniform Crime Reports.*

121. U.S. Department of Commerce, *City and County Data Book*; U.S. Department of Commerce, *Statistical Abstracts of the United States.*

122. *New York Times,* November 9, 1979.

123. Stokes, *Promises of Power*; Zannes, *Checkmate in Cleveland*; Masotti and Corsi, *Shoot-Out in Cleveland.*

124. Stokes, "Cleveland Now"; and Whelan, "Mayor Ralph J. Perk and the Politics of Decay," especially pp. 96–97.

125. Whelan, "Mayor Ralph J. Perk and the Politics of Decay," pp 96–97.

126. Ibid.

127. Holden, "Kucinich's New Urban Populism"; Whelan, "The Making of a Mayor, 1977"; Alberta Sbragia, "The 1970s: A Decade of Change in Local Government Finance," in Alberta Sbragia, ed., *The Municipal Money Chase* (Boulder, Colo.: Westview, 1983), p. 83.

128. Studs Terkel, *American Dreams* (New York: Pantheon, 1980), p. 348.

129. To see just how cohesive Cleveland's corporate community has been in the past, see *Business Week,* August 17, 1968, p. 78.

130. *Cleveland Plain Dealer,* January 16, 1978, p. 16D.

131. It is also interesting to note that many of Kucinich's speeches were covered extensively in UPI stories circulated across the state. However, they often received little to no coverage at all in the *Cleveland Plain Dealer.*

132. *Cleveland Plain Dealer,* December 10, 1978, p. 11; December 12, 1978, p. 15A; December 15, 1978, p. 5A; December 16, 1978, p. 13A.

133. Terkel, *American Dreams,* p. 348; Holden, "Kucinich's New Urban Populism," p. 19; *Playboy Magazine,* June 1979, p. 88.

134. The Federal Reserve Board ruled on March 12, 1979, and that decision was widely reported and discussed in the media for the better part of a week thereafter. For a fuller description of Cleveland Trust's interlocks and those of other major Cleveland corporations, see the U.S. House Committee on Banking and Currency, *Commercial Banks and Their Activities: Emerging Influence on the American Economy* (Washington, D.C.: Government Printing Office, 1968).

135. *Cleveland Plain Dealer,* February 16, 1979.

136. *New York Times,* November 8, 1979, p. A20.

137. *New York Times,* September 29, 1980.

138. *Cleveland Plain Dealer,* December 18, 1979, p. 1A.

PART III

The Political System

CHAPTER 7

Political Parties

To this point, we have analyzed the basic economic, social, and political structures that frame contemporary urban politics. For the next level of understanding we need to examine what Easton calls *conversion mechanisms,* those institutions most centrally involved in the city's actual governmental policy-making process. These are political parties, city councils, the office of the mayor, the bureaucracy, and the mass media. Although these institutions function primarily to reinforce existing socioeconomic hierarchies each also retains some potential for contributing to fundamental redistribution.

Political parties have been a central institutional element in urban politics. To understand their place in the urban setting, it is important to note the hostile milieu into which they were born.

POLITICAL PARTIES IN U.S. HISTORY

There is no mention of political parties anywhere in the U.S. Constitution, and that is no accident. As they sailed cautiously into the uncharted waters of democracy, a number of the founding fathers were very concerned about the possibility of "majority tyranny." James Madison spoke of it as the potentially dangerous "mischief of faction." He meant that in a democracy there was the possibility that a large group of people might unite tightly together politically and thus be able to dominate the rest of society. Many of the country's early leaders found it frightening to think that the United States might develop organized and enduring political parties that could make factional mischievousness likely.[1]

In truth, they had serious reservations about the whole concept of democracy. Of particular concern was the possibility that a nonwealthy majority might combine and use government to redistribute the wealth. In *Democracy in*

America, Alexis de Tocqueville concluded, "It is easy to see that the rich have a great distaste for their country's democratic institutions. The people are a power they fear and scorn."[2]

Some of this "fear and scorn" actually got written into the U.S. Constitution. The end result was classic conservatism: a system to help preserve the maldistribution of property and at the same time minimize popular input that could conceivably challenge it.

Alexander Hamilton

The difference of property is already great among us. Commerce and industry will increase the disparity. . . . Your government must meet this state of things, or combinations will . . . undermine your system.

The people, sir, are a great beast. . . . The same state of the passions which fits the multitude, who have not a sufficient stock of reason and knowledge to guide them, . . . very naturally leads them to a contempt and disregard of all authority.[3]

James Madison

An increase of population will of necessity increase the proportion of those who will labor under all the hardships of life, and secretly sigh for a more equal distribution of its blessings. These may in time outnumber those who are placed above the feelings of indigence. According to the equal laws of suffrage, the power will slide into the hands of the former.

. . . whenever the majority shall be without landed or other equivalent property and without the means or hope of acquiring it, what is to secure the rights of property against the danger from an equality and universality of suffrage, vesting complete power over property in hands without a share in it . . .

Landholders ought to . . . be so constituted as to protect the minority of the opulent against the majority.[4]

All of which sounds a good bit like economic philosopher Adam Smith: "Civil government . . . [is] instituted for the defence of the rich against the poor."[5]

Such sentiment also reflected the views of political philosopher John Locke, whose *Second Treatise on Civil Government* was very influential in shaping the outlooks of America's founders. Locke was so obsessed with the protection of property that his writings included provisions for rebelling against an unresponsive government but never against the sanctity of private property. If the latter were challenged, all rights were to be suspended until the threat to property had been effectively overcome.[6]

To understand better the fears of Locke, and especially those of Madison and many of his contemporaries, we must know the historical perspective. Most of the country's early leaders were men of significant personal wealth.[7] Thus, although they agreed that a strong national government made sense for the purposes of regulating their interstate commerce and protecting their property from both foreign and domestic invaders, most were highly suspicious of what the lesser propertied majority might do if given a proportionate share of the political power.

Their fears were fed by social movements beginning to surface in states like Massachusetts, Rhode Island, New Hampshire, and Pennsylvania. Small farmers, in particular, were beginning physically to resist foreclosures and forcibly free debtors from prison, while at the same time pressing for voting rights and a shift to paper currency in order to help them overcome their extensive debts.[8]

As they gathered in Philadelphia in 1776, many of the founding fathers had a good bit more on their minds than "life, liberty, and the pursuit of happiness" for all. They also set out to protect their property interests from the potentially dangerous lesser-propertied masses.

One of the most important ways Hamilton, Madison, and their cohorts succeeded in incorporating their "fear and scorn" into the Constitution was by establishing numerous roadblocks to majority rule: checks and balances within the Congress, among the three branches, and between the national and state governments. As there was no provision for national initiatives or referenda, all federal legislation would have to pass through that maze of governmental decision makers. Thus, it would become nearly impossible to use the legislative process to challenge the existing distribution of wealth and power.

Nonetheless, the preclusion of political parties, as part of this obstruction, would not endure for long. As industrialization dawned in the early nineteenth century, the first mass-based national parties began to crystallize. By the presidential election of 1828, the Democrats and the Whigs both had developed grass-roots organizations. The nation's federalistic spirit, however, also was incorporated into the political party apparatus. There would be essentially autonomous state parties loosely aligned under a national party banner.

THE POLITICAL PARTY MACHINE

Even though municipal services emerged to meet the pressing problems posed by rapid urbanization, political institutions remained weak, with services administered by a disorganized combination of boards and commissions. To bring order out of this chaos, the political party machine emerged. As Zane Miller characterized it, the machine was "an invisible bureaucracy able to cut through red tape and secure the cooperation of elected and appointed officials in the tangled maze of municipal government";[9] or in the words of Gluck and Meister, "The machine was able to unite what law and tradition had separated."[10] The fears of centralized power would gradually give way to the need to address the host of urban problems facing all city residents to varying degrees.

The first large political machine was the "Tweed Ring," which began in New York City in 1859. Then, civil unrest and a labor union movement erupted amid the economic depressions of 1873–1879 and 1893–1897, and these seemed to provide additional impetus to the growth of party mechanisms.[11] Virtually all the older big cities in the United States would have a form of centralized political party machine sometime between the Civil War and World War II. In a number of cities, vestiges of these party organizations can still be observed today.[12]

The hallmark of the political party machine was tight organization—necessary if it was to accomplish two basic things. First, it had to control a large block of votes. This was accomplished by the distribution of "divisible" patronage benefits and with mechanisms that allowed the political leaders to be sure they were getting their money's worth when the voters turned up at the polls. Second, the party bosses had to retain control over the nomination process so that the only way to attain and retain elective office was by demonstrating loyalty to the machine agenda—that agenda being primarily the provision of patronage services.[13]

Organization

At their zenith, local political party machines were the primary elements in larger state organizations. In most cases they were the key element in the state Democratic party, but cities such as Philadelphia and Cincinnati actually had a tradition of Republican political machines.

Figure 7.1 indicates the subdivisions of state parties. As most states are divided into a number of counties it was logical for each county to be a party cell. Within each county, there are a number of election districts (or wards); and those districts are further subdivided by precincts, usually with some 600 to 900 eligible voters in each.[14] Machine organizations extended even closer to the grass roots than that. At their strongest, these parties were organized down to the block level, and each community of blocks had its own party club.[15]

State political parties in machine states came to be organized hierarchically along these boundary lines, with a clear chain of command (see figure 7.2). They

FIGURE 7.1   State Party Divisions

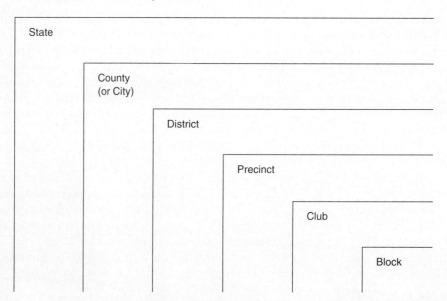

FIGURE 7.2 State Party Organization

were headed by a state executive who sat over a state committee. However, for all practical purposes this state functionary did not dominate the overall organization because most of the older industrial states had a single city that contained the lion's share of the party's membership, and thus electoral clout. As a result, the party executive in that city (or county) had the most influence. Unless the "boss" could deliver that strategic area's votes, the state party was in trouble. Therefore, the entire organization relied heavily on that person, and that position became the key party position in the state.[16]

Some of the best known of the machine bosses include New York's William Marcy Tweed (1859–1877), Kansas City's Jim Pendergast (1890–1939), Jersey City's Frank Hague (1917–1947), Boston's James Michael Curley (1914–1949), Memphis's Ed Crump (1909–1954), and Chicago's Richard J. Daley (1955–1976).

Beneath the boss was the political machine, a horde of county committee-persons, ward bosses, precinct captains, neighborhood clubs, and block captains. Within the county (or city), the ward was the typical primary unit around which most machines were organized. There were a few exceptions, however. In Michigan, for example, machines were organized around Congressional Districts, while in New York the state legislative Assembly District was the primary organizational unit.

No matter what the level, each of the machine foot soldiers had a clearly identifiable task: to turn out the maximum number of people from his or her district to vote for the party's candidates.

Operations

Politics is the art of putting people under obligation to you.[17]

At the most basic level, the machine operated on what can be termed the quid pro quo (translated from Latin as "this for that"). Party supporters made financial contributions to the machine; for example, at the turn of the century Lincoln Steffens noted that Philadelphia teachers were expected to contribute $120 of their first $141 in wages.[18] In addition, they helped during election campaigns by performing services such as canvassing voters, registering people, stuffing envelopes with campaign materials, delivering the party's candidate slate door-to-door on election day, and driving faithful voters to the polls. Finally, and most important, they provided their own votes. In return, the machine provided a sizable amount of patronage to supporters who ranged from the very wealthy to the very poor.[19] Examples of the types of patronage provided are shown in the following list.

Common Forms of Machine Patronage

Public works	hospitals, housing projects, parks
Service priorities	street paving, police patrols
Decisional biases	zoning, planning, licensing
The city's business	city contracts, disposition of property
Inside information	prior to city land acquisition
Employment	administrators, clerks, fire fighters, street sweepers
Miscellaneous goodies	baseball tickets, turkeys, coal
Intangibles	friendship, ethnic recognition

Patronage.   Patronage took a variety of forms. At the community level, the bosses built, built, and built some more—from hospitals to parks to housing projects to convention centers. Besides earning more public parks and swimming pools, loyal districts received priority in the delivery of a number of city services. Their streets were repaired first. They got more and better street lights. Their garbage was picked up more often. Police patrolled more regularly. The expansion and delivery of city services provided a tremendous opportunity for rewarding the faithful.[20]

Among individuals, reliable entrepreneurs received quick and friendly zoning, planning, and development decisions. They were first in line to receive city contracts for construction work, legal services, or foodstuffs for the jails and public school lunches. They also would be the first to receive scarce business licenses such as the liquor licenses needed to run bars and restaurants. In addition, they would be given priority when the city disposed of its property like used vehicles or abandoned lots. Just as important, they would receive inside information on pending governmental decisions such as land acquisition for a city park. With this knowledge they could buy up unused property cheaply near the park site, then sell it for a large profit when the property soared in value because of its proximity to the new park.

Party loyalists also were given the appointed administrative positions in the city, as well as a host of other city jobs—from police officers to secretaries to street cleaners to elevator operators. Most of these positions had few skill prerequisites and thus could be given to a broad cross-section of the machine's constituents.

Chicago, for instance, had more than 500 of these jobs per ward, so a Chicago boss such as Richard J. Daley had 25,000 to 35,000 positions to hand out. If the boss could count on each job generating approximately 10 votes from family, friends, and relatives of the recipient, he or she could build a healthy electoral foundation.[21]

Most voters, however, could be appeased with much smaller gifts—an occasional baseball ticket, bushel of coal, Thanksgiving turkey, loan, or "fixed" parking ticket. (Actually, such "fixing" often amounted to little more than the machine's paying the ticket rather than risking an embarrassing investigation by the state's attorney at some point were they simply to discard the summons unpaid. The voters, however, could brag that they "had connections" and did not need to be concerned about such things as parking tickets.)[22]

The machine also had at its disposal a variety of intangible psychological rewards for individuals, including friendship and ethnic recognition. In terms of friendship, the precinct captain knew his people by name and would always be there with the necessities of life when times were hard. When a breadwinner died, the family would be "looked after." If fire devastated your dwelling, the machine would be at your doorstep with food, clothing, and other help. Tammany Hall ward boss, George Washington Plunkitt, described his regular system for such assistance:

> If there's a fire in Ninth, Tenth, or Eleventh Avenue, for example, any hour of the day or night, I'm usually there with some of my election district captains as soon as the fire engines. If a family is burned out . . . I don't refer them to the Charity Organization Society. . . . I just get quarters for them, buy clothes for them if their clothes were burned up, and fix them up 'til they get things runnin' again. It's philanthropy, but it's politics, too—mighty good politics. Who can tell how many votes one of these fires brings me?[23]

Other famous ward bosses who operated in similar style included Chicago's "Bathhouse John" Coughlin, "Hinky Dinky" Kenna, and Johnny "Prince of Boodlers" Powers.

Beyond such acts of "friendship," appeals were made to cohesive ethnic groups by "balancing the ticket" (also referred to as the "politics of recognition"). This meant that party leaders were careful to have plenty of elective offices; and then they had to be sure to nominate ethnically identifiable candidates, representatives from the various groups in their constituency. In Italian wards, they ran people with names like DeMarco and Rossetti so that people could "vote for the vowel," meaning you voted for the candidates whose names ended in a vowel, often a reasonably clear indication that the person was Italian.[24]

Milton Rakove found that Chicago slates tended to include Irishmen for mayor, county assessor, state's attorney, and county clerk, a Pole for city clerk, and a Jew, Bohemian, or black for city treasurer. The judicial slate would have three or four Irishmen, two or three Jews, two or three Poles, several African Americans, a Lithuanian, a Scandinavian, several Bohemians, and several Italians. This tactic provided highly visible indicators that each ethnic group was important.[25]

All these forms of patronage had at least two characteristics in common. They were "divisible" in nature. And, they represented what Plunkitt came to call "honest graft."[26]

They were divisible in the sense that they could be handed out selectively so that only the loyal would be rewarded. A citywide environmental policy or a full-employment policy would reward all city dwellers whether they did their electoral duty or not. In addition, "indivisible" benefits often raised value issues around which party constituencies might disagree; an example is Chicago's struggle with an open housing policy beginning in the late 1940s.[27] It was much more unifying to be able to dole out a little bit for all loyal supporters. Staying in power was much simpler without the intrusion of values or ideologies.[28]

This patronage also normally came in the form of "honest graft," not to be confused with "dishonest graft." It was honest in the sense that patronage hiring, the selective lending of licenses, and the dispersal of inside information all normally occurred within existing laws. Interfering in a significant way with the impartiality of the police, prosecutors, judges, building inspectors, or tax assessors would have been clearly illegal and run the risk of state or federal investigations and possible criminal indictments. In the machine's heyday there was enough honest graft that the dishonest variety generally was not seen to be worth the risk. That is not to say, of course, that individual machine operatives did not get caught with their hands in the political till from time to time. As late as 1983, a federal jury found Chicago Alderman Tyrone Kenner guilty of ten counts of extortion, nine counts of mail fraud, and one count each of attempted extortion, conspiracy, and obstruction of justice for engaging in "dishonest graft."[29]

There was not always a clear line separating the two forms.[30] Plunkitt referred to stealing roofing materials off city buildings and selling them for junk as "dishonest graft." This he contrasted to having the building reroofed, even getting the contract himself, and then getting a good deal on the old roofing materials which could then be sold for junk. According to Plunkitt, that is the "honest" way to do it.[31]

Boss James Pendergast of Kansas City owned three businesses that thrived on city contracts.[32] Today such a practice likely would violate conflict of interest laws; but in the absence of such statutes, was that honest or dishonest graft?

Consider the following example. As Mike Royko recounts it, a small restaurant owner found himself in a bind when he attempted to put a sign in his restaurant window endorsing Ben Adamowski, an opponent of Mayor Richard J. Daley.

> The day it went up the precinct captain came around and said, "How come the sign, Harry?"
> "Ben's a friend of mine," the restaurant owner said. "Ben's a nice guy Harry, but that's a pretty big sign. I'd appreciate it if you'd take it down." "No, it's staying up."
> The next day the captain came back. "Look, I'm the precinct captain. Is there anything wrong, any problem, anything I can help with?" Harry said no. "Then why don't you take it down. You know how this looks in my job." Harry wouldn't budge. The sign stayed up.
> On the third day, the city building inspectors came. The plumbing improvements alone cost Harry $2,100.[33]

Honest or dishonest behavior? Regardless of how you categorize such machine activities, there is evidence to suggest that many city voters long have been tolerant of even some of the most sordid of these practices, provided the machines continued to deliver the goods.[34]

Boss as Broker.   Although machine governments often went into debt providing various forms of direct patronage, there were at least some fiscal limitations as to what they could spend. There were simply not enough tax revenues and kickbacks to allow them to provide favors to every city group and individual whose vote was needed. Consequently, bosses also served as brokers between various groups and individuals around the city. They utilized their positions to mediate disputes, and in the process they both curried favor and kept their coalitions together.[35]

Election Control.   The provision of patronage and brokerage services ensured that voters voted on election day. However, the bosses had to be sure they voted as directed so that the party's people got elected.

To remain on the machine's good side, the ordinary people had to deliver on their end of the bargain. They had to vote, and to vote for the party's slate of candidates. Close tabs were kept on who voted and who did not. In addition, a variety of mechanisms were used to ensure how people voted once they arrived at the polling place. For a long time there was no secret ballot; thus, it was easy. The party operative stood over their shoulder and watched them! Even after the secret ballot was introduced, there were ploys like the "Tasmanian dodge" (also referred to as the "endless chain"). Here, party representatives at each polling place would manage to filch at least one blank ballot. They would then fill it in and hand it to each loyal party member in exchange for that person's blank ballot. The blank ballot would then be filled in by the party representative and swapped with the next voter, and on and on. Not until the introduction of mechanical voting machines was it possible to reduce that form of control.

There were also far fewer voting cues available then than there are today. With no radio or television, and relatively few "newspaper districts," (where newspapers were widely read) much of what voters knew they had heard from their block captain, at the party clubhouse, or in the party press. In addition, government workers were given election day off to form a huge campaign army, passing out the party slate door-to-door and bringing "sick and lame" loyalists to the polls in government vehicles.

Election districts could be *gerrymandered,* drawing election district lines to maximize a party's electoral strength. If a city had five council districts, for instance, and 50 percent of the city's voters were loyal Democrats, district lines could be drawn in such a way as to virtually guarantee that four of the five council-members would be Democrats. That could be done by carving out an entirely Republican district, then drawing the other four districts so that there was a Democratic majority in each one.[36]

With reapportionment occurring after each decennial census, there has been plenty of opportunity to redraw district lines in this way. Actually, the practice dates to the early nineteenth century, with the term emerging in 1811 when Massachusetts governor Elbridge Gerry drew such a contorted district in Essex County that it vaguely looked like salamander. Gilbert Stuart of the *Boston Centinel* subsequently called it a "Gerry-mander."

The United States Supreme Court trod cautiously into this area in 1986. In *Davis v. Bandemer*[37] the Court ruled that gerrymandering could be unconstitutional if it "continually degraded" a group's influence and thus would violate that group's Fourteenth Amendment right to "equal protection under the law." Nevertheless, within the boundaries of the Court's ruling, the practice continues, and with an ever-greater degree of sophistication. Given the availability of computer programs that store large data bases, analyze elections, and generate maps, it is becoming possible both to predict more accurately how various areas will vote and to combine such areas into election districts, in order to achieve the desired electoral results.[38]

Much of this manipulation could still be accomplished even after the emergence of nonpartisan elections. As most places were essentially one-party towns, there was really very little practical difference between a nonpartisan election and a party primary. Thus, even though no party labels appeared on the ballot as a guide, party loyalists in nonpartisan cities like Boston, Chicago, Cincinnati, Cleveland, Kansas City, and Memphis still walked into the voting booth with their party-generated slates in hand. Much, then, depends on the partisan orientation of the voters in a particular city.[39]

Most of these practices reasonably could be called "honest graft." Most of it was legal. Of course, some of it was not. Some party goons physically intimidated people.[40] Particularly before there was a very formal registration process, people voted more than once, and occasionally the dead would rise to cast their ballot for the party until their physical disposition came to light and their names finally were expunged from the rolls. In 1844, 55,000 votes were cast in Tammany Hall's New York, even though there were only 41,000 eligible voters.[41] As late as 1984, a Brooklyn grand jury found considerable election fraud in eight separate primary elections between 1969 and 1982, including "multiple voting by teams of political workers with bogus voter registration cards."[42]

In addition, polling officials sometimes miscounted the ballots. In one gambit that survived well into the twentieth century, the vote counter would keep a piece of pencil lead under his or her fingernail so as to mar unfriendly paper ballots. For example, if both candidates' names were checked, the ballot would have to be ruled invalid. It was not uncommon for vote counters to invalidate votes for opponents by discreetly checking their own candidates' names as well. Some state laws still allow local election boards to destroy voting records after relatively short periods of time, making it hard to investigate these practices very long after the fact.

Policy Control.   Besides controlling the electoral vote in order to get the correct people into elective office, the machine also had to be able to control the elected officials once they assumed their seats of political authority. They had to be certain that those elected could be counted on to deliver the patronage that held it all together.

As Moise Ostrogorski points out, the bosses normally were interested primarily in one governmental policy, and one policy only: patronage. Describing the boss, Ostrogorski concludes:

> He does not try . . . to control all the manifestations of political life. All his designs on the commonwealth amount, in fact, to running the elections as he likes, putting his followers in all the places, keeping out his opponents . . . and realizing the material profits (patronage) attaching to these places and to the influence which they procure. The line of public policy to be adopted, in itself, is a matter of indifference to the boss.[43]

So, how did they control those elected? Outright bribery was illegal and inefficient. Far safer was nomination control.

As most older cities were overwhelmingly Democratic in voter registrations, Democratic party nomination was tantamount to general election.[44] Consequently, it was crucial to control who could run under the party banner. If the only way of attaining such a ballot position was by currying favor with the party leaders, then officeholders who wanted to retain their seats would have to deliver the patronage.

Controlling who was nominated was easier before primary elections were introduced. Party members, whether at the ward or citywide level, met in proverbial "smoke-filled rooms" and made all the nominations. However, party leaders controlled the lists of members eligible to attend and vote at these party caucuses, and they had people to cast proxies for those who were unable to attend (some of whom had actually died or moved out of town). Meetings could be called on short notice and in obscure places, often in the backrooms of saloons. The leaders controlled who could speak, and thus they could keep opposing slates off the floor and rule unfriendly motions out of order. And, of course, the leaders counted the ballots.[45]

Yet, even when nominations were turned over directly to the voters in open direct primaries, the party still often controlled the board of elections that certified nomination petitions. Independent candidates would have their petitions scrutinized closely. A misnumbered page or one ineligible name on a petition would lead to the rejection of that entire petition. Also, the party leaders minimized notification of all elections so that those turning out to vote would be disproportionately those on the party's information track. The goal was not to turn out "the" vote; the goal was to turn out "their" vote.

If all of this was done correctly, the machine boss did not necessarily have to hold any government office himself and governmental authority did not need to be centralized. He did not have to run for office if he could control the actions of the mayor, council, and commissioners by controlling who could run for office under the party banner.

As for centralized authority, many machine cities did not even have strong-mayor systems; Chicago had a weak mayor, Jersey City and Memphis had commission forms, while Kansas City actually had a council-manager system. This situation existed for a variety of reasons. A number of these cities had already undergone some structural reform. A strong-mayor arrangement was not really necessary as long as most of the governmental decision makers could be controlled. And there was no need to provide a platform whereby an individual politician could develop his or her own personal power base outside the machine apparatus.

Overall, then, nomination control was the key. It was most easily accomplished in the private caucus rooms, but more formal party conventions soon proved just about as easy to dominate. Primary elections, on the other hand, removed the nominating process from the party leaders themselves and proved to be somewhat more problematic.

Machine Demise

> Bosses cannot be judged by their sordid activities alone. They arose in an age when "respectable" industrialists and merchants trampled opponents and manipulated the public—all in the quest for dollars and power.[46]

Nevertheless, as time went by, political bosses were indeed judged by their "sordid activities," even though corporate transgressions often were overlooked —at least in part because the newspapers were private corporations themselves. While the "robber barons" gathered strength in the private economy,[47] William Marcy Tweed (Boss Tweed of New York City's Tammany Hall) built numerous streets, let transit and utility franchises, developed Central Park, and revised the city charter, leading Howard Chudacoff to conclude that "Tweed's accomplishments outdistanced those of all leaders who had preceded him in New York."[48] His administration, however, also got caught pilfering $20 million to $200 million from the public till, and it was that for which he was best known. Nonetheless, the organization managed to survive into the 1960s, at least until machine boss Carmine De Sapio finally was jailed.[49]

Antimachine journalist William Allen White described New York City's Boss Croker as "a dull, emotionless prosimian bulk of bone and sinew—a sort of human megatherium who has come crashing up from the swamps splashed with the slime of pre-Adamite wickedness!"[50] Even far more honest and reform-minded machine-era mayors, such as New York City's John Kelly, Cincinnati's George Cox, Cleveland's Tom Johnson, and Detroit's Hazen Pingree, were viciously attacked in the press. But despite the steady fire of "muckraking" journalists like White and Steffens, not to mention acerbic cartoonists such as Thomas Nast,[51] it took far more than newspaper exposés, denunciations, and ridicule to bring down the centralized political party machine. Following are a baker's dozen of interrelated factors, a combination of which account largely for the machine's demise.[52]

Nails in the Machine Coffin

Economic transformations	especially increased mobility of capital investment
Patronage restrictions	especially the civil service principle of government hiring and firing
Progressive reforms	direct primaries, nonpartisan voting
Local economic problems	fiscal stress due to suburbanization
National welfare state	Social Security, unemployment compensation, AFDC
Hatch Act	limits on electoral activities of government workers
Labor unions	greater job security, benefits in the public and private employment sectors
Mass media	increased information, campaign forums, a spotlight on selected issues
Mass education	increased public literacy and appetite for news
Enhanced vote utility	higher stakes with growth of government involvement
Homogenization	ethnic acculturation and assimilation
Immigration decline	fewer and more federally oriented emigrants
Racial divisions	African Americans and the legacies of slavery

National Economic Transformations. As capital became more mobile toward the end of the industrial period, wealthy investors no longer were as reliant on the various services provided by a specific local party machine. Actually, the extravagance of the machine gradually came to be an impediment to attracting and/or retaining the capital investment necessary for local economic growth. This was especially true when the national economy went into recession. The machines were becoming more trouble than they were worth to American capitalists, and the reform movement was soon on its way.[53]

Patronage Restrictions.   Congress struck a significant blow when it passed the 1883 Pendleton Act.[54] This established the civil service system for hiring all federal employees except those in appointive advisory roles like the secretary and under secretary of state. Beneath that level, federal hiring was to be done on the basis of merit rather than political loyalty. To get a federal job, one now had to take a standardized examination and then be ranked and appointed according to its results. A person could work for the post office, for example, regardless of political views or affiliations.[55]

States and cities proceeded to establish their own versions of civil service shortly thereafter, in part because having such a system was a mandate attached to various federal grants.[56] As a result, the machines soon lost primary control over one of their most trusted forms of patronage: the local government job.[57]

Subsequently, a string of federal court decisions have further narrowed party running room in this regard. In *Elrod v. Burns*[58] the court held that dismissals on the basis of party affiliation, even of non–civil service employees, could be an unconstitutional violation of free expression under the First Amendment, if the position did not involve public policy-making or the rendering of confidential policy advice to a policy maker. In *Branti v. Finkel,* the court extended this principle when it ruled that such firings normally would be unconstitutional, unless the elected official could prove that partisanship is "essential to the discharge of . . . the responsibilities."[59] Partisan firings would be allowed only for confidential and policy-making positions and in situations where there was a need to have election supervisors from both parties. Then in *Rutan v. Republican Party,*[60] the court extended this protection to hirings, promotions, and transfers as well.

On one hand, the bosses were losing a crucial form of patronage. Just as important, they were losing significant control over an increasingly large government bureaucracy.[61]

Progressive Reforms.   The most overt assault on the machines came in the form of what were termed *progressive* reforms. These included the introduction of secret ballots, stricter registration laws, nomination by direct primary elections, council-manager systems, at-large elections, nonpartisan voting, and so on. Nonpartisan at-large election systems, for example, were first adopted in cities such as Los Angeles (1908), Boston (1909), Akron (1915), and Detroit (1918), while direct primaries were introduced in Wisconsin (1903) and 12 other states in the next 10 years alone.[62] In addition, city accounts were subjected to more intense external auditing, and more competitive processes were designed for the letting of city contracts. The idea was to reduce both election fraud and partisan politics while increasing governmental efficiency and impartiality.

Local Economic Decline.   A combination of economic factors came together to wreak fiscal havoc on many city budgets. The Great Depression presented both soaring service needs and plummeting revenues. Consequently, a number of these cities actually went into default during this period of national economic crisis.

In addition, postindustrial phenomena were developing. Suburbanization reduced the revenues necessary to provide the level of divisible patronage services constituents had come to expect from the political machine. Also, there was a decline in the number of unskilled jobs in the private-sector's primary labor market, further reducing the machines' opportunities to arrange gainful employment for their underskilled constituents.[63]

The Welfare State.   Franklin Roosevelt's ''New Deal'' programs provided institutionalized social welfare services nationwide. A U.S. citizen could now receive emergency food aid, government employment, unemployment compensation, Social Security retirement benefits, and other services from the federal government. The federal government had preempted many of the machine's service functions, and no political quid pro quo was required. A person need not even register to vote in order to be eligible.

This shift created a certain nationalization of politics, as it placed far more importance on who was elected president than who was elected mayor. Thus, in regard to an increasing number of important social services, machine politicians were reduced to the roles of federal lobbyist and occasional intervenor—helping constituents wade through federal red tape in order to attain those externally provided services such as Social Security, veteran's benefits, Aid to Families with Dependent Children (AFDC), and unemployment compensation.[64]

The Hatch Act.   To add insult to injury, the federal government also included the Hatch Act as a rider to the Social Security Act of 1939.[65] This law precluded federal workers from taking any active part in political campaigns. They were not allowed to raise funds, distribute candidate literature, manage another's campaign, or run for office themselves. In 1985, three postal workers drew 60-day suspensions for working in Walter Mondale's 1984 presidential campaign. Congress tried to soften the restrictions in 1990 by allowing federal employees to engage in just about any type of electoral activity short of running for office, as long as they did it on their own time. President Bush vetoed the change, however, and the Senate failed to override his veto.[66]

More important yet for the urban machine, each state proceeded to establish its own version of the Hatch Act, and a number of the states enforced these limits much more aggressively than did the federal government. Thus, most state and local government workers had even less freedom than federal employees.[67]

Labor Unions.   The proliferation of labor unions, spurred by the National Labor Relations Act of 1935,[68] provided an additional substitution for services previously delivered by the machine. Instead of the ward boss helping the newly arrived immigrant find and hold a job, unions did much of this. When local government employees began to unionize in the 1960s, local-level bureaucrats became a political force even more independent from the partisan politicians who had hired them. They had their own organization, their own forms of job protection, and an ability to strike if necessary to get their way.

Mass Media.   There was also a veritable information explosion taking place. Radio and television became widely available, and the number of print sources proliferated as well. Urban residents were no longer nearly as reliant on the machine as in earlier years for their political cues. Independent candidates could now use media advertisements to speak directly to these voters without having to rely on the party apparatus to raise their money, provide their crowds, or disseminate their message.

Media also played an agenda-setting role of their own. The issues they deemed worthy of covering became issues city government would be forced to address. And one of the issues they certainly found newsworthy was corruption within the political machine. The "muckraking" press unveiled scandal after scandal in their crusade to clean up local politics.

Education.   Part of the reason media sources proliferated, particularly print sources, was because the general public was becoming much better educated. Not only were they more literate but they had an increased appetite for information, including political information. "The voter has changed," lamented Timothy Gibbons, a ward boss on Chicago's southwest side. "The Democratic Party used to be basically a blue-collar party, but the voters are getting more sophisticated. The second and third generations are going to college, the husband and wife are both working, they read *Time* and *Newsweek*. And they have a television."[69] As a result, Cook County's Thomas Carey concluded, "You don't have many precinct captains going door-to-door telling people how to vote. . . . [This generation is] more educated and they don't rely on [precinct captains] for favors or information anymore."[70]

Vote Utility.   As government at all levels came to play an ever greater role in their lives, and as their information levels increased, urban voters appeared more reluctant to barter their votes for a couple of baseball tickets. Particularly when government began to be more involved in redistributing income, people on both ends of the redistributive formulas suddenly seemed to have more at stake. Consequently, the perceived utility of the vote increased.[71]

Homogenization.   Among urban ethnic groups, long a crucial component of most political machines, the longer they were here, the more Americanized they became. First they acculturated, taking on middle-class values, accumulating appropriate work skills, and acquiring the language. This made them less dependent on either their ethnic groups or the political machine for survival in the New World. It also made them less tolerant of government inefficiency and dishonesty.

Ultimately, they began to assimilate; their ethnic identity gradually began to give way as they were increasingly likely to see themselves as Americans first and Germans or Irish second. The particular significance of this change for the machines was that the electorate was no longer as conveniently subdivided, a condition that complicated the distribution of divisible benefits.[72]

Immigration Decline.   Laws such as the Immigration Act of 1921 emerged to reduce the influx of immigrants, especially those who were not from Northern European countries. Thus, the machines were denied new infusions of needy ethnic constituents. Also, the groups who were gravitating toward the cities, Hispanics and African Americans, already were accustomed to looking to the federal government for assistance. Thus, their first stop was more likely to be the federal building than the machine clubhouse.

Racial Divisions.   American cities had long been divided into ethnic ghettos, whether these were Polish, Jewish, or Italian. These groups were often rivals, and most were held in disdain by the more assimilated natives. Nonetheless, as chapter 4 indicated, race seems to have been a far more immutable barrier to admission to mainstream life.

One indication of this uniqueness was the manner in which African Americans were treated even within the early machines. Black wards were gerrymandered to remain predominately black,[73] while blacks themselves often were relegated to parallel support roles. They were expected to turn out and vote for the machine candidates, and in return they received at least some patronage. However, normally they were not allowed to hold any party offices or have black candidates placed on the party's ballot. In New York City, this parallel structure was called the Union of Colored Democrats. African Americans were exploited in a comparable way in most other cities, with Chicago and Memphis being two of the more extensively studied besides New York.[74]

Whether it has been the unique American heritage of African Americans, their mercurial politicization in the 1960s, race-specific remediation programs like busing and affirmative action, or any of a number of other potential factors, one thing is clear. African Americans have had more trouble assimilating into American society than virtually any other group. This racial divisiveness posed problems for the local Democratic parties. As African Americans became more central components of their organizations, a variety of whites began to move away from the association. In Chicago, there are now essentially two parallel Democratic party operations—one white and one black.

Additionally, blacks were coming into their own politically after patronage and other machine tools already had been constrained severely at the local level. Thus, political organization would be more difficult for them to accomplish than it had been for their white ethnic predecessors. Such developments led the *Amsterdam News* to lament,

> Every ethnic group that has achieved political power in American cities has used the bureaucracy to provide jobs in return for political support. It's only when Blacks begin to play the same game that the rules get changed. Now the use of such jobs to build political bases becomes an "evil" activity, and the city insists on taking the control back "downtown."[75]

Indices of Decline.   For these and a number of less prominent reasons, machines began to decline in the postindustrial era. As a number of these phenomena came together in the decade following the end of World War II, some of the last powerful machines began to fade from the scene—Hague in Jersey City, Curley in Boston, Pendergast in Kansas City, McFeely in Hoboken, and Crump in Memphis. By 1976, with the death of Mayor Richard J. Daley of Chicago, the boss era was over.

This decline is visible in a variety of indicators, including a number of quantifiable ones. The proportion of big city voters registering as Republicans or independents has been increasing. A larger share of the voters are voting split-tickets, casting some votes for the candidates of one party and some for the candidates of the other.[76] The candidates endorsed by the regular Democratic party's local organization, whether it be in a primary or a general election, are faring less well.[77] There is much less competition for positions on the county committees, a clear indication of the decline in the perceived political significance of those bodies. Some of those seats actually sit vacant in what were previously strong machine cities.[78]

Another concrete indication of machine decline is their growing inability to have opponents struck from the ballot. In its heyday the machine held tight reign over the board of elections, and opponents could be struck from the ballot for relatively minor technical violations. New York City council candidate Trudy Nelson, for example, needed 1,500 signatures to get on the ballot. She turned in 4,250, but was ruled ineligible when she claimed 4,251 on her cover sheet. By 1985, however, New York mayoral candidate Herman Farrell exemplified candidates' growing ability to challenge such decisions successfully. After he had been ruled off the ballot for an incorrect cover sheet on one of his 1,000 nominating petitions, the decision was overturned by both the New York Court of Appeals and a Federal District Judge on the grounds that it was indeed an "inconsequential violation."[79]

REFORMED CITIES

In place of the machine emerged the "reformed" city governmental structure, based on the general principle that "there is no Democratic way to pave a street." The reform followed three central principles. First, there is a "public interest" in having honest and efficient government services, whether the people are aware of that or not. Second, to achieve that goal, the administration of services must be separated as far as possible from political considerations. Third, to attain that separation, administration needs to be performed by independent professional bureaucrats utilizing the most recent scientific management techniques.[80] Wealthy reform pioneer Richard Childs, founder of the National Municipal League and author of the "Model City Charter," stated, "The difficulties of democracy . . . are mechanistic, nor moral, and respond to mechanistic corrections."[81]

Commission and council-manager forms replaced many of the mayor-council arrangements for city government, and a host of appointed independent boards were established to do much of the planning and oversight. Most of the elected decision makers would be chosen at-large in nonpartisan elections with strict registration laws and short and secret ballots. Then, after election, those elected officials would hire by merit, they would have far less patronage to pass around, and their employees would be limited in their political activity. Thus, political activists soon tended to be political amateurs with very high turnover rates.[82] All of this would occur under the aggressively watchful eye of the ever present mass media establishment.

The first wave of reform tended to mirror the period in which it occurred, possessing a definite populist cast. Reform mayors such as Detroit's Hazen Pingree (1889–1897), Toledo's Samuel Jones (1897–1903), and Cleveland's Thomas Johnson (1901–1909) pressed for an end to the tight machine-corporation connection, pushing policies such as utility regulation, minimum wages, some public businesses, and more general social services such as free kindergartens.[83] Nevertheless, it was not long before the movement developed a more elitist orientation.

> Out of the clash between the needs of immigrants and the sentiments of the natives, there emerged two thoroughly different systems of political ethics . . . one, founded upon the indigenous yankee-Protestant political traditions, and upon middle-class life, assumed and demanded the constant, disinterested activity of the citizen in public affairs, argued that political life ought to be run to a greater degree than it was in accordance to general principles, abstract laws, apart from and superior to personal needs . . . .
>
> The other system, founded upon the . . . background of the immigrants, upon their unfamiliarity with independent political action, their familiarity with hierarchy and authority, and upon the urgent needs that so often grew out of their migration, took for granted that the political life of the individual would arise out of family needs, interpreted political and civic relations chiefly in terms of personal obligations, and placed strong personal loyalties above allegiance to abstract codes of laws or morals.[84]

Such a contrasting view of governmental propriety helps in part to explain the ultimate coup d'état accomplished to varying degrees by the middle- and upper-class urban gentry, regardless of the group or organization represented.[85] Even though many of them long had benefited from machine largesse, some of the behavior had become just too morally repugnant, and many blamed the corruption on the "thousands of immigrants from slums and prisons of Italy and South Europe, . . . the bogs of Ireland, the mines of Poland, the brigand caves of Italy, and from the slave camps of the South, but one remove from the jungles of Africa."[86]

Clearly, the reform was not all about high principles and efficiency. There was almost always an undercurrent of class and ethnicity prejudice as well. For example, when reform groups took power they often could be seen holding their victory celebrations in the local Masonic Temple, replacing Catholic employees with Protestants, and switching liquor licenses from neighborhood saloons to fancy downtown hotels.[87]

There has been a considerable amount of empirical analysis to learn whether these reforms, beyond achieving a "cleaner" political process, have had specific public policy implications. One rather marked conclusion is that when reformed cities are compared to less reformed ones (latitudinal analysis), reformed cities are less responsive to class, race, and religious constituencies.[88] However, when individual cities are studied before and after they adopt reform policies (longitudinal analysis), little consistent change is apparent.[89] Thus, reform similarities may be more a reflection of the type of cities at the more reformed end of the political continuum than of the impact of their adopting reform procedures.

Political Parties Today

Before assigning the political machine to the scrap heap of urban history, however, two important qualifications need to be noted.

Machine Politics Lives. First, it is the highly centralized and cohesive political party machine, and not "machine politics" that has nearly disappeared. In other words, it is the tight-knit hierarchical organization that has come unglued; but quid pro quo politics continues, only in more decentralized and somewhat less blatant ways.

Contemporary patronage is no longer distributed within a centralized machine structure. Nevertheless, individual councilpersons still deliver favored treatment for their supporters in forms such as priority for city contracts, permits, inspections, and licenses.[90] Cities continue to have a number of "provisional" jobs and consultant appointments that can be handed out on a temporary basis outside the civil service system. Politicians can tailor job descriptions to fit the desired person or can simply capture the local civil service commission politically.[91] Ethnic groups are still appealed to directly and extended both symbolic and substantive rewards for their loyalty.[92]

Parties Matter. Second, political parties still matter at the local level. They continue to play a role in the election of candidates, and party influence remains at least a minor factor in occasional policy-making decisions once candidates are elected to office and assume the reins of authority.

Elections. Party activists continue to register voters, circulate petitions so their candidates can get on the ballot, and "get out the vote" on election day.[93] But much of the organizational structure is gone, for the variety of reasons discussed above. Nonetheless, there is some evidence of organizational resurgence,[94] as the chairperson and a handful of party loyalists (often elected representatives) continue to meet periodically to conduct routine election-related tasks. Money has to be raised; poll watchers have to be found; candidates have to be recruited to "fill out the ticket"; and someone has to speak for the party, normally the chairperson. Little door-to-door canvassing occurs anymore, however, unless the canvassers are recruited and paid for by a congressional, senate, or mayoral candidate.[95]

Even though they are the exception and not the rule, a number of large cities still have fully partisan elections. In the cities of Baltimore, Cleveland, Indianapolis, Jacksonville, New Orleans, New York, Philadelphia, Pittsburgh, and St. Louis, for instance, party labels still accompany each candidate's name on the ballot. Besides those cities, some have mixed systems: Chicago's mayoral candidates appear with a partisan designation while the city councilpersons do not.

Where it is available, the party label remains an important guide to voting choices. This is particularly true in lower visibility elections such as for city councilpersons or commissioners where few other voting cues are available.[96] As most large cities continue to be dominated by those registering as Democrats, candidates affiliated with the Democratic party tend to be elected whether their partisanship is noted on the ballot or not. In addition, as many party primaries go uncontested, the party organization's endorsement is often tantamount to general election victory.

To avoid overstating the case, however, we should note that this party influence subsides significantly in more important races or if primary elections are contested. In those circumstances, individual candidates often put together their own organizations, and those organizations actively engage in fund-raising, campaign advertising, and all of the organizational functions mentioned above—from voter registration to turning out the vote on election day.[97]

Policy.   The design and implementation of a particular policy agenda, on the other hand, has seldom been a high priority for local party organizations.[98] They appear more concerned with the mechanics of getting their party representatives into office. Thus, although they do help organize elections, contemporary parties actually do little in the way of educating voters about policy matters, leading voters toward party-favored policies, or organizing government after the election for the purpose of implementing a party platform.

What is left of the political party hierarchy is more apt to intervene to assist a particular constituent or group of constituents gain a divisible policy result.[99] This situation is more likely to occur when the stakes are relatively low, the person or group played a significant electoral role, and/or the elected official owes his or her election to the party's efforts. When the stakes are higher, however, party leaders find themselves up against the bureaucracy, mass media, and powerful interest groups, all of whom appear to play a far greater role in contemporary public policy-making than do party leaders. Larger city mayors, for example, list business and civic groups as much more influential than political parties.[100]

It is realistic to think of party structure as a continuum with the full-blown political machine at one end and an archetype fully reformed city at the other. In between lies the reality for American cities at present, although admittedly they have drifted considerably from the heyday of strong centralized political party organizations.[101]

Are Strong Political Parties Desirable?

A man that'd expict to thrain lobsters to fly in a year is called a loonytic; but a man that thinks men can be tur-ned into angels by an illiction is called a ray-former . . . .[102]

—"Mr. Dooley" (1902)

Was good old Mr. Dooley correct? Were the critics too hard on the political machines? As a way of both summarizing and looking to the future, we can ask whether a return to more centralized political party organizations would be a net plus for the postindustrial city.

Arguments against Strong Political Parties. Many arguments have been made over the years condemning centralized political party organizations. Below are a half-dozen of the more prominent ones.

Arguments against Machinelike Organizations

Obsolete	Irreversible historical developments have rendered party machines unnecessary.
Biased	Selective patronage violates the democratic principle that elected officials should strive to represent all their constituents.
Corrupt	They steal elections and public monies, encourage biased law enforcement.
Inefficient	They pad payrolls and require kickbacks, as the priority is reelection and not cost-effective service delivery.
Elitist	They are self-serving and do not promote informed democracy.
Diversionary	They obscure social and economic interests.

Obsolete. Virtually all the developments discussed as reforms are irreversible. Labor unions and the federal welfare state are here to stay. Voters are too educated and information too plentiful ever to allow the machine's previous level of dominance. Ethnic groups have become assimilated, and the number of new immigrants will never again reach turn-of-the-century levels. Thus, machine legions have dwindled and most of their functions have been usurped. The centralized political party machine is a dinosaur.[103]

Biased. The American democratic creed suggests that elected officials are to represent their entire constituency, not just those who voted for them. However, the machine and its selective patronage often defied this tenet, leaving machine opponents taxed but minimally represented. The most blatant example of this was George Washington Plunkitt's "honest graft," amounting to under-the-table preferred treatment for party loyalists.

Corrupt. Beyond honest graft, there were many instances of outright illegality. The entire electoral process reeked of corruption, from multiple voting, to voting the graveyard, to miscounting returns, and on and on. Hidden away in a highly centralized and informal decision-making process, machine operatives were free to help themselves to the public purse through inflated salaries and generous "expense accounts," if not through outright stealing. Boss McFeely of Hoboken, for instance, never made more than $5,000 per year as mayor but still managed to accumulate a personal fortune of more than $3 million while in office.[104] When building code inspectors, police officers, and even judges were aware of illegalities yet looked the other way, the entire system of justice was polluted; prostitution, gambling, and other illicit businesses often flourished as long as law enforcement personnel were paid off sufficiently.[105]

Inefficient. In general, machine governments appeared far more interested in returning favors than in delivering quality services at reasonable costs. The selective letting of contracts to favored supporters without competitive bidding cost the cities more than necessary for these services. The cities' payrolls were padded with many workers whose services really were not needed, such as elevator operators on the automated elevators in Chicago's City Hall, or some who literally held "no-show" jobs (meaning they did not even have to report to a job site as a condition for being paid). City workers performed campaign duties on city time and received salaries padded enough that they could afford to make "voluntary" financial contributions to the political machine; James Bryce has estimated these contributions at approximately 1 percent to 5 percent of their salaries.[106] The machines were not even very efficient at dolling out patronage in return for electoral support, often spending far more than necessary.[107]

In the end, besides the kickbacks people were required to pay in order to receive licenses, zoning variances, city service franchises, and extra police protection, they were also subjected to high taxes needed to fund the excesses of the political machine. When the combination of kickbacks and taxes still fell short, these cities ran up massive debts: New York City's debt tripled from $30 million in 1867 to $90 million by 1871, and a number of other cities were soon running debts that ranged from 50 percent to 100 percent of their assessed property values.[108]

Elitist. Relying as they did on divisible benefits and voter ignorance concerning larger political issues, machines did little to promote informed democracy. Political elites ran the city, with the only real accountability being the need to provide ample patronage to the loyal minions. Fleeing authoritarian European regimes, unfamiliar with democracy, and having intense personal needs, the newly arrived immigrants were particularly vulnerable to machine control.[109]

In addition, Robert Michel's "Iron Law of Oligarchy" suggests that elite rulers of any large organization soon will come to be more concerned with doing what is necessary to maintain their positions of power, regardless of the purpose for which the organization was originally formed.[110] Thus, such hierarchical organizations seem destined to become ever more elitist.

Diversionary. While those on the ideological right often complained about biases and inefficiencies, those on the left complained just as loudly that the crumbs being scattered from the patronage table really did little more than mollify a number of low-income people. While being atomized politically, their class consciousness was being suppressed as they were kept reasonably content with the larger political and economic systems that exploited them.[111]

Lincoln Steffens referred to the machines as "demagogic plutocracies," a small band of political and economic elites who pandered to the insecurities of the lower classes in order to prosper themselves.[112] As an example of the cozy relationship between the boss and his business counterparts, John Jacob Astor and five other millionaires attempted to protect Boss Tweed by signing an affidavit attesting to his good character and swearing that he had never stolen a cent from New York City, while financier Jay Gould put up his $1 million bail.[113]

Machine appeals to race, ethnicity, and party identities can be seen as a diversion from underlying class interests. Speaking specifically of their moderating capacities, Alan Altschuler stated:

> Though they distributed favors widely, they concentrated power tightly. Though their little favors went to little men, the big favors went to land speculators, public utility franchise holders, government contractors, illicit businessmen, and of course the leading members of the machines themselves. . . .
>
> The bosses were entrepreneurs, not revolutionaries. They provided specific opportunities for individual representatives of deprived groups, but they never questioned the basic distribution of resources in society. Their methods of raising revenue tended toward regressivity. On the whole, the lower classes paid for their own favors. What they got was a "style" of government with which they could feel at home. What the more affluent classes got, though relatively few of them appreciated it, was a form of government which kept the newly enfranchised masses content without threatening the socioeconomic status quo.[114]

Probably the most graphic example of the point was the ease with which the machine dispatched its police to help crush early labor rallies, or at least turned their backs while the Pinkerton agents did the actual suppression.[115] The machines stifled the development of socialist parties as well.[116]

They also tended to reinforce gender and racial inequities. Machine organizations were overwhelmingly male bastions; it is interesting that non–machine states generally were quicker to provide women's suffrage.[117] In terms of race, African Americans were kept subordinate; however, their repression went beyond mere subordination. Mike Royko describes a far more recent racial incident in Chicago:

> While Daley stayed out of sight the Eleventh Ward Regular Democratic organization worked things out. While the two students were at school, the police went in the flat and carried their belongings to the corner police station. People from the neighborhood rushed in and threw the place up for grabs, smearing excrement on the walls.
>
> The real estate man who handled the move-in was summoned by the ward organization and told what to do. He listened because real estate licenses are under the control of the mayor of the city of Chicago. They told him that the two black youths were no longer tenants in the building; that two white men from the neighborhood were going to move in and were going to be given a long unbreakable lease for the apartment, and that it was all going to happen immediately. The lease was drawn up, signed, and the two white tenants moved in. The jubilant crowd joined them in the apartment for a celebration and to help clean up the mess.[118]

Arguments for Strong Political Parties.   Because they appeared so often in the popular media as well as in scholarly analyses of the machines, most of the above arguments are more familiar. Nonetheless, a number of revisionist scholars have pointed to some of the machine's redeeming qualities.[119] Below is a set of counterarguments in favor of more centralized political party organizations.

Arguments for Strong Centralized Political Parties

Democracy	Closer connection between voting and identifiable governmental rewards increases both representation and politicization.
Stability	A strong party assists in immigrant acculturation, channels political activity through the existing political system, filters out demagogues, and so on.
Security	A machine provides cradle-to-grave camaraderie and protection (as someone always will be there in times of need).
Fish bowl	The glare of today's media attention precludes most of the corruption that once plagued such organizations.

Democracy.   If democracy is seen as a process by which voters express their collective will at the polls and that will is enacted into policy after the election, a case can be made that the machines truly served to facilitate the democratic process.

INPUT   The grass-roots organization of the machine allowed constituent voices to be heard and their needs addressed. Precinct captains knew each resident personally, and they were quick to solicit help when personal or neighborhood problems arose. Party bosses often walked the wards themselves, lending an ear at least to registered voters. It was not unusual for the mayor's office itself to be open to direct citizen solicitations on a relatively regular basis.

> [Government] is an environment that in normal times is often impersonal, remote and meaningless to the people themselves until a wide-awake division leader appears before them in the flesh. He is an individual who speaks their own language and knows their own wants. He often makes warm and personal that which had been cold and distant. He "knows everybody" at City Hall, or he knows someone who does. He bridges the gap between the unseen outer world and the inadequate citizen.[120]

Contrast this situation to what has arisen in place of the machine. Without the machine apparatus to survey the constituency, disperse information, and turn out the vote, candidates often have to have money themselves or rely on wealthy individuals and interest groups for the contributions necessary to accomplish these campaign chores. It is no longer uncommon, for instance, for a large city mayoral candidate to spend millions of dollars on a single campaign, much of on short, essentially issue-less, television spot commercials.[121] In 1983, Chicago Mayor Jane Byrne spent $10 million on her election campaign. Thus, the group leaders and the wealthy have the preferred political access to supported candidates once they become elected. When a key zoning issue arises, of course the heavily contributing real estate magnate can expect to have his phone call returned. Meanwhile, the average woman or man is left to watch it all on television while the mass media in general play increasingly important king-making and agenda-setting roles by what they cover and how they cover it.

OUTPUT Besides providing more access to everyday people on the input end, the machine also was better positioned to deliver on campaign promises. When they promised that certain streets would be paved, they were paved. When they promised a housing project, it was delivered. When they promised your uncle a job on the police force, he got the job. Hours after fire destroyed a home, food, blankets, and clothing began to arrive. By providing a mechanism for sustained political power, the machine could accumulate the resources necessary to deliver on its promises. As long as the votes kept them in office, the patronage kept rolling out in return.[122]

REPRESENTATION Contrast machine politics to the reformed "amateur politics"[123] and bureaucratic state that have replaced it. Even though a variety of local interest groups, often representing the underclass, have successfully squeezed services out of "reformed" city governments, it can be argued that city residents collectively have even less control over their lives than they did in the days of the political machine.[124]

James Q. Wilson, analyzing reformed political organizations in four cities, concludes that they represent a blueprint for political failure. Democratic procedures come to take precedence over either winning elections or delivering on campaign promises. Organization is loose. Turnover is high. And turnout declines. They are essentially a weak, white, middle-class antidote for the kind of politics that more effectively represented working- and lower-class blacks and whites.[125] Meanwhile, the owning class continues to dominate the city's wealth and power.

Theodore Lowi adds that the cities may now be better "run" but not necessarily better "governed," for each bureaucratic agency has become a new machine exercising critical decision-making power; and these "islands of functional power" are more interested in maintaining their own budgets than in serving the public. Thus they have "destroyed the basis for sustained, central, popularly based [political] action."[126]

Expanding on the last point, Charles V. Hamilton argues that the more reciprocal "patron-client" relationship between city residents and the political machine (votes in return for favors) has given way to a "patron-recipient" relationship between the people and the government bureaucracy. In particular, service recipients find themselves with virtually no systematic leverage with which to affect bureaucratic decisions directly.[127] Rather, when changes are desired a "politics of protest" often is employed, but this method does not entail the type of political mobilization that will allow sustained vigilance and control. Consequently, once the protesters "cool off," a number of the benefits are gradually retracted.[128]

The community power movement is probably the closest city residents have come to recapturing some of the power lost with the demise of the political machine. Prompted by developments like the federal government's maximum feasible participation concept, there was a proliferation of community action commissions, neighborhood city halls, urban action task forces, and the like.[129] For example, in 1970 Mayor John V. Lindsay of New York City formally recognized 62 "neighborhood governments" with some 130,000 constituents each in order to improve communication between city hall and its constituent communities.[130]

Yet even though a number of local political elites felt threatened by them, these newly contrived bodies generally had little real political power. They usually lacked their own independent tax bases, and they often were not well prepared to deal with the myriad of state and federal agencies on which they would ultimately come to rely. Hamilton stresses that to institutionalize such political power, grass-roots organizing must precede external recognition and funding.[131] In this case, it seldom did. Almost as quickly as it began, the community power experiment generally was deemed to have failed and was all but totally curtailed.[132]

SERVICE   Less bound by bureaucratized rules and procedures, the machine was able to be much more flexible in its service delivery. As it normally had a good working relationship with the community involved, it could make individual adaptations. In law enforcement, for instance, the cop on the beat might well take Joey home instead of to juvenile court if the officer was certain that Joey's parents would deal with the situation effectively. Or the tax collector might give Mrs. Williams a long extension if the official was aware of her recent hospital bills.[133] Such informality allowed the system to provide the majority of honest citizens with more adaptive services, but it also made the system vulnerable to abuse, and political corruption certainly did not end with the advent of reform structures.[134]

POLITICIZATION   Most important, however, whether through community clubhouses or neighborhood city halls, the experience of acting politically and receiving concrete political benefits in return does seem to politicize people.[135] The accountability that forced government to deliver palpable services in order to receive the votes necessary to stay in office made the act of voting much more rational. Instead of voting for candidate images flashed across the television screen, people could vote for a party label that all but guaranteed certain identifiable services if that party was elected. When the public's will is spoken and answered, there is a real incentive to speak again.

Stability.   From a citywide perspective, a number of benefits were gained by having the political machine. Although not encouraged to abandon their ethnic identification, immigrants were still learning economic and political values, facilitating their adaptation into mainstream American society. Constituents' political needs were being met, and thus there was less likelihood of disruptive extrasystemic political activity such as protest marches and riots. And to reduce disruption even further, party leaders took care to sift out radicals and demagogues when making their nominations in the smoke-filled rooms.[136]

Security.   From the individual's perspective, the personalized nature of the machine made the immigrants feel welcome and cared for. If they were lonely, they could join their neighbors stuffing campaign envelopes at the local clubhouse. They did not have to worry about the future because the machine would be there to provide for their loved ones in the event that they would no longer be capable of doing so. In this sense the machine was also a convenient social vehicle as city residents struggled with the transition from rural to urban life.[137] It was one big happy family, and all you had to do to join was help keep the bosses in office. In Plunkitt's words,

> I know every man, woman, and child in the Fifteenth District, except them that's been born this summer—and I know some of them, too. I know what they like and what they don't like, what they are strong at and what they are weak in, and I reach them by approachin' at the right side.[138]

Fish Bowl.   Last, it is certain that some of the abuses of earlier bosses simply would not be tolerated today. Citizens have come to demand a higher standard of integrity and impartiality, and the mass media are there in full force to keep them informed of any deviations. Consequently, were a centralized party apparatus to revive, it would be devoid of many of its earlier warts.[139]

CONCLUSION

> Though the reformers fumed and raved, the hated political bosses were in truth buffers that taxed the one to keep the other in good humor . . . . Naturally, there were brokers' charges on the collections, but these were small as compared with the costs of riots and revolutions.[140]

For a few kickbacks, corporations were guaranteed licenses and permits and even were allowed to develop monopolies in certain lucrative industries, such as public utilities. Profits were all but guaranteed for many of them, and with cities reliant on private financiers for the loans increasingly necessary to run the city, the monied capitalists always had a firm lever with which to keep the machines in line.[141]

Rather than organizing massive numbers of pitifully poor and exploited immigrants to rise up in challenge to the economic system of free enterprise capitalism, the machine appeared to help stabilize what could have been a very unruly situation. Instead of rushing to form labor unions, or engaging in even more disruptive activities to improve life conditions in Upton Sinclair's urban "jungle,"[142] most of these immigrants seemed content with a pat on the back and an occasional Christmas turkey from the precinct captain.

The bosses stayed in power, the owners of capital continued to turn profits, the labor movement was being suppressed.[143] All was well in the world. But, if the economic elites had so much to gain by seeing to it that the political machine survived, why did they try to destroy it?

For whatever reason, it was indeed the bankers, newspaper publishers, factory owners, and other economic elites who ultimately led the charge toward reform government. On the social side of the ledger, class condescension was certainly part of the equation, as most of the party leaders had risen from rather humble origins.[144] There was also some outright nativist resentment; although some bosses such as Tweed, Cox, and Crump were actually natives themselves, their constituencies still tended to be lower-income immigrants, a situation that was distasteful to many of the better-off residents.

However, there were economic liabilities as well. Utility and other monopolies were beginning to pose unacceptable costs to other industries.[145] The tax burden created by machine expenditures had to be a sore point, particularly as the lower and working classes began to demand more redistributive benefits in the postindustrial era. In addition, the endless muckraking stories of corruption must have troubled those with such a high stake in the city's image. Machines were beginning to get out of hand. Thus, a more bureaucratized central government controlled more directly by the elites themselves had to appear increasingly attractive.[146]

As immigration slowed, machines may have outlived their usefulness to the captains of industry, now posing more of a potential threat than an advantage. Chudacoff noted that

> boss politics, with its legions of foreign-born supporters and its proclivity toward extralegal activities, posed a threat to the established classes. . . . They feared the immigrant-dominated political machines were subverting social and political order . . . and they equated bad politics with bad business.[147]

Yet, if the desire is to begin leveling the maldistribution of wealth and power that seems to plague the postindustrial city, perhaps some form of strong political parties could be a vehicle for aggregating opposition. Although not revolutionary vehicles in and of themselves, political machines could be counted on systematically to provide a reasonable degree of essential social welfare services, besides laying the organizational groundwork for more demanding political action at some later date.

NOTES

1. See James Madison, ''Federalist Paper #10,'' in Clinton Rossiter, ed., *The Federalist Papers* (New York: New American Library, 1961).
2. Alexis de Tocqueville, *Democracy in America,* ed. and trans., Phillips Bradley (New York: Knopf, 1951).
3. Quoted in Farrand, *Records of the Federal Convention* (New Haven, Conn.: Yale University Press, 1911), pp. 424, 432; Mary Jo Kline, ed., *Alexander Hamilton* (New York: Harper & Row, 1973), p. 45.
4. Quoted in Farrand, *Records of the Federal Convention,* pp. 421–423; Marvin Meyers, ed., *The Mind of the Founder* (Indianapolis: Bobbs-Merrill, 1973), pp. 504–505.
5. Adam Smith, *The Wealth of Nations* (New York: Modern Library, 1937), p. 674.

6. John Locke, "Second Treatise on Civil Government," in Maurice Cranston, ed., *Locke on Politics, Religion, and Education* (New York: Collier, 1965).

7. Charles Beard, *An Economic Interpretation of the Constitution* (New York: Macmillan, 1962).

8. Samuel Morrison, *The Oxford History of the American People* (New York: Oxford University Press, 1965), p. 274.

9. Zane Miller, *The Urbanization of Modern America* (New York: Harcourt Brace Jovanovich, 1973), p. 100.

10. Peter Gluck and Richard Meister, *Cities in Transition* (New York: Viewpoints, 1979), p. 56. Also see James Scott, "Corruption, Machine Politics, and Political Change," *American Political Science Review* 63 (December 1969), pp. 1154–1156.

11. See Dennis Judd, *The Politics of American Cities* (Boston: Little, Brown, 1988), p. 52.

12. For a general discussion of variations in machine emergence and decline, see Steven Erie, *Rainbow's End* (Berkeley: University of California Press, 1988).

13. For a classic depiction of the inner workings of the political machine, see William Riordan, *Plunkitt of Tammany Hall* (New York: Dutton, 1963); Howard Chudacoff, *The Evolution of American Urban Society* (Englewood Cliffs, N.J.: Prentice-Hall, 1975), chap. 5.

14. Demetrios Caraley, *City Governments and Urban Problems* (Englewood Cliffs, N.J.: Prentice-Hall, 1977), p. 166.

15. For a summary of club activity, see Clarence Stone, Robert Whelan, and William Murin, *Urban Policy and Politics in a Bureaucratic Age* (Englewood Cliffs, N.J.: Prentice-Hall, 1986), pp. 89–90.

16. Centralized party machines were not a uniquely urban phenomenon. Huey Long, for example, was able to construct a powerful statewide machine in Louisiana based primarily in rural areas.

17. Legendary Chicago ward boss Jacob Lavery, as quoted in the *New York Times,* July 1, 1990.

18. Lincoln Steffens, *The Shame of the Cities* (New York: McClure, Phillips, 1904; reprinted New York: Hill and Wang, 1957), p. 155. Also see Clifton Yearly, *The Money Machines* (Albany, N.Y.: SUNY Press, 1920), pp. 114–115.

19. For documentation of the patronage-participation link, see Phillip Cutright, "Activities of Precinct Committeemen in Partisan and Nonpartisan Communities," *Western Political Quarterly* 17 (March 1964): 93–108.

20. Lawrence Herson, "Pilgrim's Progress," in *Political Science and State and Local Government* (Washington, D.C.: American Political Science Association, 1973), pp. 7–9.

21. Milton Rakove, *Don't Make No Waves—Don't Back No Losers: An Insider's Analysis of the Daley Machine* (Bloomington: Indiana University Press, 1975), pp. 114–115.

22. Edward Flynn, *You're the Boss* (New York: Collier, 1962); Edward Costikyan, *Beyond Closed Doors* (New York: Harcourt, Brace and World, 1966), pp. 345–346.

23. Riordan, *Plunkitt of Tammany Hall,* pp. 27–28. Also see Robert Merton, ed., *Social Theory and Social Structure* (New York: Free Press, 1957), pp. 60–82.

24. *New York Times,* June 6, 1979.

25. Rakove, *Don't Make No Waves,* p. 96. For additional discussion of this phenomenon, see Raymond Wolfinger, *The Politics of Progress* (Englewood Cliffs, N.J.: Prentice-Hall, 1974), pp. 69–70.

26. Riordan, *Plunkitt of Tammany Hall,* pp. 3–6.

27. See Rakove, *Don't Make No Waves,* p. 12.

28. Robert Dahl, *Who Governs?* (New Haven, Conn.: Yale University Press, 1960), p. 52; Stone, *Urban Policy and Politics in a Bureaucratic Age,* pp. 93–95; Robert Lineberry and Ira Sharkansky, *Urban Politics and Public Policy* (New York: Harper & Row, 1978), p. 119.

29. *New York Times,* May 26, 1983.

30. John Peters and Susan Welch, "Political Corruption in America: A Search for Definitions and a Theory," *American Political Science Review* 72 (September 1978): 974–984.

31. Cited in Merton, *Social Theory and Social Structure,* p. 30.

32. Noel Gist and Sylvia Fleis Fava, *Urban Society* (New York: Crowell, 1974), p. 457. For more on Boss Pendergast, see Lyle Dorsett, *The Pendergast Machine* (New York: Oxford University Press, 1968).

33. Mike Royko, *Boss: Richard J. Daley of Chicago* (New York: New American Library, 1971), p. 131.

34. Esther Fuchs and Robert Shapiro, "Government Performance as a Basis for Machine Support," *Urban Affairs Quarterly* 18 (June 1983): 537–550.

35. Rakove, *Don't Make No Waves,* p. 4.

36. For a contemporary example, see *New York Times,* March 17, 1991.

37. *Davis v. Bandemer,* 106 S.Ct. 2797 (1986). Also see *Badham v. Eu,* 488 U.S. 804 (1989).

38. Frank Kuznik, "Divide and Conquer," *Common Cause Magazine,* May/June 1989, pp. 13–16.

39. Caraley, *City Governments and Urban Problems,* pp. 186–187.

40. Harold Gosnell, *Machine Politics: Chicago Model* (Chicago: University of Chicago Press, 1968), p. 88; Dorsett, *The Pendergast Machine,* p. 60; William Miller, *Mr. Crump of Memphis* (Baton Rouge, La.: LSU Press, 1964), p. 74; Alan Davis, *Spearheads for Reform* (New York: Oxford University Press, 1967), pp. 156–162.

41. See Bruce Felknor, *Dirty Politics* (New York: Norton, 1966).

42. See *New York Times,* September 5, 1984. For more examples, see Miller, *Mr. Crump of Memphis,* p. 59.

43. Moise Ostrogorski, *Democracy and the Party System* (New York: Macmillan, 1926), pp. 259–260. Also see Samuel Eldersveld, *Political Parties* (Chicago: Rand-McNally, 1964); Costikyan, *Beyond Closed Doors,* especially chap. 9.

44. Once again, it should be remembered that cities such as Philadelphia and Cincinnati were the exceptions to this rule.

45. See James Bryce, *The American Commonwealth* (New York: Macmillan, 1889).

46. Chudacoff, *The Evolution of American Urban Society,* p. 146.

47. Howard Zinn, *A People's History of the United States* (New York: Harper, Colophan, 1980), chap. 11.

48. Chudacoff, *The Evolution of American Urban Society,* p. 136. Also see Leo Hershkowitz, *Tweed's New York* (Garden City, N.Y.: Anchor Books, 1978), p. 348.

49. For good sources on Tammany Hall, see Gustavus Myers, *The History of Tammany Hall* (New York: Boni and Liveright, 1917); Seymour Mandelbaum, *Boss Tweed's New York* (New York: Wiley, 1955); Harold Zink, *City Bosses in the United States* (New York: A.M.S., 1968).

50. Quoted in Chudacoff, *The Evolution of American Urban Society,* p. 125.

51. See Lincoln Steffens, *The Autobiography of Lincoln Steffens* (New York: Harcourt Brace, 1931).

52. For a discussion of the demise of party domination in particular cities, see Jewell Bellush and Dick Netzer, eds., *Urban Politics: New York Style* (New York: Sharpe,

1990); Paul Kleppner, *Chicago Divided* (De Kalb: Northern Illinois University Press, 1985); Lawrence McCaffrey, *The Irish in Chicago* (Urbana: University of Illinois Press, 1987); Diane Pinderhughes, *Race and Ethnicity in Chicago Politics* (Urbana: University of Illinois Press, 1987).

53. Martin Shefter, *Political Crisis/Fiscal Crisis* (New York: Basic Books, 1987), pp. 23–24, 56–60.

54. Pendleton Act, 5 USC 1101 (1883).

55. The precision with which a civil service system actually can define and discern "merit," however, is a matter of debate. For example, see Albert Aronson, "State and Local Personnel Administration," in Frank J. Thompson, ed., *Classics of Public Personnel Policy* (Oak Park, Ill.: Moore, 1979); E. S. Savas and Sigmund Ginsburg, "The Civil Service," *The Public Interest* 86 (Summer 1973): 70–85.

56. The Social Security Act, 42 USC 301 (1939).

57. Raymond Wolfinger, "Why Machines Have Not Withered Away and Other Revisionist Thoughts," *Journal of Politics* 34 (May 1972): 365–398; James Q. Wilson, "The Economy of Patronage," *Journal of Political Economy* 69 (August 1961): 369–380; Melvin Holli, *Reform in Detroit* (New York: Oxford University Press, 1969), pp. 393–403; Eldersveld, *Political Parties,* 279; Costikyan, *Beyond Closed Doors,* p. 86; Robert Hirschfield, Bert Swanson, and Blanche Blank, "A Profile of Political Activists in Manhattan," *Western Political Quarterly* 15 (September 1962): 484–506.

58. *Elrod v. Burns,* 427 U.S. 347 (1976).

59. *Branti v. Finkel,* 445 U.S. 507 (1980).

60. *Rutan v. Republican Party,* 111 L.Ed. 2nd 52 (1990).

61. Michael Johnson, "Patrons, Clients, Jobs, and Machines," *American Political Science Review* 73 (June 1979): 385–398.

62. Ernest Griffith, *A History of American City Government, 1900–1920* (New York: Praeger, 1974), p. 71; Caraley, *City Governments and Urban Problems,* pp. 185–187.

63. Lineberry and Sharkansky, *Urban Politics and Public Policy,* pp. 120–121.

64. Caraley, *City Governments and Urban Problems,* p. 183.

65. Social Security Act, 5 USC 7324 (1939).

66. On June 20, 1990, the House of Representatives voted 327–93 to override the president's veto. However, the Senate failed to do so the next day, when three Republicans (Trent Lott of Mississippi, Alfonse D'Amato of New York, and Pete Domenici of New Mexico) reversed their earlier votes and provided the narrow margin of victory for the president.

67. Commission on Political Activity of Government Personnel, *A Commission Report* (Washington, D.C.: Government Printing Office, 1967), pp. 91–154; Melvin Hill, Jr., "The Little Hatch Acts," *State Government* 52 (Autumn 1979): 161–168.

68. National Labor Relations Act, 29 USC 151 (1935).

69. Quoted in *New York Times,* March 20, 1980.

70. Quoted in *National Journal,* November 3, 1990, p. 265. Also see Edward Banfield and James Q. Wilson, *City Politics* (Cambridge, Mass.: Harvard University and MIT Press, 1963), p. 123.

71. Caraley, *City Governments and Urban Problems,* pp. 183–184; Banfield and Wilson, *City Politics,* p. 121.

72. Elmer Cornwell, "Bosses, Machines, and Ethnic Groups," *Annals of the American Association of Political and Social Sciences* 423 (May 1964): 27–39.

73. James Q. Wilson, *Negro Politics* (New York: Free Press, 1960), pp. 27–32.

74. Wilson, *Negro Politics*; Ray Leo and Bill Gleason, *Daley of Chicago* (New York: Simon and Schuster, 1970); Kenneth Wald, "The Electoral Base of Political Machines: A Deviant Case Analysis," *Urban Affairs Quarterly* 16 (September 1980): 3–30.

75. *Amsterdam News,* April 1, 1978, p. A–4. Also see Banfield and Wilson, *City Politics,* pp. 123–127.

76. Walter DeVries and Lance Tarrance, *The Ticket-Splitter* (Grand Rapids: Eerdmans, 1972); Jack Dennis, "Support for the Party System by the Mass Public," *American Political Science Review* 60 (June 1966): 600–615.

77. Caraley, *City Governments and Urban Problems,* pp. 176–177.

78. Ibid.

79. *New York Times,* July 18, 1985; August 22, 1985; August 23, 1985. For a case study measuring machine decline in Detroit, see Eldersveld, *Political Parties,* pp. 103–104.

80. See Herson, "Pilgrim's Progress," p. 10; Samuel Haber, *Efficiency and Uplift* (Chicago: University of Chicago Press, 1964); Judd, *The Politics of American Cities,* p. 97; Andrew White, "The Government of American Cities," in *Forum* (1890), reprinted in Edward Banfield, *Urban Government* (Glencoe, Ill.: Free Press, 1961).

81. Childs, "Civic Victories in the United States," p. 402, as quoted in Stone, *Urban Policy and Politics,* p. 109. Childs's "Model City Charter" can be found in National Municipal League, *Model City Charter* (Chicago: National Municipal League, 1961).

82. James Q. Wilson, *The Amateur Democrat* (Chicago: University of Chicago Press, 1962); Eldersveld, *Political Parties,* pp. 276–278; Samuel Patterson, "Characteristics of Party Leaders," *Western Political Quarterly* 16 (1963): 342; Jean Sinchcombe, *Reform and Reaction* (Belmont, Calif.: Wadsworth, 1968); Joseph Lyford, *The Airtight Case* (New York: Harper & Row, 1966).

83. See Judd, *The Politics of American Cities,* pp. 73–79.

84. Richard Hofstadter, *The Age of Reform* (New York: Knopf, 1955), p. 9, as quoted in Thomas Dye, *Politics in States and Communities* (Englewood Cliffs, N.J.: Prentice-Hall, 1985), pp. 285–286. Also see James Q. Wilson and Edward Banfield, "Public-Regardingness as a Value Premise in Voting Behavior," *American Political Science Review* 58 (December 1964), pp. 876–887.

85. As for the groups involved, see James Q. Wilson, "Politics and Reform in American Cities," *American Government Annual, 1962–1963* (New York: Harcourt Brace World, 1962), pp. 37–52; Judd, *The Politics of American Cities,* pp. 85–88; W. Brooke Graves, *American Intergovernmental Relations* (New York: Scribner's, 1964), p. 795.

    As for their motives, see Richard Childs, "Civic Victories in the United States," *National Municipal Review* 44 (September 1955); Samuel Hays, "The Politics of Reform in Municipal Government," in Daniel Gordon, ed., *Social Change and Urban Politics* (Englewood Cliffs, N.J.: Prentice-Hall, 1973), p. 111; Hofstadter, *The Age of Reform*; James Weinstein, *The Corporate Ideal in the Liberal State, 1900–1918* (Boston: Beacon, 1968), pp. 99–103; George Mowny, *The Era of Theodore Roosevelt 1900–1912* (New York: Harper & Row, 1958), p. 86; Griffith, *A History of American City Government, 1900–1920,* p. 21; Paul Kantor and Stephen David, *The Dependent City* (Glenview, Ill.: Scott, Foresman, 1988), pp. 138–154; Melvin Holli, "Urban Reform in the Progressive Era," in Louis Gould, ed., *The Progressive Era* (Syracuse, N.Y.: University of Syracuse Press, 1974); Dye, *Politics in States and Communities,* pp. 288–289; John Harrigan, *Political Change in the Metropolis* (Boston: Little, Brown, 1989), pp. 85–90.

    For where they were most successful, see John Kessel, "Governmental Structure and Political Environment," *American Political Science Review* 56 (September 1962):

615–620; Robert Lineberry and Edmond Fowler, "Reformism and Public Policies in American Cities," *American Political Science Review* 61 (September 1967): 701–716; Raymond Wolfinger and John Field, "Political Ethos and the Structure of City Governments," *American Political Science Review* 60 (June 1966): 312–324; Robert Alford and Harry Scoble, "Political and Socioeconomic Characteristics of American Cities," *Municipal Yearbook 1965* (Washington, D.C.: International City Managers' Association, 1965), pp. 82–97; Thomas Dye and Susan McManus, "Predicting City Government Structure," *American Journal of Political Science* 20 (May 1976): 257–271.

86. Holli, "Urban Reform in the Progressive Era," p. 137, as quoted in Robert and Mary Kweit, *People and Politics in Urban America* (Pacific Grove, Calif.: Brooks-Cole, 1990), p. 99.

87. Harold Stone, Don Price, and Kathryn Stone, *City-Manager Government in Nine Cities* (Chicago: Public Administration Service, 1940), pp. 221–223.

88. Lineberry and Fowler, "Reformism and Public Policy in American Cities," pp. 701–716; William Lyons, "Reform and Response in American Cities," *Social Science Quarterly* 59 (June 1978): 118–132; Albert Karnig, "Private-Regarding Policy, Civil Rights Groups, and the Mediating Impact of Municipal Reforms," *American Journal of Political Science* 19 (February 1978): 91–106; Susan Blackwell Hamber, "Participation, Political Structure and Concurrence," *American Political Science Review* 69 (December 1975): 1181–1199; Terry Clark, "Community Structure, Decision-Making, Budget Expenditures and Urban Renewal, *American Sociological Review* 33 (August 1968): 576–593.

89. David Morgan and John Pelissero, "Urban Policy: Does Political Structure Matter?" *American Political Science Review* 74 (December 1980): 999–1005.

90. See Wolfinger, "Why Machines Have Not Withered." Also see Harrigan, *Political Change in the Metropolis,* chap. 4.

91. Robert Lorch, *State and Local Governments* (Englewood Cliffs, N.J.: Prentice-Hall, 1983), pp. 366–367; *New York Times,* November 28, 1976.

92. Nathan Glazer and Daniel Moynihan, *Beyond the Melting Pot* (Cambridge, Mass.: MIT Press, 1970).

93. William Crotty, ed., *Political Parties in Local Areas* (Knoxville: University of Tennessee Press, 1986); Caraley, *City Governments and Urban Problems,* pp. 188–192.

94. James Gibson, Cornelius Cotter, John Bibby et al., "Whither the Local Parties?," *American Journal of Political Science* 29 (February 1985): 139–161.

95. Frank Sorauf, *Political Parties* (Boston: Little, Brown, 1984), pp. 76–77.

96. Marcus Pohlmann, "The Electoral Impact of Partisanship and Incumbency Reconsidered," *Urban Affairs Quarterly* 13 (June 1978): 495–503.

97. James Perry, *The New Politics* (New York: Clarkson N. Potter, 1968).

98. Eldersveld, *Political Parties,* p. 127; Costikyan, *Beyond Closed Doors,* chap. 9.

99. Wallace Sayre and Herbert Kaufman, *Governing New York City* (New York: Norton, 1965), pp. 457–458.

100. David Morgan, "Municipal Expenditures and Group Influence," *Research in Urban Policy,* vol. 3 (Greenwich, Conn.: JAI, 1988).

101. For some contemporary accounts of the machine's rise and fall, particularly the Chicago machine, see Gosnell, *Machine Politics: Chicago Model*; Roydo, *Boss*; Rakove, *Don't Make No Waves, Don't Back No Losers*; Thomas Guterbock, *Machine Politics in Transition* (Chicago: University of Chicago Press, 1980); Samuel Gove and Louis Masotti, eds., *After Daley* (Springfield: University of Illinois Press, 1982); Frank S. Robinson, *Machine Politics: A Study of Albany's O'Connells* (New Brunswick, N.J.: Transaction, 1977); Erie, *Rainbow's End.*

For more general accounts of political party decline in the United States, see James McGregor Burns, *The Deadlock of Democracy* (Englewood Cliffs, N.J.: Prentice-Hall, 1963); David Broder, *The Party's Over* (New York: Harper & Row, 1972); Robert Goldwin, ed., *Political Parties in the Eighties* (Washington, D.C.: American Enterprise Institute, 1980).

102. Mr. Dooley, the fictional Irish saloonkeeper created by Chicago newspaper columnist Finley Peter Dunne, quoted in Chudacoff, *The Evolution of American Urban Society,* p. 149.

103. Murray Steadman, "Why Urban Parties Can't Govern," *National Civic Review* 61 (November 1972): 501–504.

104. See Bernard Ross and Murray Steadman, Jr., *Urban Politics* (Itasca, Ill.: Peacock, 1985), p. 63; Zink, *City Bosses in the United States,* p. 143.

105. Judd, *The Politics of American Cities,* p. 61.

106. Bryce, *The American Commonwealth,* vol. 1, p. 84. Also see Mandelbaum, *Boss Tweed's New York,* pp. 167–168; Martin Melosi, *Garbage in the Cities* (College Station: Texas A&M Press, 1981), especially p. 46.

107. Johnson, "Patrons, Clients"; Kenneth Mladenka, "The Urban Bureaucracy and the Chicago Political Machine," *American Political Science Review* 74 (December 1980): 991–998.

108. Kantor and David, *The Dependent City,* p. 115.

109. Wolfinger, *The Politics of Progress,* p. 69.

110. Robert Michels, *Political Parties* (Glencoe, Ill.: Free Press, 1949; first published 1915).

111. Robert Merton, "The Latent Function of the Machine," in Robert Merton, ed., *Social Theory and Social Structure* (New York: Free Press, 1957), pp. 71–81; Bryan Downes, *Politics, Change and the Urban Crisis* (North Scituate, Mass.: Duxbury Press, 1976), p. 112; Kantor and David, *The Dependent City,* pp. 133–138; Wolfinger, *The Politics of Progress,* p. 120.

112. Steffens, *The Autobiography of Lincoln Steffens*; Steffens, *The Shame of the Cities.*

113. See E. Barbara Phillips and Richard LeGates, *City Lights* (New York: Oxford University Press, 1981), p. 292. Also see Lineberry and Sharkansky, *Urban Politics and Public Policy,* pp. 118–120.

114. Alan Altschuler, *Community Control* (New York: Pegasus, 1970), pp. 74–75. Also see Peter Knauss, *Chicago: A One-Party State* (Champaign, Ill.: Stirpes, 1972).

115. Judd, *The Politics of American Cities,* pp. 65–73; Kantor and David, *The Dependent City,* p. 137; James Jalenak, *Beale Street Politics* (Yale University, Honor's Thesis, 1961), pp. 14–15.

116. Norman and Susan Fainstein, *Urban Political Movements* (Englewood Cliffs, N.J.: Prentice-Hall, 1974), p. 2; Kantor and David, *The Dependent City,* pp. 137–138.

117. See Harrigan, *Political Change in the Metropolis,* p. 77.

118. Royko, *Boss,* pp. 135–136.

119. See Edwin O'Connor, *The Last Hurrah* (Boston: Little, Brown, 1956); Frank Kent, *The Great Game of Politics* (Garden City, N.Y.: Doubleday, 1923; rev. ed. 1930); Sonya Forthal, *Cogwheels of Democracy* (New York: William Frederick Press, 1946); Gosnell, *Machine Politics*; Zane Miller, "Boss Cox's Cincinnati," *Journal of American History* 54 (March 1968): 823–838.

120. Jo Salter, *Boss Rule* (New York: Whittlesey House, 1957), p. 72.

121. Charles Adrian, "Some General Characteristics of Nonpartisan Elections," *American Political Science Review* 46 (September 1952): 766–776.

122. Frank Goodnow, *Politics and Administration* (New York: Macmillan, 1900); Brett Hawkins, *Politics and Urban Policies* (Indianapolis: Bobbs-Merrill, 1971), pp. 93–99;

J. David Greenstone and Paul Peterson, *Race and Authority in Urban Politics* (New York: Sage, 1973).

123. See Wilson, *The Amateur Democrat.*

124. For a general discussion of the subject, see Hamber, "Participation, Political Structure and Concurrence"; Kenneth Prewitt, "Political Ambition, Volunteerism, and Electoral Accountability," *American Political Science Review* 67 (December 1973): 1288–1307.

125. Wilson, *The Amateur Democrat*; Robert Salisbury and Gordon Black, "Class and Party in Partisan and Nonpartisan Elections," *American Political Science Review* 67 (September 1963); J. Morgan Kousser, "The Undermining of the First Reconstruction," in Chandler and Davidson, ed., *Minority Vote Dilution* (Washington, D.C.: Howard University Press, 1984); Karnig, "Private-Regarding Policy"; Lineberry and Fowler, "Reformism and Public Policy in American Cities"; Robert Lane, *Political Life* (Glencoe, Ill.: Free Press, 1959), pp. 269–271; Eldersveld, *Political Parties,* pp. 276–278; Patterson, "Characteristics of Party Leaders," p. 342; Sinchcombe, *Reform and Reaction*; Lyford, *The Airtight Case.*

Focusing specifically on turnout decline, see Albert Karnig and B. Oliver Walters, "Decline in Municipal Turnout," *American Politics Quarterly* 11 (October 1983): 491–505; Howard Hamilton, "The Municipal Voter," *American Political Science Review* 65 (December 1971): 1135–1140.

126. Theodore Lowi, "Foreword to the 2nd Edition," in Harold Gosnell, *Machine Chicago Model Politics* (Chicago: University of Chicago Press, 1968), pp. 9–10; Theodore Lowi, "Machine Politics—Old and New," in Harlan Hahn and Herbert Levine, *Urban Politics* (White Plains, N.Y.: Longman, 1980), pp. 97–104; Theodore Lowi, *At the Pleasure of the Mayor: Patronage and Power in New York City, 1898–1958* (New York: Free Press, 1964), chap. 9; Theodore Lowi, *The End of Liberalism* (New York: Norton, 1969), p. 201; Stone, *Urban Policy and Politics in a Bureaucratic Age,* part 5.

127. Charles V. Hamilton, "The Patron-Recipient Relationship and Minority Politics," *Political Science Quarterly* 95 (Summer 1979).

128. Charles V. Hamilton, "Racial, Ethnic, and Social Class Politics and Administration," *Public Administration Review* 32 (October 1972): 638–648.

129. John Donovan, *The Politics of Poverty* (New York: Pegasus, 1967); Alan Altschuler, *Community Control* (New York: Western, 1970); Milton Kotler, *Neighborhood Government* (Indianapolis: Bobbs-Merrill, 1969); J. David Greenstone and Paul Peterson, *Race and Authority in Urban Politics* (New York: Russell Sage, 1973).

130. John Lindsay, *The City* (New York: Norton, 1970); Eric Nordlinger, *Decentralizing the City: A Study of Boston's Little City Halls* (Cambridge, Mass.: MIT Press, 1972).

131. Charles V. Hamilton, "Political Costs of Participation," in Herrington Bryce, ed., *Urban Governance and Minorities* (New York: Praeger, 1976). Also see Ira Katznelson's concept of "uni-directional political relationships," in W. D. Hawley, *Theoretical Perspectives on Urban Politics* (Englewood Cliffs, N.J.: Prentice-Hall, 1976).

132. Donovan, *The Politics of Poverty,* pp. 136–139; or Daniel Patrick Moynihan, *Maximum Feasible Misunderstanding* (New York: Free Press, 1969), chap. 7.

133. Martin Shefter, "The Emergence of the Political Machine," in Hawley et al., *Theoretical Perspectives on Urban Politics* (Englewood Cliffs, N.J.: Prentice-Hall, 1976), pp. 14–44; Merton, "The Latent Function."

134. Banfield and Wilson, *City Politics,* pp. 138–150.

135. Hamilton, "The Patron-Recipient Relationship"; Paul Peterson, "The Death of Maximum Feasible Participation," in Herrington Bryce, ed., *Urban Governance and Minorities* (New York: Praeger, 1976).

136. Gosnell, *Machine Politics,* p. 183.
137. Stone, *Urban Policy and Politics,* pp. 100–101.
138. Riordan, *Plunkitt of Tammany Hall,* p. 25.
139. Caraley, *City Governments and Urban Problems,* pp. 197–198; Lowi, "Foreword."
140. James Bryce, *Modern Democracies,* vol. 2 (New York: Macmillan, 1921), pp. 209–210.
141. See Mandelbaum, *Boss Tweed's New York,* p. 78; Charles Glaab and Theodore Brown, *A History of Urban America* (New York: Macmillan, 1967), pp. 207–208; Shefter, "The Emergence of the Political Machine"; Kantor and David, *The Dependent City,* pp. 114–126.
142. Upton Sinclair, *The Jungle* (New York: Signet, 1906).
143. Kantor and David, *The Dependent City,* p. 115.
144. See Zink, *City Bosses in the United States,* pp. 3–12.
145. See David Thelen, *The New Citizenship* (Columbia: University of Missouri Press, 1972).
146. Samuel Hays, "The Politics of Reform in Municipal Government in the Progressive Era," *Pacific Northwest Quarterly* 55 (October 1964); Alfred Chandler, Jr., "The Beginning of 'Big Business' in American History," *Business History Review* 33 (Spring 1959): 1–31; Yearly, *The Money Machines*; Kantor and David, *The Dependent City,* pp. 121–125.
147. Chudacoff, *The Evolution of American Urban Society,* pp. 148–149.

CHAPTER **8**

The City Council

City councils vary in terms of their authority and power, with the larger and more postindustrially advanced cities generally having stronger mayors and weaker city councils. Thus, like the urban political party, the council is another governmental conversion mechanism whose heyday seems to have come and gone, at least in America's larger urban areas. Consider New York City as an example; remember that this is one of the nation's potentially strongest city councils, endowed with full-time salaries and considerable staff assistance.

CASE STUDY Day in [the] Life of City Council

by Molly Ivins

"This is a great day for the Bronx," Councilman Stanley Simon said during yesterday's City Council meeting.

Councilman Simon, Democrat-Liberal of the Bronx, was referring to the successful passage of a bill naming the area adjacent to Van Cortlandt Park in the Bronx Van Cortlandt Village. Councilman Simon said the passage showed "people power at work." He said several community groups had considered the question and were unanimous in their approval.

It is often said that the chief work of the City Council is changing street names. Yesterday's Council meeting produced only one street name change—changing a section of Hollis Court Boulevard in Queens to Hollis Hills Terrace—made Van Cortlandt Village Van Cortlandt Village Square and set up a Columbus Council Triangle in Brooklyn. Columbus Council No. 126 of the Knights of Columbus has its quarters near the new Columbus Council Triangle. . . .

Subcommittee Meeting Held

Yesterday was the day of the Council's fortnightly meeting, scheduled for 1:30 P.M. But official business began at 11:30 with a meeting of the Consumer Affairs Committee's Subcommittee on the City-Wide Problem of Street Peddlers, with Arthur J. Katzman, as acting chairman.

According to the day's schedule, the meeting was to discuss the scope of a bill proposing to deal with the citywide problem. In council parlance, this is known as preconsideration. After preconsideration, a bill is introduced and then undergoes consideration. However, yesterday's meeting was not to lead even to preconsideration.

Councilman Katzman, Democrat of Forest Hills, Queens, apparently has a narrow sense of the risqué. He began the meeting by announcing, "Ladies and Gentlemen, there has evidently been some foul-up, if I may use the term." He went on to explain that the purpose of this meeting was to discuss the next meeting, to wit, a public hearing scheduled for October 6 at which the proposed legislation will be given preconsideration.

Mr. Katzman then outlined the proposed bill and called for suggestions about how best to organize and whom to notify concerning the October 6 meeting. He said he proposed to notify the Commissioner of Consumer Affairs, the various Chambers of Commerce and merchants associations. He did not mention notifying street peddlers.

Councilman Henry J. Stern, Liberal of Manhattan, apparently missed Mr. Katzman's earlier announcement, and began to discuss the bill substantively. He said he particularly approved of separating vendors into food vendors and nonfood vendors, which he likened to separating the plant and animal kingdoms. Mr. Stern has a reputation for talking whenever the opportunity arises, and also for reiterating the evidence. Mr. Katzman became noticeably annoyed with him, interrupted him and silenced him.

"I didn't call upon you to paraphrase what I said," Mr. Katzman snapped.

Councilman Stephen B. Kaufman, Democrat-Liberal of the Bronx, apparently was not attending when Mr. Katzman explained that state law required that food vendors be regulated by the Health Department and said he did not think it was a good idea. Mr. Katzman treated Mr. Kaufman more kindly than he had Mr. Stern.

Councilman Frderick E. Samuel, Democrat-Liberal of Manhattan, said that the trouble with peddlers on 125th Street was very serious, and that he hadn't heard anyone mention inviting the Uptown Chamber of Commerce.

Mr. Stern suggested that members of the public present at the meeting who were under the erroneous impression that this was to be a public hearing, be allowed to introduce themselves.

"No, no, no, Mr. Stern," Mr. Katzman said. "This meeting was not intended for the public at all."

It was finally resolved to everyone's satisfaction that the October 6 meeting would be for the public. The only peddler in attendance, who refused to give his name, said the reason more peddlers hadn't shown up was because they never paid their summonses and so were afraid of drawing public attention to themselves. He also said he thought the proposed legislation was "some kind of fix." . . .

At 12:30 P.M. a meeting of the Rules, Privileges and Elections Committee was convened to give unanimous approval to the redesignation of Dr. Daniel J. Paulo as a member of the Health and Hospitals Corporation. There were several gracious speeches of approval.

Given that councils dominated mayors in the urban governmental process as recently as the mid-nineteenth century, how did the trifling council described above come to be? Is this "Day in the Life" simply an aberration? To begin answering those questions, it is important first to put the contemporary scene into historical context, and then dissect council authority and operations, before concluding as to their degree of urban power, the implications, and the alternatives.

AUTHORITY WITHOUT POWER

There was ample suspicion of strong executives following the revolutionary war against the British monarchy. Consequently, the first mayor-council systems in the United States were legislature oriented. Mayors did little more than preside over council meetings; the council initiated all legislation and their committees supervised the various administrative functions. In addition, council members often served as justices of the peace and actually sat as a court when fully assembled.

Variations of this legislative domination lasted until the cities' problems finally overwhelmed them, and power came to be centralized in the hands of the political party "boss." For a variety of reasons, reform governments emerged in the postindustrial era; and if they did not reinvigorate the council, they at least weakened political parties and the office of the mayor.

As postindustrial problems simply became too much for these more decentralized governments to bear, however, the strong mayor-council systems began to reemerge, this time without the danger of political machine domination. It was not just to the mayor that the city council was surrendering power, however;

functions also were being surrendered to external governments, and in the most extreme cases, even to corporate-dominated finance control boards. Councils also were weakened by the political clout of the local mass media and an increasingly large and independent government bureaucracy.

What is particularly peculiar is that late twentieth-century city councils still look quite powerful on paper. Most of their formal authority has remained intact.

Political Authority

City charters still routinely lodge virtually all legislative authority in the hands of the city councils, even in strong-mayor systems. The councils must approve any city regulations, laws and budgetary allocations, any taxing or borrowing, and any public condemnation of private property. They also may conduct investigations, having the legal authority to subpoena witnesses and evidence. In a recent New York City example of such an investigation, the council looked into the safety of the city's 842 bridges. When the mayor's office was not immediately forthcoming with the documents requested, and when some arrived with blanked-out portions, the council threatened to resort to subpoenas. Soon, the requested information began to arrive.[1]

In addition, where a home-rule charter is in effect, councils may have the authority to change the city's governing structure, salaries, election formats, and so on. For example, they might vote to eliminate the city's sanitation department and have the trash collected by private firms, or they might replace at-large city council seats with members elected by districts.

Where the mayor's position is weaker, the council members normally must approve mayoral appointments and dismissals. They also most likely would have primary authority for supervising the operations of the various executive departments.

Last, according to most state constitutions, any function within the city's scope of authority that is not expressly accorded to the executive or judicial branches generally is presumed to rest with the legislative branch—in this case, the city council. The council's authority is summarized in the following list.

City Council Authority

Legislation	taxing, borrowing, spending, regulating, condemning private property
Investigations	information gathering, including subpoena power
Procedural changes	altering city functions, council size, electoral process (if home rule), etc.
Ratifications	approving some mayoral appointments and dismissals
Oversight	supervising operations of various city departments
Repository	retaining authority not allocated to the executive or judicial branches

Ordinances that the council passes normally must be signed by the city's chief executive (although vetoes can be overridden), and in certain circumstances the bills even must be ratified by popular referendum. Nonetheless, on paper anyway, the city council remains a central player in the game. The reality, on the other hand, is quite another story.

Political Power

> Part of the mythology of our time is that legislative bodies do all the legislating. Actually most legislation in this country (at all levels of government) is done by administrators.[2]

As suggested by Ivins's account of a day in the life of the New York City Council, councils do not spend most of their time addressing pressing city problems such as homelessness, crime, poverty, health care, or education. Instead, council meetings generally are devoted to relatively trivial matters, such as changing the name of a street or park, deciding whether an alley is to be one-way, altering a detail in the city's building code, responding to pet control and traffic complaints, selling a small piece of city property, or postponing the condemnation of an abandoned building somewhere in one councilperson's district.[3]

But what about the raising, authorization, and appropriation of millions of dollars in government funds? What about the passage of vital laws and regulations? When does this occur, and is this not where the council leaves its most important imprint on the life of the city?

The answer is yes, they do pass all those things ultimately. However, their imprint is slight whether theirs is a strong or weak mayor system because, at least in larger cities, what they pass is almost always crafted somewhere else and essentially "rubber-stamped" by the city council. New York Councilman Henry Stein noted wryly that in reality city council members do not even qualify as rubber stamps because "at least a rubber stamp leaves an impression."[4]

Wallace Sayre and Herbert Kaufman studied 19 New York City budget proposals. In 15 of those 19 years, the council made no significant alterations whatsoever. In the other four, their changes amounted to less than .02 percent of the total money requested.[5] Despite an occasional blustery public speech opposing a mayoral proposition, this ultimate deference is a reality that appears to repeat itself year after year not only in New York City but in most other large cities as well.[6]

There are a few exceptions, of course. Council members can be expected to fight proposed structural changes that would reduce their authority or job security, such as eliminating any administrative oversight they might have (especially if the change will affect their ability to deliver services to their key electoral constituents) or introducing a new election system that might in some way jeopardize some of their remarkably safe seats. Also, when partisanship, personalities, egos, or factionalism leave the mayor and the council at odds, the council may obstruct the mayor's will—at least for a time.[7]

Overall, however, whether it be the city's various budgetary proposals, laws, regulations, or whatever, most are drafted somewhere in the executive bureaucracy and presented to the council. On almost all major items of business, the council is saddled with the executive's agenda, meaning that the executive branch proposes what they will consider. They may modify the proposal a bit, or even reject it, but they are still functioning in a reactive posture, reflecting one of the most fundamental maxims of politics: the person who controls the options considered has gone a long way toward controlling the outcome (the power of agenda-setting).[8] There are several interrelated reasons that explain why councils have been reduced to such a subordinate position; these are summarized below.

City Council Weaknesses

Part-time job	limited salaries and office space
Minimal staff	limited research and clerical help
No deficits	requirement that any increased spending must be accompanied by a corresponding revenue increase or budget cut
Factionalism	internal splits along lines of ideology, race, class, ethnicity, and gender
Invisibility	limited regular media coverage
Atomization	position security dependent on serving primarily one's own constituency
Uninterested interest groups	lack of primary access to interest groups, who take their money, information, and supporters to the executive power centers

Part-Time Job.   Most large city mayors now hold full-time, full-salary positions, as do most of their administrators. This is not the case for their city council counterparts. Except in a handful of the very largest cities—Los Angeles, New York, Chicago, Philadelphia, Detroit, Boston, Pittsburgh, and Seattle—most council positions offer only part-time employment, resulting in council members who are largely amateurs.[9] Pay is a major reason this is not a full-time occupation. In Memphis, for example, a councilperson receives only $6,000 per year; even this amount is more than a number of their counterparts receive in other cities.[10]

In sharp contrast to their administrative counterparts, councilpersons rarely even have their own individual offices. It also is seldom the norm for the council to meet as a body more than one afternoon or evening per week, unless they hold a special session; and "sunshine laws" often virtually prohibit councilpersons even from talking to one another outside formal and open committee or full-council meetings.[11]

Minimal Staff.   After studying the budgetary processes in Cleveland, Detroit, and Pittsburgh, John Crecine had little trouble determining the major reason councils have come to play such an insignificant budgetary role.

> The primary reason is more one of cognitive and informational constraints than lack of interest. The city budget is a complex document when it reaches the council. The level of detail makes it virtually impossible to consider all or even a majority of items independently. The sheer volume of information to be processed

limits the ability of a council, without its own budget staff, to consider the budget in a sophisticated or complex manner.[12]

The mayor can draw on the resources of thousands of executive bureaucrats to gather and analyze information and then utlimately draft legislative proposals. Most councils, on the other hand, have few, if any, professional or research staff and are lucky to have a handful of paid secretaries whom they all must share.[13] Even though they may have a limited budget for research work done by external agents, they are still at a significant disadvantage in any effort to challenge the mayor's conclusions or to produce alternative legislative proposals.

This situation is most obvious when juxtaposed to the complexity of much big city policy today. Designing and operating a waste management or water treatment system for a million people requires the expertise of engineers and involves sophisticated science and technology. Few individual council members come to their positions with the kind of specialized personal knowledge to question these engineers, or police, fire, finance, education, or other experts. As this "part-time" job already absorbs between 10 and 20 of their hours per week,[14] they are not in a position independently to develop the expertise needed. Thus, without their own in-house specialists in these areas, they simply cannot challenge many of the city's most important and expensive projects and practices. Instead, they will remain reliant on the information emanating from the executive bureaucracy.

No Deficits.   Further complicating the process is the prohibition against deficits in city operating budgets. Unlike Congress, city councils must confront the budgetary proposal as a zero-sum game, meaning that anything they add must be accompanied by a cut somewhere else or an increase in revenues. Therefore, they are forced to weigh the entire budget as a package, one that has been balanced carefully by the executive branch. They do not have the luxury of treating each budget item independently.[15]

Factionalism.   Another problem councils have is their inability to unite and speak with a single voice. In diverse and conflictual large cities in particular, there is a tendency for the council to factionalize, whether it be along the lines of ideology, ethnicity, or race.[16] It is difficult for a majority faction to develop and remain intact,[17] especially without strong political parties to meld the varying parochial interests. Such lack of cohesion is made even worse when the council president is separately elected rather than chosen from among the council ranks. With these internal divisions, a council can rarely rise in opposition to a mayor who brings so many structural advantages to the process.

Invisibility.   The mass media find it much easier to cover a singular mayor rather than the multiheaded city council. As a result, all media sources cover the mayor's office and are present when he or she issues a press release or calls a press conference. This attention is also given often to top bureaucratic administrators like the chief of police or the superintendent of schools. Despite often extensive reform-directed regulations requiring councils and their various committees to hold only open public meetings, the regular activities of the council receive scant attention by comparison. The city council cannot count on ready access to the headlines. Most urban residents are not likely to know much about the activities of the city council and generally cannot name more than a couple of council members.[18]

Atomization.   There is little incentive for councils to court a high public profile. City council representatives, like their state legislative counterparts, seldom lose bids for reelection.[19] If they provide adequate service to their constituents and avoid public controversy, they are seldom even seriously challenged at the polls;[20] and, as most cities place no limits on the number of consecutive terms that can be served, they can remain in office almost indefinitely if they choose to do so.[21] The disadvantages of engaging in a public confrontation with the mayor may be greater than the gains given the mayor's opportunities to criticize a council member in the media and reduce services to his or her supporters.[22]

Although some councilpersons are becoming more independent, activist, and assertive,[23] and many at least see themselves that way,[24] there are still a sizable number of them who fit legislative categories such as "ritualist"[25] or "spectator."[26]

> *Ritualists* are legislators who go through the strictly necessary motions of attending meetings, voting, and performing other parliamentary routines for their own sake without much consciousness of the policy or power implications involved. *Spectators* are passive, submissive, unambitious individuals, who lack clearly defined political aims and whose chief objectives are simply to be accepted by the legislative group and to watch the legislative process as entertainment.[27]

At the very least, most individual councilpersons can be expected to actively pursue the interests of their particular constituencies to the degree necessary to remain in office. Thus, even more problematic than factionalism is the tendency toward atomization, or "pothole politics." An exchange captured by Oliver Williams and Charles Adrian is not at all atypical. As one Michigan city councilperson declared to another, "You bastard, you had three more blocks of black-topping in your ward last year than I had, you'll not get another vote from me until I get three extra blocks."[28]

Interest Groups.   Interest groups, cognizant of these realities, often take their large campaign contributions, bundles of information, and blocs of voters to the executive branch where the action is. Thus, relatively short of money, information, interest group supporters, and media attention, individual councilpersons find it almost impossible to put together the kind of large popular coalitions that would be necessary to challenge the mayor or circumvent the bureaucracy.

However, one should not conclude that city councils are free of lobbyist pressure. The few persons attending council meetings almost always come because they want something. Listen to political science professor, turned city councilman, Robert Morlan.

CASE STUDY   The Public Hearing

The new councilman or board member soon learns that few if any visitors will attend who do not have an axe to grind. In the few moments before a meeting is formally opened, members survey the audience, recognizing certain groups and the cause they represent, jestingly speculating with one another about those they do not recognize. "What do they want?" is the standard question. . . .

Citizens participate from the audience in debate, though, of course, only when recognized to do so, and both the council and members of the audience frequently address one another by first names. Unhappily, from the board member's perspective, while groups of citizens will from time to time appear to support a favorite project, few persons attend with sufficient continuity to gain a broad understanding, and when really tough decisions have to be made, those who are sympathetic to the position of the board are prone to shy away from combat and leave the board to face its critics completely devoid of the inestimable help of visible public backing.[29]

Consequently, even though they often are denied the benefit of sustained interest group support, city councilpersons are still subject to the wrath of these blocs. At times, such narrowly focused pressure apparently can sway council votes.[30]

IMPLICATIONS

There are at least two major implications of the evolution of the weak council. Important voices are lost in the policy-making process and less popularly representative political forces tend to arise to fill the void.

Surrogates

Into the power void left by a weak city council tend to march the mayor, the bureaucracy, and the mass media. The bureaucracy, however, is made up almost entirely of insulated civil servants; and although they often live in the city, they have not been elected or in most cases even appointed by those who have been elected, and they tend to develop agency-related agendas of their own. The mass media, on the other hand, owe their livelihood to the general public, their audience. Nevertheless, these unelected agenda setters often have business-related priorities that can and do run contrary to those of the general citizenry. At least the mayor is an elected official; yet, having run citywide, he or she cannot possibly be as attuned to grass-roots interests as are district representatives. Thus, in the absence of stronger city councils, individuals and interest groups are left with far more insulated targets.

Democracy

Council representatives, particularly if they represent specific districts, are in the best position to aggregate and articulate grass-roots interests. However, when councilpersons are reduced to the role of small-time favor traders at best, their constituents' voices end up far removed from the major governmental decision making of the city. They have less opportunity to present alternative ideas. Consequently, there is the very real possibility that public alienation and hostility will build over time, particularly in lower-income neighborhoods. Some of this pent-up frustration can be heard, for instance, by listening to virtually any of the talk-radio programs that are proliferating throughout the large cities of the country.

ALTERNATIVES

If a stronger council voice is desired, there are some lessons to be learned from Washington. Congress has been able to increase its influence as a result of having larger office staffs and budgets as well as by creating its own Congressional Budget Office. With such mechanisms in place, some form of zero-base budgeting might also have its advantages. Last, weak-mayor and council-manager systems have been employed, at least in medium-sized cities, to help reestablish the interinstitutional balance of power. Some mechanisms to strengthen the council are summarized below.

Alternatives for Strengthening City Councils

Staffing	more legal counsel, researchers, accountants, pollsters, clericals, and public relations people for councilpersons and committees
Legislative budget office	professional staff to analyze executive projections and budgets, besides generating council's own
Zero-base budgeting	more comprehensive budgetary review by requiring every agency annually to rejustify both its existence and everything it does
Weak mayor-council system	assumption of more executive and legislative power
City manager	assumption of more executive and legislative power indirectly through a city manager

Staffing

To enhance city council power significantly would require sizable increases in paid staff both for individual council members and for council committees. They need more legal counsel, researchers, accountants, pollsters, public relations people, and many more clericals. Without such increases in staff or in the budgets available to hire outside professionals to do the work, councils cannot begin to compete with the vast resources a mayor has at his or her disposal. In fiscally strained postindustrial cities, however, these additional outlays may prove difficult to obtain.

Legislative Budget Office

By the early 1970s, the United States Congress was feeling rather impotent in the entire federal budget-making process. For the most part, its members were left waiting for the executive branch to compile and introduce specific budget proposals. They found themselves doing little other than incremental tinkering with those externally generated plans. In essence, their agenda was being set for them.

To gain some influence on the budget process Congress passed the 1974 Congressional Budget and Impoundment Control Act. Among other things, it set up the Congressional Budget Office (CBO). Composed of research professionals, this office was to analyze various budgetary proposals and economic projections so that Congress could generate its own independent budgetary figures and ultimately its own budgetary proposals.

At the local level, New York is an example of a city that used its charter revision process to create a Legislative Office of Budget Review with the charter commission's expressed goal of "substantially strengthening the Council." Staffed by trained professionals, in two years' time the budget office issued some 22 reports analyzing the mayor's capital borrowing, budget and tax proposals, revenue estimates, and agency requests. However, it was plagued by internal bickering between the city council and the city's board of estimate,[31] both of whom had been granted jurisdiction over the body. Five years after the voters had approved it, the council cut the budget office's funding, although it did make an effort to retain a larger professional staff of its own for the purpose of conducting similar analyses.[32]

Zero-Base Budgeting

In zero-base budgeting, all government budgets are reconsidered each fiscal year as though there were no past budget. In other words, instead of incremental tinkering around the margins of existing allocations, the legislature reconsiders whether anything at all should be spent in that area. Each year every agency must justify its very existence and everything it does. The idea is to reduce the bureaucratic momentum that tends to develop for existing programs as they proceed from one year to the next with little comprehensive review. Just how realistic this method is in dealing with large complex agencies and budgets is very much open to debate, however.[33]

Weak Mayor-Council System

A more frontal assault on the accumulated power of the strong mayor is to opt for a different governmental structure, such as eliminating the strong-mayor system altogether. Under a weak-mayor arrangement, more of the formal administrative responsibility falls to the council. The council often will appoint those agency heads not elected by the general public, and council members may serve automatically on certain administrative boards and commissions; for example, the airport commission may comprise the mayor, city treasurer, and three councilpersons. In addition, a committee of the council normally will have the responsibility of preparing the city budget, and the council even may appoint the city controller whose job is to assemble budgetary requests and monitor all city spending.[34]

This system has a number of liabilities, however, particularly in a large, complex postindustrial city. It was designed for a different era, before the introduction of modern management techniques for centralized budgeting, personnel, and purchasing. Its reliance on informality and amateurs leaves it open to abuse. As an example, if the city's purchasing agent is not a civil servant and is appointed directly by the council, that person may well slant city contracts to the wards of the councilpersons who appointed him or her regardless of the economic efficiency involved. More important, the system does not allow for the executive leadership necessary to prioritize and coordinate activities in the interests of the city as a whole, a particular dilemma in complex, problem-prone, and fiscally strapped large postindustrial cities.

Despite such weaknesses, some large cities continue to employ variations of the weak-mayor arrangement. Chicago, not yet fully adjusted to the demise of its political machine, continues to exhibit many of these characteristics. The city council remains strong; and, as it demonstrated in the first few years of Harold Washington's administration, it was capable of battling the mayor to a standstill. In addition, California cities as large as San Francisco and Los Angeles rely on a host of independent administrative boards and commissions, so independent that they even undercut the power of the city council.[35]

Charles Adrian and Charles Press speak for most contemporary urban analysts, however, when they conclude that "the structure of the weak-mayor–council plan is not regarded as being satisfactory for modern [large city] government. It is clumsy, uncoordinated, and has, for a long time, been declining in use for all but the smallest cities."[36]

City Manager

The council-manager form is currently the arrangement of choice in the majority of American cities with populations exceeding 100,000 people. These include cities as large as Dallas, San Diego, Kansas City, Phoenix, and Cincinnati. Two-thirds of those in the 100,000–200,000 population range have opted for it, and it is particularly popular in the more ideologically conservative Sun Belt and suburbs.[37]

Origins. The city manager concept formally began in 1911 with reformer Richard Childs and his National Short Ballot Association; however, a variation was first employed in Staunton, Virginia, in 1908. In 1913, Dayton, Ohio, became the first large city to introduce it, and by 1915 it had been adopted in some 49 cities. Five years later it could be found in 158 of them, and it is currently used in more than 2,000.[38]

Essentially it was a plan drawn from the corporate model, an attempt to make government run more like America's large corporations. Instead of stockholders choosing a board of directors which in turn chooses a chief executive officer to run the firm, voters choose a small city council which in turn chooses a professional manager to run the city. Ultimately the goal was to remove politics from administration.[39]

Operations.   The charters of virtually all large council-manager cities designate the manager as the chief administrative officer. Like his or her strong mayor counterpart, the manager normally may appoint and remove department heads, not only without specific council approval but also without any council interference. Unencumbered by the need (or even the authority[40]) to perform ceremonial duties and otherwise to cultivate an electoral constituency, the manager thus is freed to focus on efficient and impartial administration of policy.

Placing most of the city's administrative responsibilities in the hands of a well-compensated[41] technocrat who serves at the pleasure of the city council (and who often may not even veto their legislation) both reduces the introduction of political considerations in administration and enhances council input overall.[42] Yet, the larger the city, the more politically influential the manager is likely to become given the corresponding increase in the number and size of administrative duties. Beyond carrying out the law, for example, the manager's office also will compile and submit the city's budget. Like the mayor in the mayor-council system, the manager is the only city official who has full-time responsibility for the operations of the entire city government and who is thus positioned to field and present budgetary requests from the city's various agencies.[43]

As might be expected, city councilpersons and city managers tend to differ in their view of the appropriate policy role for the manager. As Ronald Loveridge found, managers see themselves as "expected to exert policy leadership on most demands or issues before the city," while councilpersons are far more likely to see the manager as appropriately confined to being a staff assistant or adviser.[44] Despite working at the pleasure of the council, managers continue to exert considerable legislative power and will at times even appeal to the public directly. They will, however, often stop short of publicly disagreeing with the council or upstaging a popularly elected weak mayor.[45]

When the International City Managers' Association first established a code of ethics in 1924, it explicitly stated: "No manager should take an active part in politics." By 1938, the code sanctioned the provision of "information and advice" to council, and by 1972 the code allowed the manager to "submit policy proposals to elected officials [and] provide them with facts and advice for making decisions and setting community goals." Gone entirely was any reference to staying in the background.[46]

Beyond legislative prerogatives, attention and responsibility often will turn to the city's singular voice, its chief executive, in time of crisis. In some council-manager cities, the city's charter explicitly reserves that role for the weak mayor; but just as often, if there is any formal mention of the responsibility at all, it will be reserved for the manager. In San Diego, the city charter states: "In case of general conflagration, rioting, flood, or other emergency menacing life and property, the manager shall marshall all the forces of the different Departments of the City for the maintenance of the general security, and shall have the power to deputize.''[47]

In retrospect, council weakness appears to be as much a function of city size and complexity as anything else, for whether the chief executive is independently elected and laden with considerable formal authority or is functionally subordinate to the council on the organizational chart, the end result tends to be the same. In large and complex cities, important power will gravitate to the city's number one administrator, particularly when those cities are plagued with postindustrial problems.[48]

Managerial Styles.   Managers have developed at least three different leadership styles. First there are the *technical administrators.* Generally operating in relatively homogeneous cities, they make a series of routine decisions in a very nonconflictual political atmosphere. Second, where a city has major factions but one dominates, the manager acts more as a *factional agent,* representing the wishes of the dominant faction. Finally, where a large city operates within the unstable swirl of a variety of factions, the manager must become an adept *tightrope artist,* capable of brokering conflicts and always remaining on the right bandwagon as political power ebbs, flows, and shifts.[49]

> The most persuasive line of argument supporting the critics of the council-manager system is that since even with his larger resources, an elective mayor is not often effective in leading his city to establish policies that have a significant impact in the alleviation of its ills, a city manager, with his smaller resources, lower prestige, and inability to use all the roles the mayor plays in mutually supportive combinations, must necessarily be less effective still.[50]

Problems.   Precisely because the council-manager system functions most precariously in cities with large heterogeneous populations, high levels of conflict, and shifting factional sands, we find it far less often in any of the larger American cities. Some 80 percent of the cities larger than 500,000 people have opted for the mayor-council arrangement, and the figure is nearly 100 percent for the older industrial cities with more diverse populations.

In a large city, there is a tremendous need for someone who is responsive to group demands and capable of brokering conflicting demands so that a sizable political coalition can be constructed, a coalition capable of securing both council passage and bureaucratic implementation of needed city legislation. Unfortunately, the track record in council-manager cities is not good in this regard.[51]

The manager starts with at least two key disadvantages. First, he or she was never elected, thus there is no electoral constituency to rally. Second, as the manager serves at the pleasure of the council, he or she is in no position to take on the council, or any large part of it, in a public battle. The manager lacks both the public legitimacy and the job security to be a public leader; he or she also must act within the generally accepted ethical constraints previously noted.[52]

City managers soon learn that urban problems are not only technical. Solving them is a good deal more complicated than simply being able adequately to assess the roots of the problem and determine the most cost-efficient way to deal with it. At least as important to success is an understanding of the politics involved. It may be more effective to have individual police officers walk beats than to have two-person squad car patrols, but convincing the police officers' union to adopt such a policy will be very difficult. It may make sense to concentrate virtually all the city's fire stations closest to the older, more fire-prone neighborhoods, but such a decision will bring an outcry from the better-off neighborhoods if a proposal is introduced to close their existing fire stations. Such changes require political leadership, a quality that most managers either lack or seldom dare employ. Thus, if strong mayors are proving incapable of coping with the complex dilemmas of the postindustrial city, how can we expect a city manager to handle them?

Last, questions also arise even in terms of the most basic goal of reducing politics in administration. The term *politics,* as used here, refers more to electoral politics. Not subject to periodic popular election, the manager is indeed freed of a certain amount of direct political pressure. However, inasmuch as the manager can still be lobbied after appointment, such tactics may well increase the influence of strategically located insider groups and individuals such as developers and other corporate elites while at the same time limiting the influence of the general public who are mobilized primarily through elections. Politics continues, but access has been narrowed.[53]

CONCLUSION

Overall, the size and complexity of governments in large American cities seem to dictate stronger chief executives, bureaucracies and mass media, and a weaker city council. This configuration seems particularly realistic when these governments are forced to continue to expand in order to cope with the wide range of postindustrial problems. The policial power of the mayors, bureaucrats, and media will grow while that of the city council declines.

What is less clear is whether a stronger city council is really desirable, and if so, desirable for whom. Even from a democratic perspective, it is not entirely certain that there would be gains. At any given point in time nearly one-quarter of all council-persons have been appointed to fill unexpired terms, thus they have not even been elected.[54] When they have been popularly chosen, it normally has been in an election marked by a very low turnout, and they will continue to be reelected by a comparably small electorate who knows little about them and seldom even attempts to communicate directly with them.[55] As council members hold low-paying, part-time positions, they tend to view themselves more as volunteers than representatives and to vote often according to their own personal preferences.[56]

By reducing some checks and balances, the strong-mayor arrangement actually has the potential to make corporate domination a bit more difficult. When there is a balance of power between the executive and legislative branches, such counter-vailing force tends to result in a large degree of political stasis, just as the founding fathers envisioned. It is easier to block than to pass new legislation, and powerful private groups learn quickly where the bottlenecks exist. Thus, unless conditions become so bad that civil unrest occurs, such city governments have a tendency merely to tinker around the periphery of the political-economic status quo. For those economic forces already dominating the private sector, that can be a blessing. New taxes and regulations can be blocked while at least a limited number of accumulation expenditures continue to be provided.

We are back to the same basic dilemma confronted when considering both postindustrial political realities and the value of stronger political parties. Will more centralization of political power ultimately serve more fully to empower the average urban citizen? As indicated in chapter 6, postindustrialism leaves city governments with very few alternatives, no matter who has the political authority. Mobile capital interests must be pleased or they will invest elsewhere, dooming the city. Nevertheless, given the narrowing window of social policy choices, it would seem that a more centralized political system headed by a popularly elected strong mayor stands to be more responsive to the public's interests in general. Although the track record of most mayors has not been particularly encouraging in terms of redistributing local wealth and power, a strong mayor simply seems to pose more of a potential threat to corporate domination than does a more parochial and disjointed council-dominated alternative.

Finally, as will be true for both mayors and city administrators, who holds office and under what set of political rules does matter. The political outcome is not wholly predetermined by economic realities. However, those economic realities set finite parameters on the political agenda, and it takes exceptionally strong and progressive political leadership to aggregate the popular forces necessary to press the boundaries of those parameters.

Unfortunately, the foxes are being asked to liberate the chicken coop. Like their mayoral, managerial, and administrative counterparts, although not normally drawn from the boardrooms of the city's largest corporations, most councilpersons are relatively affluent, middle-aged white men, holding full-time jobs in business, law, or one of the other professions. Admittedly, there are more exceptions as the demographics change in the postindustrial cities, but this is still a reasonably reliable profile for large cities overall.[57] Those lobbying them will be disproportionately middle and upper class as well.[58] It should come as no surprise that many of these councilpersons hold ideologically conservative views, such as anti-unionism.[59] Given these realities, redistribution of wealth and power is not likely to be very high on the city council's priority list.

NOTES

1. See *New York Times*, February 1, 1991.
2. Robert Lorch, *State and Local Politics: The Great Entanglement* (Englewood Cliffs, N.J.: Prentice-Hall, 1983), pp. 299–300.
3. For some empirical evidence of this phenomenon, see Wallace Sayre and Herbert Kaufman, *Governing New York City* (New York: Norton, 1965), pp. 611–612; Alan

Klevit, "City Councils and Their Functions in Local Government," *Municipal Year Book 1972* (Washington, D.C.: International City Managers' Association, 1972), pp. 15–54.

4. Quoted in the *New York Times*, April 15, 1981.

5. Sayre and Kaufman, *Governing New York City*, p. 614. For a general update, see Jewell Bellush and Dick Netzer, eds., *Urban Politics, New York Style* (New York: Sharpe, 1990).

6. Edward Banfield, *Big City Politics* (New York: Random House, 1966).

7. J. Leiper Freeman, "A Case Study of the Legislative Process in Municipal Government," in John C. Wahlke and Heinz Eulau, eds., *Legislative Behavior* (Glencoe, Ill.: Free Press, 1959); William H. Brown, Jr., and Charles Gilbert, "Capital Programming in Phildelphia," *American Political Science Review* 54 (September 1960): 659–668; Ed Ainsworth, *Maverick Mayor* (Garden City, N.Y.: Doubleday, 1966), p. 186; Iola Hessler, *29 Ways to Govern a City* (Cincinnati: Hamilton County Research Foundation, 1966).

8. Cortus Koehler, "Policy Development and Legislative Oversight in Council Manager Cities," *Public Administration Review* 33 (September/October, 1973): 433–441.

9. Charles Adrian and Charles Press, *Governing Urban America* (New York: McGraw-Hill, 1977), pp. 212–213; Raymond Bancroft, *America's Mayors and Councilmen* (Washington, D.C.: National League of Cities, 1974), p. 28; Kenneth Prewitt, *The Recruitment of Political Leaders* (Indianapolis: Bobbs-Merrill, 1970), p. 101; James Q. Wilson, *The Amateur Democrat* (Chicago: University of Chicago Press, 1962).

10. See *A National Survey of City Council Members* (Washington, D.C.: National League of Cities, 1980); and for further discussion of the connection between pay and part-time status, see Louise White, "Improving the Goal-Setting Process in Local Government," *Public Administration Review* 42 (January/February 1982): 78.

11. Although the entire council is not likely to meet more than one day per week, committees normally will meet between those sessions, at least in larger cities that employ more extensive committee structures.

12. John Crecine, "A Simulation of Municipal Budgeting: The Impact of a Problem Environment," in Ira Sharkansky, ed., *Policy Analysis in Political Science* (Chicago: Markham Publishing, 1970), pp. 291–292.

13. Ibid.

14. See *A National Survey of City Council Members*.

15. Crecine, "A Simulation of Municipal Budgeting."

16. For a case study of this phenomenon, see Robert Huckshorn and C. E. Young, "A Study of Voting Splits on City Councils in Los Angeles County," *Western Political Quarterly* 13 (June 1960): 479–497.

17. For a good case study, see Freeman, "A Case Study of the Legislative Process," pp. 228–237.

18. Adrian and Press, *Governing Urban America*, p. 160.

19. Marcus Pohlmann, "The Electoral Impact of Partisanship and Incumbency Reconsidered: An Extension to Low Salience Elections," *Urban Affairs Quarterly* 13 (June 1978): 495–503; John Kirlin, "Electoral Conflict and Democracy in American Cities," *Journal of Politics* 37 (February 1975): 262–269.

20. See Duane Lockard, *The Politics of State and Local Government* (New York: Macmillan, 1963), pp. 325, 333; Banfield, *Big City Politics*, pp. 22–23.

21. See Mary Schellinger, "Today's Local Policy Makers: A Council Profile," *Baseline Data Report* 20 (Washington, D.C.: International City Managers' Association, July/August 1988).

It also should be noted, however, that the turnover rate is relatively high by legislative standards. Thus, a majority of councilpersons are likely to be serving their first term at any point in time, a figure similar to what can be found in state legislatures, but considerably higher than comparable figures for the United States Congress. Apparently a sizable number of councilpersons step aside during a term or choose not to seek reelection. This may be at least in part because the position did not turn out to be nearly as powerful or prestigious as many anticipated. For example, see David Berman, *State and Local Politics* (Dubuque, Ia.: William C. Brown, 1990), p. 238.

22. Ainsworth, *Maverick Mayor*, pp. 190–191.
23. Michael Deeb "Municipal Council Members: Changing Roles and Functions," *National Civic Review* 68 (September 1979): 411–416; Kenneth Prewitt and William Nowlin, "Political Ambitions and the Behavior of Incumbent Politicians," *Western Political Quarterly* 22 (June 1969): 298–308.
24. Bryan Downes, "Municipal Social Rank and the Characteristics of Local Political Leaders," *Midwest Journal of Political Science* 12 (November 1968): 514–537; Bancroft, *America's Mayors and Councilmen*, p. 59.
25. See John Wahlke, Heinz Eulau, William Buchanan et al., *The Legislative System* (New York: Wiley, 1962), pp. 249–252.
26. See James David Barber, *The Lawmakers* (New Haven, Conn.: Yale University Press, 1965), pp. 23–66.
27. Demetrios Caraley, *City Governments and Urban Problems* (Englewood Cliffs, N.J.: Prentice-Hall, 1977), p. 245.
28. Quoted in Oliver Williams and Charles Adrian, *Four Cities* (Philadelphia: University of Pennsylvania Press, 1963), p. 264. For other examples, see White, "Improving the Goal-Setting," p. 77; Huckshorn and Young, "A Study of Voting Splits."
29. Robert Morlan, "Life on the City Council," in Robert Morlan and Leroy Hardy, eds., *Politics in California* (Belmont, Calif.: Dickenson Publishing Company, 1968), pp. 103–104. Excerpted in Berman, *State and Local Politics*, pp. 251–252.
30. Robert Horgan, "City Council Decisions," *Nation's Cities* 2 (September 1972): 57–61.
31. New York City's board of estimate is a relatively unique legislative body. It was created in part because the city actually encompasses five separate counties, and the result is a veritable bicameral legislature of sorts, similar in a way to the more common bicameral councils, many of which survived until they were streamlined in the twentieth century. But what makes this arrangement particularly unique is the presence of administrators on the board. The board, the upper house, consists of the five county (or "borough") presidents, the mayor, the city controller, and the president of city council. Among its more important prerogatives is its authority to review all budget modifications of more than $10,000.
32. *New York Times*, November 28, 1980.
33. Lance LeLoup, *Budgetary Politics* (Brunswick, Ohio: King's Court, 1977), pp. 236–237.
34. Adrian and Press, *Governing Urban America*, pp. 154–156.
35. For a study of the origins of the legislative agenda in Los Angeles, see Harry Reynolds, "The Career Public Service and Statute Lawmaking," *Western Political Quarterly* 18 (September 1965): 621–639.
36. Adrian and Press, *Governing Urban America*, p. 158.
37. For a discussion of its popularity in the suburbs, see Richard Stillman, *The Modern City Manager* (Washington, D.C.: International City Managers' Association, 1974); Robert Wood, *Suburbia: Its People and Their Politics* (Boston: Houghton Mifflin, 1959), pp. 183–186.
38. *Municipal Yearbook* (Washington, D.C.: International City Managers' Association, 1990), Table 1/8. For a general history of the plan, see Richard Childs, *The First Fifty*

Years of the Council Manager Plan of Municipal Government (New York: National Municipal League, 1969).

39. See *Model City Charter*, 6th ed. (New York: National Municipal League, 1964).

40. For a discussion of common charter constraints, see Charles Ridley, *The Role of the City Manager in Policy Formulation* (Chicago: International City Managers' Association, 1958), p. 52.

41. See Roger Lubin, "How Should Managers Be Paid?" *Public Management* 63 (1981): 2–6.

42. For a defense of council-manager systems, see James Svara, *Official Leadership in the City* (New York: Oxford University Press, 1989).

43. James Svara, "Dichotomy and Duality: Reconceptualizing the Relationship Between Policy and Administration in Council-Manager Cities," *Public Administration Review* 45 (January/February 1985): 221–232; Charles Adrian, "A Study of Three Communities," *Public Administration Review* 18 (1985): 208–214; Ridley, *The Role of the City Manager*, pp. 3–4, 19; Ronald Loveridge, *City Managers in Legislative Politics* (Indianapolis: Bobbs-Merrill, 1971), p. 112; Gladys Kammerer, "Role Diversity of City Managers," *Administrative Science Quarterly* 8 (March 1964): 434.

44. See Loveridge, *City Managers in Legislative Politics*, p. 24.

45. Robert Boynton and Deil Wright, "Mayor-Manager Relationships in Large Council-Manager Cities," *Public Administration Review* 31 (January/February 1971): 26–38; Loveridge, *City Managers in Legislative Politics*; Gladys Kammerer, *City Managers in Politics* (Gainesville, Fla.: University of Florida Press, 1962).

  The (weak) mayor has come to be popularly elected in a majority of council-manager systems, even though he or she normally will play little more than a ceremonial role, other than often also being a member of the city council.

46. See Koehler, "Policy Development and Legislative Oversight in Council Manager Cities"; Heywood Sanders, "The Government of American Cities: Continuity and Change in Structure," *Municipal Year Book, 1982* (Washington, D.C.: International City Managers' Association, 1982), pp. 180–181; Caraley, *City Governments and Urban Problems*, pp. 231–232; Charles Adrian, "Leadership and Decision-Making in Manager Cities," *Public Administration Review* 18 (Summer 1958): 208–213; Karl Bosworth, "The Manager Is a Politician," *Public Administration Review* 18 (Spring 1959): 216–222; Charles Harrell and D. G. Weiford, "The City Manager and the Policy Process," *Public Administration Review* 18 (Spring 1959); B. James Kweder, *The Roles of Manager, Mayor, and Councilmen in Policy Making* (Institute of Government, University of North Carolina at Chapel Hill, 1965).

47. San Diego City Charter, Article V, sec. 28, 1961, as quoted in Caraley, *City Governments and Urban Problems*, p. 231.

48. Actually, there is some evidence to suggest that the city's elected officials are often more than happy to see the city manager identified as the official responsible for dealing with many of these nearly intractable urban problems. For example, see John Nalbardian, "The Evolution of Local Governance," *Public Management* 69 (June 1987): 2–5; William Donaldson, "Continuing Education for City Managers," *Public Administration Review* 33 (November–December 1973): 504–508.

49. I have borrowed these conceptualizations from Demetrios Caraley, although to my knowledge they have not appeared in any of his written work.

50. Caraley, *City Governments and Urban Problems*, p. 235.

51. Delbert Taebel, "Managers and Riots," *National Civic Review* 57 (September 1968): 554–555; Robert Lineberry and Edmund Fowler, "Reformism and Public Policies in American Cities," *American Political Science Review* 61 (September 1967):

701–716; Williams and Adrian, *Four Cities*; Albert Karnig, "Private-Regarding Policy, Civil Rights Groups, and the Mediating Impact of Municipal Reforms," *American Journal of Political Science* 19 (February 1975): 91–106.

52. Ridley, *The Role of the City Manager*.
53. For a good general discussion of this phenomenon, see George Frederickson, ed., *Ideal and Practice in Council-Manager Government* (Washington, D.C.: International City Managers' Association, 1989).
54. Thomas Dye, *Politics in States and Communities* (Englewood Cliffs, N.J.: Prentice-Hall, 1985), pp. 304–309.
55. See discussion above concerning advantages of incumbency at this level, as well as Elaine Sharp, "Citizen-Initiated Contacting of Government Officials and Socio-Economic Status," *American Political Science Review* 76 (March 1982): 109–115.
56. Bancroft, *America's Mayors and Councilmen*; Heinz Eulau and Kenneth Prewitt, *Labyrinths of Democracy* (Indianapolis: Bobbs-Merrill, 1973), p. 407; Prewitt, *The Recruitment of Political Leaders*, chap. 8; Downes, "Municipal Social Rank."
    However, there is empirical evidence that suggests at least some coincidence between a community's socioeconomic characteristics, the views of its council members, and the subsequent votes of those representatives. For examples, see David R. Morgan, "Political Linkage and Public Policy: Attitudinal Congruence between Citizens and Officials," *Western Political Quarterly* 26 (June 1973): 209–223; Dye, *Politics in States and Communities*, pp. 310–312.
57. *A National Survey of City Council Members*; U.S. Department of Commerce, Bureau of the Census, "Popularly Elected Officials in 1987," in *Census of Governments* (Washington, D.C.: Government Printing Office, 1988); Schellinger, "Today's Local Policy Makers"; Downes, "Municipal Social Rank"; Sharyne Merritt, "Winners and Losers," *American Journal of Political Science* 21 (November 1977): 731–743; Klevit, "City Councils"; Deeb, "Municipal Council Members"; Delbert Taebel, "Minority Representation on City Councils," *Social Science Quarterly* 59 (June 1978): 142–152; Albert Karnig and Susan Welch, "Sex and Ethnic Differences in Municipal Representation," *Social Science Quarterly* 60 (December 1976): 467.
58. Prewitt, *The Recruitment of Political Leaders*.
59. Alan Saltzstein, "Can Urban Management Control the Organized Employee?" *Public Personnel Management* 3 (July–August 1974): 332–340.

CHAPTER **9**

The Office of the Mayor

Large city mayors have come to possess an extensive amount of authority and even more political power as their cities confront postindustrial realities. As most are "strong mayors" in strong mayor-council systems, they not only administer the cities' many programs but they also propose most of the budgetary and regulatory measures. They act, and the council reacts.

However, the advent of postindustrialism also has meant that despite the mayor's relative strength vis-à-vis the city council in the "conversion" process, the overall scope of mayoral policy discretion effectively has tended to shrink. In reality, large city mayors often are able to do little more than strategically manage retrenchment amid "street-fighting pluralism." To understand the mayor's current circumstance, it is helpful to see it in the context of historical events.

HISTORICAL CONTEXT

One identifiable characteristic of urban governance in the United States is a tendency to swing back and forth between concerns about political responsiveness and concerns about the efficient administration of governmental services. Often, there is an underlying ideological disagreement distinguishing these two positions. *Efficiency,* on a number of occasions, has meant little more than a political approach that does the least to hinder wealthy entrepreneurs. Providing the fewest governmental services at the least possible cost is especially good for those who need the services the least. Taxation extracts less money from their pockets leaving more for capital ventures. *Excessive political responsiveness,* on the other hand, often has meant a government seen by its elitist critics to be too concerned with providing ever more services to nonelite citizens, especially those who put the elected officials into office.[1]

When the urban gentry considered the city's chief executive to be excessively responsive to popular pressure, the pendulum would swing and steps would be taken to insulate him or her from politics. When the city's administration would become so insulated that the general public viewed it as blatantly nonresponsive to its will, the pendulum would swing back once again, breaking down some of those barriers so that the chief executive would again become responsive to public pressure. The governing structures reflecting these swings have varied (See figure 9.1).

Cyclical Shifts in Urban Governmental Form

Borough Form.   Many cities began under the borough form of governance, in which unelected town fathers came forward voluntarily and essentially were in an uncontested position to make the decisions they felt were in the best interests of the city. Never having to rally mass support to gain election, they were quite effectively insulated from popular pressure. The average city resident, however, could do little to sway governmental decisions.[2]

Council-Mayor.   As the populism of Andrew Jackson began to sweep the country in the early nineteenth century, suffrage was extended to most nonpropertied white men and mass-based political parties began to emerge. As industrialization and urbanization also began to stir, bringing with them some of the first severe urban problems, more formal and responsive mayor-council systems began to replace the highly elitist borough arrangements. With the memory of British monarchical rule still relatively fresh in their minds, urban residents were not yet ready to sanction strong executives. City councils remained dominant.[3]

Cities soon were growing in size, complexity, and number of services provided; and as political parties became more entrenched, town fathers rose to express their concern about the partiality and extravagance of party-based leaders. Often turning to state government for help, they argued that city council partisans were far too attentive to the popular demands of the moment, as opposed to rational and efficient long-term policies for the city as a whole.[4]

FIGURE 9.1   The Efficiency-Responsiveness Pendulum in Urban Governmental Forms

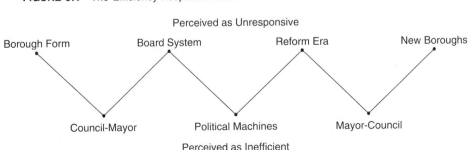

Board System.   Thus, the stage was set for the board system to begin replacing mayor-council arrangements in the mid-nineteenth century. A host of independent boards and commissions were established to handle the administrative functions previously performed by the city councils and, to a lesser extent, the weak mayors. The goal was to remove politics from service implementation by making the new administrators as independent as possible. To accomplish that, these administrators often were given either lifetime, or at least long-term, tenures.[5]

Machine Politics.   As industrialization and urbanization accelerated in the late nineteenth century, urban problems mounted and in some cities began to reach epidemic proportions. At this point, political parties once again stepped into the breach. Someone or something had to unite what formal checks and balances had kept apart. Thus, even though mayors tended to remain relatively weak in terms of formal authority, political power came to be far more centralized because of the political party machine. Urban government would become significantly more responsive to the public, showering selective patronage like rain.[6]

Reform Era.   Not long into the twentieth century, again there was concern among the urban gentry about the biases and excessiveness of city politics. Political machines were blamed, and thus came the "progressive reform" movement to protect government officials from parochial pressures. Policy would be made by stronger city councils, whose members were more likely to have been chosen in nonpartisan at-large elections, and administered by far less vulnerable commissioners or professional city managers.[7]

Mayor-Council.   Unfortunately, postindustrial problems continued to mount; and as civil unrest shook many of these cities in the 1930s, 1940s, and again in the 1960s, an increasing number of the larger ones opted for strong mayor-council structures in hopes of calming the discontent.[8] Historical trends were heading in the wrong direction for these cities, and only a strong mayor was seen as having any hope at all of providing the kind of leadership necessary to cope with the proliferation of sizable and conflicting demands. As President Lyndon Johnson's National Advisory Commission on Civil Disorders observed,

> Now, as never before, the American city has need for the personal qualities of strong democratic leadership. Given the difficulties and delays involved in administrative re-organization of institutional change, the best hope for the city in the short run lies in this powerful instrument. In most cities, the mayor will have the prime responsibility. It is in large part his role now to create a sense of commitment and concern for the problems of the ghetto community and to set the tone for the entire relationship between the institutions of city government and all the citizenry.[9]

New Boroughs.   As the dust of urban unrest has begun to settle, town fathers are once again questioning the level of governmental responsiveness to political constituencies. The case studies of New York City and Cleveland made clear that these increasingly empowered economic elites will go to almost any length to bring back governmental efficiency, even if that means extortion or the subordination of elected officials to elite-dominated finance control boards, the contemporary version of the borough system.[10]

MAYORAL ROLES

Into this vortex of public demands and increasing corporate scrutiny walks today's big city mayor. He or she will be forced to balance these various conflicting interests in order to keep the city afloat. To accomplish such mayoral governance in the postindustrial city requires the mayor to play a number of different roles simultaneously, with the particular formula depending on a given city's present socioeconomic environment and political structures as well as the mayor's personal abilities and leadership style.[11] Some of these roles, listed below, are rather traditional mayoral responsibilities, while others are more unique to the current period.

Mayoral Roles

Ceremonial Head	leads parades, cuts ribbons, greets visiting dignitaries
Chief Executive	is responsible for seeing that the bureaucracy executes the laws
Chief Legislator	formulates and presents most key legislation; has veto authority
Chief Ambassador	represents the city in negotiations, both locally and beyond
Emergency Handler	is expected to take the lead when local crises arise
Opinion Leader	has numerous opportunities to shape public opinion because of ready access to the media
Party Leader	is spokesperson for and perceived leader of his or her political party

Ceremonial Head

As ceremonial head, the mayor greets dignitaries who are visiting the city for one reason or another; in one of the more formal variations of this exercise, the mayor even may present the person with a symbolic key to the city indicating a high level of welcome as well as an invitation to return. Ceremonial duties also may include attending celebrations, throwing out the first pitch to start the baseball season, leading parades, serving as a banquet toastmaster, ground breaking when a significant construction project is begun, and ribbon cutting or christening the cornerstone when a project is complete. In these settings, the mayor is lending the symbolic support of the city to the particular project or event.

As titular head of the city, whether weak or strong in terms of authority, the mayor must play this role. No other single person is as clearly identified with the city as a whole, and thus no one else formally can represent the city in this way. Also, there are a number of political points to be scored. Unless the project is highly controversial (not many mayors can be found breaking ground for a new abortion clinic) it is a no-lose opportunity. Some of the popularity of the project is bound to rub off on the mayor, especially as he or she lends symbolic support to it. In addition, the situation may provide a very friendly setting for tactfully promoting a related mayoral policy goal or two.

In addition to avoiding certain controversial situations, however, the mayor must know when to start and stop. In a large city, there is almost no end to the number of ceremonial invitations. Once precedent has been established in a particular circumstance, it becomes hard to say no to others that are similar. If the mayor has agreed to cut the ribbon for the new Catholic church, how can he or she say no to every other denomination? What about breaking ground for the church's new baseball field, and on and on?

Chief Executive

As the city's chief executive officer, the mayor is sworn to see that the city's laws are executed. The administrative buck stops on his or her desk, just as it does on the president's desk at the federal level. If the fire department is slow responding, if a 911 operator puts an emergency call on hold, if police officers abuse a suspect, the mayor ultimately is responsible. As Wallace Sayre and Herbert Kaufman found, the mayor essentially is "held hostage for the conduct of all other officials and all employees of the city, for their personal integrity, their wisdom in policy, and their efficiency in performance."[12]

To assist in this task, the large city mayor normally will have a significant number of staffers. He or she will have aides to handle appointments, speechwriting, media relations, and liaison work with the city council and state and federal governments. There are also likely to be budget, planning, and legal staffs, not to mention the mayor's authority to hire private consultants and commission special investigations.[13]

Yet, the mayor cannot personally supervise every decision made throughout the extensive urban bureaucracy, despite all this staff assistance. Consequently, mayoral authority to appoint and remove top administrators becomes very important. These will be the people most directly responsible for such oversight. The administrative changes the mayor wants will have to be implemented by them.

In addition, such appointments can serve symbolic purposes. A classic example is the choice of police chief. In many large cities, the mayor must find someone who will be accepted by the police force, convince the African American community that race-related police brutality will be reined in, and at the same time persuade the general public that the city has chosen someone who will be aggressive in pursuing criminals. The choice in postindustrial cities often is a veteran black police officer who is identified as a tough law enforcer. Mayor Ed Koch of New York chose Benjamin Ward, Wilson Goode of Philadelphia picked Willie Williams, and Dick Hackett of Memphis tapped James Ivy.[14]

Besides appointing the right people, the mayor also must know when to let them go. If sanitation department efficiency has been deteriorating, media exposés have been increasing, and public complaints have been on the rise, it may be time to replace the appointed head of the department. However, this action must be balanced against certain political considerations. How popular is the department head with various key constituencies around the city? In particular, can the person be relieved of duty without alienating the rank-and-file members of the department to the point that cooperation will diminish and service quality decline even further?

Short of firing the department head, which may be either politically dangerous or precluded by the formal independence of the person's position in a weak-mayor arrangement, pressure still can be brought to bear through the city's budget. If the police department is slow in implementing certain high-priority mayoral reforms, the mayor can alter his or her budgetary request for the police department in order to demonstrate impatience. This could amount to not asking for additional officers in the operating budget, not requesting certain pieces of state-of-the-art equipment in the capital budget, or similar measures.

Finally, in order to free the mayor of some of the more mundane administrative chores, allowing additional time for other roles, a number of cities have opted for a chief administrative officer (CAO) and/or deputy mayors. Although the position varies considerably from city to city, the CAO generally provides the mayor with professional and technical advice as well as being delegated many of the routine administrative tasks in areas such as budgeting, personnel, liaison work and agency oversight. Essentially this person is a city manager who in this situation normally will serve at the pleasure of the mayor instead of the city council, thus allowing the benefit of such professional administration while keeping power centered in the executive branch.

The first known semblance of such an office was created in San Francisco in 1931. Following World War II, it spread to cities such as Philadelphia (1951), New Orleans (1952), and Louisville (1952).[15] Since then, a CAO or its equivalent has been utilized in a host of other cities, including Newark, Boston, Los Angeles, Memphis, and New York City. In Philadelphia, a former CAO, Wilson Goode, went on to become mayor.[16]

Variations abound, of course. Most CAOs do indeed serve at the pleasure of the mayor, meaning they can be fired at any moment without a show of cause. These persons clearly are meant to be little more than extensions of the mayor. At the other extreme, a few are career civil servants; once they are appointed they hold the job regardless of who is mayor. Between these extremes, Los Angeles requires that the city council approve the appointment and dismissal of any CAO. In New Orleans, the CAO was given the authority to appoint most department heads (with mayoral approval), besides supervising and coordinating departmental operations.[17]

New York City probably has the most involved organizational structure in this regard. After Mayor John Lindsay appointed a party crony as CAO; his successor (Abraham Beame) abolished the office and then replaced it with a nearly identical one called the first deputy mayor.[18] In a city as large and complex as New York, however, even this position became stretched to the limit. To allow the first deputy mayor to do more advising and coordinating, as well as make city hall more accessible to interest groups and department heads, other subordinate deputy mayor positions were created, such as deputy mayors for finance and economic development, policy and physical development, and operations.

Chief Legislator

With the diminishing role of the city council, the mayor often becomes the city's primary legislator, even when he or she does not even have a vote on the council. A weak mayor may preside over council meetings and a strong mayor may veto their legislation; but far more important, the strong mayor sets the council's agenda by formulating and presenting most budgetary and regulatory proposals, often under the guise of making an annual report to the council on the state of the city. These proposals are formulated at various places throughout the executive bureaucracy, then complied and forwarded by the mayor. For example, a proposal to add new sprinkler systems to the city's public golf courses will most likely be formulated in the parks and recreation department. Nevertheless, the mayor's office serves as the clearinghouse for all proposals, and it is there that they will be fit into the mayor's priority list.

Chief Ambassador

As chief ambassador the mayor represents the city in various forums within the city, across the country, and abroad. In the postindustrial era, this has become a very important mayoral task.

Within the city, the mayor often must function as a broker, serving as an intermediary between conflicting parties, helping them reach a workable solution. This function could involve providing mediation assistance in a labor dispute or convincing a private firm and its workers to reach a settlement before a strike does severe damage to the local economy; it could take place at the community level, such as when New York's Mayor David Dinkins attempted to help resolve a dispute between an African American neighborhood and a Korean grocer who was alleged to have mistreated more than one black customer.[19]

As the actions of the state and federal governments continue to have an increasing impact on city affairs, there will be a need to lobby vigorously in the state capitol as well as in Washington, D.C. Not only must the mayor keep a watchful eye on any legislation that could affect the city in a significant way but as city budgets become strained, the mayor often will be forced also to ask for financial help.

In a rather lighthearted description of his many journeys to Albany for help, New York mayor John Lindsay put it this way:

> The Mayor and the Governor have a special tradition of commemorating the major religious holidays in the Judaeo-Christian tradition. Each December,

sometime around Christmas and Chanukah, the Mayor writes the Governor a letter outlining the fiscal needs of the city for the coming year and describing the severe consequences that will result if the city does not receive a fair share of the taxes collected from the city and state. . . . In April, at about the time of Easter and Passover celebrations, the Mayor makes a pilgrimage to Albany, the state capital, to present the case for additional city money.[20]

Besides maintaining close contact with key officials in the state capital, the mayor also will visit the nation's capital with increasing frequency. New York City's Fiorello LaGuardia was one of the first large city mayors to grasp the emerging importance of such lobbying.[21] The mayor will give testimony before key committees, have discussions with top administrative officers, and so on. He or she may also choose to become actively involved in important lobbying groups such as the U.S. Conference of Mayors and the National League of Cities.[22]

Given the mobility of capital, there are always opportunities for the mayor to present his or her city as the ideal place for a venture capitalist to locate a new firm. These days, the latter pursuit even takes mayors to foreign countries, carrying a list of benefits the city has to offer: tax abatements, gas and water lines, operating subsidies, and so on.

Emergency Handler

Amid the ghetto unrest of the 1960s, Cleveland's Carl Stokes went into the riot-torn neighborhoods himself to plead for calm. John Lindsay and David Dinkins did the same thing in New York City.[23] Frank Rizzo also did it in Philadelphia, but apparently with a different message in mind. Rizzo, on one occasion, left a formal Boys Club banquet and arrived at a riot scene in his white tie and tails with a billy club tucked under his cummerbund.

Whether it be a city manager or the mayor, the city's chief executive is most likely the one who will be turned to for decisions should disaster strike. When a flood, earthquake, tornado, crime wave, terrorist attack, or ghetto disturbance occurs, the mass media spotlight will fall on city hall, asking what the city is going to do.

These occasions present both an opportunity and a risk. They provide a great opportunity to demonstrate cool but firm leadership under fire, compassion for the victims, and aggressive efforts to get financial assistance from external governments. However, when there is little that can be done or when all the choices are painful such as trying to cope with an extended drought, the mayor may be little more than the bearer of continual bad news—not an enviable political position. If handled poorly, such events ultimately may lead to significant political damage for the mayor.

Opinion Leader

With the mayor's ready access to mass media publicity, there are many opportunities to try to lead public opinion. The key generally will be to focus on a limited number of positions, on ones that can be presented succinctly in short news bites, and on ones about which the public's views are not well set. There also is the political temptation to poll the public carefully and then simply appear to lead what is already a well-established public preference.

Party Leader

With the demise of the political machine in the postindustrial era, there is no "boss" to represent the city's dominant political party. Somewhat by default, the mayor often becomes the spokesperson and perceived leader of his or her party. Except in nonpartisan settings, the mayor is the person whose name tops the party's column on the local ballot. As a result, his or her policy positions will tend to be identified as the party's. To the degree that local voters hold strong party allegiances, the mayor may be able to draw on this role to rally the party faithful behind a particular policy or candidate.

Of those various roles, which is most important for the postindustrial mayor? The answer to that question depends on the mayor's priorities. There is little doubt that a dedicated policy advocate will take full advantage of the agenda-setting opportunities available as chief legislator, opinion leader, and party leader, while using the ambassadorial role to rally all the outside help that can be found and making the most of his or her appointment power to shape policy implementation once the desired bills have been passed.

However, if the mayor's preeminent concern is reelection, and the particular direction of city policy is only secondary, he or she will spend more time on the ceremonial role and on mediating disagreements among various city forces. Given the severity of many postindustrial problems, the latter approach may become increasingly attractive. All of which brings us to mayoral leadership styles.

LEADERSHIP STYLES

Over the years, mayors have employed a variety of leadership styles, sometimes utilizing more than one in the course of their political careers and sometimes combining them to create new hybrid forms. Basically there are nine archetypes, four of which are traditional approaches; the others are more specifically tailored to postindustrial realities. All are summarized below:

Mayoral Leadership Styles

Innovator	aggressively seeks implementation of own public policy agenda
Caretaker	is primarily concerned with facilitating order, leaving agenda setting to others
Broker	remains in office by jumping in front and leading each passing political bandwagon
Broker-Innovator	mediates disputes by proposing solutions consistent with own limited policy agenda

Technical Manager	employs latest technologies and scientific management techniques to save the city
Tough Manager	maintains fiscal solvency by having various groups help in retrenchment management
New Fiscal Populist	is fiscally conservative budget balancer, but liberal on many social issues
Conflictualist	maintains position by leading large parts of the city into battle with other city groups
Cheerleader	attempts to bolster city spirit, and calls for volunteers to deliver more of the city's services

Innovator

The innovator sees a positive role for city government to play in addressing socioeconomic problems, has a definite policy agenda in mind for the city, and sets out to see that those policies are implemented. A strong advocate for specific political causes, this mayor is a highly visible activist, utilizing roles such as opinion leader and chief legislator to their fullest.[24] New York City's John Lindsay, at least in his first term, was a case in point. As one of his aides described him,

> [Mayor Lindsay] knew he'd have to take an awful lot of political heat by letting all these problems come out in the open rather than making patch-up, short-term arrangements behind the scenes which would solve nothing basically. The thing is that he and his people are making attempts—even if they're sometimes half-assed—to really come up with solutions.
>
> And the mayor is on top of those attempts. . . . He said he was elected to change the city, and that's what he went on to do because that's what he *should* be doing.[25]

Yet, more and more, the fiscal crises faced by postindustrial cities leave their mayors with ever fewer revenues with which to launch major new programmatic innovations. Instead of pondering what new programs to add, they are far more likely to find themselves trying to determine which of the existing programs can be cut without inflicting severe damage on the city. Their discretion is more concerned with whether to cut or not cut, rather than to add or not add.

Caretaker

> You know, I suppose it could be said that [we] were custodial mayors. We tried to keep the city clean and swept and policed. . . . You can't nurture flowers and good thoughts and ideas when you're living in a rat-infested squalor and your city services aren't being done.[26]

The opposite of the innovator is the caretaker. This person leaves the agenda to others and simply tries to keep the urban house in order by helping to settle disputes. Relatively passive when there are no significant disputes to be settled, this mayor spends much time on ceremonial duties and the mundane chief executive functions necessary to keep the city running as is.[27]

It is not uncommon to find such mayors at the end of their political careers, simply marking time and enjoying the limelight. This could be a multiple-term mayor in his or her lame duck years or a compromise candidate chosen to keep the seat warm until an acceptable partisan can be found. New York's Abraham Beame seems to fit the latter category rather well. Unfortunately for him, the 1975 New York City fiscal crisis arose to spoil what should have been a reasonably tranquil capstone to a long and valued political career.

Broker

Somewhere between the two styles is that of the broker, a personal opportunist who essentially jumps on whatever bandwagon seems to be gathering momentum. A pragmatist, this mayor is concerned first and foremost about remaining in office. Most of the machine bosses who also held the mayor's position appear to fall into this category. Mayor Richard J. Daley of Chicago was a classic example.[28] Describing Mayor Daley's leadership style, Edward Banfield writes:

> Wanting to do "big things" and not caring very much which ones, the [mayor] will be open to suggestions. (When Mayor Daley took office, he immediately wrote to three or four of the city's most prominent businessmen asking them to list the things they thought most needed doing.) . . . Taking suggestions from the right kind of people will help him to get the support he needs in order to win the votes of independents in the outlying wards and suburbs.[29]

As a broker, rather than a mere facilitator, this mayor will not hesitate to propose solutions to city disputes. However, those propositions are likely to be ones that will keep the mayor in power, in contrast to proposals from an innovator who ultimately would rather lose his or her seat than to surrender on issues crucial to "the cause."

Normally, this brokerage style will involve staying out of the public spotlight and trying to arrive at an alternative that gives all conflicting parties a little piece of the city's pie.[30] Nonetheless, a wise broker also knows when to widen the scope of conflict in order to achieve his or her ends by bringing other participants into the fray.[31]

Mayor Richard J. Daley's son, Chicago mayor Richard M. Daley, appears to have learned quite a lot at his father's knee. As political winds have changed in the "Windy City," the younger Daley has shifted with them. He has appointed African Americans to key posts in his administration, including press secretary. He rode in the annual gay and lesbian parade. His budget cuts generally have been seen as "even-handed."[32]

> Chicago datelines are no longer routine in the national press. Gone are the vivid television shots of rancorous, racially hostile "council wars" with aldermen in bulletproof vests. Openly hostile racial politics has subsided in what the press

has called "Beirut on the lake." Chicagoans appear to be breathing a collective sigh of relief after running through four mayors in the 14 years since the senior Daley died.[33]

Broker-Innovator

[The mayor] rarely commanded. He negotiated, cajoled, exhorted, beguiled, charmed, pressed, appealed, reasoned, promised, insisted, demanded, even threatened, but he most needed support and acquiescence from other leaders who simply could not be commanded. Because the mayor could not command, he had to bargain.[34]

Raymond Wolfinger reminds us that political systems in the United States are biased against innovation. Short of developments such as the burgeoning affluence of the years following World War II or the pressure that urban civil unrest can bring to bear, fragmented authority is the rule and deadlock tends to be the normal result. To accomplish political leadership in this milieu requires a particular set of environmental circumstances and the correct leadership approach.[35]

According to Jeffrey Pressman, an alert mayor can overcome this political fragmentation by taking advantage of it. Because authority is so fragmented, there is the built-in opportunity to intervene as a mediator. Once accepted into the game, the mayor can project his or her agenda by the integrative compromises proposed.[36]

This person has a policy agenda, but it is less pronounced and usually not as grand as that of the innovator. Rather than publicly advocating positions and trying to win converts, this mayor works in much more subtle ways. Taking full advantage of mediation opportunities, he or she will propose compromise solutions that often will nudge the result almost imperceptibly in the mayor's desired direction. For example, when an airport needs to expand and the affected neighborhood objects, the broker-innovator may propose a solution that uses city revenues to soften the economic blow for the residents while still allowing the airport expansion he or she sees as necessary for the city's economic growth. As bureaucracies grow and become more independent, tax revenues shrink, and group conflict increases in the postindustrial period, being a broker-innovator may well be the only realistic way left to achieve any sort of policy innovation.

For someone to fill the role effectively, however, requires what Pressman calls certain "preconditions of mayoral leadership." These are (1) sufficient staff resources to do the analysis, planning, liaison, and public relations work; (2) some legal jurisdiction in the matter, legitimizing the mayor's participation; (3) a full-time salary allowing him or her to devote the time necessary; (4) ready publicity vehicles; (5) existing political groups that can be mobilized behind the compromise, so that the coalition does not have to be built one person at a time; and (6) leadership skills such as charisma, public speaking ability, a personality that inspires trust, and a sixth sense for choosing issues that are likely to unite rather than divide the community.[37]

Mayor Richard Lee (1953–1969) was a pragmatic coalition-builder in this mold. Wolfinger describes how he utilized his position to accomplish massive urban renewal in New Haven, even though he had very little formal authority in the area. He effectively mediated conflicts between developers and affected neighborhoods, rallying a large popular coalition for the change. Pressman's preconditions were there, and Lee executed it all masterfully.[38]

Wolfinger does point up one area in which Lee was not nearly so successful, however. His charter reform provision, which would have increased mayoral authority, failed at the ballot box despite his best efforts. The explanation helps further explicate the principles involved here. Urban renewal was a substantive issue that could be debated in political circles, allowing compromises that provided a little something for everybody. Charter reform, on the other hand, was a procedural issue fought out in the no-compromise arena of popular referendum. Without the same opportunities to build a coalition by brokering a distributive compromise, mayoral influence declined significantly despite Lee's general popularity.[39]

Technical Manager

As the Richard Lees faded from the scene, analysts in the 1970s began to ponder why urban innovation had become so difficult. One prominent explanation was "bureaucratic inertia." City services had grown so that their huge and insulated administrative bureaucracies were effectively beyond the control of the cities' chief executives. In retrospect, Lindsay said it was like "pushing my shoulders against a mountain."[40] Often the solution was to use a technical manager style of mayoral leadership, employing more computer-assisted data analysis, organizational charts, and scientific management techniques.[41]

Clarence Stone challenges both that understanding of the problem and that solution. According to Stone, the growing complexity, or interrelatedness, of urban problems demands that they be approached in a large-scale comprehensive manner that will require considerable political skill as well as a solid technical understanding of the problems and an ability to get the service bureaucracy to respond. A real key to moving bureaucrats is knowing that bureaucracies cannot be understood separately from the constituents they serve, such as the connection between teachers and their parents and students, and fire fighters and their neighborhoods. In other words, service provider demands seldom are wholly separable from the demands of service recipients. Bureaucratic recalcitrance is not just a management problem; it is also a political one that will require political coalition building to resolve.[42]

Convincing teachers to refrain from anything resembling prayer in the public schools, for example, will require convincing parents of the potential harm. It will not be enough simply to tighten the organizational chart or increase teacher salary incentives. If the parents in that community cannot be persuaded by the city's political leadership, constitutional evasion most likely will continue.[43]

Tough Manager

As postindustrialism has spread and urban problems have deepened, there is more than just complexity to overcome. Fiscal limitations tightly constrain mayoral innovation, even if appropriately comprehensive policies can be devised and sufficient coalitions constructed. In New York City, former Deputy Mayor Kenneth Lipper estimated that that only about 5 percent of New York's operating budget was truly discretionary, not already committed to entitlements or absolutely essential services,[44] and prospects for raising new revenues are not bright.

With extremely limited leeway for policy innovation if the new policies are to cost any money, many postindustrial mayors find their only real discretion in determining where to cut existing programs as things get worse. In essence they become reduced to "retrenchment managers," and both their political careers and the health of the city will depend in large part on how well they are able to master that task.[45]

Douglas Yates suggests that such scarcity inevitably breeds political fragmentation—what he calls "street-fighting pluralism."[46] Every served constituency and their service providers become increasingly parochial as they battle each other for scarce city resources in what is essentially a zero-sum game.[47]

One possible response is the tough manager leadership style. After all external sources of assistance have been exhausted, the emphasis is on fiscal responsibility, making the cuts necessary for the city's fiscal well-being while not decimating what the public perceives to be the most necessary services. One of the ways to make this most politically palatable is to include the constituents in the decision making. Therefore the mayor establishes strict spending ceilings and then leaves many of the specific cuts to ad hoc boards that combine service recipients, service suppliers, and anti-tax groups. This action takes the specific political heat off the mayor, encourages countervailing forces in the community, and, if successful, will lead ultimately to compromises that almost everyone can live with.[48]

New Fiscal Populist

Another increasingly common response to postindustrial fiscal realities is to be fiscally conservative yet socially liberal, appeasing large numbers of urban liberals without diverting scarce revenues to additional social spending. According to Terry Clark, taxes often are reduced to try to stimulate private investment in these cities. Nonessential services are pared back first while the most desperately poor are protected as much as possible. These cities turn in part to private-sector delivery of public services in order to achieve more efficiency. Meanwhile, a liberal cover is placed on the package by strongly advocating policies such as gay rights,[49] increased protection for a variety of civil liberties, affirmative action in city hiring, and public resolutions making the city a nuclear-free zone, an official sanctuary for draft evaders, or whatever.

This style will be most successful in cities that do not have powerful existing interest groups that will insist on more than the city can provide. The appeal is from the mayor to individuals and categoric groups. In New York City, for instance, Mayor Ed Koch drew on some of this rhetoric, but entrenched interest groups and strident public service unions precluded much chance of his succeeding with this approach alone. Houston's Kathy Whitmire and Philadelphia's William Green, on the other hand, were seen as new fiscal populists who weathered considerable union opposition, while Diane Feinstein managed San Francisco by this method despite considerable pressure from various minority and gay groups.[50]

Conflictualist

> Just wait after November, you'll have a front row seat because I'm going to make Attila the Hun look like a faggot.
>
> —Frank Rizzo, 1975

Instead of brokering an accommodationist solution, mayors occasionally have seized the opportunity to lead one part of the city into battle with another. Mayor Frank Rizzo successfully directed his message primarily to the white working-class ethnics of Philadelphia. Cleveland mayor Dennis Kucinich tried to rally the city's working and lower classes against local banker "Goliaths" (see chapter 6). Most commonly done with a populist vehicle such as the approach utilized by Kucinich, conflict generation also has been employed around race, sexual preference, and other issues that deeply divide urban populations. In the near term, we may well witness more racist and homophobic appeals, as populism appears so counterproductive given the mobility of capital. However, in the long run, urban social and economic crises may lead to more populist appeals out of sheer frustration if nothing else.

Cheerleader

> A special type of mayor is emerging in big cities: one who governs more by inspiration . . . a "spiritual leader" who gets things done by persuasion.[51]

The Advisory Commission on Intergovernmental Relations estimates that some 45 states currently limit taxing and spending by their local governments following the tax revolt that swept the country in the late 1970s and early 1980s.[52] This restriction has meant additional problems for postindustrial mayors trying to serve an increasingly needy inner-city population. One result has been the proliferation of special districts, discussed in chapter 5, as well as the trend toward privatizing the delivery of public services. Another approach has been to try to cultivate more volunteerism as a way of stretching the city's social spending dollars.

The cheerleader mayor has been reduced to making seemingly endless public speeches beating the drum for volunteers. He or she then pushes public programs to facilitate their efforts. Coleman Young did this in Detroit in 1980, deputizing volunteer police officers for special occasions, re-creating the auxiliary fire department, and implementing an "adopt-a-park" program.[53] Wilson Goode made volunteerism a central part of his inaugural address in 1984.[54] Cleveland's George Voinovich developed 15 volunteer groups to provide services ranging from tending urban gardens to instituting new management techniques in the police department; like most other mayors adopting such an approach, however, he had little leverage over when and how often they would work.[55]

Such mayors also use emotive devices to bolster city spirit. They may make it a habit continually to remind city residents of all the good things they have and just how well the city actually is doing (whether it is or not). Ed Koch, New York City's highly stylistic mayor, continually asked an essentially rhetorical question, "How'm I doing?" Chicago's Jane Byrne, with little of substance to offer, showed solidarity with those suffering in decaying city housing projects by spending a couple of nights in the Cabrini-Green complex.[56] As postindustrial city crises deepen and policy options narrow, Clarence Stone and others suggest that such expressive/emotional leadership is likely to become increasingly common as a way of side-stepping the nearly intractable city problems these mayors face.[57]

MAYORAL FRUSTRATIONS

An increasing number of city services are being provided under the authority of independent commissions, special districts, intergovernmental agencies, and private and semi-private corporations (see chapters 5 and 10). Yet, even with that dispersion of responsibility, there is still too much to do. Lindsay's wife Mary described his regular routine:

> It's impossible to realize the demands of being mayor until you live it . . . . John could work twenty-four hours a day, seven days a week, and he'd never be finished. So the most important thing is to set your priorities. He's been very tough in limiting his schedule of appearances, but he still gets home late nearly every night—usually around midnight—and he brings along a folder four inches thick with just the most essential stuff he has to work on. Some of that he may do in the car riding back and forth, some he roars through with his secretary at the office, but some he has to do here. We try to work it out so he can have dinner with the children *one* night a week. . . .[58]

This is a classic burnout job. The physical and emotional stress is incredible, not only for those with some hope of implementing a helpful policy agenda but even for many caretaker mayors. There is far too much work for one person to handle and the proximity of local governance exposes the mayor to a steady barrage of lobbyists, not to mention regular and often personal criticism. Beyond the workload and the lack of insulation and personal privacy is the stress of dealing with crisis situations day in and day out. Long-term visions tend to fade away amid this swirl of immediate problems, as the mayor seeks to survive one day at a time.[59]

Besides the difficulties inherent in trying to manage thousands of job-secure civil servants scattered throughout the city, a host of socioeconomic problems have combined to make mayoral governance even more difficult in postindustrial cities. Employers move to Mexico. Middle-class whites move to the suburbs. Budgets will not balance. Revenues are insufficient to serve those left in the wake of these desertions. Social discord mounts. And amid these immense and highly consequential problems, there is also the steady stream of individual complaints about the neighbor's dog, the broken stop light, traffic congestion, potholes, and so on.[60] It is a familiar litany.

> [It's] like walking on a moving belt while juggling. Right off you've got to walk pretty fast to stay even. After you've been in office a short time people start throwing wads of paper at you. So now you've got to walk, juggle, and duck, too. Then the belt starts to move faster, and people start to throw wooden blocks at you. About the time you're running like mad, juggling and ducking stones, someone sets one end of the belt on fire.[61]

It should come as little surprise that being a large city mayor is a dead-end job for all practical purposes. Besides burnout, these mayors do not move on to higher office after the experience even if they retain the energy and desire to do so. A number have tried, and a couple actually have succeeded; but the general rule is that this will be the last political office they will hold.

After doing case studies of 20 mayors, John Kotter and Paul Lawrence concluded: "No matter where they wanted to go, it was impossible to get there from the mayor's office."[62] Boston's James Michael Curley said honestly, "Being mayor is fun and exciting, but there's no future in it."[63] Given the extent and severity of the problems faced by postindustrial cities, a mayor is unlikely to emerge looking like a success at the end of his or her mayoral term(s).

The norm is not even to run for higher office after being a large city mayor; but if a race is attempted, it most likely will result in defeat. Classic examples include the failed gubernatorial bid of New York City's Ed Koch and the two failed gubernatorial bids of Los Angeles's Tom Bradley. Since World War II, Cleveland's George Voinovich and Baltimore's William Schaefer have been the only mayors of an old, large postindustrial city to win higher offices, achieving the governorships of the states of Ohio and Maryland respectively. Minneapolis mayor Hubert Humphrey, Indianapolis mayor Richard Lugar, and San Diego mayor Pete Wilson all managed to win seats in the U.S. Senate; however, their cities had yet to experience the full brunt of postindustrialism. The norm is not to move on.[64]

Far more typical of the 20 mayors interviewed by Kotter and Lawrence was the following lament:

> I made some very real sacrifices as mayor. I worked hard, and under the circumstances, did well. Instead of praise and respect, I'm often criticized and ignored. It's not fair.[65]

Only 3 of the 20 mayors they interviewed actually could be classified as happy in the job.[66]

Why would any aspiring politician want the position? It is probably not the pay. The highest-paid mayors, holding office in some of the nation's very largest cities, scarcely make more than $100,000 per year, while the norm is closer to $70,000.[67] There is prestige and a reasonable degree of job security,[68] but both tend to fade fast when the roof starts to come down around the mayor's political ears.[69] The principal reason, other than personal ego and other psychological needs, is likely to be the challenge to try to make the city a better place to live.

AFRICAN AMERICAN MAYORS

Into this cauldron of social, economic, and political crises have walked an increasing number of African American mayors. And as Herrington Bryce notes,

> The challenges before black mayors are absolutely immense. Many of the cities they head rank with the highest rates of poverty, the most overcrowding, the lowest tax base for cities their size and even in their state. And in many, over 70% of their housing units were built before 1950, usually an indicator of very slow growth. . . . And during the last decade, nearly one half the cities with black mayors lost population, reflecting the flight of whites from the inner cities.[70]

Paul Friesema referred to their mayoral victories as "hollow prizes."[71] Nonetheless, before more fully assessing their ability to have a positive effect on urban problems, let us trace the origins and the dimensions of the phenomenon.

Historical Successes

> We've waited patiently, voted for white candidates over and over. It's our turn now.[72]
>
> —Harold Washington, 1983

Prior to 1967, no major U. S. city had had a black mayor since Reconstruction in the South. Then, a combination of circumstances came together. Many African Americans had been migrating to large cities since the turn of the century. A civil rights movement swept the country, knocking down barriers to black electoral participation and raising the level of black consciousness. At the same time, white middle- and upper-class residents were headed for the suburbs, leaving central city populations with a much higher percentage of African Americans.

It began to happen, first in Cleveland (Carl Stokes) and Gary (Richard Hatcher). Thereafter, over the course of the 1970s, blacks were elected to the mayor's office for the first time in Newark (Kenneth Gibson), Detroit (Coleman Young), Atlanta (Maynard Jackson), Los Angeles (Tom Bradley), New Orleans (Ernest Morial), Birmingham (Richard Arrington), and Washington, D.C. (Marion

Barry). Since 1980, the list has included the cities of Chicago (Harold Washington), Philadelphia (Wilson Goode), Baltimore (Kurt Schmoke), New York (David Dinkins), Seattle (Norman Rice), Kansas City (Emanuel Cleaver), Charlotte (Harvey Gantt), Oakland (Lionel Wilson), Denver (Wellington Webb), and Memphis (W. W. Herenton) (see table 9.1), not to mention smaller cities such as New Haven, Flint, Pontiac, Battle Creek, East St. Louis, Roanoke, Spokane, Richmond, Little Rock, Hartford, Pasadena, Berkeley, Camden, Tallahassee, and Atlantic City. It is highly unusual (as in Chicago, Cleveland, and Philadelphia) for a white person to hold a large-city mayor's office previously held by an African American. Once circumstances become ripe for electing a city's first black mayor, they generally appear to stay that way.

The principal determinant does not seem to be a black electoral majority. Among the largest 50 cities in the country with a strong-mayor system and a population that was even 40 percent black, only St. Louis has failed to elect a black mayor. A good many of these individuals were first elected in cities that had much smaller black populations. What was the standard formula for success?

Election Formula

Where African Americans approached numerical majorities, the results were often all but preordained. However, the elections of black mayors in predominately white cities have tended to have the following developments in common:

1. *At least two similar black candidate platform planks: pro-business growth and crime control.* These are two highly salient issues that appeal to both blacks and whites. They promise jobs and safety without implying a shift from social concerns or a crackdown on African Americans, underlying messages often heard when promised by white candidates.[73]
2. *A large voter turnout in the African American community,* approaching 75 percent of the eligible voters.
3. *Nearly all the black vote going to one strong black candidate.* Early unity helps. In Newark, Chicago, and Memphis, for example, this unity was facilitated in each case by a community conference to settle on a single black contender.

TABLE 9.1 Decade in Which Large Cities First Elected an African American Mayor

1960s	1970s	1980s	1990s
Cleveland	Newark	Chicago	Kansas City
Gary	Detroit	Philadelphia	Denver
	Atlanta	Baltimore	Memphis
	Los Angeles	New York City	
	New Orleans	Seattle	
	Birmingham	Oakland	
	Washington, D.C.	Charlotte	

4. *Roughly 20 percent of the white vote.* Here, it is advantageous if the strongest white candidate raises the issue of race prominently, as occurred in Seattle in 1989.[74] This helps rally the liberal white community.

Chicago in 1989 is a classic case of the lesson well learned. Richard M. Daley went out of his way to appeal to black voters, even though he faced a strong black opponent and had little prospect of garnering many black votes. He actually appears to have been appealing to white liberals who were less enchanted with Timothy Evans but would not support a racist. The result was that more than three-quarters of the whites who had voted for Harold Washington voted this time for Richard M. Daley.[75]

In New York City the same year, all nine mayoral candidates took a formal pledge not to appeal to prejudice based on race, ethnicity, national identity, gender, or sexual orientation.[76] Some of this agreement no doubt reflects a genuine concern for the city's social harmony. However, it would be naive to think that such restraint is not at least in part motivated by a desire to appeal to urban liberals, a highly attentive and politically active urban electoral constituency who are likely to be offended by such pandering.

5. *Two or more strong white candidates splitting the rest of the white vote,* particularly if the election is a multi-candidate primary without a run-off provision.
6. *A weak citywide party structure.* Strong party organizations tended for years to control tightly both the black political leadership and the black vote, using them to secure the election of their own white candidates. In effect, such a tradition also reduced the likelihood of the kind of electoral insurgency that could produce a black mayor.
7. *No major media opposition.* Because it was essential to extract a large bloc of votes from liberal white "bookworms" as George Washington Plunkitt called them,[77] it was important that major local media sources took the candidacy seriously and then either were supportive or at least neutral once viability was established.
8. *Large group support.* Finally, for financial contributions as well as help with turning out their voters on election day, it was very useful to have active and energetic assistance from groups like the AFL-CIO, United Auto Workers (UAW), and similar bodies.

One myth that needs to be corrected is that the large majority of the African American community automatically will vote for a black candidate over a white one no matter who the person is. There are many examples to the contrary, such as Philadelphia in 1967, Chicago in 1976, New York City in 1985, and Memphis in 1987. Far more common is a low voter turnout in the African American community if these voters are uninspired by either the black or white candidates.

On the other hand, once a black mayor has been elected for the first time, these cities rarely have elected a white mayor. Cleveland elected white mayors Dennis Kucinich and George Voinovich in the interim between black mayors Carl

Stokes and Michael White. Chicago turned to Richard M. Daley after Harold Washington died, and Philadelphia chose Edward Rendell to succeed Wilson Goode, who was precluded by law from seeking a third consecutive term. Nevertheless, these are clearly the exceptions. If trends continue, almost every large postindustrial city in the nation will have a black mayor, at least until African Americans are finally assimilated into mainstream American society to the degree that race no longer is a politically salient factor.

Unique Problems

> There is little question that the cities [black mayors] serve tend to be the most severely troubled, and their abilities to resolve the problems of these cities is affected by factors outside the control of any mayor, black or white.[78]

As indicated at the outset, African American mayors are assuming office in some of the most troubled cities in the nation. Poverty rates remain high. Homelessness continues to increase. Drug usage is rampant. Violent crime is epidemic. Health care costs have risen through the ceiling. Yet, for the most part, these are national problems that mayors with their limited budgets cannot begin to address. Their woes have been exacerbated by the absence of a liberal presidential administration in Washington since the first African American mayors took office in 1968.

The problems only start there. Not only do most all of these mayors face more than their share of poverty, crime, rundown public schools, and fiscal distress, but they initially must deal with a number of situations not faced by their more immediate white predecessors. Focusing on a city's transition to its first African American mayor, consider the words of New York City mayor David Dinkins, speaking on a black-oriented radio station:

> Let me tell you something, there are a lot of folks who are not pleased that I am Mayor . . . who don't want me to be right no how, under any circumstances.[79]

Black mayors are likely to have inherited racially divided cities, often following bitter, racially tinged campaigns. Jeffrey Hadden and others noted that these are more likely to have been defeats of inadequate discrimination rather than victories of tolerance.[80] Within that milieu, many black supporters will be looking for some immediate and clear change in policy as a tangible reward for electoral success, an expectation complicated by the reality that "the high-pitched, emotional campaigns run by black mayors frequently produce unrealistic expectations about what a black mayor can accomplish."[81] Meanwhile, wary whites will be watching closely, suitcases packed, for any sign of such a shift.[82]

Beyond the urban citizenry, a number of influential institutions also will be monitoring the mayor's first moves just as closely. Legislation will have to be steered through a predominantly white city council whose constituents are edgy; one of the worst examples was the city council wars in Chicago following the election of Harold Washington.[83] Policies will have to be implemented by enlisting the cooperation of entrenched white civil servants, a bureaucracy whose previous actions, such as those of the police department, may well have prompted some of the electoral surge in the black community.[84] Also, a predominantly white mass media will cover the transition.[85]

Finally, the white business community will have to be reassured. If that is not accomplished, capital investment will head for the suburbs even faster than it is already doing. In the case of cities under the receivership of finance control boards, these business elites may take more directly coercive action.[86]

In Atlanta, Maynard Jackson long struggled with the white business community, ultimately facing direct threats of divestment and achieving for the city the infamous reputation of being "the most difficult city in America [in which] to do business."[87] Andrew Young, on the other hand, declared that "I've made my peace with capitalism"; following that declaration with a number of pro-business concessions, he soon appeared to have overwhelming support in the Atlanta business community.[88]

As Roger Williams concludes, "Ultimately the black mayor's task comes down to balancing competing interests without losing sight of the fact that he is black and has—despite all rhetoric to the contrary—a special responsibility to black people."[89] It is a unique and sizable task to be sure, for as Rufus Browning and Dale Rogers Marshall conclude,

> The structure of ownership, financial institutions and investment that governs the economic prospects of cities . . . dominated by whites, sharply constrains the agenda of black officeholders, effectively keeping the problems of poverty and the black underclass off the agenda of city government.[90]

Policy Impact

> People have come to understand that black rule doesn't make any difference. . . . The problems still exist. Nothing is so different. Government is government with all its limitations.[91]

Is that correct? Given the swirl of conflicting pressures, do black administrations succeed in altering urban policy in any measurable way? The empirical evidence suggests a mixed record. City budgetary priorities change very little, as does the city's servility to the owners of capital. However, there have been some noteworthy procedural changes as well as symbolic gains.

When the phenomenon is studied latitudinally, meaning across various cities over the same period of time, priorities do seem at least marginally different where there are black mayors. Yet, this observation can be deceiving. Richard Hatcher, for instance, built 4,500 public housing units while Carl Stokes built 5,000; Ernest Morial succeeded in air conditioning New Orleans public housing. Cities governed by black mayors do indeed appear to spend proportionately more on social services; however, that should not be too surprising given the relatively more depressed economic circumstances of most of the cities where they have been elected.[92]

When the same phenomenon is studied longitudinally, meaning across time in individual cities, the results are more telling. Looking at overall budgetary priorities Sharon Watson and Edmund Keller found no clear indication that minority-oriented spending increased under black mayors.[93] That these budgets remained essentially the same was predictable, of course, given the very limited amount of spending discretion available in postindustrial cities, particularly outside periods of social unrest. With city services pared down to bare bones already, and with pressure actually to reduce taxes, if today's mayors are able to retain most existing services they have done a remarkable job.

Yet, when Sharon Watson asks, "Do black mayors matter?" the answer is still a resounding yes, at least when it does not require the city to spend significant additional monies.[94] Even though black mayors generally come to be seen as being tough on crime, there is a noticeable decline in the amount of conflict between the police and the black community.[95] Watson found that the ascendance of black mayors in Newark, Atlanta, and Oakland corresponded to some improvement in the minority employment picture.[96] The reasons were a marked increase in the number of city contracts going to black businesses and improved working relationships with the white business community.[97] Additionally, African Americans become more likely to receive a more proportionate share of city government jobs, especially those in the professional and administrative categories, under a black administration.[98]

Beyond improvements in the concrete life circumstances of many African Americans, there are also symbolic rewards. Role models are created and hope instilled. As a Tom Bradley appointee spoke of him,

> [Tom Bradley was] a role model . . . a man who happened to be black who could be the mayor for everyone. He was like the hopes and dreams of what I'd like to be, people relating to you as you, not your color.[99]

In addition, black pride is enhanced. The black community becomes more politicized. Black issues receive articulation to degrees they have not received before, such as special investigations of police behavior. Also, the performance of black mayors as well as the performance of appointed black administrators helps to break down a number of white stereotypes concerning what African Americans are capable of doing.[100] One white Los Angeles resident described it in these words:

> Most whites in our society have very little contact with black people. . . . So Tom Bradley welcomed into the hearth, home, and mind of a white person becomes a meaningful experience for that person.[101]

Future

> Everything has changed and nothing has changed. The statistics are still terrible. But the atmosphere is totally different.[102]

Despite the variety of advantages gained by electing a black mayor, the overall quality of life for most inner-city blacks remains bad and in a number of cases actually is getting worse.[103] In light of that condition, some critical analysis has begun to surface. Most of it does not criticize black mayors per se, but it casts a shadow over just how promising the increase in black administrations really is. Mack Jones concluded, "We are now two full decades into the period of routine black political access, and the euphoria has been tempered considerably by the chronic stagnation of the cities, particularly the inner core."[104]

William Julius Wilson has painstakingly documented that most of the black gains to date have benefited a relative few. Black appointments to city office and city preferences for black contractors tend to help the already reasonably affluent black middle class. Meanwhile, the black underclass remains essentially unaffected economically, as its standard of living remains the same or deteriorates.[105] Charles Levine observed that at best black mayors can only improve conditions at the margins of daily life.[106]

There seems to be little, if anything, black mayors can do about that. As a matter of fact, black mayors often have to go further, to be even more moderate, than their white counterparts in order to gain and hold the confidence of local corporate elites.[107] Such findings have led analysts like Friesema to conclude that local black leaders merely "dangle on white men's strings while receiving little more than crumbs."[108] As awareness of such impotence grows, so will black voter unrest.

Evidence of such unrest already may be appearing as evidenced by a look at the first generation of black mayors. Carl Stokes (Cleveland) stepped aside after one term. Richard Hatcher (Gary) and Ken Gibson (Newark) both were defeated after four or more terms in office. Coleman Young (Detroit) and Tom Bradley (Los Angeles) held on despite enormous local problems.[109] Harold Washington (Chicago) died in office and subsequently was replaced by Richard M. Daley.[110] Marion Barry (Washington, D.C.) was convicted of drug abuse and stepped aside. Atlanta, Philadelphia, and New Orleans preclude their mayors from serving more than two terms in succession. Meanwhile, the one mayor who has survived in reasonably good shape is Richard Arrington of Birmingham, and even he has been able to garner only about 10 percent of the white vote in a city that remains racially divided.[111]

Meanwhile, the "second generation" tends to be less charismatic and more technocratic in orientation. Their emphasis seems to be more on efficiency than racial solidarity and pride, more on governing than leading.[112] The end goals may be the same, but the results appear to be leaving inner-city blacks just as frustrated as before.[113]

In addition, another trend may be emerging. With the black population generally large enough to preclude a white regaining the office of mayor in the foreseeable future, white voters seem to be playing a moderating role. In New Orleans in 1986, for instance, Sidney Barthelemy, the more conservative of the two black candidates, garnered 86 percent of the white vote and only 28 percent of the black vote on his way to defeating the more racially militant William Jefferson.[114]

With mayoral elections no longer going their way, some whites have attempted to change the rules. Annexation long allowed cities like Memphis and Dallas to continue to draw in enough white voters to keep a narrow white majority in the electorate. Whether by design or not, this tactic had the effect of forestalling the election of a black mayor.

In the city of Chicago, white councilmen tried to put a referendum issue on the ballot proposing to make Chicago elections nonpartisan and require a runoff between the top two finishers in the nonpartisan primary. The reason is that Chicago retains a narrow white majority, and proponents wanted to prevent the election of another plurality mayor such as Harold Washington. Alert to the ramifications, however, Washington's supporters slipped three other nonbinding referenda on the ballot and then cited a state law that prohibits more than three referenda issues on any single ballot. White opponents had collected 150,000 signatures for nothing, at least this time around.

CONCLUSION

Not long ago, most U.S. mayors were white men from middle-class or upper-class backgrounds.[115] Now, as the rise in African American mayors indicates, urban chief executives are no longer as likely to be drawn from such a narrow stratum of American society. Besides the growing number of cities with African American mayors, cities as large as Miami (Xavier Suarez), Denver (Federico Pena), and San Antonio (Henry Ciscernos) have elected Hispanic mayors, and women have held that office in cities as prominent as Chicago (Jane Byrne), Pittsburgh (Sophie Masloff), San Francisco (Diane Feinstein), Houston (Kathy Whitmire), Dallas (Annette Strauss), Fort Worth (Kay Granger), San Antonio (Lila Cockrell), El Paso (Suzie Azer), Bridgeport (Mary Moran), Omaha (Helen Boosalis), and Washington, D.C. (Sharon Pratt Dixon).[116] West Hollywood was one of the first American cities to have an openly gay mayor (Valerie Terrigno).

As was true with city councils, who holds office does make some difference despite rather severe parameters imposed by postindustrial fiscal realities. Mayors still have a reasonable amount of discretion as to who they hire and fire, besides having opportunities to attain outside assistance, make incremental changes in the city's budget, and lead public opinion. As long as they pay proper homage to capital investors and keep a good working relationship with their bureaucracy, they can have at least some marginal personal impact on governmental policy.[117]

The chance of that policy impact taking any significant redistributive direction seems rather remote, however. Consider Detroit's Mayor Coleman Young as the classic case. An avowed socialist in his younger days, Young soon was dancing to the tune of General Motors Corporation when it wanted the city to raze the interracial Poletown neighborhood to make room for a new Cadillac plant. Given the city's desperate need for jobs, he really had very little choice. On the other hand, within those parameters, he saw to it that Detroit's public jobs and services were delivered in a reasonably equitable manner, even if redistributing the city's wealth and income was not in the cards.[118]

NOTES

1. Herbert Kaufman, ''Emerging Conflicts in the Doctrine of Public Administration,'' *American Political Science Review* 50 (December 1956): 1057–1073.
2. Ernest Griffith, *History of American Urban Government: The Colonial Period* (New York: Oxford University Press, 1938).

3. Charles Glaab and A. Theodore Brown, *A History of Urban America* (New York: Macmillan, 1976), pp. 169–170; Peter Gluck and Richard Meister, *Cities in Transition* (New York: New Viewpoints, 1979), pp. 43–46.
4. Glaab and Brown, *A History of Urban America,* pp. 170–177.
5. Ibid.
6. See chapter 7 of this volume for a more detailed discussion.
7. Ibid.
8. Demetrios Caraley, *City Governments and Urban Problems* (Englewood Cliffs, N.J.: Prentice-Hall, 1977), p. 85.
9. *Report on the National Advisory Commission on Civil Disorders* (Washington, D.C.: Government Printing Office, 1968), p. 155.
10. See chapter 6 of this volume.
11. John Kotter and Paul Lawrence, *Mayors in Action* (New York: Wiley, 1974); Edward Page, Harold Wolman, and Kathryn Shane McCarty, *America's Big City Mayors* (Washington, D.C.: National League of Cities, 1987).
12. Wallace Sayre and Herbert Kaufman, *Governing New York City* (New York: Norton, 1965), p. 659.
13. Peter Trapp, "Governors' and Mayors' Offices: The Role of the Staff," *National Civic Review* 63 (May 1964), pp. 242–249; Arnold Howitt, "The Expanding Role of the Mayoral Staff," *Policy Studies Journal* 3 (June 1975): 363–370.
14. *New York Times,* November 8, 1983.
15. Charles Adrian and Charles Press, *Governing Urban America* (New York: McGraw-Hill, 1977), pp. 162–163.
16. Lent Upson, "A Proposal for an Administrative Assistant to the Mayor," *American City* 44 (June 1931): 93; John Bollens, *Appointed Executive Local Government: The California Experience* (Berkeley: University of California Press, 1952); John Selig, "The San Francisco Idea," *National Municipal Review* 46 (June 1957): 290–295; Wallace Sayre, "The General Manager Idea for Large Cities," *Public Administration Review* 14 (Fall 1954): 253–257.
17. "New Orleans Adopts Home-Rule Charter," *National Municipal Review* 41 (May 1952): 250; "Proposed Charter for New Orleans Submitted," *National Municipal Review* 41 (December 1952): 570.
18. Sigmund Ginsburg, "The New York City Administrator," *National Civic Review* 64 (October 1975): 451–458.
19. *New York Times,* November 25, 1990.
20. John Lindsay, *The City* (New York: New American Library, 1970), p. 177.
21. *New York Times,* December 12, 1981.
22. Suzanne Farkas, *Urban Lobbying: Mayors in the Federal Arena* (New York: New York University Press, 1971); Donald Haider, *When Governments Come to Washington: Governors, Mayors, and Intergovernmental Lobbying* (New York: Free Press, 1974).
23. Sam Roberts, "On the Mean Streets, a Greater Sense of Alienation," *New York Times,* September 9, 1991, p. E6.
24. Caraley, *City Governments and Urban Problems,* pp. 210–213; Douglass Yates, *The Ungovernable City* (Cambridge, Mass.: MIT Press, 1977), chap. 6.
25. Quoted in Nat Hentoff, *A Political Life: The Education of John V. Lindsay* (New York: Knopf, 1969), pp. 273–274. Also see Yates, *The Ungovernable City,* p. 149. For discussion of another social reformer, see the analysis of Boston's Kevin White in Clarence Stone, Robert Whelan, and William Murin, *Urban Policy and Politics in a Bureaucratic Age* (Englewood Cliffs, N.J.: Prentice-Hall, 1986), pp. 219–220.

26. Cleveland Mayor Ralph Locher, quoted in Kotter and Lawrence, *Mayors in Action*, p. 111.
27. Ibid., pp. 209–210.
28. Ibid., pp. 213–215; Yates, *The Ungovernable City,* chap. 6.
29. Edward Banfield, *Political Influence* (Glencoe, Ill.: Free Press, 1961), p. 251.
30. Milton Rakove, *Don't Make No Waves, Don't Back No Losers* (Bloomington: Indiana University Press, 1975), pp. 68–75.
31. E. E. Schattsneider, *The Semi-Sovereign People* (New York: Holt, Rinehart and Winston, 1960).
32. Neal Peirce, "Mayor Daley the Younger Has Calmed Chicago," *National Journal,* March 24, 1990, p. 741.
33. Ibid.
34. Robert Dahl, *Who Governs?* (New Haven, Conn.: Yale University Press, 1961), p. 204.
35. Raymond Wolfinger, *The Politics of Progress* (Englewood Cliffs, N.J.: Prentice-Hall, 1974).
36. Jeffrey Pressman, "Preconditions of Mayoral Leadership," *American Political Science Review* 66 (June 1972): 511–524.
37. Ibid.
38. Wolfinger, *The Politics of Progress.*
39. Ibid. For more on the broker-innovator leadership style, see Dahl, *Who Governs?*; Allan Talbot, *The Mayor's Game* (New York: Harper & Row, 1967); Jewel Bellush and Murray Hausknecht, "Entrepreneurs and Urban Renewal," *Journal of the American Institute of Planners* 32 (September 1966): 289–297.
40. John Lindsay quoted in Hentoff, *A Political Life,* p. 146.
41. John Sacco and William Parks, "Policy Preferences among Urban Mayors," *Urban Affairs Quarterly* 13 (September 1977): 49–72.
42. Clarence Stone, "Complexity and the Changing Character of Executive Leadership," *Urban Interest* 4 (Fall 1982): 29–50.
43. The U.S. Supreme Court decision on the constitutionality of teacher-led prayer in the public schools can be found in *Engel v. Vitale* 370 U.S. 421 (1962).
44. *New York Times Magazine,* December 31, 1989, p. 46.
45. Charles Levine, "Organizational Decline and Cutback Management," *Public Administration Review* 38 (July–August 1978): 316–325; Charles Levine, "More on Cutback Management," *Public Administration Review* 39 (March–April 1979): p. 1; Charles Levine, *The Politics of Retrenchment* (Beverly Hills, Calif.: Sage, 1981); Jerry McCaffery, "The Impact of Resource Scarcity on Urban Public Finance," *Public Administration Review* 41 (January 1981); Mark Weinberg, "The Urban Fiscal Crisis Impact on the Budgeting and Financial Planning Practices of Urban America," *Journal of Urban Affairs* 6 (Winter 1984): 39–52.
46. Yates, *The Ungovernable City,* pp. 34–37.
47. A zero-sum game is one in which someone can gain something only if someone else loses it. The limits are fixed from the start.
48. Douglas Yates, "The Mayor's Eight-Ring Circus: The Shape of Urban Politics in Its Evolving Policy Arena," unpublished paper presented at the annual meeting of the American Political Science Association, New York City, September 1978.
49. Some 80 cities, Washington, D.C., and 4 states have gay rights laws. See *New York Time,* September 24, 1991.
50. Terry Clark, "A New Breed of Cost-Conscious Mayors," *Wall Street Journal,* June 10, 1985; Terry Clark and Lorna Ferguson, *City Money* (New York: Columbia University Press, 1983).

51. Joseph M. Davis, associate director of Cleveland's Federation for Community Planning, quoted in *New York Times,* February 19, 1984.
52. Ibid.
53. Kirk Cheyfitz, "Self-Service," *New Republic,* November 15, 1980, pp. 14–15.
54. *New York Times,* January 3, 1984.
55. *New York Times,* February 19, 1984. For more examples, see Perry Davis, ed., *Public-Private Partnerships* (New York: Academy of Political Science, 1986).
56. *New York Times,* March 23–April 2, 1991.
57. Stone et al., *Urban Policy and Politics in a Bureaucratic Age,* pp. 220–222.
58. Mary Lindsay, quoted in Hentoff, *A Political Life,* pp. 104–105.
59. Fred Powledge, "The Flight from City Hall," *Harper's Magazine,* November 1969; *Municipal Yearbook, 1982* (Chicago: International City Managers' Association, 1983), pp. 170–171; Stone et al., *Urban Policy and Politics in a Bureaucratic Age,* pp. 216–218.
60. *Municipal Yearbook, 1978* (Chicago: International City Managers' Association, 1979), pp. 8–9.
61. Kotter and Lawrence, *Mayors in Action,* p. 175.
62. Ibid., p. 239.
63. From John Galvin, *Twelve Mayors of Boston, 1900–1970* (Boston: Boston Public Library, 1970), quoted in Robert Lorch, *State and Local Politics: The Great Entanglement* (Englewood Cliffs, N.J.: Prentice-Hall, 1983), p. 295.
64. Kotter and Lawrence, *Mayors in Action,* p. 249; Russell Murphy, "Whither the Mayors?," *Journal of Politics* 42 (February 1980), pp. 277–290.
65. Kotter and Lawrence, *Mayors in Action,* p. 240.
66. Ibid.
67. *Municipal Yearbook, 1990* (Chicago: International City Managers' Association, 1991).
68. For a discussion of the numerous electoral advantages of incumbency, see Caraley, *City Governments and Urban Problems,* p. 189.
69. Jack Germond and Jules Witcover, "Why Would Anyone Want to Be Mayor?," *National Journal,* June 22, 1991, p. 1582.
70. Herrington Bryce, quoted in *New York Times,* April 4, 1975. Also see Herrington Bryce, "Problems of Governing American Cities: The Case of Medium and Large Cities with Black Mayors," *Focus* 2 (August 1974).
71. H. Paul Friesema, "Black Control of Central Cities: The Hollow Prize," *Journal of the American Institute of Planners* 35 (March 1969).
72. *Nation,* March 12, 1983, p. 295.
73. Peter Ross Range, "Capital of Black Is Bountiful," *New York Times Magazine,* April 7, 1974; Steven R. Roberts, "He's One of Us," *New York Times Magazine,* February 24, 1974; *New York Times,* June 24, 1991.
74. See Mylon Winn, "The Election of Norm Rice as Mayor of Seattle," *PS* 23 (June 1990): 159.
75. New York Times/WBBM-TV Poll, cited in the *New York Times,* April 6, 1989.
76. *New York Times,* June 13, 1989. A comparable pledge to avoid race-baiting also was taken in Birmingham in 1983. See *Washington Post,* October 13, 1983.
77. William Riordan, ed., *Plunkitt of Tammany Hall* (New York: Dutton, 1963), pp. 45–49.
78. Herrington Bryce and Eric Martin, "The Quality of Cities with Black Mayors," in Herrington Bryce, *Urban Governance and Minorities* (New York: Praeger, 1976), p. 50. Also see William Nelson, Jr., "Black Mayors as Urban Managers," *Annals of the American Academy of Political and Social Sciences* 439 (September 1978): 53–67.

79. *New York Times,* March 8, 1991.

80. Jeffrey Hadden, Louis Masotti, and Victor Thiessen, "Making of the Negro Mayors, 1967," *Trans-action* 5 (January/February 1968).

81. William Nelson, "Black Mayoral Leadership," in Lucius Barker, ed., *Black Electoral Politics* (New Brunswick, N.J.: Transaction, 1990), p. 191. And for a recent case, see Felicia Lee, "Differing Demands of Black Groups Challenge Dinkins," *New York Times,* September 1, 1991, p. E5; Roberts, "On the Mean Streets."

82. Nelson, "Black Mayors as Urban Managers," p. 63.

83. *Christian Science Monitor,* January 8, 1985.

   In terms of the more general issue of predominantly white city councils, see Albert Karnig, "Black Representation on City Councils," *Urban Affairs Quarterly* 12 (December 1976): 223–243; Thomas Dye, *Politics in States and Communities* (Englewood Cliffs, N.J.: Prentice-Hall, 1985), pp. 304–305.

   For the reasons these councils remain disproportionately white, such as by nonpartisan and at-large elections, see Thomas Dye and Theodore Robinson, "Reformism and Black Representation on City Councils," unpublished paper cited in Dye, *Politics in States and Communities,* p. 305; Richard Engstrom and Michael McDonald, "The Election of Blacks to City Councils," *American Political Science Review* 75 (June 1981): 344–354.

84. *New York Times,* April 5, 1991; March 22, 1982; *Washington Post,* April 9, 1983; Clarence Stone, *Regime Politics; Governing Atlanta, 1946–1988* (Lawrence: University of Kansas Press, 1989), pp. 156–158; Nelson, "Black Mayors as Urban Managers," p. 62; Roger M. Williams, "America's Black Mayors: Are They Saving the Cities?" *Saturday Review/World,* May 4, 1974, pp. 10–13, 66; Robert Starks and Michael Preston, "Harold Washington and the Politics of Reform in Chicago," in Rufus Browning, Dale Rogers Marshall, and David Tabb, eds., *Racial Politics in American Cities* (White Plains, N.Y.: Longman, 1989); Hadden, "Making of the Negro Mayors."

85. For example, see Nelson, "Black Mayors as Urban Managers," p. 64; for a particular example of this struggle (Mayor Richard Arrington and the *Birmingham News*), see *New York Times,* November 9, 1981.

86. Hadden, "Making of the Negro Mayors." Or, more recently, see Raphe Sonenshein, "Biracial Coalition Politics in Los Angeles," *PS* 19 (Summer 1986): 586; or *New York Times,* March 8, 1991, for some of the dilemmas faced by New York City mayor David Dinkins in this latter regard.

87. *New York Times,* October 29, 1981; Mack Jones, "Black Political Empowerment in Atlanta," *Annals of the American Academy of Political and Social Sciences* 439 (September 1978): 111–112; M. Dale Henson and James King, "The Atlanta Public-Private Romance," in R. Scott Foster and Renee Berger, *Public-Private Partnership in America* (Lexington, Mass.: Lexington Books, 1982), pp. 293–337.

88. "The Capitalist Gospel According to Reverend Young," *Atlanta Constitution,* September 22, 1983, p. 80; *Atlanta Constitution,* July 24, 1983; Susan Clarke, "More Autonomous Policy Orientations," in Clarence Stone and Heywood Sanders, eds., *The Politics of Urban Development* (Lawrence: University of Kansas Press, 1987); Adolph Reed, "A Critique of Neo-Progressivism in Theorizing about Local Policy Development," in Clarence Stone and Heywood Sanders, eds., *The Politics of Urban Development* (Lawrence: University of Kansas Press, 1987); Stone, *Regime Politics,* especially chaps. 6–7.

   William Nelson suggests that such accommodation is typical of the "second-generation" black mayors. See Nelson, "Black Mayoral Leadership," p. 191.

89. Williams, "America's Black Mayors," p. 66. For more on these conflicting pressures, see Carl Stokes, *Promises of Power* (New York: Simon and Schuster, 1973).

90. Rufus Browning and Dale Rogers Marshall, "Black and Hispanic Power in City Politics," *PS* 18 (Summer 1986): 575.

91. A former candidate for the Detroit mayoralty quoted in Peter Eisinger, *The Politics of Displacement: Racial and Ethnic Transition in Three American Cities,* (Madison, Wis.: Institute for Research on Poverty, 1980), p. 78.

92. Rufus Browning, Dale Rogers Marshall, and David Tabb, *Protest Is Not Enough* (Berkeley: University of California Press, 1984); Albert Karnig and Susan Welch, *Black Representation and Urban Politics* (Chicago: University of Chicago Press, 1981); James Button, "Southern Black Elected Officials: Impact on Socioeconomic Change," *Review of Black Political Economy* 12 (Fall 1982): 33.

93. Edmund Keller, "The Impact of Black Mayors on Urban Policy," *Annals of the American Academy of Political and Social Sciences* 439 (September 1978): 40–52; Susan Welch and Albert Karnig, "The Impact of Black Elected Officials on Urban Social Expenditures," *Policy Science Journal* 7 (Summer 1979): 707–714; Sharon Watson, "Do Mayors Matter? The Role of Black Leadership in Urban Policy," unpublished paper presented at the annual meeting of the American Political Science Association, Washington, D.C., August 1980, pp. 20–25.

94. Watson, "Do Mayors Matter?"

95. Grace Hall Saltzstein, "Police Responsiveness and the Black Community," unpublished paper presented at the annual meeting of the American Political Science Association, Washington, D.C., September 1988; Eisinger, *The Politics of Displacement*; *New York Times,* January 12, 1984.

96. Watson, "Do Mayors Matter?," pp. 12–20. Also, see Browning et al., *Protest Is Not Enough*.

97. Peter Eisinger, "Black Mayors and the Politics of Racial Economic Advancement," in Harlan Hahn and Charles Levine, eds., *Readings in Urban Politics* (White Plains, N.Y.: Longman, 1984), p. 253; Dennis Judd and Randy Ready, "Entrepreneurial Cities and the New Politics of Economic Development," in George Peterson and Carol Lewis, eds., *Reagan and the Cities* (Washington, D.C.: Urban Institute, 1986); Edmund Newton, "Taking Over City Hall," *Black Enterprise* 13 (June 1983): 159; Monte Pilawsky, "Do Black Mayors Make a Difference?," unpublished paper presented at the Southern Social Science Conference, Houston, Texas, March 1985.

   Although generally true, Huey Perry, on the other hand, found less success at routing contracts to black firms in Birmingham and New Orleans. See Huey Perry, "Black Politics and Mayoral Leadership in Birmingham and New Orleans," in Lucius Barker, ed., *Black Electoral Politics* (New Brunswick, N.J.: Transaction, 1990), pp. 158–159.

   It also should be noted, as a corporate example, that under the leadership of David Dinkins New York City adopted one of the toughest antidiscrimination policies in the nation. See *New York Times,* June 5, 1991.

98. Matthew Hutchins and Lee Sigelman, "Black Employment in State and Local Government," *Social Science Quarterly* 62 (March 1981): 79–87; Thomas Dye and James Resnick, "Political Power and City Jobs," *Social Science Quarterly* 62 (September 1981); Karnig and Welch, *Black Representation and Urban Politics*; Huey Perry, "The Impact of Black Political Participation on Public Sector Employment and Representation on Municipal Boards and Commissions," *Review of Black Political Economy* 12 (1983): 203–217; Peter Eisinger, "Black Employment in Municipal Jobs," *American Political Science Review* 76 (June 1982): 380–392;

Eisinger, "Black Mayors and the Politics of Racial Economic Advancement," p. 251; Nelson, "Black Mayoral Leadership," pp. 188–195; Ken Mladenka, "Blacks and Hispanics in Urban Politics," *American Political Science Review* 83 (January 1989): 165–191: Watson, "Do Mayors Matter?;" Peter Eisinger, *The Politics of Displacement.*

As for case studies, see Perry, "Black Positions and Mayoral Leadership," pp. 154–160; Starks and Preston, "Harold Washington and the Politics of Reform in Chicago;" Mack Jones, "Black Mayoral Leadership in Atlanta," in Lucius Barker, ed., *Black Electoral Politics* (New Brunswick, N.J.: Transaction, 1990); Sonenshien, "Biracial Coalition Politics in Los Angeles."

It also should be noted, however, that the African American share of city jobs appears to correlate more closely to the size of the black population that it does to whether or not the mayor is black. In other words, once blacks become a large enough proportion of a city's population, they will begin to receive a more proportionate share of city jobs, regardless of who is mayor. See Peter Eisinger, "Black Employment in Municipal Jobs," *American Political Science Review* 76 (June 1982): 380–392.

 99. Quoted in Raphe Sonenshein, "Bradley's People: Biracial Coalition Politics in Los Angeles," unpublished paper presented at the annual meeting of the American Political Science Association, New Orleans, August 1985, p. 22.
100. Lawrence Bobo and Franklin Gilliam, "Race, Sociopolitical Participation, and Black Empowerment," *American Political Science Review* 84 (June 1990): 377–393.
101. Ibid., p. 23.
102. C. T. Vivian quoted in Pilawsky, "Do Black Mayors Make a Difference?"
103. Marcus Pohlmann, *Black Politics in Conservative America* (White Plains, N.Y.: Longman, 1990), chap. 3.
104. Jones, "Black Mayoral Leadership in Atlanta," p. 138.
105. William Julius Wilson, *The Truly Disadvantaged* (Chicago: University of Chicago Press, 1987). And for an urban case study of the phenomenon, see Pilawsky, "Do Black Mayors Make a Difference?"

For more on the general limitations faced by African American mayors, see Michael Preston, "Limitations of Black Urban Power: The Case of Black Mayors," in Louis Masotti and Robert Lineberry, eds., *The New Urban Politics* (Cambridge, Mass.: Ballinger, 1976); Charles Levine, *Racial Conflict and the American Mayors* (Lexington, Mass.: Lexington Books, 1974).
106. Levine, *Racial Conflict and the American Mayors* p. 81.
107. Range, "Capital of Black Is Bountiful"; Roberts, "He's One of Us"; *Washington Post,* October 4, 1977, p. A2; Peter Eisinger, *The Politics of Displacement;* Peter Binzen, "Business Community Sees Reason for Hope," *Philadelphia Inquirer,* January 8, 1984.
108. Friesema, "Black Control," p. 77.
109. Bryan Jackson, "Black Political Power in the City of Angels," in Lucius Barker, ed., *Black Electoral Politics* (New Brunswick, N.J.: Transaction, 1990), pp. 169–175; Charles Bernsen, "Detroit," Memphis, *Commercial Appeal,* January 31, 1991, pp. B4–B5.
110. *New York Times,* April 3, 1989; February 28, 1991.
111. *New York Times,* August 28, 1989.
112. John Moore, "From Dreamers to Doers," *National Journal,* February 13, 1988.
113. B. Drummond Ayres, "Two Years Temper Hopes in Baltimore," *New York Times,* March 8, 1990.

114. *New York Times,* March 1, 1986.
   Also, for a discussion of the "militant" versus "moderate" distinction, see James Q. Wilson, *Negro Politics* (New York: Free Press, 1960); Charles P. Henry, "The Political Role of the 'Bad Nigger,' " *Journal of Black Studies* 2 (June 1981): 461–482.
115. Raymond Bancroft, "America's Mayors and Councilmen," *Nation's Cities* 12 (April 1974): 14–24; Albert Karnig and Susan Welch, "Sex and Ethnic Differences in Municipal Representation," *Social Science Quarterly* 60 (December 1976): 467–468; Dahl, *Who Governs?,* pp. 11–88.
116. Sharyne Merritt, "Winners and Losers: Sex Differences in Municipal Elections," *American Journal of Political Science* 21 (November 1977): 731-744; Ronald Hedlund, Patricia Freeman, Keith Hamm et al, "The Electability of Women Candidates," *Journal of Politics* 41 (May 1979): 513–525; Susan McManus, "A City's First Female Officeholder: Coattails for Future Female Officeseekers," *Western Political Quarterly* 34 (March 1981): 88–99.
117. Caraley, *City Governments and Urban Problems,* pp. 222–225; Levine et al., *The Politics of Retrenchment*; Clark and Ferguson, *City Money*; Kenneth Wong, *City Choices* (Albany, N.Y.: SUNY Press, 1990); Wen Kuo, "Mayoral Influence on Urban Policy Making," *American Journal of Sociology* 79 (November 1973): 620–638.
118. Wilbur Rich, *Coleman Young and Detroit Politics: From Social Activist to Power Broker* (Detroit: Wayne State University Press, 1989).
   For a more general discussion of this phenomenon, see Stone, *Regime Politics*; Todd Swanstrom, *The Crisis of Growth Politics* (Philadelphia: Temple University Press, 1985); Marcus Pohlmann, *Political Power in the Postindustrial City* (New York: Associated Faculties Press, 1986).

CHAPTER 10

Administrators and Bureaucrats

The urbanization explosion brought with it a host of problems that local government ultimately had to address. Streets had to be paved, sanitation systems created, schools built, police and fire protection provided, public hospitals constructed, and so on. As civil unrest rocked America's cities periodically during the postindustrial period, government has responded with a proliferation of additional public services; and given rising public expectations and the conservative nature of the political system, these services have proven difficult to scale back fully once the particular crisis has subsided.

With this increase in the services offered has come a corresponding growth in the number of people hired to provide them. A mammoth bureaucracy has emerged, and its bureaucrats have become increasingly specialized. The same person would no longer conceivably serve as both a police officer and fire fighter. Each field has become a profession, with particularized skills and training expected. Even secretaries, maintenance people, and other support staff within these fields have become specialized.

With this size and particular specializations has come a considerable degree of political power, power that progressive reforms and unionization have only enhanced. Now, the various components of this large and independent bureaucracy must be wooed rather than commanded; and the array of power resources possessed by individual bureaucrats, when taken collectively, make the bureaucracy as a whole a very formidable player in the political system.

HISTORICAL BACKGROUND

A number of historical developments have contributed to the growth and political power of the urban bureaucracy. As urbanization stirred in the mid-nineteenth century, providing city services began to emerge as a full-time occupation for more and more people; for example, the first full-time fire department appeared in 1853.[1] By the end of the industrial era, the stage was set. Political machines had padded the local governmental payrolls and progressive reforms had set these governmental workers free to a considerable extent. Then, postindustrial developments increased their ranks and enhanced their independence at the very time local governmental revenues were diminishing. The rise of bureaucratic power is summarized in the following list.

Historical Developments and Bureaucratic Power

Machine politics	The scope of governmental services expanded, increasing the size of the public work force.
Progressive reforms	These reforms insulated governmental workers from the political reach of the city's elected officials.
The liberal state	As governmental services expanded further yet, so did the number of civil servants.
Bureaucratization	A hierarchical organizational structure facilitated the emergence of parochial agency and subagency fiefdoms.
Unionization	Unionization allowed bureaucrats to increase wages and benefits, adding job security beyond civil service sureties.
Fiscal crisis	City budgetary woes finally have led to some contract showdowns with the increasingly powerful bureaucracies.

Development of Bureaucratic Power

Machine Politics.   Rapid urbanization brought with it immense political opportunities. As ever more urban services had to be provided, the political machines often were there to assign the jobs. But beyond providing traditional services such as police, fire, and sanitation, the machines also hired a host of patronage workers to build and operate schools, hospitals, public housing, and so on. Patronage jobs and public services produced the votes needed for the machine officials to remain in office. In return, public servants were expected to be faithful to the boss, providing the machine their votes, monetary contributions, and campaign services as well as cooperating by delivering more and better service to the loyal wards. Failure to demonstrate such support could cost a worker his or her city job.[2]

Progressive Reforms.   Reformers set out to trim the fat from the public payroll as well as to have services delivered more impartially. One obvious way to do this, of course, was to sever the connection between partisanship and the city worker. Nonpartisan city managers, boards, and commissions would determine which positions were necessary. Meanwhile, civil service systems were created to require hiring by merit alone, and the U.S. Supreme Court has stepped in to limit partisan firings as well. Secret ballots protected these civil servants from pressure to vote for their bosses while variations of the Hatch Act prevented them from taking an active part in the campaign process even if they wanted to. As a result, those public servants that remained had a considerable degree of autonomy from the city's elected officials, just as the reformers had intended.[3]

The Liberal State.   As civil unrest swept the postindustrial cities and governments responded at all levels, government employees would come to regulate far more aspects of the economic system. The American welfare state was also established, committing government to providing a much broader social safety net. Such governmental activity meant a sizable increase in the number of service providers. There were 4.3 million state and local government employees by 1950, 10.8 million by 1972, and more than 13.5 million by 1990.[4] At the local level, this increase meant the mayor would have even more independent civil servants to try to control.

Bureaucratization.   By the 1960s, a body of scholarly literature was developing exploring the best way to organize large institutions, public or private. In time, a consensus began to form around the bureaucracy concept. A highly professional bureaucratic hierarchy became increasingly popular in the industrial sector and gradually began to be cloned in the public sector, also.

In a bureaucratic arrangement, the organizational operation was to be broken into a series of discrete and reasonably routine tasks. Personnel were to specialize narrowly, operate according to an extensive list of written guidelines, and be hired, promoted, and dismissed strictly according to merit. Information was to percolate from bottom to top, where the decision makers could utilize it to formulate policy and then issue the necessary commands. Commands were supposed to flow from top to bottom where they were to be carried out.

Figure 10.1 presents a typical large city adaptation. At the top sit the elected officials who ultimately are answerable to city voters. At the next level are the department administrators who are appointed by the mayor in the strong-mayor systems more common to America's largest cities. Mayors appoint top administrators they believe will administer policy in much the way they themselves would if the city had not become so big and technically complex as to preclude their direct involvement in most of these decisions.

Beneath this level, the departments may be subdivided into divisions, sections, or whatever name they happen to go by, with each subdivision having its own administrators. Meanwhile, the service-providing bureaucrats are at the very bottom. These are the police officers, fire fighters, building code inspectors, teachers, nurses, secretaries, and all others who actually provide services, as opposed to supervising their delivery. Beneath the level of department administrators, virtually all the rest of the bureaucracy is made up of civil servants, career bureaucrats who are hired and promoted by a merit system and can be dismissed only for cause.

Max Weber, in his influential essay "Bureaucracy," set out the case for a hierarchical pyramid with carefully specified rules of procedure.[5] The goal was to design an operation that would function more like a machine than a

FIGURE 10.1 City Bureaucracy

conglomeration of individuals acting on their own values and biases. The end result was to be increased impartiality and efficiency.[6]

Such an arrangement would establish clear lines of responsibility so that specific individuals could be held accountable for all the organization's actions, or lack thereof. Strict, impersonal adherence to an extensive body of formal written rules also would guarantee that both the organization's personnel and their clients would be treated evenhandedly. Clients would receive services and employees would receive rewards according to the criteria established by the CEOs, board of directors, mayors, and city councils.

Peter Blau added that efficiencies also would arise as secure workers, liberated from the fear of arbitrary treatment, would exercise more initiative and innovation. In addition, the formality of the rules would reduce internal competition and pettiness, resulting in a more unified work force commonly pursuing the organization's goals.[7]

Despite the logical coherence of this arrangement on paper, it did not operate precisely as designed once the people were added. Individual workers were more than abstract cogs in a conceptual machine. Each brought his or her own biases and interests to the workplace, and no organizational structure could harness those completely.

> Modern bureaucracies . . . contain the same competitive, self-serving urges that motivated the traditional political machines. Whereas the ward bosses pursued their career goals by promoting the particular interests of neighborhood groups, modern administrators pursue their career goals by promoting the particular interests of departmental and professional specialty groups.[8]

In a number of ways and for a number of reasons, bureaucracies simply have not functioned quite as expected. Even Weber recognized that the bureaucratic form of organization posed inherent problems, such as a likely tendency for subdivisions to hoard information if doing so would serve their narrow parochial interests.[9]

Harold Wilensky, for instance, found that clear, timely, and reliable information was being obstructed at various points throughout the large bureaucratically organized institutions he had analyzed in depth. Information often was withheld or slanted in a way that served the interests of the department presenting it. In addition, those at the bottom of the organizational chart often resisted commands from above. They complained that they were closest to the actual service provision and knew best what was needed; yet important decisions tended to be made by less knowledgeable administrators a number of steps removed from the front. Therefore, if an organization is only as good as its information flow (orders from above and intelligence from below), these organizations were deficient.[10] Instead of the kind of central control that was supposed to come from a hierarchical organization such as this, the reality often amounted to parochial functional fiefdoms. Well-entrenched bureaucrats, when operating within their assigned areas of expertise, to a large extent were isolated from external interference and free to further their own organizational self-interests.[11]

Beyond the internal flow of information, bureaucracies have a penchant to expand whether anyone else will benefit from that expansion or not. Having more staff can disperse the work load. Expansion creates additional supervisory positions to which employees can aspire. Administrators' prestige and power increase with the size of their agency. Bureaucrats often come to believe in their mission and desire more resources so as better to accomplish the task—and someone else normally has to raise the revenues to pay for these increases.[12]

As C. Northcote Parkinson concluded, only partly in jest, "[Staff increases] will invariably prove to be between 5.17 and 6.56 percent [per year], irrespective of any variation in the amount of work (if any) to be done." Quite to the contrary, once the staffing is added, "work expands so as to fill the time available for its completion."[13] A bureaucratic agency will rarely say it has more resources than it needs to do its job; it almost always will complain that it does not have enough.

Service-providing bureaucrats also tend to have their own biases against change, especially technological change, as this poses a threat to the benefits they currently derive from a status quo they have helped to create.[14] The status quo allows a certain degree of "creaming" to occur, meaning that bureaucrats can opt to serve those who will be most easily served or whose serving will cast the service providers in the best possible light, such as helping blind people who can conceivably become self-supporting while ignoring the elderly blind.[15]

Robert Merton identified another bureaucratic peculiarity: a tendency for rules to develop a life of their own, to be enforced purely for their own sake. Conformity to the rules became the end rather than intelligent implementation of the particular policy.[16] Nothing can proceed, for example, if the precise forms are not filled out completely. Such slavish adherence to procedure not only makes the job easier by reducing the need to think and make decisions, but it is also a mechanism whereby the bureaucrat protects him or herself from administrative reprimand. One seldom can get into trouble when strictly "going by the book."[17] For the same reasons, there is a very real tendency for bureaucrats to avoid making decisions by passing them on to others along the bureaucratic chain of command.[18]

Thus, rather than feel efficiently and impartially served by insulated and impersonal public-sector bureaucrats, citizens often resent both the time consumed by all the red tape and the confusion created by the bureaucratic language employed.[19] They also become irritated about the bureaucrat's attitude. When run through the "bureaucratic shuffle" at the bureau of motor vehicles, an upper- or middle-class client can be enraged by the "uppity" or "arrogant" behavior of the socially inferior bureau clerk.[20] To make matters worse, the particular city agency often is the only place this specific service can be attained. Consequently, the client cannot punish the bureaucrat by switching his or her business to a competing company.[21]

Unionization. The American labor movement arose in response to capitalist excesses. Workers grew tired of the industrial jungles described by Upton Sinclair[22] and after years of turmoil and bloodshed, they finally won the governmentally guaranteed right to unionize with the passage of the 1935 National Labor Relations Act.[23] Soon industries producing coal, steel, and automobiles were virtually all under union contracts.[24]

Although there had been a few public service unions in the nineteenth century—U.S. postal workers formed the National Association of Letter Carriers in 1890—it would be years before workers in the public sector effectively began to enjoy a legal status similar to that of their private-sector counterparts. By the year 1960, for example, only the state of Wisconsin allowed public employee unions, and the federal courts consistently had upheld such governmental bans.

But in that same year, 1960, President John F. Kennedy signed Executive Order 10988 authorizing the unionization of federal workers, and soon the various states began falling into line. As a result, the number of unionized government workers grew to 3 million by 1974, when approximately two-thirds of the cities with more than 25,000 people had at least some unionized public servants.[25] The American Federation of State, County and Municipal Employees (AFSCME) became the AFL-CIO's third largest union, growing from 100,000 members in 1955 to some 1.25 million by 1990. The Service Employees International Union (SEIU), as another example, saw its numbers of government workers increase from 160,000 in 1970 to nearly 500,000 by 1990.[26] Thus, while the percentage of all workers in unions was decreasing from a 1945 peak of 35 percent to approximately one in six today, nearly 40 percent of all government workers now are unionized. More than 40 percent of these governmental workers work in jobs that are covered by union contracts (see figure 10.2), and the numbers are higher yet when only state and local government employees are considered.[27]

There was to be one fundamental difference between private-sector unions and most of their counterparts in the public sector. Calvin Coolidge stated it clearly: "There is no right to strike against the public safety by anybody,

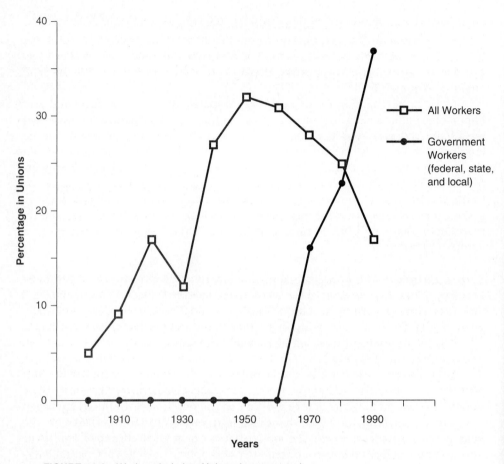

FIGURE 10.2   Workers in Labor Unions (percentages)

anywhere, anytime."[28] Thus, certain strategic groups of federal workers are not allowed to unionize, for example, the armed forces; others are allowed to unionize but not to strike, such as air-traffic controllers. The large majority of states also have various antistrike clauses in the laws that govern their public-sector unions.[29] Yet, despite such laws, most of these public employees strike anyway; and they are seldom legally reprimanded for doing so.

Fiscal Crisis.   Emboldened by unionization beyond their civil service status as well as their relative distance from the direct oversight of elected officials, these bureaucrats came to be in the strongest position they had ever known, both to protect existing budgets and to attain larger ones. On the revenue side of the equation, however, postindustrial advance had left many of their host cities squeezed for tax revenues. Fiscal crises were developing in these cities; and as talk began to turn to retrenchment, the bureaucracy was a primary target as two-thirds to three-quarters of most cities' operating budgets go to labor costs.[30]

The stage was set for what would come to be almost ritualistic showdowns between public service unions and city halls over budget allocations. In the 1980s, there were some defeats as the number of public employees began to level off;[31] but no matter how the showdowns ended, the bureaucracy remained the place where programs were formulated and ultimately implemented. They were certain to remain power centers in the local political process, even if not expanding in size and compensation.

POLITICAL POWER

The mayor's influence on the activities of the operating department is . . . marginal rather than central: Most departmental activities simply go on unchanged or with changes introduced without any reference to the mayor. Even the budgetary authority of a strong mayor . . . is limited primarily to passing on the size of proposed and normally small increases to the total amounts approved the previous year.[32]

For all practical purposes, the bureaucracy has legislative, executive, and judicial power. Its workers provide much of the information on which government policy is based and often they actually write the policy proposals themselves, such as a proposal to computerize the library system (legislative power). In the end it is up to them to carry out any policies ultimately passed by the elected officials, for example, to provide shelter for the homeless (executive power). They will have considerable discretion in determining who is in or out of compliance with existing laws, as in closing down restaurants that do not meet city health codes (judicial power).

In terms of judicial power, the courts normally will not even hear citizen appeals of bureaucratic decisions until there has been an "exhaustion of remedies" within the bureaucratic arena; even then, the appeal is heard in the court of appeals, indicating the significant legal status of agency adjudications. But as appeals can aggravate supervisors and create more work for themselves, bureaucrats often will actively and successfully discourage constituents from appealing their decisions. Thus, their decisions normally become the last word.[33]

The political power possessed by public-service bureaucracies stems from at least four separate realities. First, given their relative distance from the direct oversight of elected officials, they have considerable discretion as to the details of how specific laws actually are to be implemented. Second, as elected decision makers rely on them for information and advice, bureaucrats can shape policy by the information they choose to release and the way they frame their presentations. Third, service constituencies can be rallied to help service providers protect existing services. And, last, unionization has added another layer of protection beyond the civil service system, the Hatch Act, and other safeguards.

Application Discretion

[Bureaucrats determine] what the city government does, for whom, how quickly, by what methods and at what cost.[34]

When the city council passes a law, it almost always will contain at least some general language to allow flexibility as the law is applied by the bureaucracy. This practice saves the council from having continually to rewrite its legislation to fit each new situation that occurs. As a result, the bureaucracy issues far more interpretive regulations than the council does laws.

Besides formally filling gaps between the lines of council-passed laws, the bureaucracy also has ample opportunity to shape those laws in the course of normal implementation. Each day, these workers must decide precisely how to enforce the law and who is and is not in compliance. They have considerable leeway because most such decisions occur outside the visibility of either the council, mayor, top administrators, or most of the public.

As figure 10.1 indicated, there are multiple layers to large-city bureaucracies, and there are often opportunites for discretion at each step. The department head interprets the law for the division head, who does the same for the section head, who does the same for the service-providing civil servants in that section, whether they be police officers, social workers, or teachers.[35] It is the interpretation of the street-level bureaucrats, however, that really counts in the end, for they are the ones who actually deliver the services to the public.[36] With flexible laws and the low visibility of most of their decisions, there is considerable leeway at the street level.

Will the vice officer arrest the streetwalker, or simply suggest she keep a lower profile? Will the social worker be sympathetic to the abusive parent's pleas? Will the garbage collector reach over to pick up the paper that has fallen out of the trash can as it was dumped into the truck? How will the teacher interpret that controversial passage in the school board-approved text?[37]

CASE STUDY   Selectivity in the Ticketing of Cars

by Selwyn Raab

The [New York] State Commission on Investigation said an undercover investigation in the Little Italy section of Manhattan found that many city traffic enforcement agents routinely refrained from giving tickets to illegally parked cars of merchants and restaurateurs and their employees.

The commission said the owners of 67 vehicles were identified as "persistent violators who continually disregarded parking laws in Little Italy without being ticketed."

Restaurant owners and employees apparently avoided receiving summonses by displaying their menus inside auto windshields. Other drivers put bags over functioning meters, and agents never checked to see if the meters were working, the commission said in a report.

In one incident, the commission said, undercover investigators videotaped a restaurateur breaking a meter on Mulberry Street with a screwdriver and putting a bag over it so he could park his car there all day. The videotape has been turned over to the Police Department, the commission said.

After five months of periodic surveillance in 1988 and 1989, the commission asserted that agents in Little Italy were poorly supervised. Many shirked their duties by shopping, visiting with friends and taking two-hour lunches, the commission asserted.

> In one instance, investigators followed two agents from Little Italy to the East Village where the agents spent two and a half hours resting in a funeral home instead of patrolling. . . .
>
> Transportation Department guidelines require a traffic enforcement lieutenant or supervisor to verify the whereabouts and productivity of each agent at least twice in a work shift. According to the report, no such inspection was observed in five months of surveillance. . . .
>
> The poor enforcement in Little Italy—a congested 12-block area in lower Manhattan—cost the city about $2 million a year in parking fines, the commission said. The inquiry and financial analysis covered Little Italy, but based on these findings the commission said, "One can only imagine the loss of revenue in the entire city."
>
> *New York Times,* March 21, 1990.[38] Copyright © 1990 by The New York Times Company. Reprinted by permission.

At each discretionary juncture, bureaucrats can choose to serve one of many masters. At one end of this continuum, they can be absolutely loyal to the mayor, working to implement policy exactly as they feel the mayor would want it implemented. At the other extreme, they will serve their own interests, making decisions that will increase the likelihood of their own personal advances or make their jobs easier, safer, or more secure. In between, they may have department, division, or section loyalties as well; for example, police may make "collars for dollars" if their department or subdivision is allowed to retain some of the money garnered from the fines generated by those additional arrests.

Beyond the tremendous discretion they have in implementing policy, they also can use this discretion to bring pressure to bear on elected officials. Through *protracted obstinance* unhappy bureaucrats literally can drag their feet, sometimes just short of being fired, in order to disrupt service delivery and cause constituents to complain. Not getting the garbage collected on time can create more than unpleasantness after awhile and can lead to enough public outcry that the mayor may well be tempted to give in to the sanitation workers' demands. In Los Angeles, where public furor erupted after the police beating of Rodney King, the police responded in a defensive manner. Arrests dropped by 15 percent in the precinct of the four indicted officers.[39] In New York City, police virtually stopped writing traffic tickets in order to protest an impasse in their labor negotiations.[40] In New Haven, more than one in six police officers called in "sick" (an epidemic of what has come to be called the "blue flu") to protest both departmental disciplinary action against two officers and deadlocked contract talks.[41]

The precisely opposite way to create this political heat on elected officials is for bureaucrats to engage in *excessive compliance* with the law so as to bring comparable pressure to bear. For example, when Memphis mayor Dick Hackett wandered into a police precinct house and found too many officers watching television, the police responded to his reprimands by making nearly twice their usual number of arrests the following night. Memphis Police Association president Ray Maples vowed that the police would continue to increase their number of arrests. "We'll work hard every night," he said.[42]

There are constraints, of course. For example, there are a number of formal and informal *decision rules* to guide bureaucrats as they exercise their discretionary prerogatives. Occasionally these rules are externally generated, but normally they evolve from practices within the agency itself.[43] Following these rules to the letter is the safer way to proceed as it gives at least the appearance of neutrality. However, exceptions are reasonably common as well: a client-oriented welfare caseworker may choose to ignore certain outside income of a client if the caseworker feels the welfare payments are inadequate to begin with, or a bigoted caseworker may presume that all Hispanic clients are lazy and treat them accordingly.[44]

Beyond the discretion to make exceptions, many of the decision rules have been created by the bureaucrats to best serve their own preferred purposes. Thus, these rules often are loaded with imbedded biases. For instance, it may be standard police practice to stop any black male noticed in a white neighborhood or standard for a teacher to place African American students in the vocational track based largely on their modes of speech or cultural traits.[45] James Q. Wilson refers to these latter practices as "statistically defensible" but "individually unjust."[46]

Information and Advice

> The "political master" finds himself in the position of the "dilettante" who stands opposite the "expert" . . . [47]

If the mayor sets the council's agenda, it is the executive bureaucracy that generally sets the mayor's agenda. For the most part, what the mayor knows is what has percolated up from below. As the bureaucrats are the primary local experts in their particular field, whether it be education or law enforcement, not many in the city will be in a position to question their information, conclusions, and advice. They are the trained professionals who actually have been delivering these services over time. Given the political power inherent in making the proposals around which the legislative debate will revolve, their provision of information is a very important source of bureaucratic influence.[48]

As in the case of application discretion, bureaucrats can choose to serve any of a number of interests. They can selectively distort statistics that reflect on them or their local office; for example, a police precinct can list an ambiguous crime in the least offensive category or compare its recent crime rates to particularly bad years to create the impression that the situation has improved. On the other hand, if they are trying to get the mayor to provide them with more resources, that same precinct may leak a report to the press providing selected crime statistics to indicate just how dangerous that particular community has become.[49]

The city's fiscal circumstances may dictate that bureaucrats do not get everything they want, but if they continue to ask only for small incremental increases, these are not likely to receive much critical scrutiny.[50] Also, they can pad their budget requests to safeguard against losing anything of real importance to them. Such padding allows the mayor and council to look tough when they deny those add-on requests, but in the end the bureaucrats get essentially what they wanted from the outset, and the taxpayer picks up the tab.

This bureaucratic power, however, is not employed solely to feather their own nests. Many bureaucrats have strong feelings about the substance of policy in their areas, and they will act accordingly. An elementary school principal may be convinced of the value of a particular reading series and recommend it vigorously to the school board. A social worker may be very sympathetic to the plight of his or her clients and press for more allocations. A fire fighter may become frustrated with the number of dead children carried from burning tenement apartments and leak statistics to the press that are likely to prod the city to increase the number of fire stations in those communities.

On the other hand, a police chief may believe that family squabbles are best settled within the home and thus recommend against allocating additional police resources for preventing domestic violence. A prison psychologist may be most sympathetic to the prison's needs for internal security and thus conclude that "suicide cells" (where prisoners are stripped naked and isolated) are necessary, even when there is evidence that they are being used for disciplinary purposes. A hospital administrator may feel that most AIDS patients are "moral degenerates who got what they deserved" and thus not recommend more staff to treat them.

Constituencies

Neighborhoods get to know their police officers and fire fighters. Regular library users come to know the local librarians. Parents work with their children's principals and teachers—and so on. There is empirical evidence to suggest that bureaucrats, whether they are aware of it or not, generally are inclined to offer more and better services to existing clients rather than attempt to expand their clientele.[51]

Thus, these service constituents often will listen when their service providers tell them that the quality of service will diminish if certain cuts are made or certain budget items are not added. Constituents, then, can and do become a powerful lobbying force to help various agencies get their way. In essence, the bureaucrat-client relationship often can become reciprocal.[52]

Job Security

A combination of civil service status and unionization further insulates and empowers the bureaucracy. The overwhelming majority have attained their positions through civil service procedures. They listed their qualifications, took a written test, were ranked, and were later appointed by a separate civil service commission on the basis of their ranking and other qualifications. Not only are elected officials constrained in the hiring process, but the bureaucrats can thereafter be fired only for serious cause, such as blatant dereliction of duty.[53]

An increasingly large number of these employees have joined professional organizations such as the Fraternal Order of Police, National Education Association, International City and County Management Association, Civil Service

Assembly of the United States and Canada, and American Society of Municipal Engineers. Others have affiliated with large national unions such as AFSCME, SEIU, the Laborers International Union, and the International Fire Fighters. The larger the city, the higher will be the proportion of its public work force that is unionized.[54]

Pressure Politics.   Large group affiliation allows bureaucrats to pressure government decision makers in many of the same ways other interest groups do—through electoral campaigning, initiatives, referenda, recalls, committee testimony, and private persuasion.[55] Rather than focusing on substantive policy matters, however, these organizations normally concentrate on work place issues such as compensation, job classifications, working conditions, and decisional authority. AFSCME, for example, won a "comparable worth" provision in Los Angeles, gaining special raises for 3,900 clerks and librarians, mostly women, bringing their salaries into line with those in certain male-dominated categories.[56] In terms of choosing work place issues over policy concerns, however, there are examples to the contrary as well as ones that are difficult to categorize. When teachers press for smaller classes and more preparation time or sanitation workers achieve stricter antipollution laws, are these purely self-serving demands?[57]

Collective Bargaining.   Most states have legalized collective bargaining for their public employees. Under these provisions government workers are allowed to organize and the city must bargain in good faith with the resulting public service unions. For purposes of expediency, however, the city normally grants *exclusive recognition* to a manageable number of unions that will then bargain for the rest.

If the local unions are coordinated at all, they are likely to choose the order of negotiations very carefully in a process called *pattern bargaining.* They probably will not start with policemen or fire fighters as the public will be deeply resentful if public safety is jeopardized by a strike of one of these essential groups. They also will not start with the social workers, as a strike by that group cannot pose enough of a problem for the city as a whole. A good tactic is to have the transit workers negotiate first, assuming a city is reliant on its mass transportation system as many are. If these workers strike, they can all but shut down the city. Thus, it will be in the mayor's interest to avoid that development. Afterward, the other unions normally can "piggyback" on this initial settlement—meaning to ask for and receive much the same benefits.[58]

The Bargaining Ritual.   There is a ritual that must be undergone first, however. No matter which union is bargaining, negotiators on both sides are likely to make some unrealistic demands. Ultimately, both are hoping for an acceptable compromise somewhere in the middle; meanwhile, these exaggerated demands will allow them to appear tough to their constituencies. Both sides will use the mass media to project their positions and posturings, occasionally even using paid advertisements.[59]

Often, they will reach an impasse, with no progress being made. At that point, either voluntary or compulsory mediation usually begins. State law may call for external *fact finders* to intervene and try to sort our the disputed facts, ultimately delivering a report that includes nonbinding recommendations.[60] If there is still no agreement, state *arbitrators* may be called in to attempt to reach a compromise by using their professional negotiating skills to nudge the parties toward an acceptable alternative. Both sides may agree to *binding arbitration* in which the mediator has the authority to impose a compromise; or there may be *final offer arbitration* whereby the arbiter chooses between each party's last offer.[61] The city normally resists any binding solutions, however, as these may amount to the external imposition of tax increases. The unions would still have the ability to stage an illegal strike or otherwise disrupt city services if they did not like the mediator's package, while the city would be contractually bound to it.

The norm is for the two sides to reach an eleventh hour settlement just before the strike deadline. Yet, should the union strike, and many did between 1965 and 1975 in particular,[62] another ritual is set into motion. The city will proceed to seek a court injunction against the strike, especially if it is in a state that prohibits public-sector walkouts. Even if such an injunction is attained, the union often will strike anyway, occasionally followed by the arrest of its leadership or even some of its striking members.

Thereafter the ball is in the city's court, and the mayor actually has little choice. The city usually will make a few necessary concessions to union demands, besides agreeing not to prosecute union members and not to seek excessive fines. There are several reasons for the city's actions. First, public pressure has mounted for a return to normalcy.[63] Second, the mayor recognizes that he or she is confronted with a well-organized group of city workers whose cooperation is necessary for the effective delivery of city services. Third, this group also tends to turn out in relatively large numbers at election time, and they tend to vote as a bloc.[64] As a New York City union leader remarked, "We have a natural advantage no [private-sector] union has. We can elect our employers."[65] New York's Edward Costikyan concluded, "The best political machine in New York City is John LeLury's Sanitationmen's Union."[66] Last, such combined union pressure is likely to outweigh whatever the more atomized general public is going to think of the tax increases required later to pay for the settlement.[67]

There have been a couple of fairly standard ways for elected officials to dodge this dispersed public pressure. For one thing, they can hide and in effect defer compensation increases by agreeing to generous pension plans, shorter work hours, and more paid holidays, rather than directly increasing the operating budget by adding to wages.[68] Thereafter, an *election-taxation cycle* also can be employed whereby the city raises needed taxes in the years in which there are no city elections. The general electorate tends to have a short political attention span, and new issues will surface before the next election.[69]

The Strike Option.   Why do antistrike laws appear to be so ineffective? As previously indicated, a combination of civil service status and unionization protects these workers from arbitrary treatment. It is difficult for the mayor to fire them by proving that they have not been doing an adequate job. Given that reality, the mayor must seek their cooperation rather than attempt to command them, and it is difficult to get cooperation from workers who have been forced back to their jobs by a court order. Also, when striking workers or their leaders are arrested, they tend to become martyrs; it is bad public relations for the city to have front page pictures of little Mary's kindergarten teacher being led away in handcuffs. Finally, the unions realize that jail sentences, fines, and other punishments can be bargained away later.

There have been a few notable exceptions, however. When the Reagan administration broke the federal air traffic controllers union (PATCO) by simply firing all those illegally out on strike, many felt this action would have a chilling effect on public service unions at all levels of government. Yet, there were some unique aspects to that particular situation. The air traffic controllers had few constituents that they could rally given their relative distance from airline passengers; and they could be replaced somewhat readily by trained military controllers. They also were a small, relatively wealthy group who had regularly endorsed Republican candidates and refused to observe the picket lines of the rest of the airport unions. Thus, they received little help in their strike from other unions in the airports or anywhere else around the country.

At the city level, some of these same factors come into play. If the illegally striking group is small, relatively isolated, and not particularly difficult to replace, the mayor may well stand up to them. In New York City, for instance, 16 ferry boat operators struck in violation of state law and were subsequently fired and replaced.[70]

In Atlanta, however, it was the city's sanitation union. These predominantly African American workers had endorsed black mayor Maynard Jackson, yet they had not received a pay raise in three years despite soaring national inflation in the late 1970s. Nevertheless, when they went out on strike, Jackson was able to rally public opinion against them. Martin Luther King, Sr., for example, argued that the poor simply could not afford any more taxes. When the mayor fired them all, the public accepted the disruption in service, and there was no general strike by all city unions.[71] One of the lessons is that there are limits to how far the public can be pushed, and the public service unions must gauge those limits with considerable care.

Since that time, there have been a number of teacher walkouts, a major sanitation worker strike in Detroit in the summer of 1986, and a near general strike in Philadelphia that same summer; but for a variety of reasons, there have not been many other major strikes. Some city workers actually have been giving back previously gained benefits, acceding to certain merit pay schemes and investing union pension funds in city bonds in order to keep their cities solvent.[72] The reason is that city workers generally have fared at least as well as their private-sector counterparts, and many recognize that.[73] In addition, with most records open to the public, they are aware of the very real fiscal squeeze being experienced by their cities and they often have moderated their demands accordingly.[74]

GOVERNMENTAL IMPLICATIONS

Occasionally a mayor does intervene in the operation of a department on his own initiative. He may direct that some specific item that has come to his attention be handled in a certain way. He may demand more energetic action in dealing with an outstanding problem. Or, in a field in which he has special competence or a pet interest, he may even require a specific change in policy. . . . But given the press of all the mayor's duties, free time and energy for such interventions are rare, and when they take place by the typical mayor, it is far from certain that the desired action by the operating department will be actually forthcoming.[75]

Direct Bureaucratic Influence

The bureaucracy, taken collectively, remains one of the most powerful political entities in the postindustrial city. These workers have tremendous impact over government decisions, from policy formulation to implementation to adjudication, even though they are operating primarily on delegated authority. Thus, elected officials are put into a position where they must persuade and cajole the bureaucrats if those officials hope to shape public policy. Commanding is just not possible most of the time. Bureaucrats are generally too insulated and have too many power resources to be commanded.

There are limits to such bureaucratic power, however. Some are internal constraints. Most city workers, like workers in any other employment sector, take pride in doing a good job, delivering their services in a fair, efficient, and professionally responsible manner.[76] Most of them live in the city and they want high-quality government services just as much as any other resident. Externally, postindustrial cities have significant fiscal limitations, leaving a variety of agencies competing for many of the same scarce resources. Thus the various agencies will check one another to some degree.

The citizenry also has some recourse. Interest groups have become well aware of bureaucratic power and now lobby the bureaucracy as well as elected officials. The Atlanta example above showed that if the general public is angry enough to endure the service disruption, mayors can crack down on city workers. If nothing else, city taxpayers with enough money can vote with their feet, leaving the city with even fewer revenues. The media can expose certain noncomplying practices, and service recipients may well have recourse to appeal a bureaucrat's decision in the courts, for example, if a restaurant owner feels his or her establishment actually did meet city code.

Despite those checks, the reality is that elected officials and events come and go, but career bureaucrats remain. When the political winds currently are running against them, these career civil servants need only bide their time until a new administration comes around or new circumstances develop.[77]

Indirect Bureaucratic Influence

Bureaucratic size and power also have significant implications. The sheer size of the bureaucracy will create a significant amount of red tape, slowing down the entire governmental process.[78] Its entrenchment makes it very difficult for rapid policy change to occur. City governments tend to engage in incremental budgeting rather than large, wholesale reviews; thus, generous wage and benefit packages are hard to pare back, and cities are so labor intensive that it is difficult for them to offset labor cost increases with cuts elsewhere.

The Revolving Door

Another conservative force is the revolving door that tends to develop, whereby higher-level city employees go to work for private firms that have much to gain by utilizing their governmental connections. For example, Austin's city manager became a senior vice-president for the largest home builder in the area. The city planner in Fairfax County, Virginia, advised on the construction of a $1 billion megacenter, then joined the development's primary engineering and site-planning firm. New York City's housing development commissioner became an executive vice-president for Trump and Associates. The list goes on.[79]

Police Brutality

One of the most vexing problems facing today's postindustrial mayors is how to curb gratuitous police violence, often directed at young black males. Memphis police, for example, fired 19 shots at a man armed with a barbeque fork.[80] New York police broke Michael Stewart's neck after arresting him for drunkenness and scrawling graffiti on a subway wall.[81] Los Angeles police were captured on videotape brutally beating Rodney King, arrested for speeding; and this incident turned out to be only the tip of the much larger iceberg of police racism and brutality in Los Angeles.[82] Philadelphia police dropped a bomb on a radical group's house, killing 11 group members and burning down 61 nearby homes.[83] And that list goes on as well.

Black communities in a number of large cities have demonstrated their anger in a variety of ways, and gradually media attention has begun to focus on the problem—expanding the decisional scope outside the police department. Some cities have set up civilian review boards to hear citizen complaints about police misbehavior,[84] and in March of 1985, the U.S. Supreme Court narrowed the circumstances under which police were allowed to use deadly force.[85]

ALTERNATIVE APPROACHES

Cities have taken a variety of steps to rein in their bureaucracies. Elected officials and appointed administrators are not helpless in this process. They retain a number of measures that can encourage compliance. In addition, fiscally strapped cities have been turning to private and semiprivate agencies to deliver many of the services previously provided by the city's own bureaucracy. Such alternatives help cut costs and arguably add some administrative control.

Executive Prerogatives

The civil service and unionization protection enjoyed by bureaucrats does not make them totally free of *administrative constraints*. If recalcitrance can be uncovered, administrators may discipline underlings not only by firing them but by manipulating their pay increases, work hours, promotions, and job descriptions.[86] A variety of management techniques can be employed as well; for instance, administrators and line bureaucrats can be rotated regularly to avoid the development of entrenched bureaucratic fiefdoms, while aggressive independent budget analysts also can be utilized.[87]

The city of Detroit wanted to get a better sense of where its bureaucracy was failing as well as to elicit more responsiveness from those agencies. It hired *omsbudsmen* to serve as liaisons between citizens and the bureaucracy as well as to channel citizen complaints. Soon these intermediaries were handling thousands of calls per year and mailing formal replies in each case;[88] this response contrasts dramatically to cities like Houston where one in three queries received no reply whatsoever.[89] Elsewhere, cities have introduced civilian boards to review the behavior of the city's police officers.

To reduce the velocity of the revolving door and decrease other forms of corruption, cities can adopt their own *codes of ethics*. New York City recently used a charter revision to require that city employees who left government service not appear before their former agencies as representatives of a private business until at least one year after leaving their city jobs; they are not ever to become involved in a matter in which they "personally and substantively" participated while on the city payroll.[90]

Far more important than those devices, the real key to controlling the bureaucracy ultimately comes to two fundamental tenets. First, *administrators* must be chosen very carefully. They need to be intelligent and capable individuals who not only agree with the mayor's basic policy approaches but also will be able to generate respect up and down the ranks. As for the second tenet, it is crucial that solid *cooperative relationships* be maintained from the mayor down. There must be mutual trust and respect. The alternative is an alienated and combative work force that can do considerable political damage if they are coerced into obedience.[91]

Achieving change in bureaucratic practices may be a long and arduous administrative task, but it can be done. Mayoral leadership and administrative skills can and have made at least some difference in this regard.[92] Yet improved practices are not always best accomplished by attempting to acquire more centralized decision control. That is nearly impossible in the postindustrial city.

In order to keep the bureaucrats happy as well as to free up more time for himself and his top administrators, Mayor Abraham Beame issued Executive Order #90 in the fall of 1976. It allowed agency heads to award salary increases, hire new personnel, authorize trips, and purchase new equipment without having to have mayoral approval each time, as long as they remained within their spending ceilings. A number of other cities have experimented with various forms of neighborhood-level administration.[93] Such *decentralization* has become more the rule than the exception in cities experiencing the brunt of postindustrialism.

Public Authorities

The Problem.   A problem unique to public-sector agencies is finding a good measure of their efficiency and success. In the private sector, there is always "the bottom line." If profits are rising, the company is doing something right. If they are declining, there are problems that will have to be addressed. Unfortunately, city agencies have no such convenient measure of their progress. Because they are not profit-making businesses, they have to rely on other indices.[94]

Probably the most watched single index is the election returns. If the city's top elected officials continue to receive impressive levels of electoral support, they must be doing something right. However, this a rather crude measure for a number of reasons. It is always difficult to determine mandates from elections that revolve around multiple and complex issues. Elections are inevitably quite time bound, meaning they are affected disproportionately by the most recent events.

Another emphatic indicator is the number of people moving away. If the city is losing population, one reason is likely a relative dissatisfaction with perceived living conditions in the city, but officials are left to guess precisely why any particular individual makes such a move.

Slightly more precise are public opinion polls, although even they tend to be time bound unless the same questions are asked on a regular basis throughout the year, a practice that can be costly in pollster fees. Another problem with polls is their difficulty in capturing the intensity of the opinions being expressed. Intensity surfaces when people take the time to write letters to the newspaper, call in to local radio talk shows, or contact their elected officials or a particular bureaucratic agency. Yet, the people who do these things are not necessarily representative of the local citizenry at large.[95]

Beyond studying the equivalent of customer satisfaction, there are other ways of measuring service quality. The unit costs of providing a service, such as pounds of garbage collected per dollar expended, can be calculated over time to gauge an increase or decrease in efficiency. Such costs and trends can be compared to those of comparable agencies in other cities or to any private-sector firms that deliver comparable services.[96]

All of these are only indicators, however. It is difficult to ascertain precisely what the city spends to deliver particular services because many overhead costs often are dispersed elsewhere in the city's budget—bond interest, insurance fees, office construction and maintenance, and vehicle purchase, fuel, and maintenance.[97] Second, the indicators that can be obtained are not full output measures. Public safety cannot be measured fully by relying primarily on crime rates or arrest-to-crime ratios. Standardized tests measure only part of what is imparted in the educational process. There is much more to public health than infant mortality rates.

The measures commonly used actually can distort bureaucratic performance as service providers begin to concentrate on the measured areas. As an example, teachers are encouraged to teach to the standardized tests rather than stress class discussions and critical writing. This type of emphasis also can have an impact on who gets the public services whether they are the most in need of them or not.[98]

The Alternative.   Beyond such efforts to find adequate surrogates for bottom-line profit figures, most cities have been structuring some of their agencies in ways that allow them more closely to replicate private firms. The resulting entities tend to be called *semiprivate corporations* or *public authorities,* such as mass transit authorities or health and hospital corporations. These are quasi-public in that elected officials normally choose their directors, but they are quasi-private in that these directors normally are afforded considerable independence and the agencies are to be operated for a profit.

There are at least three possible advantages to be gained from such arrangements. First, they remove administrative decisions further from political considerations and, if successful, increase efficiency and impartiality in the process. Second, they produce a bottom-line profit figure by which to gauge success.[99] Third, although rarely admitted, such quasi-independent bodies can allow elected officials to sidestep responsibility for services that almost always generate more complaints than compliments, such as mass transportation or city hospitals. Known for his characteristic candor, New York City mayor Ed Koch smugly concluded that "[the subway system] stinks, but it's not my baby."[100]

In 1921, the Port Authority of New York and New Jersey (PATH) was the first public authority established, and it remains one of the very largest. Presently, it is responsible for three airports, six bridges and tunnels, the World Trade Center, several bus and ship terminals, and a number of other office and manufacturing buildings. It is run by a board of 12 commissioners and employs roughly 8,000 people.

Even larger is New York City's Health and Hospitals Corporation. Established in 1970, it spends more than a billion dollars annually to operate 16 hospitals with more than 10,000 beds, as well as the city's primary ambulance service. It employs roughly 40,000 people and serves approximately six million patients annually on either an inpatient or outpatient basis. The 15 members of its governing board serve staggered five-year terms and are responsible for hiring their own chief executive officer. One-third of the board is appointed by the mayor, and one-third by the city council; the final one-third are the health services administrator, the commissioner of health, the commissioner of mental health, the human resources administrator, and the deputy mayor for policy.[101]

Limitations.   Despite their attractiveness in the abstract, these public authorities are not without their inherent biases. Annamarie Walsh conducted a five-year study of 7,000 such authorities responsible for spending $27 billion annually. She found that they lacked accountability, at least in part because they tended to operate behind closed doors. She also found that they had a distinct inclination to place profits ahead of service, and that the two are not always the same thing. As an example, water authorities tended to spend available monies on power generation rather than recreation or pollution control. Housing authorities built middle- and even upper-income housing in lieu of housing for the poor.[102] She concluded that

> ideologies of laissez-faire, localism, autonomy and limited politics converge to limit the forms and ambitions of public enterprise. . . . [They] preserve the power of groups with narrow and specialized aims, and . . . relieve themselves of obligations to respond to broader interests.[103]

The hard truth is that there is a significant difference in the fundamental functions of a city and a private business. A private business has one purpose: to maximize profits for its shareholders. A city, on the other hand, has a far more complex role to play and one that is not as easily guided by a market mechanism. It must provide basic maintenance services such as police and fire protection and sanitation; these must be delivered to everyone in the city regardless of their ability to pay. The city is responsible for certain other communitywide services, such as keeping the air and water clean and the economy healthy. Finally, the city also is responsible for some wealth redistribution as well, extracting revenues from those more able to pay in order to provide additional services for those less well off, such as counseling for the jobless, food for the hungry, and shelter for the homeless.

Public authorities can pose problems even in their own right. At times they are created as a way to dodge legitimate state taxation and debt limits. In other words, when a city can no longer tax and spend for additional local services, public authorities are a convenient way to provide these services despite state law, as public authorities often will have their own debt limits and revenue-raising mechanisms. Their political insulation also can make it difficult to hold them accountable when they are inefficient or corrupt.[104]

Privatization

Since the beginning of the 1980s the prevailing political philosophy has been that governments should shed what services they can. When you add to that prevailing philosophy the fiscal imperatives that are arising in a lot of cities . . . you add a lot more momentum to the privatization process.[105]

Regardless of the service being delivered, cities have been experimenting with a wide variety of delivery mechanisms. It is no longer as simple as having all city services provided by city employees. Figure 10.3 indicates a number of possible delivery vehicles ranging from city departments to full privatization.

Full Privatization.   If city services were fully privatized, city government would provide none of them. Instead, each citizen would be responsible for hiring a private provider for the specific services he or she wanted and was willing to pay for. That citizen would shop around for the desired private school, security guards, garbage hauler, and so on. Nowhere, of course, have cities abdicated all such responsibility. It is not very practical to have individual citizens contracting for their own police and fire protection, pollution control, and health code

FIGURE 10.3 Privatizing Alternatives

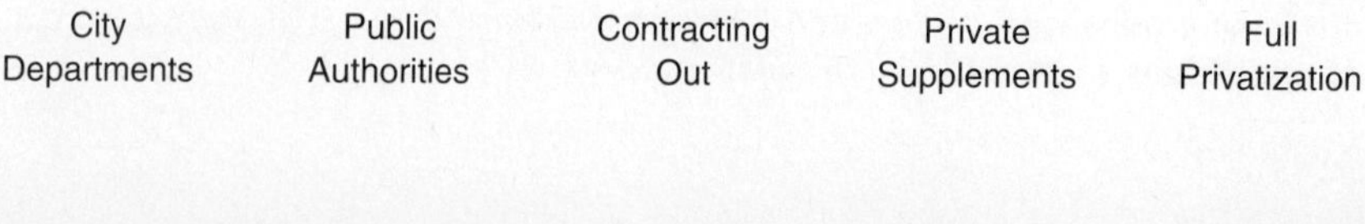

City Departments	Public Authorities	Contracting Out	Private Supplements	Full Privatization

enforcement. A number of services simply can be delivered more practically by government.

Private Supplements.   Short of full privatization is the availability of private services as a supplement for those who desire them and can afford to pay. Individuals may hire a private security agency to supplement their public police protection. Neighborhoods may collectively hire off-duty police officers to patrol their communities. Parents may hire private tutors for their children. Residential areas without street lights may pool their money and have them installed.[106] One obvious result of any degree of privatization is that the system provides more services to those with more money. Conversely, those with less money are left with fewer services. In a market economy within a hierarchical distribution of income, those with more money always will have more options.[107]

Also related to equity is the danger that cities will begin to allow these private services to substitute for public ones. Soon, inner-city residents may find reduced essential services like police, fire, health care, and education; as more affluent areas hire many of these services on a private basis, the political pressure will no longer be on elected officials to provide them at past levels. Once this process has begun there is an inclination to drift toward the full privatization end of the continuum, with subsequent negative implications for lower-income city residents.[108]

Contracting Out.   As a compromise, a growing number of cities continue to take responsibility for many citywide services, but they hire either for-profit or nonprofit private contractors to do some of them. This is a process called contracting out. Instead of placing a group of employees on the city payroll for the purpose of delivering a particular service, the city opts to sign a service contract with a private agency; or the city may give out vouchers that citizens may redeem at the service provider of their choice.[109]

Examples abound. They include hospitals in Butte, Montana, and fire protection in Knox County, Tennessee, as well as sanitation services almost everywhere. Memphis hired "ATE" to run its mass transportation system and Corrections Corporation of America to operate two juvenile detention facilities. Boston hired Boston University to run the Chelsea public schools. Milwaukee contracted with private preschools to operate six public kindergartens, Miami Beach hired a private corporation to operate an elementary school, and Duluth hired one to run an entire school district. Los Angeles uses private companies to provide a wide variety of services: hospital food preparation, embalming, water testing, data services, debt collection, record storage, custodial services, golf course operation, and much of their equipment repair. Chicago issues contracts to private firms for towing abandoned cars, tree-trimming, stump removal, engineering, and some drug treatment. The majority of American cities now contract out for major construction projects, janitorial service, and food services at public facilities.[110]

Another variation is to have both city departments and private contractors, and let them compete with each other as has been done in the education field for years. Phoenix and Philadelphia apply this method for sanitation services.

Bay County, Florida, does it for correctional facilities. Tallahassee does it for fire protection.[111]

Have these experiments been a success? If measured strictly by "bang for the buck," the answer is a qualified yes. Many of these private companies do appear to be able to deliver public services at roughly 10 percent to 40 percent less than city agencies can.[112] However, these estimates do not include many hidden costs: the expenses entailed in fielding bids, monitoring contracts, cost overruns, and employee severance. In addition, for-profit firms will choose to operate only where they have a reasonable prospect of making a profit. Therefore, they will avoid unprofitable situations like inner-city hospitals, ambulance service, and mass transit, opting instead to operate far more profitable minimum security prisons. Consequently, it is important to contract precisely, monitor carefully, and not overgeneralize from a few identifiable success stories.[113]

Prisons were privately operated in colonial America, and they became so wretched that government assumed responsibility for them after the American Revolution. Yet, with more than 40 states under court order to reduce jail overcrowding, once again we find ourselves moving back to reliance on what are perceived to be more efficient privately built and operated penal facilities.[114]

The nearly insolvent city of Philadelphia is contemplating major new contracting ventures, only 70 years since rampant corruption led to the repeal of an ordinance that had required city officials to contract out all city services.[115] As postindustrial cities labor under fiscal stress, it may become necessary for them to learn a number of lessons all over again.[116]

Overall Impact.   A result of all of these trends has been that government employment, expressed as a percentage of the overall American work force, has been declining since its peak of 15 percent in 1975.[117] That should be no surprise. Given taxpayer rebellions and federal cutbacks on top of a host of postindustrial difficulties, it was predictable that fiscally strapped cities would begin to look to the most efficient delivery systems available. Also, given the legally imposed limits on patronage hiring and firing, city officials find fewer political advantages in making all those appointments themselves.

Some efficiencies have been achieved in the process, and private competition may well improve the quality of some city-provided services.[118] Nevertheless, the trend toward privatization has raised questions concerning the overall quality of urban service and the equity of service distribution.[119] And the problems do not end there.

Increasing reliance on private services affects *worker compensation*. Public service unions are undercut while the private-sector firms often are not unionized and provide lower wages and fewer benefits. In Norfolk, Virginia, Tidewater Regional Transit charges the city half of what it previously paid for operating certain transit lines; but Tidewater pays their workers $4.50 per hour with no benefits whatsoever whereas the city had paid $10.32 per hour with an additional $3.00 per hour in benefits.[120]

There are direct *social costs* as well. Women and minority workers tend to lose ground in the transition, as government has been more inclined to hire outside the dominant white-male labor pool. About one-quarter of all African American workers are employed by government, while the same is true for only 14 percent of whites.[121] Princeton University sociologist Paul Starr, speaking of the net social result of privatization, said that while some services would cost less to provide, the city's social welfare and public health agencies would spend even more as city workers fell from the public payroll.[122]

There is always the potential for large-scale *corruption* when city contracting agents are wooed by various private firms, as has been the case in the federal government's Department of Defense. This is even more likely given the revolving door syndrome discussed earlier, whereby former government officials are hired by private firms largely because of their government contracts. Or, city decision makers may be tempted to channel contracts to firms in which they have a monetary interest themselves.[123]

Finally, there is also some indication that *over-serving* tends to occur as long as the tab is being paid out of the public coffers, such as hospitals keeping patients longer than necessary in order to collect additional fees. In other words, they treat them more efficiently but at the same time keep them longer than necessary. Once again, what is most profitable for a service provider is not always what is best for the city as a whole.[124]

CONCLUSION

Despite some fiscal pressures and increasing privatization, the bureaucracy remains politically powerful. But, does this lead to inherent biases in the delivery of public services? Do the middle-class values of public administrators and many of the line bureaucrats cause the poor to be underserved? This is a very empirically complex question, and the results are inconclusive. Francis Fox Piven and Richard Cloward have found such disparities, while Robert Lineberry is less convinced that there is a clear pattern here.[125]

A large amount of political power in the hands of unelected bureaucrats, however, does have substantial democratic implications. Michael Lipsky concludes that "accountability is the link between bureaucracy and democracy,"[126] and as we have seen, it is very difficult to hold anyone accountable for most bureaucratic behavior.

Nevertheless, at least bureaucrats are operating on authority delegated to them by officials electorally accountable to the public. The same cannot be said of private-sector elites. If a community is outraged at police brutality, it has some political recourse; but when General Motors threatens to invest elsewhere if the city of Detroit will not destroy an existing neighborhood for it, there really is not much the public, or the elected officials, or the bureaucracy can do.

The reality is that the public is not prepared to demand that the city use eminent domain to seize General Motors. Part of the reason they see the world through the blinders they do, however, has to do with the narrowness of the perspective employed by their primary source of information and ideas: the mass media.

NOTES

1. John Bollens and Henry Schmandt, *The Metropolis* (New York: Harper & Row, 1982), p. 108.
2. See Ferrel Heady, *Public Administration: A Comparative Perspective* (Englewood Cliffs, N.J.: Prentice-Hall, 1966), especially pp. 71–72.
3. For a fuller discussion of both the political machine and the reform movement, see chapter 7 of this volume.
4. U.S. Department of Commerce, Bureau of the Census, *Statistical Abstracts of the United States* (Washington, D.C.: Government Printing Office, annual).
5. Max Weber, "Bureaucracy," in H. H. Gerth and C. Wright Mills, eds., *Essays in Sociology* (New York: Oxford University Press, 1962).
6. *Efficiency* in an economic sense refers to output per resources expended. A city has become more efficient if it is getting more service, however that is defined and measured, for each additional resource expended. In political parlance, it is getting "more bang for the buck." For example, see George Washkins, ed., *Productivity Improvement for State and Local Government* (New York: Wiley, 1980).
7. Peter Blau, *Bureaucracy in Modern Society* (New York: Random House, 1971).
8. Clarence Stone, *Urban Policy and Politics in a Bureaucratic Age* (Englewood Cliffs, N.J.: Prentice-Hall, 1979), p. 14. Also see Theodore Lowi, "Machine Politics—Old and New," *The Public Interest* 78 (Fall 1967): 83–92.
9. Weber, "Bureaucracy," p. 233.
10. Harold Wilensky, *Organizational Intelligence* (New York: Basic Books, 1967). Also see Anthony Downs, *Inside Bureaucracy* (New York: McGraw-Hill, 1967).
11. Theodore Lowi, *At the Pleasure of the Mayor* (New York: Free Press, 1964), chap. 9; John Harrigan, *Political Change in the Metropolis* (Boston: Little, Brown, 1985), pp. 191–203; Douglas Yates, *The Ungovernable City* (Cambridge, Mass: MIT Press, 1977), p. 110; Thomas Schelling, "On the Ecology of Micromotives," *The Public Interest* 25 (Fall 1971): 61–98.
12. See Demetrios Caraley, *City Governments and Urban Problems* (Englewood Cliffs, N.J.: Prentice-Hall, 1977), pp. 266–267.
13. C. Northcote Parkinson, *Parkinson's Law and Other Studies in Administration* (Boston: Houghton Mifflin, 1962), p. 2.
14. Ibid.; Frank S. Levy, Arnold Meltsuer, and Aaron Wildavsky, *Urban Outcomes: Schools, Streets, and Libraries* (Berkeley: University of California Press, 1974), pp. 195–200; Wilensky, *Organizational Intelligence.*
15. Donald Schon, "The Blindness System," *The Public Interest* 18 (Winter 1970): 25–38. Also see Stone *Urban Policy and Politics in a Bureaucratic Age,* pp. 319–324.
16. Robert Merton, *Social Theory and Social Structure* (New York: Free Press, 1957), p. 197ff. Also see Robert Merton, "Bureaucratic Structure and Personality," *Social Forces* 18 (May 1940): 560–568.
17. Downs, *Inside Bureaucracy,* p. 100; Michael Lipsky, "Street-Level Bureaucracy and the Analysis of Urban Reform," in Harlan Hahn and Charles Levine, eds., *Urban Politics: Past, Present, Future* (White Plains, N.Y.: Longman, 1980), p. 222.
18. Downs, *Inside Bureaucracy,* p. 69. For a scathing general indictment of public-sector bureaucracies, see E. S. Savas, *Privatizing the Public Sector* (Chatham, N.J.: Chatham House, 1982), pp. 10–26.
19. Mary Grisez Kweit and Robert Kweit, *Implementing Citizen Participation in a Bureaucratic State* (New York: Praeger, 1981), pp. 68–72.
20. Merton, *Social Theory and Social Structure,* pp. 202–204; Susan Sheehan, "Profiles: A Welfare Mother," *New Yorker,* September 29, 1975, pp. 77–78.

21. Merton, *Social Theory and Social Structure,* pp. 202–204. For a comprehensive conservative analysis of urban bureaucracies in general, see E. S. Savas, "Municipal Monopoly," *Harper's Magazine,* December 1971.

22. Upton Sinclair, *The Jungle* (New York: New American Library, 1989; first published 1906).

23. National Labor Relations Act, 29 USC 151 (1939).

24. Philip Foner, *History of the Labor Movement in the United States,* 9 vols. (Chicago: International Publishers, 1978–1990).

25. Andrew Boesel, "Local Personnel Management," in the *Municipal Yearbook, 1974* (Washington, D.C.: International City Managers' Association, 1974), p. 87.

26. *National Journal,* December 22, 1990, p. 3082.

27. Derek Bok and John Dunlop, *Labor and the American Community* (New York: Simon and Schuster, 1970); *National Journal,* December 22, 1990, p. 3082; U.S. Department of Commerce, Bureau of the Census, *Census of Governments* (Washington, D.C.: Government Printing Office, 1990); U.S. Department of Commerce, Bureau of the Census, *Statistical Abstracts of the United States.*

28. Governor Calvin Coolidge, from a 1919 speech.

29. Lee Shaw, "The Development of State and Federal Laws," in Sam Zagoria, ed., *Public Workers and Public Unions* (Englewood Cliffs, N.J.: Prentice-Hall, 1972), pp. 32–35.

30. Bollens and Schmandt, *The Metropolis,* p. 111; Bryan Jones, *Service Delivery in the City* (White Plains, N.Y.: Longman, 1980); Kenneth Mladenka, "Rules, Service Equity, and Distributional Decisions," *Social Science Quarterly* 59 (1978): 991–998.

31. Department of Commerce, Bureau of the Census, *City Employment in 1986* (Washington, D.C.: Government Printing Office, 1988), p. viii.

32. Caraley, *City Governments and Urban Problems,* p. 202.

33. Kenneth Culp Davis, *Discretionary Justice* (Baton Rouge: Louisiana State University Press, 1969).

34. Wallace Sayre and Herbert Kaufman, *Governing New York City* (New York: Sage, 1960), p. 446.

35. Levey, *Urban Outcomes.*

36. Michael Lipsky, *Street-Level Bureaucrats* (New York: Sage, 1980).

37. Ibid.; Jeffrey Prottas, "The Power of the Street-Level Bureaucrat in Public Service Bureaucracies," *Urban Affairs Quarterly* 13 (March 1978): 285–313; Pietro Nivola, "Distributing a Municipal Service: A Case Study of Housing Inspection," *Journal of Politics* 40 (February 1978): 59–81; Martha Derthick, "Intercity Differences in Administration of Public Assistance Programs," in James Q. Wilson, ed., *City Politics and Public Policy* (New York: Wiley, 1968), pp. 243–266.

38. For other examples, see John Gardiner, "Police Enforcement of Traffic Laws," in James Q. Wilson, *City Politics and Public Policy* (New York: Wiley, 1968), pp. 151–172; James Q. Wilson, *Varieties of Police Behavior* (Cambridge, Mass.: Harvard University Press, 1968), pp. 118–139.

39. *New York Times,* April 2, 1991.

40. *New York Times,* April 4, 1991.

41. *New York Times,* September 23–24, 1991.

42. Memphis, *Commercial Appeal,* October 3, 1990, p. B1.

43. Jones, *Service Delivery in the City;* Kenneth Mladenka and Kim Hill, "The Distribution of Benefits in an Urban Environment," *Urban Affairs Quarterly* 13 (September 1977): 73–94; Robert Lineberry, *Equality and Urban Policy* (Beverly Hills, Calif.: Sage, 1977); Nivola, "Distributing Municipal Service;" Jeffrey Prottas, *People Processing* (Lexington, Mass.: Lexington Books, 1979); Levy, *Urban Outcomes;* Clarence Stone

and Robert Stoker, "Employee Inefficiency in Selected Client Service Bureaucracies," *Journal of Urban Affairs* 6 (Summer 1984): 5–18.

For depictions presented through fiction, see works such as those of Joseph Wambaugh, *The New Centurions* (New York: Dell, 1972); *The Blue Knight* (New York: Dell, 1973); and *The Black Marble* (New York: Dell, 1980).

44. Sheehan, "Profiles: A Welfare Mother," p. 59; Sharon Perlman Krefetz, *Welfare Policy Making and City Politics* (New York: Praeger, 1976); Pietro Nivola, *The Urban Service Problem* (Lexington, Mass.: Lexington Books, 1979), p. 62; Peter Manning and John Van Maaven, eds., *Policing: A View from the Street* (Santa Monica, Calif.: Goodyear, 1978).

45. Lipsky, *Street-Level Bureaucrats*; Levy, *Urban Outcomes*; Schon, "The Blindness System"; Peter Rossi, "Between Black and White: The Face of American Institutions in the Ghetto," in National Advisory Commission on Civil Disorders, *Supplementary Studies* (Washington, D.C.: Government Printing Office, 1970).

46. James Q. Wilson, "Dilemmas of Police Administration," *Public Administration Review* 28 (September/October 1968): 412.

47. Weber, "Bureaucracy," p. 232.

48. Hugh Heclo, *A Government of Strangers* (Washington, D.C.: Brookings Institution, 1977); Harry Reynolds, "The Career Public Service and Statute Lawmaking in Los Angeles," *Western Political Quarterly* 18 (September 1965): 621–639.

49. Sayre and Kaufman, *Governing New York City,* pp. 249–264.

50. Aaron Wildavsky, *The Politics of the Budgetary Process* (Boston: Little, Brown, 1974), chaps. 2 and 3.

51. Levy, *Urban Outcomes,* pp. 224–236; Nivola, "Distributing a Municipal Service."

52. Prottas, *People Processing,* pp. 1–7.

53. For a summary of this process, see Robert Lorch, *State and Local Politics: The Great Entanglement* (Englewood Cliffs, N.J.: Prentice-Hall, 1983), pp. 360–369; David Morgan, *Managing Urban America* (Pacific Grove, Calif.: Brooks-Cole, 1989), pp. 236–250.

54. See Lorch, *State and Local Politics,* p. 370.

55. Winston Crouch, *Organized Civil Servants* (Berkeley: University of California Press, 1978), pp. 200–207; Sterling Spero and John Capozzola, *The Urban Community and Its Unionized Bureaucracies* (New York: Dunellen, 1973), pp. 94–101; Lawrence Chickering, *Public Employee Unions* (San Francisco: Institute of Contemporary Studies, 1976).

56. *New York Times,* May 9, 1985.

57. Clete Bulach and William Sharp, "Teachers' Unions Blight Education," *New York Times,* May 11, 1989; Sara Silbiger, "Collective Bargaining and the Distribution of Benefits," in Dale Rogers Marshall, ed., *Urban Policy Making* (Beverly Hills, Calif.: Sage, 1979), pp. 261–279; Stone, *Urban Policy and Politics in a Bureaucratic Age,* p. 169; David Lewin, Raymond Horton, and James Kuhn, *Collective Bargaining and Manpower Utilization in Big City Governments* (Montclair, N.J.: Allenheld and Osmun, 1979), pp. 72–75; Aaron Benjamin, Joseph Grodin, and James Stern, *Public-Sector Bargaining* (Washington, D.C.: Bureau of National Affairs, 1979); Spero and Cappozzola, *The Urban Community and Its Unionized Bureaucracies,* pp. 175–185, 208–210; Zagoria, *Public Workers and Public Unions,* p. 2.

58. A. H. Raskin, "The Revolt of the Civil Servants," *Saturday Review,* December 7, 1968, pp. 27–30.

59. For an example of such a paid advertisement, see the full-page ad presented by New York's AFSCME District Council 37 in the *New York Times,* April 20, 1987. The title is "Who Wants to Work for the City?"

60. Karl Van Asselt, "Impasse Resolution," *Public Administration Review* 32 (March/April, 1972): 114–119.
61. Peter Feuille and Gary Long, "The Public Administrator and Final Offer Arbitration," *Public Administration Review* 34 (November/December 1974): 575–583.
62. Bollens and Schmandt, *The Metropolis,* p. 110; Dennis Judd, *The Politics of American Cities* (Boston: Little, Brown, 1984), pp. 206–208.
63. Harry Wellington and Ralph Winters, "The Limits of Collective Bargaining in Public Employment," in Alan Saltzstein, ed., *Public Employees and Policymaking* (Pacific Palisades, Calif.: Palisades, 1979), pp. 102–117; Jay Atwood, "Collective Bargaining's Challenge," *Public Personnel Management* 5 (January/February 1976): 24–32.
64. Thomas Dye, *Politics in States and Communities* (Englewood Cliffs, N.J.: Prentice-Hall, 1985), p. 330.
65. New York City Sanitation Workers Union leader quoted in Pietro Nivola, "Apocalypse Now?" *Polity* 14 (Spring 1982): 376.
66. Edward Costikyan, "Who Runs City Government?" *New York Times Magazine,* May 26, 1969, p. 45.
67. For good general discussions of this entire phenomenon, see David Stanley, *Managing Local Government under Union Pressure* (Washington, D.C.: Brookings Institute, 1972); Raymond Horton, "Municipal Labor Relations," *Social Science Quarterly* 52 (December 1971): 680–696.
68. George Peterson, "Transmitting the Municipal Fiscal Squeeze to a New Generation of Taxpayers," in Robert Burchell and David Listokin, *The Fiscal Crisis of Urban America* (New Brunswick: State University of New Jersey Press, 1981); David Stanley, *Cities in Trouble* (Columbus, Ohio: Academy for Contemporary Problems, 1976), p. 6; Philip Doyle, "Municipal Pension Plans: Provisions and Payments," *Monthly Labor Review* 100 (November 1977), pp. 24–31; *New York Times,* May 19, 1980; April 5, 1982; Savas, "Municipal Monopoly."
69. Donald Haider, "Fiscal Scarcity: A New Urban Perspective," in Louis Massoti and Robert Lineberry, *The New Urban Politics* (Cambridge, Mass.: Ballinger, 1976), pp. 189–192.
70. Caraley, *City Governments and Urban Problems,* p. 259.
71. A full general strike would involve all municipal unions walking out at the same time, often in support of one particular striking union.
72. Morgan, *Managing Urban America,* p. 251.
73. W. Clayton Hall and Bruce Vander Porten, "Unionization, Monopsomy Power, and Police Salaries," *Industrial Relations* 16 (February 1977): 94–100; James Freund, "Market and Union Influences on Municipal Employee Wages," *Industrial and Labor Relations Review* 27 (April 1974): 391–404; Dye, *Politics in States and Communities,* p. 332.
74. John Capozzola, "Taking a Look at Unions," *National Civic Review* 75 (July/August 1986): 205–213; Charles Levine, *The Politics of Retrenchment* (Beverly Hills, Calif.: Sage, 1981); Judd, *The Politics of American Cities,* p. 206; Stanley, *Managing Local Government under Union Pressure;* Sam Roberts, "Labor Looks for Return on Support," *New York Times,* September 3, 1990; Josh Barbanel, "Dinkins Calls on Unions to Give Up Some Gains," *New York Times,* March 21, 1991.
75. Caraley, *City Governments and Urban Problems,* p. 203.
76. Frederick Wirt and Leslie Christovich, "The Politicization of American Local Executives," unpublished paper presented at the annual meeting of the American Political Science Association, New York, September 1981.

77. Francis Rourke, *Bureaucracy, Politics and Public Policy* (Boston: Little, Brown, 1984), chaps. 2–4.
78. Sam Roberts, "Bureaucracy Delays Start of a Business," *New York Times,* January 28, 1991.
79. *New York Times,* June 24, 1986.
80. Memphis, *Commercial Appeal,* October 29, 1990, p. A2.
81. *New York Times,* November 20, 1983.
82. For a discussion of the King beating, see *New York Times,* March 5, 1991. Also see the conclusions of the independent Christopher Commission, reported in *New York Times,* July 10, 1991.
83. See *New York Times,* July 30, 1985.
84. *New York Times,* September 16–17, 1983; March 29, 1984; Memphis, *Commercial Appeal,* April 29, 1992, p. A1.
85. *Tennessee v. Garner,* 471 U.S. 1 (1985).
86. Lorch, *State and Local Politics,* pp. 356–357, 368–369.
87. *New York Times,* January 11, 1983. For background discussion, see Frederick Taylor, *The Principles of Scientific Management* (New York: Norton, 1967; first published 1911); Peter Drucker, "Managing the Public Service Institution," *Public Interest* 84 (Fall 1973): 43–59; Michael J. White, *Managing Public Systems* (North Scituate, Mass.: Duxbury, 1980); Claude George, *The History of Management Thought* (Englewood Cliffs, N.J.: Prentice-Hall, 1968).
88. Lynn Bachelor, "The Impact of the Detroit Ombudsmen on Neighborhood Service Delivery," unpublished paper presented at the annual meeting of the Midwest Political Science Association, Chicago, April 1983; Bryan Jones, *Governing Urban America: A Policy Focus* (Boston: Little, Brown, 1983), p. 350.
89. Kenneth Mladenka, "Citizen Demand and Bureaucratic Response," *Urban Affairs Quarterly* 12 (March 1977): 273–290.
90. *New York Times,* November 26, 1989. Also see the *New York Times,* November 21, 1989, for the outline of a comparable law proposed in Los Angeles.
91. For good general references, see Lowi, *At the Pleasure of the Mayor;* Herbert Kaufman, "Bureaucrats and Organized Civil Servants," in Robert Connery and Demetrios Caraley, eds., *Governing the City* (New York: Academy of Political Science, 1969).
92. George Barbour and George Sipel," Excellence in Leadership," *Public Management* 68 (August 1968): 3–5; Robert Yin, *Changing Urban Bureaucracies* (Lexington, Mass.: Lexington Books, 1980).
93. Stephen Waldhorn, "The Role of Neighborhood Government in Post-Categorical Programs," in Joseph Sneed and Stephen Waldhorn, eds., *Restructuring the Federal System* (New York: Crane, Russak and Company, 1975), pp. 149–151. And for a discussion of "community control" experiments occurring in the 1960s, see chapter 7 of this volume.
94. See Werner Hirsch, "Cost Functions of the Urban Government Service," *Review of Economics and Statistics* 47 (February 1965).
95. For methods of assessing client satisfaction, see Barbara Nelson, "Client Perceptions of Officialdom," or Brian Stipak, "Using Clients to Evaluate Programs," unpublished papers presented at the Conference on the Public Encounter, Virginia Polytechnic Institute and State University, Blacksburg, Va., January 1980; Brian Stipak, "Citizen Satisfaction with Urban Services," *Public Administration Review* 39 (1979): 46–52.
96. For a variety of measurement suggestions, see Harry Hatry, *How Effective Are Your Community Services?* (Washington, D.C.: Urban Institute, 1977); Harry Hatry,

"Measuring the Quality of Public Services," in Willis Hawley and David Rogers, eds., *Improving the Quality of Urban Management* (Beverly Hills, Calif.: Sage, 1976); Laura Irwin Longbein, *Discovering Whether Programs Work* (Santa Monica, Calif.: Goodyear, 1980); Kate Ascher, *The Politics of Privatization* (New York: St. Martin's Press, 1987); Robert Stein, *Urban Alternatives* (Pittsburgh: University of Pittsburgh Press, 1990).

97. E. S. Savas, "How Much Do Government Services Cost?" *Urban Affairs Quarterly* 15 (September 1979): 23–41.

98. Elinor Ostrom, "On the Meaning and Measurement of Efficiency in the Provision of Urban Police Services," *Journal of Criminal Justice* 1 (Summer 1978); Bryan Jones, Saadia Greenberg, Clifford Kaufman et al., "Service Delivery Rules and the Distribution of Local Government Services," in Harlan Hahn and Charles Levine, *Urban Politics* (White Plains, N.Y.: Longman, 1980), pp. 225–251; Richard Rich, ed., *The Politics of Urban Public Services* (Lexington, Mass.: Lexington Books, 1982).

99. For a good general discussion of efforts to measure the efficiency of urban bureaucracies, see Jones, *Governing Urban America,* pp. 351–365.

100. Quoted in Dye, *Politics in States and Communities,* p. 324.

101. *New York Times,* March 11, 1981.

102. Annamarie Walsh, *The Public's Business* (Cambridge, Mass.: MIT Press, 1978). Also see Robert Wood, *1400 Governments* (Cambridge, Mass.: Harvard University Press, 1961), chap. 4.

103. Walsh, *The Public's Business,* p. 6.

104. *New York Times,* March 11, 1981.

105. Anita Summers, professor of public policy and management at the Wharton School of Business, quoted in *New York Times,* May 14, 1991. Also see David Osborne and Ted Gaebler, *Reinventing Government: How the Entrepreneurial Spirit Is Transforming the Public Sector* (Reading, Mass.: Addison-Wesley, 1992).

106. *New York Times,* February 26, 1989; August 22, 1989.

107. Clifford Shearing's discussion of the "new feudalism" that seems to be developing, in *New York Times,* February 26, 1989.

108. William Woodside, "The Future of Public-Private Partnerships," in Perry Davis, ed., *Public-Private Partnerships* (New York: Academy of Political Science, 1986), pp. 150–154; Albert Shanker, "Whittle Schools," *New York Times,* May 26, 1991.

109. Gary Bridge, "Citizen Choice in Public Service: Voucher Systems," in E. S. Savas, ed., *Alternatives for Delivering Public Services* (Boulder, Colo.: Westview, 1977); John Hanrahan, *Government for Sale* (Washington, D.C.: American Federation of State, County, and Municipal Employees, 1977); Savas, *Privatizing the Public Sector*; Donald Fisk, Herbert Kiesling, and Thomas Muller, *Private Provision of Public Services: An Overview* (Washington, D.C.: Urban Institute, 1978).

110. Laurence Alexander's periodic newsletter entitled *Privatization Report*; Kirk Cheyfitz, "Self-Service," *New Republic,* November 15, 1980, pp. 14–15; *Chicago Tribune,* July 11, 1991, p. 25; *New York Times,* May 23, 1983; April 29, 1985; May 28, 1985; November 29, 1985; April 14, 1986; March 25, 1990; December 7, 1990; May 14, 1991; April 22, 1992.

111. See *New York Times,* March 25, 1990.

112. See E. S. Savas, "Public vs. Private Refuse Collection," *Journal of Urban Analysis* 6 (1979): 1–13.

113. See C. J. Hech, "Contracting Municipal Services: Does It Really Cost Less?" *National*

Civic Review (June 1983): 321–326; John Donahue, *The Privatization Decision: Public Ends, Private Means* (New York: Basic Books, 1989); *New York Times,* January 26, 1985; April 16, 1991.

114. See *New York Times,* March 2, 1985; August 3, 1990.

115. See *New York Times,* May 14, 1991.

116. See *New York Times,* March 11, 1985; March 28, 1985; May 21, 1985; March 27, 1989.
    For a general discussion on the entire "contracting out" phenomenon, see Stone, *Urban Policy and Politics in a Bureaucratic Age,* chap. 22.

117. U.S. Department of Commerce, Bureau of the Census, *Statistical Abstracts of the United States.*

118. For further discussion, see E. S. Savas, "Municipal Monopolies vs. Competition in the Delivery of Urban Services," in Hawley and Rogers, *Improving the Quality of Urban Management*; Laurence Rutter, "The Essential Community," *Municipal Year Book 1980* (Washington, D.C.: International City Managers' Association, 1980), pp. 95–97; Roger Ahlbrandt, "Efficiency in the Provision of Fire Services," *Public Choice* 16 (Fall 1973): 1–15; *New York Times,* April 26, 1988.

119. For further discussion, see John Goodman and Gary Loveman, "Does Privatization Serve the Public Interest?" *Harvard Business Review* (November–December 1991); Patricia Florestano and Stephen Gordon, "Private Provision of Public Services," *International Journal of Public Administration* 1 (September 1979): 307–327; Patricia Florestano and Stephen Gordon, "A Survey of City and County Use of Private Contracting," *The Urban Interest* 3 (Spring 1981): 22–30; *New York Times,* January 25, 1985.

120. *New York Times,* April 29, 1985; *National Journal,* December 22, 1990, p. 3082.

121. Marcus Pohlmann, *Black Politics in Conservative America* (White Plains, N.Y.: Longman, 1990), chap. 3.

122. *New York Times,* May 14, 1991.

123. Martin Tolchin, "Rewards for Public Service Are Growing," *New York Times,* May 13, 1990.

124. Paul Starr, ed., *The Limits of Privatization* (New York: Academy of Political Science, 1987); Donahue, *The Privatization Decision.*

125. Robert Lineberry, *Equality and Urban Policy* (Beverly Hills, Calif.: Sage, 1977); Francis Fox Piven and Richard Cloward, *Regulating the Poor* (New York: Pantheon, 1971), chaps. 4–5; David Jones, "The Urban Service Delivery Literature," unpublished paper presented at the annual meeting of the Western Political Science Association, Denver, April 1983; Stone, *Urban Policy and Politics,* pp. 345–347; Lawrence Herson and John Bolland, *The Urban Web* (Chicago: Nelson-Hall, 1990), pp. 415–434; Frank Levy, *Urban Outcomes* (Berkeley: University of California Press, 1974), p. 246; Frederic Bolotin and David Cingranelli, "Equity and Urban Policy," *Journal of Politics* 45 (February 1983): 209–219; David Koehler and Margaret Wrightson, "Inequality in the Delivery of Urban Services," *Journal of Politics* 49 (February 1987): 80–99; David Cingranelli, "Race, Politics, and Elites," *American Journal of Political Science* 25 (November 1981): 664–672; John Boyle and David Jacobs, "The Intra-City Distribution of Services," *American Political Science Review* 76 (June 1982): 371–379; Bryan Jones and Clifford Kaufman, "The Distribution of Urban Public Services," *Administration and Society* 6 (November 1974): 337–359; Richard Rich, "Distribution of Services," in Marshall, *Urban Policy Making*; Richard Rich, *The Politics of Urban Public Services* (Lexington, Mass.: Lexington Books, 1982).

126. Lipsky, *Street-Level Bureaucracy,* p. 160.

CHAPTER 11

The Mass Media

A journalist is the lookout on the bridge of the ship of state. He notes the passing sail, the little things of interest that dot the horizon in fine weather. . . . He peers through fog and storm to give warning of dangers ahead. . . . He is there to watch over the safety and welfare of the people who trust him.[1]

—Joseph Pulitzer

Whether consciously seeking to do so, the mass media have become an institution that long has exerted considerable influence in urban politics. Although granted no formal governing authority, they play an integral and formative role in the political system. Most significantly, they can have a major impact on the political input with which the conversion mechanisms must deal, on how their subsequent output will be perceived, and thus affect public feedback as well.

To understand the influence of the media, it is necessary to know the major sources of their political power as well as a variety of factors that limit the exercise of that power. In examining the media's actual impact on city politics today, five primary factors are important. First, mass media's mere existence and standard operating procedures have altered the urban political process in some significant ways. Second, the media form the crucial communication network linking together the entire political system. Third, their discretion allows them to affect which issues will be included in the political agenda. Fourth, although difficult to measure, their coverage appears to affect public opinion by shaping both attitudes and images. Last, in the course of both public affairs and entertainment presentations, the media do much to generate support for the existing American political-economic system.

In the context of urban politics, mass media are defined as the city's primary local television, radio, press, and magazine sources. Beyond those, however, national media coverage can have an impact as well, whether it be the *New York Times, Wall Street Journal,* CBS News, *Newsweek,* National Public Radio (NPR), or other such sources. Although our major concern is on the media's public affairs programming, the impact of entertainment elements on political culture must also be considered.

EVOLUTION

From the limited-circulation party presses of the eighteenth century, we now have thousands of media sources reaching millions of individuals from all walks of life. Figure 11.1 depicts the evolution of the media in this country.

In 1789, John Fenno established the *Gazette of the United States* "to endear the general government to the people."[2] In reality, it was an occasional press designed to propagate the views of the Federalist party, and the Republicans soon started the *National Gazette* in order to convey their own messages. Soon a limited network of these "party presses" began to develop at various localities around the country, approximately 200 by the turn of the century. By 1835, there were some 1,200 of them, and as many as 65 published on a daily basis.[3]

As urbanization dawned in the mid-eighteenth century, independent newspapers began to emerge, targeting themselves to a mass audience rather than just the party faithful. The number of newspapers reached 3,500 in 1870 and 12,000 by 1890. This proliferation also was stimulated by technological developments such as the rotary press, the telegraph, and the railroads, all of which lowered the costs of publication and circulation. Soon, schools of journalism developed, and news reporting actually became a full-blown profession.[4]

At the same time, a variety of national magazines began to appear. *Nation, Atlantic,* and *Harper's* emerged in the mid-nineteenth century, with *Scribner's, McClure's,* and *Cosmopolitan* appearing a few decades later. These often included articles by "muckrakers" such as Lincoln Steffens.

The first of the commercial radio stations began operating in 1922; today there are approximately 7,000. Television appeared in the 1940s and has grown to include some 700 local stations. The 1970s brought cable television, and there soon were thousands of cable television systems; even more options are available via the satellite dish. The Cable News Network (CNN) and C-Span offer an exclusive around-the-clock focus on public affairs. Government even got into the media business in the 1960s when Congress created the public radio and television systems.[5]

SOURCES OF INFLUENCE

Just what political power resources do the media possess? At the most fundamental level, they have explicit constitutionally protected prerogatives. In practice, they have evolved to the point that many are large, well-financed entities with access to very sizable audiences. Their power is further enhanced by the fact that the ownership of local media sources tends to be concentrated in the hands of a small number of wealthy elites.

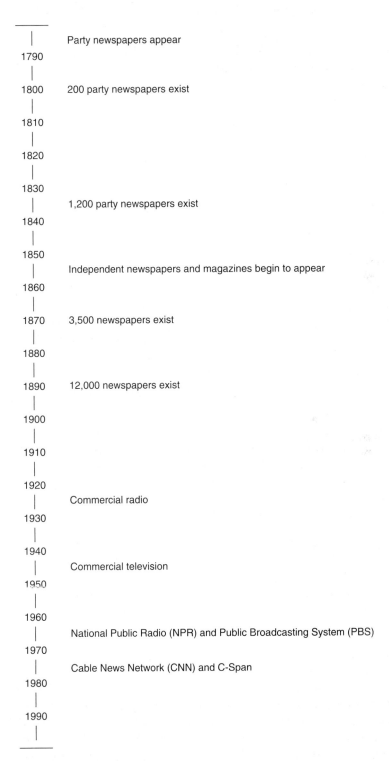

1790	Party newspapers appear
1800	200 party newspapers exist
1810	
1820	
1830	
1840	1,200 party newspapers exist
1850	
1860	Independent newspapers and magazines begin to appear
1870	3,500 newspapers exist
1880	
1890	12,000 newspapers exist
1900	
1910	
1920	
1930	Commercial radio
1940	
1950	Commercial television
1960	
1970	National Public Radio (NPR) and Public Broadcasting System (PBS)
1980	Cable News Network (CNN) and C-Span
1990	

FIGURE 11.1 Evolution of the Mass Media, 1789–1990

The First Amendment

The nation's early leaders felt strongly that a free flow of information was absolutely essential to a free society and a healthy democracy. Consequently, the First Amendment to the U.S. Constitution states: "Congress shall make no law . . . abridging the freedom of . . . the press." But the U.S. Congress was not the only institution that would have to respect the media's liberty. In 1931, the U.S. Supreme Court concluded that "it is no longer open to doubt that the liberty of the press . . . is within the liberty safeguarded by the due process clause of the Fourteenth Amendment from invasion by state action."[6] States, and by extension local governments, were not to interfere with the "freedom of the press."

In 1971 the Supreme Court outlined more clearly what it meant by noninterference. The Court concluded that government bore the "heavy burden of showing justification for the imposition of . . . [prior] restraint on publication." Such restraint would be allowed only when it was certain that a particular news story "would surely result in direct, immediate and irreparable damage to our nation or its people."[7] For all practical purposes, there was to be no direct governmental censorship.

Media Freedom from Governmental Constraints

First Amendment	"Congress shall make no law . . . abridging the freedom of . . . the press . . ."
Fourteenth Amendment	"No state shall . . . deprive any person of life, liberty, or property, without due process of law."
Near v. Minnesota (1931)	The First Amendment of the U.S. Constitution, by way of the Fourteenth Amendment, also precludes state and local governments from abridging freedom of the press.
N.Y. Times v. U.S. (1971)	Government is not to prevent publication unless such publication "would surely result in direct, immediate, and irreparable damage to our nation or its people."

The mass media can be held legally responsible for libel after the fact; however, a high standard has been established for proof. If the person claiming libel can reasonably be categorized as a "public figure," the burden is on that person to show that the story was not only untrue[8] but that the news agents presented the story "with knowledge that it was false or with reckless disregard of whether it was false or not."[9]

When operating in the realm of politics, then, mass media have extensive protection. Government is precluded from halting the release of any particular story except in the most extremely perilous of circumstances. Even if the public figure covered can prove that the story was both false and damaging, the medium cannot be punished unless the victimized public figure also can prove that the news agency either knew it was false or proceeded in "reckless disregard" of its authenticity.[10] The legal standards for libel are summarized below.

Legal Standards for Libel

Public Figure

1. Real injury occurred as a result of the story.
2. The story was false and not of "legitimate public concern."
3. The story was of legitimate public concern, but it was false and media either had knowledge that it was false or demonstrated a reckless disregard of whether it was false or not.

Private Figure

1. Real injury occurred as a result of the story.
2. The story was false.

In essence, the print media have great latitude to publish whatever they want about public events and public figures without fear of governmental interference before, during, or after the publication. This protection is generally true for electronic media transmissions as well, although some of them are subject to a few more governmental regulations than print media.[11]

Complete freedom would mean little if these media sources could not afford to gather important information, no one was listening, or they could not decide what to do with the stories once they gathered them. The way in which media have evolved, however, has all but guaranteed that none of these apply. Not only are they exceptionally free to pursue and present stories on any topic they wish, but they have accumulated considerable capacity to do so.

Audience

Television is the most pervasive of the media. More than 98 percent of all American homes currently have at least one television set, and it is turned on an average of six or seven hours each day. (By the time they are 16, most American young people will have spent more time in front of the television than at school.) *TV Guide* is one of the top-selling magazines in the country; and during peak winter viewing hours, about one-half of the American population can be found in front of their television screens.[12]

Other media sources have sizable audiences as well. More than 99 percent of American households own a radio, and the average person listens to radio 3 hours and 21 minutes per day.[13] Between two-thirds and three-quarters of all adults regularly read one daily newspaper,[14] and 9 out of 10 read at least one magazine each month.[15]

Mass Media's Audiences

Television

In more than 98 percent of all U.S. households
Turned on an average of more than 6 hours per day

Radio

In more than 99 percent of all U.S. households
Heard an average of more than 3 hours per day per person

Newspapers

Read daily by between 67 percent and 75 percent of all U.S. adults

Magazines

Read monthly by approximately 90 percent of all U.S. adults

Within the media's mass audience, there is also what James Rosenau refers to as an "attentive public." These are the "news junkies" who follow the news carefully because of particular political, social, or economic concerns. They read many stories from beginning to end and are also more likely to read editorial pieces. As they tend to be more active in the political process, the news messages they consume have an even greater impact on urban politics.[16]

Capacities

The media are capable of presenting an enormous amount of information to these huge audiences. In news coverage, technological advances and financial resources allow them to make broad, often instantaneous news presentations. The development of computers, satellites, fax machines, and videotape have enhanced worldwide coverage and reduced news deadlines significantly. Hand-held video cameras allow instantaneous presentation of television images from the immediate scene of the action.[17] Because of the large audiences, advertisers are willing to pay handsomely for the opportunity to present messages via these channels. Thus, sizable budgets have become available, allowing media both to pay more to their employees and to cover more stories.[18]

Operating Discretion

Given the variety of actual and potential events unfolding hourly in a large complex city as well as at least some limits on their own capacities, media must decide which stories to pursue and how to display what they find. By necessity, they are far more than a mirror that simply reflects everything that happens in society. They often have considerable discretion over what to cover, the placement, slant, and tone of the story, and the headlines and pictures that will accompany it. They also choose whether to pursue it with follow-up stories or let it disappear from public view. In addition, they have the option of editorial comment.[19]

Events clearly will dictate coverage in a number of cases. A presidential visit, a four-alarm fire, an extended hostage situation, an airplane crash, or the announcement of a major corporation coming or leaving the area all will require extensive and prominent presentation. On the other hand, the media will use far more discretion in deciding whether or how to portray the thousands of less dramatic events occurring across the city every day.

Monopolization of Ownership

Mass media's political influence also is enhanced by the concentration of power arising from the monopolization of ownership. Such monopolies allow a relatively small number of individual elites to circumscribe much of the important discretion outlined above, while at the same time reducing the potential for internal conflict within their particular media operation. Consider the concentration of ownership in the two politically dominant media: television and newspapers.

From the inception of television in the 1940s until well into the 1970s, CBS, NBC, and eventually ABC had almost a complete monopoly. The national networks and their local affiliates combined essentially owned the airwaves. More recently, a greater number of independent stations have emerged—especially with the advent of viewer subscription cable television. Nevertheless, the three major networks and their affiliates still attract a majority of the television audience; a good many of the independents simply play reruns of shows produced by the major networks; and the Federal Communications Commission (FCC) now permits the networks to purchase local cable units.[20]

In the press, there are also monopolies and these have been steadily increasing of late. Press chains (single companies that own a variety of different newspapers) controlled nearly one-half of all papers in 1970, and that figure grew to some three-quarters by the end of the decade, with 12 chains controlling more than one-third of all the nation's newspapers.[21] Then came the merger-mania of the 1980s.

In one three-month period, the Tribune chain purchased the *Newport News* for $130 million (104,000 circulation); the Media News Group purchased the *Dallas Times Herald* for $110 million (244, 629 circulation); Ingersoll purchased the *New Haven Register* and *New Haven Journal-Courier* for $170 million (218, 519 circulation); Times Mirror purchased the *Baltimore Sun* for $400 million (356,927 circulation); and Gannett purchased the *Louisville Courier Journal* and the *Louisville Times* for $300 million (295,965 circulation). Over a four-year time span, Gannett purchased the two Louisville papers mentioned above as well as the *Jackson Clarion-Ledger,* the *Jackson Daily News,* the *Des Moines Register,* and the *Detroit News*—spending $705 million and adding 1.3 million readers. Chains have even begun to buy up other chains; for example, Samuel Newhouse purchased Booth Newspapers for $305 million.[22]

The largest of the chains are Gannett, Knight-Ridder, Newhouse, Times Mirror, Tribune, and Dow Jones, which combined currently own nearly 200 daily newspapers and sell approximately one-third of all the individual papers purchased each day. This process has left only about 500 newspapers in the entire country that are not part of a press chain, and those tend to be in small markets and to draw all but their local stories from a handful of wire services dominated by United Press International (UPI) and the Associated Press (AP). By 1991 only 12 American communities still had fully competing newspapers under separate ownership.[23]

Not only are there heavy concentrations of ownership within the various media forms but there is growing ownership concentration across them as well. At last count, Gannett owned 91 dailies, 38 nondailies, 6 television stations, and 14 radio stations. An individual newspaper, the *Washington Post* (part of the Times-Mirror chain) owns a television station, a radio station, a news magazine, and a news wire service. The FCC places some limits on this conglomeration in that an individual company is not allowed to own more than 12 television stations or control more than one-quarter of a television-viewing market.[24] Nevertheless, the FCC recently has been considering the elimination of all such restrictions. Existing limits scarcely make a dent in the overall monopolization of the nation's media sources anyway, and because they have tended not to be applied retroactively, these efforts generally affect only new acquisitions.[25]

The end result is that three television networks, two wire services, and a handful of newspaper chains have a powerful hold on what information is made available in cities across the United States. And who actually owns these media giants? As few as 10 business and financial corporations hold the controlling shares of stock in CBS, NBC, ABC, 34 subsidiary television stations, 201 cable television systems, 62 radio stations, 59 magazines (including *Time* and *Newsweek*), and 58 newspapers (including the *New York Times, Los Angeles Times, Washington Post,* and *Wall Street Journal*).[26] WNET, the flagship channel in the Public Broadcasting Service (PBS), is heavily reliant on the Ford Foundation. And this elite control tends to cross-pollinate. Chapter 3 made it relatively clear who controls banks, financial corporations, and foundations. The owning and non-owning directors of these organizations sit on each other's boards, even within the media business. These opportunities increase their individual and collective power and mean that the number of people involved in corporate decision making is even smaller than it first appears.[27]

LIMITATIONS

Despite all of their potential political power, the media have some very real limits on their discretion, as shown in the following list.

Political Limitations of the Mass Media

Internal Constraints

Professional standards	regulate the presentation style, definition of newsworthiness, and ethics of coverage
Functional requisites	include meeting deadlines, need for visuals for TV, controlling vulnerability during live coverage
Disagreements	occur among and between reporters, editors, managers, and owners

External Constraints

Government	punishes for obscenity, slander and libel; imposes airwave regulations
Investors	demand large audiences in order to maximize profits for stockholders
Consumers	must be developed into a large and loyal audience; they can be difficult to influence
Competitors	force one another to try to be first with the story, with each attempting to get audiences to turn to that source first
Manipulation	leads savvy news subjects to strategically leak information and stage events; influence groups threaten to sponsor boycotts

The media have internal constraints created by the standards of the profession as well as functional necessities and collegial disagreements. They also have external constraints. Government regulates their behavior in the grey areas outside their constitutional protections. To some extent, they are captives of the interests of their advertisers and stockholders. They must attract and hold audiences, thus they are limited by consumer tastes and the intensity of their competition. Many of their subjects know all this and learn how to manipulate them into presenting stories as the subjects wish them to be presented.

Internal Constraints

Professional Standards.   Journalists and newscasters normally have received at least some formal professional training in the field of communications, or at very least they will have been trained intensively while on the job. They have been schooled on how to write news copy and to be as thorough and unbiased as possible; most also will have learned their profession's current standards of newsworthiness and code of ethics. Such tenets will guide them in making many of the discretionary decisions discussed above.

In terms of newsworthiness, the usual is normally not a front page story. On the other hand, the unusual may well be—the dog bites man versus man bites dog maxim.[28]

Concerning ethics, it is currently acceptable to receive and publish stolen information or to shadow a politician to see if he or she is having an illicit love affair. However, it is normally not appropriate these days to publish the names of rape victims, show pictures of dead bodies, or interview grieving relatives at the scene of a death.[29]

Functional Requisites.   Also limiting media's newsmaking discretion will be certain functional necessities. Deadlines must be met. Stories that break during a television newscast may be covered live with little opportunity to edit the results. Newspapers require greater amounts of lead time than the more instantaneous electronic media. Television needs action pictures to hold its audiences.[30]

Disagreements.   Despite concentrated ownership, no large newspaper or television station can function single-mindedly as if it were a machine made up of interchangeable parts. Many major discretionary decisions lead to considerable disagreement within the ranks.

As a typical example of such disagreement, the reporter trusts his or her source, wants to win Pulitzer prizes, and is convinced the public has a "right to know." Therefore, the reporter wants the story to run immediately. The editor, concerned about accuracy, would like verification by another source or two; otherwise the story may not be deemed fit for strong presentation on the front page. Meanwhile, the publisher is worried about the negative impact on the community if the story breaks now and receives the slant the reporter desires.

Each contributor brings his or her own personal and professional attitudes and values. Therefore, there is likely to be conflict in the newsroom. In particular, coverage of controversial events such as corporate scandals or public protests will lead almost inevitably to some internal disagreement based on these different views and agendas.[31]

External Constraints

Government.   Newspapers and magazines have no legal obligations to be responsible to anyone but themselves. Because it is relatively easy to print a newspaper or magazine, competition is supposed to guarantee an acceptable degree of variety and responsibility. Thus, one does not need to have any sort of government license (beyond a standard sales license) or to meet any sort of government standards (other than abiding by local standards of decency) to print and distribute such materials. In 1974, the U.S. Supreme Court upheld this broad latitude.[32]

Although newspapers and magazines are exempt from government licensing procedures, radio and television stations are not. They operate over public airwaves, there are a limited number of such airwaves, and their broadcast signals can enter the home with a simple flip of a switch. For such reasons these media must be licensed every three years by the Federal Communications Commission. To have their licenses renewed, stations must provide reasonable amounts of children's programming, news programming, discussion of controversial issues, and opportunities for their audiences to refute their editorial comments. They must be accessible to political candidates, providing equal time to opposing candidates if free time is given to any of them. They must keep their entertainment programs within local and national standards of decency.

Government is still deciding if and how to regulate subscription television, whether the signals come by means of a cable or a satellite dish. The 1984 Cable Communications Policy Act effectively deregulated the cable industry; however, there is growing concern about the level of monopolization of cable service that has developed in many communities. Thus, Congress has been considering a variety of different ways to regulate rates and channel availability as well as to reduce the concentration of ownership. Congressman Jim Cooper (D-Tenn.) stated that "the problem with the cable monopoly is it stifles competition, hinders innovation and abuses consumer rights."[33] In the summer of 1991, the FCC extended the authority of local governments to reduce rates;[34] but about the only other regulation of cable or satellite-transmitted programming has been an occasionally successful lawsuit challenging certain transmitions as obscene.

Congress created the Corporation for Public Broadcasting (CPB) in 1967 in order to offer some radio and television alternatives. Thus, television's Public Broadcasting System (PBS) and radio's National Public Radio (NPR) were born. They have since grown to include hundreds of affiliates and millions in their respective audiences. Their noncommercial status was designed to let them offer specialized programs that commercial stations could not afford to provide because of the relatively limited audiences for such programming. The offerings were to include cultural, public affairs, and educational programming. Congress provides nearly one-half of the funding and appoints the director of the CPB.[35]

Direct involvement is not the only way government can influence the content of the news, however. As primary players in the political game, government officials possess vast amounts of information that the media need for stories. Thus, these officials have some control over who gets what information and how soon. News releases can present all or only some of the truth. Favored reporters may be allowed in for an exclusive interview. Disgruntled officials may "leak" certain information. And despite various "sunshine laws" and public access statutes, it is not unusual for media to have to go to court to get government to comply and turn over a particular piece of information.[36]

> By default we have permitted the investor's equity to control what is basically a public-service industry.[37]

Investors. Focusing on television, Fred Friendly drew the above conclusion from his experiences as president of CBS News. As evidence, he lists his findings of the top priorities guiding television's choice of what programming will appear:

1. Nielsen ratings.
2. Effect of those ratings on advertisers.
3. Effect of those ratings on expected earnings and thus stock market position.

4. The company's corporate image in the press, among the community leaders, and at the FCC.
5. Public service and good taste.[38]

As an example of just how effective the mass media are at following these criteria, consider the economic success of the three major television networks. Advertisers pay them hundreds of thousands of dollars for each minute of prime-time advertising, adding up to over a billion dollars a year for each network. They are among the most profitable business operations in the country. They often make more than 30 percent profit on gross revenues and a 200 percent to 300 percent rate of return on invested capital. So lucrative is such access to the airwaves that local television stations sell for millions of dollars, while even individual radio stations are regularly approaching a million dollars in sale value.[39]

Highly profitable, although on a somewhat smaller scale, newspapers also rely heavily on attracting advertisers. When all newspapers are combined, they draw nearly twice as much advertising revenue as the sum total for the three major television networks. Not too surprisingly, such sponsor dependence is reflected in the allocation of newspaper space. Where roughly one-quarter of all television air time is consumed by advertisers, the standard rule of thumb in the press is that 40 percent of print space will be devoted to news and the other 60 percent will be filled with advertisements. Calling them "news" papers would actually seem to be a misnomer.[40]

The mass media, then, largely comprises private corporations whose primary reasons for being are to return maximum profits for their stockholders. As the above figures indicate, they take this responsibility seriously and are quite good at it. As the overwhelming majority of their revenues come from advertisers, they sell these sponsors a sizable share of the nation's mass communications directly and indirectly they allow the interests of those sponsors to influence most programming decisions.[41]

Consumers.   To garner this kind of advertising money requires media to locate, attract, and retain audiences for those advertisers' commercials. Consequently, they must be sensitive to what different buying audiences will and will not read, listen to, and watch. In the news business, not only must media present an attractive package that will catch and hold audience attention, but they must also remain credible enough that they will be turned to as a reliable source of information.

Yet, even after they have attracted a large and loyal audience, media cannot be sure they are having the desired impact on public opinion, whether that desire is to persuade or merely to inform to the best of their ability. This uncertainty is there because the consumer has plenty of capacity to ignore or misunderstand any particular message.[42]

Competitors.   At the outset of the twentieth century, the majority of American cities had at least two competing newspapers; today that figure has slipped to scarcely more than 2 percent. Nevertheless, thanks to radio and television, every large city has competing news sources, and government regulation tends to keep them all from being owned by the same company. Thus, in order to attract and hold a news audience, each news medium must be quick to the breaking story. While it might be nice to have that one additional source, the fear of being "scooped" by a competitor may well drive any one of them to run the story as it is. Discretion is limited to a certain extent by necessity.

> On the one side are the media, with their goals, practices, customs; on the other side are the politicians, interest groups, activists whom the media cover, who have their own goals and exert their own pressures. Out of this relationship, sometimes tempestuous, often symbiotic, emerges the media's overtly political content with its accompanying effects on power.[43]

Manipulation.   Mass media also can be manipulated by their news sources. If one understands the inner workings of the media, it is possible to take advantage of their standard operating procedures in order to have a story presented in a particular way. For example, a government official can choose to provide a press release just prior to deadline with reasonable confidence that it will be presented with very little editing or comment. By giving a speech in a highly photogenic setting, an official increases the chance of not only being covered by television but receiving a prominent placement in the subsequent news broadcast. By the same token, emotive rhetoric is also likely to catapult a story into prominence.

An additional mechanism is referred to as the strategic "leak." This involves a government employee who wants to advance his or her own policy preferences by making an unauthorized release of information designed to accomplish this. For example, if a mayor is underplaying the costs of an economic development project in order to get it approved, a budget office employee opposed to the mayor's tactics may leak the actual figures to the press as a way of reducing the likelihood that the project will be passed.

Another type of leak is the "trail balloon." A government official secretly may inform a reporter of a pending policy alternative. The source will then see how the public reacts. If the reaction is highly unfavorable, he or she can deny that it ever was seriously being considered.[44]

Interest groups also can influence editorial decisions. Aware of the media's need for revenues, they may threaten to boycott a particular television station or specific sponsors if a given story is aired. In the mid-1970s, for instance, a Scandinavian film crew did a documentary entitled "Harlem: Voices and Faces." The Scandinavians were self-described socialists bent on portraying how the American economic system was failing many in that area of New York City. Yet, a number of Harlem community leaders saw it differently. They did not deny the problems, but they resented what they perceived to be the overall negative tone of the documentary. They then proceeded to pressure WNET, a public broadcasting station, not to air the film. In the end, the station ran it but with considerable opportunity for the community leaders to respond immediately following its presentation. Subsequently, all inquiries as to film distribution were referred to the filmmakers, although no one at the station seemed to know how to contact them.[45]

POLITICAL IMPACT

In spite of their limits, the mass media are important players in the political game. They have a central role, and their decisions will affect political events whether this is intended or not. A powerful indicator is the way urban politics has conformed itself to the media's modus operandi.

Political Impact of the Mass Media

Political process	The media have increased mayoral power, required a new style of political campaigning, and provided more avenues for public input.
Communications network	They provide a less than neutral conduit through which virtually all political messages must flow.
Agenda-setting	They shape what people think about by exercising coverage discretion, such as what to cover and how to present the story.
Shaping public opinion	The media intentionally and unintentionally shape political attitudes and images by their presentation of stories and editorials.
Shaping public values	They pacify with nonoffensive political stories while reinforcing dominant values, all under the watchful eyes of investors, sponsors, and government.

Political Process

One of the most obvious ways urban politics has changed as a result of the communications revolution is the relative enhancement of mayoral power. For the reasons discussed in chapter 9, the mayor has more access to these channels than do his or her city council counterparts, and mayors have adapted to take advantage of that reality.

A second effect is the permanent alteration of campaigning styles. Spot commercials have proven far more efficient than mass rallies or attempts to make individual contact with numerous voters. Of course, their cost has affected who can run for office and to whom the successful candidate is likely to be beholden.[46]

By the same token, the power of the average citizen has been enhanced to a degree by the proliferation of public opinion polling, and talk radio provides another forum beyond the long-standing letters-to-the-editor option.[47] Local officials now have more than just a sense of what is on the public's collective mind. In addition, the audience that can be reached via predictable media coverage of sensational protests and others forms of direct political action can further enhance citizen power.[48]

Communications Network

The mass media serve as a bulletin board allowing urban residents to stay abreast of political developments. They are also a conduit through which political messages can be communicated. In particular, such a forum allows politicians to communicate with key constituencies when they wish to widen the conflict. Without the media, much of this information would have to travel by word of mouth. In essence, then, media have become the arterial network for the political system.

Yet, this is not a wholly neutral network. Not every message will be disseminated, and those that are disseminated normally will have been edited first. Therefore, although the media are an absolutely essential communications channel, they take on additional significance by virtue of how they choose to filter the political stories and messages.

Agenda-setting

In exercising discretion over what to cover, the placement and slant of the story as well as the headlines and pictures that will accompany it, mass media have become integral in the determination of the local public policy agenda (the issues to be discussed and the alternative solutions to be considered). Regardless of whether they can control what people think, they clearly have considerable influence over what the public will think about. Many problems and alternatives are not discussed seriously until they are emphasized by the media. Therefore, what the media choose to discuss will not only be a reflection of what is on the minds of government officials and urban residents, but it also can raise issues to a level of attention that will almost guarantee that they will become political agenda items. As Wallace Sayre and Herbert Kaufman noted,

> A series of articles on any aspect of [city] government . . . if treated prominently or spectacularly, is likely to cause a good deal of comment and generate a good many questions in official circles and among the general citizenry. . . . A sensational exposure, a revelation of scandal, can set off a wave of popular indignation strong enough to compel remedial or symbolic action by officials.[49]

Shaping Public Opinion

The mass media can also affect people's views of what ought to be done—directly and openly by taking positions on the editorial page or endorsing candidates with similar views or indirectly and often inadvertently by the way stories are covered. Social scientists have had a difficult time measuring the precise behavioral impact of specific media messages.[50] Obviously there are many factors that shape what we think and do. Parents, peers, teachers, preachers, and many others influence us in a variety of conscious and subconscious ways; but simply because the specific influence of any particular factor is difficult to determine empirically is no reason to ignore it—especially an informational device as pervasive as the mass media.

The media have a significant impact on opinion formation and what we think about, whether or not it actually can change what we think.[51]

Political Attitudes. Media can influence our short-term political attitudes. The placement and slant of a story clearly can affect our view of the current issue or individual involved. If the question is whether more money needs to be spent on the city's public schools, the coverage may highlight the school system's genuine inadequacies or it may play up areas where the system is overstaffed. If a candidate is speaking, will pictures of the audience show only the enthusiastic supporters or will the camera linger on empty seats and protestors?

Most responsible media sources will strive for interpretive accuracy or at least a degree of balance if the situation is difficult to interpret. Yet, as Gay Talese concluded even about the venerable *New York Times*:

> The *Times* desired no opinions within its news columns, restricting opinions to its editorial page. Realistically, this was not possible. The editor's opinions were imposed every day within the news—either by the space they allowed for a certain story, or the position they assigned to it, or the headline they ordered for it, and also by the stories they did not print, or printed for only one edition, or edited heavily, or held out for a few days. . . . The reporter's ego was also a factor in the news coverage—he wrote what he wrote best, he wrote what he understood, reflecting the total experience of his lifetime, shades of his pride and prejudice.[52]

As for editorializing, it should be remembered that few people actually read these opinion pieces.[53] Nevertheless, those who do read them are more likely to be members of Rosenau's "attentive publics," those more actively involved in politics. The mere existence of editorials may cause politicians to think twice rather than incur the wrath of the editorialists whose political orientations are relatively well known.[54]

Political Images. Media also can affect our long-term political views. If a politician is continually pictured looking confused, tripping over things, and mispronouncing names, the public may form a negative mental image of that person as a bumbling klutz. On the other hand, if the politician's political "handlers" (public relations people, speech writers, advance persons, media consultants) can keep the boss looking relaxed, comfortable, confident, and informed, the result will be a more positive political image over the long run. Consequently, more and more money is being spent by politicians carefully cultivating their media images.[55]

Media imaging is not reserved for political elites alone. Racial and ethnic groups, women, gays, and many others have long complained of their treatment in the media. Focusing on the treatment of blacks on television, for example, Jesse Jackson laments, "Television's major violation of us is a consistent combination of distortion and deletion which projects us as less intelligent, more violent, less hard-working, and less universal than we are." He concludes:

"Television's projection of us almost makes welfare, poverty, unemployment, and blacks synonymous."[56]

Michael Robinson also suggests that media's conscious orientation toward critical analysis may well create a form of "media malaise" after a while. By continually pointing up scandals, problems, and flaws in proposed alternatives, they appear to be contributing to a relatively high level of public cynicism about politics and political solutions.[57] In the long run, of course, that could help reinforce the socioeconomic status quo by offering so little hope for change through the political process.

Another potential side effect of media's critical orientation is the inclination of individuals to think twice before volunteering to become public figures. Once they toss their hat into the political ring, it is likely that some reporter will probe their personal and family backgrounds intensely. Few will feel that what they are likely to accomplish in politics is worth subjecting themselves and their families to that kind of spotlight.

Shaping Public Values

As almost the entire mass media system is privately owned and operated for a profit, it normally must first serve the investment interests of its primary stock-holders. This pursuit of profit often will result in many news and entertainment presentations that have a sort of political lobotomizing effect on the general audience. Beyond pacification, the media's profit orientation also appears to have had a noticeable impact on the political content of the news and entertainment that subtly and not so subtly shape public values.

Pacification.   Media critic John Leonard complains that "the history of the United States [is being brought to us] not by the Senate and the House, but by Occidental Bank and Weed Eater."[58] He is implying that what the public knows and considers important may be heavily affected by what large advertisers will and will not sponsor. The primary concern of corporations who spend thousands of dollars for these opportunities to circulate information about their products is almost always to reach the largest buying audience possible. In order to attract advertisers, therefore, mass media companies must be able to attract and hold large audiences with the content of what they present.

> The most serious threat to television and its claim to First Amendment freedoms is not the Federal Communications Commission or the Supreme Court, or an Imperial Presidency, but the runaway television ratings process. The current obsession with surveying the "habits" and "pulse" of television sets, rather than the response of and impact on human beings, has resulted in an industry preoccupied with short-term indicators and profits.[59]

What Fred Friendly found true for television, Gannett Publisher's Al Neuharth also found true for newspapers.[60] There is a real tendency in mass media to follow audience inclinations rather than to lead. It is not enough to attract the audience by serving them something that will catch their attention and conform to their existing values and attitudes; it is also essential to hold them. Thus, once they have been attracted, it is much safer to feed their predilections than to challenge them.

Public Affairs.   In terms of news, television gives highest priority to sensational stories that can be captured on film—auto accidents and multiple homicides. Thus, the airwaves come to be dominated by what media critic Ben Bagdikian calls, "fires, sex, and freaks."[61] Between such stories, local stations serve up a hefty portion of "happy talk" banter between the various on-camera personalities.[62] Absent, even at most newspapers, is probing, in-depth investigative reporting, especially on discomforting subjects like area workplace conditions, pollution, poverty, and product safety.

Even election coverage, essential to the functioning of a healthy democracy, tends often to be narrow, superficial, and sensational. Unable to attract and hold large audiences with extensive discussion of issues, programmers shift the focus to clichés and candidate images. Is he "strong on law and order"? Is she "fiscally responsible"? Meanwhile, what passes for investigative reporting is often voyeurism into candidates' personal lives. Then, on election day, the results are reported as if the event were a horse race.[63]

Radio and television stations are required by the FCC to devote at least 5 percent of their broadcasting time to public affairs. If it were not for that rule, there might be even less news-related programming on most of the airwaves. However, a look at the resulting public affairs broadcasts is telling. Documentaries, for example, tend to be expensive to produce and not to draw large audiences. As the three major networks gradually have lost some of their monopoly status, with cable television now in over one-half of all American households, increased competition seems to have led to even less inclination to absorb the financial losses entailed in documentaries. Instead, the viewer is given "news magazines" and early morning quasi-news programming like the "wake-up shows."

Media critic John O'Connor described television's public affairs programming as "something the FCC likes to find in the program log of stations at license renewal time as an indication, however meaningless, that the customary quest for profits was tempered by an occasional gesture toward the real world beyond old movies and sit-coms."[64]

Entertainment.   Entertainment, on the other hand, tends to be exceptionally mind numbing. Norman Lear observed, "With painful predictability, the networks putter with the same tired formats, adding more sex here and more violence there—more mindlessness."[65] Even on most of the cable stations, there is still the steady parade of game shows, soap operas, lightweight situation comedies, and police dramas.

It is not all completely mindless, however. Profit-seeking media corporations and their advertisers have a vested interest in defending a profit-based economic system. Thus, the worldview underlying most public affairs and entertainment programming is not difficult to identify.

The United States, so strongly individualist in temper and so bourgeois in appetite, has never wholly mastered the art of collective solutions, or of readily accepting the idea of a public interest, as against private gain.[66]

Conferring Values.   The mass media are an important part of American socialization. Faith in individualism, materialism, and capitalism must be reinforced, as must the illusion that the political system guarantees democratic control over the limited functions of government. This is accomplished by omission and commission in both public affairs and entertainment programming.

Public Affairs.   By omission, challenging perspectives often disappear from public affairs presentations. For example, newspapers run regular syndicated editorials by spokespersons for the extreme conservative position, such as William F. Buckley, Jr., or George Will. Absent are the regular columns by socialists such as Barry Bluestone or Noam Chomsky. In the electoral arena, third-party candidates and their potentially disruptive messages are ignored almost completely. Meanwhile, even in their heyday, documentaries tended to concentrate on subjects like incest, divorce, and youth crime, rather than taboo topics whose analysis could threaten the political-economic status quo, topics such as labor unions or the positive side of life in more socialistic countries.[67]

Apart from such omissions, news coverage itself often bears the stamp of the same underlying values. Political scientist Michael Parenti notes the way in which labor issues are twisted to make the workers look irresponsible and greedy.[68] Another example is the way political demonstrations are covered: the mass media both downplayed and apparently underestimated the size of two of the largest demonstrations in the nation's history—a half-million people marching on Washington to protest Reagan policies in September of 1981 and a full million marching in New York City to oppose nuclear weapons in June of 1982.[69]

Meanwhile, the flip side of this slant is the local media's inclination to inflate positive aspects and play down problems in their immediate communities in order to polish the community's image in the eyes of potential investors. They also may choose to lead the crusade for economic development projects like mass transportation, urban renewal, industrial parks, center-city shopping centers, and downtown parking garages. As a local business themselves, these media outlets have much at stake in the overall economic climate of their home community.[70]

Entertainment.   Similar trends can be found on the entertainment side. Erik Barnouw called television entertainment "propaganda for the status quo."[71] For example, there is no television series which has a black militant or a courageous socialist as a hero. Quite the contrary, black militants and socialists, when they do appear, are normally portrayed as dangerous caricatures. Meanwhile, police shows condition the audience to accept police repression of such dissenters, and almost all series suggest at least implicitly that one can and will advance in the United States if one simply works hard enough at it.[72]

Contributing Factors. At least four forces contribute directly to this ideological posture: media personnel, their standard operating procedures, advertisers, and government all work to foster what Ralph Miliband calls "a climate of conformity."[73]

To begin with, there is the demographic homogeneity of those in decision-making positions in the media business. They tend to be relatively well-to-do white men. In addition, all the employees are ultimately answerable to the even whiter and wealthier members of the owning class who hold the controlling shares of stock in their particular company. Both of these realities seem to encourage media's conservative content.[74] Then, there are the operational parameters that further encourage conformity, primarily the limits of time and money that prompt news journalists to feed off one another's stories.[75] Besides these internal factors, the mass media face external influences as well.

> To expect private companies to go on supporting a medium that is attacking them is like taking up a collection for money among the Christians to buy more lions.[76]

Although they are guided ultimately by the desire to maximize audience exposure and thus profits, advertisers occasionally will use their advertising money for overtly political purposes when they feel circumstances require it. At the national level, the thrust of the "Lou Grant" show came to be seen as too ideologically liberal, incurring the wrath of various right-wing organizations. Kimberly-Clark then pulled its advertising money, and the show soon dropped from the air.[77] Another example was General Electric's withdrawal of its sponsorship from an interview Barbara Walters conducted with Jane Fonda. Coming at the time of her popular film *The China Syndrome,* the sponsor feared it contained "material that could cause undue public concern about nuclear power."[78] An example at the local level is Brooklyn's Williamsburgh Savings Bank pulling its advertising money from a local newspaper that had run a story on the practice of bank "red-lining" (designating certain neighborhoods as too risky to allow investment). The tobacco industry's mere threat of withdrawing such money seems capable of censoring media coverage of that industry in Winston-Salem, North Carolina.[79]

Advertisers also draw on their stock of wealth in other ways to make certain their own perspectives are presented on important political issues of the day. They buy media time and space so they can directly present their political points of view. Such "advocacy advertising" really began to proliferate in the late 1970s and soon corporations were spending billions of dollars a year on such ads. Texaco and Mobil, for instance, have both run numerous ads extolling corporate perspectives on various issues.[80] In addition, regular commercial advertising is replete with conservative values, such as conditioning people to accept the virtues of profit-driven capitalism.[81] These same values even permeate many public-service ads, as most of these are delegated to the Advertising Council—a body largely comprising corporate owners and executives.[82] Last, these same corporations sponsor journalism prizes for outstanding work—within acceptable parameters—and they fund trips to lavish conferences at which journalists can discuss issues of interest to the corporations.

Finally, government plays a role as well. The United States Information Agency, for example, has put out pamphlets like "The Problems with Communism." Even more blatant is the "fairness doctrine"—established in the Federal Communications Act—that required all broadcasting stations to provide "balanced" coverage of controversial issues while explicitly stating that this did not include the "Communist perspective."[83] In 1987, the FCC abolished the fairness requirements altogether.[84]

CONCLUSION

Mass media were a powerful force in urban politics well before the advent of post-industrialism. During the preindustrial and industrial periods there actually were fewer media sources and ownership was even more tightly monopolistic. Yet, even though there are now more competing sources available, there are also important reasons why overall media influence has been enhanced in the postindustrial period.

Taken individually, no single media source is as powerful as in the days of veritable "one-newspaper towns." Yet, taken collectively, they have even more exposure today, as the media network has grown to encompass more people and touches their lives far more extensively. Thus, what media have lost in monopolization, they have gained in pervasiveness.

Second, as postindustrialism leaves more and more cities in precarious socioeconomic positions, these cities have less margin for error. A steady barrage of front-page stories emphasizing crimes committed by black men, or continuing exposés on the deteriorating conditions of local public services can accelerate the suburban flight of middle-class whites. Relentless pursuit of corporate scandals, revelations about polluting factories, and emphasis on business decline can reduce capital investment in the city as well. The postindustrial urban "house of cards" is particularly vulnerable to critical media analysis.

Third, government officials themselves are more vulnerable than ever to media criticism. With the decline of political party strength, every elected official essentially must operate as an individual. "Bad press" cannot be overcome by the counterefforts of the political party machine. In addition, councilpersons and bureaucrats remain secure in no small part because of their low political profiles. Thus, a media decision to shine the spotlight in their direction is one of the only ways they can be brought down.

Overall, there never have been many effective counterforces to the mass media. The old adage that one should never get into a fight with someone who "buys their ink by the barrel"[85] has always been true. Nonetheless, postindustrial developments have only enhanced that influence; and the increased influence of these privately owned sources of mass communication in practice has had the effect of further locking in the socioeconomic status quo, leaving a relatively small group of people with a disproportionate share of the city's income, wealth, and political power.

EXERCISES

Hypothetical #1: Political Power of the Mass Media

Individual students need to play the roles of newspaper reporter, editor, and publisher as well as the fictitious city's mayor and a local federal district judge. The rest of the class should feel free to interject what they think of the way the primary players are handling the scenario.

The setting is an old, large, postindustrial city sometime in the relatively near future. The city is under an air pollution alert, meaning that no one is to be on the streets unless going to or from work—particularly the elderly, children, and the chronically ill. [It is up to the faculty member to fill in any factual gaps as the exercise unfolds.]

The reporter stumbles across a reliable source at City Hall who indicates that a train has derailed just west of town. The derailment apparently has ruptured some dangerous chlorine gas tanks, with small amounts of chlorine gas already in the air. Emergency meetings are occurring in the mayor's office, and the key concern is that explosions could create a deadly chlorine gas cloud, which current wind conditions could carry into the densely populated city. Another Bhopal!

No more sources are available. Police roadblocks and airport restrictions keep you from getting anywhere near the scene. Meanwhile, unknown to the press, the mayor has been advised that the leaks and fires seem to be under control and that the primary danger is public panic.

What should the press do with the story? Does the public have a "right to know"? What are its limits? Who should decide what is in the public's best interest in such an emergency? If the mayor seeks a restraining order, will the federal judge grant it? Would the newspaper then obey such an order? Are there any other ways to restrain the press here? [Discuss implications, especially vis-à-vis the media's political power.][86]

Hypothetical #2: Economic Freedom of the Press

Individual students need to play the roles of news correspondent, assignment editor, and station manager at a local public television station. There must also be a mayor and federal district judge. The rest of the class should feel free to interject what they think of the way the primary players are handling the scenario.

The setting is an old, large, postindustrial city sometime in the relatively near future. A sizable Daisy Chemical plant is by far the largest employer in town; it also creates numerous peripheral jobs for suppliers, financiers, retailers, and others. Not only do the plant and its employees directly or indirectly generate most of the city's tax revenues, but Daisy also contributes approximately 40 percent of the public television station's revenues. Daisy Chemical is as significant to this town as GM is to Detroit. [Once again, it is up to the faculty member to fill in any factual gaps as the exercise unfolds.]

Daisy has approached the station manager with a proposal to fully underwrite a documentary on safety precautions at the plant. The plant managers hope such a program will lay to rest the persistent rumors that the company poses a variety of environmental dangers to the community. Is the station interested? Will you take their money? Will there be any provisos before you begin filming, for example, vis-à-vis access, editorial control, and other considerations?

Assuming the station's board of directors has insisted that the documentary be done, here is what your correspondent finds. There is irrefutable evidence that the plant quietly has been dumping higher levels of hazardous wastes into the environment than they are admitting publicly. In fact, they are very likely in violation of Environmental Protection Agency (EPA) standards. What will you do with this story?

Whether confronted with the material or not, Daisy learns that you have this knowledge and threatens to withdraw all of its contributions to your station if this "scurrilous misinformation" is released to the public in any form. Plant managers claim they are within EPA standards, even though those standards are "extreme" anyway. They also emphasize that "scientists differ" about the dangers posed by the release of the chemicals in question. What will the station do with this information now?

In the mayor's view, what is in the city's best interest here? Would you seek a court injunction to block the story? Would the federal judge uphold such an injunction? Would the station comply with an injunction of that type? [Discuss the implications, especially vis-à-vis "freedom of the press."][87]

NOTES

1. Joseph Pulitzer in the *North American Review* (1904), quoted in William F. Harris, "The News Story and Political Theory," unpublished paper presented at the annual meeting of the American Political Science Association, New York City, September 1978, p. 23.
2. *Gazette of the United States,* April 27, 1789, quoted in Frank Mott, *Jefferson and the Press* (Baton Rouge: Louisiana State University Press, 1943), p. 15.
3. Mott, *Jefferson and the Press,* pp. 167–168.
4. Everett Ladd, *The American Polity* (New York: Norton, 1985), pp. 486–487.
5. For good general references concerning media history, see Ladd, *The American Polity,* p. 488; Edward Chester, *Radio, Television, and American Politics* (New York: Sheed and Ward, 1969); Lawrence Lichty and Topping Malachi, *American Broadcasting* (New York: Hastings House, 1975); Michael Schudson, *Discovering the News* (New York: Basic Books, 1978).
6. *Near v. Minnesota,* 283 U.S. 679 (1931).
7. *New York Times v. United States,* 403 U.S. 713 (1971).
8. *Philadelphia Newspapers, Inc. v. Hepps,* 475 U.S. 767 (1986).
9. *New York Times v. Sullivan,* 376 U.S. 279 (1964).
10. For someone who is not a "public figure," or for a public figure when the story is not deemed to be "of legitimate public concern," the plaintiff need not prove the media's recklessness or awareness of the story's falsity. Instead, the plaintiff need only show that the story was false and damaging. See *Gertz v. Robert Welch, Inc.,* 418 U.S. 323 (1974); *Dun and Bradstreet, Inc. v. Greenmoss Builders, Inc.,* 472 U.S. 749 (1985).
11. For more on media's legally determined freedoms, see A. E. Howard, "The Press in Court," *Wilson Quarterly* 6 (Special Issue 1982): 86–93.
12. Christopher Sterling and Timothy Haight, eds., *The Mass Media* (New York: Praeger, 1982); *New York Times,* January 28, 1984; Robert Bowen, *The Changing Television Audience in America* (New York: Columbia University Press, 1984); Warren Agee,

Phillip Ault, and Edwin Emery, *Main Currents in Mass Communications* (New York: Harper & Row, 1986); Memphis, *Commercial Appeal,* February 15, 1986.

13. Kathleen Hall Jamieson and Karyn Kohrs Campbell, *The Interplay of Influence: Mass Media and Their Publics in News, Advertising, Politics* (Belmont, Calif.: Wadsworth, 1983), p. 4; *New York Times,* June 27, 1989; Frederick Williams, Herbert Dordick, and Frederick Horstman, "Where Citizens Go for Information," *Journal of Communication* 27 (Winter 1977): 95–99.

14. Doris Graber, *Mass Media and American Politics* (Washington, D.C.: Congressional Quarterly Press, 1989), p. 104; *New York Times,* May 13, 1985; September 8, 1983; Judith Sobel and Edwin Emery, "U.S. Dailies' Competition in Relation to Circulation Size," *Journalism Quarterly* 55 (Spring 1978): 145–149; Williams, "Where Citizens Go for Information," pp. 95–99.

15. *The Ayer Directory of Publications* (Fort Washington, Pa.: IMS Press, annual); *New York Times,* September 8, 1983.

16. James Rosenau, *Public Opinion and Foreign Policy* (New York: Random House, 1961). Also see Paul Lazarsfeld, Bernard Berelson, and Hazel Gaudet, *The People's Choice* (New York: Columbia University Press, 1948), pp. 151–152.

17. Graber, *Mass Media and American Politics,* pp. 373–380; Jamieson and Campbell, *The Interplay of Influence,* pp. 11–12.

18. James Boylan, "News People," *Wilson Quarterly* 6 (Special Issue 1982): 71–85.

19. Graber, *Mass Media and American Politics,* chap. 3; David Paletz and Robert Entman, *Media Power Politics* (New York: Free Press, 1981), chap. 2; Howard Kahane, *Logic and Contemporary Rhetoric* (Belmont, Calif.: Wadsworth, 1980), pp. 228–234.

20. See *New York Times,* December 24, 1990; June 19, 1992.

21. Benjamin Compaine, Christopher Sterling, Thomas Guback et al., *Who Owns the Media* (White Plains, N.Y.: Knowledge Industry, 1982).

22. *New York Times,* December 15, 1979.

23. *New York Times,* September 22, 1991; Compaine, *Who Owns the Media,* pp. 36–37.

24. As for radio, a recent FCC ruling allows a single broadcaster to own up to 30 AM and 30 FM stations while a local broadcaster can own up to 6 stations in a single media market so long as their combined audience share does not exceed 25 percent and there are at least 40 stations in that market area. See *New York Times,* March 13, 1992.

25. *New York Times,* June 2, 1991.

26. Michael Parenti, *Inventing Reality* (New York: St. Martin's Press, 1985), p. 27; *Media Report to Women,* September 1, 1981, p. 4.

27. Peter Dreier and Steve Weinberg, "Interlocking Directorates," *Columbia Journalism Review* 18 (November/December 1979): 51–53, 67–68; Thomas Dye, *Who's Running America?* (Englewood Cliffs, N.J.: Prentice-Hall, 1983), chap. 4.

28. David Altheide and Robert Snow, *Media Logic* (Beverly Hills, Calif.: Sage, 1979); Graber, *Mass Media and American Politics,* pp. 80–86; Bernard Roshco, *Newsmaking* (Chicago: University of Chicago Press, 1975), chap. 3.

29. Edmund Lambeth, *Committed Journalism: An Ethic for the Profession* (Bloomington: Indiana University Press, 1986); C. Cleveland Wilhoit and David Weaver, *The American Journalist* (Bloomington: Indiana University Press, 1986); John Merrill and Ralph Barney, *Ethics and the Press* (New York: Hastings, 1975); William Rivers and Cleve Mathews, *Ethics for the Media* (Englewood Cliffs, N.J.: Prentice-Hall, 1988); John Hulteng, *The Messenger's Motives* (Englewood Cliffs, N.J.: Prentice-Hall, 1985).

30. Edward Epstein, *News from Nowhere* (New York: Vintage, 1973); Graber, *Mass Media and American Politics,* pp. 86–93; Jamieson and Campbell, *The Interplay of Influence,* pp. 53–61.

31. John Johnstone, Edward Slawski, and William Bowman, *The Newspeople* (Champaign: University of Illinois Press, 1976). For a case in point, see Charles Whelton, "Getting Bought," *Village Voice,* May 2, 1977, p. 51.

32. *Miami Herald Publishing Co. v. Tornillo,* 418 U.S. 241 (1974).

33. Quoted in *National Journal,* December 16, 1989, p. 3058.

34. *New York Times,* June 14, 1991.

35. Graber, *Mass Media and American Politics,* pp. 39–41; *New York Times,* February 27, 1989.

36. Graber, *Mass Media and American Politics,* chap. 7; Kahane, *Logic and Contemporary Rhetoric,* pp. 239–241.

37. Fred W. Friendly, *Due to Circumstances beyond Our Control* (New York: Random House, 1967), pp. 281–282.

38. Ibid., pp. 271–272.

39. *New York Times,* August 17, 1986 (press); *New York Times,* July 6, 1988 (radio); Roger Noll, Merton Peck, and John McGowan, *Economic Aspects of Television Regulation* (Washington, D.C.: Brookings Institution, 1973), p. 16; "Broadcasting and Cable," *Broadcasting* 96 (February 12, 1979): 23.

40. For further indications of how profitable mass media have become, see Desmond Smith, "Mining the Golden Spectrum," *Nation,* May 26, 1979, pp. 595–597; *New York Times,* December 12, 1977.

41. One of the most developed examples of such delegation is a practice called "barter syndication." See *New York Times,* January 18, 1986; July 29, 1990.

42. Graber, *Mass Media and American Politics,* pp. 160–176; Doris Graber, *Processing the News* (White Plains, N.Y.: Longman, 1988); Jacob Jacoby and Wayne Hoyer, "Viewers' Miscomprehension of Televised Communications," *Journal of Marketing* 46 (Fall 1982): 12–26.

43. Paletz and Entman, *Media Power Politics,* p. 10.

44. Judy VanSlyke Turk, "Information Subsidies and Media Content," *Journalism Monographs* 100 (December 1986): 1–29; Jamieson and Campbell, *The Interplay of Influence,* pp. 78–95; William Furlong, "Manipulating the News," *TV Guide,* June 11, 1977, pp. 4–10.

45. *New York Times,* June 8, 1975. For another example, see the furor over public television's "Banks and the Poor" documentary, recounted in the *New York Times,* March 19, 1978. Also see controversies reported in the *New York Times,* June 22, 1981; April 6, 1982; March 2, 1989; Mary 27, 1990. For a discussion of interest group impact in general, see Jamieson and Campbell, *The Interplay of Influence,* chap. 9.

46. David Rosenbloom, "The Press and the Local Candidate," *Annals of the American Academy of Political and Social Science* 427 (September 1976): 12–22; Graber, *Mass Media and American Politics,* pp. 196–206; Jamieson and Campbell, *The Interplay of Influence,* chap. 11; Robert Agranoff, *The New Style of Election Campaigns* (Boston: Holbrook, 1972); Thomas Patterson, *The Mass Media Election* (New York: Praeger, 1980); Harold Mendelsohn and Irving Crespi, *Polls, Television, and the New Politics* (Scranton, Pa.: Chandler, 1970).

47. *New York Times,* February 15, 1989.

48. Michael Lipsky, "Protest as a Political Resource," *American Political Science Review* 63 (December 1968): 1144–1158; Edie Goldenberg, *Making the Papers* (Lexington, Mass.: Lexington Books, 1975); Todd Gitlin, *The Whole World Is Watching* (Berkeley: University of California Press, 1980).

49. Wallace Sayre and Herbert Kaufman, *Governing New York City* (New York: Norton, 1965), p. 491–492.

50. Jospeh Klappner, *The Effects of Mass Communication* (New York: Free Press, 1960); Sidney Kraus and Dennis Davis, *The Effects of Mass Communication on Political Behavior* (University Park: Pennsylvania State University Press, 1976); Denis McQuail, "The Influence and Effects of Mass Communication," in James Curran, Michael Gurevitels, and Janet Woolacott, *Mass Communication and Society* (New York: Sage, 1977); Graber, *Mass Media and American Politics,* chap. 5.

　　For examples of empirical studies that do link media messages to political behavior, see Lana Stein and Arnold Fleischmann, "Newspaper and Business Endorsements in Municipal Elections," *Journal of Urban Affairs* 9 (Fall 1987): 325–336; Thomas Patterson and Robert McClure, *The Unseeing Eye* (New York: Putnam, 1976); David Sears and Richard Whitney, "Political Persuasion," in Ithiel de Sola Pool, ed., *Handbook of Communications* (Chicago: Rand-McNally, 1973).

51. Graber, *Mass Media and American Politics,* p. 183.

52. Gay Talese, *The Kingdom and the Power* (New York: Bantam, 1969), p. 73.

53. Leo Bogart, *Press and Public* (Hillsdale, N.J.: Lawrence Erlbaum, 1981).

54. Demetrios Caraley, *City Governments and Urban Problems* (Englewood Cliffs, N.J.: Prentice-Hall, 1977), pp. 321–323.

55. Graber, *Mass Media and American Politics,* pp. 204–206; Mark Fishman, *Manufacturing the News* (Austin: University of Texas Press, 1980); Joel Swerdlow, "The Decline of the Boys on the Bus," *Washington Journalism Review* 3 (January/February 1981): 15–19; Joe McGinniss, *The Selling of the President, 1968* (New York: Trident Press, 1969); Dan Nimmo, *The Political Persuaders* (Englewood Cliffs, N.J.: Prentice-Hall, 1970); Joseph Napolitan, *The Election Game and How to Win It* (Garden City, N.Y.: Doubleday, 1972).

56. Quoted in Roger Hatch and Frank Watkins, eds., *Reverend Jesse L. Jackson: Straight from the Heart* (Philadelphia: Fortress, 1987), p. 320.

57. Michael S. Robinson, "Public Affairs, Television, and the Growth of Media Malaise," *American Political Science Review* 70 (June 1976): 409–432. Also see Arthur Miller, Edie Goldenberg, and Lutz Erbring, "Type-Set Politics," *American Political Science Review* 73 (March 1979): 67–84.

58. *New York Times,* December 18, 1976.

59. From *New York Times,* August 6, 1978.

60. *New York Times Magazine,* April 8, 1979, p. 52.

61. Ben Bagdikian, "Fires, Sex, and Freaks," *New York Times Magazine,* October 10, 1976, p. 40.

62. Ron Powers, *The Newscasters* (New York: St. Martin's Press, 1977).

63. Michael J. Robinson, "The Media at Mid-Year," *Public Opinion* 3 (June/July 1980): 41–45.

64. *New York Times,* June 26, 1977.

65. *New York Times,* May 20, 1984.

66. Daniel Bell, quoted in Mitchell Levita, "Homelessness in America," *New York Times Magazine,* June 10, 1990, p. 91.

67. John Culhane, "Television Taboos," *New York Times,* February 20, 1977.

68. Parenti, *Inventing Reality,* chap. 5.

69. Ibid., chap. 6.

70. Morris Janowitz, *The Community Press in an Urban Setting* (Glencoe, Ill.: Free Press, 1954); David Paletz, Peggy Reichert, and Barbara McIntyre, "How the Media Support Local Governmental Authority," *Public Opinion Quarterly* 35 (Spring 1971): 80–92.

71. Quoted in Kahane, *Logic and Contemporary Rhetoric,* p. 236.

72. See Parenti, *Inventing Reality,* chap. 1; Herbert Schiller, *The Mind Managers* (Boston: Beacon Press, 1973); Claus Mueller, *The Politics of Communication* (London: Oxford University Press, 1973).

For examples of anti-establishment television shows getting little air time, see Erik Barnouw, *The Television Writer* (New York: Hill and Wang, 1962), p. 27; Robert Cirino, *Don't Blame the People* (New York: Vintage, 1972), pp. 303–306.

73. Ralph Miliband, *The State in Capitalist Society* (New York: Basic Books, 1969), p. 238.

74. Ben Bagdikian, *The Media Monopoly* (Boston: Beacon, 1983); Herbert Gans, *Deciding What's News* (New York: Vintage, 1979); James Aronson, *The Press and the Cold War* (Boston: Beacon, 1970); Parenti, *Inventing Reality,* chap. 2.

75. Epstein, *News from Nowhere*; Timothy Crouse, *The Boys on the Bus* (New York: Ballantine, 1973).

76. Leonard Matthews, president, American Association of Advertising Agencies, quoted in *New York Times,* January 2, 1980.

77. Michael Parenti, *Democracy for the Few* (New York: St. Martin's Press, 1983), p. 193.

78. Tom Wicker, *On Press* (New York: Viking, 1978). Also see Todd Gitlin, "When the Right Talks, TV Listens," *Nation,* October 15, 1983, pp. 333–340.

79. Kahane, *Logic and Contemporary Rhetoric,* p. 212.

80. David Vogel, "Business's New Class Struggle," *Nation,* December 15, 1979, pp. 609, 625–628; *New York Times,* August 10, 1986.

81. G. William Domhoff, *The Powers That Be* (New York: Vintage, 1979); pp. 183–191; Stuart Ewen, *Captains of Consciousness* (New York: McGraw-Hill, 1976).

82. Bruce Howard, "The Advertising Council," *Ramparts,* December 1974/January 1975, pp. 25–26.

83. Communications Act of 1934, 27 USC 151 (1934).

84. For a summary of the media's socializing role, see Noam Chomsky, "Ideological Conformity," *Nation,* January 27, 1979, pp. 77–81.

85. Cited in James Q. Wilson, *American Government* (Lexington, Mass.: D C Heath, 1989), p. 249.

86. For background information on such disasters, see *New York Times,* August 2, 1989; August 8, 1989.

87. For an actual example of such economic coercion, see the controversy in Amarillo, Texas, reported in the *New York Times,* December 7, 1987.

CHAPTER 12

Alternative Futures

James O'Connor's model of governmental fiscal crisis remains instructive. In any free enterprise economy where fate is left to the winds of the economic marketplace, government will struggle with the conflicting pressures to boost capital investment and simultaneously help those who are unable effectively to compete for one reason or another. Where there is economic growth, there may be enough tax revenue to do a reasonable job of both, but where growth has slowed and available resources are scarce, these tensions may soon drive government to fiscal distress.

The latter scenario certainly appears to fit those cities furthest along in terms of postindustrial development. As their economies struggle, their inclination is to spend discretionary revenues on economic development projects. However, they also must provide services to large numbers of the nation's most hopelessly indigent people. In addition, they are saddled with the legacies of previous rounds of urban unrest. The rebellious poor periodically have struggled and won a number of governmental concessions, and they and service-providing bureaucrats often have organized themselves politically so as to resist government retrenchment. Thus, as long as these cities possibly can, they will try to fund both, hiding their subsequent fiscal stress as much as is feasible.

All cities are limited legally to the type and amount of debt they can accumulate, and sooner or later the postindustrial city will be exposed. The discovery might result from a state or federal investigation, a media exposé, an economic downturn, or any of a number of other events. But when it occurs, one of the first results will be a drop in the city's bond rating, leading to future difficulty and expense for the city in borrowing needed funds. Something will have to give.

How do fiscally strapped cities regain the confidence of the lending community? They need to exercise "fiscal responsibility," which means they will reduce legitimation expenditures in favor of accumulation ones. Of course, it is not long before the symptoms of this switch begin to appear. The number of homeless people increases. Multiple families are forced to share a single residence. The lines at the soup kitchens grow longer and longer, and violence increases, although it may be internalized and show up in self- and family abuse and crime rates. Ultimately, the outcome may well be overt urban unrest, however, and more programmatic Band-Aids most likely will be applied.

ADVANCED CASES

The advanced cases of New York City and Cleveland were discussed at length in earlier sections of this book, but other older and large cities are not far behind. Is this the future of all large cities?

Detroit

The city of Detroit has lost nearly half of its population since 1960, and three-quarters of those who remain are African Americans. Tens of thousands of high-paying manufacturing jobs have disappeared. Unemployment and poverty levels stand at twice the national average.

Symptoms of Detroit's underlying problems first surfaced in Wayne County, which includes the city. By 1979, the county had accumulated an operating budget deficit, which was illegal, of over $18 million, and it was nearly forced to miss a number of employee paydays when the governor tied further state bail-outs to the acceptance of a more centralized form of county governance. Black community leaders attacked the plan as racist for it would dilute what little political power blacks had gained; nevertheless, their opposition was relatively futile.[1]

The city of Detroit itself teetered on the brink of default in the early 1980s. The city's operating budget was more than $100 million in the red, and its bond rating plummeted. In addition, even the downtown area's symbol of hope, Renaissance Center, lost more than $100 million and went into default. To avoid default by the city government, also, Detroit voters passed a tax increase; union pension funds were invested in city bonds; and the mayor began to implement a stringent austerity program, which included job cuts by attrition as well as wage concessions. Meanwhile, the city had come to rely on the federal government for a full 20 percent of its revenues, and thus became quite vulnerable to federal cuts.[2]

Philadelphia

The City of Brotherly Love has lost more than 500,000 of its 2.1 million residents since 1950. More than 40 percent of those who remain are black. Some 150,000 of its 235,000 manufacturing jobs have left since 1970. Its tax rates are among the highest in the country. More than one-third of its residents live in poverty. As revenues decline, social problems mount; the city faces soaring costs of coping with trash collection, drug-related crime, homelessness, and AIDS patients.[3]

Meanwhile, the city's bond rating sank to "junk bond" level in 1990, prompting the state to create a finance control board (the Pennsylvania Intergovernmental Cooperation Authority). Union pension funds were forced to buy shaky city bonds; and, unable to borrow on its own, the city of Philadelphia began to run out of basic supplies and defer pension fund contributions.[4] The litany is all too familiar.

Bridgeport, Connecticut

By the mid-1980s, Bridgeport had lost most of its industrial base and much of its state and federal aid. Meanwhile, its population had shrunk to approximately 140,000 people, its welfare expenditures had increased, and it was bound by union contracts city administrators considered "onerous and economically burdensome." In 1988, when the city was faced with a $60 million operating budget deficit, the state established a finance control board so that Bridgeport could continue to borrow. The city subsequently cut nearly one-third of its municipal work force, eliminating all street sweeping, snowplowing, and recreational programs. When it simply could take no more, the city finally defied the control board and filed for bankruptcy in federal court. In response, the board voted to nullify the action, adopted a budget for the city, and raised city property taxes.[5]

East St. Louis, Illinois

East St. Louis appears to be a city that has reached the end of its resources. It gradually has become a ghostly shell of its former self. Its manufacturing plants are gone. Its population has fallen from nearly 100,000 residents, most of whom were white, to 40,000 residents, virtually all of whom are black. One-half are unemployed. Three-quarters receive some form of public assistance. Entire neighborhoods have been set on fire, leaving much of the city looking as if it has been bombed. Drug and gang problems are rampant. Garbage lies uncollected. Ruptured sewer mains spew raw sewage into the streets. Mired in debt, the city stopped paying most creditors, and the few remaining municipal employees often must wait weeks for their paychecks. Conditions there led one local professor to conclude, "I don't think there is any way you can make much out of what there is now. The best you can do is keep the patient comfortable."[6]

Mounting Crises

Enduring Problems.   Should East St. Louis completely collapse and disappear, what will have become of its urban problems? Some of the very real ones—traffic congestion, air pollution, and inadequate landfills—will have disappeared, but the plight of the low-income people will not suddenly have gone away. These people will have moved on to other cities, only to add to those cities' urban problems. In the last analysis, most "urban problems" boil down to people—often very poor people. As the urban underclass has become an ever larger percentage of post-industrial city populations, these cities have become less fiscally able to deal with the entire array of urban difficulties. This escalating urban impoverishment tends to occur in vicious cycles that lead to periodic bouts of violent social unrest.

As chapter 3 indicated, more than one out of every five postindustrial city residents lives below the federal government's poverty line. Even these figures understate the level of indigence by failing to include many who are poor and by masking the reality that inner-city residents are becoming poorer and less likely to escape their plights. They have become a permanent underclass whose ranks are growing and whose position is deteriorating even further.

They can be shuffled from slum rentals to public housing to living with relatives to heating grates on the streets and back again, even from city to city, but they do not disappear. At any point in time, some cities will have to accommodate most of them; and there are times when the various safety valves all fail.[7]

> I read that report . . . of the 1919 riot in Chicago, and it is as if I were reading the report of the investigating committee on the Harlem riot of 1935, the report of the investigating committee on the Harlem riot of 1943, the report of the McCone Commission on the 1968 Watts riot.
>
> I must again in candor say to you members of this the Kerner Commission —it is a kind of Alice in Wonderland—with the same moving picture re-shown over and over again, the same analysis, the same recommendations, and the same inaction.[8]

The Fires Return.   In the spring and summer of 1977, a number of media sources gave special coverage to the city ghettos "ten years later." What they found amid some rather cosmetic gains was continuing segregation, unemployment, housing deterioration, and incomes of blacks that were not catching up with those of whites.[9] Such findings led a task force of the National Advisory Commission on Criminal Justice Standards and Goals to conclude, "The present tranquility is deceptive. . . . Many of the traditional indicators for disorders are clearly present and need but little stimulus to activate them."[10] The commission results also led Secretary of Labor Ray Marshall to warn:

> What this leads to is an inflammable mixture in the urban areas. We have a concentration not only of a whole generation of blacks that may never have jobs, but disaffected Viet Nam vets (a high percentage of them are minorities), ex-convicts, and who knows how many illegal aliens.[11]

And then, as predicted, the urban unrest began. The following list itemizes more than 30 such disturbances that have occurred since 1977.

Urban Ghetto Unrest, 1977–1992

July 1977: A New York City power failure sets off massive looting, some beginning within 30 seconds of the blackout. Ultimately, 3,700 are arrested.

April 1980: Youths in Witchita clash with police, and in the rampage that ensues, cars are burned, bricks are thrown at passing cars, and sniping occurs. In the end, 52 are injured and 29 arrested.

May 1980: Unrest in Miami includes beatings, maimings, burnings, looting, and sniping—with 18 dead, more than 200 seriously wounded, 750 arrested, and more than $100 million in property damage.

July 1980: Violence erupts in Chattanooga, Tennessee, and Orlando, Florida, including rock throwing, sniping, and numerous fire bombings, with dozens of injuries and arrests.

December 1981: Comparable racial violence occurs in Gainesville, Florida.

December 1982: Another Miami incident involves three days of sniping, rock-throwing, beatings, robbery, lootings, and vandalism, leaving 2 dead, 25 injured, and 45 arrested.

April 1983: Crowds throw stones, bottles, and bricks at police cars in Montgomery, Alabama.

May 1983: Youths throw rocks and bottles at Miami police, besides committing sporadic vandalism.

July 1983: New York City youths rampage after a concert in Central Park, with as many as 1,000 of them robbing and assaulting concert goers as well as patrons of a posh Central Park restaurant. Arson and looting occur. Whites are advised to avoid the neighborhood or risk being violently attacked. In the end, 13 are injured and 300 arrested.

October 1985: Police face a barrage of rocks, bottles, and sniper fire in Auburn, Georgia.

February 1987: In Tampa, Florida, stores are looted, cars and trash fires are set, and stones are thrown at police.

September 1988: Rocks are hurled at whites and two stores are burned in the black Cedar Grove neighborhood of Shreveport, Louisiana.

January 1989: Angry crowds fire guns and throw rocks at police, burn cars, and loot stores in Miami.

February 1989: Rocks and bottles are hurled at Tampa police for two consecutive nights.

August 1989: Extensive vandalism and looting sweep Vineland, New Jersey.

September 1989: Thousands of black youths attack police and loot Virginia Beach stores. The National Guard is called in to restore order. The melee leaves some 50 people hospitalized and 650 arrested.

December 1990: Arson and vandalism sweep Miami's Puerto Rican neighborhood of Wynwood.

May 1991: Hispanic youths attack police and burn police cars in Washington, D.C.

June 1991: Sporadic violence once again rocks Miami's Liberty City and Overton areas. Dozens are arrested and 3 police officers are injured.

July 1991: Following a spirited protest demonstration, angry black teens smash store windows in downtown New Brunswick, New Jersey.

August 1991: Some 61 people, including 43 police officers, are injured, as racial violence envelops the Crown Heights section of Brooklyn. Rocks and bottles are thrown at police and several police cars are burned.

May 1992: Unrest in Los Angeles involves 5 days of beatings, burnings, looting, sniping, and vandalism, leaving 58 dead, 2,400 injured, and $785 million in property damage. [Other disturbances follow in cities such as New York, Washington, D.C., Las Vegas, Minneapolis, New Rochelle, Newark, Jersey City, Bridgeport, Mobile, Seattle, Atlanta, San Francisco, and Miami.]

In 1990, Milwaukee city councilman Michael McGee organized a group called the "Black Panther Community Militia," who dressed in black military fatigues. He then demanded that the city allocate $100 million to provide jobs for unemployed Milwaukee residents or his group might be forced to take violent steps within five years.[12]

As these individual incidents indicate, postindustrial city ghettos are an inflammable mixture providing a barometer of their cities' socioeconomic distress and fiscal limitations, but these events are just the tip of the iceberg. Violent crime has been soaring, racial polarization worsens, people continue to lose their middle-income jobs, tax bases decline—the list goes on.[13]

Nevertheless, not until the cities begin to burn is the situation viewed as a crisis, and even then only in the specific cities exhibiting the unrest. As a result, solutions come to be incremental and discrete. Yet if the vicious cycle continues, no one can predict just how much trauma the American fabric can withstand and how much more government can spend on placating the rebellious poor and still maintain the integrity of the present socioeconomic system.

Governmental Dilemma.   At the forefront of the battles are the postindustrial city mayors. Although their city councils will not pose much of an obstacle to their efforts in most cases, the mayors are hamstrung by other institutional developments. The bureaucracy has become very large and very independent. The mass media have become incredibly pervasive and must be finessed if the mayor is to have any chance to carry out his or her policy agenda. Meanwhile, political parties are no longer strong enough to help. Thus, not only do postindustrial cities face a plethora of socioeconomic difficulties, but the government's power to deal with them is no longer as concentrated as it once was.

> We have a number of laws on the books which give a tax preference to businesses located in the city, encourage them to stay rather than leave. . . . Some say this is subsidizing business. I say it's the name of the game. As long as we live in a society which pits workers in Mississippi against workers in Michigan, we have to make concessions.[14]
>
> —Coleman Young, mayor of Detroit

In the end, there really is little the city's elected officials can do about the underlying postindustrial problems that plague their cities. They can tinker at the margins, privatizing here and adding an accumulation expenditure or two there; but the real problems are much larger than an individual city or its elected leadership. Instead, attention turns to the federal government.[15]

Only the federal government is in a postion to begin to address the underlying dilemmas in any serious way. If a state or locality wanders far from economic development priorities, it will find itself at a competitive disadvantage in the endless competition to attract and retain the investment of highly mobile capital. The federal government, however, has to be concerned about the entire nation's international competitiveness; therefore, it has not been particularly forthcoming in terms of legitimation help, especially since the hypermobility of capital began in the late 1970s.

ALTERNATIVE FUTURES

Urban politics is deeply ideological. Decisions and policies are the product of, and must be rationalized and defended in terms of, idea systems—however tacit and inchoate—which, as a consequence of this, take on a special importance.[16]

As a number of the nation's most serious social and economic problems come to a head in its postindustrial cities, and as discord mounts, national attention must once again turn to the urban crisis. It seems that national policy is headed in one of two directions. Liberalism and conservativism appear to be part of the vicious cycle itself, with the liberals pressing for more legitimation expenditures after urban turbulence and the conservatives pressing for the substitution of accumulation spending once the unrest subsides. The cumulative effects of the present course, however, are both bankrupting government and tearing at the very fabric that holds the nation together.

When both of these paths finally appear hopeless, the alternatives are likely to be either a form of fascism further down the continuum to the right or a form of socialism further to the left (see figure 12.1). As the dilemma appears inherent in capitalism, the nation will be forced either (1) to retain capitalism—warts and all—by allowing more effective repression of the increasingly turbulent under-classes, or (2) to opt for a different economic arrangement with a gradual sociali-zation of capital ownership and the elimination of the underclasses as they presently exist. Alternatively, the country can continue to stumble along until the social order breaks down and the decision is made in the streets.

FIGURE 12.1 An Ideological Continuum

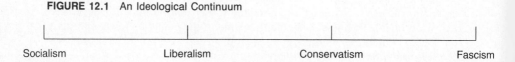

Socialism   Liberalism   Conservatism   Fascism

The question is whether or not the economic crisis will be used to reorganize society along increasingly regimented lines, or alternately, whether the crisis can be used to build a popular, socialist movement which will in the short run protect the living standard of working people and in the long run prepare the way for the eventual reorganization of our society along more humane lines.[17]

Friendly Fascism

Believe, Obey, Fight.
   —an oft-quoted fascist slogan

At the far right extreme of the ideological continuum we find a political value structure called fascism. Traditional fascism encompasses at least five important tenets: conflict theory, elitism, antirationalism, totalitarianism, and ultranationalism. These fundamental tenets are summarized in the following list.

Fundamental Tenets of Fascism

Conflict Theory. By their very nature, people strive to dominate other people, and nations strive to dominate other nations.

Elitism. People are born unequal, and thus some are capable of providing greater service to society than others. What will arise, then, is a natural grouping of political and economic elites who, on the basis of their abilities and wills, are the ones who will and should possess a disproportionate share of the nation's wealth and power.

Antirationalism. Products of the Western Enlightenment period— science, technology, and liberal democracy—have not reduced national and international problems. Life is far too complex and unpredictable for people to continue to place such faith in rationality while they search for solutions. Therefore, important truths, rather than the products of rationalism, are simply random facts that exist to serve a desired political purpose. Consequently, as Mussolini exhorted, people should "feel, not think," while the born elites discern truth by virtue of their superior instincts.

Totalitarianism. The emerging elites then should and will attempt to organize and control vitually every aspect of human existence, including lifestyles, culture, education, work, and so forth. They must crush any opposition to their quest for total control of both society and the individual.

Ultranationalism. Just as a nation is composed of a pyramid of competing people headed by whichever person has the most ability and will, the same is true internationally. In that arena, the nation with the most talent, the greatest discipline, and the strongest will to act will ultimately emerge victorious. If the citizens of a nation led by such a leader believe, unite, obey, and fight, that nation's destiny can be achieved. Consequently, national solidarity and international imperialism are signs of vitality, and war an opportunity for a spiritual creativity of sorts. Conversely, if a nation shirks this responsibility, it will be overrun by the forces of history.

Beyond the tenets of the ideology itself, it is informative to note the social context within which fascism generally has risen. Fascism has tended to emerge primarily in industrialized capitalist countries suffering from a combination of international humiliation and domestic economic difficulties. Meanwhile, left-wing social movements arise among the lower classes attempting to force some redistribution of the nation's wealth and power. Soon the combination of their militancy and the political and economic concessions they attain as a result will threaten both the status of the middle class and the dominant position of the capital-owning class. At that juncture, a charismatic leader emerges to lead a broad-based reactionary movement.

Kenneth and Patricia Dolbeare contend that fascism involves the "elaborate organization and management of daily life in the name of efficiency, mutual sacrifice, and national survival."[18] This control is accomplished by a combination of "symbolic manipulations," for example, scapegoating, ultrapatriotism in the face of a perceived external threat, and "widespread coercion, police surveillance, brutal attacks on dissidents, and deliberate arbitrariness, backed up by a network of spying and reporting on each other by citizens generally, all under the guise of national security."[19] Militarism and international imperialism are justified both as extensions of manifest destiny and as a form of self-defense.

> Before . . . the fascist upheaval, Capitalism dominates, but it is Capitalism in which there are certain mutations: it is a Capitalism with restricted limits of accumulation, where economic dead weights abound, where the destruction of capital increases, and where there are more parasitic and reactionary strata.[20]

If international respect were seriously to decline and economic hardship to mount at home, sizable components of the working, middle, and upper classes could well turn their wrath toward the societal costs involved in what many might see as overindulging a shiftless and parasitic minority of citizens wallowing in the urban ghettos. Such people also might be seen as making the streets unsafe, and their petty protests arousing senseless feelings of guilt among the hard-working majority, cutting into patriotic spirit as international challenges mount. Many in the middle and upper classes might feel that generous services for these degenerates, concocted in the rarified air of some ivory tower, were sapping needed capital away from potentially productive private investments.

The proposals for change would be rather simple as we proceeded down the ideological path ever further to the right. Accumulation expenditures would clearly need to become the top priority in governmental budgeting, from the federal to the local level. Legitimation services would be reduced so that "non-producers" would be maintained at no more than subsistence level at most, and as many of those services as possible would be provided privately—allowing private elites more control.[21] "True patriots" would be encouraged to turn in dissidents to local authorities, and those who disobeyed the law, whether as a form of social protest or for any other reason, would be dealt with swiftly and severely. The police would be "unleashed" so as more effectively to be able to enforce the law, and the judicial system would be streamlined to avoid burdensome technicalities and delays. Practices such as preventive detention would be allowed, and the rights of the accused would be reduced, in order not to interfere with the efficient prosecution of "the guilty."[22]

In addition, we would expect to see members of the repressed groups holding positions such as police officer, prison guard, mayor, and judge, with little choice but to strictly enforce these increasingly oppressive laws. Such action would convey a sense of sensitivity and impartiality while at the same time protecting the interests of the "haves." Such "local rule" is a device that has been used repeatedly by nations engaged in international colonization. At very least, it confuses the issues at hand.[23]

Prospects.   As long as the average American views urban poverty and subsequent lower-class unrest as purely ghetto problems, the situation most likely will continue to deteriorate. The response will be either to offer these people help (liberalism) or to force them to make it on their own (conservativism). If a fundamental choice must be made between the socialist direction to the ideological left and the fascist direction to the ideological right, such a narrow view of the problem, especially within the dominant American political culture that dates back to the founding fathers, may well lead at least temporarily down the road to the right.

At the national level, there are already indications of such a drift: consider the *supranationalism* aroused during the Iranian hostage crisis, the invasion of Grenada, the invasion of Panama, and the Gulf War.[24] The potential for *totalitarianism* is apparent when right-wing zealots patrol school classrooms,[25] when the United States jails a far higher proportion of its citizens than any other nation on earth, when constant dollar per capita expenditure for "police protection" nearly triples over the course of the first vicious cycle (1930–1960) and more than doubles during the second round (1960–present),[26] when police ransack newsrooms in search of evidence, journalists are jailed for refusal to reveal their sources of information, and the U.S. Treasury Department demands records of travel agents suspected of arranging "illegal" travel to Cuba. *Anti-rationalism* is evident in schoolbooks being burned, the resurgence of the Ku Klux Klan and other such groups, the blatant racism in recent presidential campaigns, and the religious right's "politics of good and evil." *Elitism* is embodied in the creation and composition of urban finance control boards and enhanced by the reduction and privatization of ever more legitimation services.

In the long run, however, the implications of such a shift may well prove unacceptable to the bulk of America's middle and working classes. If increasingly desperate poor people are repressed, particularly if some are white and elderly, the result is likely to be damage to a number of previously well-insulated consciences. If civil liberties are retracted from the ghettoized poor—the rights to assemble and protest peaceably, or the right to walk the streets without a pass of identification—there would certainly be a spillover effect. Moves such as abridging the First Amendment of the Constitution or declaring martial law would have a jarring effect on everyone else's freedom as well.

Should such a scenario transpire, the nonowning classes might soon stop blaming each other and begin to see the impositions of big government more as a surrogate for the small group of wealthy capitalists who benefit most from the existing arrangement. At that point, their socioeconomic divisions might well diminish, and they might actually begin to form a multiclass, multiracial mass movement that would seriously challenge the legitimacy and very existence of the current political-economic system.[27]

Democratic Socialism

> Every component of the forces that bear upon the American urban system, as well as the system itself, harbors twin potentials—for mass repression or for the expansion of popular freedoms. Science and technology can be directed toward war and manipulation or toward services for everyday living; the multiple ways of modern transportation can be either an escape route for the affluent or a means of expanding everyone's horizons; the service economy can be directed toward world domination or toward everyday human needs; the national network of cities can be linked only to the enrichment of local business and political elites or can become the foundation for broadened employment and equalized hiring standards; the reach and complexity of urban markets can be tied only to private profit or can provision a universal public; private and public corporations can be instruments for bureaucratic control or levers to release personal and group autonomy; the abundant land of the megalopolis can be restricted to the present unequal contest between the classes and races or can become the site of humane physical environments.[28]

Socialists argue that capitalism generates a small capital-owning class that possesses the controlling shares of the nation's wealth and power; consequently, the political and economic systems function primarily in the owners' interests. Therefore, when socialists oppose much of what government is doing, it is for quite different reasons from those offered by the conservatives. Government is seen as most concerned with stabilization—which at present amounts to stabilizing a hierarchical system. This concern leads among other things to the nearly complete subordination of those on the lower rungs of the economic ladder and the gradual abandonment of the outmoded central cities in which many of the lesser-privileged have come to live.

To deal effectively with the symptoms of the problem—such as urban fiscal crisis and popular subordination—it is necessary to face the basic underlying dilemma, which is the domination and subordination inherent in capitalism. As long as mobile capital remains concentrated in a few hands and controlled by those same people, the fate of America's cities will remain bound to the interests of those capitalists, or to what William Tabb and Larry Sawers have referred to as "situational constraints."[29] Thus capitalists can use and abandon them, leaving pollution, deterioration, unemployment, poverty, and despair in their wake.

One alternative is a form of democratic socialism. This would entail a far greater degree of individual economic security as the social safety net would be raised and reinforced. In addition, people would come to have more control over both the economic and political decisions that affect their lives. To accomplish this control, each worker would become a relatively equal stockholder in the firm where he or she works, while elected government officials would have more regulatory control, particularly over the nation's allocation of scarce resources.[30]

Economic Security.   Because of rapid changes and economic uncertainties inherent in any large and complex modern economy, both government and employers need to provide more protection for individuals. In the Milwaukee city and county governments, for example, workers enjoy pay incentives, school subsidies, parental leave, child care, and job sharing opportunities, as well as a four-day work week and flex-time options. Not only are such benefits humane, but the subsequent security seems to be contributing to the development of a cooperative and productive work force.[31]

Sweden has long guaranteed all its citizens national health insurance, virtually free education, unemployment compensation at a rate of 90 percent of income, a generous pension system, and 18 months of paid parental leave. Meanwhile, it still had barely more than a 1 percent unemployment rate most of the time, was one of the world's most competitive economies, and had a national standard of living seldom exceeded by that of any other nation.[32]

At the very least, there is absolutely no excuse for the United States, one of the world's wealthiest nations, to fail to provide all of its citizens with the necessities of life. One of the surest ways to institutionalize such protections is to write them into the nation's Constitution. For example, constitutional amendments could guarantee food, shelter, health care, transportation, a job at a living wage, and a guaranteed annual income for people unable to work, subject to a prescribed degree of effort on their part. Such subsistence policies could be funded by steeply progressive income, gift, estate, and wealth taxes as well as by using governmental taxing and licensing authority to prompt employer cooperation in the private sector.[33]

But will workers still have the incentive to work once they have been guaranteed such economic security? Contrary to the dominant ideology's myth that human beings prefer not to work and thus must be frightened into doing so by adequate economic insecurity, empirical evidence suggests the opposite. Public opinion polls actually suggest that virtually all Americans would prefer to work for a living.[34] And, as the previous examples as well as others suggest, productivity often is enhanced by such protective arrangements.[35]

Collective Control.   Beyond guaranteeing a greater degree of economic security, which could be done to some extent within the current capitalist economy, a new economic system must be fashioned that will more fully democratize the ownership of capital and thus allow everyone to have much more control over the political and economic decisions that affect their lives. Samuel Bowles and Herbert Gintis have described this control as a precondition to *self-actualization,* meaning one's own physical, emotional, aesthetic, cognitive, and spiritual development. They also see it helping society to gain more justice and democracy, as well as representing a more rational and appropriate use of its natural resources. The needs of people would begin to receive more weight than profits as the central guide to society's economic and political decisions, for what is good for General Motors is not necessarily what is good for Detroit or America as a whole.[36]

Stated more concretely, a socialist society would be distinguishable first and foremost by worker control of the means of production. That, however, has come to mean at least two different things, depending on the analyst. There are those who put their emphasis on democratizing the decisions of existing corporations, and others who maintain that the means of production must also be owned either directly or indirectly by the workers themselves.

Economic Democracy. As an example of the first position, economic democracy, Ralph Nader has proposed what he has termed his *Corporate Democracy Act,* which would require that all corporations be chartered by the federal government, that they be subject to regular independent audits, that the majority of the corporation's board of directors be chosen independently of the stockholders, and that a "community impact analysis" be undertaken and approved should an industrial enterprise intend to expand or relocate.[37] Countries like Germany, for example, already have "co-determination laws" that mandate worker representation on the boards of directors of large corporations.

That is really only a "left liberal" approach, however, as the ownership of much of the means of production would remain in the hands of the small owning class—at least at the outset. Thus, the owners of capital could still exert ultimate influence by the threat to withhold essential investments. The workers, nonetheless, would indeed have more control than they do at present, and with such control apparently comes enhanced loyalty and productivity.[38]

Worker Ownership. Conversion to a more fully socialist economic system would involve most, if not all, of the following:

1. The distribution of products would be based on people's needs, such as guaranteed rights to food, shelter, clothing, and medical and social services. [Economic Security]
2. The workplace would be democratized in the sense that worker-owners would have far greater control over such decisions as what products they were to produce, where, at what pace, under what conditions, for what wages, and under what kind of management system. [Economic Democracy]
3. Wage labor would come to an end as such, for there would no longer be a separate capital-owning class. Workers would directly, or at least indirectly (through government), own the companies where they worked—and thus work for themselves.
4. With no separate owning class, the extraction of "surplus value" would also come to an end, as those actually working in the businesses would collectively receive the full market value of what they were producing.

5. There would have to be some centralized economic planning, such as allocating scarce basic natural resources, coordinating the large state-owned primary industries, and deciding which worker-entrepreneurs receive start-up loans to form all other businesses. Nevertheless, the planners would be elected more democratically than elected representatives are at present as there would be a more equal distribution of political resources across the citizenry.
6. The role of the educational system would be to teach people to structure their personal needs more within the requirements of society, to help prepare them for a more active political life, and to help purge them of a variety of social prejudices.[39]

Implementation could include having the federal government employ the power of eminent domain to nationalize the most basic major industries, such as steel, auto, and oil. The tax system could be used to dismantle monopolies as well as to raise money to encourage and sustain cooperative businesses. As a vehicle for the latter, a governmental "consumer cooperative fund" already exists and could be significantly expanded.[40]

There are some obvious challenges here as well. For example, should these socializing efforts come to fuller fruition, critics point to the inefficiencies and repressiveness that have existed in virtually all self-styled socialist or communist states.[41] Nevertheless, there are also a number of reasons to believe that an American adaptation would not have to follow these roads.

In response to questions concerning efficiency, the American farming industry has been governmentally planned and sustained for years without any glaring problems with inefficiency. Bowles and Gintis have argued that overall American production is actually likely to improve under socialism, given the rationality of centralized planning, the increased size of the work force in a full-employment economy, and such work incentives as full partnership in the firm, more generally meaningful work, and far more leisure time.[42] Even in mixed economies like those in Germany, Japan, and Scandinavia, far less inequality is tolerated than in the United States; yet, these countries remain highly prosperous.[43]

As for repression, David Mermelstein contends that socialism in the United States could be qualitatively different from that in any other place where it presently exists. The United States is already economically well developed and thus would not require the sacrifices that have been necessary for economic development in most emerging socialist countries. Its people cherish the concepts of individual liberty and democracy, and fewer freedom-restricting security measures would be necessary as there would be no hostile capitalistic powers of any real consequence threatening the country's existence.[44]

Nonetheless, socialists are generally quick to admit that they are not promising an overnight utopia. Socialism is viewed as a gradual process, not as an immediate event.[45] Consequently, racism and other social pathologies will not cease the moment the means of production are finally controlled by the workers, nor will the frustration, anger, despair, self-hatred, and alienation that have built up over many generations disappear with the first dividend check or the first trip to the boardroom. What is promised, however, is considerably more personal security and more popular control over the economic and political decisions that affect people's lives.[46]

Socialist Trends. Actually, structural alterations are already beginning to appear in the economic system, as shown in the list presented below. A number of workers and citizens have come together to demand, and in some cases achieve, greater control over their lives.

Socialist Trends in the United States

Industrial policy	centralized governmental planning in key areas of the economy
Local content legislation	laws requiring that fixed percentages of goods sold here also be made here
Regulating plant closings	requirement for prior notification and various forms of compensation
Eminent domain	the practice of condemning and purchasing private property for public uses
Unitary taxes	taxes on the international profits of multinational corporations
Mandated corporate responsibility	demands for socially responsible investments, wages, benefits
Worker cooperatives	businesses fully owned and operated by their workers
Employee stock-ownership plans	plans allowing workers to own substantial shares of the company's stock
Worker self-management	a system in which workers help choose the managers and share in managerial decisions
Control through unions	use of unions to bargain for more information, input, job security
Mass mobilization	formation of progressive coalitions to elect socialists, press demands by lobbying and demonstrating
European models	examples of socialistic experiments

> We must speak out against plant closings that happen without prior notice; against economic royalism while thousands of workers lose their jobs; against factories fleeing to third world countries, where workers' health and safety is ignored and union organizing is forbidden.[47]

Industrial Policy. Various levels of government have been weighing industrial policies designed to allow boards of business, labor, and government officials to do more centralized planning of the economy. In particular, they would determine which industries government should assist. In all likelihood they would recommend supporting major declining industries, fast growers, large employers, exporters, and technological pioneers by such means as trade barriers, subsidies, technical assistance, favorable regulatory treatment, tax abatements, and subsidized loans. Such national planning has been done for years in agriculture and a variety of defense-related industries.[48]

As small first steps, the 1984 federal Tariff and Trade Act lists guidelines American steel companies must follow in reinvesting their capital if they want continued government protection from foreign competitors. The National Institute of Standards and Technology as well as the National Science Foundation spend millions of dollars annually to spur research and development projects. Meanwhile, a number of states have acted to protect in-state companies from hostile takeovers in order to reduce the potential for economic disruption, while both states and localities have been funding local technological development ventures.[49]

Local Content Legislation.   There also has been serious congressional discussion, as well as some action, on "local content" legislation. Such legislation requires that a fixed percentage of certain manufactured products be made in the United States if they are to be sold here. At least indirectly, one effect of such legislation would be constraint on the mobility of multinational corporations.[50]

Regulating Plant Closings.   In order to contain corporate mobility more directly, relatively strong legislation has been proposed and in some cases adopted in Wisconsin, Maine, Michigan, and at least 16 other states. One of the boldest proposals was Oregon's Employment Stability Bill of 1981, which would have required businesses with more than 50 employees (1) to give one year's notice before closing or even before any significant layoff occurs; (2) to compensate the community they leave by paying 85 percent of any "adjustment costs"; (3) to pay for the relocation of all workers; (4) to pay benefit premiums for one year after closing; and (5) to give the Oregon Bureau of Labor and Industry the first option to buy the business. Ohio's Schwarzwalder Bill would have required virtually the same types of things of its departing firms, but it called for a two-year notice.[51]

Meanwhile, at the national level, at least a half-dozen members of Congress have introduced national variants of such legislation, and in 1988 the federal government passed a law that requires a 60-day notice before any sizable plant can close.[52] In the summer of 1991, the National Labor Relations Board issued guidelines establishing when companies must negotiate with their unions before moving to new locations.[53] The U.S. Supreme Court has also upheld state-mandated severance benefits.[54]

Eminent Domain.   Eminent domain has long been available as a mechanism whereby government could forcibly acquire private property for public use. The property is simply condemned, a fair market price is paid to the owner, and the space is then used for a road, park, or whatever public purpose government has designed. The state of Hawaii has used eminent domain to acquire parts of large family estates so that land would be available for badly needed private housing construction.[55] Thus, the legal groundwork would seem to be in place for one of the newest innovations in eminent domain application.

Going a step further, cities have begun to consider the right of eminent domain as a way to prevent large corporations from deserting them. For example, the government of New Bedford, Massachusetts, designed a plan whereby it would condemn a cutting-tools plant, purchase it, and then sell it to an organization that would keep it in New Bedford, such as another company, a public-private partnership, or a group made up of plant managers and union employees. As another example, the Pittsburgh area's Tristate Conference on Steel—a combination of steelworkers, religious leaders, and other residents—designed a plan including a regional authority that could use eminent domain to allow steelworkers to buy a number of ailing steel mills in the region, modernize the mills, and run them.[56]

Unitary Taxes.   Despite considerable corporate opposition, unitary taxation has existed in more than a dozen states, has been facilitated by the Multistate Tax Commission,[57] and has been upheld by the U.S. Supreme Court.[58] In these states, all the international profits of multinational corporations are taxed according to the proportion of that corporation represented by the subsidiaries operating within the state. At very least, such taxation adds some constraints on multinational corporate investment.

Mandating Corporate Responsibility.   Governments at the federal, state, and local levels also have been taking a few tentative steps toward requiring more social responsibility on the part of private employers. Cleveland mayor Carl Stokes, for example, used $50 million in city deposits as leverage to induce banks to make small business loans to black entrepreneurs.[59] The U.S. Congress has entered the arena by introducing bills calling for mandatory benefits such as child care, health insurance, and pensions.[60]

> We want to set up worker control, not only for ourselves but for our children,
> so they'll have jobs and an economic future in our community.[61]

Worker Cooperatives.   Besides simply constraining the decisions of corporations belonging to the owning class, there are now as many as 200 fully worker-owned cooperative businesses in operation across the land. In particular, such states as Massachusetts and Maine paved the way with important legal revisions, and businesses in these states have been assisted by organizations such as the National Center for Employee Ownership and the Industrial Co-op Association.

Such collective ventures date back as far as the 1880s when the Knights of Labor first created 135 industrial cooperatives.[62] More recently, one success story has been the Workers' Owned Sewing Company of Windsor, North Carolina; primarily black women employees own and control the entire business. Other examples include Avis, Republic Engineered Steel, Inc., as well as food industry companies such as Sunkist, Ocean Spray, Agway, and Land-O-Lakes.[63]

Employee Stock-Ownership Plans.   Some ten thousand employee stock-owner-ship plans (ESOPs) exist, involving more than eight million workers, and more than one-fifth of these firms employ at least a thousand people. For example, ten thousand steelworkers in Weirton, West Virginia, agreed in September of 1983 to spend $386 million in order to buy their plant. Even though they subsequently have chosen to sell 23 percent of their stock publicly, the Weirton Works remains one of the largest worker-controlled enterprises in the United States. Workers also have purchased significant portions of companies as large as Publix Super-markets, Epic Healthcare, Science Applications, Kroger Foods, J. C. Penney, McDonnell Douglas, Ashland Oil, Colt Industries, and Pan American Airlines. The AFL-CIO has set aside an investment fund (the Employee Partnership Fund) to lend money to workers who seek to buy their factories.[64]

Worker Self-Management.   Another method of gaining at least some control in the workplace is self-management. The General Motors battery plant in Fitzgerald, Georgia, has worker-management teams that choose their leaders and help deter-mine their own budgets, schedules, and proficiency and maintenance standards. They also have had some disciplinary jurisdiction. A recent New York Stock Exchange survey found that approximately 14 percent of U.S. companies with more than 100 employees had similar plans, while a recent government study found that 44 percent of firms with more than 500 employees included their workers in discussions of plant operations.[65]

Control through Unions.   Workers are beginning to bargain collectively for even more control. The United Food and Commercial Workers recently persuaded several meat-packing companies to agree that if they closed a union plant, they would not open a nonunion one for at least five years. The United Rubber Workers convinced the four largest tire producers to guarantee that if they should shut down a plant they would give a six-month notice and grant full pensions after 25 years of work (or after 5 years if the worker was over the age of 55), assure preferential hiring at other plants, and guarantee workers the right to negotiate ways of saving the plant or the method by which it was to be closed. In another negotiation the United Auto Workers and General Motors/Toyota agreed that workers would participate in corporate decision making as well as have access to corporate financial data; and before any layoffs can occur, salaries of executives and managers must be cut, and all outside contract work must be called in. These agreements are a prelude to the kind of worker control that could emerge should organized workers begin to pool and strategically invest their hundreds of billions of dollars in pension funds.[66]

Mass Mobilization.   As for mass mobilizing, a number of labor unions joined forces in order to wage national campaigns against the anti-union postures of J. P. Stevens Company and Litton Industries.[67] Progressive laborites united with consumer advocates, liberals, and other leftists to form both the National Coalition and the All-Peoples Congress, with goals such as citizen participation in corporate decision making and severance payments from firms choosing to leave an area.[68] Various churches have backed United Steel Worker unionists in their attempts to fight plant shutdowns in Youngstown and Pittsburgh.[69] The North American Farm Alliance was established in 1983 as a coalition of farmers, union members, blacks, women, and peace, religious, and environmental groups united to fight "pro-corporate governmental farm policies."[70]

Other progressive organizations have emerged and grown, such as Fair Share, Citizens' Action, the Gray Panthers, National People's Action, the Association of Community Organizations for Reform Now (ACORN), the Institute for Policy Studies and their Conferences on Alternative State and Local Politics, various tenant groups, Detroit's League of Revolutionary Black Workers, and many more. In 1986, for instance, ACORN negotiated an agreement whereby Boatman's Bank would invest $50 million a year in home loans to residents in low-income St. Louis neighborhoods besides providing low-cost checking accounts and cashing government checks at no cost. This is only one of their more than 100 examples of such successes since 1970 alone.[71]

In addition, progressive electoral groups have sent self-proclaimed socialists into elected positions ranging from congressional representatives (Bernard Sanders of Vermont) to presidents of major industrial unions (William Winpinsinger of the International Association of Machinists). At the local level, there is a long history of socialist mayors and councilpersons as well as public ownership of capital earlier in the century in Dayton, Schenectady, Davenport, Milwaukee, Oakland, Berkeley, and dozens of other cities. In 1911, more than 70 socialist mayors and 1,200 socialist officeholders were elected in 340 American cities.[72] Most recently, socialists have been elected mayors of Burlington, Vermont, and Santa Monica, California.[73]

European Models.   European countries provide model legislation for a good deal of this transformation. Centralized industrial planning and regulation of plant relocations have existed in many of these nations for some time. In addition, many European governments have taken further progressive steps. Most have been taxing and spending at much higher rates than in the United States in order to provide a far more elaborate welfare state, including national health insurance and much more extensive mass transportation. The large majority of their public utility companies, as well as rail and air transportation, have been nationalized, as have sizable shares of their manufacturing and banking industries.

The collective farms of Czechoslovakia and Hungary provide models of economic success against great odds. Despite the privatization trend occurring across Eastern Europe following the collapse of state-centered communism, these collective enterprises endure and remain quite popular.[74]

The classic comprehensive example is Mondragon, Spain. That city pioneered worker-owned cooperatives in which employees have direct one person–one vote control over their corporations. The city developed a large cooperative complex that includes a development bank, credit unions, schools, research and development firms, leisure clubs, housing, and agricultural extension services.[75]

The Swedes even pioneered a concept that conceivably could have allowed for a gradual and peaceful transition to this type of socialism. They proposed taxing individuals and corporate profits in order to create a fund with which unions—representing 90 percent of all Sweden's workers—could gradually buy up the nation's corporate stock.[76]

> A fiscal structure that limited the contest mainly to benefits paid for by state and local taxes [and] largely succeeded in keeping the struggle confined within the lower and middle strata of American society. Schoolteachers turned against the ghetto, taxpayers against both, but no one turned against the concentrations of individual and corporate wealth in America. Local government, in short, is important, less for the issues it decides, than for the issues it keeps submerged. Of the issues submerged by the events of the urban crisis, not the least is the more equitable distribution of wealth in America.[77]

Unifying Issues.   Many issues are taking shape that may serve further to unite the nation's middle, working, and lower classes referred to above by Frances Fox Piven. There is more and more nationwide structural unemployment, and real wages are declining for those who do find work.

Structural Unemployment.   In terms of structural unemployment, corporations have been tending not to invest their profits in new construction and machinery. When they do choose to invest in productive enterprises, they are more inclined to invest in capital-intensive high-technology industries; and this shift to high-tech production appears to be causing a net decline in the number of primary labor jobs available, with displaced blue-collar workers being among those most unlikely to qualify for the new positions, which tend to require technical training and advanced educational degrees. Jeff Faux found only 3 percent of the New Englanders laid off from shoe, textile, and similar industries being rehired by high-tech firms.[78] To carry this one step further, the Japanese already have computers and robots that allow some industrial plants to run quite successfully virtually unmanned. The General Motors Corporation appears to be leading the way toward such developments in the United States. Recently, it unveiled plans for its "factory of the future," which will manufacture automobiles in Saginaw, Michigan, without any production workers.[79]

Declining Wages.   Real wages—wages in terms of constant dollars—have been declining for many of those who have found work,[80] and this phenomenon has seriously jeopardized the concept of a family-subsistence wage. Until about 1960, the general consensus was that a person's wage or salary ought to be adequate to maintain a small family. Consequently the minimum wage was set at what was deemed minimally necessary to support a family of four. By the mid-1980s, however, an adult working full-time at the minimum wage earned little more than the poverty-level income for a family of two and sank below the poverty level with a family of three. Beyond employment at the minimum wage, sociologist Caroline Bird found that only 40 percent of the jobs in the United States paid enough to support a family of four, and that two people working at the "average industrial wage" barely managed to provide their family of four with a "moderate standard of living," according to Agriculture Department estimates.[81]

Downward Mobility.   An important consequence of these two developments is that a large number of Americans have been experiencing downward mobility. *Business Week* estimated that in the five years between 1978 and 1983 nearly eight million American families dropped out of the middle class ($17,000–$41,000 annual income).[82] In addition, the longtime symbol of middle-class status, the single-family home, has become ever more difficult to acquire. Not only have the purchase price and high interest rates put such homes beyond the reach of an increasing number of Americans, but a sizable number of homeowners have also been forced to default on their payments and thus face foreclosure.[83]

Even these figures understate the declining position of the middle and working class for at least four reasons:

1. The large Baby Boom generation has begun to reach its peak earning years.
2. The number of multiple-income families has been growing markedly.[84]
3. Baby Boomers have married later and had smaller families than their predecessors, allowing for more discretionary per capita income, even when hourly wages were declining.[85]
4. Cheap Third World labor is likely to continue bidding down American wages in the postindustrial United States. South Korea, Brazil, Mexico, Hong Kong, Taiwan, and Singapore all have an average wage of less than $3.00 per hour.[86]

Thus, the present does not appear as bad as it has actually become, and the future looks even less promising for many in the next generation of middle- and working-class families.[87]

Desperation.   Terry Hatfield, aged 34, lost his job as a shipping department foreman when a Cleveland-area plant closed. When his unemployment benefits expired, he and his family were in trouble. The last source of income for Terry, his wife Susan, and their two children (ages four and five) was a welfare check of $327 a month. Unable to continue to pay their rent of $300 a month and with their electricity cut off by the utility company for overdue bills, the Hatfields sold what they could and moved into a pair of tents. "It definitely breaks your pride," Terry said. "No one could have told me when the plant closed that I'd still be out of work a year and a half later." Even after the recession started taking its toll on their neighbors, forcing them also to go on welfare and food stamps, the Hatfields still assumed that poverty was somehow the fault of those afflicted. "I used to think, What's their problem?" Susan said. "Now I realize the problem."[88]

There is also the predicament faced by a growing number of elderly people. Confronted with cuts in Social Security and Medicare, they are often compelled to rely on their children for basic subsistence needs. This shift can create economic hardship for their middle- and working-class offspring. Yet all the ederly are not even that fortunate.

Ninety-one-year-old Mattie Schultz lived in San Antonio, Texas, on a combined Social Security and Veteran's Benefit check of $233 per month. Too proud to accept public welfare or private charity, Mattie was arrested and jailed for shoplifting $15 worth of food in order to keep from starving. Humiliated, all she could say was that she just wished God would close her eyes.[89]

Or consider the case of Howard and Fannie Spears, residing in St. Louis. Howard was 93 years old and blind; his wife was 88. Unable to pay $800 in overdue utility bills, their gas was shut off. In the winter, they were forced to heat their apartment with a small electric heater; ice began to form on their floor and walls. Three days before Christmas, Howard froze to death. His wife was taken to the hospital, treated, and then released.[90]

> It is inevitable that the U.S. economy will grow more slowly . . . [and] some people will obviously have to do with less. . . . The basic health of the U.S. economy is based on the basic health of its corporations and banks. . . . Yet it will be a hard pill for many Americans to swallow—the idea of doing with less so that big business can have more. It will be particularly hard to swallow because it is quite obvious that if big businesses are the most visible victims of what ails the Debt Economy, they are also in large measure the cause of it.[91]

Not long after *Business Week* presented that assessment, a research team at the University of Michigan completed an extensive five-year study that found 7 out of every 10 Americans stood a better than even chance of falling below the poverty level at some point in their lives. The researchers concluded, "It is not merely some vague minority called 'the poor' who stand in economic peril, it is the majority of Americans."[92] The prospects look even worse given the decline in real wages and the increases in structural unemployment, poverty, homelessness, and hunger discussed above.

If present trends continue, it may not be long before more and more people identify with Mattie Schultz, the Hatfields, and the Spears, and begin to believe that there is something fundamentally wrong. It also may well be that the nonowning classes of the oldest and largest central cities, those who have been subjugated, used, and abandoned by corporations, will be the first to join forces.

> While the capitalist system can temporarily escape social dislocation by moving to the suburbs and to the Sun Belt—trading in old centers, like used cars, for new models—it cannot proceed in this manner forever. Unlike used cars, declining centers of profit cannot be removed to a junk yard, slipped into a coffin, or pushed to a controlled reservation. They remain filled with humans who are more than simply units of labor, more than "good business climates." . . . As the rising social and economic tensions of the Northeastern cities have demonstrated, the poor do not go away. They do not lose their desires for human renewal; they do not lose their frustration, discouragement, and anger.[93]

Wrack and Ruin.   In the fall of 1979, the *Cleveland Press* ran a series of articles on the removal of the Diamond Shamrock Corporation from the Cleveland area to Dallas. In the course of the series, reporters noted that the exodus of the county's largest taxpayer left in its wake a school district with 60 percent fewer funds, vast areas of Painesville Township as a chemical wasteland, a dangerously polluted Grand River, some 1,200 people without work—many of them more than 50 years old with limited prospects for future employment—hundreds dead or dying of chromate poisoning or cancer, and even more morbidity—63 percent of the workers had developed perforated nasal septums due to the chromate they had breathed in the workplace. The investigation led the *Cleveland Press* to conclude:

> In many ways it is the story of industrial America, of companies building plants, expanding, merging or taking over other companies, outgrowing the plant and community that nurtured them, and moving on. . . . And presumably if the company finds Sun Belt labor too costly, it can move its operation and jobs to a foreign country where labor is even cheaper. There is something wrong with that scenario if we are to put the interests of the nation ahead of the interests of the multinational corporations.[94]

Ideological Fissures.   Cracks already are beginning to appear in the nation's ideological armor. In a 1984 *Journalism Quarterly* article, Robert Peterson and his associates reported the answers to questions not generally asked by the established national pollsters. Interviewing a sample of more than 1,400 Americans selected to represent middle-class adults, they found that more than 25 percent of them felt "capitalism denies the masses property in life, liberty and estate"; more than 40 percent agreed that "capitalism must be altered before any significant improvements in human welfare can be realized."[95]

Interviewed by Studs Terkel, Dennis Kucinich, at that time the mayor of Cleveland, remarked:

> There are increasingly two Americas: the America of multinationals dictating decisions . . . and the America of neighborhoods . . . who feel left out. I see, in the future a cataclysm: popular forces converging on an economic elite, which feels no commitment to the needs of the people. The clash is already shaping up. The American Revolution never really ended. It's a continuing process.[96]

Kucinich is no longer mayor of Cleveland, but the echo of his words remains, and one is left with the feeling that his style may not have ended either. As the urban fiscal crisis becomes more and more severe, there are likely to be other mayors riding to power on waves of class frustration. At some point, there may be no defeating them. Meanwhile, rocket shots already are being fired across the nation, in large and small cities alike.

CONCLUSION

> Eminent domain is an attribute of sovereignty, . . . [but] when individual citizens are forced to suffer great social dislocation to permit private corporations to construct plants where they deem it profitable, one is left to wonder who the sovereign is.[97]

As Judge James L. Ryan of the Michigan Supreme Court pondered Detroit's use of eminent domain to expropriate the Poletown area for General Motors, his question can be answered directly. Under the present economic system, the interests of the capital-holding class are sovereign; for despite occasional concessions to appease the unruly poor they must ultimately take precedence over all conflicting interests, no matter who is holding political office. In order to make what have come to be seen as the necessary cutbacks at the local level, that sovereignty actually has been institutionalized. New York City and Cleveland were saddled with finance control boards, while Philadelphia; Providence, Rhode Island; Bridgeport, Connecticut; and Yonkers, New York, are among the cities that subsequently have been added to that list.

Why is this true? First, because capital is privately owned, the American citizenry and the federal, state, and local governments are left dependent upon the owners of capital in some very fundamental ways. The great majority of Americans depend upon this small capitalist class for jobs, while governmental jurisdictions require the investment of a sufficient amount of this capital if local economies are to be healthy enough to generate needed tax revenues.

Given the increasing mobility of private capital, the requisites of corporate profitability become extremely important parameters circumscribing the life decisions of most individuals as well as the political decisions of their governments. People's occupations and residential locations are often dictated by employment opportunities, and governments must do whatever is necessary to keep their jurisdictions attractive to capital investment.

As for the argument that what is good for corporate America is good for everybody, it is instructive to view that proposition against reality. Consider the declining position of the middle and working classes, not to mention the plight of the underclass residing in the inner city.[98]

Nevertheless, the collectivist trends discussed above challenge the most basic underpinnings of the present political-economic arrangement in the United States—that being the concentrated control of corporate capital. Should the tide finally turn, leading to a fundamental redistribution of economic power, the United States might well find itself moving away from urban fiscal crises, away from urban rebellions, away from neo-fascism and toward a fundamentally different political-economic form.

> Democracy in this country is a myth. . . . We don't have economic democracy. And economic democracy is a precondition to political democracy. A tremendous amount of the wealth in this country is concentrated in fewer and fewer hands. We may well have the form of a democratic society, but we don't have the substance of it. . . . If you have the great corporations of America running this country—or a city—you don't have a political democracy. If competition is destroyed and big corporations are profiting from inflation and from government programs that shun the needs of most people, what you have is a corporate dictatorship. . . . American government has an illicit love affair with the American corporate state. And when Joe Public discovers this, you can expect that there will be some fireworks.[99]
>
> —Dennis Kucinich, former mayor of Cleveland

NOTES

1. *New York Times,* October 19, 1979; November 2, 1979.
2. *New York Times,* April 28, 1980; April 27, 1981; March 18, 1981; April 3, 1981; June 23, 1981; August 13, 1981; August 15, 1981; September 17, 1981; November 1, 1981; January 13, 1983; Memphis, *Commercial Appeal,* January 13, 1991.

3. *Washington Post,* March 24, 1991, p. A6; *Time,* January 7, 1991; *National Journal,* September 22, 1990, p. 2287; December 22, 1990, pp. 3080–3085; *New York Times,* September 10, 1990; September 13, 1990; November 3, 1990; *Philadelphia Inquirer,* December 24–26, 1990.

4. Ibid.

5. *New York Times,* June 8, 1991.

6. Quoted in *New York Times,* March 23, 1989; April 4, 1991.

7. Christopher Jencks and Paul Peterson, eds., *The Urban Underclass* (Washington, D.C.: Brookings Institution, 1991); William Julius Wilson, *The Truly Disadvantaged* (Chicago: University of Chicago Press, 1987).

8. Kenneth B. Clark, quoted in *Report of the National Advisory Commission on Civil Disorders,* reprint (New York: Bantam, 1968), p. 29.

9. *New York Times,* July 24, 1977; or *U.S. News and World Report,* August 29, 1977, pp. 50–51. For an even more recent example, see *New York Times,* January 1, 1985.

10. As quoted in *New York Times,* March 3, 1977. Also see U.S. Commission on Civil Rights report on the Miami unrest, in *New York Times,* June 9, 1982.

11. As quoted in *New York Times,* May 14, 1977.

12. *New York Times,* July 1, 1990; April 6, 1990.

13. For a recent compendium, see Wesley Skogan, *Disorder and Decline* (New York: Free Press, 1990).

14. As quoted in Studs Terkel, *American Dreams* (New York: Pantheon, 1980), p. 367.

15. Paul Peterson, *City Limits* (Chicago: University of Chicago Press, 1981); Paul Kantor, *The Dependent City* (Glenview, Ill.: Scott, Foresman, 1988), pp. 406–413.

16. Peter Steinberger, *Ideology and the Urban Crisis* (Albany, N.Y.: SUNY Press, 1985), p. 129.

17. David Mermelstein, "Austerity, Planning, and the Socialist Alternative," in Roger Alcaly and David Mermelstein, *The Fiscal Crisis of the American Cities* (New York: Vintage, 1977), p. 361. Also, for wide-ranging predictions concerning the urban future, see Gary Gappert and Richard Knight, eds., *Cities in the 21st Century* (Beverly Hills, Calif.: Sage, 1982).

18. Kenneth Dolbeare and Patricia Dolbeare, *American Ideologies* (Boston: Houghton Mifflin, 1976), p. 224.

19. Ibid.

20. Renzo De Felice, *Interpretations of Fascism* (Cambridge, Mass.: Harvard University Press, 1977), p. 53.

21. Milton Friedman, *Capitalism and Freedom* (Chicago: University of Chicago Press, 1962), pp. 133–135; Theodore Lowi, *The End of Liberalism* (New York: Norton, 1979).

22. For further discussion of fascism, see De Felice, *Interpretations of Fascism,* chap. 14; Carl Cohen, ed., *Communism, Fascism, and Democracy* (New York: Random House, 1962); Kenneth Dolbeare, *Political Change in the United States* (New York: McGraw-Hill, 1974); William Ebenstein, *Fascism at Work* (New York: AMS, 1973); James Gregor, *The Ideology of Fascism* (New York: Free Press, 1969); Bertram Gross, *Friendly Fascism* (New York: Evans, 1980); Daniel Guerin, *Fascism and Big Business* (New York: Monthly Review, 1969); Paul M. Hayes, *Fascism* (New York: Free Press, 1973); Anthony James Joes, *Fascism in the Contemporary World* (Boulder, Colo.: Westview, 1978); Walter Laqueur, *Fascism* (Berkeley: University of California Press, 1976); Benito Mussolini, *Fascism* (Rome: Ardita, 1935); Benito Mussolini, *The Corporate State* (Florence: Vallechi, 1936); Franz Neumann, *Behemoth* (New York: Harper & Row, 1966); Ernst Nolte, *Three Faces of Fascism* (New York:

Holt, Rinehart and Winston, 1966); William Reich, *The Mass Psychology of Fascism* (New York: Farrar, Straus and Giroux, 1970); David Schoenbaum, *Hitler's Social Revolution* (New York: Doubleday/Anchor, 1967); and S. J. Woolf, ed., *The Nature of Fascism* (New York: Vintage, 1969).

23. *New York Times,* April 23, 1990.

24. For some documentation of the recent increases in militaristic attitudes, see Bruce Russett and Donald DeLuca, "Don't Tread on Me," *Political Science Quarterly* 96 (Fall 1981): 381–389.

25. *New York Times,* October 4, 1985.

26. Ibid., May 26, 1984.

27. For further discussion of this subject, see Robert Cherry, "Economic Theories of Racism," in David Gordon, ed., *Problems in Political Economy* (Lexington, Mass.: D C Heath, 1977), pp. 170–182; or Norman Fainstein and Susan Fainstein, *Urban Political Movements* (Englewood Cliffs, N.J.: Prentice-Hall, 1974).

28. Sam Bass Warner, *The Urban Wilderness* (New York: Harper & Row, 1972), p. 114.

29. William Tabb and Larry Sawers, eds., *Marxism and the Metropolis* (New York: Oxford University Press, 1984), p. 7.

30. For a contemporary example, see Bogdan Denitch, *The Socialist Debate: Beyond Red and Green* (New York: Pluto Press, 1990).

31. *New York Times,* October 6, 1989.

32. Daniel Pedersen, "The Swedish Model," *Newsweek,* March 5, 1990, pp. 30–31.

33. For more on this latter "linkage" concept, see Peter Marcuse, "Who Will Pay the Piper?" *City Limits,* February 12–15, 1987; Jeffrey Walker, "Privatization of Housing Programs," *Journal of Housing* 43 (November 1986): 241–253.

34. Gar Alperovitz and Jeff Faux, *Rebuilding America: A Blueprint for the New Economy* (New York: Pantheon, 1984), pp. 113–121.

35. For more examples, see Barry Bluestone and Bennett Harrison, *The Deindustrialization of America* (New York: Basic Books, 1982), pp. 232–234.

36. Samuel Bowles and Herbert Gintis, "Schooling for a Socialist America," in David Gordon, ed., *Problems in Political Economy,* (Lexington, Mass.: D C Heath, 1977), pp. 263–270; Kenneth Dolbeare and Patricia Dolbeare, *American Ideologies* (Boston: Houghton Mifflin, 1976), chap. 8.

37. *Village Voice,* September 29, 1975.

38. Karl Frieden, *Workplace Democracy and Productivity* (Washington, D.C.: National Center for Economic Alternatives, 1980); James O'Toole, *Making America Work* (New York: Continuum, 1981); Alperovitz and Faux, *Rebuilding America,* pp. 99–109.

    For further development of such "left liberal" approaches, see Samuel Bowles, David Gordon, and Thomas Weisskopf, *Beyond the Wasteland* (New York: Doubleday/Anchor, 1983); J. Morton Davis, *Making America Work Again* (New York: Crown, 1983); Martin Carnoy and Derek Shearer, *Economic Democracy* (White Plains, N.Y.: Sharpe, 1980); Neil Jacoby, *Corporate Power and Social Responsibility* (New York: Macmillan, 1973); David Mahoney of Norton Simon, Inc. in *New York Times,* February 7, 1983; Wassily Leontief, quoted in *New York Times,* April 6, 1983.

    For a counter-position, arguing that such arrangements are generally cosmetic and actually only divert workers from more radical demands, see Doron Levin, "UAW's Challenge from Within," *New York Times,* June 18, 1989; *New York Times,* January 15, 1984; February 23, 1983; February 13, 1983; June 25, 1980.

39. Bowles and Gintis, "Schooling for a Socialist America"; William Tabb, "A Pro-People Policy," in William Tabb and Larry Sawers, eds., *Marxism and the Metropolis* (New York: Oxford University Press, 1984); William Tabb, "Economic Democracy and

Regional Restructuring," in Larry Sawers and William Tabb, eds., *Sunbelt/Snowbelt* (New York: Oxford University Press, 1984); Richard Child Hill, "Fiscal Crisis, Austerity Politics, and Alternative Urban Policies," in William Tabb and Larry Sawers, eds., *Marxism and the Metropolis* (New York: Oxford University Press, 1984); Bowles, *Beyond the Wasteland.*

40. *New York Times,* June 27, 1982.
41. Friedrich Hayek, *The Road to Serfdom* (Chicago: University of Chicago Press, 1944); Friedman, *Capitalism and Freedom;* Ivan Szelenyi, *Urban Inequalities under State Socialism* (New York: Oxford University Press, 1983); Charles Lindbloom, *Politics and Markets* (New Haven: Yale University Press, 1977).
42. Bowles and Gintis, "Schooling for a Socialist America." Also Paul Bernstein, "Worker-Owned Plywood Firms Steadily Outperform Industry," *World of Work Reports,* May 1977; Bluestone and Harrison, *The Deindustrialization of America,* p. 260; Alperovitz and Faux, *Rebuilding America,* pp. 243–255.
43. Malcolm Sawyer and Frank Wasserman, "Income Distribution in the OECD Countries," *OECD Economic Outlook* (July 1976): 14; Lester Thurow, *The Zero-Sum Society* (New York: Basic Books, 1980); Lindbloom, *Politics and Markets,* chap. 20.
44. Mermelstein, "Austerity, Planning, and the Socialist Alternative," pp. 360–361.
45. Bowles and Gintis, "Schooling for a Socialist America," p. 265.
46. For further references on socialism see David McClellan, *The Thought of Karl Marx* (New York: Harper & Row, 1971); Shlomo Avineri, *The Social and Political Thought of Karl Marx* (New York: Cambridge University Press, 1969); Robert Tucker, ed., *The Marx-Engels Reader* (New York: Norton, 1978); Bruce Brown, *Marx, Freud, and the Critique of Everyday Life* (New York: Monthly Review Press, 1973); Michael Harrington, *Socialism* (New York: Saturday Review Press, 1972); David McClellan, *Marxism after Marx* (Boston: Houghton Mifflin, 1979); R. N. Berki, *Socialism* (New York: St. Martin's Press, 1975).

    As for contemporary models of urban socialism, see Tabb, "A ProPeople Urban Policy"; Hill, "Fiscal Crisis, Austerity Politics and Alternative Urban Policies"; Tabb, "Economic Democracy and Regional Restructuring." For examples of individual cities where a few such experiments have been tried, see Pierre Clavel, *The Progressive City* (New Brunswick, N.J.: Rutgers University Press, 1986).
47. *New York Times,* January 28, 1987.
48. *National Journal,* March 7, 1992, pp. 576–577; Alperovitz and Faux, *Rebuilding America: A Blueprint for the New Economy,* especially chaps. 7–16; Ira Maganizer and Robert Reich, *Minding America's Business* (New York: Harcourt Brace Jovanovich, 1982); Thurow, *The Zero-Sum Society;* Bluestone and Harrison, *The Deindustrialization of America,* pp. 244–257.
49. *New York Times,* September 16, 1983; January 12, 1984; June 10, 1984; October 14, 1984; April 19, 1990; July 30, 1991; March 2, 1992.
50. *New York Times,* November 4, 1983; November 11, 1983; February 4, 1984.
51. Bluestone and Harrison, *The Deindustrialization of America,* pp. 235–243; Bennett Harrison and Barry Bluestone, "The Incidence and Regulation of Plant Closings," in Larry Sawers and William Tabb, eds., *Sunbelt/Snowbelt* (New York: Oxford University Press, 1984), pp. 368–402; Tabb, "A Pro-People Urban Policy," p. 371.
52. *New York Times,* August 3, 1988.
53. *New York Times,* June 15, 1991.
54. *Fort Halifax Packing Company v. Coyne,* 86 U.S. 341 (1987).
55. *New York Times,* June 3, 1984.
56. *New York Times,* June 10, 1984.

57. See Bluestone and Harrison, *The Deindustrialization of America,* p. 234.
58. *Mobil Oil Corporation v. Vermont,* 445 U.S. 425 (1980).
59. Carl Stokes, *Promises of Power* (New York: Simon and Schuster, 1973).
60. *New York Times,* Aprii 13, 1987; September 20, 1984; Susan Fainstein, Norman Fainstein, and P. Jefferson Armistead, "San Francisco: Urban Transformation and the Local State," in Susan Fainstein, Norman Fainstein, Richard Child Hill et al., *Restructuring the City* (White Plains, N.Y.: Longman, 1983).
61. *New York Times,* January 25, 1980. For more coverage of the Rath Meatpacking Company buyout, see *New York Times,* November 2, 1983, p. 25.
62. Joseph Roebuck, *A History of American Labor* (New York: Free Press, 1966), p. 160; Bluestone and Harrison, *The Deindustrialization of America,* p. 257.
63. *New York Times,* April 17, 1984.
64. Corey Rosen, Katherine Klein, and Karen Young, *Employee Stock Ownership in America: The Equity Solution* (Lexington, Mass.: Lexington Books, 1985); Bluestone and Harrison, *The Deindustrialization of America,* pp. 252–262; Dotson Rader, "The Town That Saved Itself," *Parade Magazine,* April 24, 1988, pp. 8–10; *New York Times,* January 15, 1984; March 15, 1985; April 24, 1988; September 18, 1989; February 20, 1990; April 16, 1990.

    For debate concerning the risks of labor becoming co-opted in such arrangements, see Mike Slott and Dan Swinney, "Worker Ownership: Buying Control or Selling Out?" *Labor Research Review* 4 (1985); James Smith, "The Labor Movement and Worker Ownership," *The Social Report* 2 (December 1981): 2
65. Alperovitz and Faux, *Rebuilding America,* pp. 99–109; *New York Times,* June 25, 1980; February 13, 1983; February 23, 1983; January 15, 1984.
66. Jeremy Rifkin and Randy Barber, *The North Will Rise Again: Pensions and Power in the 1980s* (Boston: Beacon, 1978). Also see *New York Times,* May 23, 1980; April 7, 1981; March 17, 1991; June 6, 1991.
67. *Nation,* July 9–16, 1983, pp. 39–41.
68. *New York Times,* January 19, 1980.
69. *Washington Post National Weekly Edition,* June 4, 1984, pp. 17–18; and *New York Times,* January 1, 1985; January 18, 1985.
70. *Guardian,* June 20, 1984, p. 8.
71. *New York Times,* May 5, 1986. Also see Janice Perlman, "Grassrooting the System," *Social Policy* 7 (September/October 1976): 4–20; John Herbers, "Citizen Activism Gaining in Nation," *New York Times,* May 15, 1982; Bennett Harrison, "Regional Restructuring and Good Business Climates," in Larry Sawers and William Tabb, eds., *Sunbelt/Snowbelt* (New York: Oxford University Press, 1984), pp. 88–89; Peter Dreier, "The Tenant's Movement," in William Tabb and Larry Sawers, eds., *Marxism and the Metropolis* (New York: Oxford University Press, 1984), pp. 174–201; William Tabb, "A Pro-People Urban Policy," in William Tabb and Larry Sawers, eds., *Marxism and the Metropolis* (New York: Oxford University Press, 1984); Joe Feagin, "Sunbelt Metropolis and Development Capital," in Larry Sawers and William Tabb, eds., *Sunbelt/Snowbelt* (New York: Oxford University Press, 1984), pp. 123–124; Frances Fox Piven and Richard Cloward, *The New Class War* (New York: Pantheon, 1982); Dan Luria and Jack Russell, *Rational Reindustrialization* (Detroit: Widgetripper, 1981); Harry Boyte, *The Backyard Revolution* (Philadelphia: Temple University Press, 1980); Dan Georgakas and Marvin Surkin, *Detroit: I Do Mind Dying* (New York: St. Martin's Press, 1975).
72. James Weinstein, *The Decline of Socialism in America, 1912–1925* (New York: Random House, 1967); James Weinstein, *The Corporate Ideal in the Liberal State:*

1900–1918 (Boston: Beacon, 1968); Bruce Stave, *Socialism and Cities* (Port Washington, N.Y.: Kennikat, 1975); Frederick Howe, *The City: The Hope of Democracy* (New York: Scribner's, Sons 1905).

73. Allan Gold, "Exit a Socialist, to Let History Judge," *New York Times,* March 2, 1989; W. J. Conway, *Challenging the Boundaries of Reform: Socialism in Burlington* (Philadelphia: Temple University Press, 1990).

74. *New York Times,* October 6, 1991.

75. Anna Gutierrez-Johnson and William Whyte, "The Mondragon System of Worker Production Coops," *Industrial and Labor Relations Review* 31 (October 1977): 18–30; Carnoy and Shearer, *Economic Democracy,* pp. 149–152.

76. Reference in the *New York Times,* October 6, 1991.

77. Frances Fox Piven, "The Urban Crisis: Who Got What, and Why," in Stephen David and Paul Peterson, eds., *Urban Politics and Public Policy* (New York: Praeger, 1977), p. 338.

78. Jeff Faux, "What Now, Willy Loman?" *Mother Jones,* November 1983, p. 52. Also see *New York Times,* June 2, 1983; October 31, 1984.

79. *New York Times,* May 3, 1984; October 20, 1984.

80. Tabb, "Economic Democracy and Regional Restructuring." Also, see *New York Times,* September 5, 1981; November 3, 1981; January 15, 1984; May 26, 1991.

81. See *New York Times,* December 12, 1983.

82. *New York Times,* January 15, 1984. Also, see *New York Times,* April 14, 1992.

83. *New York Times,* June 18, 1991.

84. George Sternlieb and James Hughes, *Income and Jobs: USA* (Brunswick, N.J.: Center for Urban Policy Research, 1984), chap. 5; *New York Times,* July 31, 1987; February 6, 1991; Frank Levy, "The Vanishing Middle Class and Related Issues," *PS* 21 (Summer 1987).

85. Levy, "The Vanishing Middle Class."

86. *New York Times,* June 26, 1987.

87. *New York Times,* January 4, 1992.

88. *Akron Beacon Journal,* June 26, 1983, pp. 1, 7. For other examples, see Steven Holmes, "On the Edge of Despair When Jobless Benefits End," *New York Times,* January 28, 1991; Steven Holmes, "Many Learn the Sting of Welfare as Recession Tightens Grip," *New York Times,* March 11, 1991; John Nordheimer, "From Middle Class to Jobless," *New York Times,* April 13, 1992.

89. *New York Times,* July 30, 1979.

90. See AP story printed in *Quad City Times,* December 23, 1983, p. 5.

91. *Business Week,* October 12, 1974.

92. See James N. Morgan, "Panel Study on Income Dynamics" (Ann Arbor: University of Michigan Press, 1977). Also see *New York Times,* July 10, 1977.

93. Alfred Perry and Richard Watkins, "People, Profit, and the Rise of the Sunbelt Cities," in Joe Feagin, ed., *The Urban Scene* (New York: Random House, 1979), p. 164.

94. *Cleveland Press,* September 14, 1979, p. 84. The series ran from September 4 to 14, 1979.

95. Robert Peterson, Gerald Albaum, George Kozmetsky et al., "Attitudes towards Capitalism," *Journalism Quarterly* 60 (Spring 1984): 61. Also see Ralph Miliband, *Divided Societies: Class Struggle in Contemporary Capitalism* (New York: Oxford University Press, 1989).

96. Quoted in Terkel, *American Dreams,* p. 349.

97. Judge James L. Ryan, quoted in *New York Times,* April 30, 1981.

98. Alex Kotlowitz, *There Are No Children Here* (New York: Doubleday, 1991).

99. As quoted in Robert Scheer, "Playboy Interview: Dennis Kucinich," *Playboy Magazine,* June 1979, p. 82.

Urban Fiscal Crisis Simulation

As a useful teaching tool that can be used in conjunction with this text, consider the following role-playing simulation—not to be confused with an educational game. A game normally has an elaborate set of rules and requires participants to function within the logic of its own reality. A role-playing simulation, on the other hand, allows the participants to maintain their own personalities and values as they interact within far more general roles and rules, creating a unique reality each time. The goal of this particular simulation is to overcome a public policy problem within a simulated political environment.

Pedagogical goals include the desire not only to impart knowledge but also to stimulate critical thinking, clarity of expression, development of a political identity, and an interest in both politics and political science. The following simulation can be used as an active instructional mode to supplement the standard reading-lecture-discussion format, and can be useful in accomplishing all of the above-mentioned basic pedagogical objectives.

The simulation helps to impart knowledge in a number of ways. It focuses on substantive political issues of the day, and it helps elucidate the complexity and interrelationship of the problems involved, such as the dilemma that although programmatic cuts may be useful in helping to balance the city budget, they may also reduce the overall quality of life in the city and thus drive even more middle-class taxpayers to the suburbs.

Such an exercise lends insight into the rules, roles, and internal dynamics of the political decision-making process. Using an actual budget document increases understanding of public finance in general and city priority-setting in particular, and building coalitions and reaching strategic compromises provides invaluable lessons about the pressure under which political activists often labor. Such role-playing has the capacity to bring concepts to life, such as "power structures" or the "broker-innovator" mayoral leadership style.

The experience also helps the student approach the remaining reading and lectures with more sophistication and a better sense of what is possible. And by expanding students' understanding, such exercises often stimulate more open discussion during the most controversial portion of the course—final consideration of alternative futures.

The structural parameters faced by student decision makers prompt them to take a critical look at systemic biases as well. Beyond that, one's ability to articulate his or her positions concisely and clearly is essential given the number of participants, the complexity of the issues, and the time constraints. Competing role demands, role-personality conflicts, and the need to take positions on a variety of value-laden questions push the student toward developing a clearer and more coherent political identity. And finally, this type of role-playing captures some of the excitement of politics and generally proves to be quite enjoyable, stimulating positive feelings about the subject, and, one would hope, the discipline, too.

The student's participation serves as a test of how well he or she has understood the course material. Consequently, the simulation is probably most appropriate toward the end of the term, but before the last couple of weeks when term papers and preparation for final exams can tend to dominate student schedules. In conjunction with this particular text, the simulation should be used after consideration of urban institutions, processes, and power relationships and before analysis of policy options and alternative futures.

ACADEMIC SETTING

This urban crisis simulation was designed for undergraduates taking an advanced-level course in urban politics. Nevertheless, it may also be appropriate for certain urban studies, urban economics, and public administration courses if the students have background knowledge of the urban political process. It was first used at a residential liberal arts college on a quarter-system calendar. In that setting a full week, or one-tenth of the course, was devoted to the exercise. This translates to both a one-hour class session and roughly two hours of activity outside of class for each of the five days.

For those teaching at residential colleges on a semester calendar, the simulation itself should probably be limited to no more than three class days, particularly given the intensity of play that often develops. Many of the students become so caught up in the action that they do little else. Consequently, burnout can become a problem, not to mention the time taken from other coursework. It is suggested, therefore, that the crisis scenario be introduced at the end of the preceding class period, leaving two days for formal in-class city council sessions and the final day for debriefing. Negotiating will then occur between classes, and the instructor may wish to assist the students by designating a particular afternoon or evening hour as a nonobligatory, informal gathering time on days the class does not meet.

Commuter colleges pose some additional difficulties, in particular because many students will find it much less convenient to get together outside of the class hour. In those situations the author recommends that the entire simulation be conducted in one extended marathon session, preferably in the evening or on a Saturday. Notice should be given at the beginning of the course so work schedules and family obligations can be adjusted. The instructor may wish to reduce the number of regular class meetings to compensate for the hours of attendance that will be required for the simulation. The scenario should be distributed at the preceding class period, however, and the debriefing can occur at the subsequent one.

THE SIMULATION

Although the setting, rules, and roles can be adapted to fit a variety of city types, the city the author has used most successfully in the past is a fictitious prototype of the oldest and largest industrial cities of the United States, such as Baltimore, Cleveland, or Detroit. There is a strong mayor-council system, a sizable minority population, and a budget severely strained by the flight of industrial corporations and middle-class residents. Any other details concerning the city's specifications or past can be attained by consulting "history control"—a part usually played by the instructor and described in more detail below. A fictitious city is used to avoid lengthy debates over the realities of any actual location and to eliminate knowledge of a particular city as a variable in the simulation.

Although the simulated city will be fictitious, the budget document from an existing city government can be used. Not only does that budget provide important common information for each participant, but learning to use it adds a valuable educational component. Most cities seem more than happy to provide multiple copies so that each class member has one to use. (Or the instructor may want to limit distribution of the full budget document to a predetermined "informed elite," such as elected officials and the media, while supplying everyone else with only a general outline of the budget and an opportunity to view the full document via library reserve.) The document does not have to be a current edition as long as it contains item-by-item review and expenditure figures for at least two or three years.

The exercise can be conducted with virtually any number of students; however, there is not much purpose in trying it with fewer than four, and it is probably best to split the class into two or more identical simulations if there are more than 50. The roles are listed in approximate order of importance to the simulation: The mayor (note partisan affiliation); city councilpersons (at least three—noting partisanship, district number, and leadership position if any); lobbyists (e.g., president of the Municipal Workers Union, chairman of Ameri-Trust Bank, president of a Chrysler Assembly Plant, head of the local NAACP chapter, president of the Fraternal Order of Police, chairman of the Small Business Association, president of the Chamber of Commerce, head of the Inter-City Council of Churches, president of a B. F. Goodrich Plant, president of a Bethlehem Steel Plant, head of the local ACLU chapter, etc.); deputy mayor(s); and media representative(s) from competing news organizations.

Although the roles can be assigned randomly, it is not recommended. One of the added advantages of waiting until later in the course is that the instructor has a better sense of student personalities and abilities. It is critical, for instance, that the role of mayor be held by an outgoing, industrious individual. The instructor may also wish to teach certain lessons by the demographics of these assignments, by closely following actual patterns to remind students of those realities or by consciously making nontraditional appointments to demonstrate that members of other groups can also perform well in those positions. In addition, it helps to put talented and colorful people in some of the lobbyist roles in order to enliven those parts. It is also recommended that the instructor consult ahead of time with the students who are to be assigned to the more time-consuming roles: mayor, media representative, and city council president. If their schedules simply will not allow such a time commitment at that point in the term, it is best to find somebody else.

At least one week prior to beginning the simulation, roles should be assigned and all materials except the specific crisis scenario should be distributed and explained. That introduction can be started by summarizing the basic characteristics of the fictitious city. Besides the governmental, racial, and fiscal traits described above, the author's city has a population of 500,000 and an economy dominated by Chrysler, Bethlehem Steel, and B. F. Goodrich manufacturing plants. The budget can then be distributed and explained as to its basic organization and contents, referring to specific pages where useful. The students are instructed to familiarize themselves with the details of the document and see the instructor if they have questions.

Next, hand out a list of the role assignments and suggest that students research and think about their roles. They are to perform them as realistically as they can while at the same time trying to be true to their own personal values. Recommend that they do some rudimentary organizing along lines of obvious common interest—mayor and deputy mayor(s), party caucuses within the city council, media executives and their staffs, union leaders, corporate magnates, and so on. The author also normally adds the following limited role specifications:

City Councilpersons

Each council member is assigned a political party affiliation and is told whether he or she is also to serve as council president or a party leader. District numbers are designated and the districts are ranked by socioeconomic status, percent minority, median age, and crime rate. For example, there will be middle-income minority and white districts, as well as crime-prone districts that might be relatively youthful minority ghettos and/or made up primarily of elderly white residents.

Mayor

The mayor will be required to draw up a revised expense budget proposal and submit it to council at the first formal council meeting.

City Council President

The council president is the presiding officer of that body. Therefore, he or she will draw up the specific agendas for the two formal council meetings and make those available to the media in a timely manner. The council president also has full power of recognition, although the mayor's budgetary speech is already the first official agenda item for the initial formal council meeting. No other specific authority comes with the job, and he or she may vote only to break a tie.

Mediapersons

Each newspaper or radio/television station is to make regular news presentations at the time(s) of day established by the instructor. (If there are to be two newspapers, one can be published and available before breakfast and the other right before the dinner hour; however, competition will be increased if they report at the same time each day, e.g., shortly before the official council sessions.)

History Control

One person, normally the instructor, will supply the official answer to any questions concerning what has transpired in the past. He or she will also fill any other role that comes to be required, such as president of the United States or members of the state legislature, the general pubic, or the rank and file of a particular union. Here it is best to answer all queries in writing and to use a unique seal to designate an official response to the question.

The instructor will draw on his or her own knowledge of both American politics and the type of city involved to make general responses designed to contribute to the realism of the simulation and prove educative as well. The participants should realize, however, that their early initiatives will often determine the degree to which they will be an integral part of the simulation, such as carving out a large role for the governor. The instructor will normally avoid extensive intervention so as better to play the role of neutral arbiter. Nonetheless, he or she will carefully interject additional factors if the action bogs down or takes a turn that appears to be highly unrealistic. For cxample, one might generate a crime spree to deter an across-the-board cut that would reduce police protection, or produce a very negative public opinion poll if a public official gets too far out of line.

The author also specifies these additional rules: (1) Council may only conduct formal business during the designated class sessions. (2) Formal council meetings are open to the public. (3) If a complete budget is passed, that must be done at least 15 minutes prior to the end of the final simulation session in order to give the mayor time to consider it. At that point, the mayor may either veto it or any item(s) in it, or choose to sign it into law. If a veto occurs, it will require two-thirds of the councilpersons present and voting to override. (4) The simulation ends when a budget is finally passed and signed; when one is passed, vetoed, and the veto overridden; or at the end of the class hour on the final day scheduled for the simulation.

The introductory session closes with a discussion of the pedagogical purpose of the exercise as well as the criteria on which the participants will be evaluated. In particular, the students are told that they will be expected to develop their own goals once the crisis scenario is distributed, and from then on they are to keep a diary of their simulation-related activities. In the end, they will be expected to conclude their logs by explaining their actions vis-à-vis their goals, assessing the degree of success in achieving their goals, and indicating the ways they felt their participation was realistic or unrealistic. They will also be asked to comment on the realism of the entire simulation, discuss what they learned about urban politics and their own political values, and suggest ways for improving the exercise.

Once the students have had an opportunity to prepare, the simulation begins with the distribution of the specific scenario.

The setting is the most recent fiscal year for which you have budget figures. You are to assume that the budget has been passed by the city council and is about to be implemented. According to the budgetary figures, the city should end this year in the black. Yet, just as that year has begun, it is already certain that there have been some critical miscalculations. Inflation has remained low, which means that your expenditure figures should be pretty much on target. Nevertheless, a combination of federal cutbacks and a serious economic recession have significantly altered revenue estimates. Federal assistance has been sizably reduced and a combination of high unemployment and business sluggishness has meant fewer tax revenues. The bottom line is that the city faces a 25 percent revenue shortfall. In other words, if you spend all of the authorized money the city will end up badly in the red by the end of the fiscal year.

The mayor has sought help from every external revenue source imaginable, but to no avail. The federal and state governments are both facing their own multibillion dollar deficits and will not provide new grants, loans, or even loan guarantees. The county faces a revenue shortfall of its own. Private foundations are badly overcommitted. And local corporate leaders are once again accusing the city of overspending. Consequently, the city's state-imposed and corporate-dominated finance control board has demanded that the city cut 25 percent from its expenditure authorizations (by the end of classtime on the final day allocated to the simulation). They have also made it crystal clear that no increase in taxation will be tolerated, and that they will make the cuts where they see fit if the city government fails to do so.

Last, it is important to discuss the procedure for dispersing information between class sessions. Then just before the students begin tackling the crisis, they should be reminded that they are to be creative, form coalitions where possible, and not be afraid to make strategic compromises. The simulation then begins.

The first urge almost certainly will be quickly to negotiate an across-the-board cut. To avoid that, the instructor may wish quietly to introduce an additional factor or two. For example, a confidential memo can be sent from the chief of police to the head of the police officers' union. That memo reveals that the police force is about to be put on standby alert. Very sensitive negotiations have begun with a terroist group and must remain so completely secret that even the mayor has not been informed. However, no cuts in the police budget should be allowed, as this action might damage morale and cause disarray at a very critical juncture.

THE INSTRUCTOR

Prior to the exercise, a number of things must be done. The instructor needs to secure both an appropriately sized classroom with a blackboard as well as a bulletin board centrally located in a building accessible for as many hours as possible, such as the student union. If newspapers are to be run off and circulated, the duplication facilities and materials must be secured and a distribution box set up near the bulletin board. If duplication poses problems, however, the original can simply be posted on the bulletin board—Soviet style. (Bulletin boards and hard-copy newspapers can be avoided entirely if an electronic mail system is available on the campus.) Name tags and a gavel are nice touches. There should be at least one calculator on hand during class sessions. Budget documents must be obtained and information packets prepared. Roles have to be assigned. And, finally, introductory presentations must be prepared and delivered.

During the simulation, the instructor should be available, both to observe and to settle disputes. If he or she also plays the role of history control, accessibility is even more essential, particularly as the pace picks up toward the end. At the very least, the instructor should post the (extended) hours that he or she will be available.

Following the exercise, the debriefing session should be conducted and the logs should be graded. In the course of the debriefing, try to get as many students to speak as possible. What were their goals and strategies? What transpired? Why did those things occur? What pressures did they feel? Which interests won and lost? Why? What course lessons seemed to be reinforced? What new lessons did they learn? What, if anything surprised them? In what ways was the simulation realistic? In what ways was it unrealistic? Do they have suggestions for improving it?

Student evaluations can then be based on criteria such as the following: preparation apparent, clarity of goals, innovation, knowledge evident in goals and participation, time devoted to the role, quality of log summaries and conclusions, and a sizable deduction for any missed classes. The author has found that students take the preparation, planning, and reflective components of the exercise more seriously if their overall performance is formally graded, usually 10 percent of the final course grade or a percentage of the class participation grade.

As a case-in-point, the log of the council president may indicate that the student not only understood the previous classroom discussion of city councils but also read Robert Caro's *The Power Broker* in order to become better acquainted with various strategic political ploys. The student then carefully developed goals and tactics and devoted five hours per day to the simulation. Nevertheless, it was clear that the student inadvertently fell into a reactive posture early on in the game and was unable to accomplish any major goals. The grade would probably still be an ''A – '' if the log indicated depth of critical reflection on all of this.

Experiences with the simulation have been very positive. In particular, it provides an additional device for assessing students' understanding of important course material, with their logs indicating the amount of learning that has taken place as a result of their participation. In addition, the author has always been pleased with the level of seriousness and enthusiasm the students have displayed. They get swept up in the excitement of the competition, enjoy themselves without turning the exercise into a farce, and often produce impressive work. They also clearly appreciate the opportunity. For example, over five years of evaluating it among other course components, the average evaluation score for the simulation was 4.74 on a 5-point scale. More than three-quarters of the students rated it as a 5, and another 20 percent rated it as a 4.[1]

NOTE

1. A version of this simulation description first appeared in article form. See Marcus D. Pohlmann, American Political Science Association, *NEWS for Teachers of Political Science* 51 (Fall 1986). For further reference, also see Thomas Henderson and John Foster, *Urban Policy Game* (New York: Wiley, 1978); Charles and Anne Walcott, *Simple Simulations* (Washington, D.C.: American Political Science Association, 1976); James Woodworth and Robert Gump, *Camelot: A Role-Playing Simulation for Political Decision Making* (Homewood, Ill.: Dorsey, 1982); *Simulations and Games* (Beverly Hills, Calif.: Sage); ''Simulations/Gaming/News'' (Moscow, Idaho); *Teaching Political Science* (Beverly Hills, Calif.: Sage).

Bibliography

Adams, John. *Works*. Vol. 6. New York: AMS Press, 1971.

Adrian, Charles. "Leadership and Decision-Making in Manager Cities." *Public Administration Review* 18 (Summer 1958).

Adrian, Charles. "Some General Characteristics of Nonpartisan Elections." *American Political Science Review* 46 (September 1952).

Adrian, Charles. "A Study of Three Communities." *Public Administration Review* 18 (1958).

Adrian, Charles, and Press, Charles. *Governing Urban America*. New York: McGraw-Hill, 1977.

Advisory Commission on Intergovernmental Relations, *Metropolitan Councils of Government*. Washington, D.C.: Government Printing Office, 1966.

Advisory Commission on Intergovernmental Relations. *Regional Decision-Making*. Washington, D.C.: Government Printing Office. 1973.

Agee, Warren; Ault, Phillip; and Emery, Edwin. *Main Currents in Mass Communications*. New York: Harper & Row, 1986.

Agranoff, Robert. *The New Style of Election Campaigns*. Boston: Holbrook, 1972.

Ahlbrandt, Roger. "Efficiency in the Provision of Fire Services." *Public Choice* 16 (Fall 1973).

Ainsworth, Ed. *Maverick Mayor*. Garden City, N.Y.: Doubleday, 1966.

Alford, Robert, and Scoble, Harry. "Political and Socioeconomic Characteristics of American Cities." *Municipal Yearbook 1965*. Washington, D.C.: International City Managers' Association, 1965.

Almond, Gabriel, and Powell, G. Bingham. *Comparative Politics: A Developmental Approach*. Boston: Little, Brown, 1966.

Altheide, David, and Snow, Robert. *Media Logic*. Beverly Hills, Calif.: Sage, 1979.

Altschuler, Alan. *Community Control*. New York: Pegasus, 1970.

Anderson, Martin. *The Federal Bulldozer*. Cambridge, Mass.: MIT Press, 1964.

Anton, Thomas; Cawley, Jerry; and Kramer, Kevin. *Moving Money*. Cambridge, Mass.: Olegschlager, Gunn, and Main, 1980.

Aron, Joan. *The Quest for Regional Cooperation.* Berkeley: University of California Press, 1969.

Aronson, Albert. "State and Local Personnel Administration." In *Classics of Public Personnel Policy,* edited by Frank J. Thompson. Oak Park, Ill.: Moore, 1979.

Aronson, James. *The Press and the Cold War.* Boston: Beacon, 1970.

Ashton, Patrick. "The Political Economy of Suburban Development." In *Marxism and the Metropolis,* edited by William Tabb and Larry Sawyers. New York: Oxford University Press, 1984.

Atwood, Jay. "Collective Bargaining's Challenge. *Public Personnel Management* 5 (January/February 1976).

Bachelor, Lynn. "Urban Economic Development." *Urban Affairs Quarterly* 16 (December 1981).

Bachrach, Peter, and Baratz, Morton. Decisions and Nondecisions: An Analytical Framework." *American Political Science Review* 57 (September 1963).

Bachrach, Peter, and Baratz, Morton. "Two Faces of Power." *American Political Science Review* 56 (December 1962).

Bagdikian, Ben. "Fires, Sex and Freaks." *New York Times Magazine,* October 10, 1976.

Bagdikian, Ben. *The Media Monopoly.* Boston: Beacon, 1983.

Bahl, Roy. *Financing State and Local Government in the 1980s.* New York: Oxford University Press, 1984.

Bancroft, Raymond. *America's Mayors and Councilmen.* Washington, D.C.: National League of Cities, 1974.

Banfield, Edward. *Big City Politics.* New York: Random House, 1966.

Banfield, Edward. *Political Influence.* Glencoe, Ill.: Free Press, 1961.

Banfield, Edward. *The Unheavenly City Revisited.* Boston: Little, Brown, 1974.

Banfield, Edward, and Wilson, James Q. *City Politics.* Cambridge, Mass.: Harvard University Press, 1963.

Barabba, Vincent. "The National Setting: Regional Shifts, Metropolitan Decline, and Urban Decay." In *Postindustrial America,* edited by George Sternleib and James Hughes. New Brunswick, N.J.: Center for Urban Policy Research, 1976.

Barber, James David. *The Lawmakers.* New Haven: Yale University Press, 1965.

Barbour, George, and Spiel, George. "Excellence in Leadership." *Public Management* 68 (August 1968).

Barnouw, Erik. *The Television Writer.* New York: Hill and Wang, 1962.

Barringer, Felicity. "What America Did after the War: A Tale Told by the Census." *New York Times,* September 2, 1990.

Barth, M. C. "Dislocated Workers." *Journal of the Institute of Socioeconomic Studies* 7 (Spring 1982).

Beard, Charles. *An Economic Interpretation of the Constitution.* New York: Macmillan, 1962.

Bellush, Jewel, and Heusknecht, Murray. "Entrepreneurs and Urban Renewal." *Journal of the American Institute of Planners* 32 (September 1966).

Benjamin, Aaron; Grodin, Joseph; and Stern, James. *Public-Sector Bargaining.* Washington, D.C.: Bureau of National Affairs, 1979.

Bennet, James, and DiLorenzo, Thomas. *Underground Government: The Off-Budget Public Sector.* New York: Cato, 1983.

Bentley, Arthur. *The Process of Government.* Chicago: University of Chicago Press, 1908.

Berman, David. *State and Local Politics.* Dubuque, Ia.: William C. Brown Publishers, 1990.

Bernard, Richard, and Rice, Bradley. "Political Environment and the Adoption of Progressive Reforms." *Journal of Urban History* 1 (February 1975).

Berry, Brian. *The Human Consequences of Urbanization.* New York: St. Martin's Press, 1973.

Berry, Brian. "Islands of Renewal in Seas of Decay." In *New Urban Realty,* edited by Paul Peterson. Washington, D.C.: Brookings Institution, 1985.

Betz, Michael. "Riots and Welfare: Are They Related?" *Social Problems* 21 (Fall 1974).

Binzen, Peter. "Business Community Sees Reason for Hope. *Philadelphia Inquirer,* January 8, 1984.

Birke, Wolfgang. *European Elections by Direct Suffrage.* Layden: Sythoff, 1961.

Blake, Nelson. *Water for the City.* Syracuse, N.Y.: Syracuse University Press, 1956.

Blau, Peter. *Bureaucracy in Modern Society.* New York: Random House, 1971.

Bluestone, Barry, and Harrison, Bennett. *Capital and Communities.* Washington, D.C.: The Progressive Alliance, 1980.

Bluestone, Barry, and Harrison, Bennett. *The Deindustrialization of America.* New York: Basic Books, 1982.

Boesel, Andrew. "Local Personnel Management." *Municipal Yearbook, 1974.* Washington, D.C.: International City Managers' Association, 1974.

Bogart, Leo. *Press and Public.* Hillsdale, N.J.: Lawrence Erlbaum, 1981.

Bok, Derek, and Dunlop, John. *Labor and the American Community.* New York: Simon and Schuster, 1970.

Bollens, John. *Appointed Executive Local Government: The California Experience.* Berkeley: University of California Press, 1952.

Bollens, John, and Schmandt, Henry. *The Metropolis.* New York: Harper & Row, 1982.

Bolotin, Frederic, and Cigranelli, David. "Equity and Urban Policy." *Journal of Politics* 45 (February 1983).

Borjas, George. *Friends or Strangers: The Impact of Immigration on the United States Economy.* New York: Basic Books, 1990.

Bosworth, Karl. "The Manager Is a Politician." *Public Administration Review* 18 (Spring 1959).

Bowen, Robert. *The Changing Television Audience in America.* New York: Columbia University Press, 1984.

Bowles, Samuel; Gordon, David; and Weisskopf, Thomas. *Beyond the Wasteland.* New York: Doubleday/Anchor, 1983.

Bowman, Ann, and Franke, James. "The Decline of Substate Regionalism." *Journal of Urban Affairs* 6 (Fall 1984).

Boylan, James. "News People." *Wilson Quarterly* 6 (Special Issue 1982).

Boyle, John, and Jacobs, David. "The Intra-City Distribution of Services." *American Political Science Review* 76 (June 1982).

Boynton, Robert, and Wright, Deil. "Mayor-Manager Relationships in Large Council-Manager Cities." *Public Administration Review* 31 (January/February 1971).

Boyte, Harry. *The Backyard Revolution.* Philadelphia: Temple University Press, 1980.

Bradbury, Katherine; Downs, Anthony; and Small, Kenneth. *Urban Decline and the Future of American Cities.* Washington, D.C.: Brookings Institution, 1982.

Bratt, Rachel; Hartman, Chester; and Myerson, Ann. *Critical Perspectives on Housing.* Philadelphia: Temple University Press, 1986.

Brenner, Harvey. "Estimating the Social Costs of National Economic Policy." In Congressional Joint Economic Committee, *Achieving the Goals of the Employment Act of 1946.* 30th Anniversary Review, 1, Employment Paper no. 5. Washington, D.C.: Government Printing Office, 1976.

Bridge, Gary. "Citizen Choice in Public Service: Voucher Systems." In *Alternatives for Delivering Public Services,* edited by E. S. Savas. Boulder, Colo.: Westview, 1977.

Brown, Douglas. *Introduction to Urban Economics.* New York: Academic Press, 1974.

Brown, Harold, and Hymer, Bennett. "Racial Dualism in an Urban Labor Market." In *Problems in Political Economy,* edited by David Gordon. Lexington, Mass.: D C Heath, 1977.

Brown, William, Jr., and Gilbert, Charles. "Capital Programming in Philadelphia." *American Political Science Review* 54 (September 1960).

Browning, Rufus, and Marshall, Dale Rogers. "Black and Hispanic Power in City Politics." *PS* 18 (Summer 1986).

Browning, Rufus; Marshall, Dale Rogers; and Tabb, David, eds. *Black Politics in American Cities.* White Plains, N.Y.: Longman, 1989.

Browning, Rufus; Marshall, Dale Rogers; and Tabb, David. *Protest Is Not Enough.* Berkeley: University of California Press, 1984.

Bryce, Herrington. "Problems of Governing American Cities: The Case of Medium and Large Cities with Black Mayors." *Focus* 2 (August 1974).

Bryce, James. *The American Commonwealth.* New York: Macmillan, 1889.

Bryce, James. *Modern Democracies.* Vol 2. New York: Macmillan, 1921.

Button, James. "Southern Black Elected Officials: Impact on Socioeconomic Change." *Review of Black Political Economy* 12 (Fall 1982).

Capitman, William. *Panic in the Boardroom.* New York: Anchor Books/Doubleday, 1973.

Capozzola, John. "Taking a Look at Unions." *National Civic Review* 75 (July/August 1986).

Caraley, Demetrios. *City Governments and Urban Problems.* Englewood Cliffs, N.J.: Prentice-Hall, 1977.

Carnahan, Douglas; Gove, Walter; and Galle, Omer. "Urbanization, Population Density, and Overcrowding." *Social Forces* 53 (September 1974).

Carnoy, Martin, and Shearer, Derek. *Economic Democracy.* White Plains, N.Y.: Sharpe, 1980.

Castells, Manuel. *The City and the Grassroots.* Berkeley: University of California Press, 1983.

Chandler, Alfred, Jr. "The Beginning of 'Big Business' in American History." *Business History Review* 33 (Spring 1959).

Chester, Edward. *Radio, Television and American Politics.* New York: Sheed and Ward, 1969.

Cheyfitz, Kirk. "Self-Service." *New Republic,* November 15, 1980.

Chicago Tribune Staff. *The American Millstone.* Chicago: Contemporary Books, 1986.

Chickering, Lawrence. *Public Employee Unions.* San Francisco: Institute of Contemporary Studies, 1976.

Childs, Richard. "Civic Victories in the United States." *National Municipal Review* 44 (September 1955).

Childs, Richard. *The First Fifty Years of the Council-Manager Plan of Municipal Government.* New York: National Municipal League, 1969.

Chomsky, Noam. "Ideological Conformity." *Nation,* January 27, 1979.

Chudacoff, Howard. *The Evolution of American Urban Society.* Englewood Cliffs, N.J.: Prentice-Hall, 1975.

Cingranelli, David. "Race, Politics, and Elites." *American Journal of Political Science* 25 (November 1981).

Cirino, Robert. *Don't Blame the People.* New York: Vintage, 1972.

Clark, Kenneth. *The Dark Ghetto.* New York: Harper & Row, 1965.

Clark, Terry. "Community Structure, Decision-Making, Budget Expenditures and Urban Renewal." *American Sociological Review* 33 (August 1968).

Clark, Terry, and Ferguson, Lorna. *City Money.* New York: Columbia University Press, 1983.

Clark, W. A. U. "Residential Segregation in American Cities." *Population Residency and Policy Review* 5 (1986).

Clarke, Susan. "More Autonomous Policy Orientations." In *The Politics of Urban Development,* edited by Clarence Stone and Heywood Sanders. Lawrence: University of Kansas Press, 1987.

Clay, Philip. *Neighborhood Renewal.* Lexington, Mass.: Lexington Books, 1979.

Cleveland City Planning Commission. *Jobs and Income.* Cleveland: City of Cleveland, 1975.

Collier, Peter, and Horowitz, David. *Rockefellers: An American Dynasty.* New York: Holt, Rinehart and Winston, 1976.

Compaine, Benjamin; Sterling, Christopher; Guback, Thomas; and Noble, J. Kendrick, Jr. *Who Owns the Media?* White Plains, N.Y.: Knowledge Industry, 1982.

Cornwell, Elmer. "Bosses, Machines, and Ethnic Groups." *Annals of the American Association of Political and Social Sciences* 353 (May 1964).

Costikyan, Edward. *Beyond Closed Doors.* New York: Harcourt Brace and World, 1966.

Costikyan, Edward. "Who Runs City Government?" *New York Times Magazine,* May 26, 1969.

Courtier, J. J., and Dunn, S. E. "Federal Colonization of State and Local Government." *State Government* 50 (Spring 1977).

Crecine, John. "A Simulation of Municipal Budgeting: The Impact of a Problem Environment." In *Policy Analysis in Political Science,* edited by Ira Sharansky. Chicago: Markham Publishing, 1970.

Crouch, Winston. *Organized Civil Servants.* Berkeley: University of California Press, 1978.

Crouse, Timothy. *The Boys on the Bus.* New York: Ballantine, 1973.

Culhane, John. "Television Taboos." *New York Times,* February 20, 1977.

Curran, James; Gurevitch, Michael; and Woolacott, Janet. *Mass Communications and Society.* New York: Sage, 1977.

Cutright, Phillip. "Activities of Precinct Committeemen in Partisan and Non-Partisan Communities." *Western Political Quarterly* 17 (Spring 1964).

Dahl, Robert. "A Critique of the Ruling Elite Model." *American Political Science Review* 52 (June 1958).

Dahl, Robert. *Dilemmas of Pluralist Democracy.* New Haven: Yale University Press, 1982.

Dahl, Robert. "Further Reflections on the Elitist Theory of Democracy." *American Political Science Review* 60 (June 1966).

Dahl, Robert. *Pluralist Democracy in the United States.* Chicago: Rand-McNally, 1967.

Dahl, Robert. *Politics, Economics and Welfare.* Chicago: University of Chicago Press, 1976.

Dahl, Robert. *Who Governs?* New Haven, Conn.: Yale University Press, 1960.

Danielson, Michael. *The Politics of Exclusion.* New York: Columbia University Press, 1976.

Davis, Alan. *Spearheads for Reform.* New York: Oxford University Press, 1967.

Davis, J. Morton. *Making America Work Again.* New York: Crown, 1983.

Davis, Kenneth Culp. *Discretionary Justice.* Baton Rouge: Louisiana State University Press, 1969.

Davis, Perry, ed. *Public-Private Partnerships.* New York: Academy of Political Science, 1986.

Deeb, Michael. "Municipal Council Members: Changing Roles and Functions." *National Civic Review* 68 (September 1979).

Derthick, Martha. "Intercity Differences in Administration of Public Assistance Programs." In *City Politics and Public Policy,* edited by James Q. Wilson. New York: Wiley, 1968.

de Tocqueville, Alexis. *Democracy in America.* Edited by Phillips Bradley. New York: Knopf, 1951.

Dillon, John F. *Commentaries on the Law of Municipal Corporations.* Boston: Little, Brown, 1911.

Dolbeare, Kenneth, and Dolbeare, Patricia. *American Ideologies.* Boston: Houghton Mifflin, 1976.

Dolbeare, Kenneth, and Edelman, Murray. *American Politics.* Lexington, Mass: D C Heath, 1981.

Domhoff, G. William. *The Bohemian Grove and Other Retreats: A Study in Ruling Class Cohesiveness.* New York: Harper & Row, 1975.

Domhoff, G. William. *Higher Circles: The Governing Class in America.* New York: Random House, 1971.

Domhoff, G. William. *The Powers That Be.* New York: Vintage, 1979.

Domhoff, G. William. *Who Really Rules?* New Brunswick, N. J.: Transaction, 1978.

Domhoff, G. William. *Who Rules America Now?* New York: Simon and Schuster, 1983.

Donahue, John. *The Privatization Decision: Public Ends, Private Means.* New York: Basic Books, 1989.

Donovan, John. *The Politics of Poverty.* New York: Pegasus, 1967.

Dorsett, Lyle. *The Pendergast Machine.* New York: Oxford University Press, 1968.

Downes, Bryan. "Municipal Social Ranks and the Characteristics of Local Political Leaders." *Midwest Journal of Political Science* 12 (November 1968).

Downs, Anthony. *Inside Bureaucracy.* New York: McGraw-Hill, 1967.

Doyle, Philip. "Municipal Pension Plans: Provisions and Payments." *Monthly Labor Review* 100 (November 1977).

Dreier, Peter, and Weinberg, Steve. "Interlocking Directorates." *Columbia Journalism Review* 18 (November/December 1979).

Drucker, Peter. "Managing the Public Service Institution." *Public Interest* 29 (Fall 1973).

Dutton, William, and Northrup, Alana. "Municipal Reform and the Changing Pattern of Urban Politics." *American Politics Quarterly* 6 (October 1978).

Dye, Thomas. *Politics in States and Communities.* Englewood Cliffs, N.J.: Prentice-Hall, 1985.

Dye, Thomas. *Who's Running America?* Englewood Cliffs, N. J.: Prentice-Hall, 1983.

Dye, Thomas, and McManus, Susan. "Predicting City Government Structures." *American Journal of Political Science* 20 (May 1976).

Dye, Thomas, and Resnick, James. "Political Power and City Jobs." *Social Science Quarterly* 62 (September 1981).

Easton, David. *A Framework for Political Analysis.* Englewood Cliffs, N.J.: Prentice-Hall, 1965.

Easton, David. *The Political System.* New York: Knopf, 1953.

Easton, David, and Guddat, K. H. *Writings of the Young Karl Marx on Philosophy and Society.* New York: Doubleday, 1967.

Eisinger, Peter. "Black Employment in Municipal Jobs." *American Political Science Review* 76 (June 1982).

Eisinger, Peter. "Black Mayors and the Politics of Racial Economic Advancement." In *Readings in Urban Politics,* edited by Harlan Hahn and Charles Levine. White Plains, N.Y.: Longman, 1984.

Eisinger, Peter. *The Politics of Displacement: Racial and Ethnic Transition in Three American Cities.* Madison, Wis.: Institute for Research on Poverty, 1980.

Eisler, Benita. *The Lowell Offering: Writings of New England Mill Women, 1840–1945.* Philadelphia: Lippincott, 1977.

Eldersveld, Samuel. *Political Parties.* Chicago: Rand-McNally, 1964.

Engstrom, Richard, and McDonald, Michael. "The Election of Blacks to City Councils." *American Political Science Review* 75 (June 1981).

Epstein, Edward. *News from Nowhere.* New York: Vintage, 1973.

Eulau, Heinz, and Prewitt, Kenneth. *Labyrinths of Democracy.* Indianapolis: Bobbs-Merrill, 1973.

Ewen, Stuart. *Captains of Consciousness.* New York: McGraw-Hill, 1976.

Fainstein, Norman, and Fainstein, Susan. *Urban Political Movements.* Englewood Cliffs, N.J.: Prentice-Hall, 1974.

Fainstein, Susan, and Fainstein, Norman. "Introduction to Urban Bureaucracies." *American Behavioral Scientist* 15 (March/April 1972).

Fainstein, Susan; Fainstein, Norman; Armistead, P. Jefferson. "San Francisco: Urban Transformation and the Local State." In *Restructuring the City,* edited by Susan Fainstein, Norman Fainstein, Richard Child Hill, Dennis Judd, Michael Peter Smith. White Plains, N.Y.: Longman, 1983.

Fainstein, Susan; Fainstein, Norman; Hill, Richard Child; Judd, Dennis; and Smith, Michael Peter, eds. *Restructuring the City.* White Plains, N.Y.: Longman, 1983.

Fairchild, Halford, and Tucker, Belinda. "Black Residential Mobility." *Journal of Social Issues* 38 (1982).

Farkas, Suzanne. *Urban Lobbying: Mayors in the Federal Arena.* New York: New York University Press, 1971.

Farrand, Max, ed. *The Records of the Federal Convention of 1787.* Vol. 1. New Haven, Conn.: Yale University Press, 1937.

Feagin, Joe, and Hahn, Harlan. *Ghetto Revolts.* New York: Macmillan, 1973.

Federal Bureau of Investigation. *Uniform Crime Reports.* Washington, D.C.: Government Printing Office, 1960–1977.

Felknor, Bruce. *Dirty Politics.* New York: Norton, 1966.

Feuille, Peter, and Long, Gary. "The Public Administrator and Final Offer Arbitration." *Public Administration Review* 34 (November/December, 1974).

Fishman, Mark. *Manufacturing the News.* Austin: University of Texas Press, 1980.

Fisk, Donald; Kiesling, Herbert; and Muellar, Thomas. *Private Provision of Public Services: An Overview.* Washington, D.C.: The Urban Institute, 1978.

Florestano, Patricia, and Gordon, Stephen. "Private Provision of Public Services." *International Journal of Public Administration* 1 (September 1979).

Florestano, Patricia, and Gordon, Stephen. "A Survey of City and County Use of Private Contracting." *The Urban Interest* 3 (Spring 1981).

Flynn, Edward. *You're the Boss.* New York: Collier, 1962.

Foner, Philip. *History of the Labor Movement in the United States.* 9 vols. Chicago: International Publishers, 1978–1990.

Fossett, James. *Federal Aid to Big Cities: The Politics of Dependence.* Washington, D.C.: Brookings Institution, 1983.

Fowler, Floyd, Jr. *Citizen Attitudes toward Local Government Services and Taxes.* Cambridge, Mass.: Ballinger, 1974.

Fraser, Douglas. *Economic Dislocations: Plant Closings, Plant Relocations, and Plant Conversion.* Report prepared for the U.S. Congress, Joint Economic Committee, Washington, D.C.: Government Printing Office, 1979.

Freeman, J. Leiper. "A Case Study of the Legislative Process in Municipal Government." In *Legislative Behavior,* edited by John Wahlake and Heinz Eulau. Glencoe, Ill.: Free Press, 1959.

Fried, Edward; Rivlin, Alice; Schultze, Charles; and Teeters, Nancy. *Setting National Priorities: The 1974 Budget.* Washington, D.C.: Brookings Institution, 1975.

Frieden, Bernard, and Kaplan, Marshall. *The Politics of Neglect.* Cambridge, Mass.: MIT Press, 1975.

Frieden, Bernard, and Sagalyn, Lynn. *Downtown, Inc.* Cambridge, Mass.: MIT Press, 1990.

Friedland, Roger. *Power and Crisis in the City.* London: Macmillan, 1982.

Friedland, Roger; Piven, Frances Fox; and Alford, Robert. "Political Conflict, Urban Structure and the Fiscal Crisis." In *Marxism and the Metropolis,* edited by William Tabb and Larry Sawers. New York: Oxford University Press, 1984.

Friedmann, John. "Life Space and Economic Space." Manuscript, Los Angeles: UCLA, 1981. Quoted in Bluestone and Harrison, *The Deindustrialization of America.*

Friendly, Fred W. *Due to Circumstances beyond Our Control.* New York: Random House, 1967.

Friesema, Paul. "Black Control of Central Cities: The Hollow Prize." *Journal of the American Institute of Planners* 35 (March 1969).

Frisch, Michael. *Town into City.* Cambridge, Mass.: Harvard University Press, 1964.

Froebel, Folker; Heinrichs, Jurgen; and Kreye, Otto. *The New International Division of Labor.* Cambridge, England: Cambridge University Press, 1980.

Fuchs, Esther, and Shapiro, Robert. "Government Performance as a Basis for Machine Support." *Urban Affairs Quarterly* 18 (June 1983).

Fuchs, Victor. *Changes in the Location of Manufacturing in the United States Since 1929.* New Haven, Conn.: Yale University Press, 1962.

Fuguitt, Glenn; Voss, Paul; and Doherty, J. C. *Growth and Change in Rural America.* Madison: University of Wisconsin Press, 1979.

Furlong, William. "Manipulating the News." *TV Guide,* June 11, 1977.

Galvin, John. *Twelve Mayors of Boston, 1900–1970.* Boston: Boston Public Library, 1970.

Gans, Herbert. *Deciding What's News.* Boston: Beacon Press, 1970.

Gans, Herbert. *The Urban Villagers.* New York: Free Press, 1962.

Ganz, Alexander. *Our Large Cities: New Light on Their Recent Transformations.* Cambridge, Mass.: Massachusetts Institute of Technology Laboratory for Environmental Studies, 1972.

George, Claude. *The History of Management Thought.* Englewood Cliffs, N.J.: Prentice-Hall, 1968.

Gifford, Bernard. "New York City and Cosmopolitan Liberalism." *Political Science Quarterly* 93 (Winter 1978–79).

Ginsburg, Sigmund. "The New York City Administrator." *National Civic Review* 64 (October 1975).

Gist, Noel, and Fava, Sylvia Fleis. *Urban Society.* New York: Crowell, 1974.

Gitlin, Todd. "When the Right Talks, TV Listens." *Nation,* October 15, 1983.

Gitlin, Todd. *The Whole World Is Watching.* Berkeley: University of California Press, 1980.

Glaab, Charles, and Brown, Theodore A. *A History of Urban America.* New York: Macmillan, 1976.

Glazier, Willard. *Peculiarities of American Cities.* New York: Ferguson, 1885.

Glendening, Parris, and Atkins, Patricia. "City-County Consolidations: New Visions for the Eighties." *Municipal Yearbook, 1980.* Washington D.C.: International City Managers' Association, 1980.

Gluck, Peter, and Meister, Richard. *Cities in Transition.* New York: New Viewpoints, 1979.

Goldenberg, Edie. *Making the Papers.* Lexington, Mass.: Lexington Books, 1975.

Goldfield, David, and Brownell, Blaine. *Urban America: From Downtown to No Town.* Boston: Houghton Mifflin, 1979.

Goldsmith, William. "Bringing the Third World Home." In *Sunbelt/Snowbelt,* edited by Larry Sawers and William Tabb. New York: Oxford University Press, 1984.

Goodnow, Frank. *City Government in the United States.* New York: Century, 1904.

Goodnow, Frank. *Politics and Administration.* New York: Macmillan, 1900.

Gordon, Daniel. "Immigrants and Urban Governmental Reforms in American Cities, 1933–1960." *American Journal of Sociology* 74 (September 1968).

Gordon, David. "Capital Development and the History of American Cities." In *Marxism and the Metropolis,* edited by William Tabb and Larry Sawers. New York: Oxford University Press, 1978.

Gordon, David, ed. *Problems in Political Economy.* Lexington, Mass.: D C Heath, 1977.

Gosnell, Harold. *Machine Politics: Chicago Model.* Chicago: University of Chicago Press, 1934 and 1968.

Graber, Doris. *Mass Media and American Politics.* Washington, D.C.: Congressional Quarterly Press, 1989.

Graber, Doris. *Processing the News.* White Plains, N.Y.: Longman, 1988.

Gramlich, Edward. "Intergovernmental Grants: A Review of the Literature." In *The Political Economy of Fiscal Federalism,* edited by Warren Oates. Lexington, Mass.: Lexington Books, 1979.

Grant, Madison. *The Passing of the Great Race.* New York: Scribner's, 1921.

Grant, Robert. *The Black Man Comes to the City.* Chicago: Nelson-Hall, 1972.

Graves, W. Brooke. *American Intergovernmental Relations.* New York: Scribner's, 1964.

Greeley, Andrew. *Ethnicity in the United States.* New York: Wiley, 1974.

Greenberg, Edward S. *The American Political System.* Boston: Little, Brown, 1983.

Greenhut, M. L., and Colberg, M. R. *Factors in the Location of Florida Industry.* Tallahassee: Florida State University Press, 1962.

Greenstone, J. David, and Peterson, Paul. *Race and Authority in Urban Politics.* New York: Sage, 1973.

Griffith, Ernest. *History of American City Government.* New York: Praeger, 1974.

Gutman, Herbert. "Work, Culture, and Society in Industrializing America, 1815–1919." *American Historical Review* 78 (June 1973).

Haber, Samuel. *Efficiency and Uplift.* Chicago: University of Chicago Press, 1964.

Hadden, Jeffrey; Masotti, Louis; and Thiessen, Victor. "Making of the Negro Mayors, 1967." *Transaction* 5 (January/February 1968).

Hagan, Duane; Ahlburg, Dennis; and Shapiro, Morton. In *Hospital and Community Psychiatry.* (May 1983).

Haider, Donald. "Fiscal Scarcity: A New Urban Perspective." In *The New Urban Politics,* edited by Louis Massotti and Robert Lineberry. Cambridge, Mass.: Ballinger, 1976.

Haider, Donald. "The New York City Congressional Delegation." *City Almanac,* March, 1973.

Haider, Donald. *When Governments Come to Washington: Governors, Mayors, and Intergovernmental Lobbying.* New York: Free Press, 1974.

Hall, W. Clayton, and Vander Porten, Bruce. "Unionization, Monopsony Power, and Police Salaries." *Industrial Relations* 16 (February 1977).

Hamber, Susan Blackwell. "Participation, Political Structure and Concurrence." *American Political Science Review* 69 (December 1975).

Hamilton, Alexander. *The Federalist Papers.* Edited by Clinton Rossiter. New York: New American Library, 1961.

Hamilton, Charles V. "The Patron-Recipient Relationship and Minority Politics." *Political Science Quarterly* 94 (Summer 1979).

Hamilton, Charles V. "Political Costs of Participation." In *Urban Governance and Minorities,* edited by Herrington Bryce. New York: Praeger, 1976.

Hamilton, Charles V. "Racial, Ethnic, and Social Class Politics and Administration." *Public Administration Review* 24 (October 1972).

Hamilton, H. C. "The Negro Leaves the South." *Demography* 1 (January 1964).

Hamilton, Howard. "The Municipal Voter." *American Political Science Review* 65 (December 1971).

Hamilton, Richard. *Class and Politics in the United States.* New York: Wiley, 1972.

Hanrahan, John. *Government for Sale.* Washington, D.C.: American Federation of State, County, and Municipal Employees, 1977.

Harrell, Charles, and Weiford, D. G. "The City Manager and the Policy Process." *Public Administration Review* 18 (Spring 1959).

Harrigan, John. *Political Change in the Metropolis.* Boston: Little, Brown, 1985.

Harrigan, John, and Johnson, William. *Governing the Twin Cities Region.* Minneapolis: University of Minnesota Press, 1978.

Harrington, Michael. "The Betrayal of the Poor." *Atlantic,* January, 1970.

Harrison, Bennett, and Bluestone, Barry. "The Incidence and Regulation of Plant Closings." In *Sunbelt /Snowbelt,* edited by Larry Sawers and William Tabb. New York: Oxford University Press, 1984.

Hatch, Roger, and Watkins, Frank, eds. *Reverend Jesse L. Jackson: Straight from the Heart.* Philadelphia: Fortress, 1987.

Hatry, Harry. *How Effective Are Your Community Services?* Washington, D.C.: The Urban Institute, 1977.

Hatry, Harry. "Measuring the Quality of Public Services." In *Improving Urban Management,* edited by Willis Hawley and David Rogers. Beverly Hills, Calif.: Sage, 1976.

Hawkins, Brett. *Politics and Urban Policies.* Indianapolis: Bobbs-Merrill, 1971.

Hays, Samuel. "The Politics of Reform in Municipal Government." In *Social Change and Urban Politics,* edited by Daniel Gordon. Englewood Cliffs, N.J.: Prentice-Hall, 1973.

Hays, Samuel. "The Politics of Reform in Municipal Government in the Progressive Era." In *Urban Politics: Past, Present and Future,* edited by Harlan Hahn and Charles Levine. White Plains, N.Y.: Longman, 1980.

Heady, Ferrel. *Public Administration: A Comparative Perspective.* Englewood Cliffs, N.J.: Prentice-Hall, 1966.

Hech, C. J. "Contracting Municipal Services: Does It Really Cost Less?" *National Civic Review* 72 (June 1983).

Heclo, Hugh. *A Government of Strangers.* Washington, D.C.: Brookings Institution, 1977.

Hedlund, Ronald; Freeman, Patricia; Hamm, Keith; and Stein, Robert. "The Electability of Women Candidates." *Journal of Politics* 41 (May 1979).

Helig, Peggy, and Mundt, Robert. *Your Voice at City Hall.* Albany, N.Y.: SUNY Press, 1984.

Henretta, James. "Economic Development and Social Structure in Colonial Boston." *William and Mary Quarterly* 22 (January 1965).

Henry, Charles P. "The Political Role of the Bad Nigger." *Journal of Black Studies* 2 (June 1981).

Henson, M. Dale, and King, James. "The Atlanta Public-Private Romance." In *Public-Private Partnership in America,* edited by R. Scott Foster and Renée Berger. Lexington, Mass.: Lexington Books, 1982.

Hentoff, Nat. *A Political Life: The Education of John V. Lindsay.* New York: Knopf, 1969.

Herbers, John. *The New Heartland: America's Flight beyond the Suburbs and How It Is Changing Our Future.* New York: Times Books, 1986.

Hershkowitz, Leo. *Tweed's New York.* Garden City, N.J.: Anchor Books, 1978.

Herson, Lawrence. "Pilgrim's Progress." *Political Science and State and Local Government.* Washington, D.C.: American Political Science Association, 1973.

Herson, Lawrence, and Bolland, John. *The Urban Web.* Chicago: Nelson-Hall, 1990.

Hessler, Iola. *29 Ways to Govern a City.* Cincinnati: Hamilton County Research Foundation, 1966.

Higham, John. *Strangers in the Land*. New York: Atheneum, 1963.

Hilaski, Harvey. "Unutilized Manpower in Poverty Areas of Six Major Cities." *Monthly Labor Review* 91 (August 1968).

Hill, Melvin, Jr. "The Little Hatch Acts." *State Government*. 48 (Autumn 1979).

Hirsch, Werner. "Cost Functions of the Urban Government Service." *Review of Economics and Statistics* 47 (February 1965).

Hirschfield, Robert; Swanson, Bert; and Blank, Blanche. "A Profile of Political Activists in Manhattan." *Western Political Quarterly* 15 (September 1962).

Hofstadter, Richard. *The Age of Reform*. New York: Knopf, 1955.

Hofstadter, Richard. *Social Darwinism in American Thought*. Rev. ed. New York: George Braziller, 1955.

Hogan, Lloyd. "Blacks and the American Economy." *Current History* 67 (November 1974).

Holden, Bob. "Kucinich's New Urban Populism." *Seven Days,* March 16, 1979.

Holli, Melvin. *Reform in Detroit*. New York: Oxford University Press, 1969.

Holli, Melvin. "Urban Reform in the Progressive Era." In *The Progressive Era*, edited by Louis Gould. Syracuse, N.Y.: University of Syracuse Press, 1974.

Hoover, Edgar, and Vernon, Raymond. *Anatomy of a Metropolis*. Garden City, N.Y.: Anchor Books, 1959.

Horgan, Robert. "City Council Decisions." *Nation's Cities* 2 (September 1972).

Horton, Raymond. "Municipal Labor Relations." *Social Science Quarterly* 52 (December 1971).

Howard, A. E. "The Press in Court." *Wilson Quarterly* 6 (Special Issue 1982).

Howard, Bruce. "The Advertising Council." *Ramparts* (December 1974/January 1975).

Huckshorn, Robert, and Young, C. E. "A Study of Voting Splits on City Councils in Los Angeles County." *Western Political Quarterly* 13 (June 1960).

Hughes, James. *Suburbanization Dynamics and the Future of the City*. New Brunswick, N.J.: Center for Urban Policy Research, 1974.

Hughes, Langston. *The Panther and the Lash*. New York: Knopf, 1951.

Hulteng, James. *The Messenger's Motives*. Englewood Cliifs, N.J.: Prentice-Hall, 1985.

Hunter, Floyd. *Community Power Structure*. Chapel Hill: University of North Carolina Press, 1953.

Hutchins, Matthew, and Sigelman, Lee. "Black Employment in State and Local Government." *Social Science Quarterly* 62 (March 1981).

Iacocca, Lee. *Iacocca: An Autobiography*. New York: Bantam, 1984.

Jackson, Kenneth T. "Metropolitan Government versus Suburban Autonomy." In *Cities in American History,* edited by Kenneth Jackson and Stanley Schultz. New York: Knopf, 1972.

Jacobs, Jane. *The Economy of Cities*. New York: Random House, 1969.

Jacoby, Jake, and Hoyer, Wayne. "Viewers' Miscomprehension of Televised Communications." *Journal of Marketing* 46 (Fall 1982).

Jacoby, Neil. *Corporate Powers and Social Responsibility*. New York: Macmillan, 1973.

Jamieson, Kathleen Hall, and Campbell, Karyn Kohrs. *The Interplay of Influence: Mass Media and Their Publics in News, Advertising, Politics*. Belmont, Calif.: Wadsworth, 1983.

Janowitz, Morris. *The Community Press in an Urban Setting*. Glencoe, Ill.: Free Press, 1954.

Jhabvala, Firdaus. "The Economic Situation of Black People." In *Problems in Political Economy: An Urban Perspective,* edited by David Gordon. Lexington, Mass.: D C Heath, 1977.

Johnson, Michael. "Patrons, Clients, Jobs, and Machines." *American Political Science Review* 73 (June 1979).

Johnstone, John; Slawski, Edward; and Bowman, William. *The Newspeople.* Champaign: University of Illinois Press, 1976.

Jones, Bryan. *Governing Urban America: A Policy Focus.* Boston: Little, Brown, 1983.

Jones, Bryan. *Service Delivery in the City.* White Plains, N.Y.: Longman, 1980.

Jones, Bryan, and Bachelor, Lynn. "Local Policy Discretion and the Corporate Surplus." In *Urban Economic Development,* edited by Richard Bingham and John Blair. Beverly Hills, Calif.: Sage, 1984.

Jones, Bryan, and Bachelor, Lynn. *The Sustaining Hand.* Lawrence: University of Kansas Press, 1986.

Jones, Bryan, and Kaufman, Clifford. "The Distribution of Urban Public Services." *Administration and Society* 6 (November 1974).

Jones, Mack. "Black Political Empowerment in Atlanta." *Annals of the American Academy of Political and Social Sciences* 439 (September 1978).

Jones, Victor. "Local Government Organization in Metropolitan Areas." In *The Future of Cities and Urban Redevelopment,* edited by Coleman Woodbury. Chicago: University of Chicago Press, 1953.

Judd, Dennis. *The Politics of American Cities.* Boston: Little, Brown, 1988.

Judd, Dennis. "Urban Revitalization." In *The Changing Structure of the City,* edited by Gary Tobin. Beverly Hills, Calif.: Sage, 1979.

Judd, Dennis, and Ready, Randy. "Entrepreneural Cities and the New Politics of Economic Development." In *Reagan and the Cities,* edited by George Peterson and Carol Lewis. Washington, D.C.: The Urban Institute, 1986.

Kahane, Howard. *Logic and Contemporary Rhetoric.* Belmont, Calif.: Wadsworth, 1980.

Kammerer, Gladys. *City Managers in Politics.* Gainesville: University of Florida Press, 1962.

Kammerer, Gladys. "Role Diversity of City Managers." *Administrative Science Quarterly* 8 (March 1964).

Kantor, Paul, and Stephen, David. *The Dependent City.* Glenview, Ill.: Scott, Foresman, 1988.

Karnig, Albert. "Black Representation on City Councils." *Urban Affairs Quarterly* 12 (December 1976).

Karnig, Albert. "Private-Regarding Policy, Civil Rights Groups, and the Mediating Impact of Municipal Reforms." *American Journal of Political Science* 19 (February 1975).

Karnig, Albert, and Walters, B. Oliver. "Decline in Municipal Turnout." *American Politics Quarterly* 11 (October 1983).

Karnig, Albert, and Welch, Susan. *Black Representation and Urban Politics.* Chicago: University of Chicago Press, 1981.

Karnig, Albert, and Welch, Susan. "Sex and Ethnic Differences in Municipal Representation." *Social Science Quarterly* 60 (December 1976).

Kasarda, John. "Caught in the Web of Change." *Society* 21 (November/December 1983).

Kasarda, John. "Urban Change and Minority Opportunities." In *New Urban Reality,* edited by Paul Peterson. Washington, DC.: Brookings Institution, 1985.

Katznelson, Ira. *City Trenches.* Chicago: University of Chicago Press, 1981.

Katznelson, Ira. "Uni-Directional Political Relationships." In *Theoretical Perspectives on Urban Politics,* edited by W. D. Hawley. Englewood Cliffs, N. J.: Prentice-Hall, 1976.

Katznelson, Ira, and Kessleman, Mark. *The Politics of Power.* New York: Harcourt Brace Jovanovich, 1975.

Kaufman, Herbert. "Bureaucrats and Organized Civil Servants." In *Governing the City,* edited by Robert Connery and Demetrios Caraley. New York: Academy of Political Science, 1969.

Kaufman, Herbert. "Emerging Conflicts in the Doctrine of Public Administration." *American Political Science Review* 50 (December 1956).

Kessel, John. "Governmental Structure and Political Environment." *American Political Science Review* 56 (September 1962).

Kessner, Tom. *The Golden Door.* New York: Oxford University Press, 1977.

Kheel, Theodore. "A Strategy for Survival. *New York Magazine,* September 1, 1975.

Klappner, Joseph. *The Effects of Mass Communication.* New York: Free Press, 1960.

Kleniewski, Nancy. "From Industrial to Corporate City: The Role of Urban Renewal." In *Marxism and the Metropolis,* edited by William Tabb and Larry Sawers. New York: Oxford University Press, 1978.

Klevit, Alan. "City Councils and Their Functions in Local Government." *Municipal Year Book 1972.* Washington, D.C.: International City Managers' Association, 1972.

Kline, Mary Jo, ed. *Alexander Hamilton.* New York: Harper & Row, 1973.

Knauss, Peter. *Chicago: A One-Party State.* Champaign, Ill.: Stirpes, 1972.

Koehler, Cortus. "Policy Development and Legislative Oversight in Council Manager Cities." *Public Administration Review* 33 (September/October 1973).

Koehler, David, and Wrightson, Margaret. "Inequality in the Delivery of Urban Services." *Journal of Politics* 49 (February 1987).

Kolko, Gabriel. *Wealth and Power in America.* New York: Praeger, 1972.

Kotter, John, and Lawrence, Paul. *Mayors in Action.* New York: Wiley, 1974.

Kousser, Morgan J. "The Undermining of the First Reconstruction." In *Minority Vote Dilution,* edited by Chandler Davidson. Washington, D.C.: Howard University Press, 1984.

Kraus, Sidney, and Davis, Dennis. *The Effects of Mass Communication on Political Behavior.* University Park: Pennsylvania State University Press, 1976.

Krefetz, Sharon Perlman. *Welfare Policy Making and City Politics.* New York: Praeger, 1976.

Kuo, Wen. "Mayoral Influence on Urban Policy Making." *American Journal of Sociology* 79 (November 1973).

Kuznik, Frank. "Divide and Conquer." *Common Cause Magazine,* May/June 1989.

Kweder, B. James. *The Roles of Manager, Mayor and Councilmen in Policy Making.* Chapel Hill: University of North Carolina Press, 1965.

Kweit, Mary Grisez, and Kweit, Robert. *Implementing Citizen Participation in a Bureaucratic State.* New York: Praeger, 1981.

Kweit, Robert, and Kweit, Mary Grisez. *People and Politics in Urban America.* Pacific Grove, Calif.: Brooks-Cole, 1990.

Ladd, Everett. *The American Polity.* New York: Norton, 1985.

Lakeman, E. *How Democracies Vote: A Study of Majority and Proportional Electoral Systems.* London: Faber and Faber, 1974.

Lambeth, Edmund. *Committed Journalism: An Ethic for the Profession.* Bloomington: Indiana University Press, 1986.

Lane, Robert. *Political Life.* Glencoe, Ill.: Free Press, 1959.

Larson, Calvin, and Nikkel, Stan. *Urban Problems: Perspectives on Corporations, Governments, and Cities.* Boston: Allyn and Bacon, 1979.

Laska, Shirley Broadway, and Spain, Daphne, eds. *Back to the City.* New York: Pergamon, 1980.

Latham, Earl. "The Group Basis of Politics." *American Political Science Review* 46 (June 1952).

Lazarsfield, Paul; Berelson, Bernard; and Gaudet, Hazel. *The People's Choice.* New York: Columbia University Press, 1948.

Lehman, Nicholas. *The Promised Land.* New York: Knopf, 1990.

LeLoup, Lance. *Budgetary Politics.* Brunswick, Ohio: King's Court, 1977.

Leo, Ray, and Gleason, Bill. *Daley of Chicago.* New York: Simon and Schuster, 1970.

Levine, Charles. "Economic Maturity and the Metropolis' Evolving Physical Form." In *The Changing Structure of the City,* edited by Gary Tobin. Beverly Hills, Calif.: Sage, 1979.

Levine, Charles. "More on Cutback Management." *Public Administration Review* 39 (March–April 1979).

Levine, Charles. "Organizational Decline and Cutback Management." *Public Administration Review* 38 (July–August 1978).

Levine, Charles. *The Politics of Retrenchment.* Beverly Hills, Calif.: Sage, 1981.

Levine, Charles. *Racial Conflict and the American Mayors.* Lexington, Mass.: Lexington Books, 1974.

Levitas, Mitchell. "Homelessness in America." *New York Times Magazine,* June 10, 1990.

Levy, Frank S.; Meltsner, Arnold; and Wildavsky, Aaron. *Urban Outcomes: Schools, Streets, and Libraries.* Berkeley: University of California Press, 1974.

Levy, Paul, and McGrath, Dennis. "Saving Cities for Whom? *Social Policy* 10 (November/December 1979).

Lewin, David; Horton, Raymond; and Kuhn, James. *Collective Bargaining and Manpower Utilization in Big City Governments.* Montclair, N.J.: Allenheld and Osmund, 1979.

Lewis, Eugene. *The Urban Political System.* Hinsdale, Ill.: Dryden, 1973.

Lichty, Lawrence, and Topping, Malachi. *American Broadcasting.* New York: Hastings House, 1975.

Lindbloom, Charles. "The Market as a Prison." *Journal of Politics* 44 (May 1982).

Lindbloom, Charles. *Politics and Markets.* New York: Basic Books, 1977.

Lindsay, John. *The City.* New York: New American Library, 1970.

Lineberry, Robert. *Equality and Urban Policy.* Beverly Hills, Calif.: Sage, 1977.

Lineberry, Robert, and Fowler, Edmund. "Reformism and Public Policy in American Cities." *American Political Science Review* 61 (September 1967).

Lineberry, Robert, and Sharansky, Ira. *Urban Politics and Public Policy.* New York: Harper & Row, 1978.

Lipsky, Michael. "Protest as a Political Resource. *American Political Science Review* 63 (December 1968).

Lipsky, Michael. "Street-Level Bureaucracy and the Analysis of Urban Reform." In *Urban Politics: Past, Present, Future,* edited by Harlan Hahn and Charles Levine. White Plains, N.Y.: Longman, 1980.

Lipton, Gregory. "Evidence of Central City Revival." *Journal of the American Institute of Planners* 45 (April 1977).

Lockard, Duane. *The Politics of State and Local Government.* New York: Macmillan, 1963.

Locke, John. "Second Treatise on Civil Government." In *Locke on Politics, Religion, and Education,* edited by Maurice Cranston. New York: Collier, 1965.

Lockwood, Charles. "Gangs, Crime, Smut, Violence." *New York Times,* September 20, 1990.

Longbein, Laura Irvin. *Discovering Whether Programs Work.* Santa Monica, Calif.: Goodyear, 1980.

Lorch, Robert. *State and Local Politics: The Great Entanglement.* Englewood Cliffs, N.J.: Prentice-Hall, 1983.

Lovell, Catherine. *Federal and State Mandating on Local Governments.* National Science Foundation, Contract No. NSF/RA-790138. Washington, D.C., 1979.

Lovell, Catherine, and Tobin, Charles. "Mandating—A Key Issue for Cities." *Municipal Yearbook, 1980.* Washington, D.C.: International City Managers' Association, 1980.

Lovell, Catherine, and Tobin, Charles. "The Mandating Issue." *Public Administration Review* 41 (May/June 1981).

Loveridge, Ronald. *City Managers in Legislative Politics.* Indianapolis: Bobbs-Merrill, 1971.

Lowe, Jeanne. *Cities in a Race with Time.* New York: Random House, 1967.

Lowi, Theodore. *At the Pleasure of the Mayor: Patronage and Power in New York City, 1898–1958.* New York: Free Press, 1964.

Lowi, Theodore. *The End of Liberalism.* New York: Norton, 1969.

Lowi, Theodore. "Machine Politics—Old and New." In *Urban Politics,* edited by Harlan Hahn and Herbert Levine. White Plains, N.Y.: Longman, 1980.

Lubin, Roger. "How Should Managers Be Paid?" *Public Management* 63 (1981).

Lubove, Roy. *The Progressives and the Slums.* Pittsburgh: University of Pittsburgh Press, 1962.

Lyford, Joseph. *The Airtight Case.* New York: Harper & Row, 1966.

Lyons, William. "Reform and Response in American Cities." *Social Science Quarterly* 59 (June 1978).

Lyons, William, and Morgan, David. "The Impact of Intergovernmental Revenue on City Expenditures." *Journal of Politics* 39 (1977).

Mack, Raymond. "Economic Factors in an Industrial Shop." *Social Forces* 32 (May 1954).

Madison, James. "Federalist Paper #10." In *The Federalist Papers,* edited by Clinton Rossiter. New York: New American Library, 1961.

Main, Jackson Turner. *The Social Structure of Revolutionary America.* Princeton, N.J.: Princeton University Press, 1965.

Mandel, Ernest. *Late Capitalism.* London: New Left Books, 1975.

Mandelbaum, Semour. *Boss Tweed's New York.* New York: Wiley, 1955.

Manley, John. "Neo-Pluralism." *American Political Science Review* 77 (June 1983).

Manning, Peter, and Van Maaven, John, eds. *Policing: A View from the Street.* Santa Monica, Calif.: Goodyear, 1978.

Mansbridge, Jane. *Beyond Adversarial Democracy.* New York: Basic Books, 1980.

Marable, Manning. *How Capitalism Underdeveloped Black America.* Boston: South End Press, 1983.

Marshall, Harvey, and Lewis, Bonnie. "Back to the City." *Journal of Urban Affairs* 4 (Winter 1982).

Marx, Karl. Preface to "A Contribution to the Critique of Political Economy." Quoted in Robert Tucker, ed. *The Marx-Engels Reader.* New York: Norton, 1978.

Marx, Karl. *Das Kapital.* Edited by Frederick Engels. Moscow: Progress Publishers, 1965.

Marx, Karl. *The Grundrisse.* Translated by Martin Nicolaus. Baltimore: Penguin, 1973.

Marx, Karl. *The Poverty of Philosophy.* Edited by Frederick Engels. Moscow: Progress Publishers, 1966.

Marx, Karl, and Engels, Frederick. *Articles from the Nene Rheinische.* Translated by S. Rvazanskava, edited by B. Isaacs. Moscow: Progress Publishers, 1964.

Marx, Karl, and Engels, Frederick. *The German Ideology.* Translated and edited by S. Rvazanskava, Moscow: Progress Publishers, 1964.

Masotti, Louis, and Corsi, Jerome. *Shoot-Out in Cleveland.* Washington, D.C.: Government Printing Office, 1969.

Massey, Douglas, and Denton, Nancy. "Hypersegregation in United States Metropolitan Areas." *Demography* 26 (August 1989).

Massey, Douglas, and Denton, Nancy. "Trends in Residential Segregation of Blacks, Hispanics, and Asians, 1920–1980." *American Sociological Review* 52 (December 1987).

Massey, Douglas, and Eggers, Mitchell. "The Ecology of Inequality." *American Journal of Sociology* 96 (March 1990).

McCafferey, Jerry. "The Impact of Resource Scarcity on Urban Public Finance." *Public Administration Review* 41 (January 1981).

McGinniss, Joe. *The Selling of the President, 1968.* New York: Trident Press, 1969.

McKelvey, Blake. *American Urbanization.* Glenview, Ill.: Scott, Foresman, 1973.

McKelvey, Blake. *The Urbanization of America, 1860–1915.* New Brunswick, N.J.: Rutgers University Press, 1963.

McKenzie, Roderick. *The Metropolitan Community.* New York: McGraw-Hill, 1933.

McLellan, David. *The Thought of Karl Marx.* New York: Harper & Row, 1971.

McManus, Susan. "A City's First Female Officeholder: Coattails for Future Female Office Seekers." *Western Political Quarterly* 34 (March 1981).

McMurtry, John. *The Structure of Marx's World View.* Princeton, N.J.: Princeton University Press, 1978.

McQuail, Denis. "The Influence and Effects of Mass Communication." In *Mass Communication and Society,* edited by James Curran, Michael Gurevitch, and Janet Woolacott. New York: Sage, 1977.

Meier, August, and Rudwick, Elliott. *From Plantation to Ghetto.* New York: Hill and Wang, 1969.

Menchik, Paul. *Conference on Research in Income and Wealth.* New York: National Bureau of Economic Research, 1979.

Mendelsohn, Harold, and Crespi, Irving. *Polls, Television and the New Politics.* Scranton, Pa.: Chandler, 1970.

Mermelstein, David. "Austerity, Planning, and the Socialist Alternative." In *The Fiscal Crisis of the American Cities,* edited by Roger Alcaly and David Mermelstein. New York: Vintage, 1977.

Merrill, John, and Barney, Ralph. *Ethics and the Press.* New York: Hastings, 1975.

Merritt, Sharyne. "Winners and Losers: Sex Differences in Municipal Elections." *American Journal of Political Science* 21 (November 1977).

Merton, Robert. "Bureaucratic Structure and Personality." *Social Forces* 18 (May 1940).

Merton, Robert. "The Latent Function of the Machine." In *Urban Government,* edited by Edward Banfield. New York: Free Press, 1969.

Merton, Robert, ed. *Social Theory and Social Structure.* New York: Free Press, 1957.

Meyers, Marvin, ed. *The Mind of the Founder.* Indianapolis: Bobbs-Merrill, 1973.

Michels, Robert. *Political Parties.* Glencoe, Ill.: Free Press, 1949.

Milbraith, Lester, and Goel, M. L. *Political Participation.* Chicago: Rand McNally, 1977.

Miliband, Ralph. *The State in Capitalist Society.* New York: Basic Books, 1969.

Miller, Arthur; Goldenberg, Edie; and Erbring, Lutz. "Type-Set Politics." *American Political Science Review* 73 (March 1979).

Miller, Gary. *Cities by Contract.* Cambridge, Mass.: MIT Press, 1981.

Miller, William. *Mr. Crump of Memphis.* Baton Rouge: Louisiana State University Press, 1964.

Miller, Zane. "Boss Cox's Cincinnati: A Study in Urbanization and Politics. *Journal of American History* 54 (March 1968).

Miller, Zane. *The Urbanization of Modern America.* New York: Harcourt Brace Jovanovich, 1973.

Mills, C. Wright. *The Power Elite.* New York: Oxford University Press, 1956.

Mills, Edwin S. *Urban Economics.* Glenview, Ill.: Scott, Foresman, 1972.

Mladenka, Kenneth. "Blacks and Hispanics in Urban Politics." *American Political Science Review* 83 (January 1989).

Mladenka, Kenneth. "Citizen Demand and Bureaucratic Response." *Urban Affairs Quarterly* 12 (March 1977).

Mladenka, Kenneth. "Organizational Rules, Service Equality and Distributional Decisions in Urban Politics." *Social Science Quarterly* 59 (June 1978).

Mladenka, Kenneth, and Hill, Kim. "The Distribution of Benefits in an Urban Environment." *Urban Affairs Quarterly* 13 (September 1977).

Mohl, Raymond. "Poverty in Early America." *New York History* 50 (January 1969).

Mollenkopf, John H. *The Contested City.* Princeton, N.J.: Princeton University Press, 1983.

Mollenkopf, John. "The Crisis of the Public Sector in American Cities." In *The Fiscal Crisis of the American Cities,* edited by Roger Alcaly and David Mermelstein. New York: Vintage, 1977.

Moore, Joan. *Mexican-Americans.* Englewood Cliffs, N.J.: Prentice-Hall, 1971.

Moore, John. "From Dreamers to Doers." *National Journal,* February 13, 1988.

Morando, Vincent. "City-County Consolidation." *Western Political Quarterly* 32 (December 1979).

Morando, Vincent. "The Politics of City-County Consolidation." *National Civic Review* 64 (February 1975).

Morando, Vincent, and Thomas, Robert. *The Forgotten Governments.* Gainesville: University of Florida Press, 1977.

Morgan, David. *Managing Urban America.* Pacific Grove, Calif.: Brooks-Cole, 1989.

Morgan, David. "Political Linkage and Public Policy: Attitudinal Congruence between Citizens and Officials." *Western Political Quarterly* 26 (June 1973).

Morlan, Robert. "Life on the City Council." In *Politics in California,* edited by Robert Morlan and Leroy Hardy. Belmont, Calif.: Dickenson Publishing Company, 1968.

Morrison, Samuel. *The Oxford History of the American People.* New York: Oxford University Press, 1965.

Mowny, George. *The Era of Theodore Roosevelt 1900–1912.* New York: Harper & Row, 1958.

Moynihan, Daniel Patrick. *Maximum Feasible Misunderstanding.* New York: Free Press, 1969.

Mueller, Claus. *The Politics of Communication.* London: Oxford University Press, 1973.

Mumford, Lewis. *The City in History.* New York: Harcourt Brace, 1961.

Murphy, Russell. "Whither the Mayors?" *Journal of Politics* 42 (February 1980).

Myers, Gustavus. *The History of Tammany Hall.* New York: Boni and Liveright, 1917.

Napolitan, Joseph. *The Election Game and How to Win It.* Garden City, N.Y.: Doubleday, 1972.

Nathan, Richard, and Adams, Charles. "Four Perspectives on Urban Hardship." *Political Science Quarterly* 104 (Fall 1989).

National Advisory Commission on Civil Disorders. *Report.* New York: Bantam Books, 1968.

National Commission of Urban Problems. *Building the American City.* New York: Praeger, 1969.

National Municipal League. *Model City Charter.* Chicago: National Municipal League, 1961.

Nelson, William, Jr. "Black Mayoral Leadership." In *Black Electoral Politics,* edited by Lucius Barker. New Brunswick, N.J.: Transaction, 1990.

Nelson, William, Jr. "Black Mayors as Urban Managers. *Annals of the American Academy of Political and Social Sciences* 439 (September 1978).

Newfield, Jack, and DuBrul, Paul. *The Permanent Government.* New York: Pilgrim Press, 1981.

Newton, Edmund. "Taking Over City Hall." *Black Enterprise* 13 (June 1983).

Newton, Kenneth. "Feeble Governments and Private Power." In *The New Urban Politics,* edited by Louis Masotti and Robert Lineberry. Cambridge, Mass.: Ballinger, 1976.

Nice, David. *Federalism.* New York: St. Martin's Press, 1987.

Nimmo, Dan. *The Political Persuaders.* Englewood Cliffs, N.J.: Prentice-Hall, 1970.

Nivola, Pietro. "Apocalypse Now?" *Polity* 14 (Spring 1982).

Nivola, Pietro. "Distributing a Municipal Service: A Case Study of Housing Inspection." *Journal of Politics* 40 (February 1978).

Nivola, Pietro. *The Urban Service Problem.* Lexington, Mass.: Lexington Books, 1979.

Noll, Roger; Peck, Merton; and McGowan, John. *Economic Aspects of Television Regulation.* Washington, D C: Brookings Institution, 1973.

Nordlinger, Eric. *Decentralizing the City: A Study of Boston's Little City Halls.* Cambridge, Mass.: MIT Press, 1972.

Noyelle, Thierry. "The Implications of Industrial Restructuring for Spatial Organization in the United States." In *Regional Analysis and the New International Division of Labor,* edited by Frank Moulaert and Pokius Wilson-Salimas. Boston: Kluwer-Nijhoff, 1982.

O'Connor, Edwin. *The Last Hurrah.* Boston: Little, Brown, 1956.

O'Connor, James. *The Fiscal Crisis of the State.* New York: St. Martin's Press, 1973.

Ostrogorski, Moise. *Democracy and the Party System.* New York: Macmillan, 1926.

Ostrom, Elinor. "On the Meaning and Measurement of Efficiency in the Provision of Urban Police Services." *Journal of Criminal Justice* 1 (Summer 1978).

Palen, J. John. *The Urban World.* New York: McGraw-Hill, 1987.

Palen, J. John, and London, Bruce, eds. *Gentrification, Displacement, and Neighborhood Revitalization.* Albany, N.Y.: SUNY Press, 1983.

Paletz, David, and Entman, Robert. *Media Power Politics.* New York: Free Press, 1981.

Paletz, David; Reichert, Peggy; and McIntyre, Barbara. "How the Media Support Local Governmental Authority." *Public Opinion Quarterly* 35 (Spring 1971).

Palley, Marian, and Palley, Howard. *Urban America and Public Policies.* Lexington, Mass.: D C Heath, 1977.

Parenti, Michael. *Democracy for the Few.* New York: St. Martin's Press, 1983.

Parenti, Michael. *Inventing Reality.* New York: St. Martin's Press, 1985.

Parenti, Michael. "Power and Pluralism." *Journal of Politics* 32 (August 1970).

Park, Robert. "The City: Suggestions for the Investigation of Human Behavior in the Environment." *American Journal of Sociology* 20 (March 1916).

Park, Robert; Burgess, Ernest; and McKenzie, Roderick. *The City.* Chicago: University of Chicago Press, 1925.

Parkinson, C. Northcote. *Parkinson's Law and Other Studies in Administration.* Boston: Houghton Mifflin, 1962.

Patterson, Samuel. "Characteristics of Party Leaders." *Western Political Quarterly* 16 (June 1963).

Patterson, Thomas. *The Mass Media Election.* New York: Praeger, 1980.

Patterson, Thomas, and McClure, Robert. *The Unseeing Eye.* New York: Putnam, 1976.

Peirce, Neal. "Industrial Blackmail in the Cities." *L.A. Times,* December 1, 1980.

Peirce, Neal. "Mayor Daley the Younger Has Calmed Chicago." *National Journal,* March 24, 1990.

Perry, David, and Watkins, Alfred. "People, Profit, and the Rise of the Sunbelt Cities." In *The Urban Scene,* edited by Joe Feagin. New York: Random House, 1979.

Perry, Huey. "The Impact of Black Political Participation on Public Sector Employment and Representation on Municipal Boards and Commissions." *Review of Black Political Economy* 12 (1983).

Peters, John, and Welch, Susan. "Political Corruption in America: A Search for Definitions and a Theory." *American Political Science Review* 72 (September 1978).

Peterson, George. "Finance." In *The Urban Predicament,* edited by William Gorham and Nathan Glazer. Washington, D.C.: The Urban Institute, 1976.

Peterson, George. "Transmitting the Municipal Fiscal Squeeze to a New Generation of Taxpayers." In *The Fiscal Crisis of Urban America,* edited by Robert Burchell and David Listokin. New Brunswick: State University of New Jersey Press, 1981.

Peterson, Paul. *City Limits.* Chicago: University of Chicago Press, 1981.

Pettigrew, Thomas. *Racially Separate or Together.* New York: McGraw-Hill, 1971.

Pfiffer, James. "Inflexible Budgets, Fiscal Stress, and the Tax Revolt." In *The Municipal Money Chase,* edited by Albertia Sbragia. Boulder, Colo.: Westview, 1983.

Phillips, Barbara, and LeGates, Richard. *City Lights.* New York: Oxford University Press, 1981.

Phipps, Peter. "How the City Withers Away." *Cleveland Magazine,* June, 1972.

Piven, Frances Fox. "The Urban Crisis: Who Got What and Why." In *Urban Politics and Public Policy,* edited by Stephen David and Paul Peterson. New York: Praeger, 1977.

Piven, Frances Fox, and Cloward, Richard. *Poor Peoples' Movements.* New York: Vintage, 1979.

Piven, Frances Fox, and Cloward, Richard. *Regulating the Poor: The Functions of Public Welfare.* New York: Vintage, 1971.

Piven, Frances Fox, and Cloward, Richard. "The Urban Crisis: Who Got What, When, and Why." In *The Politics of Turmoil,* edited by Frances Fox Piven and Richard Cloward. New York: Pantheon, 1974.

Plotnick, Robert, and Skidmore, Felicity. *Progress Against Poverty.* New York: Academic Press, 1975.

Pohlmann, Marcus. *Black Politics in Conservative America.* White Plains, N.Y.: Longman, 1990.

Pohlmann, Marcus. "The Electoral Impact of Partisanship and Incumbency Reconsidered: An Extension to Low Salience Elections." *Urban Affairs Quarterly* 13 (June 1978).

Pohlmann, Marcus. *Political Power in the Postindustrial City.* New York: Stonehill, 1986.

Polsby, Nelson. *Community Power and Political Theory.* New Haven, Conn.: Yale University Press, 1980.

Porter, Paul. *The Recovery of American Cities.* New York: Sun River, 1976.

Porter, Phillip. *Cleveland, Confused City on a Seesaw.* Columbus: Ohio State University Press, 1976.

Powers, Ron. *The Newscasters.* New York: St. Martin's Press, 1977.

Powledge, Fred. "The Flight from City Hall." *Harper's Magazine,* November 1969.

Pred, Alan. *The Spatial Dynamics of United States Urban-Industrial Growth.* Cambridge, Mass.: Harvard University Press, 1966.

President's Urban and Regional Policy Group Report. *A New Partnership to Preserve America's Communities.* Washington, D.C.: Government Printing Office, March 1979.

Pressman, Jeffrey. "Political Implications of the New Federalism." In *Financing the New Federalism,* edited by Warren Oates. Baltimore: Johns Hopkins University Press, 1975.

Pressman, Jeffrey. "Preconditions of Mayoral Leadership." *American Political Science Review* 66 (June 1972).

Preston, Michael. "Limitations of Black Urban Power: The Case of Black Mayors." In *The New Urban Politics,* edited by Louis Masotti and Robert Lineberry. Cambridge, Mass.: Ballinger, 1976.

Prewitt, Kenneth. "Political Ambition, Volunteerism and Electoral Accountability." *American Political Science Review* 64 (March 1970).

Prewitt, Kenneth, and Nowlin, William. "Political Ambitions and the Behavior of Incumbent Politicians." *Western Political Quarterly* 22 (June 1969).

Prottas, Jeffrey. *People-Processing.* Lexington, Mass.: Lexington Books, 1979.

Prottas, Jeffrey. "The Power of the Street-Level Bureaucrat in Public Service Bureaucracies." *Urban Affairs Quarterly* 13 (March 1978).

Rainwater, Lee. *What Money Buys.* New York: Basic Books, 1974.

Rakove, Milton. *Don't Make No Waves—Don't Back No Losers: An Insider's Analysis of the Daley Machine.* Bloomington: Indiana University Press, 1975.

Range, Peter Ross. "Capital of Black Is Beautiful." *New York Times Magazine,* April 7, 1974.

Raskin, A. H. "The Revolt of the Civil Servants." *Saturday Review,* December 7, 1968.

Reich, Robert. *The Work of Nations.* New York: Knopf, 1990.

Reynolds, David. "Progress Toward Achieving Efficiency and Responsible Political Systems in Urban America." In *Urban Policy Making and Metropolitan Dynamics,* edited by John Adams. Cambridge, Mass.: Ballinger, 1976.

Reynolds, Harry. "The Career Public Service and Statute Lawmaking in Los Angeles." *Western Political Quarterly* 18 (September 1965).

Rich, Richard. *The Politics of Urban Public Services.* Lexington, Mass.: Lexington Books, 1982.

Rich, Wilbur. *Coleman Young and Detroit Politics: From Social Activist to Power Broker.* Detroit: Wayne State University Press, 1989.

Ridley, Charles. *The Role of the City Manager in Policy Formulation.* Chicago: International City Managers' Association, 1958.

Riordan, William. *Plunkitt of Tammany Hall.* New York: Dutton, 1963.

Rivers, William, and Matthews, Cleve. *Ethics for the Media.* Englewood Cliffs, N.J.: Prentice-Hall, 1985.

Roberts, Barbara. *The Dynamic West: A Region in Transition.* Portland, Oreg.: Westrends, 1989.

Roberts, Sam. Labor Looks for Return on Support." *New York Times,* September 3, 1990.

Roberts, Steven V. "He's One of Us." *New York Times Magazine,* February 24,1974.

Robinson, Michael J. "The Media at Mid-Year." *Public Opinion* 3 (June/July 1980).

Robinson, Michael, S. "Public Affairs, Television and the Growth of Media Malaise." *American Political Science Review* 70 (June 1976).

Rogin, Michael. *The Intellectuals and McCarthy.* Cambridge, Mass.: MIT Press, 1967.

Roof, Wade, ed. "Race and Residence in the United States." *Annals of the American Academy of Political and Social Sciences* 441 (January 1979).

Rose, William Gamson. *Cleveland: The Making of a City.* Cleveland: World Publishing, 1950.

Rosenau, James. *Public Opinion and Foreign Policy.* New York: Random House, 1961.

Rosenbloom, David. "The Press and the Local Candidate." *Annals of the American Academy of Political Science* 427 (September 1976).

Rosenthal, Donald, ed. *Urban Revitalization.* Vol. 18, Urban Affairs Annual Reviews. Beverly Hills, Calif.: Sage, 1980.

Roshco, Bernard. *Newsmaking.* Chicago: University of Chicago Press, 1975.

Ross, Bernard, and Stedman, Murray. *Urban Politics.* Itasca, Ill.: Peacock, 1985.

Rossi, Peter. "Between Black and White: The Face of American Institutions in the Ghetto." In National Advisory Commission on Civil Disorders, *Supplementary Studies.* Washington, D.C.: Government Printing Office, 1970.

Rossi, Peter. *Down and Out in America.* Chicago: University of Chicago Press, 1989.

Rossi, Peter. "The Urban Homeless: A Portrait of Urban Dislocation." *Annals of the American Academy of Political and Social Sciences* 501 (January, 1989).

Rourke, Francis. *Bureaucracy, Politics and Public Policy.* Boston: Little, Brown, 1984.

Royko, Mike. *Boss: Richard J. Daley of Chicago.* New York: New American Library, 1971.

Rutter, Laurence. "The Essential Community." *Municipal Year Book 1980.* Washington, D.C.: International City Managers' Association, 1980.

Ryscavage, Paul, and Willacy, Hazel. "Employment of the Nation's Poor." *Monthly Labor Review* 91 (August 1968).

Sacco, John, and Parks, William. "Policy Preferences among Urban Mayors." *Urban Affairs Quarterly* 13 (September 1977).

Sacks, Seymour. "The Cities as the Center of Employment." In *Urban Governance and Minorities,* edited by Herrington Bryce. New York: Praeger, 1976.

Salins, Peter. "The Limits of Gentrification." *New York Affairs* 5, no. 4 (1979): 61.

Salsbury, Robert, and Black, Gordon. "Class and Party in Partisan and Nonpartisan Elections." *American Political Science Review* 67 (September 1973).

Salter, Jo. *Boss Rule.* New York: Whitlessey House, 1957.

Saltzstein, Alan. "Can Urban Management Control the Organized Employee?" *Public Personnel Management* 3 (July–August 1974).

Samuelson, Paul, and Nordhous, William. *Economics.* New York: McGraw-Hill, 1985.

Sanders, Heywood. "The Government of American Cities: Continuity and Change in Structure." *Municipal Yearbook, 1982.* Washington, D.C.: International City Managers' Association, 1982.

Sanders, Heywood. *Voters and Urban Capital Finance.* Unpublished paper presented at the annual meeting of the American Political Science Association, San Francisco, September 1990.

Savas, E. S. "How Much Do Government Services Cost?" *Urban Affairs Quarterly* 15 (September 1979).

Savas, E. S. "Municipal Monopoly." *Harper's Magazine,* December 1971.

Savas, E. S. *Privatizing the Public Sector.* Chatham, N.J.: Chatham House, 1982.

Savas, E. S. "Public vs. Private Refuse Collection." *Journal of Urban Analysis and Public Management* 6 (1979).

Savas, E. S., and Ginsburg, Sigmund. "The Civil Service." *The Public Interest* 32 (Summer 1973).

Sayre, Wallace. "The General Manager Idea for Large Cities." *Public Administration Review* 14 (Fall 1954).

Sayre, Wallace, and Kaufman, Herbert. *Governing New York City.* New York: Norton, 1965.

Sbragia, Alberta. "The 1970's: A Decade of Change in Local Government Finance." In *The Municipal Money Chase,* edited by Alberta Sbragia. Boulder, Colo.: Westview, 1983.

Schattsneider, E. E. *The Semi-Sovereign People.* New York: Holt, Rinehart and Winston, 1960.

Schelling, Thomas. "On the Ecology of Micromotives." *The Public Interest* 25 (Fall 1971).

Schellinger, Mary. "Today's Local Policy Makers: A Council Profile." *Baseline Data Report* 20. Washington, D.C.: International City Managers' Association, July/August 1988.

Schiller, Herbert. *The Mind Managers.* Boston: Beacon Press, 1973.

Schnore, Leo. "Urban Structure and Suburban Selectivity." *Demography* 1 (January 1964).

Schon, Donald. "The Blindness System." *The Public Interest* 18 (Winter 1970).

Schudson, Michael. *Discovering the News.* New York: Basic Books, 1978.

Schultze, Charles; Fried, Edward; Rivlin, Alice; and Teetes, Nancy. *Setting National Priorities: The 1973 Budget.* Adapted in Roger Alcaly and David Mermelstein, eds., *The Fiscal Crisis of American Cities.* New York: Vintage, 1977.

Schultze, William. *Urban Politics.* Englewood Cliffs, N.J.: Prentice-Hall, 1985.

Schwartz, Barry. *The Changing Face of the Suburbs.* Chicago: University of Chicago Press, 1976.

Scott, James. "Corruption, Machine Politics, and Political Change." *American Political Science Review* 63 (December 1969).

Sears, David, and Whitney, Richard. "Political Persuasion." In *Handbook of Communications,* edited by Ithiel de Sola Pool. Chicago: Rand-McNally, 1973.

Selig, John. "The San Francisco Idea." *National Municipal Review* 46 (June 1957).

Senate Subcommittee on Antitrust and Monopoly. *Economic Concentration.* Washington, D.C.: Government Printing Office, 1979.

Shannon, Charles P. "The Rise and Emerging Fall of Metropolitan Area Regional Associations." In *Intergovernmental Relations and Public Policy,* edited by J. Edward Benton and David Morgan. New York: Greenwood, 1986.

Sharp, Elaine. "Citizen-Initiated Contacting of Government Officials and Socio-Economic Status." *American Political Science Review* 76 (March 1982).

Sheatsley, Paul, and Greeley, Andrew. "Attitudes towards Racial Integration." *Scientific American* 238 (June 1978).

Sheehan, Robert. "Proprietors in the World of Big Business." *Fortune,* June, 15, 1967.

Shefter, Martin. "The Emergence of the Political Machine." In *Theoretical Perspectives on Urban Politics,* edited by Willis Hawley. Englewood Cliffs, N.J.: Prentice-Hall, 1976.

Shefter, Martin. "Organizing for Armageddon." Unpublished paper presented at the annual meeting of the American Political Science Association. Washington, D.C., August 1980.

Shevciw, Terry. "Canadian Experience with Metropolitan Government." *Municipal Yearbook, 1973.* Washington, D.C: International City Managers' Association, 1973.

Silbiger, Sara. "Collective Bargaining and the Distribution of Benefits." In *Urban Policy Making,* edited by Dale Rogers Marshall. Beverly Hills, Calif.: Sage, 1979.

Sinchcombe, Jean. *Reform and Reaction.* Belmont, Calif.: Wadsworth, 1968.

Sinclair, Upton. *The Jungle.* New York: Signet, 1906.

Shaw, Lee. "The Development of State and Federal Laws." In *Public Workers and Public Unions,* edited by Sam Zagoria. Englewood Cliffs, N.J.: Prentice-Hall, 1972.

Sheehan, Susan. "Profiles: A Welfare Mother." *New Yorker,* September 29, 1975.

Sheingold, S. *Dislocated Workers.* Washington, D.C.: Budget Office, 1982.

Skogan, Wesley. *Disorder and Decline.* New York: Free Press, 1990..

Smith, Adam. *The Wealth of Nations.* New York: Modern Library, 1937.

Smith, Desmond. "Mining the Golden Spectrum." *Nation,* May 26, 1979.

Smith, James D., and Franklin, Stephen, D. "The Concentration of Wealth, 1922–1969." *American Economic Review* 64 (May 1974).

Sobel, Judith, and Emery, Edwin. "U.S. Dailies' Competition in Relation to Circulation Size." *Journalism Quarterly* 55 (Spring 1978).

Sonenshein, Raphe. "Biracial Coalition Politics in Los Angeles." *PS* 19 (Summer 1986).

Spero, Sterling, and Capozzola, John. *The Urban Community and Its Unionized Bureaucracies.* New York: Dunellen, 1973.

Stanbeck, T. M., and Noyelle, T. J. *Cities in Transition.* Totowa, N.J.: Allanheld and Osman, 1982.

Stanley, David. *Cities in Trouble.* Columbus, Ohio.: Academy for Contemporary Problems, 1976.

Stanley, David. *Managing Local Government under Union Pressure.* Washington, D.C.: Brookings Institution, 1972.

Starks, Robert, and Preston, Michael. "Harold Washington and the Politics of Reform in Chicago." In *Racial Politics in American Cities,* edited by Rufus Browning, Dale Rogers Marshall, and David Tabb. White Plains, N.Y.: Longman, 1989.

Starr, Paul, ed. *The Limits of Privatization.* New York: Academy of Political Science, 1987.

Steadman, Murray. "Why Urban Parties Can't Grow." *National Civic Review* 61 (November 1972).

Steffens, Lincoln. *The Autobiography of Lincoln Steffens.* New York: Harcourt Brace Jovanovich, 1931.

Steffens, Lincoln. *The Shame of the Cities.* New York: McClure, Phillips, 1904; reprint New York: Hill and Wang, 1957.

Stein, Lana, and Fleischmann, Arnold. "Newspaper and Business Endorsements in Municipal Elections." *Journal of Urban Affairs* 9 (Fall 1987).

Steinberger, Peter. *Ideology and the Urban Crisis.* Albany, N.Y.: SUNY Press, 1985.

Sterling, Christopher, and Haight, Timothy, eds. *The Mass Media.* New York: Praeger, 1982.

Sternleib, George. "The City as a Sandbox." *Public Interest* 25 (Fall 1971).

Sternleib, George, and Ford, Kristina. "Some Aspects of the Return to the Central City." In *Revitalizing the Cities,* edited by Herrington Bryce. Lexington, Mass.: D C Heath, 1979.

Sternleib, George, and Hughes, James. "Back to the Central City: Myths and Realities." In *America's Housing: Prosperity and Problems,* edited by George Sternleib and James Hughes. New Brunswick, N.J.: Center for Urban Policy Research, 1980.

Sternleib, George, and Hughes, James. *Income and Jobs: USA.* New Brunswick, N.J.: Center for Urban Policy Research, 1984.

Sternleib, George, and Hughes, James. "New Regional and Metropolitan Realities of America. *Journal of American Institute of Planners* 21 (July 1977).

Sternleib, George, and Hughes, James, eds. *Revitalizing the Northeast.* New Brunswick, N.J.: Center for Urban Policy Research, 1978.

Sternleib, George, and Hughes, James. "The Uncertain Future of the Center Cities." *Urban Affairs Quarterly* 18 (June 1983).

Still, Bayard. "Patterns of Mid-Nineteenth Century Urbanization in the Midwest." *Mississippi Valley Historical Review* 28 (September 1941).

Stillman, Richard. *The Modern City Manager.* Washington, D.C.: International City Managers' Association, 1974.

Stipak, Brian. "Citizen Satisfaction with Urban Services." *Public Administration Review* 39 (January/February 1979).

Stokes, Carl. "Cleveland Now." *American City* 84 (September 1968).

Stokes, Carl. *Promises of Power.* New York: Simon and Schuster, 1973.

Stone, Clarence. "Citizens and the New Ruling Coalition." In *Urban Governance and Minorities,* edited by Herrington Bryce. New York: Praeger, 1976.

Stone, Clarence. "Complexity and the Changing Character of Executive Leadership." *Urban Interest* 4 (Fall 1982).

Stone, Clarence. *Regime Politics: Governing Atlanta, 1946–1988.* Lawrence: University of Kansas Press, 1989.

Stone, Clarence, and Stoker, Robert. "Employee Inefficiency in Selected Client Service Bureaucracies." *Journal of Urban Affairs* 6 (Summer 1984).

Stone, Clarence; Whelan, Robert; and Murin, Wiliam. *Urban Policy and Politics in a Bureaucratic Age.* Englewood Cliffs, N.J.: Prentice-Hall, 1986.

Stone, Harold; Price, Don; and Stone, Kathryn. *City-Manager Government in Nine Cities.* Chicago: Public Administration Service, 1940.

Storper, Michael. "Toward a Structural Theory of Industrial Location." In *Industrial Location and Regional Systems,* edited by John Rees, J. D. Geoffrey, and Howard Hewings. Brooklyn: J.F. Bergin, 1981.

Storper, Michael, and Walker, Richard. "The Spatial Division of Labor." In *Sunbelt/Snowbelt,* edited by Larry Sawers and William Tabb. New York: Oxford University Press, 1984.

Svara, James. "Dichotomy and Duality: Reconceptualizing the Relationship between Policy and Administration in Council-Manager Cities." *Public Administration Review* 45 (January/February 1985).

Swanstrom, Todd. *The Crisis of Growth Politics.* Philadelphia: Temple University Press, 1985.

Swerdlow, Joel. "The Decline of the Boys on the Bus." *Washington Journalism Review* 3 (January/February 1981).

Szatmary, David. *Shay's Rebellion: The Making of an Agrarian Insurrection.* Amherst: University of Massachusetts Press, 1980.

Tabb, William. "Economic Democracy and Regional Restructuring: An Internationalization Perspective." In *Sunbelt/Snowbelt,* edited by Larry Sawers and William Tabb. New York: Oxford University Press, 1984.

Tabb, William, and Sawers, Larry, eds. *Marxism and the Metropolis.* New York: Oxford University Press, 1984.

Taebel, Delbert. "Managers and Riots." *National Civic Review* 57 (September 1968).

Taebel, Delbert. "Minority Representation on City Councils." *Social Science Quarterly* 59 (June 1978).

Taeuber, Karl. *Racial Segregation, 28 Cities, 1920–1980.* Center for Demography and Ecology, University of Wisconsin, Working Paper 83-12, March 1983.

Takaki, Ronald. *Strangers from a Different Shore.* Boston: Little, Brown, 1989.

Talbot, Allan. *The Mayor's Game.* New York: Harper & Row, 1967.

Talese, Gay. *The Kingdom and the Power.* New York: Bantam Books, 1969.

Taueber, Alma. *Negroes in the Cities.* Chicago: Aldine, 1965.

Taylor, George Rogers. *The Transportation Revolution, 1815–1860.* New York: Rinehart, 1951.

Teaford, John C. *The Municipal Revolution in America.* Chicago: University of Chicago Press, 1975.

Terkel, Studs. *American Dreams.* New York: Pantheon, 1980.

Thelen, David. *The New Citizenship.* Columbus: University of Missouri Press, 1972.

Thernstrom, Stephen. *The Other Bostonians.* Cambridge, Mass.: Harvard University Press, 1973.

Thompson, Wilbur. "A Preface to Suburban Economics." In *The Urbanization of the Suburbs,* edited by Louis Masotti and Jeffrey Hadden. Beverly Hills, Calif.: Sage, 1973.

Thurow, Lester. *Zero-Sum Society.* New York: Basic Books, 1980.

Till, Thomas. "Manufacturing Industry: Trends and Impact." In *Nonmetropolitan America in Transition,* edited by Amos Hawley and Sarah Mills. Chapel Hill: University of North Carolina Press, 1981.

Tobin, Gary. "Suburbanization and the Development of Motor Transportation." In *The Changing Face of the Suburbs,* edited by Barry Schwartz. Chicago: University of Chicago Press, 1976.

Tobin, Gary, and Judd, Dennis. "Moving the Suburbs to the City." *Social Science Quarterly* 63 (December 1982).

Tolchin, Martin. "Rewards for Public Service Are Growing." *New York Times,* May 13, 1990.

Trapp, Peter. "Governors' and Mayors' Offices: The Role of the Staff." *National Civic Review* 63 (May 1964).

Truman, David B. *The Governmental Process: Political Interests and Public Opinion.* New York: Knopf, 1971.

Tucker, Robert. *The Marx-Engels Reader.* New York: Norton, 1978.

Turk, Judy Van Slyke. "Information Subsidies and Media Content." *Journalism Monographs* 100 (December 1986).

Twentieth Century Fund Task Force on Municipal Bond Credit Ratings. *The Rating Game.* New York: Twentieth Century Fund, 1974.

Upscon, Lent. "A Proposal for an Administrative Assistant to the Mayor." *American City* 44 (June 1931).

U.S. Congress, Joint Economic Committee. *Trends in the Fiscal Conditions of Cities, 1978–80.* Washington, D.C.: Government Printing Office, 1980.

U.S. Department of Commerce, *Census of Manufacturers.* Washington, D.C.: Government Printing Office, 1958 and 1972.

U.S. Department of Commerce. *City and County Data Book.* Washington, D.C.: Government Printing Office, Annual.

U.S. Department of Commerce, Bureau of the Census. "Characteristics of American Children and Youth." *Current Population Reports.* Washington, D.C.: Government Printing Office, 1982.

U.S. Department of Commerce, Bureau of the Census. "Occupational Changes in a Generation Survey." *Current Population Reports.* Washington, D.C.: Government Printing Office, 1973.

U.S. Department of Commerce, Bureau of the Census. "Persons of Spanish Origin in the United States, March 1982." *Current Population Reports.* Series P-20, #396. Washington, D.C.: Government Printing Office, 1965.

U.S. Department of Commerce, Bureau of the Census. *Poverty in the United States, 1985.* Washington, D.C.: Government Printing Office, 1985.

U.S. Department of Commerce, Bureau of the Census. *Statistical Abstracts of the United States.* Washington, D.C.: Government Printing Office, 1986–1989.

U.S. Department of Commerce, Social and Economic Statistics Administration, Bureau of the Census. *Low Income Families in 1969, by Type, Age, and Race of Head: 1970.* Washington, D.C.: Government Printing Office, 1970.

U.S. Department of Housing and Urban Development, Office of Policy Development and Research. *Displacement Report.* Washington, D.C.: Government Printing Office, 1979.

U.S. Department of Justice. *Criminal Victimization in the United States.* Washington, D.C.: Government Printing Office, 1974.

U.S. House Committee on Banking and Currency. *Commercial Banks and Their Activities: Emerging Influence on the American Economy.* Washington, D.C.: Government Printing Office, 1968.

Ucko, Peter; Tringham, Ruth; and Dimleby, G. W., eds. *Men, Settlement and Urbanism.* Cambridge, Mass.: Schenkman, 1972.

Van Asselt, Karl. "Impasse Resolution." *Public Administration Review* 32 (March/April, 1972).

Verba, Sidney, and Nie, Norman. *Participation in America.* New York: Harper & Row, 1972.

Vernon, Raymond. *Storm over the Multinationals.* Cambridge, Mass.: Harvard University Press, 1977.

Vogel, David. "Business's New Class Struggle." *Nation,* December 15,1979.

Wade, Richard. "The City in History—Some American Perspectives." In *Urban Life and Form,* edited by Werner Hirsch. New York: Holt, Rinehart and Winston, 1963.

Wade, Richard. *The Urban Frontier.* Chicago: University of Chicago Press, 1959.

Wahlke, John; Eulau, Heinz; Buchanan, William; and Ferguson, LeRoy. *The Legislative System.* New York: Wiley, 1962.

Wald, Kenneth. "The Electoral Base of Political Machines: A Deviant Case Analysis." *Urban Affairs Quarterly* 16 (September 1980).

Waldhorn, Stephen. "The Role of Neighborhood Government in Post-Categorical Programs." In *Restructuring the Federal System,* edited by Joseph Sneed and Stephen Waldhorn. New York: Crane, Russak and Company, 1975.

Walsh, Annmarie. *The Public's Business.* Cambridge, Mass.: MIT Press, 1978.

Wambaugh, Joseph. *The New Centurions.* New York: Dell, 1972.

Warner, Sam Bass. *The Private City.* Philadelphia: University of Pennsylvania Press, 1968.

Warner, Sam Bass. *Streetcar Suburbs.* Cambridge, Mass.: Harvard, University Press, 1962.

Warner, Sam Bass. *The Urban Wilderness.* New York: Harper & Row, 1972.

Washkins, George, ed. *Productivity Improvement for State and Local Government.* New York: Wiley, 1980.

Watkins, Alfred. *The Practice of Urban Economics.* Beverly Hills, Calif.: Sage, 1980.

Watson, Sharon, and Fowler, Edmund. "Impact of Black Mayors on Urban Policy." *Annals of the American Academy of Political and Social Sciences* 439 (September 1978).

Weber, Adna Ferrin. *The Growth of Cities in the Nineteenth Century.* New York: Macmillan, 1899.

Weber, Max. "Bureaucracy." In *Essays in Sociology,* edited by H. H. Gerth and C. Wright Mills. New York: Oxford University Press, 1962.

Weinberg, Mark. "The Urban Fiscal Crisis Impact on the Budgeting and Financial Planning Practices of Urban America." *Journal of Urban Affairs* 6 (Winter 1984).

Weinstein, James. *The Corporate Ideal in the Liberal State, 1900–1918.* Boston: Beacon, 1968.

Welch, Susan, and Karnig, Albert. "The Impact of Black Elected Officials on Urban Social Expenditures." *Policy Science Journal* 7 (Summer 1979).

Wellington, Harry, and Winters, Ralph. "The Limits of Collective Bargaining in Public Employment." In *Public Employees and Policymaking,* edited by Alan Saltzstein. Pacific Palisades, Calif.: Palisades, 1979.

Whelan, Edward. "The Making of a Mayor, 1977." *Cleveland Magazine,* December, 1977.

Whelan, Edward. "Mayor Ralph J. Perk and the Politics of Decay." *Cleveland Magazine,* September 1975.

Wheltan, Charles. "Getting Bought." *Village Voice,* May 2, 1977.

White, Louise. "Improving the Goal-Setting Process in Local Government." *Public Administration Review* 42 (January/February 1982).

White, Michael J. *Managing Public Systems.* North Scituate, Mass.: Duxbury, 1980.

Wicker, Tom. *On Press.* New York: Viking Press, 1978.

Wildavsky, Aaron. *The Politics of the Budgetary Process.* Boston: Little, Brown, 1974.

Wilensky, Harold. *Organizational Intelligence.* New York: Basic Books, 1967.

Wilhoit, Cleveland, and Weaver, David. *The American Journalist.* Bloomington: Indiana University Press, 1986.

Williams, Frederick; Dordick, Herbert; and Horstman, Frederick. "Where Citizens Go for Information." *Journal of Communication* 27 (Winter 1977).

Williams, Oliver, and Adrian, Charles. *Four Cities.* Philadelphia: University of Pennsylvania Press, 1963.

Williams, Roger M. "America's Black Mayors: Are They Saving the Cities?" *Saturday Review/World,* May 4, 1974.

Wilson, James Q. *The Amateur Democrat.* Chicago: University of Chicago Press, 1962.

Wilson, James Q. *American Government.* Lexington, Mass: D C Heath, 1989.

Wilson, James Q. "The Economy of Patronage." *Journal of Political Economy* 69 (August 1961).

Wilson, James Q. *Negro Politics.* New York: Free Press, 1960.

Wilson, James Q. "Politics and Reform in American Cities." *American Government Annual, 1962–1963.* New York: Harcourt, Brace and World, 1962.

Wilson, James Q. *Varieties of Police Behavior.* Cambridge, Mass.: Harvard University Press, 1968.

Wilson, James Q., and Edward Banfield. "Public-Regardingness as a Value Premise in Voting Behavior." *American Political Science Review* 58 (December 1964).

Wilson, William Julius. *The Truly Disadvantaged.* Chicago: University of Chicago Press, 1987.

Winn, Mylon. "The Election of Norm Rice as Mayor of Seattle." *PS* 23 (June 1990).

Wirt, Frederick. *Power in the City: Decision-Making in San Francisco.* Berkeley: University of California Press, 1974.

Wolfinger, Raymond. *The Politics of Progress.* Englewood Cliffs, N.J.: Prentice-Hall, 1974.

Wolfinger, Raymond. "Why Machines Have Not Withered Away and Other Revisionist Thoughts." *Journal of Politics* 34 (May 1972).

Wolfinger, Raymond, and Field, John. "Political Ethos and the Structure of City Governments." *American Political Science Review* 60 (June 1966).

Wood, Robert. *1400 Governments.* Garden City, N.Y.: Doubleday Anchor, 1964.

Wood, Robert. *Suburbia: Its People and Their Politics.* Boston: Houghton Mifflin, 1958.

Woodside, William. "The Future of Public-Private Partnerships." In *Public-Private Partnerships,* edited by Perry Davis. New York: Academy of Political Science, 1986.

Wright, Deil. *Understanding Intragovernmental Relations.* Monterey, Calif.: Brooks-Cole 1982.

Yates, Douglas. *Neighborhood Democracy.* Lexington, Mass: Lexington Books, 1973.

Yates, Douglas. *The Ungovernable City.* Cambridge, Mass.: MIT Press, 1977.

Yearly, Clifton. *The Money Machines.* Albany, N.Y.: SUNY Press, 1920.

Yin, Robert. *Changing Urban Bureaucracies.* Lexington, Mass.: Lexington Books, 1980.

Zannes, Estelle. *Checkmate in Cleveland.* New York: University Press Book Service, 1972.

Zeitlin, Maurice. "Who Owns America?" *The Progressive* 42 (June 1978).

Zilg, Gerald. *Du Pont: Behind the Nylon Curtain.* Englewood Cliffs, N.J.: Prentice-Hall, 1974.

Zink, Harold. *City Bosses in the United States.* New York: AMS, 1968.

Zinn, Howard. *A People's History of the United States.* New York: Harper Colophon, 1980.

Zorbaush, Harvey. *The Gold Coast and the Slum.* Chicago: University of Chicago Press, 1929.

Index

Accumulation function, 26, 27
Acquired immune deficiency syndrome (AIDS), 97
Adamowski, Ben, 183
Adrian, Charles, 219, 223
Advertising Council, 314
African American mayors
  election formula of, 250–252
  future for, 254–256
  historical successes of, 249–250
  policy impact of, 253–254
  problems of, 252–253
African Americans
  difficulty in counting, 78–79
  impact of Reagan administration policies on, 149
  machine politics and, 191
  median age among, 81
  migration to North by, 67, 71, 73–75
  policy brutality toward, 273, 280
  regional distribution of, 74
  single-parent families, 81
  socioeconomic status of, 87–88
  suburbanization of, 75, 84, 85
  violence against, 68, 86, 88–90
Agglomeration, 38
Aid to Families with Dependent Children (AFDC), 141, 149
Akron, Ohio, 152

All-Peoples Congress, 339
Almond, Gabriel, 16
Altschuler, Alan, 198
American Federation of State, County, and Municipal Employees (AFSCME), 269, 276
American Patriotic League, 68
American Protective Association, 68
Antirationalism, 329, 331
Arab Americans, 78
Arrington, Richard, 249
Asian Americans, 71, 77–78
Associated Press (AP), 302
Association of Bay Area Governments (San Francisco), 121
Association of Community Organizations for Reform Now (ACORN), 340
Astor, John Jacob, 198
At-large elections, 122, 123
Azer, Suzie, 256

Bachelor, Lynn, 152
Bachrach, Peter, 18
Bagdikian, Ben, 312
Baker v. Carr, 110
Baltimore, Maryland, 143
Banfield, Edward, 85, 242
Baratz, Morton, 18
Barnouw, Erik, 313